AMERICAN COURT SYSTEMS

AMERICAN COURT SYSTEMS

Readings in Judicial Process and Behavior

EDITED AND WITH INTRODUCTORY ESSAYS BY

Sheldon Goldman

UNIVERSITY OF MASSACHUSETTS, AMHERST

Austin Sarat

UNITED STATES DEPARTMENT OF JUSTICE

W. H. Freeman and Company
San Francisco

Library of Congress Cataloging in Publication Data

Main entry under title:

American court systems.

   1. Courts—United States.   2. Judicial process—United
States.   3. Judges—United States—Attitudes.   I. Goldman,
Sheldon.   II. Sarat, Austin.
KF8700.A7A46   347'.73   78-19160
ISBN 0-7167-0061-1
ISBN 0-7167-0060-3 pbk.

Printed in the United States of America

10 9 8 7 6 5 4 3 2 1

CONTENTS

PREFACE

Our objective in this book is to present to the student, within a broad dispute-processing framework, some of the best materials available to illuminate various facets of American courts. We also aim, in our introductory essays to each chapter, not only to set the stage for the readings that follow but to complement those selections so that the student is given a general view of the judicial process. To be sure, there are some topics we have left out. For example, we have not dealt much with the technical issues of judicial administration, nor have we considered the prison and parole systems. These subjects are worthy of separate extensive treatment, but they tend to diverge from the central concerns of our analysis.

Initially our intention was to update an earlier reader, *The Federal Judicial System: Readings in Process and Behavior,* edited by the late Thomas P. Jahnige and Sheldon Goldman (New York: Holt, Rinehart and Winston, 1968). However, as our work progressed it became clear that we were creating an entirely new work that was worthy of its own identity. Of the 54 selections in this book, only 9 appeared in the earlier reader. In addition, this book is organized differently, state judiciaries are considered, and the introductory essays for each chapter were written especially for this book. There is no explicit treatment of systems analysis because it seems to us that the broad outlines of the systems framework are widely understood and that the interrelationships of the diverse materials presented in this book are apparent. Instead, our perspective on the judicial process is one that has been identified with students of the sociology of law. Simply put, we focus our attention on courts as dispute-processing institutions, and "dispute" is the basic unit of analysis.

Although we worked together on the entire manuscript and share responsibility for its contents, we must acknowledge the helpful comments and suggestions we received from several scholars who read the portions of the manuscript that were specially written for this book. In particular we wish to thank Professors Larry Baum, Jay Casper, David Danelski, Joel Grossman, William McLauchlan, and Harold Spaeth. Richard Lamb, political science editor at W. H. Freeman and Company and fellow political scientist, deserves our special thanks for his encouragement and great help with this project. We are also appreciative of the fine editing job done by Ms. Jeanne Duncan. Ms. Vera Smith did an outstanding job of typing the original material for the book and retyping some of the edited selections. Finally, we are grateful to the authors and publishers of the works we have included for allowing us to reprint them.

April 1978   *Austin Sarat*
                                                          Sheldon Goldman

AMERICAN COURT SYSTEMS

INTRODUCTION

Alexis de Tocqueville, perhaps the most perceptive of all commentators on American social life, noted early in the nineteenth century what he believed to be a distinctive tendency of Americans to transform almost every important political question into a legal question. The spirit of American democracy is, according to Tocqueville, the spirit of spontaneity, energy, creativity, and perhaps even anarchy. Tocqueville saw in the early experience of America the potential for great achievement and, at the same time, the possibility of great peril. He looked to law and to its spirit to provide a guiding, stabilizing, and limiting force, a force that would channel the vitality of American life into creative paths. Especially important in this role would be the part played by courts and judges. What is remarkable about American courts, Tocqueville noted, is that judges are invested with the power and responsibility to supervise the contests of a majoritarian political system, to protect an essentially democratic polity and society from the excesses of democracy. Courts are unique among political and social institutions in that they embody the spirit of reason and reasoned judgment. They provide a forum in which the strength of argument rather than the strength of numbers is decisive.[1]

1

Tocqueville's observations about the special character of American courts have been echoed throughout the nineteenth and twentieth centuries, but not always with Tocqueville's spirit of admiration. Our judicial system has been variously criticized for being irresponsible, abusing its power, for failing to uphold the central tenets of democracy, and for being costly and inefficient.[2] Recently, for example, sociologist Nathan Glazer advanced the argument that we have developed an "Imperial Judiciary"— that is, that courts and judges now have so much power, play so much of a role in regulating the way Americans conduct their lives, that they pose a threat and a challenge to the vitality of our political system. Too much power, wrote Glazer, has moved from the elected, representative branches of government to the largely nonelective judiciary. Furthermore, he argued that the judicial system is no less political than are the other branches of government. Judges use their positions to carry out specific policy preferences rather than to provide neutral judgment. They do so without being accountable for their actions.[3]

Whether the power of American courts is too great or whether it is appropriate and necessary to the maintenance of democratic politics, there can be little doubt that courts have played and continue to play a major role in shaping and influencing political and social life in the United States. Perhaps more than in any other nation, courts in this country have been and remain a barometer of the morals, problems, and aspirations of the citizenry.

Glazer's position is important in that it represents a wide variety of contemporary concerns about the operation of American courts. These concerns have developed in recent years along with the increase in the number of things subject to government regulation. The law now regulates and prescribes standards for what we wear, what we eat, how we conduct our business dealings, how we educate our children and are educated ourselves, and most other aspects of our daily lives.[4] As the scope of law has expanded, so have the activities of the American judiciary. Whereas most courts, particularly at the lower levels, were once largely concerned with settling narrowly drawn conflicts between private parties, courts in the 1970s are often concerned with the broadest issues of public policy—for example, school desegregation, environmental pollution, and the rights of people on welfare.[5] In dealing with these issues the courts have been doing more than simply making declarations of the legal rights of the particular parties involved in the litigation. Because of their apparent perception of governmental agencies as being unable or unwilling to satisfactorily implement such judicial declarations, judges, in a number of legal areas affecting large numbers of people, have become increasingly involved in devising detailed positive plans for enforcing the law as they determine it. For example, in recent years there have been a number of school desegregation cases where judges, finding that local officials have been unable or unwilling to draw up satisfactory plans to desegregate urban school districts, have themselves drawn up such plans. They have gone beyond simply deciding whether districts are illegally segregated and have attempted to devise remedies that in practice tell communities how their schools should be organized. This positive kind of judicial policy making has raised questions in the minds of many people—questions as to whether it is fair for judges rather than the elected representatives of the citizenry to make such decisions and, even more importantly, whether judges are competent to decide such complex issues of public policy.

Other critics maintain that the major problem with contemporary courts is not that judges are engaged in policy making, but that the policy made is unjust.[6] This criticism, often from the political left, suggests that American courts are simply tools of an inegalitarian social order and that they are used as an instrument to repress the legitimate political grievances of the poor and the powerless. These criticisms, focusing as they do on questions of fairness, competence, and justice, have placed the courts at the center of strident political controversy about the nature of American politics and law.

The major issues of American political life, perhaps even more so today than in Tocqueville's time, frequently find their way into court. Abortion, the conduct of the police and the rights of criminals, obscenity, the powers of the President, the way we conduct and finance elections—these and other issues are argued in American courts. We know that courts are important in our lives, but it is fair to say that most of us are not sure why they are or how they came to be that way or what difference it makes that courts are so important. An underlying assumption in this book is that the fact that our courts are active and frequent makers of public policy makes a great deal of difference in the quality of American life. It makes a difference in terms of the nature and quality of our democracy and of our private lives as well. It makes a difference because courts are distinctive types of institutions; they operate in ways that are quite unlike the ways in which other political and social institutions operate. Our concern in this book is to try to understand how courts operate and why they operate as they do, and to compare, although more often implicitly than explicitly, their operation with the workings of other public institutions (such as legislatures and administrative agencies) and private institutions (such as marriage counseling and labor arbitration). We do this in the context of what, for lack of a better term, might be called the *political sociology of the judicial process.* What this means is that we are concerned with the institutional characteristics of courts. We ask what courts are, what they do, and what effect their activities have. It also means that we believe that one cannot understand courts and their role in American life without understanding what makes them distinctive—that is, without having some sense of their relation to and place in the range of public and private institutions that deal with important social and political issues.

What do American courts do? The most direct, if not the simplest, answer is that courts hear lawsuits; they decide cases in which two or more individuals, organizations, or government officials argue about their rights, obligations, and responsibilities under the law. A lawsuit is a particular type of dispute. A dispute may be defined as a particular set of behaviors marked by competition, aggression, and more or less open displays of hostility that may focus on material or nonmaterial values.[7] Thus it might be said that courts hear disputes, that is, that what courts do is to try to decide between or among those who have some disagreement, misunderstanding, difference, or conflict. Disagreements might involve, for example, who should pay for the damage in an automobile accident, whether money must be paid for an appliance that is defective, whether a father can exclude his child from his will, whether a student has to wear his hair in a particular way, or whether the police can legally search a car stopped for a traffic offense. These types of events or disputes are the source of the material upon which courts work. Yet, as we will suggest in Part One, these kinds of disputes do not have to end up in court. People, when they have a disagreement or problem, generally can do many things to deal with it without resorting to law or using the courts. However, it is only in the course of deciding a dispute between two parties that a court can make a broad public policy decision. Thus, the dispute that was actually heard and decided by the Supreme Court in the abortion decision of *Roe* v. *Wade*[8] involved one woman and the district attorney of one city.

What courts do is to hear and decide disputes. Another way of putting this is to say that courts are a particular kind of dispute-processing institution.[9] When we say that courts process disputes, we mean to caution against the widespread belief that a court decision represents the last word in a dispute. Most people think that when a decision is handed down by a court, it puts an end to the particular problem in dispute. Thus if two people go to court to get a divorce, we may have the impression that the granting of the divorce terminates their relationship; in fact, it may simply move the relationship to a new phase. Instead of fighting over who should do what in the house or fighting over money, the former spouses may continue to argue, but now they argue about visiting rights for the children, about the things that each one says to former friends, or about how to treat each other in public. Rarely do the actions or decisions of courts fully terminate the social problems that are brought before them. Think about the experience of northern cities that have, in recent years, been ordered to desegregate their schools. In some cities the court decision ordering desegregation did not resolve the issue of where children should go to school, to say nothing of the more enduring interracial problems. In fact, at times the court decisions increased feelings of racial hostility and racial conflict. Whether the disputes that courts hear involve only the two parties who bring the case or whether they have broader ramifications, court decisions are rarely the final events or the last words in a dispute.

The role of courts is to process disputes, not to end them—to render a decision informing citizens as to that to which they are legally entitled. To say that courts do not end disputes is not to say that what they do is insignificant. The conflicts and disputes that come to court are seldom simple.[10] To bring a case to court requires a substantial investment in time and money, an investment that ensures that people whose disputes are decided have an intense commitment to their cause that will not easily dissipate once a court decision has been made. Decisions may serve only, as in the divorce example, to help to alter the nature of the dispute giving rise to the lawsuit. Just as judges react to the presentation of facts and evidence in the course of a lawsuit, so do the individuals involved in a suit react to the operations of the court. Judicial decisions may represent the legal termination of a dispute but they may not reach the underlying problem. This is generally true when, as in the United States, courts do not process disputes with an eye toward reconciling the disputants. In most cases a judge is concerned only with what is desirable from the perspective of law or public policy, not what will restore harmony to the relations of the litigants.

To say that courts process disputes is not to suggest that they can or will process any and all disputes. American courts do not actively seek out the disputes with which they deal. Instead it may fairly be said that our courts are passive and reactive.[11] They wait for disputes to be brought to them. If a citizen is involved in a dispute in which he or she is entitled to some help or remedy, the courts will be able to do nothing unless the citizen initiates a lawsuit. Courts do not set their own agendas. However, courts are able to exert some control over the cases they hear by selecting among those which are brought to them. Only disputes that are framed as a contest over legal rights and responsibilities and for which there are remedies specified by law are eligible for judicial action.[12] However, this restriction is one that is, except in its broadest outline, growing increasingly less significant. Given the vast reach and high level of inclusiveness that characterizes modern legal systems like our own, almost any dispute can be so framed as to give it the form of a contest over legal rights and responsibilities. This has led to what some analysts consider the overburdening of American courts. It is this easy transformation of disputes to cases that leads us to view the sociological category of "dispute" rather than the legal category of "case" as the appropriate unit for understanding the functions of judicial systems. To talk about cases is to talk about the ritualized and stylized presentation of disputes rather than about any distinctive, substantive subtype of social conflict. It is not unimportant, as we shall see, that courts require disputes to take the form of cases but not so important and fundamental as to alter the fact that courts process essentially the same kinds of disputes that are processed by a wide range of public and private institutions. This book is organized to enable us to trace the way in which disputes are translated into cases and the way in which cases are translated into judicial decisions. In short, we believe that the best way to understand what courts do is to examine how and why they process disputes as they do.

There are three important categories of disputes that provide the bulk of the work of American courts.[13] The first is what we will call the *private dispute*. Private disputes are defined by the absence of any initial participation by public authorities. For example, when a husband and wife quarrel, when two automobiles collide, when two businessmen disagree about the terms of a contract, these events are likely to give rise to private disputes. Such disputes may occur in public places or they may involve competing interpretations of public norms, but they remain private so long as the government is not a party. These types of disputes arise more or less spontaneously in the normal course of social life. Because they arise out of purely private relations, they are also typically processed and managed without the intervention of government. Most private disputes are unknown to anyone except those who are immediately involved; they are most often dealt with within the general context of ongoing relationships or through an ad hoc and temporary framework of bargaining and negotiation.[14] Yet these kinds of disputes may vary in intensity to the extent that the intervention of outside parties may be required to help structure and interpret the dispute. Private disputes typically have the widest range of options insofar as their processing is concerned.

The two other types of disputes with which American courts most often deal are public in that both involve the participation of some agency of government as a disputant.[15] The first of these categories, which we will call the *public-initiated dispute,* occurs when government seeks to enforce norms of conduct or to punish individuals who breach such norms. These kinds of public disputes arise as governments attempt to control and channel social behavior through the promulgation of binding legal norms. Such attempts at control cannot proceed solely in the abstract, that is, government cannot rely simply on the promulgation of norms to ensure that citizens will conduct themselves in accordance with governmental desires. Enforcement is necessary. The most appropriate model of the public-initiated dispute is the ordinary criminal case in which the state or some official acting on its behalf seeks to use the courts to determine whether a particular breach of legal norms has occurred and whether sanctions ought to be applied. The public-initiated dispute is distinctive in that it always involves and is governed by the law of the entire community. These kinds of disputes are public in terms of both their participants and their substantive bases. What this means is that, at least formally, dispute processing must occur in a public forum. No stable society allows or could allow the development of private mechanisms for the enforcement of breaches of public norms. This is not to suggest that all public-initiated disputes are resolved or processed by means of judicial action. A variety of informal devices ranging from the warnings that a policeman may give to a speeder to the prosecutor's decision not to proceed with a criminal case to the practice of plea bargaining may be employed to deal with breaches of public norms.[16] Furthermore, there is evidence to suggest that many disputes that involve such breaches are not brought to the attention of public authorities. For example, the husband who beats his wife may have committed a breach of public norms. However, their dispute remains private unless and until a complaint is lodged with law enforcement authorities. Looked at from the perspective of all of the disputes that might involve a breach of public norms, the percentage of public-initiated disputes is rather small; however, from the perspective of the judiciary such disputes are of major quantitative and qualitative importance.

A third type of dispute that frequently finds its way into American courts is what might be called the *public defendant dispute.* Unlike the public-initiated dispute, in this type the government participates as a defendant. These kinds of disputes typically involve challenges to the authority of some government agency or challenges of the propriety of some government action, challenges that may be initiated by a private individual or organization. In these types of cases courts are called upon to review the action of other branches of government. This is the kind of judicial quality control that Tocqueville recognized as characteristic of our constitutional system and that Nathan Glazer believes has gone too far in the modern age. Public defendant disputes often involve claims that the government has not abided by its own rules or followed procedures that it has prescribed. For example, parents of school children in racially segregated public schools might claim that public school officials violated the Constitution's guarantee of equal protection of the laws. Or a landowner might complain that he was wrongfully denied a property tax exemption to which he believes himself entitled under a city's zoning regulations. Public defendant disputes generally come to court only after the aggrieved party has failed to remedy his grievance either through the political process or through remedy procedures provided by the offending government agency. Public defendant disputes provide an especially important staple of the business of American courts, even though such disputes make up a significantly smaller number of the cases on any court's docket than do either private- or public-initiated disputes. Their importance lies in the fact that they provide the courts with an opportunity to affirm the rule of law, to ensure that the government will act according to its own rules and that such rules conform to the most basic principles of constitutional government.

Private-initiated, public-initiated, and public defendant disputes constitute the workload of American courts. However, dispute processing in
America does not typically result in an easy or uniform flow of disputes
into the judicial system. American courts are expensive, slow, and difficult
to use. Their decisional style, that is, their tendency to focus narrowly on
particular elements of law and the compatibility of social action and legal
norms, means that as dispute-processing institutions, they may be more
costly and inefficient than other, comparable institutions. In the United
States courts are part of an innumerable array of individuals and institutions that perform dispute-processing functions. Such individuals and institutions range from marriage counselors and religious or community
leaders to organized arbitration services. All employ wide-ranging techniques and procedures for dealing with disputes.

To understand what courts do, how they operate, and what their role is
in American life, it is necessary to determine what distinguishes courts
from other dispute-processing institutions, that is, to establish standards
for judging whether or not and to what extent courts function in a distinctive manner and to apply those standards in judging the performance of
American courts. Ultimately our concern is evaluative. We want to be able
to measure the performance of courts against those standards of performance which give courts special claim to authority and a legitimacy in
American life.

Four aspects of the judicial process seem especially important in establishing the standards necessary to understand and judge how courts operate: the ways in which courts acquire their business, the types of people
who participate in the judicial process, the way in which judicial decisions
are made, and the nature of the results produced by those decisions. First,
as we have already suggested, courts, unlike other dispute-processing institutions, are reactive. Judges can, in theory, act only when they are called
upon to do so by parties with no official connection to the judiciary. Legislative institutions, in contrast, do not wait nor do they need to wait for
problems to be brought to their attention. They can and frequently do
undertake to define and investigate situations before those situations give
rise to problems. In this sense they are able to set their own agenda. The
judiciary is passive; courts do not seek out disputes. "When it is called
upon to repress a crime, it punishes the criminal; when a wrong is to be
redressed, it is ready to redress it; when an act requires interpretation, it is
prepared to interpret it; but it does not pursue criminals, hunt out wrongs
or examine evidence of its own accord."[17]

The passivity of courts is itself a product of America's commitment to
individualism, that is, it is a product of a value system that stresses the
importance of personal privacy and self-sufficiency. The passivity of courts
places the burden on citizens to recognize and define their own needs and
problems and to decide which of those needs and problems require legal

judgment. As sociologist Donald Black puts it, this method of acquiring cases ". . . assumes that each individual will voluntarily and rationally pursue his own interests. . . ."[18] The courts are indifferent to those problems or disputes that citizens fail to notice or wish to ignore. The reactive nature of the courts has the further effect of narrowing and isolating problems. Since disputes are processed on a case-by-case basis, it is difficult for many disputants or other participants in the judicial system to perceive underlying patterns and common problems.[19] Furthermore, the reactive nature of courts ensures that they deal with disputes after injuries have occurred and problems have matured. This in turn ordinarily limits the ability of courts to become important agents of basic social change.

Accompanying and part of the liberal underpinnings of the manner in which courts get their cases is an ideological commitment to equal protection of the law that determines the types of people who participate. Courts are, in theory, different from other kinds of dispute-processing institutions in that they are available to all citizens. Any citizen having a dispute for which there is a potential legal remedy ought to be able to use the courts. Unlike other dispute-processing institutions that are available only to specific kinds or groups of people (for example, religious tribunals), courts are public in the broadest sense. Furthermore, they allow for the participation of a peculiar mix of ordinary citizens and legal experts. Judicial processing of disputes involves both the application of legal knowledge and the interpretation of factual events. Thus, there is a division of labor in which disputants and jurors on the one hand and lawyers and judges on the other play equal roles. Participants in court proceedings bring diverse interests and skills to a forum in which their skills are, in theory, equally valued.

A third element that distinguishes courts from other dispute-processing institutions is the way in which decisions are made. Courts are *legal* institutions. Their role in the political and social system is to interpret and apply law—to use legal norms to process disputes. Furthermore, their legitimacy is thought to be dependent on their tie to such norms. Unlike other branches of American government that may claim to derive their authority through the electoral process, courts claim distinctive competence in matters of law. Judicial interpretation of legal norms is expected to be neutral, that is, those making judicial decisions are expected not to base their interpretation of legal norms on their own private interests or policy preferences. Their decisions are expected to be governed by legal principle and not by political pragmatism.[20] Judges are not supposed to do what is best for the disputants; instead they are charged to do right in accord with *legal* definitions of what is right. In practice, however, it is clear that the process of interpreting and applying law is quite complex. Laws are ambiguous and rules of interpretation are themselves open to interpretation. No two cases are exactly alike. Yet judges are expected to decide cases on the basis of the facts insofar as they can be established and specific legal rules and principles insofar as they can be determined and reasonably applied. To the extent that judges do not fulfill this expectation they abandon their distinctive claim as dispute processors, and courts become indistinguishable from other dispute-processing institutions.

The fourth and final distinguishing characteristic of courts is the nature of the results of their activity. Simply put, those results are expected to be impartial. Equal justice requires that the merits of fact and law, rather than the characteristics of the disputants, determine the result. The results of judicial decision making differ from the results of decision making by other branches of government to the extent that they do not favor particular types or categories of litigants. Furthermore, the results of court decisions ought to have a special claim on the individuals or groups involved in disputes. By providing a neutral and unbiased forum, the courts invite good sportsmanship; they invite people to submit to a process of judgment that is fair, and expect that their decisions will be accepted by those who lose as well as by those who win.

We believe that in order to understand American court systems it is necessary to deal with the issues of access, participation, decision making, and result. This book is organized to facilitate the examination of the evidence that suggests the extent to which courts operate in a distinctive manner. It is about the ways that the disputes that occur in society find their way into courts, the ways that they are transformed into cases, the ways that cases become court decisions, and the ways that decisions affect the environments in which courts operate. We have selected readings that address concerns relevant to the politics of the judicial process and that we believe provide a key to understanding and assessing the role of courts in American life.

Notes

1. Alexis de Tocqueville, *Democracy in America,* Vol. 1 (New York: Vintage Books, 1954), Chaps. 6 and 8.

2. See, for example, Henry S. Commager, *Majority Rule and Minority Rights* (New York: Peter Smith, 1943); Herbert Wechsler, "Toward Neutral Principles of Constitutional Law," *Harvard Law Review* 73 (1959), 1–35; and Leonard Downie, *Justice Denied* (New York: Praeger, 1971).

3. Nathan Glazer, "Toward an Imperial Judiciary?," *The Public Interest* 41 (1975), 104–123. Also see Raoul Berger, *Government by Judiciary* (Cambridge, Mass.: Harvard University Press, 1977).

4. This expansion is discussed and criticized by Thomas Ehrlich in "Legal Pollution," *New York Times Magazine,* February 8, 1976.

5. Compare Francis Laurent, *The Business of a Trial Court* (Madison: University of Wisconsin Press, 1959) and Donald Horowitz, *The Courts and Social Policy* (Washington: Brookings Institution, 1977).

6. See, for example, Howard Zinn, "The Conspiracy of Law," and Edgar Friedenberg, "The Side Effects of the Legal Process," in *The Rule of Law*, edited by Robert Paul Wolff (New York: Simon and Schuster, 1971), pp. 15–53.

7. Vilhelm Aubert, "Competition and Dissensus," *Journal of Conflict Resolution* 7 (1963), 25.

8. 410 U.S. 113 (1973).

9. Richard Abel, "A Comparative Theory of Dispute Institutions in Society," *Law and Society Review* 8 (1974), 229.

10. Even those involving relatively little in the way of tangible resources may present complex legal and factual problems. See Barbara Yngvesson and Patricia Hennessey, "Small Claims, Complex Disputes," *Law and Society Review* 9 (1975), 219–274.

11. See Donald Black, "The Mobilization of Law," *Journal of Legal Studies* 2 (1973), 128.

12. The standards courts use in selecting the cases they hear are discussed in David Rohde and Harold Spaeth, *Supreme Court Decision Making* (San Francisco: W. H. Freeman, 1976), pp. 9–20.

13. See Lawrence Friedman, "The Functions of Trial Courts in the Modern World," paper presented to the Conference on the Sociology of the Judicial Process, Bielefeld, Germany, 1973.

14. Austin Sarat, "Alternatives in Dispute Processing: Litigation in a Small Claims Court," *Law and Society Review* 10 (1976), 339–375.

15. We recognize that there may be some blurring of these categories since government officials or agencies are often involved in what appear to be private disputes. This occurs when the government is not trying to enforce or is not being held accountable to a public norm. The government, for example, may seek to enforce the terms of a contract with someone doing work for it or it may seek to recover damages done to government property. Nevertheless, we think it most useful to categorize disputes along a public-private dimension.

16. See James Eisenstein and Herbert Jacob, *Felony Justice* (Boston: Little, Brown, 1977).

17. Tocqueville, *op. cit.*, note 1, pp. 103–104.

18. Black, *op. cit.*, note 11, p. 138.

19. See Stuart Scheingold, *The Politics of Rights* (New Haven: Yale University Press, 1974).

20. See Wechsler, *op. cit.*, note 2.

PART ONE
INPUT

CHAPTER ONE

COURTS AND
THEIR ALTERNATIVES

"Tell me how you got here," asked the interviewer. "Well, it is a long and not happy story," answered the rather plump, middle-aged man seated in a large, noisy courtroom in New York City. "At first I didn't know what to do. I wasn't even sure that there was a problem, let alone something worth going to court about. I talked to my wife about it and eventually we decided to call and see if we couldn't get it fixed or get our money back." The "it" in this man's description was a used television set; the problem was that it had a faulty picture tube.

"I bought the set without really paying too much attention. We needed to replace our old one and it was cheap so I figured that we were getting a good deal. It wasn't until a few days after we had it at home that the picture began to fade out. You'd have it on for a few minutes and then it would lose the picture. Well, eventually I called the store and talked with the salesman. He said that he was sorry but that all sales were final and that there was no guarantee. We talked for a while and finally he said that he would take it up with his boss and get back to me. I never heard from him. After much trying I managed to contact his boss, who gave me pretty much the same story. Now I didn't want to cause trouble for this guy, but what good is a television set if you can't watch it? After thinking a bit I called the

Better Business Bureau. They are always advertising on the radio and when I told my brother what was going on he suggested that they might be able to do something. Well, I guess they talked to the guy who owns the store and asked him to do something. They called back to tell me that there was nothing they could do but record the complaint and advise people not to buy from him. I was pretty upset and disgusted. I didn't want to buy another TV, but I didn't know what I could do. I'd pretty much made up my mind to forget the whole thing when my brother told me that I should go to court. I didn't want to make a federal case out of it. But, when I found out that I could go to small claims court and not have to pay a lawyer or miss work, I decided to sue."[1]

In this man's story we have a rather typical profile of the process whereby individuals translate disputes into lawsuits. This process is characterized by several distinct stages. First, there is the stage of "recognition," that is, of coming to understand that there is a problem. This stage is, of course, just the beginning, but it is, in some ways, the most important stage. Most people do not relish trouble, problems, or conflict; most of us have an ingrained inability to distinguish from among all the events of daily life those which are, in fact, troublesome. This reluctance and inability to identify trouble stems in part from a desire to think of our lives as relatively comfortable and rewarding. The theory of cognitive dissonance, developed by psychologists, indicates the tendency of most people to try to minimize or ignore conflicts or problems that might disturb their psychic tranquility.[2] Furthermore, people are generally reluctant to take on the role of troublemaker, to risk the stigma of appearing to cause trouble for someone else even though that other person may be directly responsible for the trouble. It is only after an individual decides to shoulder this burden that the processing of a dispute begins.

In the second stage of the process, a decision is made whether to "lump it."[3] This decision occurs after an individual acknowledges the existence of trouble; it involves a calculation as to whether the benefits of seeking to deal with the trouble are outweighed by the costs of doing so. The choice is between accepting a loss and risking a greater loss (the original loss compounded by the time and energy invested in pursuing a remedy) in seeking to solve the problem. Yet the decision whether to initiate action to deal with the problem is not totally an unemotional one. As law professor Arthur Leff has suggested, "spite," as much as any other variable that figures into the calculus of costs and benefits, is what spurs much disputing and dispute-processing behavior.[4] An individual, once he comes to see himself as aggrieved, may act simply out of a desire to complicate the life of the individual who he believes has injured him.

Once an individual recognizes the problem and decides to do something about it, dispute processing can commence. The kind of unpleasantness that is part of this process is, from the perspective of the judiciary, both the source and the object of action. The job of American courts is to provide a means of managing such unpleasantness. However, in any society, there is a wide variety of institutions or mechanisms for dealing with disputes, of which the courts are just one.

The simplest and most frequently employed remedies do not require third-party intervention. As in the case of the man with the broken television set, an individual faced with a problem involving another individual or organization typically begins the process of dealing with that problem by dealing directly with the other party. There may be an informal contact in which all that transpires is the exchange of information; that is, the aggrieved party notifies the other party that trouble exists. Frequently, such notification prompts remedial action. Yet the form of such action may itself become the subject of discussion. Should the set be repaired, a replacement be provided, or money returned? This is the classic bargaining situation: a problem is acknowledged to exist and some degree of responsibility is conceded. There are, however, frequent occasions in which neither occurs; the putative defendant refuses to admit that trouble exists or, having done so, refuses to take responsibility. Two-person dispute processing is likely to be successful only when both parties perceive a need for settlement. The process of negotiation may itself be understood as attempting to foster such a perception when it is absent in one of the parties.[5] Quite often one party desires a solution, but the other does not. The latter party may not care or may hope to gain by inaction or may simply be intransigent. Generally, it is only after attempts to deal directly with the other party have failed that third parties (such as judges, mediators, arbiters) will be called in. When two people find that they cannot settle a dispute between themselves, they may seek some other respected person, someone with no stake in the dispute, to listen to their problem and give them advice. The way in which this third-party intervention may occur is highly variable.

The forms of third-party intervention are described and discussed in the three readings in this chapter. Each of the readings describes the range of third-party dispute-processing alternatives in a somewhat different manner. The first selection, by Sarat and Grossman, categorizes these alternatives along two dimensions—the relative formality of their procedures and their degree of publicness. Sometimes the intervention of third parties in a dispute will be formal. The third party will devise or employ regularized procedures, rely on ritual, and tend to employ, exclusively and rigidly, one style of decision making. Sometimes third parties act informally. Sometimes third-party intervention involves the government. The third party may exercise and employ the coercive power of public authority in carrying out and enforcing any decision; or it may have no connection to the state and be private.

Eckhoff, in the second selection, suggests that one can distinguish among third-party alternatives in terms of their reliance on rules and norms to guide decisional behavior. Some third parties deal with disputes by employing common sense, but others try to find rules on which to base decisions. For example, a sports official must apply a set of rules in making decisions. Similarly judges, Eckhoff argues, must decide disputes in accord with prescribed and articulated general rules, in contrast with mediators, who seek to reconcile disputants rather than to apply norms. Judges tend to make decisions in an all or nothing manner, to deal with disputes by examining the past, and to narrow and focus the definition of the problems with which they must deal. Mediators, on the other hand, seek compromise and try to anticipate the future by providing a broader definition of the trouble. Administrators, like mediators, look to the future but, like judges, can impose a resolution of the dispute.

The third selection, by Lon Fuller, suggests yet another approach. Fuller differentiates among the various ways of dealing with social problems in terms of the degree and nature of the participation that each affords the parties involved.

No matter how dispute-processing alternatives are described, it is clear that the way in which they are organized and structured affects the way people deal with their problems. The way in which courts and other third-party alternatives operate helps to determine the way in which individuals perceive and interpret their problems. Third parties, which, like umpires at sporting events, are positioned in anticipation of conflict, facilitate both the perception of trouble when it occurs and its resolution. Such remedy systems regularly supervise the execution of potentially troublesome events. This is exemplified by the supervision by the National Labor Relations Board of elections in which workers decide whether they wish to be represented by a labor union. Should trouble occur, should questions be raised about the propriety of someone's performance or about the interpretation of an event, these kinds of remedy systems will already have at hand information gathered in the course of their normal monitoring activity that can provide the basis for settlement. These kinds of third parties are already present before disputes occur. They do not have to be called in. The dispute does not have to be explained to them because they have already observed it. Furthermore, the very positioning of these third parties with regard to relationships and situations prior to the occurrence of trouble facilitates its identification and declaration by expressing, in a symbolic way, the expectation that trouble is a normal part of those relationships and situations. In baseball, the positioning of umpires at every base indicates a general expectation that disputes will regularly occur and that judgments will regularly be required. The fact that such an expectation exists means that people will feel less hesitant about making a fuss than they would if third parties had to be sought out and informed about the problem.

When disputants have to seek out third parties, the significance of their declaration of trouble is magnified both in their minds and in the minds of others. Reactive procedures force the troubled party to come forward in a visible way, to step out of the normal trend of the troubled relationship.[6] They also impose costs special to each case by requiring the parties involved in a problem to describe and interpret the transaction or the context in which the problem developed. Courts, as a third-party dispute institution, thus deter the declaration of trouble by emphasizing its disruptive effects and manage the trouble by placing the burden of fact finding and interpretation on the parties themselves.

Different third parties see disputes in different ways. Whether any disagreement is seen and dealt with as an isolated incident or as part of a pattern of similar incidents may influence whether disputants will seek one or another kind of third-party help. Third parties who operate in a private and informal manner generally mediate disputes, that is, they see any single dispute in a broad context; they try to shape trouble, problems, or conflict into "disagreements" and to restore order by getting the parties to the trouble to come to an agreement. Public, formal alternatives, like courts, attempt to transform personal problems into disputes over questions of fact or over competing interpretations of rights and rules; they try to produce a more limited version of the dispute and render verdicts that are in conformity with those rights and rules—verdicts that the parties may or may not find agreeable. As a result, parties who desire to retain control over the ultimate resolution of their problem will try to avoid third-party remedy systems that are public and formal.[7] When a dispute is brought to court, the parties are, in essence, agreeing to abide by a decision before they know what that decision is.

The way in which third-party remedy systems account for the emergence of trouble in a relationship also influences the way people will deal with that trouble. Those which try to settle troubles by determining whether someone violated a social norm and by assigning causal or moral responsibility will not be attractive to people who have long-standing personal relationships. These people will generally see greater ambivalence in the evolution and continuance of their trouble than such a settlement procedure recognizes. Typically, in a marital dispute, the spouses may find it difficult to accurately trace the blame. So complex is their relationship that there are no clear causes of any single dispute. Furthermore, when remedy systems focus on the question of who did what and who is at fault, they may exacerbate the original trouble that needed to be settled. Relationships can best survive the trauma of an open declaration of trouble if the procedure invoked to deal with that trouble places it in the context of the complex moral history of the parties' relationship and thus serves to obscure partially whatever particular incident gave rise to the present trouble.

The resolution of troubles in public by formal remedy systems like courts generally has formal institutionalized precedent value. Decisions in one case become the basis for subsequent decisions in similar cases; this means that when the "judge" attempts to resolve a particular trouble in the present, that "judge" must fashion a settlement with an eye toward what other parties in future cases may make of it.[8] For example, when parties bring problems to court they lose control over the context in which their problems are perceived. Present problems are placed in a context of the past and the future, which may be entirely divorced from the needs and interests of the parties themselves. Furthermore, their troubles become important to a wider audience. Their problems are played out before a public that is interested because of the bearing the decision may have on the future adjudication of its own problems. The court forces litigants to present their problems in such a way as to give them meaning in the context of a past and future with which judges must deal and in such a way that outside parties can read its meaning for themselves and their problems. A settlement that occurs in private is, in contrast, relieved of this burden of publicity; the parties are under no obligation to be "other directed" in their interpretation of their own problems.

By choosing to employ different third-party remedy systems, the parties to a troubled relationship express different things about themselves and their interactions. People who employ private, informal alternatives, alternatives that promote negotiation and compromise, acknowledge some potential community of interest. Their choice implies that they recognize that there is more to their relationship than the trouble itself. It further signifies that they have greater trust in each other than in the type of normative systems that usually govern public, formal procedures. When the parties choose a public, formal alternative, they express a shared belief in the reasonableness of the intervener and in the validity of the normative system that is represented. They express greater faith in the reasonableness and ability of the third party to make distinctions between them than in their own ability to come to a mutually satisfactory agreement. When parties have had no prior relationship, and when they expect none to develop in the future, they have no basis for believing in their mutual reasonableness and ability to compromise. When they have had prior relations, the kind of context that makes compromise feasible is more likely to be present.[9]

One cannot accurately understand the way in which courts function or the way in which disputes are processed and sometimes translated into lawsuits without taking account of the alternatives that are available to disputants. Furthermore, like the man with the broken television set, most people move reluctantly, if at all, into third-party arenas and especially reluctantly into courts. To understand this reluctance it is necessary to understand the structure and operation of third-party dispute-processing institutions, which compete with courts for society's dispute-processing business. The readings facilitate such an understanding.

Notes

1. This man was interviewed as part of a research project on small claims courts. See Austin Sarat, "Alternatives in Dispute Processing: Litigation in a Small Claims Court," *Law and Society Review* 10 (1976), 339.

2. See Leon Festinger, *A Theory of·Cognitive Dissonance* (Evanston, Ill.: Row, Peterson, 1957).

3. For a discussion of the costs of "lumping it," see Richard Danzig and Michael Lowy, "Everyday Disputes and Mediation in the United States," *Law and Society Review* 9 (1975), 675.

4. Arthur Leff, "Ignorance, Injury and Spite," *Yale Law Journal* 80 (1970), 1.

5. See Philip Gulliver, *Neighbors and Networks* (Berkeley: University of California Press, 1971).

6. Donald Black, "The Mobilization of Law," *Journal of Legal Studies* 2 (1973), 125.

7. Martin Shapiro, "Courts," in *The Handbook of Political Science*, Vol. 5, Fred Greenstein and Nelson Polsby eds. (Reading, Mass.: Addison-Wesley, 1975), pp. 321–371.

8. Martin Shapiro, "Toward a Theory of Stare Decisis," *Journal of Legal Studies* 1 (1972), 125.

9. On the importance of the prior relationship among disputants, see Sarat, *op. cit.*, note 1, and Donald Black, "The Social Organization of Arrest," *Stanford Law Review* 23 (1971), 1087.

1

Courts and Conflict Resolution: Problems in the Mobilization of Adjudication

Austin Sarat and Joel B. Grossman

If, as Edward Banfield and James Wilson suggest, politics ". . . arises out of conflict and . . . consists of the activities by which conflict is carried on,"[1] then political science should be concerned with the way conflicts are defined, interpreted for public consumption and managed in society. . . .

Two generic types of conflict-resolving tendencies in political institutions have been identified. The first, with which political scientists are most familiar, is *nonadjudicative*. Institutions which are primarily nonadjudicative are concerned with the formulative and prescriptive aspects of lawmaking. Conflict resolution in nonadjudicative institutions, such as legislatures, tends to be universalistic—more concerned with general rules or standards for future application than with the equities between two or more parties currently in dispute. Additionally, nonadjudicative institutions deal with the needs of broad and un-named classes or groups rather than of individuals, with "issues and symbols" rather than specific pronouncements, and with general, often imprecise, claims of deprivation or need. They are concerned with individual problems only insofar as these are symptomatic of social problems which are visible, intense and broad in scope.

Institutions which are primarily *adjudicative* deal with conflicts through third party intervention. Often the parties in dispute participate in its resolution through presentation of reasoned arguments. Adjudicative institutions such as courts are particularistic in form and process, and most often concerned with individual level disputes. The impact of adjudicative decisions initially extends only to the parties in dispute, although it may also have much broader policy implications. Theoretically, adjudicative institutions are more concerned with enforcing existing norms than with creating new ones. Furthermore, they are almost totally "reactive." Unlike nonadjudicative bodies, which also search out or try to anticipate problems before they arise, adjudicative institutions rely on private individuals or groups or other government agencies to bring problems to their attention. They rely on the initiative of private parties to set the agenda of issues on which public officials act. They can take no part in defining, interpreting, and managing conflict until they are

Reprinted by permission of the American Political Science Association from *American Political Science Review* 69 (1975), 1200-1217. Most footnotes have been omitted.

"mobilized."[2] As a result, adjudicative institutions are not well suited to resolving problems that private parties do not or cannot perceive, or wish to ignore.

. . .

In this paper, we explore the management of conflict by a variety of adjudicative institutions, both public and private. We look for a common thread of dispute-solving techniques in institutions with different legal statuses and formal structures, varying degrees of visibility and extending over a wide range of substantive areas. Our comparison of courts to other types of adjudicative bodies is designed to show both similarities and differences of task, and to underscore the interrelated nature of their functions. Additionally, since all types of adjudicative institutions are dependent ultimately on the initiative of outside parties, we examine the conditions which facilitate or inhibit their involvement in defining, interpreting and managing conflict. Our intention is to highlight the consequences of judicial resolution of some disputes, but not others, by describing the kind of institutions which deal with these "other" disputes, how such disputes are settled, and why people choose (or are required to use) particular adjudicative mechanisms when the need for dispute settlement arises.

Courts and Other Adjudicators

The very attributes which distinguish courts from other political institutions—their particularized focus and their reactive nature—are most useful in connecting judicial functions and those of nongovernmental dispute-resolving institutions. Yet adjudicative bodies also differ among themselves. Their differences, as we shall suggest, may be especially important in determining the conditions under which courts and other adjudicators are mobilized and involved in conflict and conflict resolution.[3]

With any particular dispute settlement institution comes a special set of participants, perhaps a different set of rules, and a distinctive style. Each alternative may provide its own kind of "justice"; some proceed without reference to general rules which are known and articulated in advance; others operate according to such rules. Some provide a process of judgment in which it is the status of the parties in dispute, or the preferences of the judge, which determine the outcome; others require impartiality. Courts, for example, generally emphasize greater procedural regularity than do other adjudicative institutions. Furthermore, public adjudicative decision making is, in theory, supposed to encompass the marshaling of reasons and justifications by an impartial arbiter. Yet reasoned decisions and equitable results are not the uniform product of public dispute settling, nor are they uniquely found in the public arena.

The structure of a dispute-resolving institution may have an important influence on the way the dispute is presented; indeed it may affect the basic nature of the dispute itself. This is as true in moving from informal to more formal means of conflict resolution as it is recognized widely to be true in moving from the trial to appellate stages of litigation. Finally, any particular institution may also carry with it some limitations on the available remedies, and thus indirectly affect the nature of the settlement which is possible. Participants have to agree to play by the rules of the institution; often this requires that they redefine their interests, goals and strategies.

Variables which have been used to distinguish among adjudicative institutions include the level of coerciveness, the scope and severity of available sanctions, the applicable

TABLE 1-1
A Typology of Adjudicative Dispute Resolution

	Formal	Informal
Public	Court trials/some types of administrative agency procedures, e.g., wage-price boards	Police in family quarrels/plea bargaining/administrative agency inquiries (hearing examiners) and consent agreements, such as the resolution of most tax disputes and anti-trust actions/pre-trial conferences/parole boards/state civil rights commissions/juvenile courts pre-*Gault*/police review boards
Private	College disciplinary boards/rabbinical or other ecclesiastical courts/arbitration of labor disputes/some bar association grievance committees	Settlement of automobile accident claims/marriage counseling/debt adjustment/reconciliation by family, community, or religious leader

norms, and the extent of third party intervention. We have chosen two other variables which appear to differentiate particularly well among the most common adjudicative alternatives. These variables are the level of formality in the procedures used and the degree of "publicness." The level of formality is defined by the presence of a specialized judicial role, specialized rules of evidence and procedure, written records, established channels of appeal and the swearing in of witnesses. An institution is considered public if it is part of the established government apparatus and if the coercive power of the state can be used to enforce its decisions.

The four-cell table presented above depicts, somewhat artificially, four "ideal types" of adjudicative dispute-settling alternatives; each represents a combination of our key variables, hence the cell labels: Private-Formal, Private-Informal, Public-Formal, and Public-Informal. The categories are not pure types, merely regions sliced from a graph of two continuous variables. We are looking for the predominant characteristics of each type of adjudicative alternative while recognizing the impurities in the forms which we have assigned to each. Below we elaborate on these characteristics and we illustrate the way differences among adjudicative institutions may help account for differences in the way they are mobilized and involved in conflict and conflict management.

Private-Informal Dispute Settlement

The simplest form of private-informal dispute settlement occurs in the interaction between two individuals or groups.[4] Conflicts generally arise in these dyadic settings, and the first attempts at resolution also generally occur at this level, usually in the form of direct negotiation and two-party bargaining. Only if such efforts prove unsuccessful, or if the expectation of failure in this context is so great that no attempt at direct negotiation is made, does third party resolution within an adjudicative context become relevant. When a third party is called into the dispute he may act as a "judge," or mediator, but may not necessarily be bound by any formal, codified rules.

Of course there are rules which he must follow, but they will not predominate; at most they may provide a context of expectations in which private, informal settlements may occur. The adjusters of disputes in a private, informal setting will not have any formal connection with the state, although in some cases they may have to be licensed by the state or by a quasi-private organization of professionals which exercises a delegated licensing function. The third-party mediator may be chosen because he has status, position, respect, power, money or the alleged power to invoke sanctions in behalf of a deity or some other supra-human force. Or he may have none of these but simply be the designated agent of an organization set up to handle specific disputes. The technique of bringing disputes to a third party may be the choice of both disputants, or of one but not the other party to a conflict, or it may be the result of private norms or expectations of a subcultural group which "require" that disputes be settled, as much as possible, within the group.[5]

Private-informal dispute resolution is found in all societies. In the United States, it is found in religious and ethnic communities, in the work of trained professionals such as marriage counselors, in various commercial relationships, and even in supermarkets. In all of these settings, private-informal adjudication is based on the assumption that the parties to a dispute will agree about what matters are in dispute and will trust the person called upon to act in an adjudicative role.

Societies differ in the extent to which private, informal modes of dispute settlement predominate, and in the extent to which the norms of private settlement affect the operations of more public and formal institutions. Japan, for instance, seems marked by the ubiquity of such private-informal conflict resolving devices. Henderson reports that private adjudication in Japan has been and still is effective ". . . in settling the vast majority of disputes."[6] The third party is generally a man of higher social status than the disputants, and the role of the adjudicator or mediator is enhanced by the persistence of remnants of traditional social deference. It is promoted by a strong cultural preference for harmony and saving face over claiming one's "rights." In Japan, in contrast to the United States, law and right are entirely different concepts and not just two sides of the same coin. . . .

. . .

Public-Informal Dispute Settlement

Adjudication of disputes also proceeds through public-informal methods. These methods involve the informal intervention by agents of the state to solve disputes. Such dispute resolution is utilized to complement the needs of public, formal institutions by reducing their operating burdens through the delegation of discretion to actors whose behavior in working out disputes is less often guided by standardized norms or procedures than by role relevant routines. Likewise, dispute settlement in this context reflects not only official norms of substance and procedure but also, within broad limits, the organizational commitments of the public agents involved. Thus, the needs of the police to maintain order have been shown often to be incompatible with the norms of enforcing the law, and both are not necessarily consistent with due process rights of arrested persons and rules defining proper police behavior. Wilson argues that when a choice must be made, most policemen will choose the order maintenance orientation, which gives them "substantial discretion over matters of greatest importance in a situation that is, by definition, one of conflict."[7] This choice is perhaps best illustrated when police are called upon to act as resolvers of marital disputes. More often than not the officer acts to "cool things off" rather than to make an arrest. He does not see it as his primary duty to determine who is right and who is wrong; indeed to do so might only exacerbate the disturbance he is trying to quell. Rather his main concern is to restore calm and find a way "of mollifying everyone." He can act this way because his presence carries with it the authority of state power and the threat of arrest, although he does not follow the procedural regularities that would be observed in a more formal setting.

Avoidance of procedural regularity in the pursuit of more immediate and more efficient conflict resolution is also characteristic of plea bargaining, of what used to be the norm of informality in juvenile courts before the United States Supreme Court's *Gault* decision,[8] and in the pretrial conference which has come to play an increasing role in facilitating the settlement of civil suits in the United States. In the case of plea bargaining and juvenile justice, the defendant is induced to settle his "conflict with the law" through an informal, bargaining process. Thus plea bargaining may be less like other types of adjudication, in which the roles of "judge" and adversary are clearly separated, than the kind of dyadic negotiations which often precede resort to adjudication. . . .

The emerging institution of the pretrial conference performs essentially the same function for civil cases. If the parties are unable to resolve their differences privately, the judge, in chambers, will informally discuss the case with both sides in the hope that a compromise will emerge. The judge cannot announce in advance of trial how he would decide the case. But, based on his experience, he can suggest possible outcomes which would ensue if the case went to a jury or suggest the limits of damages "normally" awarded in similar types of cases. The judge has no power to compel an agreement, but "helping" the parties to do so is certainly in his interest. The pretrial conference is considerably less ritualized and the role of the judge as mediator less managerial than that of the prosecutor in plea bargaining. But it serves a comparable function in allowing the judge to keep up with his caseload while reducing the costs and risks to the disputants. . . .

The common thread connecting all public-informal methods of dispute resolution is their proximity to the formal arena of the courts and to third-party adjudication by a judge or other public official, as well as their reliance on private bargaining within this context. There are no formal "rules," but a set of norms and mutual expectations gives these processes some structure. Indeed, in some cases, of which plea bargaining is the best example, the process by which informal settlements are reached has itself become bureaucratized. A relatively small group of actors is involved in any one jurisdiction, regularized relationships and mutual dependencies develop, and the needs of the bureaucracy for compromise and accommodation frequently predominate.

. . .

Private-Formal Dispute Settlement

In this category the dispute settlers remain private actors but they carry out their functions in accord with certain agreed upon and standardized procedures. They are more likely to act as "judges" than mediators, although role definitions may be fluid. Such formal but private tribunals are found within the confines of private organizations or associations, professional groups, as well as within certain subcultural groups. These tribunals exist to settle conflicts between group members, conflicts which cannot be settled informally but which, for some reason, the parties are reluctant to move into the public arena. Where group membership is conditioned by a voluntary or imposed acceptance of certain norms, or a code of conduct, the enforcement of such norms will typically be handled at several levels within the group. Those breaches which cannot be settled or sanctioned informally will usually have to be settled by more formal means. Although the rules and procedures followed by such tribunals may bear some resemblance to those of the courts, those rules and procedures remain private and often diverge substantially from those employed in the public sector.

Many trade associations have established their own formal arbitration machinery for the settlement of disputes among members. Similarly, labor-management disputes are often brought before arbiters, designated in advance, whose decisions are binding by mutual consent of the disputants and ultimately enforceable by private sanctions and by the courts. Agreement to submit disputes to private but formal arbitration is characteristic of parties whose relationship involves long-term performance or other aspects of permanence.

· · ·

Private-formal dispute-settling devices share some similarities but also vary widely. What they have in common is a court-like procedure for settling disputes among group members (even the complaint of an "outsider" about the conduct of a group member, e.g., a legal or medical malpractice accusation, is considered as the occasion for an inquiry rather than as a strict adversary proceeding. Thus it becomes a dispute between a group and one of its members). Decision makers are not agents of the state, but may be regarded by group members as possessing some sort of jural authority based on the stipulations of a prior contract or flowing from delegated state authority. Compliance may be purely voluntary, as in the case of a religious court, or induced by potential sanctions (e.g., loss of license, loss of hospital privileges for a doctor, etc.) or the ultimate threat of a spillover into the public courts with greater potential consequences. . . .

Public-Formal Dispute Settlement

The final arena of adjudicative conflict resolution is both public and formal, and is best exemplified by courts. Although there is a wide gap between the highest appellate courts and the now nearly extinct justice of the peace courts, certain characteristics are shared. All are agencies of the state and vested with its coercive power. Most judicial personnel are trained in the law. Though individual discretion is a significant factor in the operation of courts, on the whole they are expected to operate congruently with procedural norms such as those described by Lon Fuller as the "inner morality" of the law.[9] Nonjudicial public bodies are frequently held to comparable, if not identical, standards in their adjudicative functions.

Whereas the optimal goal of dispute resolution at a simpler level is the mutual satisfaction of the parties, at this level the emphasis falls more heavily on rights and duties. Moreover the institutional self-interest of adjudicative bodies which are public and formal plays some role in the outcome of disputes they help to settle. A concern to do justice to the parties while maintaining institutional power and prestige often requires preference for one or the other. This potential internal conflict is but one expression of the traditional ambivalence of Americans toward law and the judicial system. The conflicting demands we make of our courts also require them to balance considerations of state with considerations of private justice. Though technically they must be particularistic, in fact they cannot function legitimately without paying some attention to a broader universe of concerns. This is particularly true as one moves up the judicial ladder, where the specific grievances of the original disputants are rarely the sole focus of attention.

The rules which govern access and establish the procedural framework of adjudicative bodies are variables of critical importance. What kinds of disputes are to be decided, who can bring these disputes, and what kinds of solutions are possible are among the most important determinants of the involvement of public-formal adjudicators in defining, managing, and interpreting conflict. In contrast to private, informal mechanisms, the "rules" for decision in courts do not come from the parties themselves. Their sources are many—statutes, prior decisions governed by the rule of precedent, and evolving policy considerations responsive to current demands. Recent relaxation of the rules of standing and class actions, and those governing habeas corpus challenges to criminal convictions, have opened new channels of access. Changes in the substantive law also promote increased use of the courts as interests seek to take advantage of newly favorable rules.

Unlike other adjudicative institutions, those that are both public and formal generally require, either explicitly or implicitly, that parties in dispute be represented by legal specialists, people who claim unique knowledge of the procedural and substantive rules which govern access to and the operation of public-formal adjudicative institutions.[10] These specialists act on behalf of the parties to try to shape and structure the issues presented to these institutions and the way the issues are perceived and handled by them. Legal specialists play a critical "gatekeeping" role. They can influence and often determine the conditions under which courts and similar types of adjudicative institutions become involved in conflict management; and they will play a crucial role in defining the goals and objectives of litigation.

Public-formal dispute mechanisms are usually more oriented toward zero-sum decisions than are the less formal mechanisms we have noted. Additionally, they generally require disputants to narrow their definitions of issues in such a way as to identify unambiguously, if sometimes artificially, the nature of their problems. One example is in divorce cases, where the courts may focus on one incident in what is a complex and often not very clear-cut series of problems. In spite of the zero-sum nature and formality of many of their procedures, public-formal adjudicators occasionally do seek compromise and flexibility. Since they are substantively more concerned with right or wrong, and with enforcing general norms, than with the resumption of "normal" relations between the parties, the processes through which this flexibility is introduced may be quite unique. A number of means have been devised for reconciling new experiences and expectations with past values, while at the same time preserving at least the illusion that the law is consistent over time. The development of equity is one well-known technique of providing "justice" to the parties where a strict application of the law would be unjust. Furthermore, the formal adjudication of disputes is, at least in some countries, an essential if somewhat awkward means of reinforcing or changing public policy. This is bound to have an important effect on the way in which essentially private or localized disputes are settled. For those who seek to bring public norms to bear in essentially private disputes, and thus broaden the range of perspectives relevant to their problem, litigation is an attractive mode of participation. For them the "public regardingness" which is attached to all disputes brought to the courts is an advantage which outweighs group ties or cultural norms designed to discourage this form of political participation.

We have described and analyzed a variety of adjudicative alternatives which disputants employ to resolve particular disputes. As a general rule, we, like Herbert Jacob, believe that the likelihood that parties will bring disputes to courts varies inversely with the availability of less formal, and less public alternatives.[11] Where informal public or private remedies of all types are available they generally provide less costly means (in the psychological as well as material sense) of settling disputes and as such will be more attractive than formal, public bodies. . . .

. . .

The Impact of Adjudicative Mobilization

The various types of adjudicative processes we have discussed may exist separately or in combination; where they do exist in the same society their functioning is not clearly insulated or distinct. This is true both with respect to structure and methods of operation. Adjudication often is only a phase or tactic in ongoing processes of conflict resolution. Settlements reached through adjudication are not always definitive. Indeed, a common strategy of adjudication is to prolong and widen a dispute rather than settle it. Frequently, adjudication is only conclusive for the parties but not for the issue.

Even after "settlement," conflict and the need for conflict resolution often continue. Current solutions become part of future problems which, in turn, may involve a return to some of the adjudicative alternatives which we have discussed previously; or they may involve the displacement of conflict into a nonadjudicative setting. The processes by which disputes are resolved result in the fragmentation of some conflicts. This fragmentation is often required by the norms and procedures of the various agencies of dispute resolution. If an agency is equipped to handle only certain types of issues, conflicting parties are forced to sublimate or divert parts of their dispute which go beyond those issues. As a result disputes are often settled piecemeal. The phenomenon of fragmentation certainly is not unique to the judicial process, but it may help to account for the lack of finality often associated with court decisions.

In terms of the structure of dispute-settling alternatives, where a society possesses the full range of conflict-resolving devices, they can be depicted best in the form of a pyramid, with the more numerous private-informal mechanisms composing the foundation and the least numerous and more residual public and formal devices congregated at the top.[12] There is no strict hierarchical relationship intended here. The dimensions of publicness and formality, while they clearly increase as one approaches the top of the pyramid, do not always go together in the same proportion. Symmetry would be a poor guide to understanding this pyramid, yet it is not formless or without structure.

. . .

Notes

1. Edward Banfield and James Q. Wilson, *City Politics* (New York: Vintage, 1963), p. 7.

2. Mobilization refers to the process through which adjudicative institutions become involved in the definition, interpretation and management of conflict. Litigation refers exclusively to the mobilization of courts.

3. The similarities and differences among courts and other dispute-settling institutions have been the subject of an extensive treatment by Richard Abel, "A Comparative Theory of Dispute Institutions in Society," *Law and Society Review* 8 (Winter 1974), 217–347.

4. We recognize that many "potential" disputes are either suppressed by the individual feeling aggrieved or are displaced onto others not directly involved. This self-suppression or displacement is often practiced by people who fear being labeled as troublemakers.

It is exemplified when people complain about family life while at work and about work life while at home but never make their feelings known in the appropriate setting.

5. For a description of this phenomenon as it applies to organized crime in the United States, see Donald R. Cressey, *Theft of a Nation: The Structure and Operations of Organized Crime in America* (New York: Harper & Row, 1969), Chaps. 8 and 9.

6. Don Henderson, "Law and Political Modernization in Japan," in *Political Development in Modern Japan,* ed. Robert Ward (Princeton: Princeton University Press, 1969), p. 449.

7. James Q. Wilson, *Varieties of Police Behavior* (Cambridge: Harvard University Press, 1968), p. 21.

8. *In Re Gault,* 387 U.S. 1 (1967).

9. Lon Fuller, *The Morality of Law* (New Haven: Yale University Press, 1964), Chap. 2.

10. This requirement is not adhered to in all courts. In fact, some courts have been established so as to avoid the need to rely upon legal specialists. For a discussion of one type of court where lawyers are generally not employed, see Barbara Yngvesson and Patricia Hennessey, "Small Claims, Complex Disputes: A Review of the Small Claims Literature," *Law and Society Review* 9 (Winter 1975), 219-274.

11. See Herbert Jacob, *Debtors in Court* (Chicago: Rand McNally, 1969), p. 20.

12. . . . Our use of the metaphor is descriptive only. Certainly it would be contrary to much that we say elsewhere in this paper to endorse a top-down view of the legal system. Morton Grodzins's "Marble Cake" metaphor, by which he described the federal system, might almost be more appropriate. Grodzins, "Centralization and Decentralization in the American Federal System," in *A Nation of States,* ed. Robert Goldwin (Chicago: Rand McNally, 1963), pp. 1-4.

2

The Mediator, the Judge and the Administrator in Conflict-Resolution

Torstein Eckhoff

I. Introduction

Conflicts between people are sometimes resolved by a third party who helps to bring about a reconciliation or makes a decision by which they abide. The conflict-resolver, who in the following will be referred to as the "third party," can be a father or mother who stops a quarrel between children, or a woman who chooses one of two rival suitors, or a court which settles a legal dispute or the United Nations which resolves an international conflict. The purpose of this article is to discuss some of the conditions for attempting such third party intervention and for bringing about positive results.

· · ·

II. Conditions for the Participation of a Third Party in Conflict-Resolution

There can be various reasons for the participation of a third party in the resolution of conflicts.

Sometimes he controls the object about which the parties are disputing. He is, for instance, an employer who is going to fill a position for which two applicants are competing, or a woman who has two suitors to choose from. It is conceivable enough that such a third party leaves the two parties to resolve the conflict on their own, but the fact that he controls the object is in any case a condition which increases the probability that he will make the decision.

The third party's interest in having the conflict resolved is also an important factor. In those cases where he controls the disputed object, his interest will often consist of being able to secure, through the decision, services in return, for instance, the performance of work by the person he employs. The value of the compensation often depends on how the conflict is resolved. I assume that the third party, all else being equal, will be less inclined to leave the decision to others the stronger his interest in the outcome is.

Reprinted by permission from *Acta Sociologica* 10 (1966), 148–172. Footnotes and references have been omitted.

The third party can be interested in having the conflict resolved even if he does not control the good which is in dispute. He has, for instance, interests in common with one or both parties, or he suffers injury or inconvenience in some way if the conflict continues. Parents' interest in adjusting disputes between children and the state's interest in settling conflicts between citizens may be mentioned as examples. There are also cases where desires or demands to settle a dispute do not come (or not solely) from the third party, but (also) from others, e.g., from the relatives, friends, neighbors or colleagues of the parties, from the state or another organization, etc. As a common designation for all these I use the expression "the environment." The environment may have many different ways of forcing or convincing the parties to bring the conflict before a third party. Sometimes organized force can be applied and sometimes various kinds of unorganized influence (threats, persuasion, etc.). Whether or not the power will be used depends on many things, among others on how strongly the environment considers its interests threatened if the conflict situation continues. All other things being equal, I assume that a conflict will be more threatening for the environment the stronger the competing interests and the disagreement of the parties are. I assume that pressure from the environment will point more strongly in the direction of third party intervention the less possibility the parties have for resolving the conflict in another way.

So far I have only spoken about the forces which affect the parties from outside. But also the attitude of the parties themselves is of significance. In the first place, it is possible to conceive of cases where none of the parties is interested in having the conflict resolved, but where the third party or the environment demands it of them. Mother has decided, for instance, that one of the children shall do an errand, and a discussion develops between the children as to who shall do so. None of them is interested in coming to any result because both of them enjoy the quarrel and would like to have the displeasure of going to do the errand postponed as long as possible. In the second place, it often happens that one party, but not the other, is interested in having the conflict resolved. He demands, for instance, that the other party should be punished or surrender the good, and the latter party finds nothing to lose and everything to gain by resisting a settlement. It is conceivable that the one who makes the demand is strong enough to force a solution on his own. But if he is not, it may become urgent for him to seek support in the environment or in a third party, in order to reach a settlement. Both the environment's, the third party's and the parties' attitudes to the conflict and their relative strength will in that case be significant.

A third situation, which I shall discuss in more detail, occurs when both parties are interested in having the conflict resolved. This will often be the case when the third party or another outsider controls the disputed object. The parties have for instance, both applied for the same position, proposed to the same girl, made claims to the same inheritance, or in some way come into conflict over some good which none of them can have any part of unless the dispute is settled. Both parties can also have other reasons for desiring a solution. They are, for example, negotiating about an exchange which will be advantageous for both of them, but cannot agree on the conditions. Or they are faced with a disastrous or, at least, an unpleasant situation if the conflict is not resolved. The parties in a labour-dispute may, for instance, be interested in avoiding a long strike from which both would lose, and in international conflicts the danger of war may have the same effect. Whether it is a question of attaining some good or avoiding some evil, the parties may operate with more or less long-range calculations. There are, for instance, cases where one party has no immediate interest in having the conflict resolved. He has, for instance, control over some good which his adversary claims, and without the intervention of a third party there is no possibility for taking it from him by force. But consideration for his future relationship to his opponent may nevertheless make him interested in resolving the conflict.

Even if both parties are interested in having the conflict resolved, they still have competing interests with respect to *what* the solution should be. Sometimes it even happens that the stronger the parties' *common* interest in resolving the conflict, the stronger are also their *competing* interests in the outcome. This is the case, for instance, where there is a dispute about the division of some good of which the parties can have nothing before the conflict is resolved. The more valuable the good is, the more important it is for both of them to have it divided in one way or another, and the more there is to win by ensuring the greatest possible share for himself at the expense of his opponent. . . .

. . .

The parties' common interest in finding a solution will in some cases make it superfluous to bring in a third party because they will manage on their own to come to agreement. Sometimes this happens so painlessly that a conflict-situation does not arise. Two children, for instance, get a chocolate-bar together and take it for granted that each of them shall have half, or both buyer and seller assume without further ado, that the market-price is the basis of a sale. Naturally, there also exist cases where there has been a conflict right from the beginning, but where this is settled by the parties gaining knowledge of the market-situation or of norms which both accept (for instance, a legal provision which regulates the relation between them and of which they were originally unaware). In such cases one can perhaps say that the market or the norm serves the function of a third party.

Cases also occur, however, in which the parties negotiate an agreement in spite of the fact that the relationship between them is not regulated by market-mechanisms or by norms which both accept and apply in the same way. A compromise which to some extent considers the interests of both, is the most likely solution in such a case. . . . But it is not always possible to reach a compromise through negotiations. In the following, I shall point to certain factors which can prevent or impede this form of conflict-resolution. It is important to consider these factors because it must be assumed that the probability for drawing a third party into the conflict is increased if the parties do not manage to resolve the conflict on their own, in spite of their both being interested in doing so.

There are cases where a compromise solution is excluded because the object of dispute is indivisible. The dispute, for instance, is about who should be the first to go through the door or into the life-boat, or who should perform a dangerous assignment for which only one person is needed. It may be that the parties come to an agreement in such a case by finding a method for resolving the conflict which both can accept, for instance, drawing lots. Or one may sacrifice himself for the other. He considers it his duty, for example, to be the last to abandon ship because he is the captain. In general, however, we may assume that the parties' possibilities for resolving conflicts on their own are reduced if compromises are excluded. This applies to a greater extent the stronger the competing interests the parties have and the greater emphasis they place on maintaining their interests.

. . .

I have, in what precedes, mentioned a number of examples to show that norms which one or both parties accept can facilitate conflict resolution. The norms may indicate directly how the difference should be treated, for instance, that the bar of chocolate should be divided equally between the children and that the captain should leave the ship last.

Or they may have indirect significance as, for example, the norm that promises should be kept, which can contribute to the creation of mutual confidence and thereby facilitate negotiations between the parties.

Disagreement about normative factors which the parties consider relevant for the solution, for instance, who is right or who is to blame, have, generally speaking, the opposite effect. Such disagreement can in certain cases be cleared away for instance, by one party arguing so strongly that he convinces his opponent, or by referring to written rules or presenting evidence (e.g., a written contract) to which the other yields. But often this does not succeed, so that negotiations which aim to find a compromise are the only manner in which the parties can resolve the conflict. Such negotiations present special difficulties when the parties disagree about the normative relations. As a rule there will be greater reluctance to renounce what one considers his right than to be accommodating on a mere question of interests. The reluctance may be due to a belief that "right will win in the end," so that it is unnecessary to give in, or it may be based on a feeling that it is morally more acceptable to "fight for one's right" than to "compromise" or to "make a deal" about it.

In the preceding, various factors which can create a need in the parties or others for bringing in a third party as a resolver of conflicts have been pointed out. The main points of view can be schematized as shown in Figure 2-1, where the following propositions are indicated (the numbers in parentheses refer to the arrows in the figure):

The greater the agreement between the parties concerning normative factors which they consider relevant for the solution, the greater is the probability of their being able to resolve the conflict on their own and the less need is there for bringing in a third party (1).

The greater the common interests of the parties for having the conflict resolved, the more probable is it that they will engage in resolving the conflict *either* on their own, *or,* if that leads to difficulties, by bringing in a third party (2 and 3).

The stronger the competing interests the parties have in the outcome, and the more they disagree on normative factors which they consider relevant, the less probable is it that they will be able to resolve the conflict on their own, and the greater need they have for bringing in a third party, presuming that they have common interests in having the conflict resolved (4 and 5).

The relationship of antagonism between the parties can make their environments interested in having the conflict resolved—if necessary with the help of a third party (6, 7 and 8). The third party may himself be interested in the conflict being resolved (9). His reactions and those of the environment may have the consequence that the parties become more interested in the conflict being resolved (10).

In the diagram it is also indicated that market-mechanisms facilitate conflict-resolution by the parties themselves and reduce the need for third party intervention (11), whereas the circumstance that a disputed good is indivisible operates in the opposite direction (12).

Even if the parties (or their environments) have a *need* to have the conflict resolved by a third party, it is not certain that they find someone suited to undertake the assignment. And if they find someone, it may *cost* so much (in terms of economic expenditures, delays, loss of prestige, etc.) that it does not pay. It is, naturally, also possible to conceive of cases where a third party—either on his own initiative or because the parties or their environments ask him—tries to resolve the conflict but does not succeed. A third party's potenti-

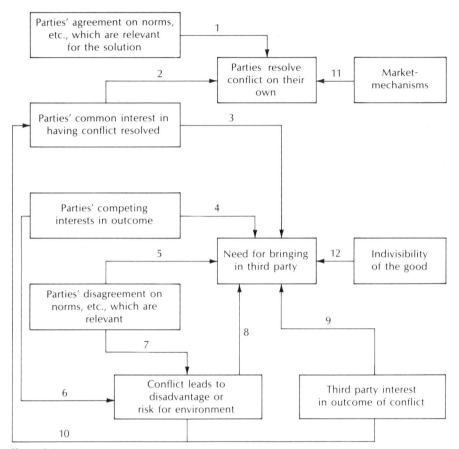

Figure 2-1.

alities for resolving conflicts and the parties' (or others') opinions of his suitability, depend both on characteristics of the conflict and of the third party and the procedure he follows. The connection between these factors will be discussed in the next section.

I distinguish in what follows among three different kinds of third parties, who are characterized by the methods which each of them uses: to mediate, to judge and to administer. They are described here as pure types ("ideal types" in Max Weber's sense). The resolvers of conflicts one meets in the world of reality can belong partly in one category, partly in another. A mother who resolves conflicts between children may, for instance, alternate by acting as a "mediator," a "judge" and an "administrator." She may also combine the methods in such a way that the single conflict-resolution has ingredients of more than one of them. And the person who is judge in a court of law does not have to be an outright "judge" in our meaning of the word, but may act occasionally as mediator or administrator. But even if many resolvers of conflicts are not fully covered by any of the ideal types, they may to a lesser or greater degree approach one of them.

Mediation consists of influencing the parties to come to agreement by appealing to their own interests. The mediator may make use of various means to attain this goal. He may work on the parties' ideas of what serves them best, for instance, in such a way that he gets them to consider their common interests as more essential than they did previously, or their competing interests as less essential. He may also look for possibilities of resolution which the parties themselves have not discovered and try to convince them that both will be well served with his suggestion. The very fact that a suggestion is proposed by an impartial third party may also, in certain cases, be sufficient for the parties to accept it. . . . The mediator also has the possibility of using promises or threats. He may, for instance, promise the parties help or support in the future if they become reconciled or he may threaten to ally himself with one of them if the other does not give in. A mediator does not necessarily have to go in for compromise solutions, but for many reasons he will, as a rule, do so. The compromise is often the way of least resistance for one who shall get the parties to agree to an arrangement. . . .

In order that both parties should have confidence in the mediator and be willing to cooperate with him and listen to his advice, it is important that they consider him impartial. This gives him an extra reason to follow the line of compromise. . . . For, by giving both parties some support, he shows that the interests of one lie as close to his heart as those of the other. Regard for impartiality carries with it the consequence that the mediator sometimes must display caution in pressing the parties too hard. That the mediator, for instance, makes a threat to one of the parties to ally himself with the opponent unless compliance is forthcoming, may be an effective means of exerting pressure, but will easily endanger confidence in his impartiality. This can reduce his possibilities for getting the conflict resolved if threats do not work and it can weaken his future prestige as a mediator.

The conditions for mediation are best in cases where both parties are interested in having the conflict resolved. The stronger this common interest is, the greater reason they have for bringing the conflict before a third party, and the more motivated they will be for cooperating actively with him in finding a solution, and for adjusting their demands in such a way that a solution can be reached.

. . .

That normative factors are considered relevant for the solution, can in certain cases be helpful during mediation. By referring to a norm (e.g., concerning what is right and wrong) the mediator may get the parties to renounce unreasonable demands so that their points of view approach each other. Even if the parties do not feel bound by the norms, it is conceivable that others consider it important that they be followed and that the mediator can therefore argue that a party will be exposed to disapproval if he does not accommodate.

. . .

If, however, the parties consider the norms as giving answers to the questions being disputed, but disagree on what the answers are, the possibilities for mediation will, as a rule, be weakened. In the first place, the probability that the conflict will at all be made the object of mediation is reduced, among other reasons, because bringing it before a judge will often be possible and more likely in these cases. Secondly, mediation which has been begun may be made difficult because of the parties' disagreement concerning the norms or the relevant facts. This is the more true the more inflexibly the opinions are opposed to each other and the more value-laden they are. . . .

. . .

The *judge* is distinguished from the mediator in that his activity is related to the level of norms rather than to the level of interests. His task is not to try to reconcile the parties, but to reach a decision about which of them is right. This leads to several important differences between the two methods of conflict resolution. The mediator should preferably look forward, toward the consequences which may follow from the various alternative solutions, and he must work on the parties to get them to accept a solution. The judge, on the other hand, looks back to the events which have taken place (e.g., agreements which the parties have entered into, violations which one has inflicted on the other, etc.) and to the norms concerning acquisition of rights, responsibilities, etc. which are connected with these events. When he has taken his standpoint on this basis, his task is finished. The judge, therefore, does not have to be an adaptable negotiator with ability to convince and to find constructive solutions, as the mediator preferably should be. But he must be able to speak with authority on the existing questions of norms and facts in order to be an effective resolver of conflicts.

The possibility for judging in a dispute presupposes that the norms are considered relevant to the solution. The norms may be more or less structured. They may consist in a formal set of rules (e.g., a judicial system, the by-laws of an organization or the rules of a game), in customs or only in vague notions of what is right and just. The normative frame of reference in which a decision is placed does not have to be the same—and does not even have to exist—for all those who have something to do with the conflict. What one person perceives as a judgment another may perceive an arbitrary command. If, however, *none* of those involved (the parties, the third party, the environment) applies normative considerations to the relationship because all consider it a pure conflict of interests, decision by judgment is excluded.

A decision may be a "judgment" (in the sense in which the term is used here) even if the parties do not comply with it. But the greater the possibility that a judgment will be lived up to, the more suitable judgment will be as a method of conflict-resolution, and the better reason will the person who desires a solution have for preferring that procedure. It is therefore of significance to map out the factors which promote and hinder compliance to judgments.

The parties' interests in the outcome play an important role in this connection. If the main thing for them is to have the dispute settled, and it is of secondary importance what the content of the solution is, it will require very little for them to comply with the judgment. If, on the other hand, there are strong and competing interests connected with the outcome, so that submission to the judgment implies a great sacrifice for one or both of the parties, the question of compliance is more precarious.

That one party (voluntarily or by force) submits to a judgment in spite of the sacrifice it means for him, may be due in part to norms and in part to the authority of the judge. There may be many reasons for the parties' respect for those *norms* on which the judge bases his decision, for instance, they may be internalized, or one fears gods' or people's punishment if one violates them, or one finds it profitable in the long run to follow them (e.g., because it creates confidence in one's business activities if one gains a reputation for law-abidance or because it makes the game more fun if the rules are followed). If the parties are sufficiently motivated to comply with the norms and these give exhaustive answers to the question under dispute, then relatively modest demands are made on the *judge's* authority. If he is regarded as having knowledge of the norms and as having ability to find the facts, this will be sufficient to assure that his judgments are respected. Sometimes this is a simple assignment which many can fulfill. . . .

If the parties are not sufficiently strongly motivated to comply with the norms which regulate their mutual rights and duties, or if they do not regard these as giving exhaustive answers to the matter of dispute, the judgment must appear as something more than a conveyance of information in order to command respect. The parties must, in one way or another, be bound or forced to adhere to it. One condition which may contribute to this is that, in addition to the primary norms which define the parties' mutual rights and obligations, there is also a set of secondary norms of adjudication which single out the judge as the proper person to settle the dispute and which possibly also impose upon the parties the duty to abide by his decision. That the judge is in this way equipped with *authority,* is in many cases sufficient reason for the parties to consider themselves bound to live up to his decision. But the establishment of authority often presupposes power, and even if the authority-relationship is established, it may sometimes be necessary to press through a decision by force. The power can reside with the judge, with someone he represents (e.g., the state) or with others who are interested in the decision being respected (e.g., the winning party or his relatives or friends). And it can have various bases: physical or military strength, control of resources on which the parties are dependent, powers of sorcery, etc. How *much* power is necessary depends partly on what other factors promote and hinder compliance, and partly upon the relative strength of the enforcing authority and the disobedient party.

That the parties and others have confidence in the judge's impartiality, promotes compliance to judgments. It strengthens the belief that the decisions he makes are right and it facilitates enforcement by making the application of force more legitimate. As mentioned before, it is also important for the mediator to appear impartial, but the manner of showing impartiality is different for the two kinds of third parties. To a certain extent the judge can display that he gives equal consideration to both parties, for instance, by giving both the same possibilities for arguing and for presenting evidence. But he cannot, like the mediator, systematically endeavour to reach compromises, because the norms sometimes demand decision in favor of one of the parties. If he finds that one party is completely right, he must judge in his favor, and the outcome of the case will not in itself be a testimony to his giving equal consideration to both.

But the judge has other possibilities for appearing impartial. Sometimes his person gives sufficient guarantee. He is, for instance, because of his high rank, his contact with supernatural powers, or his recognized wisdom and strength of character, regarded as infallible, or at least freed from suspicion of partisanship. The privilege of the judge to assume a retired position during the proceedings and not to engage in argumentation with the parties, makes it easier to ascribe such qualities to him than to the mediator. Another significant factor is that there are, as a rule, small possibilities for checking the rightness of a judgment because this presupposes knowledge of both the system of norms and the facts of the particular case. To maintain a belief that certain persons are infallible can, nevertheless, present difficulties, especially in cultures characterized by democratization and secularization. To reduce or conceal the human factor in decision-making will therefore often be better suited to strengthening confidence in the decisions. Letting the judge appear as a "mouthpiece of the law," who cannot himself exert any influence worth mentioning on the outcome of the cases tends to remove the fear that his own interests, prejudices, sympathies and antipathies may have impact on his rulings.

Tendencies to overestimate the influence of the norms, and underestimate the influence of the judge, may also have other functions than strengthening confidence in the judge's impartiality. Firstly, these tendencies contribute to the transmission of authority from the norm system to the individual decisions. Secondly, the conditions are favorable for a gradual and often almost unnoticeable development of a norm system through court practice, so that the resistance to change is reduced. And thirdly, the judge will be less exposed to criticism and self-reproach when he (both in his own and others' eyes) avoids appearing as personally responsible for his decisions. This is important because it might otherwise involve great strain to make decisions in disputes where the parties' contentions are strongly opposed to each other, where there are perhaps great interests at stake for both, and where it may be extremely doubtful who is right. It is therefore not surprising that many techniques have been used in the various judicial systems for the purpose of eliminating, limiting or concealing the influence of the judge. The use of ordeals and drawing of lots in the administration of justice may be mentioned as examples of this, and the same is true for the technique of judicial argumentation which gives the decisions the appearance of being the products of knowledge and logic, and not of evaluation and choice.

· · ·

The activity of judging is in these respects quite different from the activity of mediating. As mentioned before, the task of the mediator becomes more difficult the more emphasis the parties place on the normative aspects of the conflict (presupposing that there is disagreement about these, as there usually will be in conflict situations). The mediator, therefore, must try to "de-ideologize" the conflict, for instance, by stressing that interests are more important than the question of who is right and who is wrong, or by arguing that one ought to be reasonable and willing to compromise. The use of mediation in certain types of disputes, may tend to create or reinforce the norm that willingness to compromise is the proper behavior in conflict situations and thereby to reduce the significance of such norms as judges base their decisions on.

The contrasts between the two types of third party intervention make it difficult to combine the role of the judge and the role of the mediator in a satisfactory way. Indeed it does happen that a third party first tries to mediate between the parties and if that does not succeed, passes judgment. Also the reverse is conceivable: that a third party first passes judgment and then proceeds to mediate when he sees that the judgment will not be respected. But in both cases attempts to use one method may place hindrances in the way of the other. By mediating one may weaken the normative basis for a later judgment and perhaps also undermine confidence in one's impartiality as judge; and by judging first, one will easily reduce the willingness to compromise of the party who was supported in the judgment, and will be met by suspicion of partiality by the other.

· · ·

The *administrator* has in common with the judge that he *decides* how the conflict should be resolved. He does not, as the mediator, leave this to the parties. But in contrast to the judge, who merely pretends to determine what already *is* right, the administrator establishes an arrangement which has the character of being new. The administrator can indeed give certain consideration to existing normative positions, but his most important concern is what the rights and duties should be in the future. In this respect he has more in common with the mediator than with the judge.

Which considerations the administrator emphasizes in making his decision may otherwise vary. It may be his own interests he seeks to promote, or some organizational or social aim, for instance, to increase a company's sales, to maximize the national product or to strengthen the country's defense-preparedness. It is also possible to conceive of cases where he aims to promote the interests of the parties, but does not want to leave the decision to them because he considers them lacking in insight concerning what is in their best interest or because he knows that they have difficulty in reaching an agreement.

The person who will be able to resolve conflicts administratively must have sufficient power or authority to be able to force his will upon the parties. As mentioned before, this holds also for the judge at times, but for him it is not always necessary and, as a rule, so much will not be required because his decisions have stronger support in normative ideas than do the administrator's.

Sometimes the administrator's power depends on his control of the good about which the parties are disputing. . . . The administrator's influence may also have other bases, for instance, physical strength, personal leadership qualities, or norms which give him authority to decide over the parties. Several of these factors may be present at the same time and they may also be combined with control over material resources. Sometimes the administrator stands in a permanent relation of superiority to the parties and has many means of power at his disposal. We may, for example, think of the relationship between parents and children, school and pupils, management and employees, institutional staff and inmates, a public agency and its clients, or a state and its citizens.

In such social systems of which I have mentioned examples, the superior has many other tasks in relation to his inferiors besides resolving conflicts between them. And when he must resolve a conflict, he can, because of his position of power, often choose whether he will act as mediator, judge or administrator. For example, if children submit a question of dispute to their father he may say that: "You have to manage to reach an agreement on this yourselves," and restrict himself to mediating between them, or he may act as a judge and decide which of them is right, or in his capacity as administrator, give them an order about what the arrangement should be. Within certain limits the leadership of a company, an institution or a state has corresponding possibilities for choice and will act partly as administrator, partly as judge and partly as mediator in conflicts between inferiors.

Many factors may influence the choice among these procedures. On the one hand, it is of significance whether the superior is interested in the conflict being resolved in a particular direction. The stronger his interest in the outcome is and the less certainty he has that the desired result will be reached through mediation or judgment, the greater reason he has to act as administrator. But on the other hand, the question of costs also plays a role. If the inferiors are opposed to the superior intervening too actively in their differences, or if they have normative ideas which they think ought to be decisive for the solution, it is conceivable that they will react so strongly against being directed that their superior resigns himself to this. He may perhaps have sufficient power to enforce an administrative decision, even if the parties find it arbitrary, but he understands that this will demand so much effort on his part that it does not pay, or he is afraid that it will lead to new conflicts and unpleasantness. It often happens, for instance, that a superior in a company tries to mediate between his inferiors, even though he has authority to decide how the dispute should be resolved. The national authorities sometimes follow a similar practice, for instance, when business organizations or employer- and employee-organizations are in conflict on questions of prices, subsidies or wages. A government may find it wise, in such cases, to content itself with acting as mediator even if it could have resolved the conflict with injunctions or regulations and even if it has an interest in what the solution is.

Changes which occur in a social system may sometimes lead to the replacement of one method of resolution by another in certain types of conflicts. If, for instance, the power of the conflict-resolver increases or if his interest in the outcome becomes greater, it is conceivable that he begins to decide as administrator conflicts which he previously resolved by judgment or mediation. . . .

The development may also go in the opposite direction, so that the resolver of conflicts passes from being an administrator to being a judge or mediator in certain types of disputes. The reason for this may be that his interest in the outcome becomes smaller, or that the resistance against his administrative decisions increases because, for instance, norms have developed and the parties will only accept a judge. As an example we may think of a bureaucracy in which the leadership yields to the constant demands that promotion shall be based on seniority: instead of deciding freely who should advance, the leadership must restrict itself to evaluating who has the *right* to advancement.

. . .

In the preceding main section (II) attention was drawn to relationships which create the need (in the parties or others) for having a third party as a resolver of conflicts. In this section, the analysis is brought a step further by a comparison of three different methods for considering this need: mediation, judgment and administrative decision. The main points may be summarized as follows:

Administrative decision is more probable the greater interest the third party has in the outcome and the better the possibilities for enforcing his decision are. The stronger the resistance and the greater the costs the more is this probability reduced. Interplay among the factors mentioned here may sometimes lead to differentiation within an organization so that its leadership supports with its power of enforcement the decisions that it has left to independent judges.

Factors which counteract administrative decision increase the probability for judgment or mediation, yet in such a way that possibilities for enforcement in certain cases are a presupposition for conflict-resolution by judgment. It will normally be a condition for mediation that both parties are interested in having the conflict resolved. Otherwise the choice between judgment and mediation is determined primarily by how relevant norms are considered for the solution.

3

The Forms and Limits of Adjudication

Lon L. Fuller

The subject matter of this essay is adjudication in the very broadest sense. As the term is used here it includes a father attempting to assume the role of judge in a dispute between his children over possession of a toy. At the other extreme it embraces the most formal and even awesome exercises of adjudicative power; a Senate trying the impeachment of a President, a Supreme Court sitting in judgment on the power of the government of which it is a part, an international tribunal deciding a dispute between nations. . . .

As the term adjudication is used here its application is not restricted to tribunals functioning as part of an established government. It includes adjudicative bodies which owe their powers to the consent of the litigants expressed in an agreement of submission, as in labor relations and in international law. . . .

The problems that are the concern of this paper are those suggested by the two terms of the title, the *forms* and *limits* of adjudication. By speaking of the *limits* of adjudication I mean to raise such questions as the following: What kinds of social tasks can properly be assigned to courts and other adjudicative agencies? What are the lines of division that separate such tasks from those that require an exercise of executive power, or that must be entrusted to planning boards or public corporations? What tacit assumptions underlie the conviction that certain problems are inherently unsuited for adjudicative disposition and should be left to the legislature? More generally, to borrow the title of a famous article by Roscoe Pound, What are the limits of effective legal action?—bearing in mind that legislative determinations often can only become effective if they are of such a nature that they are suited for judicial interpretation and enforcement.

By the *forms* of adjudication I refer to the ways in which adjudication may be organized and conducted. . . . In general the questions posed for consideration are: What are the permissible variations in the forms of adjudication? When has its nature been so altered that we are compelled to speak of an "abuse" or a "perversion" of the adjudicative process?

Questions of the permissible forms and the proper limits of adjudication have probably been under discussion ever since something equivalent to a judicial power first emerged in

Reprinted by permission of the author from an unpublished manuscript, "The Forms and Limits of Adjudication," pp. 1-3, 6-9, 15-19, 21-22, 24-31, 34, 38-39, 43, 47-48, 51-53, 57-59, 61-63, 68-69, 74-78.

primitive society. In our own history the Supreme Court at an early date excluded from its jurisdiction certain issues designated as "political." This exclusion could hardly be said to rest on any principle made explicit in the Constitution; it was grounded rather in a conviction that certain problems by their intrinsic nature fall beyond the proper limits of adjudication, though how these problems are to be defined remains even today a subject for debate. . . .

[W]e shall have to begin our inquiry with an attempt to define "true adjudication," or adjudication as it might be if the ideals that support it were fully realized. In doing so we shall of necessity be describing something that never fully exists. Yet it is only with the aid of this nonexistent model that we can pass intelligent judgment on the accomplishments of adjudication as it actually is. Indeed, it is only with the aid of that model that we can distinguish adjudication as an existent institution from other social institutions and procedures by which decisions may be reached.

I.   The Two Basic Forms of Social Ordering

It is customary to think of adjudication as a means of settling disputes or controversies. This is, of course, its most obvious aspect. The normal occasion for a resort to adjudication is when parties are at odds with one another often to such a degree that a breach of social order is threatened.

More fundamentally, however, adjudication should be viewed as a form of social ordering, as a way in which the relations of men to one another are governed and regulated. . . . [A]n adjudicative determination will normally enter in some degree into the litigants' future relations and into the future relations of other parties who see themselves as possible litigants before the same tribunal. Even if there is no statement by the tribunal of the reasons for its decision, some reason will be perceived or guessed at and the parties will tend to govern their conduct accordingly.

If, then, adjudication is a form of social ordering, to understand it fully we must view it in its relation to other forms of social ordering. It is submitted that there are two basic forms of social order: *Organization by common aims* and *organization by reciprocity.* Without one or the other of these nothing resembling a society can exist.

These two forms of order represent the two basic ways in which men may, by coming together, secure an advantage for all participants. We may illustrate these forms very simply by assuming, first, that two men share an objective which neither could achieve without the aid of the other or could not achieve so easily without that aid. A roadway connects two farms with a highway; it becomes blocked by a boulder. Neither farmer is strong enough to remove the boulder by himself. When the two join forces to remove the boulder we have, obviously, organization or association by common aims. Now let us suppose that our two farmers are to a considerable extent engaged in "subsistence" farming. One of them has a large crop of onions, the other an abundance of potatoes. A trade of a portion of their respective crops may make each richer; to the potato-raising farmer the "last" potato is not so valuable as the "first" onion, and, of course, a surfeit of onions will put the other farmer in the reverse position. Here we have illustrated in its crassest and most obvious form organization or association by reciprocity.

It should be noticed that the conditions which make these two principles of order effective are directly opposite to one another. To make organization by reciprocity effective the participants must want different things; organization by common aims requires that the participants want the same thing or things.

In order to bring these forms of order into closer relation with adjudication let us now consider briefly their *forms* and *limits*. With respect to reciprocity the form of the relationship may run all the way from a tacit perception of the advantages of an association, scarcely rising to consciousness, to a highly formalized written contract or treaty. . . .

Association by common aims also varies over a wide range in the degree of its formality. At the one end of the spectrum, we have the small group all actively sharing and all understanding the same objectives. Such is the case of our farmers uniting to remove a roadblock. At an intermediate point on the scale of formality, we have the voluntary association, the political party, the labor union, the benevolent society. Here some general aims will commonly be shared actively by most intelligent members; other aims will be promulgated by the leaders which will not in any real sense be shared or even understood by most members; finally, some aims will be pursued by the leaders in the name of the association that will not even be known outside a small circle. In considering this constellation of objectives, it would not be forgotten that it is, in the long run, the actively shared and at least vaguely understood aims that give the association its motive power. Ascending farther along the scale of increasing formality, we finally encounter the nation or state. Here we have what may be truly called an involuntary association, in the sense that there is no readily available procedure by which the member may resign or effectively disclaim his membership. At the same time he is bound by rules enacted to secure certain objectives whether or not he approves of these objectives or even understands them. The extent to which he and other citizens actively share the objectives pursued by their government is something that varies from nation to nation and over time within a given nation. . . .

These remarks may seem something of a digression from adjudication. But since the analysis presented in this paper discerns an intimate connection between adjudication and what I have called the two basic forms of social ordering, it was thought wise to forestall at the outset at least the more obvious misunderstandings that may be engendered in the course of the discussion. It is now time, however, to place adjudication in its proper relation to the two basic forms of social organization.

II.   Adjudication as a Form of Social Ordering

In discussing reciprocity and organization by common aims I point out that these two forms of social ordering present themselves along a scale of varying formal explicitness. To some extent the same thing is true of adjudication. We talk, for example, of "taking our case to the forum of public opinion." Or, two men may argue in the presence of a third with a kind of tacit hope that he will decide which is right, but without any explicit submission of their dispute to his arbitrament.

On the very informal level, however, forms of social ordering are too mixed and ambiguous to make comparisons fruitful. It is only when a particular form or ordering explicitly controls a relationship that it can be set off clearly against alternative forms of ordering. For this reason, therefore, I am here employing *contract* to represent reciprocity in its formal and explicit expression. I shall take elections as the most familiar formalization of organization by common aims.

Adjudication, contract, and elections are three ways of reaching decisions, of settling disputes, of defining men's relations to one another. Now I submit that the characteristic feature of each of these forms of social ordering lies in the manner in which the affected party participates in the decision reached. This may be presented as follows:

Form of Social Ordering:	Mode of Participation by the Affected Party:
Contract	Negotiation
Elections	Voting
Adjudication	Presentation of proofs and reasoned arguments

It is characteristic of these three ways of ordering men's relations that though they are subject to variation—they present themselves in different "forms"—each contains certain intrinsic demands that must be met if it is to function properly. We may distinguish roughly between "optimum conditions," which would lift a particular form of order to its highest expression, and "essential conditions," without which the form of order ceases to function in any significant sense at all.

. . .

Now much of this paper will be concerned in carrying through with an analysis of the optimum and essential conditions for the functioning of adjudication. This whole analysis will derive from one simple proposition, namely, that the distinguishing characteristic of adjudication lies in the fact that it confers on the affected party a peculiar form of participation in the decision, that of presenting proof and reasoned arguments for a decision in his favor. Whatever heightens the significance of this participation lifts adjudication toward its optimum expression. Whatever destroys the meaning of that participation destroys the integrity of adjudication itself. Thus, participation through reasoned argument loses its meaning if the arbiter of the dispute is inaccessible to reason because he is insane, has been bribed or is hopelessly prejudiced. The purpose of this paper is to trace out the somewhat less obvious implications of the proposition that the distinguishing feature of adjudication lies in the mode of participation which it accords to the party affected by the decision.

But first it will be necessary to deal with certain objections that may be raised against my starting point, against the proposition, namely, that the "essence" of adjudication lies in the mode of participation it accords to the affected party.

III.   Adjudication and Rationality

It may be said that the essence of adjudication lies, not in the manner in which the affected party participates in the decision but in the office of judge. If there is a judge and a chance to appear before him, it is a matter of indifference whether the litigant chooses to present proofs or reasoned arguments. He may, if he sees fit, offer no argument at all, or pitch his appeal entirely on an emotional level, or even indicate his willingness that the judge decide the case by a throw of the dice. It might seem then, that our analysis should take as its point of departure the office of judge. From this office certain requirements might be deduced, for example, that of impartiality, since a judge to be "truly" such must be impartial. Then, as the next step, if he is to be impartial he must be willing to hear both sides, etc.

The trouble with this is that there are people who are called "judges" holding official position and expected to be impartial who nevertheless do not participate in an adjudication in any sense directly relevant to the subject of this paper. Judges at an agricultural fair or an art exhibition may serve as examples. Again, a baseball umpire, though he is not called a judge, is expected to make impartial rulings. What distinguishes these functionaries is not that they do not hold governmental office, for the duties of a judge at a livestock fair would scarcely be changed if he were an official of the Department of Agriculture. What distinguishes them from courts, administrative tribunals, and boards of arbitration is that their decisions are not reached within an institutional framework that is intended to assure to the disputants an opportunity for the presentation of proofs and reasoned arguments. The judge of livestock may or may not permit such a presentation; it is not an integral part of his office to permit and attend to it.

If, on the other hand, we start with the notion of a process of decision in which the affected party's participation consists in an opportunity to present proofs and reasoned arguments, the office of judge or arbitrator and the requirement of impartiality follow as a necessary implication. . . .

Adjudication is, then, a device which gives formal and institutional expression to the influence of reasoned argument in human affairs. As such it assumes a burden of rationality not borne by any other form of social ordering. A decision which is the product of reasoned argument must be prepared to meet itself the test of reason. We demand of an adjudicative decision a kind of rationality we do not expect of the results of contract or of voting. This higher responsibility toward rationality is at once the strength *and the weakness* of adjudication as a form of social ordering.

In entering contracts, men are of course in some measure guided by rational considerations. The subsistence farmer who has a surfeit of potatoes and only a handful of onions acts reasonably when he trades potatoes for onions. But there is no test of rationality that can be applied to the result of the trade considered in abstraction from the interests of the parties. Indeed, the trade of potatoes for onions, which is a rational act by one trader, might be considered irrational if indulged in by his opposite number, who has a storehouse full of onions and only a bushel of potatoes. If we asked one party to the contract, "Can you defend that contract?" he might answer, "Why, yes. It was good for me and it was good for him." If we then said, "But that is not what we meant. We meant, can you defend it on general grounds?" he might well reply that he did not know what we were talking about. Yet this is precisely the kind of question we normally direct toward the decision of a judge or arbitrator. The results that emerge from adjudication are subject, then, to a standard of rationality that is different from that imposed on the results of an exchange.

. . .

Now if we ask ourselves what kinds of questions are commonly decided by judges and arbitrators, the answer may well be, "Claims of right." . . . If, then, we seek to define "the limits of adjudication," a tempting answer would be that the proper province of courts is limited to cases where rights are asserted. On reflection we might enlarge this to include cases where fault or guilt is charged (broadly, "the trial of accusations") since in many cases it is artificial to treat the accuser (who may be the district attorney) as claiming a right. . . . The proper province of adjudication [then] is to make an authoritative determination of questions raised by claims of right and accusations of guilt. . . . [However,] it is not so much that adjudicators decide only issues presented by claims of right or accusations. The point is rather that *whatever* they decide, or *whatever* is submitted to them for decision tends to be converted into a claim of right or an accusation of fault or guilt. . . .

Let me spell out rather painstakingly the steps of an argument that will show why this should be so: (1) Adjudication is a process of decision that grants to the affected party a form of participation that consists in the opportunity to present proofs and reasoned arguments. (2) The litigant must therefore, if his participation is to be meaningful, assert some principle or principles by which his arguments are sound and his proofs relevant. (3) A naked demand is distinguished from a claim of right by the fact that the latter is a demand supported by a principle; likewise, a mere expression of displeasure or resentment is distinguished from an accusation by the fact that the latter rests upon some principles. Hence, (4) issues tried before an adjudicator tend to become claims of right or accusations of fault.

. . .

If the analysis presented here is correct, three aspects of adjudication that seem to present distinct qualities are in fact all expressions of a single quality: (1) the peculiar mode by which the affected party participates in the decision; (2) the peculiarly urgent demand of rationality that the adjudicative process must be prepared to meet; and (3) the fact the adjudication finds its normal and "natural" province in judging claims of right and accusations of fault. So, when we say that a party entering a contract, or voting in an election, has no "right" to any particular outcome, we are describing the same fundamental fact that we allude to when we say that adjudication has to meet a test of rationality or of "principle" that is not applied to contracts and elections.

. . .

I have suggested that it is not a significant description of the limits of adjudication to say that its proper province lies where rights are asserted or accusations of fault are made, for such a statement involves a circle of reasoning. If, however, we regard a formal definition of rights and wrongs as a nearly inevitable product of the adjudicative process, we can arrive at what is perhaps the most significant of all limitations on the proper province of adjudication. Adjudication is not a proper form of social ordering in these areas where the effectiveness of human association would be destroyed if it were organized about formally defined "rights" and "wrongs." Courts have, for example, rather regularly refused to enforce agreements between husband and wife affecting the internal organization of family life. There are other and wider areas where the intrusion of "the machinery of the law" is equally inappropriate. An adjudicative board might well undertake to allocate one thousand tons of coal among three claimants; it could hardly conduct even the simplest coal-mining enterprise by the forms of adjudication. Wherever successful human association depends upon spontaneous and informal collaboration, shifting its forms with the task at hand, there adjudication is out of place except as it may declare certain ground rules applicable to a wide variety of activities.

. . . [T]he incapacity of a given area of human activity to endure a pervasive delimitation of rights and wrongs is also a measure of its incapacity to respond to a too exigent rationality, a rationality that demands an immediate and explicit reason for every step taken. Back of both of these incapacities lies the fundamental truth that certain kinds of human relations are not appropriate raw material for a process of decision that is institutionally committed to acting on the basis of reasoned argument.

. . .

IV.   Adjudication and the Rule of Law

So far a point of crucial importance and difficulty has not been reached in this discussion. It has been repeatedly asserted that adjudication is institutionally committed to a "reasoned" decision, to a decision based on "principle." But what is the source of the "principle" on the basis of which the case is to be argued and decided? Where do the parties and the adjudicator get their respective "reasons"?

. . .

All are agreed that courts are essential to "the rule of law." The object of the rule of law is to substitute for violence peaceful ways of settling disputes. Obviously peace cannot be assured simply by treaties, agreements, and legislative enactment. There must be some agency capable of determining the rights of parties in concrete situations of controversy. Beyond this point, however, disagreement begins.

. . . The essence of the rule of law consists in being assured of your day in court. Courts can be counted on to make a reasoned disposition of controversies, either by application of statutes or treaties, or in the absence of these sources, by the development of rules appropriate to the cases before them and derived from general principles of fairness and equity.

Critics of this view assert that it does disservice to a great and valid ideal. It dodges the whole issue of "justiciability" and assumes there can be no problem or controversy that lies beyond the limits of adjudication. It substitutes for critical judgments a naive trust in good intentions. It forgets that you cannot be fair in a moral and legal vacuum. It ignores the fact that adjudication cannot function without some standard of decision, either imposed by superior authority or willingly accepted by the disputant. Without some standard of decision the requirement that the judge be impartial becomes meaningless. Similarly, without such a standard the litigants' participation through reasoned argument loses its meaning. Communication and persuasion presuppose some shared context of principle.

. . .

. . . We need, I believe, to keep two important truths before us: (1) It is sometimes possible to initiate adjudication effectively without definite rules; in this situation a case-by-case evolution of legal principle does often take place. (2) This evolution does not always occur and we need to analyze more clearly than we generally have what conditions foster or hinder it.

. . .

I suggest more generally that where adjudication appears to operate meaningfully without the support of rules formally declared or accepted in advance, it does so because it draws its intellectual sustenance from the two basic forms of social ordering I have already described. It has done this historically with most notable success in the field where the accepted objective is to develop a regime of reciprocity or exchange. Students of comparative law are often struck by the fact that in the area of commercial transactions courts operating in entirely different environments of legal doctrine will often reach identical or similar results in the decision of actual cases.

But the possibility of a case-by-case development of principle is by no means confined to the field of commercial transactions. For example, the demands of a viable system of federalism are by no means immediately obvious. In gradually discovering and articulating the principles that will make federalism work, the courts may exemplify [this] process. . . .

It should be made clear that the view expressed here is radically different from the one which it superficially resembles that threatens to become commonplace in sociology. I refer to the conception that in a sufficiently homogenous society certain "values" will develop automatically and without anyone intending or directing their development. In such a society it is assumed that the legal rules developed and enforced by courts will reflect these prevailing "values." In our own discussion, however, we are not talking about disembodied "values," but about human purposes actively, if often tacitly, held and given intelligent direction at critical junctures. In working out the implications of federalism or of a regime of exchange, a court is not an inert mirror reflecting current mores, but an active participant in the enterprise of articulating the implications of shared purposes.

. . .

The view taken in this paper is that adjudication is a form of social ordering institutionally committed to "rational" decision. This follows from the only mode of participation it accords to the affected party, the litigant. . . . It is apparent that adjudicators seldom rest their decisions directly on matters of empirical fact. When they seem to do this the "facts" . . . are generally human faults or shortcomings. To "find" such a "fact" is to express a condemnation. . . . This leaves logical deduction. Now it is apparent that when adjudication proceeds by previously established rules, at least one aspect of the tribunal's task involves something akin to logical deduction. If this is the only significant area of rationality permitted to adjudication, then it can act rationally only insofar as it applies previously established rules. . . .

V.   The Forms of Adjudication

. . .

[I]n most of the practical manifestations of adjudication the arbiter's function has to be "promoted" by the litigant and is not initiated by himself. . . .

. . .

Certainly it is clear that the integrity of adjudication is impaired if the arbiter not only initiates the proceedings but also, in advance of the public hearing, forms theories about what happened and conducts his own factual inquiries. In such a case the arbiter cannot bring to the public hearing an uncommitted mind; the effectiveness of participation through proofs and reasoned arguments is accordingly reduced. Now it is probably true that under most circumstances the mere initiation of proceedings carries with it a certain commitment and often a theory of what occurred. . . . In most situations the initiation of proceedings could not have the same neutral quality, as, for example, where the occasion consisted simply in the fact that a corporation had gone two years without declaring a dividend.

There is another reason which justifies the common conception that it is not normal for the adjudicative process to be initiated by the deciding tribunal. If we view adjudication in its widest extension, as including not only the work of courts, but also that of arbiters in labor, commerce, and international relations, it is apparent that the overwhelming majority of cases submitted to adjudication involve the assertion of claims founded directly or indirectly on *contract* or *agreement*. It seems clear that a regime of contract (more broadly, a regime of reciprocity) implies that the determination whether to assert a claim must be left to the interested party.

. . .

We tend to think of the judge or arbiter as one who decides and who gives reasons for his decision. . . . By and large it seems clear that the fairness and effectiveness of adjudication are promoted by reasoned opinions. Without such opinions the parties have to take it on faith that their participation in the decision has been real, that the arbiter has in fact understood and taken into account their proofs and arguments. A less obvious point is that where a decision enters into some continuing relationship, if no reasons are given the parties will almost inevitably guess at reasons and act accordingly. Here the effectiveness of adjudication is impaired, not only because the results achieved may not be those intended by the arbiter, but also because his freedom of decision in future cases may be curtailed by the growth of practices based on a misinterpretation of decisions previously rendered.

Obviously the bond of participation by the litigant is most secure when the arbiter rests his decision wholly on the proofs and arguments actually presented to him by the parties. In practice, however, it is not always possible to realize this ideal. Even where all of the considerations on which the decision rests were touched on by the parties' arguments, the emphasis may be very different. An issue dealt with only in passing by one of the parties, or perhaps by both, may become the headstone of the arbiter's decision. This may mean not only that, had they foreseen this outcome, the parties would have presented different arguments, but that they might also have introduced evidence on very different factual issues.

If the ideal of a perfect congruence between the arbiter's view of the issues and that of the parties is unattainable, this is no excuse for a failure to work toward an achievement of the closest approximation of it. We need to remind ourselves that if this congruence is utterly absent—if the grounds for the decision fall completely outside the framework of the argument, making all that was discussed or proved at the hearing irrelevant—then the adjudicative process has become a sham, for the parties' participation in the decision has lost all meaning. We need to analyze what factors influence the desired congruence and what measures may be taken to promote it.

One circumstance of capital importance is the extent to which a particular process of adjudication takes place in a context of established rules. In branches of the law where rules have become fairly settled and certain, it may be possible for lawyers to reach agreement easily in defining the crucial issue presented by a particular case. In such an area the risk is slight that the decision will fall outside the frame of reference set by the proofs and arguments. On the other hand, in areas of uncertainty, this risk is greatly increased. There are, to be sure, dangers in a premature crystallization of standards. On the other hand, one of the less obvious dangers of a too long delayed formulation of doctrine lies in the inevitable impairment of the integrity of adjudication that is entailed, for the reality of the parties' participation is reduced when it is impossible to foretell what issues will become relevant in the ultimate disposition of the case.

. . .

In practice both the decision of courts and the award of arbitrators are retrospective, both as to their effect on the litigants' rights and their effect as precedents for the decisions of other cases. . . .

The philosophy underlying the retrospective effect of the judicial decision can be stated somewhat as follows: It is not the function of courts to create new aims for society or to impose on society new basic directives. The courts for various reasons analyzed previously are unsuited for this sort of task. Perhaps the most compelling objection to an assumption of any such function lies in the limited participation in the decision by the litigants who (1) represent generally only themselves, and (2) participate in the decision only by proofs and arguments addressed to the arbiter. On the other hand, with respect to the generally shared aims and the authoritative directives of a society, the courts do have an important function to perform, that of developing (or even "discovering") case by case what these aims or directives demand for their realization in particular situations of fact. In the discharge of this function, at times the result is so obvious that no one thinks of a "retroactive effect." Theoretically, a court might distinguish between such decisions, and those which announce a rule or standard that seems "new," even though it may represent a reasoned conclusion from familiar premises. But if an attempt were made to apply such a distinction pervasively, so that some decision would be retrospective, some prospective in effect only, the resulting confusion might be much less bearable than the situation that now obtains.

VI.   The Limits of Adjudication

Attention is now directed to the question, What kinds of tasks are inherently unsuited to adjudication? The test here will be that used throughout. If a given task is assigned to adjudicative treatment, will it be possible to preserve the meaning of the affected party's participation through proofs and arguments?

This section introduces a concept—that of the "polycentric" task—which has been derived from Michael Polanyi's book, "The Logic of Liberty," 1951. In approaching that concept it will be well to begin with . . . [an example]:

. . . [S]uppose in a socialist regime it were decided to have all wages and prices set by courts which would proceed after the usual forms of adjudication. It is, I assume, obvious that here is a task that could not successfully be undertaken by the adjudicative method. The point that comes first to mind is that courts move too slowly to keep up with a rapidly changing economic scene. The more fundamental point is that the forms of adjudication cannot encompass and take into account the complex repercussions that may result from any change in prices or wages. A rise in the price of aluminum may affect in varying degrees the demand for, and therefore the proper price of, thirty kinds of steel, twenty kinds of plastics, an infinitude of wood, other metals, etc. Each of these separate effects may have its own complex repercussions in the economy. In such a case it is simply impossible to afford each affected party a meaningful participation through proofs and arguments. It is a matter of capital importance to note that it is not merely a question of the huge number of possibly affected parties, significant as that aspect of the thing may be. A more fundamental point is that each of the various forms that award might take (say, a three cent increase per pound, a four cent increase, a five cent increase, etc.) would have a different set of repercussions and might require in each instance a redefinition of the "parties affected."

We may visualize this kind of situation by thinking of a spider web. A pull on one strand will distribute tensions after a complicated pattern throughout the web as a whole. Doubling the original pull will, in all likelihood, not simply double each of the resulting tensions, but will rather create a different complicated pattern of tensions. This would certainly occur, for example, if the double pull caused one or more of the weaker strands to snap. This is a "polycentric" situation because it is "many-centered"—each crossing of strands is a distinct center for distributing tensions.

. . .

Now, if it is important to see clearly what a polycentric problem is, it is equally important to realize that the distinction involved is often a matter of degree. There are polycentric elements in almost all problems submitted to adjudication. A decision may act as a precedent, often an awkward one, on some situation not foreseen by the arbiter. Again, suppose a court in a suit between one litigant and a railway holds that it is an act of negligence for the railway not to construct an underpass at a particular crossing. There may be nothing to distinguish this crossing from other crossings on the line. As a matter of statistical probability it may be clear that constructing underpasses along the whole line would cost more lives (through accidents in blasting, for example) than would be lost if the only safety measure were the familiar "Stop, Look & Listen" sign. If so, then what seems to be a decision simply declaring the rights and duties of two parties is in fact an inept solution for a polycentric problem, some elements of which cannot be brought before the court in a simple suit by one injured party against a defendant railway. In lesser measure concealed polycentric elements are probably present in almost all problems resolved by adjudication. It is not, then, a question of distinguishing black from white. It is a question of knowing when the polycentric elements have become so significant and predominant that the proper limits of adjudication have been reached.

. . .

The final question to be addressed is this: When an attempt is made [at adjudicating] . . . a problem that is essentially polycentric, what happens? As I see it, three things can happen, sometimes all at once. *First,* the adjudicative solution may fail. Unexpected repercussions make the decision unworkable; it is ignored, withdrawn, or modified, sometimes repeatedly. *Secondly,* the purported arbiter ignores judicial proprieties—he "tries out" various solutions in post-hearing conferences, consults parties not represented at the hearings, guesses at facts not proved and not properly matters for anything like judicial notice. *Thirdly,* instead of accommodating his procedures to the nature of the problem he confronts, he may reformulate the problem so as to make it amenable to solution through adjudicative process.

Only the last of these needs illustration. Suppose it is agreed that an employer's control over promotions shall be subject to review through arbitration. Now obviously an arbitrator cannot decide whether when Jones was made a Machinist Class A, there was someone also more deserving in the plant, or whether, in view of Jones' age, it would have been better to put him in another job with comparable pay. This is the kind of allocative problem for which adjudication is utterly unsuited. There are, however, two ways of obtaining a workable control over promotions through arbitration. One of these is through the posting of jobs; when a job is vacant, interested parties may apply for promotion into it. At the hearing only those who have made application are entitled to be considered and of course only the posted job is in issue. Here the problem is simplified in advance to the point where it can be arbitrated, though not without difficulty, particularly in the form of endless arguments as to whether there was in fact a vacancy that ought to have been posted, and whether a claimant filed his application on time and in the proper form, etc. The other way of accommodating the problem to arbitration is for the arbitrator to determine, not who should be promoted, but who *has* been promoted. That is, the contract contains certain "job descriptions" with the appropriate rate for each; the claimant asserts that he is in fact doing the work of Machinist A, though he is still assigned the pay and title of a Machinist B. The controversy has two parties—the company and the claimant as represented by the union—and the single factual issue, Is the claimant in fact doing the work of a Machinist A?

In practice the procedure of applying for appointment to posted jobs will normally be prescribed in the contract itself, so that the terms of the agreement keep the arbitrator's function with respect to promotion within manageable limits. The other method of making feasible a control of promotions through arbitration will normally result from the arbitrator's own perception of the limitations of his role. The contract may simply contain a schedule of job rates and job classifications and a general clause stating that "discharges, promotions, and lay-offs shall be subject to the grievance procedure." If the arbitrator were to continue such a contract to give him a general supervision over promotions, he would embark himself upon managerial tasks wholly unsuited to solution by any arbitrative procedure. An instinct toward preserving the integrity of his role will move him, therefore, to construe the contract in the manner already indicated, so that he avoids any responsibility with respect to the assignment of duties and merely decides whether the duties actually assigned make appropriate the classification assigned by the company to the complaining employee.

. . .

In closing this discussion of polycentricity, it will be well to caution against two possible misunderstandings. The suggestion that polycentric problems are often solved by a kind of "managerial intuition" should not be taken to imply that it is an invariable characteristic of polycentric problems that they resist rational solution. There are rational principles for building bridges of structural steel. But there is no rational principle which states, for example, that the angle between girder A and girder B must always be 45 degrees. This depends on the bridge as a whole. One cannot construct a bridge by conducting successive separate arguments concerning the proper angle for every pair of intersecting girders. One must deal with the whole structure.

Finally, the fact that an adjudicative decision affects and enters into a polycentric relationship does not of itself mean that the adjudicative tribunal is moving out of its proper sphere. On the contrary, there is no better illustration of a polycentric relationship than an economic market, and yet the laying down of rules that will make a market function properly is one for which adjudication is generally well-suited. The working out of our common law of contracts case by case has proceeded through adjudication, yet the basic principle underlying the rules thus developed is that they should promote the free exchange of goods on a polycentric market. The court gets into difficulty, not when it lays down rules about contracting, but when it attempts to write contracts.

. . .

CHAPTER TWO

DEMANDS MADE ON COURT SYSTEMS

In 1976 Thomas Ehrlich, former dean of the Stanford Law School, wrote that America was suffering from "legal pollution." As Ehrlich put it, "We have far too many laws; we rely too heavily on law as an instrument of social change; we depend too much on courts, legislatures and administrative agencies to resolve our woes." Speaking specifically about courts, Ehrlich cited statistics describing a pattern of rapid growth in the number of cases that have in recent years been brought into both the state and federal judicial systems.[1] There is, in fact, no doubt that the workload of American courts has expanded steadily, if not uniformly, in the last seventy years. Yet it remains true that being involved in litigation is an experience not shared by the vast majority of the American people.[2]

The steady expansion of the workload of the courts can be explained in several ways. First, it is possible that there has been an increase, although perhaps not great, in the number of people who have at one time or another been involved in litigation. An expanded volume of litigation may result from even a small increase in the total number of litigants. Such an expansion may be produced by changes in the social and political conditions that promote or facilitate the translation of disputes into lawsuits. Recent increases in the number of cases reaching the courts may mean that the courts are taking on a greater share of society's dispute-resolution business. The increases may also be related to decreases in the costs of litigation. Litigation is a relatively expensive way of processing disputes. A substantial investment of time and money is required to bring and sustain a lawsuit. However, in recent years numerous attempts have been made to reduce or redistribute such costs through such devices as the provision of free legal services. As a result of the reduced costs, the amount of litigation may have increased, because people who formerly were unable to afford to bring disputes to court are now able to do so, and because those already able to afford litigation are simply able to afford more of it.[3]

The second explanation for the increase in the number of cases reaching the courts may be that the number of litigants has not increased but rather that the relatively few people who typically use courts to process disputes have, in recent years, simply found more occasions to do so. This may provide the basis for a third explanation of the growth of litigation, an increase in the range of legally actionable problems. As the scope of law expands, as more legal rights and remedies are created, the amount of litigation increases as a result of the new opportunities for court action.[4] As new rights are created, litigation may be necessary to clarify the way in which those rights will be defined and understood by the courts. Furthermore, the creation of new rights may direct the attention of organized interest groups to the judiciary. Interest groups may come to perceive litigation as a viable strategy for stimulating group mobilization to achieve the groups' political goals.[5] This type of explanation focuses attention on the ways in which legislatures and courts themselves may be responsible for the "legal pollution" described by Ehrlich.

Thus, it seems that one can identify three generic factors that may explain litigation. The first is what we call social development. Variation in the amount of litigation is a function of changes in the level of complexity, differentiation, and scale of the society in which courts operate. Increased reliance on courts to process disputes results from changes in the nature of typical social relationships that appear to accompany processes of social development and changes in the structure of society. In less developed societies, individuals have relatively stable and enduring contacts with a limited range of other individuals. Disputes in such settings are easier to resolve informally. The framework of trust and the context of ongoing relationships generally found in such societies mean that resort to supposed impartial third parties can be avoided.[6] As a result, courts play a less important role in processing disputes.

In more complex, industrialized societies individuals generally have a wider range of social relationships, but this expansion is accompanied by a diminution in their depth and intensity. Relationships typically are of a more transitory nature; disputes often occur between strangers, between people who have nothing more in common than the dispute itself. Under such circumstances informal dispute processing is impractical. The social development argument suggests that courts will play a more important role in dispute processing in developed societies than in underdeveloped societies because of the proliferation of impersonal relationships. We are not suggesting that courts replace other dispute-processing mechanisms in developed societies, but rather that their share of society's dispute-processing business increases.

The second factor that explains why disputes are translated into demands for judicial services is subjective cost/benefit calculations on the part of disputants. The decision to employ courts to process disputes is for some disputants a relatively objective, well-thought-out decision. For others, however, the decision to go to court may be an act that has value because of its cathartic effect, even though it may not produce tangible, material benefits. Those who use the court frequently tend to use it for more clearly instrumental purposes than do those who are occasional users.[7] The major distinction between those who use courts and those who use other mechanisms to process disputes may be less attitudinal than financial. As a general rule, the costs of using various dispute-processing institutions rise as one moves from informal, private institutions to formal, public institutions.

Since courts process disputes by clearly declaring who is entitled to what from whom, disputants must calculate a "risk" factor and weigh what they might lose against the possible benefits of doing nothing or of using different devices for dispute processing. Thus, courts encourage settlements that might not otherwise occur by conveying to disputants the idea that they have more to gain by trying to reach an informal settlement of differences, a settlement that allows them to exercise some control over the result.

A third factor is that legislatures and courts are creating more legally actionable rights and remedies. The greater the reach and scope of the legal system, the higher its litigation rate will be. The recent expanded use of American courts is attributable to some extent to the expansion of rights and remedies fostered by an activist Supreme Court under Earl Warren. An expanded scope of law increases litigation by implicitly if not directly expanding the jurisdiction of the courts. The creation of new legal rights is likely to stimulate litigation designed to vindicate or protect those rights. This sequence is illustrated by the "criminal rights explosion" of the 1960s, which followed the logic that the creation of new rights would stimulate further litigation, which in turn would produce new rights, which would require further litigation. Since judicial dispute processing must proceed in accordance with the law, courts and legislatures are able to alter the amount of litigation by creating or changing law.

The three readings that follow are particularly relevant and contribute to our understanding of the impact of social development and individual cost/benefit calculations. Each focuses on a different type of court. Friedman and Percival, in their analysis of two trial courts in California (selection 5), challenge the idea that the dispute-processing function of courts has increased in recent years. Atkins and Glick, in their analysis of state supreme courts (selection 6), and Grossman and Sarat, in their study of federal district courts (selection 4), explore the way in which the frequency and nature of judicial dispute processing vary with the characteristics of the environments in which courts operate. These three readings thus provide an interesting comparative picture of the development of litigation at different court levels.

Notes

1. Thomas Ehrlich, "Legal Pollution," *New York Times Magazine*, February 8, 1976.
2. Barbara Curran and Francis Spaulding, *The Legal Needs of the Public* (Chicago: American Bar Foundation, 1974).
3. On the importance of cost see Lawrence Friedman, "Legal Rules and the Process of Social Change," *Stanford Law Review* 19 (1967), 786.
4. Karen Orren, "Standing to Sue: Interest Group Conflict in the Federal Courts," *American Political Science Review* 70 (1976), 723.
5. Stuart Scheingold, *The Politics of Rights* (New Haven: Yale University Press, 1974).
6. Richard Abel, "A Comparative Theory of Dispute Institutions in Society," *Law and Society Review* 8 (1974), 217.
7. Marc Galanter, "Why the 'Haves' Come Out Ahead: Speculations on the Limits of Legal Change," *Law and Society Review* 9 (1974), 95.

4

Litigation in the Federal Courts: A Comparative Perspective

Joel B. Grossman and Austin Sarat

Introduction

. . .

Litigation is a special case of the more general and pervasive category of legal activity. By legal activity we refer generally to the invocation of substantive and procedural rules and formal processes established in the legal system to regulate, order, guide and legitimate private social, economic and political relationships. Legal activity, as we have defined it, is not always visible, or recognizable as such. It is not always conflictual, nor does it always involve lawyers. The acquisition and sale of property and the transfer of goods and services in the marketplace are all dependent, to some extent, on current or former legal activity. The extent of legal activity might be measured by the use of common forms of licensing, contracting, and entitling.

While resort to the courts remains a costly, often traumatic, and rare experience, most other types of legal activity of the kind just described are routine and less openly conflictual. But the importance of litigation to the workings of the legal system, and to the resolution of disputes throughout the society, may be far out of proportion to its relative infrequency.

In this paper . . . we are interested in the determinants of legal activity and litigation over time, and in explaining cross-sectional differences in different areas of the United States.[1] At our macro-social level of analysis it is possible to identify two sets of aggregate, environmental factors likely to encompass many of the major determinants. We refer to these simply as the Social Factor and the Political Factor. We also recognize the importance of what might be called "internal" factors, such as changes in substantive and procedural law; but our focus in this paper is on variables formally external to the legal system.

Reprinted by permission of the Law and Society Association from *Law and Society Review* 9 (1975), 322-329, 331-335, and 337-343. Copyright © 1975. Most footnotes and references have been omitted. The *Law and Society Review* is the official publication of the Association.

The Social Factor

Much writing on law and society proceeds from the assumption that the use of law in a society reflects the level of social and economic development in that society. The literature suggests, generally, that in societies in which the level of economic development is relatively low and in which social relationships are close and interdependent, customary devices of social control and mechanisms of conflict resolution seem to predominate and make unnecessary the development of formal legal institutions. Increased reliance on formal law and its processes appears to parallel changes in the complexity of a society which are produced by economic growth and development. Close, interdependent relations which facilitate informality are replaced by relationships in which interests diverge; new kinds of social organizations emerge which are more dependent on competition than cooperation. . . . [This, in turn, is associated with a vast increase in legal activity.]

Does the economic and social development of a society, manifest in increased legal activity, mean that there will also be a greater utilization of courts to solve disputes and make public policy? Available evidence . . . suggests a disjunction between legal activity and litigation: social and economic development does not necessarily lead to higher rates of litigation. Friedman suggests that the effect of social development on litigation may be curvilinear. In the early stages of development there may be a marked increase in the litigation rate; but with industrial maturity the litigation rate levels off. . . . Friedman presents data from England which seem to support his argument. These data show that litigation has, for most of this century, remained static even as the population has grown rapidly.

. . . In Spain, in spite of the dramatic increase in legal activity, the litigation rate "has remained remarkably constant and at a relatively low rate . . . the process of economic change does not seem to have affected the rate of litigation . . ."[2] . . . Early phases of industrial development . . . [are] accompanied by higher rates of litigation, but . . . increases . . . cease as a point is reached where there is simply more to be gained by continuing the economic relationships which litigation might disrupt. Economically advanced societies may develop alternatives to litigation which impose fewer social and economic costs.

Studies of the social context of litigation suggest the following hypotheses. First, the litigation rate will be higher in more developed societies than in less developed societies. Second, development leads to an increase in legal activity, without a corresponding increase in the litigation rate. Finally, within any society the effect of social change and social development on litigation will not be uniform, but will reflect internal variations in the pattern of development. . . .

The Political Factor

Litigation is political in the sense that the very act of involving the formal, public authority of the courts in dispute resolution inescapably is part of the political process and likely to have important political consequences. Litigation is a form of political participation even if the individual who enters the judicial arena is not fully cognizant of the political ramifications of his act. Although individual motivation in such matters may be more situation specific than broadly political, the decision to litigate may be influenced by key political variables. For example, whether participation in public affairs is encouraged in a society and whether the organization of political institutions facilitates such participation may be important determinants of the rate at which citizens "consume" the services which courts provide.

Political cultures which encourage participation in politics are often characterized as "modern"; those which discourage public participation are often labeled "traditional." In "modern cultures" we expect that there will be a higher litigation rate; "traditional cultures," on the other hand, characterized by a reluctance to acknowledge publicly the existence of conflict and by a parallel emphasis on private dispute resolution, should display a lower litigation rate. Herbert Jacob has observed that in more traditional political cultures,

> . . . there is greater reliance on private dispute settling processes. . . . people will make greater efforts to negotiate settlements between themselves . . . because they feel they know one another on a personal footing, they have greater opportunity to settle conflicts within the confines of established personal relationships.[3]

Yet there are two reasons to consider seriously the converse hypothesis that higher litigation rates will be found closer to the traditional than to the modern end of the political culture continuum. First, if litigation is a form of political participation it is generally privatized and individualized in form. At least in theory, litigation does not require the building of coalitions, alliances and the attraction of public support which is characteristic of other forms of participation and competition. As a result, it may not be . . . incompatible with the norms of a "traditional culture." . . . Second, litigation may be an alternative to "orthodox" political participation and hence an inverse relationship would be expected.

A critical problem with this "political" explanation is its overlap with the social development theory which we discussed above. One would expect a relationship between social and economic development, and political modernity. Therefore, in studying these influences, it is necessary to determine if the relationship of political factors to litigation rates persists when we control for the impact of social and economic development.

The Data

We have utilized three major types of data in this study. First, to serve as a rough indicator of levels of legal activity we have constructed a simple ratio of lawyers to the general population. . . . On both a state and national basis the number of lawyers was recorded at ten-year intervals, from 1900 to 1970. Data on the incidence of lawyers is drawn from the Census Bureau Reports, as is Population data.

We have used two indices of litigation—total civil cases and total private civil cases filed in the United States District Courts at ten year intervals, from 1902 to 1972. (This data comes from the Annual Reports of the Administrative Office of the Federal Courts, and from the Attorney General's Reports for the years before 1942.) To facilitate analysis of the social, economic and political influences on litigation we have aggregated district court data to the state level. For any category and reporting year, the litigation reported for a state is the total number of cases filed in all of the federal district courts in that state. Alaska, Hawaii, the District of Columbia, and all territorial courts are excluded from our cross-sectional comparisons. In this paper we refer both to litigation and to litigation rate. The former consists of raw totals. Litigation *rate*, on which we rely primarily, is a ratio of litigation to population, expressed as the number of cases per 100,000 population. Thus, a litigation rate of 19.9 indicates that many cases for every 100,000 persons.

In carrying out our analysis of social, economic and political influences on litigation, we rely on federal court case filings because comparable data from state courts simply are not available. Not every state compiles such data, even today. And only a few states compiled such data prior to 1950. One of our main goals was to observe the longitudinal development of litigation, and this could be done only with federal data.

. . .

The third major source of data for this paper is provided by the work of Richard Hofferbert.[4] Hofferbert has gathered data on the social, economic, cultural and political characteristics of the American states, for the years 1890–1960. (We have added comparable data for 1970.) Included among Hofferbert's measures are percent employed in manufacturing, urbanization, income per capita and two multivariate factors labeled industrialization and cultural enrichment or affluence. We have used such indices in our cross-sectional analyses, and in describing changes in litigation and legal activity. We are interested both in the development of broad, historical trends, and also in a more precise delineation of differences among the states.

The Findings

Indicators of Legal Activity

We begin our analysis with the simple hypothesis that in the 20th century there would be an increase in the level of legal activity greater than what might be expected from population growth alone. It is not just population growth, but increased economic and social complexity which affects the pace of legal activity. . . .

. . . Lawyers are not involved in all legal activity, but they play at least an indirect role in almost all significant legal affairs. . . . One weakness of a lawyer-based index of legal activity is that the work focus of many lawyers, paralleling the organization of business enterprises, cuts across geographic boundaries; the lawyers practicing in a particular state do not encapsulate the legal business of that state. Also one cannot assume that the prevalence of lawyers is due exclusively to the demand for legal services.[5] But acknowledging these distortions in our index (and others such as the unequal workload of lawyers) it still appears to be the best available indicator of legal business.

. . .

[We found] a slight decrease (of 10.7 percent) in the level of legal activity in the United States from 1900 to 1970. During the first two decades of the century, if our measure is accurate, the rate of legal activity declines sharply, by 23.2 percent. This does not indicate an absolute decline in legal activity but a growth in population disproportionate to the growth of the lawyer population. From 1900 to 1920 the population increased by nearly 40 percent; the total number of lawyers also increased, but only by 7.5 percent.[6] After World War I, there is a reversal of this trend and a relatively steady increase in the rate of legal activity. The decade 1940–1950 again shows a decline in our indicator of legal activity, followed by a leveling off in the 1950s and a sharp increase from 1960 to 1970.

The slight overall decrease in legal activity from 1900–1970 is somewhat surprising given the continuing urbanization and industrialization of the United States during that

TABLE 4-1
Changes in Legal Activity (1900–1970) by States,
Grouped by Level of Industrialization in 1960*

		Legal Activity (Lawyers per 100,000 Population)		
		1900	1970	% Increase 1900–1970
I	Most Industrialized	133.8	152.8	+14.2%
II	Industrialized	140.2	106.4	−24.1%
III	Semi-Industrialized	160.1	109.9	−31.4%
IV	Least Industrialized	170.0	109.4	−35.6%

* The quartile groupings were derived from Hofferbert's industrialization factor scores for 1960. They express only relative levels of industrialization. We have relied only on the 1960 scores because changes in rankings of the states from 1900 to 1960 were not significant. . . . The groupings on the industrialization factor are as follows: *Group I:* New Jersey, Connecticut, New York, Massachusetts, Illinois, Pennsylvania, Rhode Island, Delaware, Ohio, California, Michigan, Maryland. *Group II:* Indiana, Wisconsin, Missouri, New Hampshire, Washington, North Carolina, Virginia, Tennessee, Minnesota, Georgia, South Carolina, Louisiana. *Group III:* Iowa, Maine, West Virginia, Oregon, Texas, Vermont, Alabama, Florida, Kentucky, Kansas, Colorado, Utah. *Group IV:* Nebraska, Oklahoma, Mississippi, Arkansas, Arizona, Nevada, Idaho, Montana, New Mexico, South Dakota, Wyoming, North Dakota.

same period. The decline which we have noted may reflect the peculiarities of our measure. The highly irregular character of the development of legal activity from 1900–1970 makes interpretation difficult. For example, while legal activity appears to grow substantially during the post-war period of the 1920s, a roughly comparable period of war and recovery during the 1940s is associated with a downturn in our measure of legal activity. Only the decade of the 1960s, which has, by most accounts, witnessed a striking legalization of many previously private areas of life, produces an interpretable pattern of growth in nationwide legal activity.

When we look at the development of legal activity in the states over the course of this century, as reflected in Table 4-1, we find that it has grown only in the most industrialized states.[7] In the others it declined between 25 and 35 percent. We expected such a growth in legal activity among the most industrialized states, but the decline recorded among the other states is surprising.

. . .

Indicators of Litigation

From 1902 to 1972 there has been a dramatic overall increase in the absolute number of cases filed in the federal district courts, and a relatively smaller increase in the litigation rate.[8] In 1902 there were 19.9 cases filed per 100,000 persons; in 1972 43.9 cases per 100,000, an increase over the period of 120 percent. On the other hand, the absolute number of cases filed rose nearly 500 percent.

The observed increases have not been uniform, as shown in Figures 4-1 and 4-2. The largest component of the dramatic increase following World War I was in the category of government cases and reflected the era of Prohibition. In 1920 there were 92 civil liquor cases; by 1932 there were nearly 16,000 (as compared to nearly 14,000 other government cases). During this decade the number of government cases rose from 9,455 in 1922 to 33,311 in 1932 while the number of private cases increased by less than 3,000. The end of Prohibition and the Depression brought a reversion to more "normal" litigation rates, followed by another rapid increase following World War II.[9] With the exception of the decade beginning in 1952, both litigation and litigation rates increased, the former at a consistently higher rate. This was true for all cases, and for private and government cases considered separately. Beginning in 1952 private cases began to exceed government cases, reverting to the pattern at the beginning of the century.

. . .

We expected a positive correlation between litigation rates in the federal courts and industrialization. Using the division of the states, by level of industrialization, employed in Table 4-1, we found that the most highly industrialized states did not have the highest litigation rates.[10] Nor did they demonstrate the highest rates of litigation rate growth. In 1972, for example, the most industrialized states had the lowest litigation rates in all

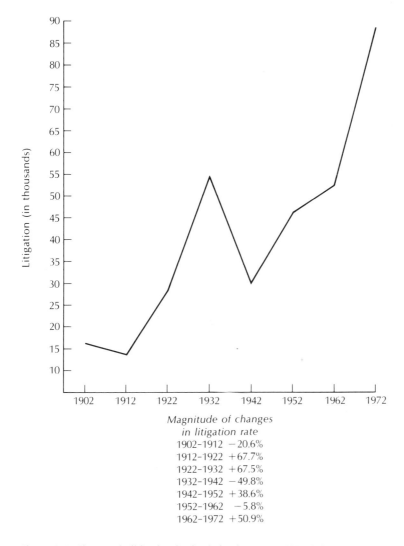

Magnitude of changes
in litigation rate
1902–1912 −20.6%
1912–1922 +67.7%
1922–1932 +67.5%
1932–1942 −49.8%
1942–1952 +38.6%
1952–1962 −5.8%
1962–1972 +50.9%

Figure 4-1. Changes in litigation in the federal courts, 1902-1972.

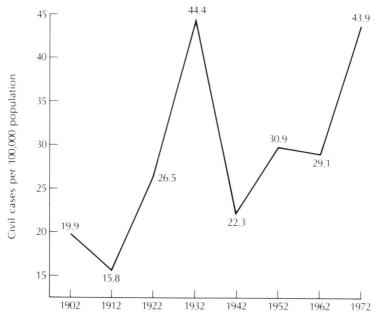

Figure 4-2. Changes in litigation rates in the federal courts, 1902–1972.

categories, although they showed moderately high rates of increase in litigation rates from 1912 to 1972. The greatest increase in total civil litigation is in the Category II states. The impact of industrialization on litigation displays a curvilinear form. Growth in litigation rates moves from lowest to highest in a steady progression as one moves from Category IV to Category II states, and declines somewhat in the most industrialized states. The pattern of litigation growth seen here thus seems similar to what Friedman suggests is to be expected.

Because of the large component of government cases, some bias may be introduced by relying exclusively on total civil cases in relating litigation rate to socio-economic factors. To be sure, the government's use of the courts may also be responsive to economic factors, but perhaps it is not as reflective of cross-sectional differences. Table 4-2, however, demonstrates that the impact of industrialization is no more in line with our original hypothesis when private cases alone are examined.

. . .

. . . Like Herbert Jacob we are forced to conclude that, while socio-economic factors may be useful in explaining variations in voting turnout or state budget expenditures, they may play only a secondary role in explaining litigation rates in the federal courts.

Jacob then suggested, as we have already noted, that political culture variables might provide an explanation. Specifically he hypothesized that in traditional cultures, litigation rates would be low.[11] Using two common "indicators" of political culture—level of inter-party competition and turnout in gubernatorial elections—we find no support for Jacob's hypothesis. As shown in Table 4-3, in most of the years encompassed by our study, neither

TABLE 4-2
Changes in Mean Litigation Rate, 1912–1972, by States Grouped by Level of Industrialization*

States by Level of Industrialization	Mean Litigation Rate: Total Civil Cases (# of Cases per 100,000 Pop.)			Mean Litigation Rate: Private Cases (# of Cases per 100,000 Pop.)			Mean Litigation Rate: Government Cases (# of Cases per 100,000 Pop.)		
	1912	1972	% Increase	1912	1972	% Increase	1912	1972	% Increase
I Most Industrialized	14.5	37.9	161.4%	11.1	28.4	155.9%	3.4	10.4	206.0%
II Industrialized	15.0	51.1	241.0%	10.2	35.8	250.0%	4.9	14.6	198.0%
III Semi-Industrialized	17.3	46.4	168.0%	15.3	31.2	104.0%	3.6	13.7	281.0%
IV Least Industrialized	20.9	47.6	128.0%	12.4	31.2	152.0%	8.1	16.5	104.0%

* As defined in Table 4-1.

Note: For this table we are using 1912 instead of 1902 as a base year, owing to the imprecision of reported data for the earlier year. The mean litigation rate for government cases for 1912 in category II excludes Indiana; in that state there were only 2 reported "government" cases and thus an aberrantly low litigation rate.

TABLE 4-3
Correlations* between (Surrogate) Political Culture Measures and Litigation Rate
(Total Civil Cases) 1902–1972

	Litigation Rate (Cases per 100,000 Population)							
	1902	1912	1922	1932	1942	1952	1962	1972
Index of competitiveness gov. elect.**	.197	.228	−.021	.079	−.190	−.076	−.596	.060
Turnout gov. elect.**	−.041	.044	−.214	.150	−.279	−.017	−.522	−.275

* Pearson's R.
** We are using Hofferbert's measure of gubernatorial elections which is based on the most recent previous election.
.000—Those correlations which are underlined are statistically significant. Significant ($\Sigma \leq .05$).

of these indicators displayed significant correlations with our measure of litigation rate. More than half of the correlations are negative, but most are weak and only two are statistically significant. Only in 1962 do political variables appear important. In that year, litigation rates were higher in states characterized by lower levels of political participation and competition, states which we would label "traditional" in their political cultures. For the most part, however, litigation in the federal courts shows only the most tenuous relationships with our political culture variables. These results must be regarded as inconclusive. Our earlier stated alternative hypothesis that litigiousness might well be found in more traditional cultures is neither proved nor disproved. Further testing will be required to determine if, in more traditional cultures, litigation functions as an alternative and more privatized form of political participation.

. . .

Summary and Conclusions

We began this inquiry with what we believed were a set of well established hypotheses. However, few of our expectations were confirmed. For example, only in the Category I (high industrialization) states did *both* legal activity and litigation increase over time; furthermore, while Category I states experienced such increases, their rate of increase on both our legal activity and litigation measures was not, as we had expected, higher than the rate of increase among other groups of states. In the remaining categories of states we found a decline in legal activity *and* an increase in litigation. Neither of these patterns is consistent with what Toharia found in Spain and what Friedman argues is the case in Great Britain.

It is difficult to explain why we found that legal activity has declined in most parts of the United States. What we know of current trends toward legalization points toward a contrary conclusion. During the 70 years covered by our study, the growth in the number of lawyers has not kept pace with the growth in population; the result is a decline in the level of legal activity as we have measured it. At the same time, there appears to have been a narrowing of the gap between legal activity and litigation. More legal business ends up in federal court at present than was the case at the beginning of this century, and this increase cannot be accounted for exclusively by population growth.[12] We have no way to estimate what proportion of the legal business in a society is litigated. The causes of an increased federal litigation rate are thus not entirely clear. Certainly one possible explanation is an increase in litigiousness. Another may be a rise in the complexity and range of potentially conflictual problems which are perceived to require some form of legal action.

Industrialization is a useful predictor of levels of legal activity but not of litigation rates; legal activity but not litigation rates appears to be greater in more industrialized areas. The most industrialized and economically developed states have experienced more rapid growth in legal activity but not in litigation. States lower in their level of industrialization appear to be somewhat more litigious. . . .

The counter intuitive nature of our findings suggests the need to identify the conditions under which the original hypotheses might be expected to hold. Precise measures of industrial growth, rather than levels of industrialization, ought to be obtained for all states. And certainly a more precise specification of political culture—or perhaps "legal culture"—variables is required. Data on individual dispositions to litigate are also needed. The degree to which decisions to litigate are situation specific, or related to a wider range of attitudes toward, and contacts with, the legal system, remains largely unexplored.

. . .

Notes

1. The determinants of legal activity and litigation are unquestionably more complex than appear from this paper. Our intention is not to provide a comprehensive explanation, but to test several important hypotheses discussed in previous research.

2. Jose Toharia, "Economic Development and Litigation: The Case of Spain," a paper presented at the Conference on the Sociology of the Judicial Process held at the Zentrum für interdisziplinäre Forschung at the University of Bielefeld, F.R.G., September 24-29, 1973, to appear in Jahrbuch für Rechtsoziologie und Rechtstheorie (forthcoming), p. 14.

3. Herbert Jacob, *Debtors in Court* (Chicago: Rand McNally, 1969), p. 92.

4. Richard Hofferbert, "Socio-Economic Dimensions of the American States," 12 *Midwest Journal of Political Science* 401 (1968).

5. Our legal activity indicator implicitly assumes a supply and demand model. . . . but we concede its imperfections. It does not take account of the efforts of the organized bar to control entry into the profession, or to create a favorable balance between lawyers available and law work. Nor does it account for a variety of other social forces which have affected entry into law school and the legal profession.

6. This finding of a decline in legal activity may be spurious, caused by the cumulative effects of licensing and law school accreditation requirements. . . .

7. By 1900 the United States had passed through its industrial revolution. Subsequent differences among the states in industrialization must be viewed as differences within an advanced industrial economy.

8. The volume of civil litigation pending in the federal courts remained quite constant from 1873, when statistics were first recorded, until 1904, when the additional calculation of a category of "cases commenced" was begun (American Law Institute, *A Study of the Business of the Federal Courts, Part II, Civil Cases,* 1934, pp. 32 ff.).

9. Frankfurter and Landis assert that the business of the federal courts has come "from the interests that at different periods have been predominant in our national life. The range and intensity of governing political, social and economic forces are accurately reflected in the volume and variety of federal litigation." They also note the similarity between the post Civil War and post World War I increases in litigation in the federal

courts. [See Felix Frankfurter and James M. Landis, *The Business of the Supreme Court* (New York: Macmillan, 1928), p. 56.]

10. In fact, litigation rates among the most industrialized states in 1972 range from a high of 71.7 cases per 100,000 persons in Massachusetts to a low of 25.0 cases per 100,000 persons in Connecticut.

11. Political culture is a difficult concept to operationalize. It is common to utilize surrogate variables, such as turnout and party competition, a practice we have followed in this study.

12. Gregory J. Rathjen, "Population Growth and the Federal Judicial System," in Virginia Gray, ed., *Political Issues in U.S. Population Policy* (Lexington, Mass.: Lexington Books, 1974).

5

A Tale of Two Courts: Litigation in Alameda and San Benito Counties

Lawrence M. Friedman and Robert V. Percival

. . .

This paper reports on a study of the *civil* load of two trial courts in California between 1890 and 1970. One court sits in an urban county, the other in a rural county. We tried to measure how the work of these courts changed over time. We expected to find that trial courts have come to do less and less work in settling disputes and that most of their labor is now routine, administrative, cut-and-dried. This hypothesis was confirmed. We also expected to find major differences between the rural and the urban court. But here, it turned out, we were surprised. A common fate overtook both courts; and essentially, our data tell a single story, which holds for city and country alike.

. . .

The raw materials of the study are the civil casefiles of the Superior Courts in two California counties. These files were sampled at twenty-year intervals from 1890 to 1970, that is, in 1890, 1910, 1930, 1950, and 1970. Eighteen-ninety was chosen as the starting point, partly because it was the first census year after the court reform that established the system of Superior Courts. In 1890, California was still a young state, compared to the states of the Eastern seaboard. It was yet to experience its greatest urban growth and industrial development.

[I.] The Counties

Alameda and San Benito are the two counties of the study. Although their borders are less than fifty miles apart, at opposite ends of the Santa Clara Valley in west-central California, they are profoundly different in demographic character. Alameda County is densely populated, part of a sprawling megalopolis. It fronts on the eastern shore of San Francisco Bay, directly across from San Francisco and its peninsula. The county has an area of 840 square miles, stretching from the Contra Costa foothills on the northeast to the Santa Clara County border on the south. Oakland, the county seat and largest city, is located along San Francisco Bay in the county's northwest corner. From this point, a string of suburb-cities, some with populations over 100,000, now sprawl along freeway paths to the north and south, engulfing the western portion of the county in the Bay Area megalopolis.

San Benito County is bounded on the north by the Pajaro River and the southern edge of Santa Clara County. The county extends seventy miles to the south, averaging twenty-five miles in east-west width. Hollister is the county seat and only town of size. It is set in a lowland area at the southern end of the Santa Clara Valley, in the northern part of the county. Nearly everyone in the county lives and works in this area, between the hamlet of Tres Piños eight miles to the southwest and San Juan Bautista, an equal distance to the west. The rest of the county is mountainous, except for one small lowland area, along the east-central edge of the county. . . .

. . .

[II.] The Study

As we have mentioned, the basic materials for this study were drawn from civil casefiles of the superior courts of the two counties, for the years 1890, 1910, 1930, 1950, and 1970. The case load of San Benito is small, and hence every case was examined in each of these years. In Alameda, with its enormous caseloads, a sample had to be taken. One hundred cases were taken at random from the files in 1890, 1910, and 1930. In 1950 and 1970, sufficient cases were taken to represent 2% of the cases. In all, 1176 cases were included in the study—677 from Alameda and 499 from San Benito.

[Table 5-1] records the number of cases filed in the two counties, for the years in question, and also gives the caseload per 1,000 population. This last figure is, however, difficult to interpret, because, as we shall see, there are other courts that handle civil litigation, and the concept of a "case" requires some elucidation, too.

Throughout the period, the Superior Courts were not exclusively trial courts. At all times between 1890 and 1970, inferior trial courts functioned in the counties and the Superior Courts had jurisdiction over appeals from certain of these courts. In all, more than 97% of the cases in the two courts were original. Less than 3% were appeals, and all of these were tried *de novo* in the Superior Court. The records of these inferior courts are

TABLE 5-1
Superior Court Caseload per County

	1890	1910	1930	1950	1970
Alameda					
Cases	716	3,320	5,112	7,049	11,811
Population	93,864	246,131	474,883	740,315	1,073,184
Cases per 1,000 population	7.6	13.5	10.8	9.5	11.0
San Benito					
Cases	31	29	101	150	188
Population	6,412	8,041	11,311	14,370	18,226
Cases per 1,000 population	4.8	3.6	8.9	10.4	10.2

very incomplete, and the Superior Court has always had a far broader jurisdiction. Still, these courts—small claims courts, police courts, municipal courts, justice courts—handle, and have handled, a tremendous volume of work. For example, for the fiscal year 1969-70 (California judicial statistics are gathered on this basis), the municipal courts of the state disposed of 424,247 civil cases (not counting parking cases). In the Oakland-Piedmont municipal court (the district is the most populous in Alameda County), there were 8,275 small claims filings, 1,724 tort filings, and 8,652 miscellaneous civil filings.

The presence of these inferior courts, and the fact that jurisdictional limits have changed with the years, means that one cannot compare the caseload of Superior Courts over time as strictly and as rigorously as one would like. Their presence makes it difficult to tell how much the actual functions of the courts have changed between 1890 and 1970. The jurisdictional floor of the Superior Court has gone up over the years from $300 to $3,000. Claims for small amounts, which once appeared in Superior Court, would now show up in one of the inferior courts. Of course, the value of the dollar has also changed. But even if we converted the jurisdictional floor into constant dollars, the correspondence between the two sets of figures would still be inexact over time. Indeed, the presence of these courts means that our data can not conclusively demonstrate that there are no courts in which genuine "disputes" among ordinary people may be heard, and rather cheaply and efficiently. But other studies suggest that the inferior courts too are not functioning in any way as "people courts." . . .

One other possible alternative should be mentioned. The United States is a federal system. Is it not conceivable that important cases are funneled into the federal courts? The federal courts handle cases arising under federal laws; they may also hear cases between residents of different states. The business world is increasingly interstate; perhaps important business cases overwhelmingly gravitate into federal courts.

There is no doubt that federal courts are an important part of the judicial system, and that the volume of work they do is increasing. This is largely due to the fact that federal regulation is ubiquitous in the 20th century. It seems extremely doubtful that much ordinary civil litigation has been lost to the federal courts. . . .

A. The Docket

What kind of cases do the two courts hear? How has the docket changed over time? A number of broad trends become apparent upon examining the incidence of types of cases in our study (Figures 5-1 and 5-2).

In both counties the percentage of *family* and *tort* cases filed rose dramatically from 1890 to 1970: the proportion of *property* and *contract* cases fell quite drastically. The family cases are primarily uncontested divorces in which the court basically does nothing except to stamp its approval on arrangements which the parties have already agreed to before coming to court. Contemporary *tort* cases generally stem from automobile accidents. At first glance, there seem to be substantial disputes in some of these cases, but the defendant's insurance company will settle almost all of them before they go to trial (Figure 5-6). Neither in family nor in tort cases do courts often resolve a true "dispute" between two contending parties. . . .

In both counties, contract and property cases were the most frequent kinds of litigation in 1890. Not by any means were all of these cases contested even then (see Table 5-2). Property cases fell from around a quarter of all cases in 1890 to less than 4% of each

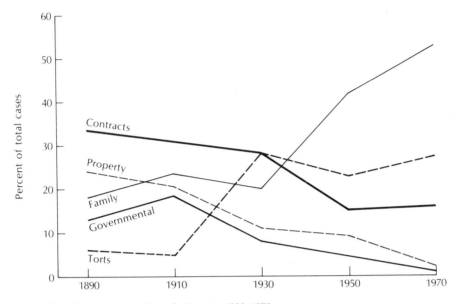

Figure 5-1. Type of case—Alameda County, 1890–1970.

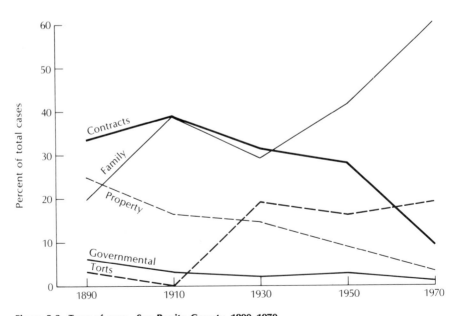

Figure 5-2. Type of case—San Benito County, 1890–1970.

TABLE 5-2
Percent of Cases Tried

	1890	1910	1930	1950	1970
Alameda					
All cases	36.0	25.0	48.0	29.1	16.1
Contracts	30.3	22.6	57.1	19.0	27.0
Property	54.2	55.0	63.6	53.8	33.3
San Benito					
All cases	25.8	37.9	19.8	20.0	11.7
Contracts	40.0	18.2	19.4	17.1	17.6
Property	12.5	100.0	33.3	33.3	50.0

county's cases in 1970. In Alameda County in 1890, 57% of the cases were classified as contract or property. Such cases constituted only 18% of the 1970 docket, a difference significant at the .1% level. The trend appears even more marked in San Benito. Three-fifths of San Benito's 1890 docket were property or contract cases. By 1970, such cases amounted to about one in eight; the difference here too is significant at the .1% level. Three of every five cases were routine family matters. Nearly half of all the "cases" in San Benito in 1970 were routine petitions for dissolution of marriage. Corporation or labor cases rarely occur.

Yet we feel confident that, as the economy develops, the volume of *private* transactions which use legal forms, or which take account of legal rules and processes, rises tremendously. Contracts are made, corporations formed, and property changes hands. The law (statutes, decisions of appellate courts, administrative proceedings) may significantly affect the form and legitimacy of these private transactions; yet in both counties we find a decline in formal resort to courts, to adjudicate disputes arising out of legal transactions. Surprisingly, San Benito (rural, non-industrial) and Alameda (urban, industrial) differ not at all in these regards. In both, the incidence of cases of economic disputes has fallen off, and the incidence of routine cases has risen.

B. Case Disposition

Another indication of the role courts play is provided by examination of how cases are resolved (Figures 5-3 and 5-4). As uncontested judgments—mostly judgments by default—rise, in both counties the percentage of contested judgments for defendants falls, dropping from 32.0% to 14.2% in Alameda (significant at the .1% level) and from 22.6% to 8.3% in San Benito (although because of the small number of 1890 cases in the sample, this result is not statistically significant). San Benito has a higher incidence of dissolution petitions; here the proportion of cases disposed of by uncontested judgments rises to over half of all cases. This is evidence of the shift toward administration, away from dispute settlement. The trend is equally striking if we take the percentage of *judgments* which are contested. In Alameda, the proportion of judgments which are uncontested has risen from 47.5% in 1890 to 71.9% in 1970 (significant at the .2% level). In San Benito 86.7% of the judgments are now uncontested, as opposed to 65% in 1890 (significant at the .2% level). Here, too, Alameda seems, surprisingly enough, less routinized and perfunctory than San Benito, where less than one case in ten is contested.

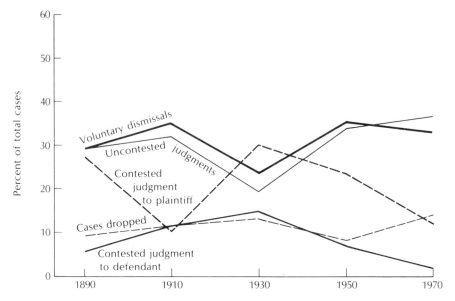

Figure 5-3. Case disposition—Alameda County, 1890–1970.

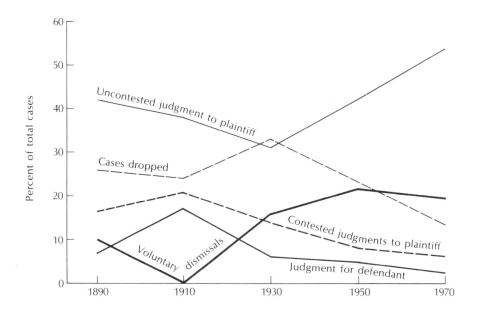

Figure 5-4. Case disposition—San Benito County, 1890–1970.

C. Proportion of Plaintiff Victories

We suggested that the percentage of cases which plaintiffs win is an indicator of degree of routinization of judicial process. Where there are genuine disputes, one might still expect plaintiffs to win most of their cases; but not 90 to 95 percent. In Alameda, plaintiffs won 96% of the judgments in 1970; in San Benito, 97%. Similar findings have been reported in other jurisdictions. This too indicates movement towards a routine administrative role. In San Benito, the percentage of plaintiff victories was slimmest in 1910 (77%); in Alameda it was slimmest in 1930 (77%), perhaps indicating a greater dispute-settlement role than in 1890 when the ratio is greatest for Alameda. In Alameda, contested cases were most frequent and voluntary dismissals least frequent in 1930 (44.5% contested judgments, 23.5% voluntary dismissals); in San Benito in 1910 (37.9% contested judgments, 0% voluntary dismissals).

D. Percent of Cases Brought to Trial

One index of dispute settlement is the percentage of cases brought to formal trial. In both counties the incidence of trials has substantially declined between 1890 and 1970 (Figure 5-5). In 1890, more than one out of every three cases filed in Alameda County was brought to trial. Today less than one in six has such a life cycle (a difference significant at the .1% level). The trend is also pronounced in San Benito; trial incidence fell from one in four in 1890, to only one of nine today (significant at the 5% level). Again, this is a strong trend away from dispute settlement; and, again, the incidence of dispute settlement—represented here by percent of cases tried—is lower in the rural county.

Figure 5-5 indicates that the decline in the rate of trials has not been continuous; it rose briefly in San Benito in 1910, sharply in Alameda in 1930. This pattern resembles that of the case disposition statistics. It was in 1930 that automobile accident cases first appeared

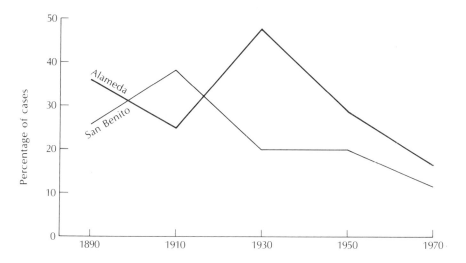

Figure 5-5. Percent of cases brought to trial or hearing, Alameda and San Benito Counties, 1890-1970.

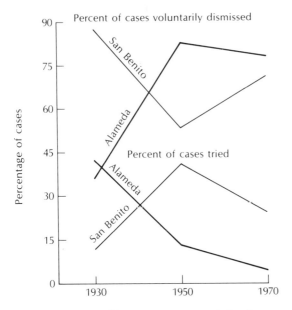

Figure 5-6. Auto accident cases—percent tried and percent voluntarily dismissed, Alameda and San Benito Counties, 1930-1970.

in the data in substantial numbers. In Alameda, in 1930, these cases were brought to trial more often than they were settled out of court; today less than one in ten is brought to trial there (Figure 5-6). Auto accident cases, however, do not account completely for the sharp rise in trials in 1930; this remains, for the present, unexplained.

E. Percent of Trials with Formal Opinions

A rough indicator of the extent of dispute settlement by courts is the proportion of cases tried in which the court writes a formal opinion, or makes formal findings of fact or law. The incidence of such cases is quite similar to the incidence of trials themselves. . . . With the exception of Alameda in 1930, formal opinions or findings in non-jury trials have declined steadily in both counties. In 1890, in both counties, judges made such opinions or findings in over 70% of non-jury trials. Today they are made in only 34% of such cases in Alameda and 29% in San Benito (the change from 1890 is significant at the .4% level for Alameda, and the .6% level for San Benito). Courts feel less necessity to justify their actions formally, perhaps because of the increased routinization of their work. Again, differences between the two counties are small; if anything, the rural court works in a slightly more perfunctory way.

F. Costs of Litigation—Time and Delay

Delays and costs may be important factors that act to discourage litigation in modern courts. Formal litigation today is much slower than before . . . despite the increase in routinization of procedures and results. Delays are greater in the densely populated county of Alameda than in San Benito (three-month final disposition difference between counties; significant at the .1% level). In 1890, 44% of the cases in Alameda and 52% of the cases in San Benito reached their final outcome within three months after filing. In 1970, in Alameda, only 9% of the cases now reach such an outcome (the difference is significant at the .1% level); in San Benito, only 26% (significant at the 2% level) are cleared from the docket within three months. Most San Benito cases take between six months and a year to reach their final outcomes; in Alameda delays up to one to two years are more frequent. Delays are particularly great for cases which go to trial. In 1890, 72% of such cases in Alameda were tried within six months after filing. In 1970, only 13% were brought to trial within six months (significant at the .1% level). The actual trials also take longer. Only 6.1% of the trials in Alameda took longer than one day in 1890. Today, 27% of the Alameda trials—63% of San Benito trials—take longer than one day.

G. Volume of Litigation

Studies in a number of counties suggest an inverse relationship between economic growth and volume of formal litigation. That is, highly developed economic systems do *not* show growth in their litigation rates; on the contrary, rates tend to stabilize or decline in the face of rapid economic growth.

Why should this be so? The idea is that formal court processes are slow, expensive, technical. Court process is, from the economic standpoint, inefficient; and society will take no steps to encourage it for ordinary civil disputes. That formal court processes are inefficient and irrelevant to economic life, is quite consistent with our data. But it is not so clear that the two counties confirm the prediction that litigation declines as an economy develops. The rate of cases per 1,000 population in the two counties was shown in Table 5-1. A number of interesting facts emerge from this table. One is the convergence of the counties. In 1890, urban Alameda was more litigious than rural San Benito; differences today are very small.

Compared to 1890, both counties show an apparent rise in cases per 1,000 population. But the rate in Alameda in 1910 was higher than it is today; and San Benito's ratio declined slightly between 1950 and 1970. And the figures are too crude to be used as indicators of litigation rates. For one thing, they do not take into account either the federal courts or the inferior trial courts. For another thing, they do not take into account the nature of the cases litigated. Before we can speak of "litigation rates" we must define litigation: is an uncontested divorce "litigation"? To test the hypothesis of declining litigation, we would really need some valid measure of dispute settlement, for all courts, in a community. "Litigation" would mean a proceeding containing elements of dispute, that were not resolved before one party filed a complaint, or perhaps not resolved without the intervention of a judge. Perhaps such a "true" rate would show a decline since 1890; but our figures do not permit us the luxury of a guess.

[III.] Conclusion

Quantitative indicators of court performances in these two counties confirm one general hypothesis: the dispute settlement function in the courts is declining. In general, the trial courts today perform routine administration; dispute settlement has steadily shrunk as a proportion of their caseload. Most cases today are quite routine. In 1890, a higher percentage of cases involved genuine disputes, and the work of the courts was on the whole less stereotyped. The rate of uncontested judgments has multiplied while the incidence of contested judgments has fallen. A smaller percentage of cases are brought to trial today, and courts issue formal opinions or findings in far fewer cases. Court delays have significantly lengthened.

What factors account for the routinization of the work of modern courts? One possibility is that uncertainty—a prime breeder of litigation—has declined in the law; that rules are more "settled" than in 1890. Some kinds of dispute (over land titles for example) have been largely resolved, or reduced to order by new social arrangements, such as the use of title insurance, and improvement in county record-keeping. But there is no easy way to measure this factor in the aggregate. Our assumption is that some areas of law do become "settled"; but as they do, new uncertainties replace old ones. Land titles were less chaotic in 1930 than in 1890; but as this problem faded, the automobile accident more than replaced it, creating a new and complex field of law.

For another possible explanation, one may point to factors associated with *urbanization* and the particular brand of economic development that has occurred in the United States. The population in 1970 is mobile and rootless. Overwhelmingly, people live in metropolitan areas. They deal primarily with strangers. The ordered social relations of small towns and traditional courts—a world of face to face relations—has vanished.

In this light, we might expect the modern court in San Benito to resemble its 1890 ancestor, and traditional courts, more closely than we would expect of the Alameda court. Surprisingly, however, the data of 1970 do not show much difference between the counties. On the contrary, San Benito's courts play, if anything, a more routinized role than the courts in urban Alameda. In San Benito, more cases involve routine matters, a larger proportion are uncontested, fewer are brought to trial, and courts more rarely issue formal opinions or findings.

There is a general assumption in the literature that "modernization" brings about a general shift from social-harmony litigation to a more formal style of dispute-settlement. Our data suggests a rather different kind of evolution. To be sure, in 1890 it was already true that precious little of the work of the court conformed to the social harmony style. That had perhaps already virtually vanished in the United States, unless one were to find it in the justice courts, which is doubtful. Did it ever exist? The records of colonial courts suggest that at the very dawn of American history there were institutions that came closer to the anthropologists' model. But by 1890, the Superior Court of Alameda was already an urban court; and as for San Benito, while it was a small community, it was hardly a tightly knit, traditional community. On the contrary, it was a raw and new community—a community of recent arrivals, transients, strangers. If anything, it is more of a face-to-face community today; and yet the social harmony style is even more absent.

The evolution, then, does not go from social harmony to legalistic style, and find a resting point. Rather, dispute settlement vanishes completely from the courts; it is replaced by routine administration. Whether the legalistic style was an intermediate phase, or whether the development was directly from social harmony style to routine, our data do not allow us to state with confidence.

Our evidence shows, then, that in the two California courts—one sitting in a bustling urban metropolis, the other not—the dispute settlement function has shriveled to almost nothing; the routine administrative function has become predominant.

This seems on the surface rather curious. Certainly, disputes still arise in society, and they probably must be settled. Yet for some reason, they are not settled in court. Of course, it *is* theoretically possible that fewer disputes go to court than in an earlier period because the *number* of disputes has fallen. We have no way to measure the number of disputes that *might* go to court, if court were costless and freely accessible. Nor do we have any information about the *relative* number of disputes in San Benito County, compared to Alameda, now or in any other period. It is barely possible that, when genuine disputes do occur in San Benito, a larger proportion of them may actually be taken to court than in Alameda. But there is no obvious reason why the number of actual "disputes" should be so low in the two counties; and the most likely assumption is that the court itself—its style, its mode of operation—discourages its use for dispute settlement, rather than that the number of issues or disputes has declined.

. . .

6

Environmental and Structural Variables as Determinants of Issues in State Courts of Last Resort

Burton M. Atkins and Henry R. Glick

A considerable body of research published in the last several years has demonstrated the important effects of socioeconomic and political diversification upon political processes and policy outputs. Yet little research has been conducted on the impact of environmental differences on judicial processes and policy. This is not to suggest, however, that the linkage between environmental conditions and courts has been totally ignored. On the contrary, most models of the judicial processes make some reference to this linkage, and the systems model in particular underscores the effects of the flow of demands and conflict from the environment towards the judicial system. However, while reference is often made to these relationships, the literature is still devoid of empirical research that systematically examines the impact of environment upon judicial action. To remedy this omission, the present study will offer a comparative examination of the relationship between socioeconomic and political conditions within the fifty American states, on the one hand, and issues decided by state courts of last resort on the other.

Our focus is upon issues resolved by state supreme courts, since the types of controversies that political institutions confront is an important component among the factors that determine the types of policies courts make. While processes that determine which issues will be considered and which will be ignored are important for all institutions, they are particularly relevant for courts, since whether or not judicial action will be invoked is greatly dependent upon the types of demands and conflicts brought to them by participants and processes beyond the institution itself. This is not to suggest, of course, that appellate courts cannot exercise any discretion over the types of issues they will resolve. However, the discretion exercised is normally negative rather than positive, with the parameters of the issue universe set by actors often far from the courtroom. Thus, since courts are passive rather than active policymakers, the characteristics of the socioeconomic and political environment which generate demands and conflicts may be particularly important predictors to the kinds of issues resolved by judicial institutions.

Reprinted from Burton M. Atkins and Henry R. Glick, "Environmental and Structural Variables as Determinants of Issues in State Courts of Last Resort," *American Journal of Political Science,* vol. 20, no. 1 (1976), pp. 97–114, by permission of the Wayne State University Press. Copyright © 1976. Footnotes and references omitted.

We are choosing state supreme courts as the focus of the study, given their important role as courts of last resort within state political systems. While the powers and roles of these courts vary somewhat, they are nevertheless analogous to the United States Supreme Court in terms of their functional relationship with the political system. By examining these courts, we can also tap the comparative dimension and take advantage of the socioeconomic and political diversity among the fifty states.

By selecting these systemic characteristics as our independent variables, we are not necessarily implying that contextual variables are either the only or most important predictors of issues found in state courts of last resort; nor need we specify that certain levels of statistical explanations will be achieved. Rather, we posit the general hypothesis that contextual variables establish parameters within which judicial policymaking occurs, and our goal is to determine what portion of the variance can be accounted for by socioeconomic and political environments. Moreover, by examining the impact of these forces we can draw upon several cognate bodies of research being conducted by political scientists and begin to examine whether or not the forces that shape public policy within the fifty states have a similar impact upon judicial decisionmaking.

Research Design

The Dependent Variables

State supreme court decisions filed with full opinions during 1966–67 formed the data base for this study. Since considerable variation exists in the number of decisions rendered each year by state supreme courts, two criteria were used to determine how many decisions from each court would be coded. If the total number of decisions on the merits was less than one hundred, all cases were included in the data set; however, if the N for a court was considerably larger, a sample was taken so that at least one hundred cases were included. This procedure created a data set of 4,974 cases, with a mean for each state of 99.8.

An important feature of many state supreme courts that distinguishes them from the United States Supreme Court is that they generally decide an enormous variety of issues, many of which hardly ever appear at all in Supreme Court decisions. Besides criminal appeals, found frequently in most state courts of last resort, economic controversies such as wills, trusts, estates, contract disputes, and real estate litigation constitute a large proportion of decisions on the merits. Other issues found frequently in state supreme courts are divorce, motor vehicle accident, and personal injury suits. The coding format used to collect these data obviously had to be sufficiently flexible to capture the range of litigation found in fifty courts of last resort, yet when data collection was completed, the code sheet provided for more than fifty categories of issues.

In order to facilitate data analysis, these categories were reduced to five. The first includes criminal appeals with or without a concomitant constitutional claim. Civil rights litigation, defined as cases raising questions under the First and Fourteenth Amendments of the federal Constitution, or similar provisions in state constitutions, were coded in a second category. Though relatively uncommon in state courts, civil rights issues are an important component of the decisions rendered by the United States Supreme Court, and thus provide a basis of policy comparison between the state courts of last resort and their federal counterpart.

A third category contains cases that raise issues concerning regulation and redistribution of economic resources. For the most part, cases in this category are tax appeals or appeals from state regulatory agencies and commissions in which the supreme courts review decisions associated with the redistribution of wealth, implicitly requiring the court to balance the ethic of governmental intrusions into the business sector against the ethic associated with a free marketplace. As with civil liberties and rights, these issues parallel those found frequently in the United States Supreme Court.

The last two categories include private litigation, cases in which both parties are individuals, as opposed to corporations, criminal defendants, or state agencies. On the assumption that some judges may view questions concerning the distribution of economic resources as more important than noneconomic problems, these cases were separated on the basis of whether or not an economic dispute was involved. Private economic settlements include various claims associated with contests over wills, trusts, estates, landlord-tenant controversies, and disputes over property titles and sales. The primary distinction between private economic and private noneconomic litigation is that the former directly involves conflict over control of economic resources, whereas the latter, while often involving money, does not necessarily stem from economic conflicts. Among the private noneconomic conflicts are personal liability suits, wrongful death actions, and malpractice suits.

Cases that could not be identified as belonging in any of the above categories were omitted from the data analysis since they lacked any apparent common dimension. Of the original 4,974 cases, approximately 81% (4,045) were retained. The distribution of these issues in state supreme courts is reported in Table 6-1.

Environmental Variables

State environmental characteristics . . . measuring six aspects of state socioeconomic and political settings [are employed]. Also employed to measure state characteristics are two policy factors. . . . Since courts share policymaking with legislatures and administrative agencies, the types of decisions made by these branches of state government help to shape the types of issues involved in court litigations. For our purposes, therefore, the public policy orientation of the state is conceptualized as one of the contextual variables accounting for variations among issues found in court decisions.

Political Characteristics. These are measured by two factors, one labeled Professionalism-Local Reliance, and the other, Competition-Turnout. The factor scores are based on an original set of 53 items which measure participation and party competition, characteristics of the legislative, executive, and judicial branches of the states, and individual and mutual aspects of the state, local, and intergovernmental fiscal structures. Professionalism-Local Reliance primarily concerns salaries of judges and legislators, legislative staff budgets, and local tax effort. Competition-Turnout primarily concerns measures of gubernatorial election turnout and one-party domination. . . .

Socioeconomic Characteristics. The industrialization factor taps economic and occupational activity and has the proportion of the population engaged in manufacturing and the value added per capita by manufacturing loading highly on it. Affluence, the second factor, is heavily regional along a North-South axis. States loading high on the positive end of this dimension are characterized by high education and generally are indicative of modern, affluent cultures.

TABLE 6-1
Issues in State Supreme Courts (Percent of Caseload)

State	Criminal	Civil Liberty	Economic Regulation	Private Economic	Private Noneconomic
Alabama	24.5	1.1	16.0	23.4	21.3
Alaska	41.9	0.0	4.8	22.6	14.5
Arizona	48.5	1.0	4.1	20.6	7.2
Arkansas	19.6	2.1	10.3	37.1	14.4
California	44.8	4.2	13.5	9.4	6.3
Colorado	18.6	2.1	17.5	22.7	9.3
Connecticut	20.9	2.3	22.1	14.0	8.1
Delaware	26.1	5.7	19.3	13.6	12.5
Florida	36.0	0.0	8.0	6.0	2.0
Georgia	21.2	2.0	16.2	24.2	3.0
Hawaii	14.9	4.5	16.4	31.3	1.4
Idaho	21.6	1.0	6.2	32.0	14.4
Illinois	57.3	1.0	13.5	3.1	5.2
Indiana	71.7	1.0	6.1	4.0	4.0
Iowa	29.3	3.0	13.1	24.2	9.1
Kansas	33.3	1.0	9.1	32.3	13.1
Kentucky	20.2	0.0	10.2	21.2	22.2
Louisiana	53.5	2.0	8.1	15.2	9.1
Maine	45.5	0.0	14.8	17.0	9.1
Maryland	5.0	5.0	20.0	41.0	15.0
Massachusetts	18.6	4.9	20.6	34.3	16.7
Michigan	24.4	4.4	21.1	25.6	16.7
Minnesota	40.0	4.0	2.0	29.0	19.0
Mississippi	15.6	2.1	4.2	19.8	20.8
Missouri	50.0	3.0	11.0	17.0	15.0
Montana	27.1	2.1	10.4	19.8	17.7
Nebraska	32.0	3.0	13.0	23.0	13.0
Nevada	43.3	0.0	9.3	18.6	11.3
New Hampshire	14.1	0.0	9.8	28.3	25.0
New Jersey	28.3	1.0	13.1	18.2	13.1
New Mexico	48.0	2.0	4.1	29.6	9.2
New York	23.4	2.1	9.6	26.6	11.7
North Carolina	40.0	1.0	5.0	27.0	21.0
North Dakota	12.1	0.0	15.5	20.7	29.3
Ohio	23.7	2.1	32.0	14.4	17.5
Oklahoma	45.9	0.7	6.4	20.3	11.1
Oregon	33.0	1.0	9.3	22.7	14.4
Pennsylvania	34.3	2.0	13.1	17.2	15.2
Rhode Island	22.0	1.0	18.0	24.0	20.0
South Carolina	22.2	0.0	9.1	34.3	23.0
South Dakota	27.4	0.0	9.6	26.0	15.1
Tennessee	26.5	1.0	14.3	38.8	11.2
Texas	52.0	0.5	6.0	25.0	7.5
Utah	26.3	0.0	12.6	26.0	15.8
Vermont	28.0	0.0	4.0	33.3	17.3
Virginia	28.7	3.2	13.8	25.5	20.2
Washington	45.7	1.1	12.0	17.4	9.8
West Virginia	16.7	0.0	9.3	27.8	24.1
Wisconsin	29.0	3.2	8.6	24.7	18.3
Wyoming	23.5	0.0	4.4	26.5	25.0
	$\bar{X}=31.12$	$\bar{X}=1.70$	$\bar{X}=11.60$	$\bar{X}=23.12$	$\bar{X}=14.30$
	SD=13.52	SD=1.55	SD=5.85%	SD=8.25	SD=6.15
	CV=43%	CV=91%	CV=50%	CV=35%	CV=43%

Public Policy Factors. . . . The first factor is Welfare-Education, and separates states on the basis of amount of welfare payments, the likelihood of high school pupils to remain until graduation, and student success on nationwide examinations. The second factor is Highway-Natural Resources, and is characterized by measures of rural highway mileage and highway expenditures, measures of fish and wildlife services and expenditures for natural resources. Since the political conflicts that flow to the judiciary are essentially one component of the distribution of conflicts in the environment, these measures are useful in assessing the relationship between issues decided by the state courts of last resort and the policy orientation of other institutions within the state. . . .

Method of Analysis

Multiple regression models were used to examine the relationship between environmental variables and the issues decided by state supreme courts. The first model tests the total effects of environmental variables upon the distribution of issues and assumes a linear effect of the independent variables on each of the issue categories. This model hypothesizes that much of the variation in issues decided by state supreme courts can be accounted for by the state's environmental characteristics which shape the conflicts requiring political and judicial resolution. Moreover, it is hypothesized that criminal law, civil liberties, and government economic regulation decisions will be positively related to economic development and political competition, positively related to expenditures on health and welfare services, but negatively related to expenditures on Highways-Natural Resources. Private litigation, both economic and noneconomic, should occur most frequently in states low on Affluence and Industrialization, low on Professionalism and Competition, low on Welfare, but high on Highways-Natural Resources.

These hypotheses, however, do not presume that there is a direct correspondence between socioeconomic and political conditions on the one hand, and issues resolved by state courts on the other; numerous processes can divert certain types of controversies from the judicial system and thereby skew the distribution of issues. Insofar as a state supreme court is concerned, one particularly important variable is whether or not the court system of which it is a part contains an intermediate appellate court.

Intermediate appellate courts are usually established to reduce the case load of courts of last resort. In practice, however, the effect of intermediate appellate courts is not so much to reduce the case load as it is to redistribute the types of issues decided by the court of last resort. Cases not raising fundamental issues are left to the intermediate appellate court, thus allocating the supreme court's time more effectively by reserving their attention to issues perceived to be more critical to the political system. The second regression model tests for effects of state intermediate appellate courts upon the distribution of issues decided by courts of last resort by adding Court System as a dummy variable to the equation, with a value of zero when no intermediate appellate court exists, and a value of 1 when the intermediate appellate court does exist.

For the purposes of this study, criminal law issues were analyzed in a third regression model. While we have hypothesized that the distribution of criminal cases decided by state supreme courts is a function of environmental variables and the court structure, one would obviously expect that the amount of criminal litigation would be a reflection of the number of cases prosecuted by the state. Since information on the number of prosecutions was not available, a measure of reported crime in the states was used as a surrogate and added as a separate variable in the regression equation.

The final regression model tested for an interaction effect between crime rate and the presence or absence of an appellate court upon the distribution of criminal law cases decided by state supreme court. This was done because the continued increase of criminal litigation in state and federal judicial systems, recognized as placing severe strains upon the legal systems, has spawned attempts to shield state supreme courts from routine criminal appeals. One tactic often used to divert criminal appeals is to create an intermediate appellate court between trial and supreme courts. Thus, the joint effects of high crime rates and intermediate appellate courts were added to the stepwise model as a separate interaction term.

Results of Regression Analysis: Model 1

The data in Table 6-2 report the contribution of each of the three pairs of indicators as well as the explanatory power of all six. The correlation between each environmental component and each issue, it should be observed, is the R between the two factors comprising the dimension and each issue. For example, the R representing the relationship between economic conditions and civil liberties decisions (.20) is the multiple correlation between affluence and industrialization, on the one hand, and civil liberties decisions on the other. Likewise, the R representing the relationship between the political dimension and civil liberties decisions (.31) reflects the multiple correlation of each of the two dimensions within that environmental descriptor and that issue. Since the two dimensions within each environmental component are uncorrelated, there is no statistical redundancy within this multiple correlation. Also reported in Table 6-2 are the regression coefficients for each environmental dimension. Finally, at the bottom of each column are the R and statistical significance for each model. These data show that no one set of environmental factors is primarily responsible for the variance on the issues, although the economic descriptors are marginally stronger correlates with private litigation and government economic regulation suits.

Another basis for comparing the relative effects of the environmental indicators is their explanatory contribution in the regression equations. Table 6-2 shows that affluence is the most important variable affecting civil liberties, private economic, and private noneconomic litigation, whereas industrialization is the most important predictor of economic regulation controversies, and almost as important as affluence in the civil liberties equation.

Additional information concerning the impact of environmental variables is provided by the multiple R for all six factors in the Model 1 equations. These correlations range from a low of .21 for criminal law to .60 for private noneconomic suits. While the average amount of explained variance in the five equations is not very high, the data do indicate that environmental variables are an important component in the configuration of processes that shape issues decided by state courts of last resort. Yet the fact that the multiple R's vary as much as they do, especially among issues that are fairly comparable, such as private economic and private noneconomic controversies, not only indicates substantial differences in the impact of environment from one issue to the next, but also suggests redundancy among the independent variables. Part of the problem stems from the fact that while each pair of factors comprising an environmental component is uncorrelated . . . there are several high interdimensional correlations. For example, . . . Professionalism is correlated .72 with Industrialization, Competition .67 with Affluence, and Competition

TABLE 6-2
Regression Coefficients of Six Environmental Variables on State Supreme Court Decisions

	Civil Liberties					Private Suits (Noneconomic)					Private Suits (Economic)				
		Model 1		Model 2			Model 1		Model 2			Model 1		Model 2	
	R	b	Beta	b	Beta	R	b	Beta	b	Beta	R	b	Beta	b	Beta
Economic Component	.20					.35					.34				
Affluence		.81	.33	.95	.39		−6.63	−1.01	−6.19	−.94		−5.31	−.58	−4.93	−.54
Industrialization		−.85	−.33	−.80	−.33		1.52	.23	1.70	.26		.12	.01	.27	.03
Political Component	.31					.29					.29				
Professionalism		.71	.30	.96	.41		.78	−.12	.02	.003		−.48	−.05	.21	.02
Competition		.00	.00	−.01	.00		.87	.14	.81	.12		−1.92	.22	−1.98	−.22
Policy Component	.25					.21					.20				
Highways		−1.04	−.45	−1.20	−.52		4.28	.68	3.77	.60		3.56	.41	3.12	.35
Welfare		−.20	−.08	−.46	−.19		2.85	.45	2.01	.32		3.56	.41	2.84	.32
Court System				−1.37	−.28				−4.46	−.34				−3.82	−.21
		R = .40		R = .47			R = .60		R = .67			R = .44		R = .47	
		p = .27		p = .162			p = .003		p = .001			p = .15		p = .14	

Economic Regulation

	R	Model 1 b	Model 1 Beta	Model 2 b	Model 2 Beta
Economic Component	.47				
Affluence		2.46	.406	3.76	.619
Industrialization		3.53	.581	2.56	.421
Political Component	.26				
Competition		-.918	-.158	-.952	-.164
Professionalism		-1.86	-.316	-1.43	-.243
Policy Component	.42				
Highways		-2.82	.487	-3.09	-.533
Welfare		-.922	-.158	-1.36	-.234
Court System				-2.34	-.195
		R = .575		R = .598	
		p = .008		p = .009	

Criminal Law

	R	Model 1 (Environmental) b	Beta	Model 2 (Court Structure) b	Beta	Model 3 (Crime Rate) b	Beta	Model 4 (Interaction) b	Beta
Economic Component	.16								
Affluence		2.11	.146	.379	.026	-6.21	-.43	-6.175	-.42
Industrialization		-.520	-.036	-1.22	-.085	-1.68	-.11	-1.626	-.11
Political Component	.19								
Competition		2.56	.186	2.82	.204	4.62	.33	4.265	.33
Professionalism		.937	.067	-2.19	-.157	-3.10	-.22	3.11	-.22
Policy Component	.13								
Highways		-1.61	-.117	.358	.015	1.23	.08	1.25	.09
Welfare		1.55	-.112	1.70	.123	4.00	.29	3.92	.28
Court System				17.32	.608	14.56	.51	13.57	.47
Crime Rate						.158	.45	.155	.44
Crime Rate × System								9.56	.03
		R = .210		R = .551		R = .63		R = .63	
		p = .925		p = .03		p = .006		p = .01	

TABLE 6-3
Zero Order Correlations, Environmental Factors by Issues

	Criminal Appeals	Civil Liberties	Economic Regulation	Private Economic	Private Noneconomic
Affluence	.15	.11	.11	−.27	−.30
Industrialization	.07	.16	.46	−.20	−.18
Professionalism	.08	.30	.25	−.19	−.28
Competition	.17	.02	.03	−.22	−.02
Welfare	.13	.14	.16	−.17	−.11
Highways-Natural Resources	−.01	−.21	−.39	.11	.17

.70 with Welfare. This multicollinearity is not damaging to the analysis so long as we are aware of the relative importance of each environmental component. However, the problem is compounded when several of the independent variables have higher correlations among themselves than they have with the dependent variables. . . . [I]n Table 6-3 the zero order correlations between the factors and issues, shows that this is indeed the case. As a result of these patterns, the magnitudes, and especially the signs of the regression coefficients in the equations, are affected, thus obscuring potentially important relationships in the data.

Some of this ambiguity can be removed by more closely examining the zero order correlations between the environmental characteristics and issues. While these data cannot show the unique contributions made by each variable, they will show any patterns between environmental conditions and issues in the supreme courts unencumbered by the multicollinearity in the regression equations. While none of the relationships in Table 6-3 are strong, several patterns do emerge. Private litigation is more likely to appear in less affluent, less industrialized, and less politically diversified states. The appearance of these decisions is also negatively correlated with high expenditures for welfare policies (a positive correlate of affluence and industrialization), and positively related to high expenditures for highways and natural resources (a negative correlate of industrialization but a positive correlate of affluence). In other words, supreme courts within more rural, and politically undifferentiated states tend to decide greater proportions of private litigation. By contrast, civil liberties and government economic regulation decisions appear in states that score higher on affluence, economic development, and political professionalism. Criminal appeals do not show any strong correlations with any of the environmental characteristics.

While our research design is not longitudinal, the data do suggest that the emergence of conflicts in supreme court decisions may be hierarchical. In other words, the fact that environmental diversification is related to the appearance of certain issues in supreme courts does not imply that other litigation is not appearing at all in the state judicial system. Rather, it would seem that as political and economic diversification generates alterations in the universe of litigation, supreme courts restructure their decisional priorities to meet changing demand patterns. Thus, supreme courts within rural, less affluent, and less politically competitive states are not relegated to secondary status because they decide substantial portions of private litigation. Since their role is determined in part by the types of conflict generated by the environment, these courts of last resort would naturally decide few civil rights or economic regulation cases until economic and political diversification develops to the point where it generates litigation that would have de facto priority in the supreme courts. This developmental process would have the effect of "bumping" private litigation from the court of last resort to some lower court. Once we presume that courts of last resort resolve issues perceived to be of fundamental importance within a political system, it follows that the appearance of larger proportions of civil liberties, criminal law, and particularly economic regulation cases may be indicative of judicial systems which have remained attuned to changing patterns of demands entering the political system from the differentiated political and socioeconomic environment.

Besides reflecting changing patterns in the environment, the distribution of issues resolved by supreme courts also indicates, in some instances, how certain groups perceive the benefits of judicial action. For example, it is well recognized that civil rights groups avoided southern supreme courts and sought judicial remedies in federal courts instead. Similarly, other groups, particularly business or labor litigants, might avoid a certain supreme court because of perceived bias in its prevailing ideology. Thus the appearance of groups in court decisions may be closely related to the types of decisions made by supreme courts.

Effects of Intermediate Appellate Courts: Model 2

Since economic and political development is associated with an increase in litigation, intermediate appellate courts would presumably be established in states having complex socioeconomic and political structures. To test this hypothesis, Table 6-4 compares the mean factor scores of states with and without intermediate appellate courts. As anticipated, the characteristics of the states do differ. In particular, states with intermediate appellate courts tend to score high on Professionalism, high on Industrialization, and low on Highways-Natural Resources (a negative correlate of economic development).

The fact that the establishment of intermediate appellate courts is related to socioeconomic and political diversification suggests a certain restructuring of issues in supreme courts with an appellate court below. In particular, it would be expected that supreme courts with the appellate court below would decide fewer cases involving personal justice, these having been siphoned away by the lower appellate court, and would decide larger proportions of criminal law, civil liberties, and government economic regulation cases.

The regression coefficients for the Court System variable entered into the equations for each issue show the effect of intermediate appellate courts upon the distribution of issues. Some of the results are startling. The negative signs of the coefficients indicate that the appearance of four of the issues is inversely related to the presence of an intermediate appellate court. However, supreme courts with intermediate appellate courts below are

TABLE 6-4
Mean Factor Scores by Type of Court System

	States with Inter-mediate Appellate Court	States Without Inter-mediate Appellate Court
Professionalism	.561	−.310
Competition	−.271	.173
Welfare-Education	−.121	.084
Highways-Natural Resources	−.528	.322
Affluence	−.172	.092
Industrialization	.455	−.250

not necessarily deciding fewer cases, since the sign and magnitude of the regression coefficient for Court System on criminal appeals (17.32) shows that the existence of an intermediate appellate court is associated with substantial increases of criminal decisions rendered by the supreme court. The effect of intermediate appellate courts on the appearance of criminal law decisions is also apparent in the substantial increment of the R from .210 to .551 when that variable is added to the regression equation. The empirical significance of the marked increase in criminal litigation decided by supreme courts with intermediate appellate courts below is difficult to ascertain without data on the flow of litigation at all tiers of the state judicial systems. In other words, it is impossible to ascertain whether or not these court systems have so much criminal litigation that the intermediate appellate courts cannot effectively shield the supreme court from them, or whether or not the appearance of these cases represents a policy by the supreme courts to devote their attention to criminal law cases. In either event, the data do show that some supreme courts, by necessity or design, are functioning primarily as criminal courts of last resort.

Some evidence concerning the environmental conditions that transform some state supreme courts into de facto criminal courts of last resort can be obtained by adding the Crime Rate variable and the interaction term representing the joint effects of crime rate and the presence or absence of an intermediate appellate court to the regression equations. The results show that the addition of Crime Rate (Model 3) increases the multiple R to .63. More importantly, however, the new regression coefficient indicates that while Crime Rate is an important predictor to the percentage of criminal appeals decided by a state supreme court, Court System remains the most critical variable in the regression equation. However, the Model 4 equation shows that the interaction term does not add substantially to the explained variance, and that Court System and Crime Rate remain as important determinants of criminal appeals.

It thus appears that one reason why large numbers of criminal appeals are resolved by supreme courts with intermediate appellate courts below is that the environment within which these judicial systems operate generates considerable criminal litigation. Although the data are not currently available, it may be that intermediate appellate courts in the very same states are also besieged with criminal appeals, and thus can only minimally shield the court of last resort. This suggests, in turn, that although a court may have certiorari discretion, a device that seeks to allow the court reasonable initiative over which issues it will decide, environmental stress may dictate the parameters within which the discretion is exercised. Though intermediate appellate courts are created to restore the initiative within courts of last resort beleaguered by litigation, our data suggest that their presence may not have the intended effect when environmental conditions effectively set the agenda for the court of last resort. It seems that supreme courts may remain sensitive to environmental stress only at the cost of deferring the resolution of certain issues to courts below.

Conclusions

The data reported in this study demonstrate that environmental variables are important predictors to the types of issues resolved through state supreme court decisions. Court System, it has been shown, is an important structural variable shaping the distribution of issues as they emerge in state courts of last resort. Although our emphasis has been upon the effects of the environmental variables, the fact that the presence or absence of an intermediate appellate court affects the distribution of issues on supreme courts suggests the need to incorporate additional court system variables into models seeking to account for the types of conflicts found in courts of last resort. By examining aggregate relationships between judicial decisions and environmental conditions, we naturally bypass some of the more subtle relationships between courts and other governmental institutions and environmental conditions that bear upon the types of issues resolved by supreme courts. . . .

CHAPTER THREE

DEMAND REGULATION: TRIAL COURTS

American courts are reactive institutions; that is, they become involved in dispute processing at the initiative of parties who are not members of the judiciary. To say that courts are reactive is not, however, to say that they are defenseless. Not every dispute that is brought to court receives a full and formal judicial hearing. American courts employ a variety of mechanisms, some of which they control directly and some of which are controlled externally, to refuse to decide disputes or to encourage the settlement of disputes without a judicial decision. The selections in this chapter concern the most important of these mechanisms in both criminal and civil litigation.

Disputes between the state and any of its citizens over alleged violations of the criminal law begin with the decision to arrest.[1] This decision is of substantial interest and importance but it is rather remote from the interests of someone concerned with the activities of American courts. It is remote because intervening between arrest and appearance in court are several screening stages that substantially reduce the number of criminal cases reaching the courts.[2] One might imagine a progressively smaller number of cases flowing through a funnel until one reaches the theoretical end, the formal trial.

The two most important screening decisions that reduce the number of criminal cases reaching court are the prosecutor's decision to charge and the defendant's decision whether to waive the right to a formal trial by pleading guilty.[3] There are other screening stages such as indictment by a grand jury, arraignment, and pretrial or motion hearings, but none are as significant or as obvious as the charging and pleading decisions.

The prosecutor is a public official who is given the responsibility for deciding which suspects arrested by the police should be formally charged with having committed a crime and what the charges should be. In making decisions, the prosecutor in theory considers two basic questions. First, is there a reasonable probability of the suspect's factual guilt? Second, is there enough legally admissible evidence to establish guilt in a trial? If the answer to either of these questions is no, then, at least in theory, the prosecutor ought not to charge a suspect with a crime.[4] Given that the reason why the police make an arrest may have little or nothing to do with the task of enforcing the criminal law, what frequently happens is that the prosecutor is faced with the necessity of releasing many of those arrested. The police arrest people for a variety of reasons, such as harassment of "undesirables," protective detention of drunks, or merely to allow disputants time to cool their tempers. Thus prosecutors may have neither the necessary evidence nor the inclination to charge.

The considerations that influence the charging decision may have less to do with the evidence of a suspect's guilt than is generally assumed. Five such influences should be noted. First, prosecutors, especially in large cities, typically carry a heavy workload, or at least they perceive their workload to be burdensome. They believe that they have more cases to handle than they can reasonably process in an efficient and effective way. To the extent that this is true, prosecutors have an incentive to be lenient in cases where the evidence is not strong—that is, to use the decision not to charge as a way of maintaining control over their own workload.

A second influence affecting the decision to charge is the prosecutor's need or desire to achieve a high conviction rate. This is often assumed to be an extremely important part of a prosecutor's professional orientation. We think, however, that its importance may be overestimated. To the extent that a concern for maintaining a high conviction rate *does* influence the prosecutor, it may lead to a refusal to charge in cases in which there may be enough evidence to go to trial but not enough evidence to make conviction a sure thing.

A third influence on the charging decision is the expressed interest of criminal court judges regarding the disposition of particular kinds of criminal cases. Judicial resources are scarce and judges frequently communicate to prosecutors the manner in which they desire to expend them—that is, the kinds of cases they think ought to be emphasized. Thus, prosecutors may not charge people who are arrested for committing the kinds of offenses that judges believe to be trivial or insignificant.

The prosecutor's sense of "substantive justice" is a fourth influence on the charging decision. Prosecutors may use their power to charge as a way of imposing sanctions on those who they believe deserve punishment. They may do so even though they may not believe that a case can be made in court or even though they are confident that no guilty plea will be forthcoming. In this sense the charging decision is the prosecutor's way of dealing with people who may be factually but not legally culpable for violating the criminal code. The charging decision, by threatening a suspect with trial and by establishing a formal record of prosecution, imposes sanctions even on those who the prosecutor knows cannot be convicted.

Finally, prosecutors may charge in anticipation that a suspect will plead guilty even in cases in which the prosecutor does not believe there is sufficient evidence to convict. Each of these influences may also be important in encouraging prosecutors and judges to dismiss cases even after the initial charging decision. Each of the five influences is as important as the official determination of factual or legal guilt. The reading by Cole (selection 7), which is based on a case study of a prosecutor's office, illustrates several of these points.

Once an individual is charged with a serious crime the commission of which the prosecutor believes can be proven in court, all that stands between the suspect and a formal trial is the decision whether to claim innocence or to plead guilty. In most American courts the overwhelming majority of criminal cases are terminated by a plea of guilty. This perhaps indicates, first, that the charging decisions made by prosecutors are so accurate that those who are in fact innocent tend to be screened out of the judicial process without being charged. Second, the high percentage of criminal cases terminated by guilty pleas may result from the particular cost/benefit calculations of individuals charged with crimes. The costs of going to trial include lawyers' fees, time that may or may not have to be spent in jail, uncertainty, and the risk of incurring a more severe penalty than would be imposed should the individual voluntarily acknowledge guilt. Each defendant must decide whether the chances of success at trial are worth incurring such costs.[5]

Third, it is often argued that the high incidence of guilty pleas is a direct result of "bargain justice." This phrase implies that no one in the criminal justice system has an incentive to pursue cases through to trial. Prosecutors seek a rapid and certain disposition of cases and attempt to reduce the workload for both the prosecutor and the judge. They may do so by offering concessions to those accused of crimes in return for confessions of guilt. These concessions typically take the form of reduced or dropped charges or promises to recommend leniency in sentencing. It should be recognized, however, that guilty pleas do not necessarily result from an explicit process of bargaining between prosecutor and defendants. Bargaining can take place tacitly with no direct exchange of concessions. A plea of guilty may be entered in anticipation of a leniency recommendation or a dropped charge.

As both the Heumann (selection 8) and Feeley (selection 9) articles point out, it is important to recognize that the high incidence of guilty pleas is not a recent phenomenon. It is not simply a result of the pressures of heavy caseloads but reflects instead the kind of calculations that defendants have always had to make about the costs and benefits of protesting their innocence.

In criminal cases the regulation of demands is largely controlled not by the judges but rather by the prosecutors and defendants. In contrast, in civil litigation the role of the judge in diverting cases from court is frequently more direct. As in the criminal process many civil cases are not filed with any expectation that they will proceed to a formal trial. Filing a lawsuit may simply be a strategic device designed to promote or facilitate out-of-court settlements. In this sense there is a specifiable level of natural "fall-out" that will occur between the filing and the disposition stages in civil litigation. As in the criminal process, most civil cases never go to trial.

In order for a dispute to be processed by a court, it must meet certain formal qualifications. First, it must involve an actionable legal right and an available legal remedy. However, given the wide scope of legal regulation in America today, almost any dispute can be framed as a contest over legal rights. Second, a dispute must fall within the court's geographic or subject matter jurisdiction. Third, the parties must have standing to sue, that is, their dispute must be real, must involve a recognizable conflict of interest and a direct and substantial injury to one of the parties. Traditionally courts have allowed litigants to sustain actions to protect their own personal or property rights. These and other formal requirements provide courts with limited, but nevertheless useful, ways in which they may avoid hearing particular disputes or particular categories of disputes. The requirements are useful to courts precisely because they are broad and flexible; they allow judges wide latitude in deciding which cases will or will not be heard.

One of the many factors that determine which cases persist and go to trial is the pretrial conference. The pretrial conference is of relatively recent vintage and is not employed by all courts or in all civil cases.[6] In some states it is a formal requirement for particular kinds of cases, but in most courts its use is informal and at the discretion of the judge. During pretrial conferences the judge meets with lawyers for both parties and seeks to promote a mutually satisfactory settlement. The judge may suggest what, if anything, a case is "worth" or may try to narrow the differences between the parties in such a way as to increase the likelihood that they themselves can reach a settlement. The reading by federal judge Skelly Wright (selection 10) describes the way in which pretrial conferences operate.

The process of demand regulation in civil and criminal cases ensures that trial courts will give full and formal consideration to a select but not necessarily representative sample of the disputes that they are called upon to deal with. Those cases which receive such consideration will provide courts with the occasion for the most visible exercise of their dispute-processing responsibilities. Therefore, the process of regulating demands deserves special attention.

Notes

1. Wayne Lafave, *Arrest: The Decision to Take a Suspect into Custody* (Boston: Little, Brown, 1965), and Jerome Skolnick, *Justice Without Trial* (New York: Wiley, 1966).

2. By "screening stages" we mean the major occasions when cases once filed in a criminal court are disposed of, resolved, or diverted.

3. See James Eisenstein and Herbert Jacob, *Felony Justice* (Boston: Little, Brown, 1977).

4. Frank Miller, *Prosecution: The Decision to Charge a Suspect with a Crime* (Boston: Little, Brown, 1970). Also see John Hagan, "The Parameters of Criminal Prosecution," *Journal of Criminal Law and Criminology* 65 (1974), 536.

5. Donald Newman, *Conviction: The Determination of Guilt or Innocence Without Trial* (Boston: Little, Brown, 1966). Also see Arthur Rosett and Donald Cressey, *Justice by Consent: Plea Bargains in the American Courthouse* (Philadelphia: Lippincott, 1976); John Klein, *Let's Make a Deal* (Lexington, Mass.: Lexington Books, 1976); and Milton Heumann, *Plea Bargaining: The Experiences of Prosecutors, Judges, and Defense Attorneys* (Chicago: University of Chicago Press, 1978).

6. Maurice Rosenberg, *The Pretrial Conference and Effective Justice* (New York: Columbia University Press, 1964).

7

The Decision to Prosecute

George F. Cole

This paper is based on an exploratory study of the Office of Prosecuting Attorney, King County (Seattle), Washington. . . . An open-ended interview was administered to one-third of the former deputy prosecutors who had worked in the office during the ten-year period 1955–1965. In addition, interviews were conducted with court employees, members of the bench, law enforcement officials, and others having reputations for participation in legal decision-making. Over fifty respondents were contacted during this phase. A final portion of the research placed the author in the role of observer in the prosecutor's office. This experience allowed for direct observation of all phases of the decision to prosecute so that the informal processes of the office could be noted. Discussions with the prosecutor's staff, judges, defendant's attorneys, and the police were held so that the interview data could be placed within an organizational context.

The primary goal of this investigation was to examine the role of the prosecuting attorney as an officer of the legal process within the context of the local political system. . . . By focusing upon the political and social linkages between these systems, it is expected that decision-making in the prosecutor's office will be viewed as a principal ingredient in the authoritative allocation of values.

The Prosecutor's Office in an Exchange System

While observing the interrelated activities of the organizations in the legal process, one might ask, "Why do these agencies cooperate?" If the police refuse to transfer information to the prosecutor concerning the commission of a crime, what are the rewards or sanctions which might be brought against them? Is it possible that organizations maintain a form of "bureaucratic accounting" which, in a sense, keeps track of the resources allocated to an agency and the support returned? How are cues transmitted from one agency to another to influence decision-making? These are some of the questions which must be asked when decisions are viewed as an output of an exchange system.

Reprinted by permission of the Law and Society Association from *Law and Society Review,* Vol. 4, No. 3 (1970), pp. 331–343. Copyright © 1970. Footnotes and most references have been omitted. The *Law and Society Review* is the official publication of the Association.

The major findings of this study are placed within the context of an exchange system. This serves the heuristic purpose of focusing attention upon the linkages found between actors in the decision-making process. In place of the traditional assumptions that the agency is supported solely by statutory authority, this view recognizes that an organization has many clients with which it interacts and upon whom it is dependent for certain resources. As interdependent subunits of a system, then, the organization and its clients are engaged in a set of exchanges across their boundaries. These will involve a transfer of resources between the organizations which will affect the mutual achievement of goals.

The legal system may be viewed as a set of interorganizational exchange relationships analogous to what Long (1962: 142) has called a community game. The participants in the legal system (game) share a common territorial field and collaborate for different and particular ends. They interact on a continuing basis as their responsibilities demand contact with other participants in the process. Thus, the need for the cooperation of other participants can have a bearing on the decision to prosecute. A decision not to prosecute a narcotics offender may be a move to pressure the United States Attorney's Office to cooperate on another case. It is obvious that bargaining occurs not only between the major actors in a case—the prosecutor and the defense attorney—but also between the clientele groups that are influential in structuring the actions of the prosecuting attorney.

Exchanges do not simply "sail" from one system to another, but take place in an institutionalized setting which may be compared to a market. In the market, decisions are made between individuals who occupy boundary-spanning roles, and who set the conditions under which the exchange will occur. In the legal system, this may merely mean that a representative of the parole board agrees to forward a recommendation to the prosecutor, or it could mean that there is extended bargaining between a deputy prosecutor and a defense attorney. In the study of the King County Prosecutor's Office, it was found that most decisions resulted from some type of exchange relationship. The deputies interacted almost constantly with the police and criminal lawyers, while the prosecutor was more closely linked to exchange relations with the courts, community leaders, and the county commissioners.

The Prosecutor's Clientele

In an exchange system, power is largely dependent upon the ability of an organization to create clientele relationships which will support and enhance the needs of the agency. For, although interdependence is characteristic of the legal system, competition with other public agencies for support also exists. Since organizations operate in an economy of scarcity, the organization must exist in a favorable power position in relation to its clientele. Reciprocal and unique claims are made by the organization and its clients. Thus, rather than being oriented toward only one public, an organization is beholden to several publics, some visible and others seen clearly only from the pinnacle of leadership. As Gore (1964: 23) notes, when these claims are "firmly anchored inside the organization and the lines drawn taut, the tensions between conflicting claims form a net serving as the institutional base for the organization."

An indication of the stresses within the judicial system may be obtained by analyzing its outputs. It has been suggested that the administration of justice is a selective process in which only those cases which do not create strains in the organization will ultimately reach the courtroom (Chambliss, 1969: 84). As noted in Figure 7-1, the system operates so

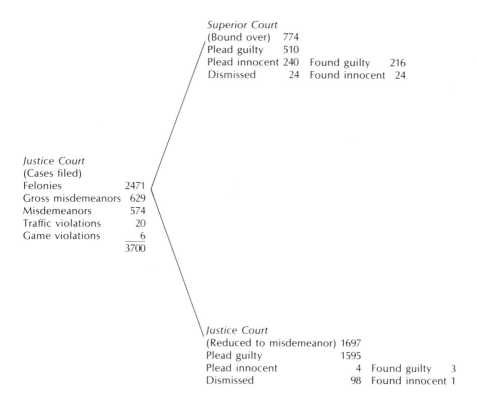

Superior Court
(Bound over)   774
Plead guilty   510
Plead innocent 240   Found guilty   216
Dismissed   24   Found innocent   24

Justice Court
(Cases filed)
Felonies   2471
Gross misdemeanors   629
Misdemeanors   574
Traffic violations   20
Game violations   6
                                    3700

Justice Court
(Reduced to misdemeanor) 1697
Plead guilty   1595
Plead innocent   4   Found guilty   3
Dismissed   98   Found innocent 1

Figure 7-1. Disposition of felony cases—King County, 1964.

that only a small number of cases arrive for trial, the rest being disposed of through reduced charges, *nolle pros.*, and guilty pleas. Not indicated are those cases removed by the police and prosecutor prior to the filing of charges. As the focal organization in an exchange system, the office of prosecuting attorney makes decisions which reflect the influence of its clientele. Because of the scarcity of resources, marketlike relationships, and the organizational needs of the system, prosecutorial decision-making emphasizes the accommodations which are made to the needs of participants in the process.

Police

Although the prosecuting attorney has discretionary power to determine the disposition of cases, this power is limited by the fact that usually he is dependent upon the police for inputs to the system of cases and evidence. The prosecutor does not have the investigative resources necessary to exercise the kind of affirmative control over the types of cases that are brought to him. In this relationship, the prosecutor is not without countervailing power. His main check on the police is his ability to return cases to them for further investigation and to refuse to approve arrest warrants. . . . As noted by many respondents, the police, in turn, are dependent upon the prosecutor to accept the output of their system; rejection of too many cases can have serious repercussions affecting the morale, discipline, and workload of the force.

A request for prosecution may be rejected for a number of reasons relating to questions of evidence. Not only must the prosecutor believe that the evidence will secure a conviction, but he must also be aware of community norms relating to the type of acts that should be prosecuted. . . .

Factors other than those relating to evidence may require that the prosecutor refuse to accept a case from the police. First, the prosecuting attorney serves as a regulator of case loads not only for his own office, but for the rest of the legal system. Constitutional and statutory time limits prevent him and the courts from building a backlog of untried cases. In King County, when the system reached the "overload point," there was a tendency to be more selective in choosing the cases to be accepted. A second reason for rejecting prosecution requests may stem from the fact that the prosecutor is thinking of his public exposure in the courtroom. He does not want to take forward cases which will place him in an embarrassing position. Finally, the prosecutor may return cases to check the quality of police work. . . . Rather than spend the resources necessary to find additional evidence, the police may dispose of a case by sending it back to the prosecutor on a lesser charge, implement the "copping out" machinery leading to a guilty plea, drop the case, or in some instances send it to the city prosecutor for action in municipal court.

In most instances, a deputy prosecutor and the police officer assigned to the case occupy the boundary-spanning roles in this exchange relationship. Prosecutors reported that after repeated contacts they got to know the policemen whom they could trust. . . .

Sometimes the police perform the ritual of "shopping around," seeking to find a deputy prosecutor who, on the basis of past experience, is liable to be sympathetic to their view on a case. At one time, deputies were given complete authority to make the crucial decisions without coordinating their activities with other staff members. In this way the arresting officer would search the prosecutor's office to find a deputy he thought would be sympathetic to the police attitude. . . .

An exchange relationship between a deputy prosecutor and a police officer may be influenced by the type of crime committed by the defendant. The prototype of a criminal is one who violates person and property. However, a large number of cases involve "crimes without victims." This term refers to those crimes generally involving violations of moral codes, where the general public is theoretically the complainant. In violations of laws against bookmaking, prostitution, and narcotics, neither actor in the transaction is interested in having an arrest made. Hence, vice control men must drum up their own business. Without a civilian complainant, victimless crimes give the police and prosecutor greater leeway in determining the charges to be filed.

. . .

Courts

The ways used by the court to dispose of cases is a vital influence in the system. The court's actions affect pressures upon the prison, the conviction rate of the prosecutor, and the work of probation agencies. The judge's decisions act as clues to other parts of the system, indicating the type of action likely to be taken in future cases. . . . Under such conditions, it would be expected that the prosecutor would respond to the judge's actions by reducing the inputs to the court either by not preferring charges or by increasing the pressure for guilty pleas through bargaining. The adjustments of other parts of the system could be expected to follow. For instance, the police might sense the lack of interest of the prosecutor in accepting charges, hence they will send only airtight cases to him for indictment.

The influence of the court on the decision to prosecute is very real. The sentencing history of each judge gives the prosecutor, as well as other law enforcement officials, an indication of the treatment a case may receive in the courtroom. The prosecutor's expectation as to whether the court will convict may limit his discretion over the decisions on whether to prosecute. . . . Since the prosecutor depends upon the plea-bargaining machinery to maintain the flow of cases from his office, the sentencing actions of judges must be predictable. If the defendant and his lawyer are to be influenced to accept a lesser charge or the promise of a lighter sentence in exchange for a plea of guilty, there must be some basis for belief that the judge will fulfill his part of the arrangement. Because judges are unable formally to announce their agreement with the details of the bargain, their past performance acts as a guide.

Within the limits imposed by law and the demands of the system, the prosecutor is able to regulate the flow of cases to the court. He may control the length of time between accusation and trial; hence he may hold cases until he has the evidence which will convict. Alternatively, he may seek repeated adjournment and continuances until the public's interest dies; problems such as witnesses becoming unavailable and similar difficulties make his request for dismissal of prosecution more justifiable. Further, he may determine the type of court to receive the case and the judge who will hear it. Many misdemeanors covered by state law are also violations of a city ordinance. It is a common practice for the prosecutor to send a misdemeanor case to the city prosecutor for processing in the municipal court when it is believed that a conviction may not be secured in justice court. As a deputy said, "If there is no case—send it over to the city court. Things are speedier, less formal, over there."

. . .

Defense Attorneys

. . .

In a legal system where bargaining is a primary method of decision-making, it is not surprising that criminal lawyers find it essential to maintain close personal ties with the prosecutor and his staff. Respondents were quite open in revealing their dependence upon this close relationship to successfully pursue their careers. The nature of the criminal lawyer's work is such that his saleable product or service appears to be influence rather than technical proficiency in the law. Respondents hold the belief that clients are attracted partially on the basis of the attorney's reputation as a fixer, or as a shrewd bargainer.

There is a tendency for ex-deputy prosecutors in King County to enter the practice of criminal law. Because of his inside knowledge of the prosecutor's office and friendships made with court officials, the former deputy feels that he has an advantage over other criminal law practitioners. All of the former deputies interviewed said that they took criminal cases. Of the eight criminal law specialists, seven previously served as deputy prosecutors in King County, while the other was once prosecuting attorney in a rural county.

Because of the financial problems of the criminal lawyer's practice, it is necessary that he handle cases on an assembly-line basis, hoping to make a living from a large number of small fees. Referring to a fellow lawyer, one attorney said, "You should see ———. He goes up there to Carroll's office with a whole fist full of cases. He trades on some, bargains on others and never goes to court. It's amazing but it's the way he makes his living." There are incentives, therefore, to bargain with the prosecutor and other decision-makers. The primary aim of the attorney in such circumstances is to reach an accommodation so that the time-consuming formal proceedings need not be implemented. . . . One of the disturbing results of this arrangement is that instances were reported in which a bargain was reached between the attorney and deputy prosecutor on a "package deal." In this situation, an attorney's clients are treated as a group; the outcome of the bargaining is often an agreement whereby reduced charges will be achieved for some, in exchange for the unspoken assent by the lawyer that the prosecutor may proceed as he desires with the other cases. . . .

The exchange relationship between the defense attorney and the prosecutor is based on their need for cooperation in the discharge of their responsibilities. Most criminal lawyers are interested primarily in the speedy solution of cases because of their precarious financial situation. Since they must protect their professional reputations with their colleagues, judicial personnel, and potential clientele, however, they are not completely free to bargain solely with this objective. As one attorney noted, "You can't afford to let it get out that you are selling out your cases."

The prosecutor is also interested in the speedy processing of cases. This can only be achieved if the formal processes are not implemented. Not only does the pressure of his caseload influence bargaining, but also the legal process with its potential for delay and appeal, creates a degree of uncertainty which is not present in an exchange relationship with an attorney with whom you have dealt for a number of years. As the Presiding Judge of the Seattle District Court said, "Lawyers are helpful to the system. They are able to pull things together, work out a deal, keep the system moving."

. . .

Summary

By viewing the King County Office of Prosecuting Attorney as the focal organization in an exchange system, data from this exploratory study suggests the market-like relationships which exist between actors in the system. Since prosecution operates in an environment of scarce resources and since the decisions have potential political ramifications, a variety of officials influence the allocation of justice. The decision to prosecute is not made at one point, but rather the prosecuting attorney has a number of options which he may employ during various stages of the proceedings. But the prosecutor is able to exercise his discretionary powers only within the network of exchange relationships. The police, court congestion, organizational strains, and community pressures are among the factors which influence prosecutorial behavior.

References

Chambliss, W. J. (1969) Crime and the Legal Process. New York: McGraw-Hill.
Gore, W. J. (1964) Administrative Decision Making. New York: John Wiley.
Long, N. (1962) The Polity. Chicago: Rand McNally.

8

Plea Bargaining Systems and Plea Bargaining Styles: Alternate Patterns of Case Resolution in Criminal Courts

Milton Heumann

I. Introduction

The study of local criminal justice has emerged in the past several years as a major concern for the student of public law. The fall of the "upper court myth" and the result-ant realization of the importance of the "trial" court has spurred research into the dispo-sitional processes of criminal courts. In the forefront of the results yielded by these efforts is a model of case disposition very different from the familiar Perry Mason courtroom interaction, a model predicated on negotiated dispositions rather than adversary combat, in short, a plea bargaining model.

. . .

I will be primarily concerned with three sets of plea bargaining-related issues. First, I will examine the proposition that plea bargaining is a relatively new phenomenon neces-sitated by the increased volume of cases coming to the local criminal court. Second, I will present evidence suggesting variations in plea bargaining processes across courts of differ-ent jurisdictions and within courts of equal jurisdiction. . . .

II. Research Methods

Six courts in three cities in Connecticut were chosen for study. Each of the three cities is the site for a Circuit and Superior Court. The former have criminal jurisdiction over all misdemeanors and felonies punishable by up to five years imprisonment, while the Supe-rior Courts have concurrent jurisdiction over any Circuit Court matters, and exclusive jurisdiction over felonies punishable by more than five years imprisonment.

From June 1973 to March 1974 in-depth interviews were conducted with seventy-one individuals working in these six courts. Almost every prosecutor (State's attorney in the

Paper delivered at the 1974 annual meeting of the American Political Science Association, pp. 1–3, 5, 7–10, 13–18, 20–26, 33. Reprinted by permission of the author. Footnotes have been omitted.

Superior Courts) and public defender in each of the courts is included in this sample. Additionally, private attorneys with a reputation for handling criminal cases in the three cities were interviewed, as were those judges assigned to the courts during my stay in the particular locality.

. . .

In addition to the interviews, quantitative data on case dispositions were collected from both published State reports and from the files of the public defenders in one of the Circuit and one of the Superior Courts. As is the case with the qualitative evidence, these data cover only Connecticut criminal cases. . . .

III. The Trial: A Straw Man

Plea bargaining can be defined as the process by which the defendant agrees to relinquish his right to go to trial in exchange for a reduction in charge and/or sentence. Case pressure imputably weighs heavily on the mind of the prosecutor and he willingly enters into such an agreement to save the state the time and expense of a trial. The figure most frequently bandied about as indicative of the pervasiveness of plea bargaining is something to the effect that roughly only 10% of all criminal cases go to trial.

. . . [I]n recent years recourse to trial has been the exception rather than the rule in Connecticut's Superior Courts. In not one of the [last] seven years [from 1966-1973] . . . [have] the trials [as a proportion of the] total cases disposed . . . exceeded 9%. The trial perceived by many as the touchstone of our legal system accounted for the final outcome of only 114 of the 2244 cases resolved in one fashion or another by the Superior Courts in 1972-73.

. . .

Thus far we have not encountered any novel ground—as indicated above the 10% trial figure is quite well advertised. But what is not commonly realized, though critical for an appreciation of the reality of plea bargaining, is that the relative lack of trials versus alternate modes of disposition is not a recent phenomenon. . . . The mean percentage trial/total disposition over [the] 75 year period [from 1880-1954] is 8.7%. From 1880 to 1910 the ratio was slightly above 10%; from 1910 to 1954 it reached the 10% plateau only three times. Overall, the trial ratio does not differ to any great extent from the current figures. Historically it appears that the trial, as far back as 1880, did not serve as a particularly popular source of case dispositions.

The exaggerated ability of appellate courts to rectify trial court error was labeled an "upper court myth." The belief that most cases in the trial court were tried, and the overemphasis on trial procedures to the exclusion of guilty pleas, both recently outmoded ideas, should properly be viewed as forming a "lower court myth." . . .

The "discovery" of plea bargaining sounded the death knell for the "lower court myth." However, I think yet a third myth has arisen from the ashes of the "lower court myth"—a "plea bargaining myth." This is the assumption that case pressure is predominantly responsible for the low trial rate in the criminal courts. We are led to believe that crowded urban courts, obsessed with "moving the business," forsake the trial and in its stead plea bargain. This line of thought implies that if case pressure was lessened, trials would be the name of the game.

A partial test of this proposition is made possible by comparing trial rates in low volume Superior Courts with trial rates in the high volume courts. This test is at best "rough"

TABLE 8-1
Rank Ordering of Connecticut Superior Courts by Mean Number Cases
Disposed Annually, 1880–1954

Superior Court	Total Cases	Mean	Standard Deviation
Tolland	2468	34	21
Middlesex	4143	56	20
Windham	5362	73	25
Litchfield	6235	85	51
Waterbury*	6655	95	171
New London	8553	117	43
Fairfield	19,043	261	71
New Haven	20,326	278	104
Hartford	24,212	332	158

* Data missing for 1897 and 1900. The Waterbury Superior Court was established in 1893, thus the N is 70 for Waterbury and 73 for the others.

because without staffing data no control over the number of prosecutors and judges working in the court is possible. Nevertheless these data should yield some clues concerning the ability and desire of local court officials to try cases.

Connecticut's nine Superior Courts were arrayed on the basis of the mean number of total cases disposed of annually between 1880 and 1954. The rank order based on these means can be found in Table 8-1. For purposes of further analysis, Tolland, Middlesex and Windham, the three courts with the lowest mean number cases per year were called "low volume courts"; Fairfield, New Haven and Hartford were similarly labelled "high volume courts." The ratio of trials/total dispositions for each of these six courts was calculated, and the mean of these ratios for the low and high volume groupings for each year was determined. The summary statistics over the 75 year period for each court are presented in Table 8-2. . . .

. . . [The findings] indicate that over this 75 year period the low volume courts did not try a substantial percentage of their cases, and did not try substantially more cases than the high volume courts. Though in certain years and certain time periods (particularly 1894–1904) the predicted greater rate is found and is pronounced, I think it fair to conclude, especially from 1910 and on, that despite the large difference in actual case pressure which was used to dichotomize the groupings, trial rates between them varied minimally, and indeed often the low volume courts tried proportionately fewer cases.

. . .

I think it beneficial at this point to offer a recapitulation, clarification, and explanation of the data presented thus far. We have seen that trials are not now, nor have they been

TABLE 8-2
Means of Annual Trial to Total Cases Ratio for Low and High Volume
Superior Courts, 1880–1954

	Low Volume Courts			High Volume Courts		
	Tolland	Middlesex	Windham	Fairfield	New Haven	Hartford
Mean Trials/Cases	.16	.14	.11	.07	.12	.07
Standard Deviation	.12	.07	.07	.05	.06	.04

since 1880, the predominant method of case resolution in the local criminal court. This fact emerges from both the annual aggregate statistics for all the Superior Courts, and from breakdown by court. Furthermore, we have seen that variations in case pressure do not directly and appreciably affect trial rates—low volume courts historically have not tried significantly more cases, and recent decreases in volume have not led to markedly greater rates of trial.

Guilty pleas, and to a lesser extent, nolles [dismissals], have always been the best traveled routes to case disposition. Today we know, and this is well documented by my observations and interviews, that these guilty pleas are the product of discussion and negotiation between the defense attorney and the state's attorney. We can attribute the low trial rate, and the high percentage of guilty pleas to plea bargaining. This is fine and well, except that by implication it suggests that plea bargaining has always played a role in the local court, and if this is true, it casts doubt upon the efficacy of proposals to eliminate so well entrenched a process.

One cannot speak with assurance about the procedures followed in the "old days" to obtain the high percentage of guilty pleas. However, several clues harvested from my interviews lend credence to the argument that plea bargaining is no "Johnny come lately." "Oldtimers," court personnel, and private attorneys who have been active in criminal courts since the 1930's—scoffed at the current clamor about plea bargaining. Though indicating that some of the steps followed in negotiating dispositions have changed, these "oldtimers" maintained that the core notion of arranging a deal with the state's attorney in return for a guilty plea was always central to the practice of criminal law.

This evidence is admittedly piecemeal, and subject to the problem of selective recall. But when juxtaposed with several other findings, I think the contention of these "oldtimers" is supported, and further insight into the reality of plea bargaining is gained. Almost every respondent accepted the three following propositions as being empirically correct: 1. Somewhere between 80-90% of the defendants in the Superior Court are factually, but not necessarily, legally guilty; 2. Of these, a sizable percentage have no substantial grounds to contest the state's case—i.e., they are factually and legally guilty, and their trials would be barren of any contentions likely to produce an acquittal; 3. If a defendant pleads guilty he is likely to be rewarded in terms of a reduction in charge and/or sentence. These perceptions do not necessarily add up to a negation of the legal tenet of presumption of innocence. Court personnel and defense attorneys simply recognize the factual culpability of many of the defendants, and the fruitlessness, in terms of case outcome, of a trial. From these perceptions flows the notion—and it cannot be emphasized enough that this third component in particular is not normatively subscribed to by all court personnel, but is accepted by them as the empirical reality—that if the obviously guilty defendant "cops a plea" he will receive some reward. . . .

Assuming that the criminal justice system has always processed a substantial number of defendants who were factually guilty and who did not stand a very good chance for acquittal at trial, the low rate of trials historically, and the reliance on the guilty plea, becomes more understandable. Regardless of whether or not actual discussions took place between prosecutors and defense attorneys as the oldtimers asserted, the plea of guilty itself probably earned the defendant—or was perceived as likely to earn the defendant—a more favorable disposition than if he insisted on trial. Pleading guilty was (and is) tantamount to engaging in "implicit plea bargaining." Today perhaps defense attorneys are more forceful in insuring that the reward is forthcoming, and perhaps their efforts in the "explicit plea bargaining" encounter yield even greater rewards, but the difference is one of degree and not of kind.

To state the argument in stark terms, plea bargaining appears to be as integral and inevitable in the local criminal court (whether high or low volume) as is something like the committee system of the Congress. Once concessions are made for the defendant who pleads guilty, or penalties exacted from the defendant who does not—even if these can be justified in terms other than saving the state time and money—the slippery slope from implicit to explicit plea bargaining is being traversed. Gradually, the defense attorney seeks assurances from the prosecutors that the expected implicit reward will be forthcoming, and as these discussions increase the full fledged plea bargaining system emerges.

. . .

The "plea bargaining myth"—the belief that case pressure variations explain trial rates—implies that plea bargaining will vary almost directly with case volume. It should now be evident that guilty pleas will be proffered and accepted for reasons other than case volume, and that at a minimum, implicit plea bargaining will be the norm even in those courts that handle few cases annually.

Let me stress, though, that the argument that case pressure can be removed and plea bargaining remain does not mean that case pressure is without its effects on plea bargaining processes. It merely suggests that the relationship is far more complex than a simple dichotomization between trial and plea implies. For example, there is probably a critical ratio between volume and staff . . . i.e., when volume increases beyond a certain point and staff remains constant, changes in the plea bargaining process may become manifest. Final dispositions may not change much, but they become easier to obtain; or the prosecutor may nolle the marginal case which he might have pursued for a plea earlier. He may offer to reduce more charges and recommend lighter sentences, or he may simply push for more severe sentences after trial, and remain as firm as he ever was on his plea bargaining offers. Innumerable additional hypotheses along these lines can be posited, but I think these few make plain that not much is plain about the very involved relationship between volume and plea bargaining. . . .

IV. Plea Bargaining Systems: Notes Toward Classification

In developing the argument that plea bargaining is inextricably bound to the local criminal court, that it is the lowest common denominator crosscutting criminal courts, we ignored distinctions amongst plea bargaining systems and orientations. But once we move beyond this position—i.e. we accept as given the centrality of plea bargaining—differences amongst systems and actors blossom. Plea bargaining after all is not a homogeneous process with identical connotation and denotation for all criminal systems and the individuals involved in them. Indeed, I think one explanation for the confusion that surrounds plea bargaining is directly attributable to the failure to note these distinctions.

. . .

One obvious "break point" falls between the Circuit and Superior Courts. Though the Circuit Court now has felony jurisdiction of up to five years, the overwhelming majority of its cases stem from misdemeanor offenses, such as breach of the peace, found intoxicated, violations of town ordinances, and disorderly conduct. As would be expected, the Circuit Courts' case volume is substantially higher than that of the Superior Court.

. . . [Study of] the disposition figures for non-motor vehicle criminal cases in Connecticut's eighteen Circuit Courts in 1972 . . . [reveals] the almost complete absence of recourse to the jury trial in both the high and low volume courts, and indicate the extensive use of the nolle to dispose of charges levelled against the defendant. . . .

There are many aspects of the plea bargaining process in both the Circuit and Superior Courts that could not be readily quantified in any event. The milieu surrounding the actual plea bargaining negotiations and the nature of the discussions themselves, differ greatly. Typically, in the Circuit Court, a line forms outside the prosecutor's office in the morning before court is convened. Defense attorneys shuffle into the prosecutor's office, and in a matter of two or three minutes dispose of the one or more cases "set down" that day. Generally, only a few words have to be exchanged before agreement is reached. The defense attorney mutters something about the defendant, the prosecutor reads the police report, and mutual concurrence on "what to do" generally, but not always, emerges.

. . .

"Plea bargaining," then, for many Circuit Court cases is simply this rapid consensual agreement that the facts dictate certain dispositions—be it a reduced charge, a nolle, a nolle of a few counts for a plea to one charge, etc. Long ago the legal realists seemed to have put the mechanical jurisprudential school, and its slot machine theory of justice, to rest. It can now be reported that the slot machine is alive and well in Circuit Court.

. . .

Plea bargaining in the Superior Court, on the other hand, is a less hurried and less sloppy process. Lengthier discussions take place in the office of one of the assistant state's attorneys. The facts of the case as well as the defendant's background and prior record (if any) are more thoroughly reviewed. Less room for post-plea discussion "hustling" is available. Witness the remarks of an attorney who practices in both the Circuit and Superior Court:

IN THE SUPERIOR COURT YOU PLEA BARGAIN JUST LIKE YOU DO IN THE CIRCUIT COURT?
No, no, all your cards are out on the table, it's not very much of a hustle, not a hustle at all . . . you don't prosecutor shop, there's a lot more at stake, it's totally different. It's like night and day.

The seriousness of the charges in the Superior Court case weigh against too heavy a reliance on pure gamesmanship. Delay and prosecutor shopping will only get you so far; the facts of the case will not disappear, and ultimately they will have to be confronted. Unlike the Circuit Court in which "time," i.e. a jail or prison sentence, is a rarity, "time" is what it is all about in the Superior Court. This is to say that the single most important question that state's attorneys and defense attorneys in the Superior Court confront is whether or not the defendant will have to "do time." If the answer is a mutual "no," but agreement exists on the defendant's guilt, the disposition of the case is a relatively simple matter; some combination of a suspended sentence and probation can be worked out with little difficulty. But "if you are talking time" negotiations become strained.

Defendants in the Superior Court generally have more than one charge outstanding in their files. Of the 88 defendants whose files I examined in one Superior Court public defender's office, only 12 were charged with a single count of a single offense, while the remaining 76 defendants had a total of 288 charges against them. The piling on of charges, when combined with mandatory five year minimum sentences for offenses such as Sale of Heroin, and Robbery With Violence, and with repeated offender statutes which double the exposure for the second offender in particular crimes, provide ample years for the state's attorney to "play with" in negotiations. In the Superior Court "charge bargaining" becomes far less important than "sentencing bargaining." Charges can be dropped without reducing the realistic range of years within which the defendant will be sentenced. For the most part, charge bargaining retains its significance only when a mandatory minimum sentence would be necessitated by a plea to a particular charge, or when the charge can be reduced from a felony to a misdemeanor. In almost all other situations, the state's attorney can appear to yield much in the way of charges without really giving much in the way of "time."

The agreement that emerges from the sentence bargaining can take several forms, all of which relate to what will, or will not, be said to the judge on sentencing day. The defense attorney and state's attorney may agree that the state's attorney will simply present the charges and read the facts but will not make any sentence "rec" (recommendation). This leaves the defense attorney free to make his "pitch" to the judge, and leave the final sentencing decision up to the judge. A second pattern allows the attorney to make any "rec" he desires, and the defense attorney can again respond with his pitch. This is commonly employed when the state's attorney "gives a lot" on charge but refuses to budge on sentence. The third form of agreement as to sentence is the "agreed rec." This is by far the most controversial form of sentence bargaining, and the one that best distinguishes amongst Superior Courts. In two of the Superior Courts, the "agreed rec" means that the state's attorney will not ask for more than a specified in advance number of years; the defense attorney remains free to "pitch" to the judge for less. The expectation is that the judge will almost never go above the state's attorney recommendation, that he will most likely follow it, but that he may occasionally be swayed by the "pitch" and go below it. . . .

. . . It ought to now be evident that Circuit and Superior Court plea bargaining differ in several significant respects; actual physical location for the negotiations, extent of time accorded each case, "hustle factor," charge and sentence bargaining, etc. Similarly, variations exist within courts of equal jurisdiction, e.g., with regard to sentence recommendation patterns in the Superior Courts. No claim to an exhaustive or conclusive cataloguing of these differences is being made.

. . .

V. Some Final Comments

Plea bargaining is central to the process of allocating justice within the local criminal court. The very nature of the guilty plea itself leads inevitably to negotiated dispositions. Factually guilty defendants without much hope at trial will be disposed to plead guilty and avail themselves of the reward imputably accorded the contrite and cooperative defendant.

The centrality and importance of plea bargaining requires that we eschew the simplistic trial/plea bargaining dichotomization and work toward a more realistic appreciation of the dynamics and patterned differences that characterize plea bargaining systems and plea bargainers. . . .

9

The Effects of
Heavy Caseloads

Malcolm M. Feeley

[The paper begins with an exploration of the arguments that are frequently made concerning the effects of heavy caseloads on the ways courts operate. These arguments suggest that heavy caseloads are responsible for the infrequency of trials, the great reliance on plea-bargaining, the tendency to shortcut the process by failure of lawyers to file motions, and the harsh and arbitrary treatment of defendants that inevitably results from mass production justice.]

One important feature of these arguments is that they all cut two ways. That is, each of them implies an opposite; in the absence of heavy caseloads, there will be more trials, less reliance on plea bargaining, an increase in motions, and different types of outcomes. Consequently this paper will examine the arguments by contrasting [the state of Connecticut's] high volume, heavy caseload Sixth Circuit with a neighboring court, the low volume, lighter caseload Eighth Circuit court. If the assertions about caseload are supported, there should be some differences in the ways cases are handled in the two settings. If on the other hand there are no substantial differences, one can begin to question the importance of caseload and begin to look elsewhere for explanations for the observed practices in criminal courts.

. . .

I. The Caseload Hypotheses Explored

The core of the heavy caseload-cursory disposition argument focuses on the degree of "adversariness" in the system. In its most general form this position argues that criminal cases should be resolved through combat between the two parties, with the state having to prove beyond a reasonable doubt to the judge or jury that the defendant did commit the particular offense with which he was charged. The defendant, on the other hand, is

Paper delivered at the 1975 annual meeting of the American Political Science Association, pp. 4, 8-13, 15-18, 23, 28-30, 33-39, 41-42. Reprinted by permission of the author. Footnotes have been omitted.

presumed to be innocent and should be able to invoke the available procedures to protect himself.

An examination of this position, however, poses serious problems for any researcher. At the outset it raises important conceptual questions—what precisely is an adversarial relationship? What is the minimum that the criminal process requires? To what extent must adversariness be characterized as a zero-sum game where one player's victory is another's loss? A mixed strategy game where both players can lose something but both can also gain?

Neither critics nor defenders of the general lack of trials or other combative features available in the criminal process have developed an explicit yardstick against which to judge actual practices. For the most part available standards are very general and discussions tend to proceed by assuming the obviousness of their claims. . . . A perusal of the various discussions of the problems of administering criminal justice leads to no clear consensus as to the precise nature of an "acceptable" or "typical" adversarial relationship. For instance, while some seem to suggest that anything less than a full-fledged jury trial is a departure from the ideal resolution of criminal charges, others adopting an implicit civil law analogy, seem to view the very inability to resolve cases by a negotiated settlement or through informal motion practices as unprofessional. My purpose here . . . is to identify at least several practices commonly associated with this process in order to determine how they may be affected by a variation in caseload.

Trials and Motions

Turning to the central concern of the adversary argument—that there is a relationship between heavy caseloads and lack of trials—the Connecticut data do not support the position. In fact, none of the cases in the samples of the two circuit courts was decided either by a jury or by a court trial. This pattern is not a result of a bias in sampling but represents the typical pattern in these two—and the other sixteen—circuit courts in Connecticut. A separate check of the annual reports of the state's Judicial Department also indicated a paucity of trials in any of the circuits. . . . Thus not only is there a lack of trials in the busier and more rushed courts, there is also a corresponding lack of them in the smaller lower caseload circuits as well.

A trial, however, is only one of several possible indicators of an adversary relationship. Another more subtle indication is use of formal motions by the defense. Motions test the prosecutor's case against the defendant and require him to take seriously the defense effort. A defense attorney can use these as ways of forcing prosecutors to demonstrate the strength of their evidence and to confront the possibility of reducing the charges or abandoning prosecution altogether. Thus motions serve many of the same functions as trials, including the central one of making the prosecution "prove" its case.

There are a variety of motions available to the defense. Pleas in abatement, motions to dismiss, motions to suppress illegally seized evidence, probable cause hearings all attack the sufficiency of evidence and the grounds for arrest. Motions of discovery and bills of particulars both aid the defense in learning more about the charges and circumstances of the arrest. . . . A successful motion to have the court handle the charges under the state's youthful offender statute protects the defendant, if convicted, from having a public record of conviction. The frequency with which formal motions are filed then is another and perhaps more subtle measure of adversariness. Here too, then, one would have expected that the smaller caseload circuit would have produced a higher rate of motions. However, a comparison of the two circuits reveals no substantial differences between them. In the Eighth Circuit, most—90% of the cases—were resolved without the filing of any motions. In 9% more of the cases, one motion was filed and in only 1% of the cases were two or more filed. These figures are almost identical with the rates for the Sixth Circuit. In 92% of the cases no motions were filed, in another 7% one was filed and in only 1% of the cases were two or more filed. Thus by this indicator, as well, there is no significant difference between the degree of adversariness in the two circuits.

Plea Bargains

Plea bargaining occupies a central place in discussions of heavy caseloads. The standard argument holds that plea negotiations are a necessary evil reluctantly accepted by an overworked court, and by implication a reduction of caseload will result in less or perhaps no plea bargaining. However, such an argument is extremely difficult to either support or refute because it too is usually not stated with much precision and the logic of decision-making as it responds to the press of a heavy caseload is not clear. This lack of precision may stem from the ambiguity surrounding the central concept. Are *all* pleas of guilty *prima facie* evidence of plea bargaining? Are all nolles? Would critics of the very idea of plea bargaining expect to resolve *all* cases by trial? It is difficult to imagine such a position being taken although no doubt there may be some support for it. Thus the absence of trials need *not* be taken, by itself, as an indicator of plea bargaining—if bargaining implies actual give and take and acknowledged agreement to compromise by both parties before a final decision is arrived at.

. . .

One measure that has often been used to examine the magnitude of plea bargaining is the frequency with which the most serious charge(s) has been reduced. While defendants may plead guilty for a variety of reasons, pleas to *reduced* charges are much more likely to be the result of an explicit agreement between the defense and prosecution and represent a significant concession by both parties. They are then more likely to be a more meaningful indicator of plea bargaining than the rate of guilty pleas or the rate of cases with other types of charge reductions. Even more important are the cases in which original felony charges are disposed of by pleas of guilty to misdemeanors. From the defendant's perspective, escaping a felony record is extremely desirable. It keeps his record "clean." On the other hand prosecutors are reluctant to reduce a felony charge to misdemeanors since by doing so a relatively important and serious offense is reclassified for the record as just another routine misdemeanor. These types of reductions, then, are cases in which both the prosecution and the defendant have the most to gain and lose.

By the first measure, the percent of *total* charge reductions, the two circuits differ significantly. Thirty percent of all guilty pleas in the Sixth Circuit involve a plea to a lesser (or substituted) charge, while this is the case for only eleven percent of the guilty pleas in the low volume Eighth Circuit. The inference then is that at least in the lower volume circuit, there is less need or pressure to settle cases by resort to reduction of the charges.

Even more startling differences were found when only felony charges which eventually led to misdemeanor convictions were considered. Eighteen percent of the original class D felony charges in the Eighth Circuit were reduced to less serious charges, while in the Sixth Circuit the figure was seventy percent. Thus on this one crucial indicator it does appear that caseload is strongly related to at least charge reductions. The heavier caseload court appears much more willing to reduce charges than does the court with the lighter workload.

. . .

Pretrial Processing

One complaint about high volume systems is that . . . important early decisions must be made on the basis of incomplete and inadequate information . . . and thus . . . [they are] more likely [than low volume courts] to have . . . "restrictive" pretrial releasing policies.

Looking at release practices in the two circuits, however, this proposition is *not* borne out . . . [B]oth in terms of total numbers released and in numbers released without money bail, the high volume [court] fares slightly better than the low volume circuit. Over 89% of those in the former are released prior to trial, while only 86.9% of those in the low volume circuit are released. Furthermore, of those released, the high volume Sixth Circuit is more likely to release the accused on his own recognizance (52.4% to 47.2%).

Turning from the type of release conditions to the actual amount of money bond, the same pattern is seen. Overall the Eighth Circuit Court sets higher bonds than the Sixth. Not only is the high volume court slightly more willing to release arrestees, it also tends to set lower bonds. 18.5% of those having money bond set in the Sixth Circuit have a bond of $50 or less, as opposed to only 2.7% for the Eighth Circuit. . . .

One possible explanation for the more lenient release conditions in the Sixth Circuit is that the defendants are charged with less severe offenses. This, however, is not the case. When controls for seriousness of offense were introduced, still no significant differences appeared. Defendants in the high volume Sixth Circuit were still more likely to receive liberal release conditions.

Another important aspect of the pretrial process is the length of time an arrestee is held in pretrial custody. Conventional wisdom would expect the setting with the heavier caseload to have the longer delay in processing and releasing arrestees. Again, however, the data *do not* support the claim. Table 9-1 indicates that the heavy caseload Sixth Circuit has the larger percentage of arrestees released within three hours (60.4% to 49.7%), although the picture becomes mixed when the remainder of the table is considered. In both circuits around two-thirds of all arrestees are eventually released within seven hours, and only a handful are held beyond twenty-four. In sum, despite variations in workload there are no major pretrial releasing differences between the two settings. Both release in about the same way and at about the same rate.

. . .

TABLE 9-1
Time Spent in Pretrial Custody

	Circuit	
Time	Sixth (high)	Eighth (low)
0–3 hours	60.4%	49.7%
4–7 hours	5.7	21.3
8–12 hours	6.4	7.8
13–24 hours	21.4	17.0
Two or more days	6.1	3.6
	100.0%	100.0%
	(1436)	(141)

Historical Support

The heavy caseload-cursory disposition argument contains a strong historical dimension as well. Some observers of contemporary courts speak of a "decline" of the adversary system due to the press of cases, while others speak of the crisis of criminal justice. However, while it is a rhetorical convenience to speak of greener pastures or better days of a bygone era when smaller caseloads and greater deliberation in criminal courts prevailed, it is not at all clear that this is an accurate comparison. Rather what is seen in the records and description of American Courts fifty and seventy-five years ago is a process easily recognized by contemporary students of criminal courts.

[What follows is a discussion and excerpts from: (1) a study published in 1922 describing the heavy caseload-cursory disposition situation in Cleveland; (2) another early study of Connecticut; and (3) one study of the criminal courts of Chicago. Also discussed are additional data from Connecticut and from New York City.]

. . .

In summary, . . . historical findings . . . while sketchy and incomplete, all point in the same direction and reinforce the findings for the Sixth and Eighth Circuits. Obviously strict comparisons between the periods and courts is not possible due to a host of intervening and confounding conditions. The explosive changes in criminal procedure affect the comparisons in major and undeterminable ways, as do changes in the definitions and understanding of offenses and offenders. Nevertheless the similarities in the findings of these various courts and periods offer considerable support for the position that there has not been any particularly noticeable "decline" in or "twilight" of the adversary system, but rather that it has remained at a more or less constant level despite changes and variations in the magnitude of workload. Although some of the evidence dealt with felony cases, most of the evidence and discussions including the two circuit comparison, referred exclusively to misdemeanor and "minor" felonies, not all cases, particularly major felonies. Consequently while all conclusions and findings should be read and interpreted gingerly, the caseload argument appears strongest as it applies to minor cases in "lower" courts. . . . Lastly it should be emphasized that this caseload argument is also limited by the extremes found in the courts under study. Greater extremes in either direction may produce more noticeable differences. Keeping these caveats in mind it is of interest to ask why there has been such little actual change and why so many commentators have singled out spiralling caseloads to account for "recently" *observed* problems.

While there are some important differences between these two Connecticut circuit courts, there are few differences between them that tend to support the heavy caseload-cursory disposition position under primary consideration in this paper. Virtually all of this and the additional evidence challenges the ability of the heavy caseload theory to account for differences in the ways defendants are "processed" in lower courts. This conclusion of no effect, however, is by itself inadequate. A basic question still remains: are there alternative explanations which account for this seeming paradox? Why is there a belief in their importance in lower courts? And why are they less important than generally believed? There are, in fact, several arguments which when taken together provide a convincing explanation. They raise issues about the *ways* the problem is characterized and also point to some important features of the unique organization of lower courts.

II.   Why Caseload Is Stressed

The Implications [for] Due Process

The thinking underlying the heavy caseload position is a pervasive but implicit assumption that is so ingrained in the thinking and ideology of American criminal justice that it frequently goes undetected and unexamined. This assumption holds that in the unimpeded course of events, each case brought into the criminal courts will "naturally" be resolved by means of heavy combat in the adversary arena. The idea of the adversary system—the basic instrument for protecting the innocent—is extended to mean that the sophisticated procedures and techniques for truth detection and rights preservation not only are available if desired, but will be desired and relied upon in every case. While this position is reinforced by popular presentations of the operation of criminal justice, historically there is no strong tradition or legal presumption that these devices are to be used in each and every case or in any proportion of them. Rather the *full-fledged* adversary process is only one of *several alternatives* available to the participants. Other more expeditious alternatives also enjoy a well institutionalized position in the criminal law. For instance, never has the right to plead guilty been seriously challenged, and while the United States Supreme Court has been somewhat squeamish about putting its formal stamp of approval on plea bargaining, through its traditional inaction and more lately through its explicit rulings, plea bargaining has been gaining a legally acceptable and honorable position in the administration of criminal justice.

Thus a major assumption implicit in much of the literature examining the nature and function of lower criminal courts and commenting on the infrequency of trials rests on a premise that at best can be characterized as idealized myth. Despite this, much of the analysis of the criminal court system has been undertaken with an underlying premise that a full-fledged adversarial relationship is the most obvious and desirable form of proceeding. Thus the actual observed processes are frequently measured against an unexplored ideal of complete combat that has no firm basis in legal theory.

. . .

Non-reactive "Causes"

Whenever there is discontent there is a search for someone to blame. Social organizations are not immune from this, and indeed can function only because they are successful in assigning specific duties to designated individuals who can then be held accountable for their performance. Countering this, there is also a tendency for those with such responsibilities to develop techniques to protect themselves, devices which allow them to accept credit for successes but disavow responsibility for failures. In large complex organizations these practices can be refined to a high art. Specialization, minute division of labor, and the corresponding inability for any one person to see "the whole picture" make it difficult to trace the ultimate impact of a particular action, and hence facilitate the diffusion and transfer of responsibility.

Transferring responsibility is not, however, any easy task. Not surprisingly there is a tendency for those in whose arms the blame is cast to want to reject or pass on the unwanted burden. Also, blaming someone else creates the prospect that the allegation can be returned at some later date. It is a risky business at best. Not surprisingly then one solution to this dilemma is to find a more reliable culprit, a *non*-reactive agency on whom blame can be placed without fear of reciprocity. Perhaps the most common way to do this is to place blame not on any person but on a *process*. Pointing to factors beyond *anyone's* control is one way to avoid not only personal responsibility but also the possibility of retaliation and recrimination engendered by pointing to someone else. Such an explanation proves to be both safe and convenient. The culprit can neither defend itself nor query its accusers. Furthermore, it is difficult to contradict such assertions.

In the administration of criminal justice, three types of non-reactive factors have emerged as "the cause" of many problems confronting the system. Heavy caseloads, understaffing, and inadequate funding are all "enemies" which everyone can safely point to as causes for poor performance. They are culprits that neither speak back nor have any defenders. . . .

So far this discussion has examined why heavy caseloads are *not* so important in accounting for the way cases are processed in lower criminal courts. If it is not the heavy caseload, however, then what does explain this ubiquitous practice of rapid and perfunctory processing of cases? There are two inter-related sets of factors that seem to account for it, factors which while affected by caseload are constantly present regardless of the magnitude of the caseload. Both sets of factors have to do with the nature of the organization of the court system. The first focuses on the peculiar and perhaps unique way the court's workload is distributed and the other is a consequence of the mutually advantageous practices that are inherent in a system of justice where the stakes are not very high in comparison to the costs of going through the system.

III.   Alternative Explanations

The Organization of the Court's Business

The working hours in a lower court are scheduled in a distinctive if not unique way. Participants are interested in getting through the calendar as quickly as possible so that they can leave the courtroom for the day. If it is completed by noon, many of them can leave at that time. For others the incentive is not to go home but to get back to an office and other work. Prosecutors have to prepare the following day's cases. Defense attorneys have other clients to meet, cases to prepare, and records to file, and clerks have the day's work to record and file. Whatever the precise reasons for wanting to "move the day's business" in court, almost everyone, save perhaps the frequently bewildered defendant, seems anxious to go through the work as quickly as possible in order to get someplace else.

Concomitant with this desire to press through the work, is the general irritation at any of a variety of events that can disrupt the usually smooth and steady routine and extend the length of time court is in session. An attorney new to the court and unfamiliar with its workings is viewed as a minor irritant by the regulars. A defense attorney who raises more than the normal and perfunctory arguments in behalf of his client may be interrupted and prodded by the judge and urged to rush through his statement. At times a judge may indicate his displeasure at even having to listen to such additional arguments and will make a ruling before the attorney completes his argument. . . . There is a set of half-conscious norms about what one can and cannot do, and violation of them is met with disapproval.

[Disapproval] is not reserved wholly for uncooperative defense attorneys. There may be grumbling among defense attorneys and prosecutors when a judge new to a court conducts business at a much more leisurely pace than his predecessor. Usually, however, the judges will soon learn the norm of that courtroom and adjust to it. They may begin their rotation taking their time, carefully warning defendants of their rights, explaining procedures to them, and inquiring into any deals arranged with the prosecutor. But within a short time they too are like everyone else—running through the docket as quickly as possible.

A moment's reflection will lead to the conclusion that the common interest in the rapid processing of defendants goes far beyond simply the attempts of the various actors to keep their heads above the rising waters in an overburdened court. Stated more bluntly, regardless of caseload, there will always be *too many cases* for many of the participants in the system since most of them have a strong interest in being some place other than in court. Court personnel and others in the extended court organization have a distinctive if not unique work arrangement. They are neither required to be at their jobs from nine to five (in which case it could be argued they might as well spend the hours carefully handling the cases) nor do they get paid by the piece (other than private defense attorneys), in which case while there would be an incentive to move cases rapidly, there would also be an incentive to work longer hours. Rather, they are presented with a predetermined total daily workload, everyday, and when this task is completed, many of them can leave. While a court with a heavier load may adjourn for the day at 4:00 p.m. and take only brief recesses and the smaller court may adjourn at 12:30 p.m., the incentive for rapid processing remains. In each instance, the faster the work is done the sooner court can be adjourned and many people can go home or back to their offices. This simple feature of the way the court's business is organized—a predetermined workload scheduled on a daily basis—goes a long way in explaining why there will always be a strong incentive to move through cases at a rapid pace. While related to the total court workload in some ways, the connection is far from direct and immediate since there is a strong incentive for rapid processing regardless of caseload.

Mutual Advantages and Substantive Justice

Coupled with the peculiar nature of the daily organization of the court's workload is a much more fundamental feature of the court life, and one that provides a convincing explanation for the lack of trials and other time consuming and costly adversarial proceedings. It is the belief that disputes settled through negotiation and/or pleas of guilty provide mutually advantageous benefits for *all* the involved parties.

The savings in time and effort for the prosecutor and defense attorney are obvious. . . .

The normative stance that facilitates this "short circuiting" of the elaborate process is a consensus by nearly everyone involved in most every case that the defendant is, in fact, responsible for *some* wrongdoing which is connected with the charges. The question before the prosecutor and defense attorney then is not whether the defendant is innocent or guilty of the offenses charged, but rather "how should we dispose of this case?" and "what should we settle for?" "What is appropriate for this type of conduct?" The very phrasing of these questions presumes a *joint* enterprise rather than a warring set of parties, and presumes a consensus on the "verdict" on the actions which precipitated the arrest. Any stance other than this cooperative one is . . . almost inconceivable in a setting where there is such a pervasive belief in the defendant's guilt.

. . . [T]he emphasis is on an "equitable" disposition of the case. If the defendant is unfairly charged, or over-charged according to the prevailing norms of the courthouse, the defense counsel finds it more productive to "work with" the prosecutor to obtain an appropriate reduction in the charges or to quietly argue for a lenient sentence recommendation rather than to openly fight in court. Most defense attorneys defend this position as benefiting defendants both in the long run and in individual cases. By dispensing with the trappings of formal procedure, they argue, it allows them to provide efficient and equitable "substantive" justice.

. . .

There is still one more aspect of the process to be considered. Like both defense attorneys and prosecutors, defendants are also subject to decision making costs. . . . While it is clear that defendants rarely ever "manage" their cases or are even fully appraised of all the legal alternatives open to them, it is not at all clear that the defendants in circuit court are unwitting dupes who would much prefer to have their attorney go into full battle for them. Given the certainty of the small sanction, the defendant too has much to lose in extending his case and engaging in full fledged combat. Interviews with his attorney, corralling favorable witnesses, and repeated court appearances all take their toll on the defendant's resources as well as the prosecutor's and defense counsel's.

The defendant in a minor criminal case is much like a party in a civil suit; frequently the most economical course of action is to forego principle and settle in order to minimize the costs of pursuing a decision by means of a formal process, a process which entails expenses that can quickly come to outweigh the magnitude of the sentence itself. While the defendant who retains his own counsel must pay for this service, in most instances the costs of simply having to make repeated court appearances and visit the attorney during regular working hours in order to participate in the construction of the defense more than overshadows the magnitude of the eventual sentence. The loss of just one day's wages is likely to be greater than the typical fine imposed in circuit court.

Ironically the cost of *invoking* one's rights frequently is greater than the loss of the rights themselves. Given this one can see why so many defendants accept a guilty plea without a battle. This situation poses a major paradox for the administration of criminal law since this calculus applies equally well to those defendants who are or consider themselves to be innocent as well as to those who readily acknowledge their guilt.

This dilemma poses serious questions about the efficacy of the adversary process as an institution for protecting individual rights and assuring justice in lower criminal courts. When the costs of invoking the safeguards of the process are likely to be greater than the eventual criminal sentence there is little incentive to engage this process in an effort to vindicate oneself or to avoid or minimize the eventual sanction. Thus, the nearly standard response to problems of American criminal justice—to expand "due process" of the adversary system—may produce negligible results or worse yet may be counterproductive. Not only does expansion of the process give the illusion of improvement when none in fact may have taken place, it also contributes to a set of standards and controls so remote from the existing bureaucratic-cooperative system as to be inapplicable and meaningless in all but the occasional case. . . .

10

The Pretrial Conference

J. Skelly Wright

I believe that the administration of justice means what the term implies. The administration of justice does not mean merely dispensing justice, merely having a judge referee a fight between two lawyers. The administration of justice means administration; a judge has to get into these cases and administer them. The lawyers are likely, in their advocacy, to run off in different directions; it's the judge who brings them back to the issues, it's the judge who shows them where the point of the case is, where the issues are.

In that way he can bring the case into proper focus and keep these cases from getting out of hand.

So, unless the judge moves into the picture actively, to some extent like an advocate himself, at least in the pretrial state of the case, we will be likely to continue to have the kind of administration of justice that we have had up until the adoption of the new rules of civil procedure.

. . .

Pretrial was intended to make these cases easier, to save lawyers' time, to save litigants' expense. It wasn't intended that pretrial be just another layer on the judicial cake. . . . Now, I am going to take up the pretrial as we have it in our district, with some comments on how it can be improved on. I will first refer to pretrial of the routine case, which is the type of case we deal in day in and day out and which most judges deal with all the time.

In the regular routine case we send out a notice requiring that the trial lawyer be present, and bring with him his documents, and that he be prepared to make stipulations, and to do whatever is necessary to advance the trial of the case.

We require that he have one paper with him in addition to his file. We require that he have one sheet of paper on which he has a list of all of his witnesses, and a list of all of his documents; on one sheet of paper.

Now, the first reason for having that requirement is to make certain that a lawyer goes through his file before he comes to the pretrial conference and seeks out his witnesses, and takes out his documents.

Reprinted by permission of West Publishing Company from *Federal Rules Decisions* 18 (1962), 141–147. This is the edited text of a talk delivered by Judge Wright before a conference of lawyers and judges.

The second reason for that requirement is that at the pretrial conference the work is expedited by this list. The list is distributed to the other side, and if the other side sees all the witnesses on it and knows all the witnesses, knows what each witness is going to testify to (and a good lawyer would, after discovery and what-not), there is no need to discuss anything the witnesses are going to say, or all the witness is going to say.

So, at this pretrial conference, then, we begin by having each side briefly state the issues of the case. Then the judge formulates the issues. He tells the lawyers what he thinks the issues are from their statements.

We don't have anybody at the pretrial conference except the lawyers and the judge. We have it in chambers. If you bring the lawyers' litigants in there, the clients, well the lawyers will begin to act like thespians, in front of their clients.

. . .

So we just sit there with the lawyers. They are free; they are informal. And they talk about their lawsuit.

So we understand the issues in these simple negligence cases, or whatever type of case you want that is routine.

After we understand the issues, we have the lawyers ask each other any questions they want to about the case including, as I said, the witnesses and the documents. We make each side disgorge completely and absolutely everything about its case. There can't possibly be surprise, if the lawyers know what they are doing. . . .

So then we set the case for trial. Now, we don't take a long time to pretry these cases, either, because we are busy. We set the case for trial. After we set the case for trial, we talk about settlement. I say, "Well, have you exhausted the possibility of settlement?" . . .

Then I say to the plaintiff's lawyer: "You brought this suit, how much is it worth?" And then they begin to talk; and then I actually find out that they have discussed settlement, and they have reached a stand-off with reference to the offer of settlement: One having made an offer in X amount, and the other having countered in Y amount.

So, if it's a personal injury case, I look at the doctors' reports—just the last paragraph, where they show the extent of injury—I tell them, "This case is worth $20,000 for the settlement," and I tell them why; and I tell them further to go tell their clients that I said so.

And the funny thing is, the lawyers in our district want the judge to do that. They want to be able to go back to their clients and have some of the load taken off their shoulders. They say, "This is what I think, but the judge says this."

And, by and large, these cases are settled.

. . .

Now, we don't stop with one pretrial conference. After we set the case for trial, which is usually about six weeks to two months in advance; if the case is coming on for trial, a week before the trial we see it's still on that calendar, we send for the lawyers again.

In the meantime we have required the lawyers, twenty days before trial, to file in the record a list of their witnesses with an indication of the type of testimony they will give. In other words, just "eye-witness" if it's an accident case. And then a list of their documents, with copies attached, properly numbered, with their trial numbers.

So that at the time of the second pretrial conference, if one is held, you have already in the record all the witnesses, which limits the area in which the lawyers may go in proving their lawsuit. All the documents are already there. . . .

At the second pretrial conference we check the record, see that the noted evidence is all intact, and we ask the lawyers, "Any questions?" And there are usually some few questions. They are ready for trial; they are ready to go. They are really prepared at this stage. And they are also ready to talk settlement.

They are ready to talk settlement then, because they know this is the last time they can get any help from the court in settling the case.

We go over the procedure again, and do the best we can to assist them in settling the case. And we try to take the load, as I say, off the lawyers' back by telling them what we think the case should settle at, if it's a personal injury case, a case that we can look at and see about what it's worth.

And what it's worth is usually midway between what the lawyers think it's worth, anyway. So there is no chance of really grave injustice in telling what these personal injury cases are worth.

Now, in other types of cases, we are a little more tentative about even the settlement discussion; we discuss the settlement, but we are much more tentative about it, because other issues may arise that you can't appraise at a pretrial conference very well, and probably the trial of the case is required for resolution of such issues.

But, generally speaking, we do touch upon settlement in any case. But in these personal injury cases, and our calendar is made up about forty per cent of them, we try to settle and we try to get rid of them. And, as I say, we do.

Now, that's what happens in the routine cases.

. . .

CHAPTER FOUR

DEMAND REGULATION: APPELLATE COURTS

Within American court systems another type of court exists above the trial level. These courts are commonly called appellate courts. Typically in state judicial systems and in the federal system, any party not fully satisfied with the decision of a trial court may, by right, file an appeal. An appeal may take one of two forms: a trial *de novo* or a more limited review of specific aspects of a trial proceeding. The number of cases that are, in fact, appealed in any court system is usually only a portion of all of those which might possibly be appealed. For example, in the federal system in fiscal 1970, the rate of civil appeal of appealable district court decisions was only about one in four.[1] What this means is that the role of appellate courts is typically limited to reviewing cases that are not necessarily representative, in either their content or the issues that they raise, of the range of cases heard by trial courts.

As one would expect, the cases that are appealed are likely to be more complex than those that are not, and they are cases that frequently raise broad general questions of legal policy. The cost of the process of appeal in terms of both time and money serves to regulate the number and types of cases appealed. Monetary costs include filing fees (which are generally not very substantial and which may be waived for indigents), attorneys' fees, and the cost of transcription and reproduction of the trial proceedings. There may also be psychological costs of appeal that can be as important as the monetary and time costs. The delays associated with the process of appeal may impose substantial "uncertainty costs." In some cases the losing party may prefer the certain knowledge of defeat to the continued uncertainty that is part of the process of appeal. However, this is more likely to be true in civil cases than in criminal cases, where filing an appeal may be a strategic device to delay implementation of a prison sentence. Delay and uncertainty may, however, differentially affect different types of litigants. Those for whom litigation is a routine matter may be better able to endure the costs of delay and uncertainty than those whose involvement in litigation is exceptional and those for whom the investment in each case is very great.

The style of dispute resolution found in appellate courts varies significantly from that typically found in trial courts. The former have a quite different and restricted cast of characters and a more limited interest in the dispute, and tend to be more formal and stylized in their procedures. Trial court proceedings typically bring together a diverse mixture of amateurs and professionals. In addition to judges and lawyers who are specifically trained in the law, participants with no legal training may play an important part. Litigants, witnesses, and jurors all act to democratize the trial court proceeding. Dispute processing in trial courts involves them in a process of clarifying events and interpreting norms.

As a dispute moves from the trial to the appellate level it is typically transformed. It becomes almost exclusively a dispute about law or procedure. Issues of law or questions about the way in which the trial was conducted are argued in appellate courts. It is assumed that findings of fact produced by the trial proceedings are correct. Whereas the matters at issue in a trial are almost always subject to extensive oral argument, the time allotted for such argument before appellate courts is limited. The dispute is conducted largely through briefs, motions, and memoranda. What all this means is that disputing in appellate courts is a "lawyer's game." Only those trained in law are permitted to play; the amateur participants found in trial courts are eliminated.

In trial courts decisional responsibility lies with a single judge or is shared by a judge and a jury. In appellate courts decision making is generally collegial and involves only judges. Disputing in appellate courts is far removed in time and substance from the events that gave rise to the original disagreement. The original parties, their dispute, and its specific resolution become less important than the legal context into which they are placed.

In the federal system and in many states there are two levels of appellate courts. The first level, intermediate appellate courts, stands between the trial level and the highest appellate or supreme court level. In theory, intermediate appellate courts are courts of review, whereas supreme courts may go beyond review and act as policy making bodies. However, this distinction is very difficult to make because all types of appellate courts both review and make policy. Furthermore, it may be very difficult to determine whether, in any particular appeal, the decision reached involved either review or policy making. Nevertheless, when appellate courts do review decisions of trial courts they serve in a supervisory or quality control capacity to ensure that the actions of trial courts are in conformity with the law. When they make policy they use the cases that are appealed to them as vehicles for developing the broad outlines of legal policy. Review tends to be concerned with the past, with ensuring that what was done at the trial level was fair. Policy making is forward looking. Although courts are constrained to decide within the context of particular cases, when they make policy their decisions are intended to provide guidelines for future action. The issue of the representativeness of the cases that are appealed is of less concern, for in policy making what is at issue is not general supervision. In fact, appellate courts are frequently equipped with devices that allow them to screen out even those cases which are appealed to ensure that only the most important and controversial ones are given full attention. Appellate courts, like trial courts, are reactive but not defenseless.

In the first selection of this chapter (selection 11), Lawrence Baum reviews the variety of techniques that appellate courts may employ to avoid giving full consideration to cases that are appealed to them. Some of these techniques accrue to appellate courts as formal legal mechanisms of demand regulation. Others develop informally through the practices and decisions of the courts. One of the most important of the formal legal techniques is the *certiorari* power of the United States Supreme Court. The papers by Tanenhaus *et al.* (selection 12) and by Casper and Posner (selection 13) examine that power. The former explains what *certiorari* is and how it is employed by the Supreme Court; the latter examines the impact of the use of that power to determine the kinds of disputes that find their way to our highest court.[2]

Notes

1. Jerry Goldman, "Federal District Courts and the Appellate Crisis," *Judicature* 57 (1973), 211.

2. Russell Wheeler has suggested that the arguments of Casper and Posner concerning the caseload size of the Supreme Court do not obviate the need for contingency planning to handle what is likely to be continued caseload growth. Some devices that could be utilized are also discussed in his paper, "The Supreme Court's Workload and the Demands on the Federal Appellate Courts," delivered at the annual meeting of the Midwest Political Science Association, 1975.

11

The Judicial
Gatekeeping Function:
A General Analysis

Lawrence Baum

In recent years social scientists have shown an increasing interest in litigation as a political process. On the civil side of the law, scholars have examined such subjects as the decision to take disputes to court, the use of litigation to obtain policy change, and the role of the lawyer in litigation decisions. In the study of criminal litigation, extensive work has been done on the police decision to arrest, the prosecutor's decision to initiate prosecution, and the pretrial settlement of cases through plea-bargaining.

. . .

The setting of judicial agendas is a function which litigants share with judges themselves. Courts possess and utilize a variety of what may be called gatekeeping powers, powers with which they help to determine which demands they will address and how fully they will consider the demands they do address. These powers provide the basis for gatekeeping activities as diverse as the exercise of discretionary jurisdiction by the Supreme Court, the judicial manipulation of rules of jurisdiction, and the encouragement of pretrial settlement by trial courts.

. . .

Inattention to institutional gatekeeping activities has been particularly unfortunate in the study of the judiciary, for it has reinforced a long-standing view of the courts as virtually powerless to determine what demands they will address. With the exception of the Supreme Court, courts tend to be seen as agencies which must respond to agendas established by litigants, and even the Court's ability to help set its agenda sometimes is minimized. I believe that this conception of the courts' role is inaccurate and misleading. Courts possess significant powers to help determine what they will decide, and their use of these powers plays an important part in determining the outcomes of the judicial process. More specifically, two arguments on judicial gatekeeping may be put forward.

First, the holding of important gatekeeping powers is almost ubiquitous among courts, and the use of these powers substantially increases the difficulties faced by potential litigants in obtaining desired outcomes from the judicial system.

Reprinted by permission of the author from "The Judicial Gatekeeping Function: A General Analysis and a Study of the California Supreme Court," paper presented at the 1975 annual meeting of the American Political Science Association, pp. 1–11. Footnotes have been omitted.

Second, there is an important purposive element in the use of gatekeeping powers by at least some courts. These powers are employed as instruments to achieve policy goals. As a result, decisions in the gatekeeping process contribute to the same judicial ends as decisions "on the merits." This purposive use of gatekeeping powers increases their significance for litigants seeking certain policy outcomes, for policy-oriented gatekeeping creates systematic rather than random roadblocks to the achievement of favorable results.

I. Gatekeeping Powers: Their Forms and Importance

As indicated . . . , gatekeeping powers may be defined as those with which courts help to determine which demands they will address and how fully they will consider those that they do address. This rather broad and ambiguous definition requires some explication. Litigants may be considered political actors who wish to obtain favorable responses to their demands. To achieve this end, they seek first to get these demands before judges and to have them considered fully and officially. Gatekeeping powers represent means by which courts help to determine litigants' success in achieving this intermediate goal. The decision whether or not to hear a case, the shunting of some cases to a category receiving limited consideration, the establishment of rules of access to the court, and the encouragement of litigation or of alternative paths of action all constitute types of gatekeeping. To understand the nature of judicial gatekeeping, it will be useful to examine briefly some major forms of judicial activity which may be classified as gatekeeping practices.

1. Discretionary Jurisdiction

Perhaps the most clearly delineated form of judicial gatekeeping is the exercise of discretionary jurisdiction. The Supreme Court's *certiorari* power has its counterpart in most of the states, where the highest appellate courts possess the power to refuse decision on the merits to some or all classes of appeals. In the 23 states with intermediate appellate courts, typically the supreme court is required to hear certain kinds of appeals but has discretionary jurisdiction over most appeals from the intermediate level. Several states without intermediate appellate courts give their supreme courts discretion in the hearing of some cases; most notably, Virginia and West Virginia allow no appeals as a matter of right. Procedures for decision on the acceptance of cases and the proportions of cases accepted both vary considerably. In each court, however, discretionary jurisdiction serves as a device by which a large number of appellants are denied formal consideration of their demands on the merits.

2. Summary Disposition

Siblings of discretionary jurisdiction, some of illegitimate birth, are the practices of summary dismissal of appeals and summary affirmance of lower-court decisions in cases which appellate courts legally must hear. These practices are widespread as means by which appellate judges dispose rapidly of appeals which they do not wish to accord full consideration. The federal courts of appeals have used statutory powers as bases for summary dismissal of *habeas corpus* cases involving state prisoners and of pauper appeals, and under court rules some have adopted procedures for summary disposition of other appeals. The Supreme Court summarily affirms and dismisses appeals under its mandatory jurisdiction in a procedure similar to its *certiorari* decisions. Some state supreme courts have adopted similar procedures. In Nebraska, for instance, the appellee may move for summary affirmance under court rule. Summary disposition differs in legal form from discretionary jurisdiction, but its impact on appellants is virtually the same.

3. Truncated Procedure

Cousins of the first two forms are the procedures increasingly used by appellate courts to classify certain cases as worthy of less than the court's full procedure for their consideration. In some state courts, a staff director classifies some appeals as easy to decide and assigns them to a staff member, who writes a memorandum on the case, proposes the court's decision, and writes a draft *per curiam* opinion for the court. These materials then go to the judges responsible for the case, who reach final decision without oral argument. Other kinds of truncated procedure, with and without extensive staff involvement, exist in both federal and state systems.

Like summary disposition, truncated procedure represents a kind of substitute for discretionary jurisdiction, but it constitutes a more ambiguous form of gatekeeping. It involves gatekeeping in two senses. First, most of the "easy" cases assigned to the group receiving limited consideration inevitably will be those in which the appellant's demand is perceived as having little merit, so that the assignment in itself serves as a signal to limit the seriousness with which that demand is considered. Second, the adoption of truncated procedure, particularly the avoidance of oral argument, limits the appellant's ability to overcome the presumption of lower-court correctness. In contrast with discretionary jurisdiction and summary disposition, however, the appellant retains a chance for victory even if his case has been screened out of the mainstream.

. . .

4. Manipulation of Costs

Both trial and appellate courts can manipulate the financial costs of litigation, costs which may be crucial in a potential litigant's decision whether to go to court. Thus, the relaxation of rules of form for appeals by indigent appellants in the Supreme Court and other courts has eliminated a major financial barrier to the appeal of criminal convictions. An example of another kind is the imposition of financial penalties for appeals judged frivolous in the intermediate appellate courts of California, intended to discourage groundless appeals. Whether directed specifically at indigents or at the general population, the manipulation of financial costs inevitably has a differential impact on groups of different economic status. What serves as an important gatekeeping device in regard to some segments of the population may have no effect on others.

5. Manipulation of Courts' Right to Decide

A variety of characteristics of a case may deprive a court of the legal power to hear and to decide it, including lack of jurisdiction, mootness, and lack of adversariness. Many of the rules establishing restriction on courts' power to decide cases were created by courts themselves. Moreover, those "imposed" on the courts by constitutions and legislatures are subject to considerable leeway in their interpretation. As a result, these rules have served as judicial gatekeeping devices, manipulated in their general form and in individual cases to open or close access to litigants. The Supreme Court's use of such devices as rules of standing and the doctrine of political questions as gatekeeping procedures is part of the folklore of the judiciary. Thus, for instance, the requirement of adversariness is adhered to when the Court wishes to avoid decision, relaxed when the Court wishes to decide.

Manipulation of rules concerning a court's right to decide cases serves two rather separate gatekeeping functions. The rules in themselves constitute factors influencing potential litigants' decisions whether to go to court. In addition, their application in particular cases allows courts to determine whether particular litigants will obtain full consideration. The two functions together make this a significant form of gatekeeping.

These [five] forms of judicial gatekeeping, probably the most significant, provide a basis for some general conclusions about this form of judicial action. First, gatekeeping powers are used primarily to narrow access to judicial decision. Courts may relax or fortify barriers to litigants, and many gatekeeping powers are used for both purposes. But the emphasis of gatekeeping activity is one of making it more difficult for litigants to go to court and to obtain full consideration of their demands. This emphasis follows from the major purposes for the adoption of gatekeeping practices, the limitation of court workloads to improve court functioning and to ease judges' responsibilities.

Second, the possession of significant gatekeeping powers is not limited to a small number of fortunate courts. Relatively few courts possess highly formal, explicit gatekeeping powers like discretionary jurisdiction, but judges on other courts have made use of less explicit powers to achieve the same ends. Gatekeeping should be seen as a nearly universal function in the judicial system, an integral part of the judicial process at all levels.

Third, gatekeeping practices differ in some significant characteristics. One is the identity of the ultimate decision-maker in the gatekeeping process. In "court-centered" gatekeeping like the exercise of discretionary jurisdiction, the court determines whether or not each case will receive full consideration. In "court-litigant" gatekeeping, exemplified by encouragement of pretrial settlement, the court influences the *litigant's* decision whether to seek court decision. . . . [M]anipulation of the courts' right to decide cases involves both types of gatekeeping.

Another distinction among gatekeeping practices concerns the impact of the gatekeeping decision. In most forms of gatekeeping this action determines whether a case will be decided on the merits or dropped. In this sense the impact of gatekeeping is "absolute." Truncated appellate procedure . . . [is a] device of "limited" impact; even after a case is screened out a decision on the merits . . . remains to be made.

The gatekeeping devices which have been discussed may be characterized on these two dimensions in the way shown in Table 11-1.

TABLE 11-1
Characteristics of Major Forms of Judicial Gatekeeping

		Impact	
		Absolute	Limited
	Court-centered	Discretionary jurisdiction Summary disposition	Truncated procedure
Locus of decision-making	**Combined**	Manipulation of right to decide	
	Court-litigant	Manipulation of costs Encouraging civil settlement	Encouraging criminal settlement

. . . It is clear that judicial gatekeeping creates barriers to success for litigants. This fact is clearest in the case of discretionary jurisdiction, by which some courts turn back the vast majority of demands which are brought to them. But it is also true of very different forms of gatekeeping such as the manipulation of financial costs. Litigants face other barriers to success in the courts—including, of course, judges' decisions on the merits in those cases which get past the gatekeeping stage. The existence of gatekeeping powers simply adds to the difficulty of getting to court and securing favorable outcomes. The agenda-setting powers of courts are real and significant, and students of the litigation process must take these powers into account in examining the tasks faced by those who would use the courts for political or other action.

. . .

12

The Supreme Court's
Certiorari Jurisdiction:
Cue Theory

Joseph Tanenhaus, Marvin Schick,
Matthew Muraskin, and Daniel Rosen

1. Introduction

. . .

Ever since the effects of the Judiciary Act [of 1925] came to be fully felt, *certiorari* has provided the bulk of the cases that go to oral argument each term [before the Supreme Court.] According to data reported by Schubert, for example, 465 cases were decided after oral argument during the 1953–1956 terms. Of these cases 76.6 per cent reached the Court via the *certiorari* route.

Certiorari petitions are of two types: those submitted *in forma pauperis*, which, since 1947, have been placed on the Miscellaneous Docket, and other (not *in forma pauperis*) petitions, which go on the Appellate Docket. Applications of both kinds are very numerous. During the 1950–1959 terms, 695 appellate docket and 571 *in forma pauperis* petitions were disposed of, on the average, per term.

Appellate docket petitions for the writ are fairly standardized in format. They are printed documents, usually 10 to 30 pages in length, that must set forth the basis for the Court's jurisdiction, frame the questions presented for review, state the facts material to a consideration of those questions, and, in the words of the late Chief Justice Vinson, "explain why it is vital that the question involved be decided finally by the Supreme Court." The opinions and judgments of the tribunals below, and any administrative agencies involved, are appended to the petitions, as well as at least one copy of the record. Respondents may counter with briefs in opposition seeking to show why *certiorari* should be denied, and petitioners may file supplementary briefs in reply. Individual copies of all these documents, with the frequent exception of copies of the record, go to each member of the Court. Most justices ask their clerks to prepare a memorandum on each application before attacking the documents themselves.

Applications *in forma pauperis* are very different in nature. Usually the petitioner submits but a single copy of a typewritten document prepared without legal assistance and without access to the complete record of his case. As a result the petitions follow no particular form, tend to contain much that is irrelevant, and omit materials essential for a thorough understanding of the facts and issues involved. When only a single copy of an application is filed, it goes to the Office of the Chief Justice. Its processing there seems to be as follows. The Chief's clerks prepare memoranda analyzing each application and send copies to every Justice. The petitions themselves tend to be circulated only if a prisoner's life is at stake or if some matter of particular interest and importance seems to be involved.

Both appellate docket and *in forma pauperis* petitions are handled in much the same way in conference. Every petition is placed on the agenda of at least one conference and will be discussed if even a single justice so desires. What makes the system manageable at all is that normally half of the appellate docket certioraris and an overwhelming majority of the *in forma pauperis* petitions receive little or no conference discussion. In fact, Chief Justice Hughes, in an effort to expedite the processing of *certiorari* applications, initiated a practice which has apparently been carried on by Chief Justices ever since. He prepared and circulated to the members of the Court before each conference a special list of petitions that in his judgment did not merit conference discussion. Only rarely did a justice exercise his right to have a petition removed from these "blacklists" and discussed.

It has long been the practice of the Court to grant *certiorari* if as many as four justices so desire. If *certiorari* is granted, the Court may either decide the case on its merits on the basis of the documents in hand, or earmark it for argument in open court.

Although applications for *certiorari* provide a large share of the cases that go to oral argument, these successful applications make up only a small proportion of the total applications for discretionary review. The Administrative Office of the United States Courts reports that 6946 appellate docket applications for *certiorari* were disposed of during the 1950-1959 terms. Of these, 15.5 per cent were granted, ranging from a low of 13.0 per cent for 1953 to a high of 16.9 per cent for 1954. Petitions *in forma pauperis* for the 10-term period were almost as numerous: 5708. Only 4.1 per cent of these petitions were granted, however, ranging from a low of 1.9 per cent for 1953 to a high of 6.9 per cent for 1959. It must be noted, moreover, that the percentages of applications granted include a goodly number that were decided without going to oral argument.

Both the importance of *certiorari* as an avenue of access to the Court and the rather small proportion of *certiorari* applications granted have been widely known for many years. It is small wonder, then, that there has been a substantial interest in the standards the Court uses in evaluating applications for the writ.

2. Rule 19

The most important official statement of the standards used by the Court in granting or denying *certiorari* is Rule 19.[1] This Rule has remained largely unchanged for more than three decades. Its opening sentences state:

> A review on writ of certiorari is not a matter of right, but of sound judicial discretion, and will be granted only where there are special and important reasons therefor. The following, while neither controlling nor fully measuring the court's discretion, indicate the character of reasons which will be considered.

The reasons mentioned may be summarized as follows:

1. A Court of Appeals decides a point of local law in conflict with local decisions.
2. A Court of Appeals departs from or sanctions departure from the usual course of judicial proceedings.

3. A lower court ruling conflicts with a ruling of the Supreme Court.
4. A conflict in circuits exists.
5. An important question has been decided on which the Supreme Court has not yet ruled.

Other than Rule 19 there is only the group of rules on technical requirements such as format, the number of copies of documents to be submitted, and filing dates.

Analyses of the utilization of Rule 19 reveal that it does not constitute a very adequate explanation of the standards the Court uses in evaluating applications for *certiorari*. The first analyses were undertaken by Frankfurter and his associates for the 1934-1936 terms.[2] Apparently these early studies had been prompted by Chief Justice Hughes' 1934 address to the American Law Institute in which he suggested that the Court would not be so deluged with frivolous petitions for the writ if lawyers paid more careful attention to the contents of the Rule. Harper made an analysis roughly similar to Frankfurter's for the 1952 Term, and we have followed suit for the 1956-1958 terms. Our data appear in Table 12-1. While these analyses are not comparable in all respects, because of somewhat differing methods of data collection, they do warrant a number of conclusions about the Court's employment of the Rule.

For one thing, only rarely does the Court give any reason for refusing to grant the writ. In fact, our data for these reasons for denying *certiorari* span the 1947-1958 terms. On less than 40 occasions in a systematic sample of more than 3000 unsuccessful applications for the writ during those 12 terms did the Court explain why it had denied *certiorari*. And then the most commonly offered explanation was that a petition had been dismissed on the motion of one or both parties. Another reason sometimes offered was that the application was not filed in time. It should be noted, what is more, that these are not Rule 19 explanations.

Explanatory comments in cases decided with opinion are more frequent. They appeared in about one case in three for the 1934-1936 terms and in more than 66.8 per cent of the opinions of the Court during the 1956-1958 terms. It might seem at first glance, then, that the widespread criticism of the Court for its failure to explain why *certiorari* was granted has been extraordinarily effective. More careful analysis substantially discounts any such conclusion. For as Table 12-1 shows, the reason offered in 20.1 per cent of the Court's opinions for the 1956-1958 terms was simply "to decide the issue presented"— and this in reality is no different from offering no reason at all. Realistically, then, the Court gave reasons of the type mentioned in Rule 19 in only 46.7 per cent of its opinions during the 1956-1958 terms. This is, to be sure, something of an increase over the 32.4 per cent for the 1934-1936 terms. But the increase, while statistically significant at the 0.01 level of confidence ($X^2 = 11.65$), is not very impressive when one bears in mind the repeated scholarly pressures on the Court to disclose more fully its reasons for granting review.

The several analyses of the utilization of Rule 19 further disclose that the first three items on the list of five reasons summarized above are rarely cited. Only a conflict in circuits, the importance of the issue, or a combination of the two are referred to very often. Importance is cited somewhat more frequently than conflict in circuits. If one considers only cases in which Rule 19 reasons were actually given, importance alone was cited 48.5 per cent of the time during the 1935-1936 terms, 55.1 per cent during the 1952 Term, and 56.9 per cent during the 1956-1958 terms. Using this same group of cases as a universe, conflict in circuits (whether alone or in combination with other reasons) was

TABLE 12-1
Reasons Offered by the Supreme Court for Granting Review
in *Certiorari* Cases Decided after Oral Argument: 1956-1958 Terms*

Reason	1956 Term		1957 Term		1958 Term		Three-Term Total	
	N	Per Cent	N	Per Cent	N	Per Cent	N	Per Cent
1. None	28	31.4	43	43.9	21	23.1	92	33.1
2. To Decide Issue Presented	12	13.5	12	12.2	32	35.2	56	20.1
3. Importance of Issue	26	29.2	28	28.6	20	22.0	74	26.6
4. Importance and Circuit Conflict	13	14.6	4	4.1	5	5.5	22	7.9
5. Circuit Conflict: Actual	9	10.1	11	11.2	7	7.7	27	9.7
6. Circuit Conflict: Alleged	1	1.1	0	—	2	2.2	3	1.1
7. Conflict with Supreme Court	0	—	0	—	4	4.4	4	1.4
Total	89	99.9	98	100.0	91	100.1	278	99.9

* Opinions deciding more than one case have been counted only once.

mentioned 40.6 per cent of the time during the 1935-1936 terms, 40.0 per cent during the 1952 Term, and 40.0 per cent during the 1956-1958 terms. The increase in the frequency of Rule 19 reasons cited in more recent terms, it thus appears, is almost entirely attributable to Reason 3, "the importance of the issue."

Although importance was officially cited more frequently than any other reason, it is not of much assistance in enabling students of the Court to understand the basis of its exercise of its *certiorari* jurisdiction. This is so because the Court has sedulously avoided providing any metric for determining what is or is not important—other than that which at least four justices wish makes it so.

Conflict in circuits is another matter. There has been, it is true enough, some controversy as to whether the Court has granted *certiorari* in every case of direct conflict without exception. But there is no question but that a clear conflict in circuits usually leads to a grant of the writ. In fact universal recognition of the importance of this ground for access to the Court is reflected in the heroic efforts of skilled lawyers to work in some sort of conflict angle, however tenuous. A few terms back the Court seemed to be encouraging this practice by stretching the concept of conflict in circuits to cover sweeping ground. "Alleged conflict," "apparent conflict," and "seeming conflict" began to be cited as reasons for granting *certiorari.* But during the 1956-1958 terms such reasons were mentioned on only three occasions.

However, the most serious limitation of conflict in circuits as a satisfactory explanation for the way the Court exercises its *certiorari* jurisdiction is neither that sometimes [clear] conflicts do not result in *certiorari,* nor that the Court sometimes stretches the concept to cover cases where the existence of direct conflict is most doubtful. Rather the most serious limitation of conflict of circuits as a key to the Court's *certiorari* behavior is that conflict is cited as a reason for granting *certiorari* in less than 20 per cent of the *certiorari* cases decided with full opinion: 14.3 per cent during the 1935-1936 terms, and 18.7 per cent during the 1956-1958 terms.

. . .

3. The Cue Theory

The theory that underlies our study . . . [w]e call . . . "the cue theory of *certiorari.*" In constructing it we have proceeded from three assumptions, each of which is grounded in established knowledge. The first assumption, that Rule 19 does not provide a very satisfactory explanation for the Court's exercise of its *certiorari* jurisdiction, has already been discussed at length. . . .

Our second assumption is . . . that *certiorari* petitions are so sizable and so numerous that justices saddled with many other heavy obligations (e.g., hearing argument, attending lengthy conferences, doing necessary research, and drafting and redrafting opinions) can give no more than cursory attention to a large share of the applications for *certiorari.* . . .

Our third assumption is that a substantial share of appellate docket petitions for *certiorari* are so frivolous as to merit no serious attention at all. Chief Justice Hughes estimated that 60 per cent of the petitions for *certiorari* were of this character. The usefulness of the earlier-mentioned "blacklists" is additional evidence of the total lack of merit in many petitions, as are statements by other members of the Court.

These three assumptions have led us to hypothesize that some method exists for separating the *certiorari* petitions requiring serious attention from those that are so frivolous as to be unworthy of careful study. We further hypothesized that a group of readily identifiable cues exists to serve this purpose. The presence of any one of these cues would warn a justice that a petition deserved scrutiny. If no cue were present, on the other hand, a justice could safely discard a petition without further expenditure of time and energy. Careful study by a justice of the petitions containing cues could then be made to determine which should be denied because of jurisdictional defects, inadequacies in the records, lack of ripeness, tactical inadvisability, etc., and which should be allotted some of the limited time available for oral argument, research, and the preparation of full opinions. Those remaining could then be disposed of by denying *certiorari* or by granting it and summarily affirming or reversing the court below.

A number of possible cues have occurred to us. These concern the parties seeking review, the reputations of the attorneys of record, the reputations of the judges who wrote the opinions below, several types of dissension (conflict in circuits, conflict in a given case within a court below, and conflict in a given case between the courts and agencies below), and subject matter. Our limited resources permitted us to assemble the data necessary for testing only some of these.

Our justification for selecting the cues we did use for testing, and the methods employed both in collecting the requisite data and in testing hypotheses about the cues, will be discussed in detail in Sections 4 and 5. . . . But in general terms our approach has been to examine lower court reports for the presence of selected cues and then determine whether the incidence of writs granted was in fact greater (to a statistically significant degree) when cues were present than when they were not.

4. Technical Problems and Procedures

. . .

The data used in this study were drawn from the published records of the United States Supreme Court and the lower courts and administrative agencies in which the cases were litigated. No use was made of the *certiorari* documents themselves. A codebook was used in assembling the data for a systematic sample of applications for review for the 1947-1958 terms. Since both the codebook and sample were prepared for several purposes in addition to this study, something needs to be said in detail about each.

The sample was drawn as follows: Every fifth petition was coded for the ten terms 1947-1951, 1953-1955, and 1957-1958, and every petition for the two terms 1952 and 1956, with the exception of:

1. Original docket entries
2. Petitions for change of counsel, permission to submit *amicus* briefs or additional briefs and statements, postponement of consideration, etc.
3. Applications for rehearing
4. Entries on the Miscellaneous Docket other than petitions for *certiorari* carrying lower court citations

When two or more applications for review arose from a single lower court decision, each was counted separately. We should also point out that initial disposal only was coded; amended decisions and rulings were ignored.

The sampling design was established for purposes largely unrelated to this study, but the size of the sample was not. A sample as large as this one (more than 3500 cases) was deemed necessary because we were committed in this study to test with nominal data several independent variables, not all of which can be dichotomized. This meant, of course, a heavy reliance on cross-tabulation—a technique notorious for its appetite in consuming cases. In fact, the original design called for coding the 1948 Term in the same manner as the 1952 and 1956 terms, and for larger samples than one case in five from several of the other terms. However, those persistent inhibitors of overly ambitious research projects, time and money, forced us to modify our initial sampling plans.

An indication of the extent to which the sample mirrors the universe can be gained from Table 12-2. The differences between the sample and universe are slight and fall well within the usual limits of sampling error.

Data coded included case name and citation, docket and docket number, court immediately below and citation to it, agreement within the court immediately below, agreement among the courts and agencies below, parties involved, mode of application for review, disposition by the Supreme Court, exceptions taken by individual justices to the Supreme Court's handling of the case, and subject matter. Several of these classifications required more than 50 mutually exclusive categories.

No difficulties were experienced in using some classifications, such as the citations, courts below, and agreement within and among lower courts. Certain others proved more troublesome. We found it necessary to expand and refine some subject matter and party categories even after hundreds of cases had been coded.

Emending the categories after coding had begun increased the danger of unreliability even though we undertook all the coding ourselves. To compensate for this danger, most

TABLE 12-2
Appellate Docket *Certiorari* Cases Disposed of During 1947-1958 Terms:
Comparison of Study Sample and Actual Universe

	Granted		Denied		Total	
	N	Percentage	N	Percentage	N	Percentage
Universe	1279	15.7	6860	84.3	8139	100.0
Sample	445	16.9	2186	83.1	2631	100.0

of the first 1500 cases coded were subsequently checked by a second coder. In addition, all problem cases in the entire sample—about one in six—were coded at least twice, and many were coded three times. After the data had been punched into IBM cards and verified, they were machine-processed for internal consistency, and the errors thereby uncovered were corrected. As a result of these measures we believe that all systematic errors that might have affected this analysis were removed. Whatever errors remain are, we think, random and do not exceed 1 per cent for any one of the variables to be used.

5. Hypotheses and Data

The cue theory of *certiorari* maintains that the justices of the Supreme Court employ cues as a means of separating those petitions worthy of scrutiny from those that may be discarded without further study. If the theory is valid, it should follow that:

Proposition I: Petitions that contain no cues will be denied.
Proposition II: Petitions that contain one or more cues will be studied carefully, and 25 to 43 per cent of them granted.

We estimate the percentage of petitions which contain cues and which are granted in the following manner. Previously cited statements by the members of the Court lead us to believe that 40 to 60 per cent of the appellate docket petitions have some merit, and therefore receive more or less careful attention. Since, furthermore, the Court grants the writ in 15 to 17 per cent of all appellate docket petitions, those granted should constitute from 25 per cent to 43 per cent of all meritorious *certioraris*.

It hardly needs to be said that we cannot expect to find the requirements of the cue theory completely fulfilled, if only because not all the hypothesized cues have been included in our analysis. But if we have accounted for most of the major cues, these requirements should be fairly well satisfied. At the very least, we should find a sizable and statistically significant correlation between the presence of one or more cues and the granting of *certiorari*. Before this relationship can be measured, however, it is necessary to determine whether each of the several possible cues about which we have collected data can properly be regarded as a cue. One method of doing this is to take cases involving none of the hypothesized cues and compare them in turn with those cases containing a given cue but no other. If a given cue is present, the likelihood of *certiorari* should be greater (to a statistically significant degree) than when none of the cues is involved. Whenever this turns out in fact to be the case, we shall accept it as satisfactory evidence that the hypothesized cue does exist. Because the large number of petitions involved causes rather small differences to produce large *Chi* squares, we have set the confidence level necessary to accept an hypothesis at 0.001.

The hypotheses concerning the several cues we wish to test may be stated as follows:

A. *Party as a Cue.* When the federal government seeks review, but no other cue is involved, the likelihood of *certiorari* is greater (to a statistically significant degree) than when other parties seek review and no other cue is involved.

B. *Dissension as a Cue.* When dissension has been indicated among the judges of the court immediately below, or between two or more courts and agencies in a given case, but no other cue is involved, the likelihood of *certiorari* is greater (to a statistically significant degree) than when no such dissension is present and no other cue is involved.

C. *Civil Liberties Issues as Cues.* When a civil liberties issue is present, but no other cue is involved, the likelihood of *certiorari* is greater (to a statistically significant degree) than when no civil liberties issue is present and no other cue is involved.

D. *Economic Issues as Cues.* When an economic issue is present, but no other cue is involved, the likelihood of review is greater (to a statistically significant degree) than when no economic issue is present and no other cue is involved.

We turn now to our reasons for selecting each of these hypotheses for testing, the procedures used in classifying the petitions, and the data we have developed.

Hypothesis A: Party as a Cue

This hypothesis finds some support in the literature. Frankfurter and Landis, in two of their early articles, observed that the Solicitor General speaks with special authority. They pointed out that during the 1929 and 1930 terms the federal government was extremely successful in having *certiorari* granted when it was appellant and denied when it was respondent. More recently Justice Harlan and the authors of a law review note made similar observations.

There are several reasons why the position of the federal government may be regarded as an important cue. For one thing, many of the persons who prepare petitions for *certiorari* are sorely lacking in the required expertise. This is decidedly not the case with the Solicitor General's staff and the other government attorneys who practice before the Court. They have the talent, the resources, and the experience fully to exploit the strong aspects of their own cases, and in reply briefs to expose the most glaring weaknesses of their opponents. We do not mean to imply that government attorneys are grossly unfair in seeking or opposing writs of *certiorari*. In fact, we place credence in the widely circulated gossip that when a clerk or justice wants to get to the nub of a complex case in a hurry he turns to the government's brief. Still, it is surely not invidious to suggest that government attorneys generally turn their assets to the government's advantage.

Another consequence of the government lawyers' expertise is its tendency to prevent them from deluging the Court with applications that they know the Court has no interest in reviewing.

Still another reason why the petitions for review submitted by the lawyers for the government tend to be meritorious is that only rarely are they under pressure to carry cases to the Court solely to satisfy a client who insists upon leaving no stone unturned in his search for vindication. Nor is the government lawyer tempted to pursue a case regardless of merit in the hope that he may gain the prestige of having argued once before the highest court in the land.

Finally, we suspect that the Court's deference for the opinions of the executive branch tends to make it especially solicitous of the government's judgment that particular cases do or do not warrant review.

The data used to test Hypothesis *A* appear in Table 12-3. We have included in the group of cases "federal government favors review" not only those in which the United States and its agencies and officials were petitioners, but also others if they clearly indicated that review should be granted—e.g., official declarations that review would not be opposed, and cases in which the federal government intervened on the side of the appellant. Cases involving the District of Columbia and the territories were not included unless a federal judge was a party. Cases dismissed for technical reasons, such as the petitioner

TABLE 12-3
Party as a Cue

	Certiorari Granted		Certiorari Denied		Total	
	N	Percentage	N	Percentage	N	Percentage
Federal Government Favored *Certiorari*, Cue Involved	8	47.1	9	52.9	17	100.0
No Cues Involved	39	5.8	637	94.2	676	100.0
Total:	47	6.8	646	93.2	693	100.0
	$\phi = +0.25$		$\chi^2 = 44.72$		$P < 0.001$	

withdrawing the case or mootness, and cases for which data on the parties were inadequate have been excluded from the analysis altogether.

The data reveal that when the federal government favored review and no other cue was involved the writ was issued 47.1 per cent of the time. On the other hand, when all other parties sought review, and no other cue was involved, only 5.8 per cent of the petitions were granted. Since these differences are statistically significant at the .001 level of confidence, Hypothesis *A* is confirmed. We accept these data as satisfactory evidence that party is a cue.

Hypothesis B: Dissension as a Cue

Hypothesis *B* was formulated to determine whether dissension may be regarded as a cue. By dissension we mean disagreement among the judges in the court immediately below (one or more concurring opinions, dissenting votes, or dissenting opinions) or disagreement between two or more courts and agencies in a given case. We have employed the term dissension rather than conflict to avoid any possible confusion between the concept we are testing and conflict in circuits. We have not sought to test conflict in circuits, not because we do not regard it as an important cue, but because there was no systematic way to assemble the necessary data without going to the *certiorari* papers themselves. And this we were not in a position to do.

The justification for deciding to test dissension as a cue was suggested by Chief Justice Vinson when he said: "Our discretionary jurisdiction encompasses, for the most part, only the borderline cases—those in which there is a conflict among the lower courts or widespread uncertainty regarding problems of national importance." When lower court judges and quasi-judicial administrators disagree strongly enough officially to reveal their differences, petitions for *certiorari* concerned with these disagreements are, we think, bound to be studied closely by the members of the highest appellate tribunal in the land. This feeling was buttressed by an examination of the *certiorari* cases decided with full opinion during the 1947–1958 terms. At least 52 majority opinions during that period contained specific references to dissension within the court immediately below.

Table 12-4 contains the data used to test Hypothesis *B*. All appellate docket applications for *certiorari* were included, except the handful decided on the technical grounds referred to just above.

TABLE 12-4
Dissension as a Cue

	Certiorari Granted		*Certiorari* Denied		Total	
	N	Percentage	N	Percentage	N	Percentage
Dissension Only Cue Present	37	12.8	253	87.2	290	100.0
No Cues Involved	39	5.8	637	94.2	676	100.0
Total:	76	7.9	890	92.1	966	100.0

$$\phi = +0.12 \qquad \chi^2 = 13.69 \qquad P < 0.001$$

The data disclose that 12.8 per cent of the petitions in which dissension, but no other cue, was present were granted. As earlier noted, *certiorari* was granted in only 5.8 per cent of the petitions without any cue at all. While the phi coefficient shows that the correlation between the presence of dissension and the grant of *certiorari* is rather weak, these differences are significant at the .001 level of confidence, and Hypothesis *B* is confirmed. We accept these data as satisfactory evidence that dissension is a cue.

Hypotheses C and D: Civil Liberties and Economic Issues as Cues

Hypotheses *C* and *D* were formulated to determine whether certain types of subject matter can be regarded as cues. They will be considered together.

The supposition that subject matter is a major ingredient of what the Court refers to as "important" has been made so frequently that hypothesizing it as a cue needs no special justification. In fact, much data about subject matter appear in the literature. Petitions for *certiorari* granted and denied have been classified by subject matter by Frankfurter and his associates for the 1929-1938 terms, by Harper for the 1952 Term, and by the editors of the *Harvard Law Review* for all terms since 1955.

We settled upon two subject matter groups (with four subcategories each) as the most likely to attract the interest of the justices when scanning the mountainous piles of *certiorari* papers. In the civil liberties group we included petitions pertaining to (1) alien deportation, (2) racial discrimination, (3) military justice, and (4) miscellaneous civil liberties.[3] Our second group, economic issues, contain (5) labor, (6) regulation of economic life, (7) financial interest of the federal government, and (8) benefit and welfare legislation. Some of these categories are self-explanatory; others require a comment.

Miscellaneous civil liberties includes church-state relations, permits and licenses for the use of the streets and parks, postal and movie censorship, state and local censorship of reading matter, loyalty oaths, problems arising from the investigations of legislative committees, disbarment proceedings, regulation of occupations and professions, picketing— free speech, and right to work litigation. The financial interest of the federal government includes excise, gift, income, and excess profit tax cases, and government contract disputes in time of peace and war. The benefit and welfare category refers to litigation concerned with civil service rights, wage statutes, the Federal Employers Liability Act, seamen and longshoremen welfare legislation, servicemen's benefits, workmen's compensation, social security legislation, tort claims, agricultural benefit regulations, and unemployment insurance. About 1 per cent of the applications for *certiorari* could not be classified with satisfac-

TABLE 12-5
Civil Liberties Issue as a Cue

	Certiorari Granted		*Certiorari* Denied		Total	
	N	Percentage	N	Percentage	N	Percentage
Civil Liberties Issue Only Cue Present	57	32.9	116	67.1	173	100.0
No Cues Involved	39	5.8	637	94.2	676	100.0
Total:	96	11.3	753	88.7	849	100.0
	$\phi = +0.35$		$\chi^2 = 101.46$		$P < 0.001$	

tory precision because insufficient data were available. These cases have been omitted from the analysis.

Table 12-5 contains the data used to test the civil liberties issue hypothesis (Hypothesis *C*). These data show that about one petition in every three containing a civil liberties cue, but no other, was granted. The differences between the treatment of the petitions with civil liberties cues and petitions without any cues are significant at the 0.001 level of confidence. Hypothesis *C* is therefore confirmed, and we accept these data as satisfactory evidence that the presence of a civil liberties issue constitutes a cue.

The data used to test Hypothesis *D* (economic issue as a cue) appear in Table 12-6. As the contents of this table make clear, the likelihood of review when only an economic issue is present is not much greater than when no cue at all is involved. The *Phi* coefficient shows the correlation between the presence of an economic issue and the grant of *certiorari* is only slightly positive. Nor can a *Chi* square of the magnitude attained be regarded as impressive for an *N* of nearly 1400 cases. Hypothesis *D* is not confirmed, and we cannot regard the presence of an economic issue as a cue.

Now that we have determined that party, dissension, and civil liberties issues are cues, we can return to the two propositions set forth. . . . We then pointed out that if the cue theory were valid, it should follow that: *(Proposition I)* petitions which contain no cue will be denied, and *(Proposition II)* petitions which contain one or more cues will be studied carefully and 25 to 43 per cent of them granted. Data giving some indication of the extent to which these propositions are satisfied by the data in our sample appear in Table 12-7.

Table 12-7 makes it quite evident that the requirements of *Proposition II* are satisfied. Of the petitions containing at least one cue, 27.5 per cent were granted. In addition, the petitions containing cues constituted 47.2 per cent of all appellate docket petitions. This

TABLE 12-6
Economic Issue as a Cue

	Certiorari Granted		*Certiorari* Denied		Total	
	N	Percentage	N	Percentage	N	Percentage
Economic Issue Only Cue Present	59	8.5	637	91.5	696	100.0
No Cues Involved	39	5.8	637	94.2	676	100.0
Total:	98	7.1	1274	92.9	1372	100.0
	$\phi = +0.05$		$\chi^2 = 4.11$		$0.05 < P < 0.01$	

TABLE 12-7
Petitions Containing One or More Cues and Petitions Containing No Cue Compared

	Certiorari Granted		*Certiorari* Denied		Total	
	N	Percentage	N	Percentage	N	Percentage
One or More Cues	337	27.5	889	72.5	1226	100.0
No Cues	98	7.1	1274	92.9	1372	100.0
Total:	435	16.7	2163	83.3	2598	100.0
	$\phi = +0.27$		$\chi^2 = 192.20$		$P < 0.001$	

falls within the estimate that 40 to 60 per cent of all appellate docket petitions contain some merit.

Proposition I is not fully supported, since 98 petitions containing no cues (7.1 per cent) were granted. But these 98 deviant cases do not in our judgment invalidate the cue theory, since all hypothesized cues have not been tested. Our judgment is reinforced by reading the opinions of the Court in those deviant cases decided with full opinion. In 19 instances the Court specifically pointed to a conflict in circuits, a cue we were unable to test. In one case, the Court pointed to dissents by intermediate appellate judges, and in another to the fact that the federal government did not oppose review. Still another case had civil liberties overtones which had been missed when the case was coded. More painstaking analysis would, we are convinced, still further reduce the number of deviant cases not readily accounted for by the cue theory.

We feel justified in concluding, therefore, that the cue theory of *certiorari* is valid.

6. [Predictions]

. . . [W]e had no theoretical or empirical bases for hypothesizing in advance of data processing about the interrelationships among the several cues and their usefulness as predictors of what the Court will do with sets of *certiorari* petitions containing given characteristics.

Insofar as the cue theory itself is concerned, the relative magnitude of the correlations between established cues and the grant or denial of *certiorari* (outcome) is of no particular consequence. All the cue theory requires is that the presence of a cue is enough to insure that a petition for *certiorari* will be studied with care. Hence, the presence of more than one cue, or for that matter the fact that one established cue may be more or less strongly correlated with outcome than another, will not alter the likelihood that a petition will be scrutinized. However, these relationships do have enough intrinsic interest to warrant analysis.

In testing Hypotheses *A, B,* and *C,* ϕ coefficients were computed and included in the appropriate tables. The correlation between outcome and party was $+0.25$, outcome and dissension $+0.12$, and outcome and civil liberties $+0.35$. But these correlations are not very adequate measures of the relationship between the individual cues and the outcome because cases containing more than one cue were not taken into account. A more satisfactory method for determining the magnitude of the association between outcome and any given cue, when all other cues are held constant, is to compute the portion of the variance

TABLE 12-8
Multiple Correlation and Regression Data

		X_1	X_2	X_3	X_4
	X_1	—	0.28	0.17	0.19
Intercorrelations	X_2	0.28	—	0.16	−0.03
	X_3	0.17	0.16	—	−0.06
	X_4	0.19	−0.03	−0.06	—
		X_1	X_2	X_3	X_4
$\overline{M}$		0.176	0.076	0.401	0.116
σ		0.379	0.266	0.490	0.319

$\beta_2 = 0.264$ $B_2 = 0.375$ $A = 0.076$
$\beta_3 = 0.140$ $B_3 = 0.108$
$\beta_4 = 0.206$ $B_4 = 0.245$
$r^2 1.234 = 0.138$
$(\beta_2)(\phi12) = 0.074$ $r\,1.234 = 0.37$
$(\beta_3)(\phi13) = 0.024$
$(\beta_4)(\phi14) = 0.039$

$$X_1 = 0.375X_2 + 0.108X_3 + 0.245X_4 + 0.076$$

Legend for Variables

X_1 = Outcome (*certiorari* granted vs. *certiorari* denied) X_3 = Dissension
X_2 = Party (federal government favored *certiorari* vs. other cases) X_4 = Civil liberties issue

explained by each. The portion of the variance accounted for by a given cue is obtained by multiplying the coefficient of correlation between outcome and the cue by its standard partial regression (β) coefficient.

The β's were obtained by Doolittle's method and appear, together with the data necessary for their computation, in Table 12-8. Since only cases for which adequate information about all three cues were available could be utilized, the number of cases used in this analysis was 2293.

As the data in Table 12-8 show, 7.4 per cent of the variance is explained by the party cue, 3.9 per cent by the civil liberties cue, and 2.4 per cent by the dissension cue. In our sample, therefore, party was relatively three times as important as dissension and almost twice as important as civil liberties in explaining outcome. Since the several contributions to the variance are additive, one may quickly determine the relative importance of the several cues in combination. For example, party alone was slightly more important than dissension and civil liberties combined, and all three cues taken together account for nearly twice as much of the variance (13.7 per cent) as party taken alone.

However, these data on the percentage of the variance explained by the three cues, independently and in combination, do not in themselves enable us to predict the likelihood of *certiorari* grants in sets of cases containing various assumed proportions of cues. Such predictions are made possible by solving the regression equation $X_1 = B_2X_2 + B_3X_3 + B_4X_4 + A$, where outcome is the dependent variable (X_1) and the independent variables are party (X_2), dissension (X_3) and civil liberties issues (X_4). The equation and the data used in computing it appear in Table 12-8.

One can now substitute any set of means desired for the independent variables in the regression equation and solve for outcome. To illustrate, if in a given set of *certiorari* petitions the federal government sought review in 75 per cent, dissension was present in 50 per cent, and civil liberties issues were involved in 40 per cent, the following substitutions would be made:

$$X_1 = 0.375\,(0.75) + (0.108)(0.50) + (0.245)(0.40) + 0.076$$

Solving for outcome, $X_1 = 0.434$. Therefore, 43 per cent of the set of petitions will be granted.

TABLE 12-9
Predicted Percentages of *Certiorari* Petitions That Will Be Granted
When All Cases in a Set Contain Indicated Cues

Cues			Predicted Percentage of
Party	Civil Liberties	Dissension	*Certioraris* to Be Granted
+	+	+	80
+	+	0	70
+	0	+	56
+	0	0	45
0	+	+	43
0	+	0	32
0	0	+	18
0	0	0	7

Legend
0 = Absence of a cue in all cases in set   + = Presence of a cue in all cases in set

Since our particular interest is to determine the predictive powers of the cues if every case in a set contains them in a given combination, we need to substitute 1.00 if we wish to include a cue and 0.00 if we wish to exclude it. For example, for a set in which every case contains all three cues, the following substitutions are made:

$$\chi_1 = (0.375)\,(1.00) + (0.108)\,(1.00) + (0.245)\,(1.00) + 0.076$$

Therefore, $\chi_1 = 0.804$, and 80 per cent of the petitions in the set will be granted. Similar substitutions provided the other results reported in Table 12-9.

We consider it important to reemphasize that the relationships discussed in Section 6, unlike those in Sections 3–5, were not hypothesized in advance of processing. As a result, we do not regard them as established, but only as useful bases for formulating hypotheses that need to be tested with fresh data. . . .

Notes

1. Prior to the 1954 revision of the Court's Rules, the contents of Rule 19 were contained in Section 5 of Rule 38. For reasons of style both the old 38 (5) and the new 19 will be referred to as Rule 19.

2. . . . Felix Frankfurter and Henry M. Hart, Jr., "The Business of the United States Supreme Court at October Term, 1934," *Harvard Law Review* 49 (1935), 83. . . .

3. We decided at the outset not to include applications for review by criminal defendants in the civil liberties category even though the allegation of a deprivation of constitutional rights is usually involved. Our reason for the decision was our belief that such petitions tend to be so completely frivolous that the justices will ignore them unless some other cue is present.

13

A Study of the Supreme Court's Caseload

Gerhard Casper and Richard A. Posner

I. Introduction

The annual number of applications for review (mainly petitions for certiorari) received by the U.S. Supreme Court has doubled since the late 1950's and has increased fourfold since the late 1930's (Table 13-1). The growth of the caseload has been quite steady since the Court's 1950 term.

On the assumption that the Justices were probably not underemployed in the 1950's— or for that matter in the 1930's—it is natural to wonder whether the increase in the caseload may not have overburdened the Court. The widespread belief that it has is behind the many recent proposals for reducing the Court's caseload, the best known being the proposal of the Study Group on the Caseload of the Supreme Court, headed by Professor Paul Freund, to establish a new court to screen out unmeritorious applications for Supreme Court review and to resolve conflicts among the federal courts of appeals.

The Freund Report has touched off a lively debate, in which a central issue is the significance to be ascribed to caseload statistics such as those presented in Table 13-1. We believe that statistical data and analysis are highly relevant to the workload issue but that more data, and a more detailed analysis of data, than available in the Freund Report or elsewhere are required in order to study the workload problem competently. We present additional data, plus additional analysis of existing data, in this article. In particular, by using a readily available source of information about the subject matter of cases filed with the Court—*United States Law Week*—we have been able to produce new statistics concerning the caseload that help us to understand changes over time within specific subject-matter areas. And we have developed a theory to account for the differential growth pattern across areas that we observe.

. . .

Although the Supreme Court is the most frequently studied institution of American government, statistical analysis of the Court's workload is in a primitive state. The official

Reprinted by permission of authors and publisher from *Journal of Legal Studies* 3 (1974), 339-375. Most footnotes have been omitted.

TABLE 13-1
Cases Filed in Supreme Court—1935–1972

Term	Number	Term	Number
1935	**983**	1954	1,397
1936	950	**1955**	**1,644**
1937	981	1956	1,802
1938	942	1957	1,639
1939	981	1958	1,819
1940	**977**	1959	1,862
1941	1,178	**1960**	**1,940**
1942	984	1961	2,185
1943	997	1962	2,373
1944	1,237	1963	2,294
1945	**1,316**	1964	2,288
1946	1,510	**1965**	**2,774**
1947	1,295	1966	2,752
1948	1,465	1967	3,106
1949	1,270	1968	3,271
1950	**1,181**	1969	3,405
1951	1,234	**1970**	**3,419**
1952	1,283	1971	3,643
1953	1,302	1972	3,749

Sources: Report of the Study Group on the Caseload of the Supreme Court, p. A2 (Fed. Judic. Center, Dec. 1972); Office of the Clerk, U.S. Supreme Court.

statistics are inadequate because they offer no subject-matter breakdown at all. . . . There has been no systematic study of the Court's caseload since 1928.[1]

. . . The last major effort to reduce the workload was made when, at the urging of the Supreme Court, Congress passed the Judiciary Act of 1925. A principal purpose of the Act was to diminish what was considered an excessive burden by further limiting the categories of cases that the Court was required to decide (*i.e.*, by enlarging the Court's discretionary jurisdiction). . . . Table 13-2 . . . reveals that the 1925 Act did reduce substantially the number of cases that the Court was obliged to review.

. . .

The shift to an almost completely discretionary jurisdiction has made it difficult to determine how serious the Court's workload problem is and whether the Court is doing an adequate job of screening applications for review. . . .

. . .

What has become a perennial debate over the implications of a rising Supreme Court caseload is, we believe, unlikely to be resolved until the caseload problem is subjected to a more searching theoretical and empirical scrutiny than heretofore attempted.

II.   Why Has the Court's Caseload Increased?

A. A Theory of Caseload Change

Why do judicial caseloads change over time? Many lawyers and students of judicial administration apparently regard such change as a process of mysterious but inexorable

TABLE 13-2
Supreme Court's Obligatory and Discretionary Jurisdictions, 1923-1930

Term	Cases Filed	Percentage Obligatory	Percentage Discretionary
1923	637	39%	61%
1924	724	40	60
1925	781	36	64
1926	817	32	68
1927	812	20	80
1928	788	19	81
1929	778	14	86
1930	874	15	85

Sources: Computed from Felix Frankfurter, The Supreme Court under the Judiciary Act of 1925, 42 Harv. L. Rev. 1 (1929); Felix Frankfurter & James M. Landis, The Business of the Supreme Court at October Term, 1928, 43 Harv. L. Rev. 33 (1929); *id.,* 1929, 44 Harv. L. Rev. 1 (1930); *id.,* 1930, 45 Harv. L. Rev. 271 (1931).

growth akin to and perhaps caused by the growth of population. The process is more complex. A number of factors can be expected to influence the demand for a court's services and they do not all work in the same direction. We seek here to identify those factors and to discuss in a preliminary way their interaction.

First, it seems reasonable to expect a positive relationship between the volume of an activity—crime, or highway accidents, or retail sales, or marriages, or whatever—and the number of cases arising out of that activity. Other things being equal—a very important qualification—an increase over time in the volume of an activity should give rise to an increase in the number of legal disputes, including the number of those disputes that are litigated, arising from the activity.

Second, the number of litigated disputes can be expected to vary inversely with the certainty (predictability) of the law. The more certain the law, the fewer will be the number of legal disputes and the smaller will be the fraction of those disputes that are litigated, especially at the appellate level where legal rather than factual issues predominate. And, other things being equal, legal certainty within a given subject area should increase over time, at least up to a point, as precedents accumulate. Thus our first and second factors will often work in opposite directions. The volume of an activity will often be growing over time but the effect on the number of cases may be offset by an increase over time in the number of precedents, which, by increasing the certainty of the law, reduces the amount of litigation.

. . .

Third, the creation of new or the expansion of existing substantive legal rights should produce an increase in the number of cases. The effect is analogous to that of the growth of an activity. The creation of a new legal right—the right of privacy, or the right to exclude illegally obtained evidence from a criminal trial, or the right to be free from pollution—is tantamount to bringing a new activity within the reach of the law and thereby creating a new class of legal disputes. The extinction of a right would have the opposite effect.

Changes in legal procedure can have similar consequences. A relaxation of the standing requirement, or a change in the law of damages that makes it easier for a claimant to obtain a substantial recovery, increases the value of the underlying substantive legal right and thereby makes it more likely that the right will be asserted. This means an increase in the number of legal disputes, some fraction of which are litigated.

Fourth, the availability or cost of legal services may change over time and these changes may affect the number of cases brought. For example, a decision to subsidize legal services for a particular class of claimants will, by reducing the costs of litigation to those claimants, increase their demand for litigation.

Fifth, we may expect secular caseload changes to be self-limiting to some extent. Changes in caseload affect the value of a court to the litigants and hence their demand for its services. If the caseload of a court increases faster than its ability to process its cases, the court will respond either by increasing the waiting period for litigants or by reducing the fraction of cases that it accepts for review. The former has been the usual response of courts—most courts are not empowered to refuse to review cases within their jurisdiction. The Supreme Court has the power to refuse review and has used it, rather than delay, to prevent an imbalance between the demand for and the supply of its services. Whether delay or refusal to review is used as the method of rationing access to the court, the value of the court's services to the applicant for review is reduced. Other things being equal, this should reduce the number of applications filed. Conversely, if over time a court shortens the queue or accepts an increasing fraction of cases for review, the value of review will rise and this should induce an increase in the number of cases filed.

The analytical framework developed in this subpart can be used to generate hypotheses concerning changes in the Supreme Court's workload during the relevant period. These hypotheses are examined in the following subpart. One hypothesis is that the growth of the caseload will not be distributed uniformly over the different types of cases. Some types will show no growth over time, or even a decline, even though the activity giving rise to the type of case may be increasing. We hypothesize a more rapid growth in constitutional than in nonconstitutional cases because of the Court's creation during our period of many new constitutional rights and because of its progressive abandonment of various procedural techniques for avoiding the decision of constitutional cases. We hypothesize that the criminal docket will grow more rapidly than the civil docket, not only because of the Warren Court's activity in enlarging both the substantive and procedural rights of the criminally accused, but also because of increased subsidization of the legal services provided to criminal defendants and the disproportionate increase in the volume of criminal activity compared to other activities. We hypothesize that at some point the rate of increase in the Court's caseload will begin to decline.

B. Statistical Analysis

Table 13-3 presents the statistics of new cases filed in the 1957–1958 through 1971–1972 Supreme Court terms by major categories of case. We obtained our information about each case from the case summaries published in *United States Law Week*. The statistics in Table 13-3 are limited to the Court's appellate docket (*i.e.*, paid cases) because cases on the miscellaneous docket (the indigent cases) are not summarized in *Law Week*. We present statistics on pairs of terms rather than single terms for simplicity and to reduce the influence of random factors.

As expected, caseload growth is uneven across categories—some have grown dramatically, some insignificantly or not at all. . . .

TABLE 13-3
Increase in Cases Filed, Appellate Docket, and Proportion Constitutional

Type of Case	Terms of Court[a] and Numbers of Cases Filed/Proportion Constitutional							
	1957-58	1959-60	1961-62	1963-64	1965-66	1967-68	1969-70	1971-72
Civil cases	1408/.29	1348/.26	1457/.30	1523/.33	1710/.32	1865/.36	2090/.44	2273/.46
From lower federal courts	1077/.15	1035/.11	1112/.15	1152/.18	1296/.17	1413/.21	1605/.31	1726/.32
Federal government litigation	537/.13	517/.15	535/.14	520/.16	627/.14	648/.18	646/.27	646/.26
Review of administrative action	176/.14	204/.12	193/.15	230/.16	284/.10	310/.12	282/.16	245/.18
Taxation	147/.15	137/.04	139/.06	118/.10	126/.08	100/.05	109/.14	99/.24
Other	214/.18	176/.24	203/.19	172/.20	217/.23	238/.32	255/.44	302/.33
State or local government litigation	70/.46	63/.56	70/.50	95/.71	89/.71	131/.70	296/.77	386/.68
Private litigation	470/.11	456/.07	507/.10	537/.12	580/.11	634/.13	663/.15	694/.18
Federal question	275/.08	275/.04	315/.08	344/.09	358/.08	417/.09	447/.10	483/.13
Diversity	195/.16	181/.13	192/.14	193/.17	222/.17	217/.21	216/.25	211/.27
From state courts	331/.76	313/.73	345/.76	371/.79	414/.81	452/.83	485/.85	547/.89
State or local government litigation	194/.91	191/.91	195/.92	228/.86	258/.89	273/.86	295/.93	354/.94
Private litigation	137/.53	122/.53	149/.56	143/.68	155/.67	178/.74	188/.75	193/.81
Criminal cases	338/.69	409/.71	443/.74	537/.74	717/.78	779/.81	1007/.86	1201/.81
Federal criminal cases	221/.55	239/.54	245/.56	320/.58	383/.64	386/.68	573/.79	705/.73
State criminal cases	117/.97	170/.96	198/.95	217/.96	334/.95	393/.94	444/.95	496/.91
Total	1746/.37	1757/.36	1900/.40	2060/.44	2427/.46	2644/.49	3097/.57	3474/.58

[a] Pairs of terms.

Source: Computed from *U.S. Law Week* summaries of new cases filed in Supreme Court.

Table 13-3 also reveals the proportion of cases in each category that are constitutional. We classify as constitutional any case in which the applicant for review tenders at least one constitutional issue, but we exclude cases in which the only such issue is preemption under the Supremacy Clause—such cases involve the interpretation of federal statutes rather than of the Constitution.

Table 13-3 indicates that constitutional cases have increased at a faster rate than nonconstitutional cases. Constitutional cases have increased by 214 per cent since the 1957-1958 terms, nonconstitutional cases by only 32 per cent.

The increase in constitutional cases could reflect simply an increase in categories of cases that by their nature involve a higher-than-average proportion of constitutional issues—such as criminal cases from state courts, almost all of which raise constitutional issues. This is certainly part of the explanation. . . . But it is not the complete explanation. A glance back at Table 13-3 will show a much more broadly based increase in constitutional cases. Every category shows an increase in the proportion of constitutional cases between the beginning and end of the period except the "saturated" category of state criminal cases.

These results suggest at first glance that the caseload increase is largely, perhaps entirely, of the Court's own creation. There was no important constitutional amendment during our period, nor evidence of a trend toward greater disregard of constitutional rights by government officialdom. But before one concludes that the Court's caseload increase is solely the result of its greater willingness to reinterpret the Constitution, there are other possible explanations to be considered. Changes in the political, social, and economic environment may lead to attempts by people to reopen apparently settled issues (such as "separate but equal") or to raise new ones (equality for women). In addition, . . . the percentage of cases that the Court accepts for review has fallen steadily over the relevant period; building on the discussion of the self-limiting character of caseload changes in the previous subpart, we shall argue that a likely consequence has been to reduce the number of marginal cases in the pool of applications. If nonconstitutional cases are, in general, more marginal from the standpoint of the Supreme Court than constitutional cases, one would expect the decline in the percentage of cases accepted for review to be accompanied by an increase in the ratio of constitutional to nonconstitutional cases in the applications for review. A related point is that the assumed decline in the willingness of the Court to review nonconstitutional cases may induce applicants to attempt to clothe the issues they raise in a constitutional garb; these cases would show up in our statistics as constitutional cases.

. . . [C]riminal cases have increased more rapidly than civil cases on the appellate docket. . . .

Table 13-4 shows that, if one may judge by applications for review, at the outset of our period the Supreme Court was already primarily a criminal court of appeals. The primacy of criminal cases has grown since then. Today three-fifths of the applications for Supreme Court review are criminal. The increase in the number of civil applications between the beginning and end of the period is 89 per cent; in criminal applications, 131 per cent. However, all of the increase in the ratio of criminal to civil cases occurs between the first and second pairs of terms analyzed.

. . .

Let us now examine caseload changes in finer subject-matter or issue categories. Table 13-5 lists the major categories of cases in which there was no substantial increase, or an actual decline, in the number of cases over the period covered by the study. In several

TABLE 13-4
Composition of Docket, Miscellaneous Cases Included

Type of Case	Terms of Court,[a] and Numbers/Proportions of Cases of Each Type Filed							
	1957-58	1959-60	1961-62	1963-64	1965-66	1967-68	1969-70	1971-72
Civil	1556/.45	1552/.40	1752/.38	1828/.40	2125/.38	2412/.38	2682/.39	2941/.40
Criminal	1931/.55	2308/.60	2857/.62	2754/.60	3425/.62	4007/.62	4188/.61	4463/.60
Total	3487/1.00	3860/1.00	4609/1.00	4582/1.00	5550/1.00	6419/1.00	6870/1.00	7404/1.00

[a] Pairs of terms.

TABLE 13-5
Areas Where Appellate-Docket Caseload Either Did Not Increase Substantially or Declined

Area	Terms of Court and Numbers of Cases			
	1957 and 1958 Terms		1971 and 1972 Terms	
Civil	735		617	
Civil action from lower federal court		674		577
Taxation		147		99
FPC		21		17
FTC		18		9
ICC		34		25
Immigration and Naturalization Service		21		8
Antitrust (Department of Justice)		13		19
Eminent domain		17		8
Federal tort claims		11		12
Priority of government liens		13		8
Federal government personnel		16		21
Public (federal) contracts		24		10
FELA		15		12
Interstate Commerce Act (private)		18		8
Jones Act		29		23
Patents, copyrights & trademarks		68		72
Railway Labor Act		14		15
Diversity cases		195		211
Civil action from state courts		61		40
Taxation of interstate commerce		23		21
FELA		16		8
Labor relations		22		11
Federal criminal cases	11		13	
Contempt		11		13
Total	746		630	

categories the explanation for the lack of growth appears to lie in the decline or stagnation of the underlying activity. The railroad and maritime industries were declining during our period so it is not surprising to find the number of FELA, Jones Act, ICC and other Interstate Commerce Act, and Railway Labor Act cases declining (or not increasing significantly), especially given the absence of other factors, such as major changes in substantive or procedural rights in these areas, that might have offset the effect of the decline in the underlying activity on the number of cases. Similarly, since the number of cases brought by the FTC and the number of antitrust cases brought by the Department of Justice did not increase significantly during our period, it is not surprising that the number of cases in these areas on the Supreme Court's docket did not increase substantially either.

In several of the areas analyzed in Table 13-5, such as federal government personnel and public (federal) contracts, the underlying activity was growing—the federal government expanded very rapidly over the period covered by the study—but there were no significant legal or other changes, besides the growth in the activity, operating to increase the number of cases. In these circumstances, a decline over time in the number of cases is quite possible, since the effect of the growth of the underlying activity in increasing the number of cases could be dominated by the effect of time in reducing legal uncertainty (and hence litigation) through the accumulation of precedents. An important example is federal taxation. The last major revision of federal tax law prior to the Tax Reform Act of

TABLE 13-6
Major Growth Areas, Civil Cases on Appellate Docket

Area	Terms of Court, and Number of Cases	
	1957 and 1958 Terms	1971 and 1972 Terms
Military	14	68
NLRB	30	89
Civil rights acts	8	111
Racial discrimination (not elsewhere classified)	27	67
Education	1	40
Reapportionment	0	29
Elections	2	63
Health/welfare	10	49
Private antitrust	19	72
Private SEC	3	33
Government personnel (state)	26	90
Regulation of attorneys	12	32
State liquor control	4	16
Domestic relations	16	34
Zoning	10	22
Property	7	26
Torts	11	39
Total	200	880

1969 (the effects of which are too recent to influence our statistics) was the Internal Revenue Code of 1954. The accumulation of precedents under the 1954 Code, coupled with the activity of the Treasury in issuing rulings and regulations designed to clarify and particularize the application of the Code, would operate to reduce uncertainty about federal tax law during the period embraced by the study. This effect might well offset the effect on the number of cases of the increase over time in the number of taxpayers and the amount of taxes (corrected for inflation) collected.

The major areas of growth in the appellate docket are presented in Tables 13-6 (civil) and 13-7 (criminal). . . .

Some of the increases shown in Table 13-6 seem explicable in terms of the creation of new substantive rights—in particular the enactment of civil rights statutes and the expansive interpretation of the equal protection clause adopted by the Court during this period with respect to legislative apportionment and other matters. The increases in the number of private antitrust and private securities cases reflect the removal of various procedural obstacles to the maintenance of such actions. Consistently with our theoretical analysis of caseload change, the most dramatic growth is found in areas, notably military activities (including induction) and civil rights, where rapid increases during the period in the underlying activities (due to the Vietnam War and the civil rights movement, respectively), themselves rather novel, coincided with an expansion in the relevant legal rights.

Table 13-7 presents the major growth areas on the criminal side of the appellate docket. This table contains double counting because the major categories in the table are issue categories and criminal defendants typically raise more than one issue in their applications for review. The statistics provide reliable indications of the trends within

TABLE 13-7
Major Growth Areas, Criminal Cases on Appellate Docket

Issue	Terms of Court and Number of Times Issue Was Raised [a]	
	1957 and 1958 Terms	1971 and 1972 Terms
Federal cases	186 (221)	825 (705)
Due process	27	135
Evidence	53	193
Judicial administration	8	46
Procedure	38	141
Right to counsel	6	42
Search and seizure	38	143
Self-incrimination and immunity	12	54
Speedy trial	4	32
Right to confrontation	0	39
State cases	63 (117)	432 (496)
Evidence	11	59
Jury	10	49
Procedure	22	99
Right to counsel	8	47
Search and seizure	10	115
Obscenity	2	63
Total	249 (338)	1257 (1201)

[a] Numbers in parentheses are total number of cases in category (from Table 13-3).

categories but do not enable an estimate of how much of the growth in the number of cases can be ascribed to the increases shown in Table 13-7.

The major areas of growth in Table 13-7 are ones where an expansion in substantive rights occurred during the relevant period. Good examples are the speedy-trial and right-to-confrontation categories in the federal cases and the right-to-counsel, search-and-seizure, and obscenity categories in the state cases. However, it is unlikely that expansion in substantive rights can explain the whole or even a large part of the growth in the number of criminal cases. . . .

That growth may be due to an increase in the provision of free legal services to federal criminal defendants, and possibly to a perceived increase in the likelihood of the Supreme Court's ruling favorably on a criminal defendant's claim. These factors were also operative with respect to state criminal defendants, but in addition their access to the Court was increased by the Court's landmark habeas corpus decisions during the period as well as by the recognition of important new substantive rights of accused state criminal defendants. Furthermore, the number of state criminal convictions grew much more rapidly than the number of federal convictions—by 121 per cent compared to 43 per cent. Thus it is not surprising that the increase in the number of the state criminal cases on the appellate docket during our period was much greater than the increase in the number of federal cases—324 per cent compared to 219 per cent.

. . .

To summarize, it would appear that the increase in the Court's caseload since 1957 has been a consequence in major part of the Court's substantive and procedural rulings, and to a lesser extent of new legislation. In addition, the provision of legal services to indigent defendants has probably played a major role in the growth of the caseload, but this factor is not completely independent of the first—it is partly a consequence of the Supreme Court's expansive interpretation of the constitutional right to counsel. There is no evidence at all that the caseload increase is the inexorable result of increases in population, national income, or other indices of social activity. Had there been no expansion of the rights and court access of litigants, the Court's caseload might not have increased.

. . .

Note

1. Felix Frankfurter and James M. Landis, *The Business of the Supreme Court* (1928).

CHAPTER FIVE

SUPPORT FOR THE COURTS

Whether an individual involved in a dispute will turn to the courts for help is to some extent a function of his or her attitudes and beliefs about the efficacy, fairness, and competence of judicial institutions. What this means is that one ought to have some understanding of such attitudes and beliefs to better comprehend which disputes reach the courts. It is possible to think about American attitudes toward courts in many ways. Do Americans approve of what courts do, of how they process cases and make decisions? Do they respect and trust judges? Do they think they will get a fair deal from courts? These and other questions are discussed in the selections that follow in the language of political support. That language differentiates *diffuse support,* that is, support for an institution without consideration of its decisions or output, from *specific support,* which is based on approval of those decisions.[1]

Although most studies of support for the courts, including our selections, deal with support for the Supreme Court, some useful empirical research has been conducted that highlights the issues and questions important to an understanding of the way the public thinks about courts at all levels of the judicial system. Such studies provide impressive evidence that courts are not particularly conspicuous in the minds of the American people. Public knowledge about courts, court personnel, and court decisions is slight.[2] This is no less true for the Supreme Court than it is for local trial courts. The theoretical significance of this lack of awareness is uncertain. However, there is some evidence that suggests an important and interesting paradox about public attitudes toward the courts. It appears that there is an inverse relationship between knowledge about courts and support for them; the more citizens know about courts the less happy many are with their operation and performance.[3] Although most surveys report general, if not intense, positive diffuse support for courts, they also indicate that that support is eroded by information and that this erosion is especially dramatic for those whose information is gained through firsthand experience as a litigant.

Two other variables seem important in shaping attitudes toward local courts. First, among people who believe courts to be too lenient in dealing with criminals, support for courts is greatly reduced. It appears that people typically blame the courts rather than the police or social conditions for the crime problem.[4] Second, there is a strong relationship between the way in which people expect to be treated by courts and their support for judicial institutions. Those who believe that some individuals or groups receive better treatment than others are almost uniformly more negative in their feelings about courts than are those who believe that the courts treat people equally.[5]

Insofar as the Supreme Court is concerned, these findings, especially the inverse relationship between knowledge and support, are important. The Supreme Court, like the lower courts, seems to benefit from widespread ignorance of its decisions. Political scientists William Daniels (selection 14), Walter Murphy, and Joseph Tanenhaus (selection 15) report that less than one half of the respondents in each of two national surveys could think of anything specific that they liked or disliked about what the Supreme Court had done. Furthermore, the decisions that were most visible to the public tended to be those which were most controversial, dramatic, and unpopular. The public usually becomes aware of a Supreme Court decision only when there is a campaign of criticism against it. Nevertheless, although neither public knowledge nor public approval of specific decisions is very great, many people, including substantial numbers of those who disapprove of specific decisions, accord the Court high levels of diffuse support. Respect for the institution is not based on approval of its specific decisions.[6]

Rather, there appear to be two other bases for such respect. The first is the rather widespread diffusion of myths about the way in which the Supreme Court makes its decisions. The article by Gregory Casey (selection 16) describes the impressive public endorsement of myths and beliefs associated with symbols of the Court and the Constitution. Fully 60 percent of those of Casey's respondents who were able to describe the operation of the Supreme Court described it in mythic terms. Other scholars have found a similarly strong adherence to the theory of "mechanical jurisprudence"—the theory that judicial decisions can be fully explained by reference to the facts of a case and to the relevant law, mechanically applied.[7] They also argue that this adherence accounts for the widespread diffuse support for the Supreme Court. Those who have a mythic or highly idealized notion of what the Court does and of how it operates are more likely than others, whose perception is more accurate, to support the Court.

Another frequent explanation for the diffuse support of the Supreme Court posits an indirect flow of sentiment from the public to the Court. According to this argument the basis of support is citizens' attitudes toward what has been called the "governing coalition" at the federal level. If individuals identify with the party of the President, if they trust the federal government as a whole or the President in particular, they are likely also to support the Supreme Court. This explanation, along with several others, is discussed in selection 15. The relationship of attitudes toward the Supreme Court and attitudes toward other national government institutions is reflected in the facts that in the 1960s Congress was trusted by more people than the Supreme Court and that support for Congress was an important determinant of support of the Supreme Court. Additional data from surveys conducted in the 1960s suggest that the Court benefited from being associated with the prevailing liberalism of the national executive.[8]

Since most of the empirical research on public attitudes toward the courts was carried out during the 1960s, our knowledge of the way in which the public thinks about courts may be particularly time bound and subject to change. Two studies, one by Jack Dennis[9] and the other by Murphy and Tanenhaus,[10] have presented longitudinal data spanning the period of the late 1960s and early 1970s. Dennis found that in this period, support for the Supreme Court as well as for the entire national government suffered a significant decline. Murphy and Tanenhaus challenged the prevailing governing coalition hypothesis by suggesting that even after the Republicans gained the presidency, Democrats and liberals remained most supportive of the Supreme Court. The implication of this finding is that the governing coalition argument may only be applicable when the President and the majority of the Supreme Court are of the same political party or of the same general ideological bent.

Perhaps as much as anything else the literature on public attitudes toward the courts provides a hint as to why the courts do not play a greatly expanded dispute-processing role. Courts are respected, yet they are also feared. Survey studies are also valuable simply because they reveal beliefs about the distribution of benefits resulting from court decisions. The three selections in this chapter present a wide range of information and discussion about the nature of public support for American courts.

Notes

1. For a discussion of this distinction as it applies to the federal judiciary, see Sheldon Goldman and Thomas P. Jahnige, *The Federal Courts as a Political System,* 2d ed. (New York: Harper & Row, 1976), pp. 138–154.

2. See Darlene Walker *et al.,* "Contact and Support: An Empirical Assessment of Public Attitudes Toward the Police and Courts," *North Carolina Law Review* 51 (1972), 43; and Wesley Skogan, "Judicial Myth and Judicial Reality," *Washington University Law Quarterly* (1971), 309.

3. Jack Dennis, "Mass Public Support for the U.S. Supreme Court," paper presented at the 30th Annual Conference of the American Association of Public Opinion Research, 1975; and Kenneth Dolbeare, "The Public Views the Supreme Court," in *Law, Politics and the Federal Courts,* edited by Herbert Jacob (Boston: Little, Brown, 1967).

4. See Monica Blumenthal *et al., Justifying Violence* (Ann Arbor: Institute for Social Research, University of Michigan, 1972).

5. Austin Sarat, "Studying American Legal Culture: An Assessment of Survey Evidence," *Law and Society Review* 11 (1977), 427–488.

6. See Goldman and Jahnige, *op. cit.,* note 1, pp. 140–148.

7. Skogan, *op. cit.,* note 2; and Richard Engstrom and Micheal Giles, "Expectations and Images: A Note on Diffuse Support for Legal Institutions," *Law and Society Review* 6 (1972), 631–636.

8. See Dennis, *op. cit.,* note 3.

9. *Ibid.*

10. Walter Murphy and Joseph Tanenhaus, "Patterns of Diffuse Support: A Study of the Warren and Burger Courts," paper presented at the 10th World Congress of the International Political Science Association, 1976.

14

The Supreme Court
and Its Publics

William J. Daniels

The United States Supreme Court is "regarded as the font of . . . near infallibility. . . ."[1] Its justices occupy the most prestigious positions in the United States. "Americans find in the Supreme Court a sense of security not unlike that instilled by the British Crown."[2] And the Court in invalidating some laws, lends a general air of legitimacy to all governmental acts. On a contrary note, it has been observed that the Supreme Court is not unique, it is one governmental agency among many, and its work is equally mundane because all judicial activity is "interest group" activity.

. . .

Considering the assumptions about public attitudes toward the Supreme Court noted above and other prevailing notions, several questions are dominant in these studies. First, to what extent does the Court have visibility to the general public? Second, assuming the Supreme Court is visible as a governmental institution, what is the degree and quality of public knowledge of its actions? Third, how is information about the Court evaluated by the public? That is, is the Court perceived and evaluated as are other political bodies or do neutralizing components mold perceptions? Fourth, will respondents' comments tend to be specific and related to actual Court decisions or will they tend to be vague generalities? Fifth, is the central tendency of attitudes toward the Court favorable or critical in nature? Sixth, what characteristics tend to be dominant as structuring components for resulting perceptions of the Supreme Court? And finally, what requisites must be present for the Court to fulfill effectively the function of invalidating unconstitutional behavior of governmental officials?

It is important that the diffuse research findings relating to these crucial questions be synthesized and collated. This article constitutes such an effort. The findings, which respond to the crucial questions above, as well as several related residual questions, are presented as a collection of propositions. . . . Section (I) . . . denotes the public's level of awareness of the Court; . . . (II) relates the disposition of Court perceptions; (III) considers the concept of "role" and the Supreme Court; (IV) reviews the substantive contents of Court comments; (V) contains a composite of characteristics of the Court's critics; and (VI) presents summary comments.

. . .

Reprinted by permission of author and publisher from *Albany Law Review* 37 (1973), 632–661. Most footnotes have been omitted.

(I) Public Awareness

How visible is the Supreme Court? Or, stated differently, do persons generally pay attention to the activities of the Supreme Court of the United States? Until recently, little evidence was available to respond to this question, but numerous arguments prevailed which were grounded on assumptions about the nature of public response to the Court. These assumptions generally supported the notion that the public possessed sufficient knowledge of the Court to react to unpopular decisions. Some findings relevant to this position can be found in surveys designed to measure the extent of public awareness of the Court.

In 1945 the American Institute of Public Opinion found that only 40% of a national sample could accurately note the number of Supreme Court justices. A less difficult (AIPO) question in a 1949 national sample revealed that 86% of the respondents knew the name of the highest Court of the land.

In 1964 the Survey Research Center national sample found in response to the question, "Have you had time to pay attention to what the Supreme Court of the United States has been doing in the past few years?" that 41% of the sample indicated they had paid attention to the activities of the Supreme Court. In addition, as a measure of the extent of attention paid the Court, those respondents who paid attention were asked to comment further. Most made only one comment and none, more than four. The exact percentages are: one comment, 57%; two comments, 34%; three comments, 8%; and four comments, less than 1%. In another section of the 1964 SRC survey, respondents were permitted to make several comments about the political parties, candidates, and issues. Those who made the greatest number of comments about party, candidates, and issues also made the greatest number of comments on the Court. This finding suggests that persons who are politically aware also tend to have reactions to the decisions of the United States Supreme Court.

The 1965 survey of residents of two congressional districts in Seattle, Washington, found that 21% of the respondents were unable to articulate any opinion about the Supreme Court. In fact, nearly two-thirds of the respondents with no opinion frankly stated they possessed too little information to form an opinion about the Supreme Court.

In 1966, 627 Wisconsin adults were asked whether the Supreme Court had made decisions in eight subject areas, and an Index of Knowledge based on responses to the question was devised. Three classifications of knowledge were reported: 15% "high knowledge" persons with five or more correct answers; 36% "medium knowledge" persons with three and four correct answers; and 50% "low knowledge" persons (all others). The high-knowledge persons in the sample were generally better educated and wealthier. Political party affiliation showed them to be about half Republican, 5% Independents, and the remainder Democrats. A characteristic all share in common was a high sense of political efficacy.

. . .

It should be noted that the awareness of the Supreme Court in 1966 was not especially lower than general political awareness in the United States. For example, 76% of the persons for whom the Supreme Court was not visible in 1966 could not name candidates for the House of Representatives for their districts. Moreover, 70% could not identify a single issue of the campaigns that divided the two major parties. . . .

. . .

(II)   Attitudes Toward the Court

In this section, the fundamental question may be phrased: Will persons for whom the Supreme Court has visibility tend to be favorably or critically disposed toward its activities? In addition to this essential question, additional questions of the reviewed studies seek to ascertain respondents' evaluations of the Court's performance, the level of respect which exists for the Court, the degree of trust and confidence respondents have in the Court as an institution, and attitudinal changes which have occurred in evaluations of the Court's work.

The first cluster of attitudes, labeled "like-dislike" perceptions, are based on the 1964 SRC survey. The majority—63%—of the 600 persons who reported they paid attention to the Supreme Court made only statements critical of the Court's work, 25% made only favorable comments, and 12% of the respondents were in agreement with some decisions and critical of others. Of the 916 separate comments made by respondents, 71% were unfavorable comments. The 1966 SRC survey findings were identical to the 1964 SRC results: again, the ratio was 71% unfavorable to 29% favorable comments.

The February, 1965, survey in Seattle revealed that positive attitudes toward the Court were expressed by the largest proportion of respondents, with students holding the most favorable attitudes. There was a tendency for positive attitudes that the Court was doing its job well to be "fairly strongly held," while "strongly held" attitudes were expressed by persons critical of the Court. Overall, the specific comments of respondents showed a fairly low level of informational support for their attitudes.

In a preliminary report, "The U. S. Supreme Court and Its Elite Publics," the perceptions of five specific Court publics are discussed.[3] In this study four observations fundamental to an understanding of public reactions to the Supreme Court are duly indicated. First, it is observed that "Support" for the Court can be "positive" or "negative." Examples of "positive" support are Presidential enforcement of Court decisions, implementation by lower courts, and defense in law reviews. Support can be "negative" when Supreme Court decisions are attacked by presidential candidates, circumvented by lower courts, or ignored by local officials. Second, support for the Court may be in the nature of observable behavior of respondents and therefore "overt," or support may be merely reflected in attitudes or sentiments and in this sense be a form of "covert" support. Third, perceptions of the Court can be diffuse and generalized or specific and concrete. Finally, this study recognizes that the Supreme Court has a variety of publics. Two basic court publics are identified as "mass" and "elite." Four of the included groups, namely, administrative assistants to U. S. senators and congressmen, lawyers, students of Princeton University's class of 1968, and attentive public are included in the "elite" category. These respondents tend to be well-educated and more knowledgeable and active politically, and they possess other high status characteristics which set them apart from the mass public which is the fifth group included in the study.

The principal concern of this study is perceptions of the Court by the "elite publics"; the mass public data are utilized as a basic line for comparison. Examination of the response pattern to a pair of open-ended questions, designed to indicate recent likes or dislikes about Court actions, revealed that a majority of the Court's mass public was unable to respond, but those who did were inclined to indicate dislikes rather than actions of the Court they liked. The group with the highest "like only" responses was students with 28%, followed by administrative assistants with 21%. The three remaining groups are clustered at 9% "like" responses for the attentive public and 7% each for the lawyers and mass public.

Percentages for "dislikes only" responses were higher for four of the five groups, ranging from a high of 43% for the attentive public to a low of 6% for lawyers. Falling between these extremes were the mass public (26%), administrative assistants (22%), and students (19%). When both like and dislike responses are considered, the attentive public is most critical of the Court followed by the mass public.

When both likes and dislikes responses for the 1966 SRC survey were cross-tabulated with responses to the question of whether the Court was doing its job well, it was found that a little more than half the respondents who made only critical comments about the Court said the Court was not doing its job well. This finding seems to indicate the existence of a reservoir of residual respect or a consensus of acceptance for the Court, even though respondents may be critical of specific Court decisions. . . .

. . .

The study of the elite public . . . included survey questions to ascertain "diffuse support" or the general esteem for the Supreme Court as an institution. The analysis was based principally on responses to the fundamental questions, "How well is the Court doing its job?" and "Do you trust Congress or the Supreme Court more?" as interpreters of the Constitution. It is inferred that, while the correlation between diffuse and specific support is high, the Supreme Court receives more of the former than the latter. A distinct minority in each group sampled expressed the opinion that the Court was performing its basic task poorly. The greatest dissatisfaction with the Court's performance was registered by the lawyers, followed by the attentive public, administrative assistants, the mass public, and students. Nearly all respondents who made only favorable comments about the Court when asked to express specific likes and dislikes expressed satisfaction with the Court's general performance. Interestingly, the same overall favorable view was expressed by many respondents who voiced only dislikes.

In addition to noting diffuse support for the Court for the five groups, the relationship between level of knowledge about the Court and evaluation of the Court was analyzed and presented with the groups divided into attentive and mass publics. The result, cautiously stated, was a tendency for diffuse support of the Court to decrease somewhat as specific knowledge of the Court's activities increased. For example, 86% of the attentive public rated the Court was doing its job very well, but only 50% of those who made specific mentions gave the Court this rating. Similarly, the percentage of "Court does job very well" opinions for the mass public drops from 81% for those without specific comments to 53% for those with specific comments.

. . .

(III) The Role of the Court

Several survey questions are directed at determining how the public perceives the role of the Supreme Court. Generally, survey findings relate to perceived roles, preferred roles, actual roles, or potential roles. Specifically, in order of discussion below, are survey results for the following questions: Has the Supreme Court taken on more authority than the Constitution intended? What do you think the job of the Supreme Court should be? What should be the main job of the Court? Should judges be free from political pressures to insure their decisions be impartial? Should judges in a democracy be accountable to the people for their official actions? What representational roles are performed by the Supreme Court? What conditions must prevail for a Supreme Court decision to effectively fulfill a legitimating role for controversial decisions?

The question of whether the Court was exceeding its constitutional authority was asked of respondents in the 1956 AIPO survey. The results, when categorized by the respondents' political party affiliations, were striking in their similarity. Only 18% of the Democrats and 20% of the Republicans expressed a belief that the Court was taking on more authority than the Constitution intended. The majority of respondents of both parties (58% of the Democrats and 57% of the Republicans) did not share this belief. It was expected that Republicans would be more critical than Democrats, in response to this question, in a manner consistent with past levels of disapproval of the Court. A possible explanation for the virtually indistinguishable party perceptions in 1956 is that partisan attitudes toward the Supreme Court seem to be related to the party affiliation of the President. That is, respondents tend to view the Court favorably when their party controls the White House.

An understanding of the Court's work was indicated by nearly 80% of the 1965 Seattle study. In describing the Supreme Court's "proper" job, nearly half of the respondents mentioned two issues: to interpret the law or the Constitution, and to act as Court of final appeal. Six additional preferred roles were stipulated: continue exercising present responsibilities, protect our freedoms, settle cases impartially, settle questions affecting the entire country, and check other branches of government. The scope and distribution of these responses are notable in that collectively they reflect tasks which are conceded to be within the Court's domain.

A significant 61% of the persons who responded to the question about the "main" job of the Court in the 1966 SRC survey made comments which show awareness of the Court's role in interpreting the Constitution. For example, observations that the Court "decide(s) on the constitutionality of laws" or "maintain(s) balance in government" clearly show that many respondents are aware that the Court has the authority to review and, if in violation of the fundamental law, declare legislative or executive action invalid.

. . .

. . . [C]onstitutional courts, e.g., the United States Supreme Court, do in fact perform several representative functions. . . . Three particular representative functions may be performed by . . . [them]. First, courts are representative bodies in the sense that they are selected by popularly elected governmental officials and quite typically represent the country's major geographical areas and ethnic, economic, and religious groupings. Second, a function of providing access to governmental power for minority groups has been performed by constitutional courts. Such groups frequently lack political resources which afford meaningful roles in selecting, having access to, or influencing popularly elected legislators. Third, important decisions protecting the integrity of the electoral process or political rights, such as the full ramifications of the one man, one vote doctrine, have been rendered by constitutional courts.

The final question on the role of the Court involves generally the role which might be performed by the Court when deciding whether or not governmental actions are constitutional. . . . [C]onstitutional court validation of controversial policies fulfills a "legitimating" role and tends to promote the stability of representative government. The central issue thus centers on the conditions which must obtain for legitimation to occur, four of which are the following. First, constitutional courts must have visibility in order for one to be aware of a potentially legitimizing decision. Second, there must be a recognition that resolving constitutional conflicts is a proper function of the Constitutional Court. Third, one must generally approve of the overall operation of the Court even if critical of specific rulings. And fourth, the Court must be trusted at least as much as the institution it is asked to judge.

One must conclude, after analyzing SRC data for 1964 and 1966, that the Supreme Court performs a legitimating role for only a small proportion of the sample respondents. In fact, the data show that this function is fulfilled for about one person in thirteen; this proportion, however, was not dismissed as being trivial. . . .

(IV) Issues and the Court

General dispositions of public perceptions have been outlined; the substantive contents of perceptions or the specific issues mentioned in response to open-ended survey questions are the subject here. First, a range of perceived issues is presented; secondly, the dependent variables are denoted; and thirdly, the observed relationships between the specific issues mentioned and demographic as well as other characteristics of respondents are discussed.

The 1964 SRC survey included the first open-ended questions which enabled respondents to indicate if they liked or disliked anything in particular the United States Supreme Court had done. The range of issues mentioned, either favorably or critically, included civil rights of blacks with 38% of the respondents noting this as the most salient issue; school prayer, 30%; rights of criminal defendants, 6%; reapportionment, 5%; and other issues, 20%. The favorable and critical comments for the four salient issues are given in Table 14-1.

Respondents in the 1965 Seattle survey were asked if they heard or read anything about the Supreme Court during the past year. Three of the four issues of 1964 were dominant in this smaller sample. Also three-fourths of the survey respondents mentioned the four issues of civil rights, with a 42% response rate; school prayer, approximately 20%; reapportionment, 8%; and communism, approximately 5%.

In 1966 the SRC again included an open-ended question which permitted the identification of specific issue perceptions. The character of the dominant issues was strikingly similar to that of the 1964 SRC survey and the 1965 Seattle survey. There were, however, some notable changes in the percentages of total comments. The "residual" category of other issues increased 14% to 34%; rights of criminal defendants up ten per cent to 16%. Three other issues were less visible: civil rights of blacks decreased 13% to 25%; school

TABLE 14-1
Dominant 1964 Issues

Issue	Favorable %	Critical %
Civil Rights	77	36
Prayer	12	50
Reapportionment	8	5
Criminal Defendants	3	9
	100	100

TABLE 14-2
Dominant 1966 Issues

Issue	Favorable %	Critical %
Civil Rights	75	25
Prayer	11	45
Reapportionment	3	1
Criminal Defendants	11	29
	100	100

prayer was down six points to 24%; and reapportionment received an 8% response rate which was down approximately 5% from the 1964 rate.

In addition to changes in the percentages of total comments, there was also slight change in the favorable and critical reactions to the dominant issues as shown in Table 14-2.

The favorable comments remained basically the same. However, unfavorable comments were down for all issues excepting one. There was a dramatic increase in the percentage of unfavorable comments on the issue of rights of criminal defendants. Other notable changes were variation in the issue of civil rights for blacks which received considerably fewer unfavorable remarks, and reapportionment barely retained visibility in 1966 with one per cent.

. . .

At this point, at least four observations about the substantive content of perceptions can be made. First, essentially the same issues were noted by respondents in the several surveys. Second, even the dominant issues tended not to be visible for the majority of respondents. Third, the issues likely to be mentioned were those which could be perceived in an intensely personal manner. And fourth, perceptions of particular issues seem to warrant mentioning. The issue of reapportionment, which received much attention and seriously affected the balance of power in state legislatures, had very low salience in 1964 and 1966. Public attention to the issue of rights for criminal defendants, on the other hand, experienced dramatic increases in visibility during the years 1964-1968.

. . .

(V)   Criticism of the Court

The preponderance of the evidence suggests that, at least in terms of response to open-ended Court evaluation queries, critics of the Court outnumber its supporters. It seems appropriate therefore to attempt to extract findings from opinion studies to confront a crucial question. What factors tend to account for or predispose critical attitudes toward the United States Supreme Court?

Anthony Lewis has noted that Supreme Court criticism falls essentially into three categories. The first is "result oriented" criticism which is focused on the decisions reached by the Court rather than with the reasons given for such action. This criticism is loud and great in volume but signifies nothing more than disagreement with Court decisions. . . . A second category of criticism is predicated on assumptions about the proper relationships between governmental bodies and generally presents the point of view that the Court has exceeded its power to review the constitutionality of legislation. It is further stated that unfettered use of judicial review violates the separation of powers and the Court thereof has become a third legislative chamber. The third group of critics are primarily law professors, and their criticism has been labeled by Lewis as the "new academic criticism." These critics are not concerned with results or the proper role of the Court, but maintain that the "process" through which the Court reaches a result is most important. The academic critics are concerned that the Court adequately and sufficiently bridge the gap between the authorities they cite and the results they reach. Often it is said that the Court is saying too little or that, in other instances, the Court's workmanship is not solid or strong and therefore does not command confidence or support.[4]

. . .

Generally, there is a low level of public awareness and knowledge about the Supreme Court. This tends to be significant in that high knowledge and high status are related to greater disapproval of the Court. Nevertheless, when high-knowledge, high-status respondents were grouped as Republicans and Democrats, it was found that Republicans were far more critical of the Court. That is to say, political party was a more consistent indicator of attitudes critical of the Court than were high status or high knowledge. However, political party identification may, in turn, be an indicator of issue dispositions, or more importantly, ideological predilections. A court decision may intrude upon public awareness, and the specific issue or Court decision may at that time become dominant in structuring an attitude. But behind issue orientation may be a propensity toward conservatism which causes one's reaction to the issue decided by the Court. . . . In any case, one can say with confidence that basic political factors are powerful determinants in accounting for critical perceptions of the Court.

(VI)   Summary and Conclusions

Public opinion survey perceptions of the United States Supreme Court have been presented. What do we make of them? In this concluding section a portrait of perception observations which represent dominant findings will be drawn. Needless to say, the findings of the surveys in several respects are not congruent, and this collated presentation contains an element of distortion. However, the development of a theory of public reactions to Supreme Court decisions requires a far more substantial data base, and therefore the following suppositions and propositions ought to be taken as generalizations in need of further verification.

Adequate and accurate communication of Supreme Court decisions will not bring about the millennium, but it is a necessary condition for informed public reactions to the work of the Court. In any event, no matter what criteria of knowledge one selects, the public is not politically attentive. As a result, there is a very low level of knowledge about the Court. Only a minority of the public is sufficiently aware to name individual justices or to comment on recent Court decisions. It seems that one must be aware politically for the Court to have visibility.

Respondents who accepted the mechanistic jurisprudence proposition or who believed the Court is limited in its discretion when deciding cases tended to give higher ratings to the Court. But survey findings are less conclusive as to whether there is widespread acceptance of the myth of judicial divinity or the notion that the Court is less fallible than are other bodies of government.

At the lowest level of public knowledge, persons were simply aware of the Court's existence, and they generally perceived it as something more than just another governmental institution. A measure of understanding of the Court's important governmental function as well as its constitutional court function exists for a significant portion of the aware public. The perception of the Court's governmental role notwithstanding, the Court is not only the object of fluctuating levels of trust and confidence, but the several studies seem to show a decrease in esteem for the Court between the years 1946 and 1966. However, the level of esteem for the Court may not fluctuate for the Court's less attentive public; indeed, for this group, the level of esteem for the Court may be constant and overall favorable.

The data tend to show, with one notable exception, an inverse relationship between knowledge and support for the Court. The excepted case is black respondents. Whereas greater knowledge generally decreases support for the Court, for blacks the more knowledge, the greater the support for the Court. These findings seem to cast doubts on the assumption that making the Court's actions more visible will increase support for it.

In broad perspective, reactions to the Court were policy-oriented. That is, the public tended not to react to the niceties of the decision-making process, but to what the Court in fact decided. The reactions were in large measure critical in disposition. When the public has become engaged, it has tended to be in opposition to issues that can be viewed in an intensely personal fashion.

Basic demographic, *e.g.*, race, and political variables, *e.g.*, political party affiliation, are powerful determinants of support for or antipathy toward the Court. The configuration of variables and the nature and extent of their interaction in accounting for variance in perceptions of the Court differs slightly from survey to survey. Generally, of lesser significance in structuring approval and disapproval have been specific issues or Court decisions, knowledge, status, education, and place of residence. . . .

General public support plays a considerable role in the effectiveness of laws, and there seems to be substantial agreement that a reservoir of residual respect or diffuse support exists for the Supreme Court. However, the precise nature of this diffuse support, in view of observations found in the literature, warrants further investigation. Could it be that, on balance, Court decisions during the period of the surveys have merely followed prevailing public sentiments on the issues decided and that the jurisprudence of the Warren Court was compatible with a working majority of private citizens. On the other hand, it could be that general public ignorance, lack of awareness, and public acquiescence are accountable for general compliance. Additional probes, however, will be necessary to determine the plausibility of this contrary notion.

. . .

A theory may be defined as a symbolic construction of component propositions in an identifiable configuration which converge on some central point. Applying this definition to the substantive area of public opinion and judicial decisions there are two possible points of conversion, namely public reaction to specific court decisions or judicial decisions as reflections of public opinion. Moreover, we postulate that at least seven component propositions interrelate in an identifiable pattern and are applicable at both points of conversion. These components may be labeled thusly: (1) visibility, (2) focus, (3) direction, (4) intensity, (5) belief, (6) information, and (7) context.

The components may pertain to the points of conversion in the following manner. *Visibility.* Any reactions to public opinion or judicial decisions requires that they be known. Court decisions may or may not be visible to the public; judges may not be aware of public opinion. *Focus.* The issue, a judicial decision or public reaction to a decision, may not be sharply or clearly defined. The more specific the focus, the greater the potential for understanding the issue. *Direction.* Relates to the emotional quality of the issue. Public opinion may be critical of a judicial decision; judges may be favorably disposed toward public opinion. *Intensity.* To say one is favorably or critically disposed toward public opinion or a judicial decision is not sufficient; such dispositions must also be accompanied by measures of intensity or the strength of one's commitment. *Belief.* One's beliefs affect the evaluation of information received. For example, the orientation of the judge is important; he may not consider it proper to submit to public opinion in the execution of judicial functions. Or a person's respect for the judiciary might tend to mute his criticism of judicial actions. *Information.* Of crucial importance to the process of assessing public opinion or a specific court decision is the accuracy of the information one receives. Moreover, one's subsequent activity can only be effective if the information received is reliable. *Context.* This component relates to important variations in the environment. For example, the type of court, level of the proceeding, and the nature of the case, are important variables in evaluating potential judicial reactions to public opinion. On the other hand, the attentiveness of the public, the socio-economic status of groups within the affected public, and political party and ideological configurations of the public have an important bearing on the impact and evaluation of judicial decisions. Of course, this discussion does not exhaust all possible interrelationships between the components outlined, but the variables noted are measurable, and our synthesis strongly suggests that they can be useful in the formulation of a theory of public opinion and judicial decision-making.

. . .

Notes

1. T. Arnold, *The Symbols of Government* 196 (1935).
2. Mason, "Myth and Reality in Supreme Court Decisions," 48 *Va. L. Rev.* 1386 (1962).
3. Murphy and Tanenhaus, "The United States Supreme Court and Its Elite Publics: A Preliminary Report," paper read before 1970 International Political Science Association Congress. . . .
4. Lewis, "The Supreme Court and Its Critics," 45 *Minn. L. Rev.* 305 (1961).

15

Public Evaluations of Constitutional Courts: Alternative Explanations

Walter F. Murphy, Joseph Tanenhaus, and Daniel L. Kastner

. . .

The major theoretical concerns of this . . . work center around constitutional courts as stabilizers and educators. To analyze these capacities requires an understanding of the different abilities of judges to reach audiences in their countries and of the different levels of support with which judges operate. Of necessity, then, a considerable part of any such investigation must concentrate on the ways in which general publics and particular elites perceive and esteem their courts as well as the underlying causes for prevailing patterns of perception and support. . . .

This paper focuses on the results of interviews with a national sample of 1,285 Americans of voting age conducted by the Survey Research Center of the University of Michigan in November 1966. . . . The first part of this paper presents a brief summary of the patterns of support that have emerged. . . . The second part uses these data to choose among competing explanations of patterns of support. We use a variant of what John R. Platt calls "strong inference." That aspect of the monograph thus may have a methodological as well as substantive interest.

The third part of the paper discusses, albeit tentatively, some of the implications for the roles of constitutional courts suggested by explanations for those patterns of support.

I. Patterns of Support

The concept of political support is intuitively clear. In common parlance it refers to supplying assistance through action or promises of action, perhaps a vote, a campaign contribution, a loan, a sale of surplus arms, or a treaty of alliance. In less overt but not necessarily less significant terms, support may also refer to psychological aid and comfort. Just being there, quiet but sympathetic, may be as important in public as it often is in private life. Indeed, support in the sense of widespread acceptance of the legitimacy of certain substantive and procedural rules is a critical element in the functioning of any

These excerpts from "Public Evaluations of Constitutional Courts: Alternative Explanations," by Walter F. Murphy, Joseph Tanenhaus, and Daniel L. Kastner, Volume 4, No. 01-045 *Sage Professional Paper in Comparative Politics Series* © 1973, are reprinted by permission of the Publisher, Sage Publications, Inc.

society. Without such acceptance—or perhaps even if support had to be created for every significant decision—political stability would vanish. . . .

Yet for all its apparent clarity and simplicity, political support is typically difficult to measure. . . . More commonly . . . the indicia from which analysis must infer support for a political system or an institution—as opposed to an individual candidate or official—are negative: the absence or impotence of revolutionary movements or the feebleness and infrequency of efforts to change fundamental norms or structures of authority. And a dearth of frontal challenges poses a host of substantive as well as methodological problems, since silence can cloak a range of emotions varying from seething resentment to semi-euphoric delight. Moreover, even a seeming host of critics may supply misleading signs of widespread absence of support, since speakers can create noise more readily than they can understanding and sympathy.

In this study we have used a questionnaire to try to tease from respondents verbal—and positive—evidence of support for the Supreme Court of the United States. We are sorely aware that strong words are seldom fungible into the hard currency of brave deeds, and we return to problems of exchange in the concluding part of the paper. . . .

Following a well worn path, we have divided the concept of support into two categories, specific and diffuse, but shall be much more concerned with the latter than the former in this paper. Variations in diffuse support form the dependent variable, the thing to be explained, in this study. In part II, we shall try to use specific support, along with a bevy of other variables, as a means of accounting for variations in diffuse support. Specific support, as Easton defines it, refers to a set of feelings about a polity, an institution, process, or one or more officials generated as "a quid pro quo for the fulfillment of demands." As we use the term, specific support will refer to the critical or favorable reactions to what the Court or individual justices have recently done. In contrast, diffuse support refers to a generalized attachment. That broader kind of support (or its converse, alienation turned to revolution) may be the result of a number of factors acting singly or in combination: calculations that short-run costs may purchase long-run benefits; less thoughtful but not necessarily less selfish analyses of debits and credits; more emotional reactions because of continuations of attitudes installed during childhood; or perhaps fear, blind rage, patriotism, or some form of neurosis.

We have constructed a scale of diffuse support from replies to four questions asking: (1) how well the Court was doing its basic job(s)—preceded by a filter in the form of an open-ended query asking what the respondent thought was the Court's primary task or tasks; (2) whether the Court was too much involved in partisan politics; (3) whether it was basically fair in its decisions; and (4) what was the relative degree of trust in Congress as opposed to the Court. We use two measures here. Tables and discussions in the text employ a simple Likert scale summating responses to these questions. That kind of scale has the advantage of an intuitively obvious midpoint, allowing readers easily to classify scores as supportive or unsupportive. The scale goes from a low of 1 for those who were least supportive to a high of 5 for the most supportive; the midpoint of course is 3. On the other hand, for regressions and scatterplots, we use factor scores because of their greater capacity to discriminate among respondents. As one would guess, these four questions load heavily on a single axis; and the Likert and factor scores correlate strongly ($r = .91$).

A total of 1,072 respondents were able to answer one or more of the questions probing diffuse support. On two of those queries, how well the Court did its job and how fair it was, favorable replies outnumbered critical comments by more than two to one. To the questions about the Court's possibly being excessively involved in partisan politics, a bare majority replied that the Court was not too much involved. The fourth question, that

TABLE 15-1
Replies to the Questions About Diffuse Support (in percentages [a])

	Response				
	Favorable	Pro/Con	Unfavorable	%	(n)
How Court Does Job?	63	11	27	101	(720)
Court Fair?	69	2	29	100	(865)
Court Too Political?	51	5	44	100	(784)
Trust Congress/Trust Court?	37	12	51	100	(861)

[a] Percentages may exceed 100 because of rounding.

about relative trust in Congress and the Court, was the only one in which the justices did not fare well. Those preferring Congress substantially outnumbered those choosing the Court. For some purposes even that pattern of replies need not be considered critical of the Court, but we have so treated it here because of interest in the ability of judges to perform stabilizing and educating functions in the face of possible legislative opposition.

Table 15-1 collapses various levels of response into three categories for each of the questions and reports the replies of those people who were able to answer each query. As one would have guessed from these data, the Likert scale shows that the Court received a modest amount of diffuse support. The mean score for the entire sample was 3.3, but with a rather wide standard deviation of 1.9. Figure 15-1 shows the patterns of distribution along that scale. The most crowded section of the figure is at the very peak of support.

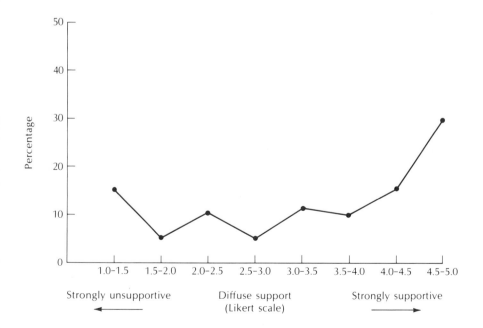

Figure 15-1. Full sample: distribution along scale of diffuse support.

Exactly 30% of the 1,072 people scored in that range. Nevertheless, the number of people scattered about the lower end of the scale indicates (as does the rather slim margin by which 3.3 exceeds the midpoint of 3.0) that the Court had a fair share of critics as well as admirers. Analysis of the wording of the actual replies shows an almost complete absence of that reverence with which some writers have claimed the Court is commonly viewed. Even its strongest admirers tended to speak with respect rather than awe.

II.   Tests of Competing Explanations

That the Warren Court in 1966 enjoyed a modest amount of diffuse support is interesting and important, but it is also important (and more interesting) to be able to account for the variations in support pictured by Figure 15-1, for only then can one begin to understand what that level of support implies either for the polity or the Court itself. Simple cross-tabulation of the data reveals certain relationships. Blacks were the most supportive of all ethnic groups. Jews were more supportive than Catholics who, in turn, were more supportive than Protestants. On the average, Republicans scored lower on the scale than did Democrats, southerners scored lower than nonsoutherners, and older people scored lower than young adults. None of these findings is unexpected or unimportant, but neither do they collectively or individually move very far toward understanding.

. . .

We have searched the literature dealing with courts and public opinion and extracted (following the judicial example, on occasion we indulged in creative extrapolation) a number of credible explanations about why some people do and others do not support the Court. We have deduced one or more narrow and more testable hypotheses from these more general explanations—propositions that would have to obtain were the more general explanations valid. We use our data to test these propositions as fairly as possible, to indicate what is useless, and to try to refine what seems promising. Because of constraints on time, money, and imagination, the questionnaire was specifically designed to test only some of these propositions; thus, we shall be unable to test a few of the hypotheses at all, others only indirectly, and still others imperfectly.

The size and character of the sample pose a number of problems. Most immediately, the extent of knowledge about the Court varied widely. It is apparent from reading the protocols that some respondents gave informed and thoughtful answers, while others freely offered evaluations based on almost total ignorance. As would be expected from other research, the views of the uninformed can charitably be described as rather unstructured and pretty much invulnerable to current techniques of mass survey research, although perhaps not to longer, more intensive interviewing, or to more refined modes of calibrating responses. Further complicating the situation is a presumption implicit in some of the propositions of rational self-interest that must be based on at least a modicum of knowledge about the Court.

To cope with, without being able to conquer, these difficulties, we have divided the sample into three groups in increasing order of knowledge about the Court: (1) those 1,072 people who could answer one or more questions relating to diffuse support (the full sample); (2) a subset of 919 persons from the 1,072 whose answers to another battery of questions revealed at least moderate knowledge about the Court (a culled sample); and (3) the 590 members of the culled sample who were sufficiently informed to reply to one or more open-ended queries about the recent work of the Court (the knowledgeables).

More often than not, we shall use the culled sample to test various propositions, since its members have at least moderate knowledge and the size of the group is sufficiently large to allow analysis that holds constant such factors as race, religion, income, or party identification. . . .

A. The Court as Guardian of the Defeated and Alienated

Among the functions that scholars as well as political activists have ascribed to constitutional courts is that of protecting the interests of those people so defeated in the political processes as to become highly distrustful of or even alienated from the regime. These people can go to the Courts for a rematch in an arena with different (perhaps "nonpolitical") rules.

An explanation that holds that variations in support can be accounted for by the extent to which the politically disenchanted, disaffected, or alienated see the Court as the protector of their interests against a hostile government must make the assumption that the Court is perceived not merely as separate in terms of institutional independence from the other branches of government but also that people (at least those who are disgruntled) see judges as able to pursue very different policies from those espoused by the legislature and executive. As section C will point out, there is some, but only some, evidence to the contrary; we take up that matter later.

If support for the Court is higher among the disaffected and alienated, then the following and somewhat overlapping propositions should hold:

(1) Those respondents who were more alienated from, or distrustful of, the federal government should have expressed much stronger support for the Court than those who were less alienated or not at all alienated.

. . .

(2) Those respondents who basically disagreed with the general course of domestic public policy followed by the federal government should have expressed stronger support for the Court than those who less basically disagreed and even stronger support than those who agreed with that course.

There is a third proposition that, while it does not ineluctably follow from the general proposition, is a reasonable inference:

Those respondents who felt less effective politically should have been more supportive than those who felt more politically effective.

Tests

(1) Support and alienation from the federal government. The Survey Research Center asked four questions about general attitudes toward the federal government. We have used factor analysis to construct a scale of responses to those queries which can be used as a rough measure of alienation from national government or, if one prefers less controversial terminology, distrust of the national government. The correlation between that scale and diffuse support was $-.32$. That is, the more alienated from or less trustful of the federal government respondents were, the less supportive of the Court they turned out to be. There is a relationship here, not awesome but still not weak. It runs, however, in the opposite direction from that predicted by the first proposition.

. . .

(2) Reactions to federal domestic policies. Section F takes up in detail the relationships between support and opinions toward federal domestic policies. It is sufficient to note here that those we have labeled as liberals, that is, respondents who were most favorably disposed toward the cause of black civil rights, were least concerned about the growth of federal power, and voted for Lyndon Johnson in 1964, tended to be the strongest supporters of the Court. Those who voted for Barry Goldwater in 1964, were concerned about federal power, and less favorably disposed toward civil rights of blacks, were apt to be least supportive of the Court. In short, these data stridently shout down the proposition, at least for the mid-1960s.

. . .

(3) Efficacy and support. We have been able to construct two measures of respondents' own evaluations of their political efficacy, one designed by Almond and Verba the other by the Survey Research Center. For present purposes the scale developed by Almond and Verba provides the more useful yardstick, since it more directly taps self-perceptions of ability to affect politics and records specific efforts to do so. That scale shows no substantively or statistically meaningful relationship between how politically effective a respondent believed himself to be and how he evaluated the Court as an institution. Indeed, for the culled sample, the relationship $(r = .001)$ is about as close to random as one is apt to come in the real world. The correlation barely increased in either girth or pulchritude for particular groups, such as blacks and southern whites.

Proponents of the proposition can scarcely find more comfort in SRC's measure of political efficacy. The correlation there was a slender .09, hardly enough to stir the blood or even muddy the waters. The data simply lend no credence whatsoever to the third proposition.

Conclusions

These tests make it difficult to accept, for the period covered by the interviews, an explanation that asserts support for the Court will increase as alienation from or distrust of the federal government increases. Indeed, the opposite tendency is quite noticeable. These tests also lend scant reinforcement to an explanation linking support for the Court with alienation from local government. It must be conceded, however, that the congruence between jurisprudence of the Warren Court and the domestic policies of the Kennedy and Johnson Administrations makes 1966 an especially difficult year for such explanations; for those unhappy with national politics and knowledgeable about the Court could realistically have expected little succor from the justices. But the results of these tests at minimum throw the burden of proof onto those who assert the explanation for other periods.

. . .

B. The Court as Comforter of the Afflicted

An explanation for patterns of support that is akin to, but different from, that of the Court as the guardian of the interests of the alienated pictures the Court as comforter of the severely disadvantaged and deprived in society. In this context, "the afflicted" would include those "discrete and insular minorities" to whom Harlan Stone referred in paragraph three of his *Carolene Products* (*United States v. Carolene Products*, 304 U.S. 144, 1938) footnote, those who had not merely been defeated in the other political processes but who lacked enough political clout even to have had a fair chance of winning on their own. More broadly, it includes those who are not receiving anything like a full share of society's benefits. These deprivations may be economic, social, or political. The severely disadvantaged may have received some payoffs (or side payments) from the polity, but these would have been sops rather than prizes—for instance, an increase in welfare benefits rather than meaningful programs to train them for well paying jobs, or a few arrests of pushers rather than an effective campaign to stamp out drug abuse.

. . .

(1) In any event, if it is a valid explanation for variations in support for the Court that the more severely disadvantaged in society look to the justices for help and thus give them more support than do the less disadvantaged, then the following proposition should have held:

> Those who were most disadvantaged in American society, blacks and the poor, for example, should have been more supportive than were those who were relatively advantaged by the social and political structures.

Tests

One faces a dilemma in testing this hypothesis. On the one hand, to exclude the less knowledgeable from analysis would be to exclude a potentially substantial share of the most disadvantaged respondents. On the other hand, the proposition contains a strong, although implicit, assumption that people, especially the disadvantaged, will react in line with their self-interests; and, unless a respondent demonstrates some knowledge, an analyst has no way of telling whether that person had any conception at all about where his self-interest lay. We meet this dilemma by reporting the tests as run against the full

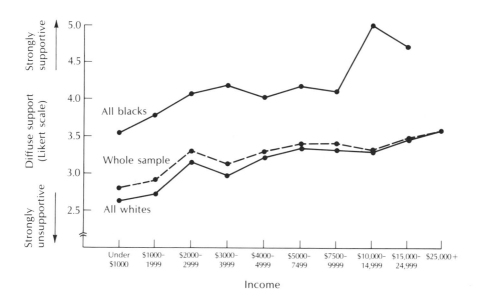

Figure 15-2. Diffuse support by income (full sample).

TABLE 15-2
Comparison of Mean Scores of Diffuse Support

	Mean Score
All whites in the full sample:	3.2
All blacks in the full sample:	4.1
All whites in the culled sample:	3.3
All blacks in the culled sample:	4.4
All whites in the 590:	2.9
All blacks in the 590:	4.5

sample of 1,072 people, the culled sample of 919, and then again against the smaller group of 590 knowledgeables.

(a) *The full sample.* We need not repeat here how very positively disposed toward the Court blacks were. The responses of the poor tell a somewhat different story, but one which can be unraveled only with great care because SRC asks for ranges of income rather than exact figures and also because those ranges broaden as income increases. Moreover, even enthusiasts of survey research concede that a question about money touches an area in which an interviewer is likely to be given misleading information. With those caveats in mind, we can look at Figure 15-2. It shows that people in the lowest income brackets were less supportive on the whole than were the most affluent, although the relationship does not proceed in neat steps. One can also see the way in which blacks, especially the more numerous poorer blacks, inflate diffuse scores. Among whites, support was not only uniformly—and sometimes sharply—lower, but it also followed a more even course.

. . .

(b) *The 590 knowledgeables.* Blacks in this group were more supportive than blacks generally and much more supportive than whites among the 590. Table 15-2 presents the data. But, in the full and culled samples, there was no discernable association between income and support among the knowledgeables ($r = .03$).

(2) One can shift the emphasis in the basic explanation for the pattern of support to read that those people who believe strongly that it is the function of the Court to protect the severely disadvantaged in society will voice more support than will those people who believe less strongly or do not believe at all in the propriety of such a function. If this revised explanation is valid, then the following pair of propositions should hold:

   (a) Those people sympathetic to the cause of the underdog—those, for example, who in 1966 were more favorably disposed toward civil rights of blacks and federal protection of those rights—should have been more supportive than were those who were less sympathetic to charges of racial injustice in American society.

   (b) More specifically, those who voiced concern about the Court's decisions in the field of criminal justice should have been much less supportive than those who approved of such rulings.

Tests

(a) *Infracanophilia and support.* The 1966 survey contained no questions regarding general attitudes toward underdogs, but it did include three queries regarding civil rights of blacks

TABLE 15-3
Diffuse Support and Opinions of Criminal Justice Decisions

Criminal Justice Decisions	Mean Score on Diffuse Support	
Mentioned among dislikes	2.8	($n=138$)
Mentioned among likes and dislikes	—	($n=0$)
Mentioned among likes	4.0	($n=20$)
Had likes or dislikes but no mention	3.0	($n=432$)
Had no likes or dislikes	3.6	($n=482$)

and federal protection of those rights. Certainly blacks had no monopoly on being disadvantaged in American society; but most of them, at least in 1966, could produce solid reasons for being included among the flock of the unelect. Responses to the three questions about black civil rights produced strong if not conclusive evidence for the revised proposition. For all of the 1,072 respondents on whom we had data, the correlation between sympathy for civil rights and support for the Court was .37 among the full sample and .40 among the culled sample. For the 590 knowledgeables the correlation went up to .49. . . .

(b) *Concern about criminal justice.* One might look on concern for the rights of the criminally accused, especially for accused who were poor and ignorant, as another indicium of sympathy for the underdog. Certainly the decisions of the Warren Court insisting on procedural fairness for those who could not afford to hire counsel or buy transcripts or were too uninformed even to be aware of their rights can be reasonably classified as helping the disadvantaged. Thus the second proposition predicts a much higher degree of support from respondents who approved of the Court's recent decisions in the field of criminal justice than from those who disapproved.

Logically, the second hypothesis would also predict that those who knew of the decisions but were neither favorably nor unfavorably disposed toward them would fall in between the pros and the cons on the scale of support. Table 15-3 shows that in fact those few people ($n = 20$) who approvingly mentioned the criminal justice decisions were far more supportive than respondents who commented critically on these rulings. Those two subsets of people who did not refer to criminal justice (both those who could not answer the question and those who answered it but mentioned other matters) fell in between the other two groups. While one can conclude that Table 15-3 offers evidence, hard if not powerful, for the second proposition insofar as those commenting on criminal justice are concerned, one cannot draw any firm conclusion about the other two subsets because it is impossible to tell if those respondents knew about the decisions at all. Indeed, the most rigorous presumption would be that they did not know.

Conclusions

The evidence bolsters both propositions, but even taken together the two propositions leave much to be desired as surrogates for the basic explanation linking support to a belief that the Court should protect the underdog. Still, this explanation should not be discarded. It has a firm empirical base even if one cannot now tell how extensive that base is.

. . .

C. The Court as a Facet of a Single Governmental System

Logically contradicting the first hypothesis regarding alienation and support, a third explanation holds that people will tend not to make fine distinctions among makers of national public policy. They will view government as a unit and evaluate policies together, bestowing blame or praise pretty much alike on the President, the Congress, and the Court. Indeed, a few respondents held the justices responsible for various civil rights statutes, for Medicare, and even for the war in Vietnam. More extreme were those people with little education who, in the fashion of younger school children, referred to government simply as a monolithic "he." At the other end of a spectrum of sophistication would be those who accept Robert A. Dahl's thesis that the Court is typically a part of the ruling coalition—a view that, in terms of the jurisprudence of the Warren Court and the avowed egalitarian goals of the Kennedy Administration and more especially that of Lyndon Johnson, had considerable justification in the mid-1960s. That congruence loads the dice in favor of the explanation. Thus even if the data vindicate this explanation, one might still retain grave reservations about its value in other periods. With that caveat, we proceed to the propositions.

If a substantial portion of the public did view the Court as an integral and largely undifferentiated aspect of a national government and base support on such a perception, then:

(1) Support for the Court should have been strongly and positively associated with trust in the federal government.

(2) Support for the Court should have been strongly and negatively associated with alienation from or distrust of the federal government. That is, those people most alienated from the federal government should have been very unsupportive of the Court and those who experienced little or no alienation should have been quite supportive.

(3) Support for the Court should have been strongly and positively associated with approval of the general course of public policy followed by the federal government.

. . .

Tests

Since it is not necessary to make any assumptions about knowledge here, one can use data from the full sample.

(1) Support and trust in the federal government. What was said in the first section applies here. As trust in the federal government increased, so, on the whole, did support for the Court. The relationship was not powerful but it was clearly visible. The correlation was −.24. (The sign is negative because the scales score strong support high and strong alienation—or distrust—high.)

Replies to the question regarding concern about the growth of federal power produced a stronger linkage. As reported earlier, the correlation for the full sample was −.36. As anxiety decreased, support increased noticeably if not dramatically.

Together the two measures provide a solid purchase, if not vindication, for the first proposition. It stands as a tenable statement if modified to read: Support should have been "rather" strongly and positively associated with trust in the federal government.

(2) Support and alienation. Again the opening section laid out the basic analysis. The more alienated (or distrustful) displayed a marked, although not an habitual, tendency to be

less supportive of the Court. The correlation was −.30 for the full sample. The strength of these associations, once again, does not indicate a vigorous relationship, but it does offer evidence that the second proposition points in the right direction, even though it does not lead the way itself.

(3) Support and public policy. We need do no more here than state that general outlook toward politics and public policies as measured by a scale of Liberalism/Conservatism was positively and rather strongly associated with diffuse support. Section F supplies the details; for the full sample the correlation was .45.

. . .

Conclusions

All three propositions have solid support in the data. Moreover, one can use multiple regression to push the case further. When the explanatory power of alienation from government is combined with that of reactions to public policy as measured on the scale of Liberalism/Conservatism, the multiple correlation stands at .49 for the full sample. Manifestly we have to classify the basic explanation linking support and general attitudes toward the federal government as worth additional exploration. . . .

D. The Court as an Object of Partisan Allegiance

In 1956 Richard Nixon spoke of Earl Warren as "a great Republican Chief Justice." Although Nixon soon had cause to repent his remark, both because of the furor it stirred and the later course of the Warren Court, the vice president had touched on an important fact of American political life. Among the most common characteristics historically shared by the justices of the Supreme Court, other than their all (through 1972) having been male lawyers who were citizens of the United States, is that they have been members of the same political party as the president who nominated them. Furthermore, in selecting new justices a president and his advisers try their best to pick people who will agree with the administration on critical issues. The problem, as Abraham Lincoln stated it, is that "we cannot ask a man what he will do, and if we should, and he should answer us, we should despise him for it." Lincoln's solution, as has been that of most chief executives, was straightforward: "Therefore, we must take a man whose opinions are known"— known and tested in the crucible of practical, partisan politics.

. . .

More specifically, Robert Dahl has argued that, because American presidents have frequent opportunities to nominate new justices, the United States Supreme Court is likely to be an integral part of the ruling coalition that controls the White House and attempts to run Congress. Thus one explanation of patterns of support for the Court asserts that citizens tend to perceive the Court as Dahl pictures it (albeit without either Dahl's clarity or sophistication), and predicts that when Democrats are in power in Washington, Democrats will be more pro-Court than Republicans; and when Republicans are in power, their adherents will be more supportive of the Court than will Democrats.

If this general explanation is true, then the following proposition should have held in 1966:

Democrats should have been much more supportive than Republicans.

TABLE 15-4
Comparison of Diffuse Support by Party Identification

Percentage Who Were:	(n)	Strongly Supportive	Supportive	Neutral	Unsupportive	Strongly Unsupportive	NA/DK
Strong Democrats	(171)	42	21	11	8	14	4
Strong Republicans	(109)	25	16	3	21	36	0
Democrats	(249)	37	23	9	10	16	6
Republicans	(150)	31	27	5	13	20	4
Independents leaning toward Democrats	(92)	40	28	4	15	10	2
Independents leaning toward Republicans	(76)	26	21	5	11	34	3
Firm Independents	(107)	37	20	5	10	19	9

Tests

For the time being we pass over the question of how much is very much and look at the relationship between party allegiance and diffuse support. Two measures are readily available here. The first is subjective party identification, obtained through responses to the following set of questions:

> Generally speaking, do you usually think of yourself as a Republican, a Democrat, an Independent, or what? (If Republican) Do you think of yourself as a strong Republican or a not so strong Republican? (If Democrat) Do you think of yourself as a strong Democrat or a not so strong Democrat? (If Independent, no preference, or other) Do you think of yourself as closer to the Republican or the Democratic party?

The correlation between diffuse support and answers to that cluster of questions, as conventionally scaled by SRC, was a slender $-.20$ for the culled sample. (The correlations were negative because strong support was scored high, and strong Democrats, who turned out to be very supportive, were scored low.) Table 15-4 shows that Democrats proportionately outnumber Republicans in the upper ranges of support, and Republicans outnumber Democrats in the lower ranges. But a large share of Democrats, about one-quarter, were unsupportive, and an even larger share of Republicans were supportive.

We devised a second measure of party allegiance, a factored scale that we labeled partisanship. It combines the questions about party identification with a respondent's presidential vote in 1964. The linkage between partisanship so defined and support for the Court was still not robust ($r = -.28$ for the culled sample), but it was stronger than for party identification alone. Those respondents who were better informed about the Court showed a more structured political outlook. Among the 590 knowledgeables, the correlation between support and partisanship went up to $-.31$.

Part of the reason neither party identification nor partisanship can account for much support lies in the complicated nature of the party system itself. Many white southerners, who called themselves Democrats, evidenced on the whole much less support than did nonsouthern Democrats and somewhat less than did Republicans outside the South. Table 15-5 reports these data for the culled sample.

Dropping white southerners from analysis increases somewhat the ability of partisanship to account for support. The correlation is $-.29$ for the full sample, $-.30$ for the culled sample, and $-.35$ for the knowledgeables, indicating at least an interesting association.

Conclusions

Party allegiance did vary to some extent with support for the Court, and that variation was stronger as one went up the steps of sophistication from the full sample to the knowl-

TABLE 15-5
Mean Scores on Diffuse Support (Culled Sample)

Group	(*n*)	Mean Score
White southern Democrats	(92)	2.4
White southern Republicans	(49)	2.3
White nonsouthern Democrats	(319)	3.7
White nonsouthern Republicans	(272)	3.1

edgeables. Standing alone, then, party allegiance provides a step toward understanding the bases of support. We return to this explanation in part III.

E. To Understand Is to Support the Court

Often defenders of the Court and sometimes the justices themselves have caustically noted the uninformed character of much of the criticism (and critics) of the Court. The implication of such laments is that if people would only take the time and effort to understand the way the Court operates, they would be far less critical. In sum, the argument is that to know the Court is to respect it, if not to love it. If differences in degree of knowledge can account for variations in support, then the following proposition should have held:

> Respondents who were better informed about the Court should also have been more supportive than respondents who were less well informed.

Tests

SRC put to the 1966 sample a number of questions whose replies we used to construct an index of knowledge about the Court. The correlation between that index and the scale of diffuse support was frail for the full sample ($r = -.13$), for the culled sample ($r = -.15$), and trivial for the 590 knowledgeables ($r = -.02$). Insofar as any relationship at all exists here, it runs in the opposite direction from that predicted by the proposition.

. . .

. . . For certain subsets, [however,] knowledge about the Court was rather strongly associated with support. Among blacks, for example, there was a powerful connection. . . . For blacks with low knowledge, support varied almost randomly around the middle of the scale. As soon, however, as knowledge increased beyond a minimal threshold, support among blacks leaped close to the maximum measured by the scale. Given our questions, there was no way that more knowledgeable blacks could register much more support than those with a modicum of information. For blacks, to know anything at all about the Court was to love it.

Among southern whites, the situation was quite different. In linear terms, there was a negative association between knowledge and support ($r = -.33$). That relationship, however, is more accurately described by a bow shaped curve. . . . As among blacks, support among uninformed southern whites fluctuated near the midpoint. But there the similarity ends. Some of the more knowledgeable southern whites were quite supportive; a somewhat larger proportion of the more knowledgeable were very unsupportive. These relationships among blacks and southern whites indicate that additional knowledge increases support only if the respondent learns something that pleases him. That was not what the proposition predicted.

. . .

F. The Court as a Maker of Desirable Public Policy

Another general explanation for variations in support holds that evaluations of the Court are largely functions of preferences among public policies. Those people who agree with the implications of the Court's jurisprudence for practical policies will esteem the Court more highly than those who are neutral toward such policies and much more highly than those who are opposed to the political implications of the Court's work.

TABLE 15-6
Distribution of Likes and Dislikes (in Percentages)

	Likes	Dislikes
Criminal Justice	7	19
Civil Rights of Blacks	44	17
School Prayers	7	30
Reapportionment	1	1
Other	41	33
Total	100	100
(n)	(310)	(765)

Without question, the decisions of the Court for at least a decade prior to the survey in 1966 had been quite liberal. Thus, if the characterization of support as essentially instrumental and pragmatic is valid, then:

(1) Respondents who approved the particular decisions of the Court should have been more supportive than those who were neutral and much more supportive than those who were opposed to the rulings.

(2) Respondents whose basic political outlook was more congruent with the liberal trend of decisions of the Court should have been much more supportive than those whose outlook was opposed to that trend.

· · ·

Tests

At the outset we again confront the problem of choosing which subset of respondents to use to test the propositions. In some respects the situation is easier to cope with because when we talk about reactions to particular decisions we can speak only about the 590 knowledgeables. The choice among sets of respondents is less clear when we talk about support and political attitudes. . . . A person might well have a general feeling that the Court was liberal without being able to recall any specific decision. It is even possible, though not probable, that a respondent who knew almost nothing about the Court might have associated it with liberal policies. To avoid these snares, we report on each of the three divisions of the sample.

(1) Support and evaluations of recent actions of the Court. The opening pages of this paper spoke of dividing support into the standard categories of specific and diffuse. Attention so far has centered on diffuse support, but we can also measure specific support from replies to the open-ended questions asking whether the Court had done anything recently that the respondent liked or disliked. Only 590 people could answer either of these questions; but, since interviewers deliberately pushed for as many comments as possible from each respondent, the total number of likes and dislikes came to 1,075. In contrast to answers to the questions probing diffuse support, the replies here were decidedly negative. Critical comments outnumbered favorable by a ratio of more than two to one. Table 15-6 summarizes the major categories of both likes and dislikes.

· · ·

The correlation between respondents' scores on the scale of specific support and scores on the measure of diffuse support was .53. For survey research, that indicates a rather strong relationship. But a correlation often obscures as much as it reveals. And here it is necessary to be very clear about what the correlation does and does not mean. The

TABLE 15-7
Cross Tabulation of Specific and Diffuse Scores (in percentages)

Diffuse Support	Specific Support		
	Positive	Neutral	Negative
Positive	88	66	37
Neutral	5	5	8
Negative	7	29	55
Total	100	100	100
(n)	(123)	(65)	(402)

correlation does not mean that those who were negative on the specific scale also scored negatively on the diffuse scale. All that the correlation says is that those respondents who stood higher on the specific scale tended to score higher on the diffuse scale than did respondents who scored lower on the specific scale. A glance at Table 15-7 should cut through verbal obscurities. It shows that a substantial minority of those who were negative on the scale of specific support still registered positive scores on the diffuse scale. Indeed, only a little more than half of those who voiced negative specific support were also unsupportive on the diffuse scale.

The point to be stressed here is that opposition to particular decisions did not necessarily imply a negative reaction to the Court as an institution. What opposition to particular decisions did imply was a probability of lower support than from people who were pleased by the decisions. . . .

(2) Support and general political outlook. Section C spoke briefly of a strong connection between diffuse support and general political orientation as measured by a scale that we labeled liberalism/conservatism. . . .

The association between this truncated scale of liberalism and diffuse support was strong and positive. For the full sample it was .45, for the culled sample .47, and for the 590 knowledgeables .55. . . .

. . . Scatterplots convey[ed] the same message [as previously suggested]: Congruence between respondents' political outlooks and the jurisprudence of the Warren Court meant, on the whole, increased support for the Court. Dissonance meant that the level of support was likely to be lowered, but a large number of conservatives still strongly supported the Court. As in the case of specific support, the justices enjoyed a residuum of diffuse support even among their ideological opponents.

. . .

Conclusions

The two hypotheses . . . provide solid evidence for the utility of the basic explanation linking support to what may be loosely termed ideology. . . .

. . .

III. Conclusions

Generalizing from a single time in a single country is a hazardous enterprise; still, if we are to move beyond case studies toward broader explanations, it is worthwhile to spell out some of the implications of this analysis both for future research and for political systems.

TABLE 15-8
Would an Adverse Decision Lower Your Opinion of the Supreme Court?

	Views on Sales of "Indecent" Magazines (in Percentages)			
Change Opinion?	Would Not Ban (Feel Strongly)	Would Not Ban	Would Ban	Would Ban (Feel Strongly)
No	54	72	69	41
Depends	2	1	1	2
Would lower	39	18	18	50
Couldn't be lower	3	5	4	3
DK, NA	3	4	9	4
Total	101a	100	101	100
(n)	(134)	(133)	(83)	(806)

a Percentages may exceed 100 because of rounding.

The implications for the latter are especially important. If our findings are valid across time in the United States and (what is far less likely) across national boundaries, then the first message is that constitutional courts have quite limited capacities to reach the general public. The American tribunal is the oldest of constitutional courts and during the years immediately preceding these interviews had been engaged in one of its more active and controversial periods. The Warren Court had handed down a torrent of decisions regarding race relations, church and state, criminal justice, and voting rights, and had endured several crises in its relations with Congress. Yet in the face of these dramatic events, only 46% of the sample in 1966 could recall anything at all that the Court had recently done.

Indirectly, of course, a constitutional court may reach much wider audiences through the mediating processes of columnists, news analysts on television, lawyers, high school teachers, college professors, public officials, and informed private citizens. Doctrines inherent in recent decisions could thus have been received and accepted or rejected by many people who did not at all associate these ideals with a court. Thus the judges could have been educating and performing a legitimating function for huge numbers of people and doing so in ways that are almost invulnerable to survey research. While admitting the possibility (but not necessarily the reality) of such a mediated process, one can still fairly say that the American Court had a limited ability directly to reach large segments of the population.

. . .

Second, a belief that increased public knowledge of what a constitutional court is doing will bring increased support has a slim evidentiary basis. . . .

Another set of questions put to the American national sample provides additional evidence. SRC asked each respondent whether he thought that newsstands should be allowed to sell to adults magazines that some people thought obscene. Next, SRC instructed each respondent to imagine that the Supreme Court had decided the issue in precisely the opposite fashion that the respondent had thought proper; then SRC asked if that decision would lower the respondent's respect for the Court. Table 15-8 reports the results. First of all, that table shows that an overwhelming majority, of those who answered the question favored a form of censorship. Second, a large number of people (about 43% of those responding) said that an adverse decision would lower their respect for the Court. To be sure, one should always take at a considerable discount replies to hypothetical questions; but, even with such a discount, it appears that the Warren Court would have lost support had its decisions against censorship of movies and magazines been more widely known. (Incidentally, only twelve of the 1,075 references to recent decisions could even be remotely connected to this issue.)

It is also possible that the Court might have picked up support if other decisions had been more widely known; but that possibility only emphasizes the basic point that the effects of increased knowledge about a court or its actions may be either to raise or to lower support. What would be most important to learn are, first, how the extent of knowledge about the American Court would differ in periods when the Court was not so active and the Court and president were not pursuing such parallel courses; and, second, the extent to which knowledge and support are linked in other systems. If what we have found is generally true, then greater familiarity with the operations of the newer constitutional courts is about as likely to create dissatisfaction as support, unless the court has the good fortune to decide mainly issues that do not divide the public and to decide them in a popular way.

Third, and more broadly, the linkage between political views and support indicates a rather soft base for judicial power. Any constitutional court is apt to hand down a series of decisions that are unpopular both with the general public and the government in power. One critical element in determining the ability of a court to weather such crises is the depth of the residuum of support that we found in the United States. . . .

Somewhat paradoxically, in the United States the link between political views and support also offers an ancillary protection for the Court and a partial explanation for the fact that unpopular decisions create many threats but few retaliatory acts from Congress. To attack the American Court is almost inevitably to attack or defend certain public policies. These assaults and defensive maneuvers usually also mobilize both sides and subject the legislative and administrative processes to a variety of pressures. An absence of party discipline and the consequent autonomy of committee chairmen in the American Congress confer a great advantage on those who wish to preserve the status quo. Thus a small minority of supporters of the Court can normally bloc counterattacks. If the Court's defenders can also convince those who oppose the Court's policies but support it as an institution, then successful attacks become even more difficult.

. . .

A related and important matter concerns the amount of support a constitutional court enjoys and the amount that it needs to function. Before we began our research, we had expected a higher level of support than that registered by the national sample. . . . Obviously, however, this level of support was sufficient not only to maintain the American Court but also to allow it to operate as an active, even aggressive agency of government. Yet it does not at all follow that newer constitutional courts in different and not always hospitable institutional and cultural settings can long remain vital ruling bodies without a considerably higher level of support than the Warren Court had. To be sure, one should approach this kind of problem with a degree of humility appropriate to his ignorance. Social scientists have little hard data on how even the American Supreme Court was esteemed by the public during its various historic crises. As the introduction pointed out, one cannot extrapolate from fiery newspaper editorials or impassioned political speeches to broader based public opinions. In any case, one must also keep in mind the possibility that political scientists have overestimated the amount of support that an institution—or a polity—needs to survive in the absence of a clear-cut challenge and alternative.

16

The Supreme Court and Myth: An Empirical Investigation

Gregory Casey

The mass public is often depicted as indifferent to and unaware of many facets of political life which elites deem essential to understanding the political process. Yet despite its indifference to political reality as defined by elites, the general public does hold its own version of political reality—albeit a more emotional, more symbolic, and less concrete reality than elites view. Popular perceptions of the United States Supreme Court follow this pattern: on the one hand, most observers take for granted that the public appreciates the Court on a symbolic or mythical plane while, on the other hand, most research concludes that the masses lack factual information on this institution.

Works on the Supreme Court have almost unanimously contended that the American public views it as more legitimate than other branches and agencies of government. Indeed, the term "legitimate" is only a mild expression in comparison with the exuberant terms to be encountered in this literature which often calls upon words such as "sanctify," "deify," "worship," and "sacerdotalize" to describe the public's regard for the Court. The foundation for the Court's purported legitimacy can aptly be examined under the rubric of political myth. . . . Myth comprises two facets: a political doctrine and miranda. The political doctrine consists of beliefs, or credenda, which specify and serve as rationale for the structure of power; the miranda are symbols of sentiment and identification which kindle enthusiasm and emotional support for power. Myth captivates by impressing people with the mystique of power; it makes acceptable the displeasing, demanding, and forceful face of power by transfiguring it with a halo of ideology and ceremony which gives the public a sense of security, participation, and aesthetic satisfaction. In brief, political myth transforms political institutions from instruments of naked power to legitimate authorities capable of proclaiming and implementing policies without use of force.

It is a commonplace that the Supreme Court's lack of means of enforcing its edicts makes legitimacy, and hence myth, particularly crucial for it. In commenting on public opinion toward the Court, most authors have assumed that the public's perspectives amount to a myth, but for the most part their observations have been based more on impressions of what the public thinks than on systematically collected data. This study uses survey data to examine the views which the public expresses about the Court, and to evaluate whether or not those views constitute a myth. The data set is taken from a survey which the Public Opinion Survey Unit of the University of Missouri-Columbia conducted in May and early June, 1968. Professionally trained interviewers polled a probability cluster sample of adults in the state of Missouri ($N = 866$). . . .

While commentators have maintained that Americans' view of the Supreme Court is mythic, survey research has contrastingly shown that the mass public is generally unaware of basic facts on the Court's structures and activities. . . .

. . .

Diverse commentators . . . have asserted that the Supreme Court's relative invisibility is responsible for the endurance of its legitimacy. These scholars' common thesis is that the High Court's myth together with its essentially non-democratic ideology of judicial review flourish in the shade, but might wither in the bright glare of public attention. In their view, visibility would jeopardize the Court's mystique and cause a decline in its legitimacy. . . .

. . .

In theorizing on how visibility affects the public's beliefs in the judicial myth (and hence the Court's legitimacy) most scholars and jurists have not had the benefits of systematically-collected survey data. Many of their ideas on the prevalence and qualities of the judicial myth have perforce been derived from notions of the Supreme Court popular in their own social milieu—i.e., the attitudes of their colleagues, families, friends and other opinion leaders (including trusted journalists). Unfortunately, these sources are not necessarily a reliable indicator of mass opinion of the Court, and dependence on them may have led some academic observers far astray from the reality of the public's perspectives. Analysis of survey data can test three assumptions, pervasive in this literature, which have heretofore been based in large measure on impressions of what the public thinks.

First, scholars have assumed that the mass public holds mythic orientations toward the High Court, whereas such orientations may be current only in the social and cultural circles frequented by scholars and opinion elites. Secondly, they have assumed that their reconstructions of the content of the judicial myth adequately reflect the thought patterns of the public. Yet various authors have reconstructed the myth quite differently and there is little agreement on which symbols represent the Court to the public and on which political formulas legitimate its power at popular levels. Survey data can serve to check these reconstructions; this survey uses an open-ended question (which permitted respondents to associate freely various roles and qualities with the Supreme Court) to tap public perceptions of this institution. Thirdly, discussion of whether judicial visibility undermines or weakens the myth depends on the first two assumptions of the myth's existence and of its qualities. These data measure the Court's visibility to the public by measuring awareness of its involvement in politically controversial issues; visibility's effect on myth can thus be explored empirically.

To test these assumptions on judicial myth, the analysis follows four paths of investigation. (1) The first concerns how widely myth is diffused throughout society: does it reach the mass public, or is it less widespread, perhaps reaching only elites? (2) Secondly, if not all hold mythic views, among which social sectors are they accepted? (3) To what degree are the non-symbolic aspects of the Supreme Court—that is, the institution which on occasion formulates public policy—visible to the mass public? Further, for which social sectors is this reality more visible? (4) Finally, is invisibility of the powerful facet of the Supreme Court functional for acceptance of the judicial myth, and is visibility detrimental thereto? The following four sections of this paper address each of these four questions in turn.

I. Diffusion of Myth

Socialization studies indicate that knowledge of elements of judicial myth is widely diffused among youth. . . . Though these socialization studies provide important insights on how the Court fits into other values in American political culture, they leave unanswered how the broader public visualizes and conceives of the Court.

The survey data analyzed here are a representative sample of the broader public and can address this question. These data can also test some of the theories on the content of the Supreme Court's myth. Various scholars' reconstructions of the myth have placed emphasis on different credenda and miranda. . . .

This poll used the following open-ended question to tap the public's notions of the Supreme Court:

> What would you say the Supreme Court's main job in government is? That is, what is it supposed to do?

Probes allowed each respondent a maximum of three comments. This item allowed the subjects to express freely their thoughts on the Court's role. Most answered descriptively, telling what the Court seemed to them to do, but some responded normatively, speaking about what the Court ought to do (and occasionally upbraiding it for failing to abide by its assigned role). A preliminary scan of 250 of the responses made clear that most could be sorted easily into fairly distinct categories. Some comments made no mention of any element of myth, while others associated the Court with a general class of symbol or credendum, such as the Constitution, law, judicial miranda/credenda, or civil rights/liberties. Within these broad categories, subtler nuances suggested subcategories; a few alterations and additions resulted in 28 code categories which accommodated all 958 comments made by respondents. Three persons coded all comments; in the few instances of intercoder disagreement, the response in question was moved from a more specific to a less specific subcategory within the same general class of response. Table 16-1 gives the broad response categories with frequencies and examples.

[Max] Lerner's theory on the Constitution's importance as a legitimating symbol for the Supreme Court seems incorrect for Missourians in 1968—only 8.1% of the responses associated the Court with the Constitution (Category A). Some respondents brought up the quality of constitutionality or constitutional fitness as a criterion for good laws without direct reference to the document itself (Examples B1, B2). If these comments, amounting to 8.5% of the total ($N = 81$), are also considered to invoke the Constitution as a mirandum, a total of only 16.6% of the responses would associate the Supreme Court with the American system's premier political symbol.

Lerner had also maintained in 1937 that the popular mind believed in mechanical jurisprudence. One tenet of mechanical jurisprudence has it that the Court compares statutes to the Constitution and rejects those not in accordance, a view which necessitates a static concept of the Constitution. To see whether mechanical jurisprudence endures, responses using the word "Constitution" were further broken down into those with wording indicating a static conception of it (example A1) and those expressing a more dynamic interpretation (example A2). More than half the remarks (5.0% of total, $N = 48$) mentioning the Constitution were static in their conception of it, indicating that the credendum of mechanical jurisprudence lives on.

"Law" loomed large in the public's understanding of the Court, although not necessarily in the way that theorists have specified. Fully 30.2% of the comments associated the Court with this symbol (category B). Of these, 8.5% (examples B1 and B2) talked of law in the light of its constitutional qualities, linking the Court to two mutually reinforcing

TABLE 16-1
Comments on the Supreme Court

In answer to the question: "What would you say the Supreme Court's main job in government is? That is, what is it supposed to do?"

Comment Category	Meaning of Comment	Frequency	
A.	Invokes the Constitution "To enforce the Constitution of the United States." (A1) "To interpret the Constitution." (A2)	8.1%	(78)
B.	Invokes law "It's supposed to see that the laws are constitutional." (B1) "What laws are constitutional and what are not." (B2) "Enforce laws." (B3) "They are supposed to give an interpretation of the laws." (B4) "Interpret the actions of Congress; yes, serve as the balance." (B5) "Uphold the laws of the land." (B6)	30.2%	(289)
C.	Invokes judicial functions, court-like miranda/credenda "No matter how many courts a trial goes through, the Supreme Court has the final say." (C1) "I think they settle matters other courts can't." (C2) "Handles the cases that no one else can decide." (C3) "Wise and fair judgment of cases that are brought before them." (C4)	30.4%	(291)
D.	Invokes civil rights, liberties, freedoms to safeguard people "Not favor certain majorities like big wheels; all have equal rights in the Constitution and see that the people are protected, look into the laws, rights of individuals." (D1) "The main job is to see that equal rights is performed." (D2) "Protect rights of individual against infringement by Congress and the states." (D3) "When it renders decision-point of national law—they have final decision. It's our last stand. The individuals and groups' last recourse to justice in this country." (D4)	7.3%	(70)
E.	Invokes ceremony, rectitude, need for qualifications. "It's a position demanding the utmost in morality, guidance, integrity, and legal training." (E1) "When they inaugurate President, the Chief Justice does that." (E2)	1.0%	(10)
F.	Invokes general decision-making functions "I guess they're supposed to rule everything." (F1) "See that everything goes all right." (F2) "Sets the laws for the government." (F3) "Makes decisions concerning the welfare of the people." (F4) "I think it should pass laws." (F5)	23.0%	(220)
	Total	100.0%	(958)

(N.B.: This table is a frequency distribution of respondents' comments on the Court's role. Some respondents made no comments and some gave multiple responses, so the total of comments does not correspond to the total of respondents.)

positive symbols. The remaining 21.7% invoked only the notion of law. Of these, 9.8% alluded to law in vague, general terms only (example B3), 5.9% described it as dynamic and adaptive (B4), 3.2% saw it as making the Supreme Court the source of balance (B5), and only 2.7% referred to law in wordings which indicated a static conception (B6). . . .

The next category of comments (30.4%) dwelled on the High Bench's court-like features and functions (category C). Most of these remarks described the Supreme Court as the highest court, as an appeals court, as a court which steps in to settle questions which other (or lower) courts cannot, or as a court making final decisions. Some 5.0% were vaguer, conceiving of the Court as a trial courtroom of sorts (such comments described the Court's activities as involving "big trials" or simply stated that it decided cases brought before it). [Some commentators] had suggested that the majestic image of a hushed, temple-like appellate courtroom contributed to the Supreme Court's legitimation. But these comments do not support this view, for none brings up the mirandum of the appellate courtroom atmosphere. Instead, either they refer to court-like qualities of the Supreme Court abstractly, without invoking the concrete imagery that would indicate that respondents have in mind the symbolic appurtenances of the appellate courtroom, or they speak of the Supreme Court as a court like any trial court. The Supreme Court is the least physically visible branch and television cannot broadcast images of it in its glorious setting, but television series such as *Perry Mason* may have popularized images of the trial courtroom which unsophisticated people may project onto the Supreme Court.

This set of comments also fails to relate the Supreme Court with the notions of legal certainty and predictability. Instead of yearning for reassurance that the Supreme Court will ascertain how a stable corpus of pre-existing law fits new situations, people making these remarks appear unconcerned with the substance of law. They seem instead to be looking to the Supreme Court as a source of final answers to quash conflicting viewpoints and to settle unresolved questions. They want the reassurance that there will be an authority to provide solutions—but there is no indication that they expect the solutions to derive from earlier solutions already honored as law, or from natural or organic law. It should be noted that comments in category C validate the Supreme Court by defining it as a court, rather than by adorning it with other symbols (*e.g.*, the Constitution, law, or the quality of constitutionality). For people making category C comments, the Court (and lower courts) may symbolize the continuity of society itself, playing an architectonic role by integrating all institutions in a meaningful whole. For the respondents making comments in categories A and B, the Constitution or "law" may symbolize this continuity.

Some comments (category D) referred to the Court's policy outputs in recent years in broad terms, describing its function as protecting minority rights and freedoms, civil rights and/or liberties, and generally watching out for individuals and the "people." . . . It is notable that comments on civil rights far outnumbered comments of problems of federalism ($N = 5$, 0.6%; these remarks not tabulated separately in Table 16-1), suggesting that people associate the Court much more with current trends in policy output than with issues it handled prominently in an earlier constitutional era but which are no longer as exposed to public view.

One other small category of comments also associated positively vested symbols with the Court. Some respondents saw the Supreme Court in the light of the ceremonial facet of its work or of the integrity of its personnel (category E). The comments in category E came the closest of any to referring specifically to the prestige of the position of Justice, but the infrequency of their occurrence casts some doubt on . . . [the] suggestion that the popular mind confers the "charisma" of judges on courts as institutions.

Finally, 23% of the comments (category F) did not associate the Court with miranda. These remarks attributed to the Supreme Court such general decision-making roles as passing bills/laws, making key decisions, keeping the wheels of government turning, ruling everything, and solving problems. Although crude and inarticulate in comparison to comments in other categories, these responses should not be dismissed as qualitatively inferior. Their significance lies primarily in that they indicate awareness of the Supreme Court but stop short of symbolizing or mythifying it. They are also notable in that they indicate an impression of the Court primarily as a political institution, an institution openly and visibly making political decisions and exercising social choices, comparable to the Congress or other institutions of government. . . .

Altogether, 77.0% of the comments (categories A through E) associate the Court with miranda and/or credenda. Of these, about three-fifths (categories A, B, D, and E; 46.7% of the total) relate the Supreme Court to a symbol external to it (the Constitution, law, liberties, equality, or balance), while the remaining two-fifths (category C; 30.4% of the total) mention no symbols other than the judicial function itself, justifying the Court on its own terms. If comments making no mention of other symbols (category C) are combined with the comments making no mention of symbols at all (category F), a slim majority (53.4%) of the remarks can be said to invoke no external miranda in conceptualizing the Supreme Court, which suggests that the Court may be able to stand on its own rather well. Only a minority (46.7%) of the responses (categories A, B, D and E) gives expression to the available positive symbols which have been regarded as legitimators of the Court's authority. Academic observers' reconstructions of the judicial myth thus appear to be poor characterizations of the mosaic of popular conceptions of the High Bench. In return for their acceptance of its authority, many members of the general public may quest after credenda and miranda much less than elite commentators have been prone to believe. . . .

Up to this point, statistics have been based upon the total number of responses rather than on the total number of respondents. (Using the total number of comments as the statistical base facilitated discussion of the various symbols and beliefs associated with the Court while avoiding the complex problem of single respondents making multiple comments.) At this juncture, the statistical base shifts to the total number of respondents for two reasons. First, this shift makes it possible to assess the diffusion of the judicial myth. Secondly, it also makes possible comparison of the results of this poll with those reported by [others]. . . .

Diffusion of the Myth

Comments on the Court were ventured by 74.4% of the respondents; the remaining 25.6% (222) declined to answer or pled ignorance. The latter respondents are considered largely oblivious to the Court—it is for them an invisible branch of government, not a salient reality. Do then all 74.4% of the sample making comments hold a mythic perspective on the Supreme Court? Fully 50.2% ($N = 435$) of the sample associated the Court only with miranda or credenda (giving only responses in categories A–E). Another 14.3% ($N = 124$) did not view the Court in connection with its miranda or credenda (giving only category F responses). A final, small group of respondents (9.8%, $N = 85$) "crossed planes" by giving multiple responses, at least one of which made mention of miranda/credenda and at least one of which did not. All respondents who mentioned miranda or credenda at all were considered to mythify—i.e., to partake of the mythic perspective on the Supreme Court. Thus a majority of 60.0% ($N = 520$) sees the Supreme Court in the glow of its symbols and credenda. Since three-fifths of this representative sample freely give expression to some manifestation of the judicial myth when asked about the Supreme Court's place in the scheme of things, the conclusion that the Court's myth enjoys widespread diffusion is certainly justifiable.

. . .

II. The Social Bases of Myth-Holding

Lerner's classic interpretation in 1937 distinguished between lower and middle class perceptions of the Court. At that time, the "common man's" attitude struck him as more reverential, while the attitudes of the propertied classes and (to a lesser extent) of the middle class seemed more blasé and coldly realistic. He saw the Court as a symbol which helped subdue the lower classes by keeping them in a state of awe while it worked as an institution to enrich the middle and upper classes who realized its bias and saw through its pretenses. Lerner also expressed the foreboding that the working class was on the verge of rebelling against the High Bench as a symbol. Some survey evidence suggests that his premonition may even then have been in the process of becoming true. Throughout the period 1935-37, labor union members, reliefers, Democrats, and Roosevelt supporters were much likelier than lawyers, Republicans, and Roosevelt critics to favor limiting the Court, to feel that it had gotten in the way of the people's will, and to favor Roosevelt's Court-packing plan. The Court may have at an earlier point beguiled the lower more than the middle class, but by the mid-1930's the lower class seems to have been disenchanted while the middle class apparently closed ranks behind this institution. . . .

For the purpose of exploring its demographic correlates, mythholding was treated as a nominal variable having four values. The first of the four types of orientation towards the myth was mention of only credenda or miranda (*i.e.,* giving only category A–E responses); as seen earlier, half the sample held this exclusively mythic view of the Court. The second orientation was a mixed mythic and non-mythic view for the 9.8% who "crossed planes," both associating the Court with its credenda/miranda and expressing the non-mythic outlooks in category F. These respondents, though positively attuned to the myth, were not pooled with the group holding exclusively mythic views because their voicing category F comments indicates awareness of the Court as a political institution which might dilute their appreciation of its mythic qualities. They were kept in a separate category in case they might be less supportive of the Court than other respondents. Third were the 14.3% of the respondents making only non-mythic comments, and fourth were the oblivious respondents who made no remarks on the Court at all. The relation between this variable and a battery of other factors was then investigated, with the results given in Table 16-2.

Education emerged as the strongest correlate of mythifying; as expected, it works to inculcate the myth and to stamp out ignorance and disregard for the Court. In one sense this confirms the results of the socialization studies—if grade school implants the myth, further education should root it even more deeply. But in another sense it throws doubt on the durability of the judicial myth as transmitted in grade school, for the sooner people quit school, the likelier they seem to consign the Supreme Court to oblivion.

Higher social status also makes myth-holding likelier, which casts doubt on Lerner's proposition that the lower classes are more awestruck. Those who see themselves as lower or working class are much less likely to mythify the Supreme Court, mildly likelier to

TABLE 16-2
Correlates of Myth-Holding

Variable	Cramer's V
Education[a]	.240
Subjective Social Class[b]	.207
Politicization[c]	.199
Newspaper Readership[d]	.156
Location of Residence[e]	.134
Gender	.126
Generation[f]	.101
Partisan Identification[g]	.080
Ideology[h]	.059 } X² not significant
Race	.058

[a] Educational attainment is trichotomized into: those with a grade school diploma or less, those with some high school experience or high school completion, and those with some college experience or beyond.

[b] Subjective social class is a dichotomous variable: those who classify themselves as middle or upper class, and those who describe themselves as lower or working class.

[c] Politicization is a four-point scale; see Appendix A for details on its derivation.

[d] Newspaper readership is a four-fold category: those who do not read a newspaper regularly, those who read only a weekly regularly, those who read an outstate daily regularly, and those who read a metropolitan daily or a prominent out-of-state daily regularly.

[e] Residence is a trichotomous variable: St. Louis and Kansas City metropolitan dwellers (both suburban and city); outstate medium-sized city inhabitants and small town folk; and farm dwellers.

[f] Generation is a five-fold category: those above 75 (in 1968), and those in the age ranges 60-74, 45-59, 30-44, and 18-29.

[g] Partisan identification is trichotomized into Democrats, Republicans, and Independents. Independents include "leaners," those who feel slightly closer to the Democratic or Republican party.

[h] Ideology is a four-point scale of liberalism-conservatism; see Appendix B for derivation.

express only a non-mythic perception, and much likelier to be oblivious. Moreover, at all levels of education and politicization, lower class identifiers mythify less than middle class identifiers. Although the breakdown in the Supreme Court's spell over the common man which Lerner foresaw may simply have occurred in the intervening years, these data taken together with the survey data from the 1930's make it more likely that Lerner was mistaken in 1937: the middle and upper classes then, as now, may have been the conscious repositories of the judicial myth. . . .

Education's influence on myth-holding presents a particular problem. Some college experience enhances the tendency to mythify. Yet . . . adults in this sample with less than a college education are in large measure not even consciously aware of the institution. Either these adults never learned about the Court in school (suggesting ineffective teaching or different curricula when they were of school age), or they acquired only such superficial and shallow beliefs that they were prone in the absence of reinforcement to forget what once they knew.

It is possible to test the forgetting hypothesis by controlling for the recency of formal instruction—*i.e.*, age or generation. Respondents between 60-74 had been somewhat less likely than younger cohorts to mythify the Court and those in the 75+ bracket were much less likely to do so; if myth-holding lessens for all elderly regardless of educational attainment, forgetting must be taking place. Similarly, if forgetting is causing ignorance of the myth, the less-educated young will have had less time to forget and so should mythify more than their elders with equal levels of educational attainment. On the other hand, if ignorance derives from failure ever to learn about the Court while in school, both the less-

TABLE 16-3
Educational Level and Generation by Mythic Images of the Supreme Court
(Cell Figures are Percent Expressing Only Mythic Images of the Supreme Court)

Generation (Age Cohort)	Educational Level				
	Low (Grades 0-8)		Medium (Grades 9-12)		High (Grade 13+)
18–29	28.6%		37.1%	**	76.1%
	(2)		(33)		(25)
30–44	34.8%		46.5%	**	77.0%
	(16)		(67)		(47)
45–59	32.0%	*	57.7%	*	77.1%
	(24)		(64)		(37)
60–74	33.6%	**	73.0%		60.0%
	(36)		(27)		(18)
75+	37.0%		58.3%		60.0%
	(17)		(7)		(6)

  * Difference of proportions significant at .05 level.
  ** Difference of proportions significant at .001 level.

educated young and old should be less aware than the better-educated of their generations. The results, in Table 16-3, disconfirm the forgetting hypothesis: the less educated
young and old both mythify less than the better-educated middle-aged and elderly, and
those over sixty do not mythify notably less than younger persons with equal educational
attainment. Generation is thus seen to be an extraneous factor, and grade school training
appears unavailing in implanting a *lasting* mythic appreciation of the Court. Despite the
findings that grade schoolers grasp several mythic judicial qualities, these data suggest
that they forget if not reinforced by a continued education (or by other conducing factors,
such as high politicization). Indeed, middle-aged people at the medium educational level
(some or all high school) mythify more than similarly educated youth, which hints that
settling down and experience may transmit the judicial myth better than educational
institutions.

Reviewing the findings in Parts I and II, it can be seen that, although the judicial myth
by no means extends to the entire public, it does reach the great majority of people aware
in any way of the High Bench. Moreover, those who accept the judicial myth are disproportionately from the more advantaged strata of society—socially, politically, and educa-
tionally. Acceptance by these influential societal sectors undoubtedly gives the myth its
cultural dominance and explains the emphasis on the Court in the (only superficially
effective) civics curricula of grade schools. Furthermore, the myth's cultural eminence
puts respondents not expressing mythic views squarely in their place: these are *not* extraordinarily perceptive observers who have on their own reached the view of the Court held
by the many political scientists who have unmasked the "true" Supreme Court and found
there a political branch. Instead, they are only imperfectly socialized individuals who
have failed to absorb society's symbols and beliefs. Given the predominance of mythic
perceptions of the Court in better educated circles, it is also little wonder that many
scholars have believed the myth more widespread and elaborately articulated than these
data show it to be. From their social vantage point they have only had to look for myth-
holders to find them.

What is perhaps most interesting is that no single socializing factor appears able to
bring about an enduring absorption of the Supreme Court's myth. Education is the posi-

tive force which probably puts most effort into inculcating the myth, yet grade school training does not socialize pupils permanently. Other favorable influences seem necessary if an appreciation of the Court's role is to take root, and these data suggest that these other influences are successful even in teaching the myth to adults untouched by their schools' attempts to indoctrinate them in childhood. The overall social environment is crucial: high political interest, middle-class identification, daily newspaper readership, and some college experience admit people to a social world for which the cult of the Supreme Court is real. This social world appears better able to transmit and sustain the myth than formal institutions of education.

III.   The Visibility of the Supreme Court

This section examines the visibility to the public of the Supreme Court's policy-making facet, which involves it in controversial decisions and behavioral demands on the people and their leaders. The visibility of judicial decisions is defined conceptually and operationally and correlates of visibility are sought.

. . .

Visibility and Its Correlates

Knowledge of the Supreme Court's work is cumulative—*i.e.*, people aware of its lesser-known decisions are highly likely to be informed on its better publicized ones, and people unmindful of its better known decisions are highly likely to be unaware of its lesser-known ones. Accordingly, many acceptable Guttman scales (*i.e.*, coefficient of reproducibility > .9, coefficient of scalability > .6) could be created by using different subsets of the items measuring awareness of the Court's decisions, and it was possible to define visibility as a single dimension of perception. The three item subset whose CR (coefficient of reproducibility) and CS (coefficient of scalability) were highest (CR = .966, CS = .870) was chosen to represent visibility operationally. This scale put awareness of the school segregation decision(s) in the position of least difficulty, awareness of the defendant's rights case(s) next in difficulty, and correct awareness that the Supreme Court had not ruled on medicare in the most difficult position. Scale scores ranging from "0" (for lowest awareness/familiarity) through "3" were then assigned each respondent.

The relationships of a series of other factors to knowledge of the Supreme Court's activities was then investigated. . . .

The data in Table 16-4 confirmed . . . that politicization and education enhance attentiveness to Court decisions. Moreover, greater general attentiveness to current events, measured by extent of newspaper readership, coincides with greater heed for judicial activities. However, many non-readers (64%) know of at least one decision (*i.e.*, score "1" or higher), indicating that issues which gain the Court renown (or notoriety) are so salient that they come through even to people virtually isolated from the printed word—perhaps by stirring conversations and/or by being memorable even when transmitted by the electronic media. This may be in the nature of status issues. Lerner's hypothesis was also confirmed: the middle class is more aware of what the Court is doing, while the working/lower class is more in the dark.

The last two factors canvassed, partisan identification and race, bore no relation to knowledge of court decisions. Missouri Republicans in 1968 are not significantly better

TABLE 16-4
Correlates of Knowledge of the Supreme Court's Decisions

(Low score = low knowledge, high score = high knowledge)

Variable	Kendall's Tau
Politicization (high score = high politicization)	+.328
Education (high score = high education)	+.248
Subjective Social Class (low score = middle class)	−.190
Newspaper readership (high score = reader of a daily; low score = non-reader)	+.171
Gender (low score = male)	−.149
Location (high score = metropolitan dweller)	+.109
Generation (low score = youth)	−.092
Ideology (high score = liberal; low score = conservative)	−.062
Partisan identification (low score = Democrats; high = GOP)	+.053
Race	Not significant

informed than Democrats . . . and Missouri blacks are not significantly less aware than whites. . . . Since metropolitan dwellers were more aware and blacks more likely to live in the metropolitan centers, suspicions arose that blacks might be as aware as whites because of their location. Contrasting urban whites with urban blacks canceled out the effects of location, yet brought out no racial differences, from which it can be concluded that none existed in Missouri in 1968, even though racial differences had appeared nationally in 1966.

The factors which enhanced the visibility of Supreme Court decisions were themselves inter-correlated, inviting further investigation with control variables. Most combinations of predispositional factors were cumulative, *i.e.,* two factors together would heighten or depress visibility more than one factor working alone. This aided in specifying the most attentive sectors of the population. Males who are highly politicized, well-educated, who think of themselves as middle-class, and who read daily newspapers are most likely to be well-informed on the Court's decisions. By contrast, apolitical, poorly educated females who consider themselves working class and who read no daily newspapers are most likely to be oblivious to decisions. The sexual differences did not disappear with other correlates held constant: in most categories of politicization, education, subjective social class and even generation, women remained less aware than men.

This exploration largely corroborates the relationships reported in the literature. . . . [T]he most notable result turned up in this section is that the social strata most likely to mythify the Supreme Court are also the strata most likely to be familiar with its controversial decisions.

IV.   Does Visibility Dispel Myth?

The many commentators who have recommended restraint to the Supreme Court have done so largely out of fears of the consequences of activism for the judicial mystique and ultimately for the legitimacy of judicial review. Are their fears grounded? Does familiarity with the controversial rulings which the Supreme Court has issued undermine its myth?

The process which would engender disbelief is cognitive dissonance or imbalance: one cognitive element, the positive association of the Supreme Court with miranda such as the

Constitution, law, etc., would clash with the other, the negative association of the Court with substantial and painful demands for social and behavioral change in the here and now. Two means for people aware of this clash to reduce their dissonance would leave the myth intact: some might strengthen their association between the Court and cherished symbols, allow this association to dim their realization the Court has made controversial rulings, and eventually convert to a favorable opinion of the rulings; others might reconcile a controversial ruling with their symbol-laden vision of the Court by differentiating the ruling, viewing it as an exception. Another means of relieving the dissonance would not, however, leave the myth intact: here, people would form the opinion that the Court is meddling in politics and dissociate it from the valued symbols, dispelling the myth. This last pattern would produce part of the outcome that the commentators who recommend restraint have worried about.

Although their greatest concerns have been about judicial activism causing the mass public to reject the judicial myth, an important consideration about the nature of mass public opinion suggests that dissonance (and its feared result) might not even afflict the mass public. . . . The multitude of humans are quite capable of simultaneously holding two logically (or otherwise) contradictory beliefs without realizing or bringing to a head the conflict between them. Elites are by contrast much likelier to realize the conflict and to agonize over it in the course of trying to reduce their dissonance, while the masses may never even reach a state of dissonance. Thus, even if the general public does not dissociate the Supreme Court from its credenda and miranda upon discovering that it makes controversial decisions, elites may do so, which would justify the worries that have been expressed.

. . .

Awareness of Court activism is operationally defined as recall knowledge of its rulings and is measured by the same Guttman scale used in Part III to measure the visibility of controversial court decisions. Myth holding is defined as associating the Court with its miranda and credenda. The data in Table 16-5, showing the relation between visibility and myth for the entire sample, provide [no] support for the . . . original hypothesis. The respondents most knowledgeable about judicial decisions are most rather than least likely to mythify the Court; and as knowledgeability declines, mythifying declines instead of rising. Obliviousness to the Court rises as knowledgeability falls. . . . Since respondents less aware of its decisions are less likely to mythify, clarity in perceiving what the Court is doing cannot be said in and of itself to undermine a mythic view of the Court.

Are elites bothered by this conflict? Defining elites as the most politicized respondents, visibility's effect on myth-holding was examined for two subsets: (1) the more politicized 39.6% ($N = 343$) of respondents, a category made up of those who scored either "2" or "3" on the politicization scale; and (2) the most politicized 11.3% ($N = 98$), including only those scoring "3" on politicization. For neither subset was the relationship between visibility and myth materially altered. Even elite respondents very aware of the Court's politically controversial decisions mythify the Court, and with declining awareness, elite respondents mythify less and become more oblivious. In sum, neither the mass public nor elites seem disturbed by the purported conflict between judicial activism and retention of the myth.

. . .

The judicial myth . . . is both socially and governmentally cued: acquisition of the myth, as has been seen, is more a product of social environment than of education, and

TABLE 16-5
Supreme Court Visibility and Myth-Holding

	Respondent's Orientation to the Judicial Myth				
Level of Supreme Court Visibility to Respondent	Mythic Only	Mixed: Mythic and Non-Mythic	Non-Mythic Only	Oblivious	Total
Unaware (score "0")	22.7% (35)	6.5% (10)	11.7% (18)	59.1% (91)	100% (154)
Low (score "1")	39.5% (115)	10.7% (31)	18.2% (53)	31.6% (92)	100% (291)
Medium (score "2")	65.1% (237)	11.3% (41)	13.5% (49)	10.2% (37)	100% (364)
High (score "3")	84.2% (48)	5.3% (3)	7.0% (4)	3.5% (2)	100% (57)
	Cramer's V = .267				N = 866

the Supreme Court is itself part of governmental authority. Moreover, elite acceptance of the myth makes the judicial miranda and credenda the basis for public discourse about the Court, providing further reinforcement throughout concerned and attentive sectors of society.

Loosening the people's inertial acceptance of the myth would, . . . become possible if governmental leadership were to present an alternative set of symbols—but in recent times the people have seldom been given this opportunity. Proposals to curb the Court have tended away from bills broadly aimed at diminishing its powers toward measures which would bound it only incrementally. Each successive Court-curbing era has seen more mellowed proposals, as though the past failures of broader bills have cooled the political branches' zeal to tame the Court. Unsuccessful attempts at Court-curbing may actually strengthen the myth as their protagonists withdraw from the field of battle, leaving the Court's dominion unharmed and its authority undiminished.

In one instance when governmental leadership made so bold as to introduce a plan to adjust the High Court's status, it enlisted fairly widespread (though by no means consensual) public support. President Franklin Roosevelt is the only popular leader in recent times even to approach offering an alternative, though his Court-packing plan stopped far short of shearing the Court's authority away. Acceptance of the myth may have been waning at this time, as Lerner feared and as the Fortune poll discovered when it asked twice in 1936–37: "Do you think the Supreme Court has recently stood in the way of the people's will or do you think it has protected the people against rash legislation?" An average of 41.2% believed the Court had protected the people, an average of 22.4% thought it had gotten in the people's way—indicating not inconsiderable disillusionment with the myth. From this beginning, and using different tactics with Congress, Roosevelt might have been able to provide enough anti-Court cues to shape an anti-Court movement which could have dethroned the existing myth by forcing it to compete with a new system of beliefs and symbols about the Court. But he drew back, leaving the Court's authority basically unchallenged (possibly thus cuing greater respect for it). Government cues in 1937 started reinforcing the Court's aura once again and the myth, though probably ruffled, emerged safely.

Barring collapse of the attitudes and structures in society and government which emit cues favorable to it, the judicial myth has good prospects. The mosaic of specific popular beliefs which elevate the Court may change (a current Court's policy specialization, such as the Warren Court on civil rights, is likely to work its way into the myth) or even wither somewhat (the current crisis in legal machinery might imperil the sanctity of some of the associated symbols), but does not appear likely to suffer from the Court's future meanders in political thickets. This is apparently another case in which scholars, jurists, and other elite commentators have searched for justifications and validations for authority in symbols (hence the scholarly output on the particular symbolic configurations which edify the Court) and in strict role definitions (hence the controversy on neutral principles) while the general and even the politicized public accept authority and its legitimating myth as givens.

Appendices

A. Politicization Scale

A Guttman scale of politicization was developed from responses to three questions on political interest and activities. The least difficult item was passed if respondent had entered into a discussion of the war in Viet-Nam with anyone; the middle item was the extent of respondent's interest in the presidential campaigns (those very much interested passed, those only somewhat or not much interested failed); the most difficult item was passed if respondent had tried to convince someone to change his position on Viet-Nam. The CR and CS were acceptable (CR = .923, CS = .697). Respondents were assigned scale scores ranging from "0" for lowest politicization through "3." Respondents with one inconsistent or missing response were given the perfect scale score which altering their inconsistent or missing response would have yielded, except in the case of the response patterns $(-+-)$ and $(-+0)$, where a score of "2" was assigned. Frequencies for each score were: "0"—113 (13.0%); "1"—405 (46.8%); "2"—245 (28.3%) and "3"—98 (11.3%). Five respondents could not be assigned scale scores because they had more than one missing response.

B. Ideology Scale

A Guttman scale of ideology (liberalism-conservatism) was constructed from responses to items tapping preferences for increased, unchanging, or decreased federal involvement in three areas. Respondents passed the least difficult item if they thought federal aid to education should be increased or continued as is, but failed if they wanted it decreased. The middle item was passed if respondents wanted federal job training for the unemployed increased or continued, failed if they wanted it decreased; the most difficult item was passed if respondents wanted federal expenditures for slum clearance and housing increased, failed if they wanted it continued unchanging or decreased.

The CR and CS were acceptable (CR = .961, CS = .817). Respondents were assigned scale scores ranging from "0" (for most conservative) through "3" (for most liberal). Those with one inconsistent or missing response were given the perfect scale score which altering their inconsistent or missing response would have yielded except in the case of the response patterns $(- + -)$ and $(- + 0)$ where a score of "2" was assigned. Frequencies for each score were: "0" (most conservative)—26 (3.0%); "1"—72 (8.3%); "2"—277 (32.0%); "3"—(most liberal) 408 (47.1%). Eighty-three respondents could not be assigned scale scores because they had more than one missing response. This scale was used despite its obvious tilt toward liberalism because the subset of items used to construct it had both the highest CR and CS and the lowest number of respondents to whom scores could not be assigned.

PART TWO
PARTICIPANTS

CHAPTER SIX

LITIGANTS AND LAWYERS

Courts, as dispute-processing institutions, bring together a relatively distinct, if shifting, group of participants—legal specialists as well as people without such expertise. Furthermore, these participants bring to judicial proceedings diverse and divergent interests, values, and perspectives that exert important influences on the way in which disputes are processed.

Since the business of courts is to process disputes, the most obvious participants must be the disputants. Private citizens, private organizations, and government officials attempt to manage their own interpersonal relations and to regulate their own behavior and the behavior of others. They are the ones who initiate judicial proceedings. It is their inability to manage conflict successfully in private or informal ways that gives courts an agenda of dispute-processing business. However, not all citizens, organizations, or officials are equally able or willing to use courts. Problems of cost, efficiency, and appropriateness differentially affect potential consumers of court services. The result is that there are two distinct types of litigants.

Marc Galanter, in what is sure to become a classic article, labels these two types of litigants "one-shotters" and "repeat-players." They are distinguished, as the labels suggest, by the relative frequency with which they are involved in litigation. As Galanter suggests, "Because of differences in their size, differences in the state of the law and differences in their resources, some of the actors in society have many occasions to utilize the courts . . . to make . . . claims; others do so only rarely."[1] Repeat-players are typically, according to Galanter, large units whose investment in or interest in a particular case is relatively small. Automobile insurance companies are a clear example of a type of repeat litigant that conforms with Galanter's description. Such companies are frequently involved in disputes with their policyholders or with those who have been injured by a policyholder. These disputes frequently end up in court. Because of the frequency of their participation in judicial proceedings, such companies have distinctive interests in litigation; for example, they have an interest in structuring judicial rules so as to provide advantages for themselves in subsequent cases.[2] Parties that have only a "one-shot" interest in litigation are typically more interested in the substantive result of their case than in the way in which the decision may in the future affect the disposition of other cases.

Nathan Hakman's article on lobbying the Supreme Court (selection 18) demonstrates how a long-run interest in rules may lead private organizations to sponsor cases and to invest resources in an attempt to influence the way in which courts deal with particular types of cases (although interest groups do not do this to the extent commonly assumed). Not only do repeat-players have distinctive interests, but their frequent appearances in court enable them to develop expertise. Such expertise is reflected in the way in which they select cases for litigation as well as in the manner in which they carry on disputes that have been transformed into lawsuits. Their participation can be contrasted with that of the infrequent participant, whose interest in litigation is more substantive and whose expertise is minimal.

If Galanter is correct, organizations and government officials, because of the nature of their activities and their access to resources, should participate much more frequently in judicial proceedings than private individuals. In selection 17, Galanter summarizes the results of numerous empirical studies of litigants and litigation. These results confirm his hypotheses about types of litigants. Furthermore, the findings reveal that a particular configuration of participants is typical of most types of courts. The most frequent configuration includes organizations as plaintiffs and individuals as defendants.[3] The result of differences in activities and resources is a pattern of participation in which governmental and nongovernmental organizations are the most frequent initiators of court proceedings and in which they typically employ courts to process disputes between themselves and private individuals with whom they have dealings.

The fact that courts operate or are supposed to operate in accordance with standards and rules established by law means that participation in judicial proceedings is participation in a particular and special kind of process—a process of "discovering" and applying applicable rules. This process requires special knowledge, training, and expertise, all of which are provided by members of the legal profession. Lawyers stand between disputants and the judicial system. Disputants, before they can bring their problems to court, typically need to enlist the help of trained legal practitioners who advise disputants as to the state of legal rules and the ways in which those rules might apply to the issues in dispute. They do so by predicting how courts will interpret the law and find facts. Thus they screen out some types of disputes and, at the same time, promote the movement of other disputes into the judicial process.[4]

Lawyers are not, however, neutral technicians. They have their own interests and values, which affect the advice they give and their own performance in court. Lawyers are, to use Galanter's term, particular kinds of repeat-players. But not all lawyers are directly involved in litigation. Most lawyers in the United States are primarily givers of advice or technicians primarily responsible for carrying out certain routine transactions (such as writing wills). Relatively few lawyers regularly argue cases in court. Some of these litigating lawyers specialize in particular areas of law (such as criminal or divorce law); some represent only particular kinds of parties, and some limit themselves to representing particular parties within particular areas of law.

The most important distinction that can be made among types of litigating lawyers is the manner in which they perceive their clientele. This distinction has been discussed by a political scientist, Jonathan Casper.[5] Casper argues that some lawyers, admittedly a small although perhaps a growing number, see themselves primarily as representatives of the interests of the public as a whole. Individual cases are simply vehicles for achieving broad public objectives generally requiring significant changes in the law. This type of lawyer is interested in the issues of public policy raised by a case rather than in the case itself. Such lawyers typically take only cases that they believe involve issues of major importance.[6] The article on the new public interest lawyers (selection 19) describes this segment of the bar.

Another type of lawyer is identified as a representative of particular interests or organizations. For example, some private organizations establish their own in-house counsel whose function is to represent members of the organization in cases of importance to that organization.

The third type of lawyer, most commonly criminal defense lawyers, perceive their clientele as coextensive with the court in which they typically practice and their most important function as the maintenance of the efficiency and productivity of the court organization with which they deal. Since they generally practice before the same judges and prosecutors, it is in the professional interest of these lawyers to maintain good relations with those members of the court organization. This interest may, as selection 20 by Blumberg indicates, conflict with the interests of the individuals whom they nominally represent.[7]

The fourth and last type of litigating lawyer we call the "client advocate." These lawyers approximate the stereotypic Perry Mason model. They see their role primarily as serving individuals. Client advocates are interested solely in the cases in which they are involved; they will do everything that they can to ensure favorable results for their clients. In the view of the client advocate the lawyer is merely a technician put in the service of a case, not a cause.

The different types of lawyers behave differently in advising disputants whether to litigate and in developing and employing strategies of litigation. The readings in this chapter that deal with lawyers analyze these differences and their consequences for disputants and for courts as dispute-processing institutions.

Notes

1. Marc Galanter, "Why the 'Haves' Come Out Ahead: Speculations on the Limits of Legal Change," *Law and Society Review* 9 (1974), 95.

2. See Laurence Ross, *Settled Out of Court* (Chicago: Aldine, 1970).

3. See Craig Wanner, "The Public Ordering of Private Relations: Part II," *Law and Society Review* 9 (1975), 293.

4. See Douglas Rosenthal, *Lawyers and Clients: Who's in Charge?* (New York: Russell Sage Foundation, 1974).

5. See Jonathan Casper, *Lawyers Before the Warren Court* (Urbana: University of Illinois Press, 1972).

6. Also see Philip Selznick, "Social Advocacy and the Legal Profession in the United States," *Juridicial Review* 1974 (1974), 113.

7. It is important to recognize that the largest number of lawyers in this category are employed by or work for government.

17

. . . Explaining Litigation

Marc Galanter

. . . [T]he character and impact of litigation might be best understood if, rather than starting from consideration of rules or of institutional processes, we began by looking at the parties and their relation to dispute institutions. . . . [It is possible to distinguish] between those actors in society who have many occasions to utilize the courts (in the broad sense) to make (or defend) claims and those parties who do so only rarely. Parties who have only occasional recourse to the courts I call one-shotters (henceforth, OS) and parties engaged in a large number of similar litigations over time repeat-players (RPs). I . . . argue that an RP might be expected to play the litigation game differently from an OS and that the RP

TABLE 17-1
A Taxonomy of Litigation by Strategic Configuration of Parties

		Plaintiff, *Initiator, Claimant*	
		One-Shotter	**Repeat Player**
Defendant	**One-Shotter**	OS vs. OS I	RP vs. OS II
	Repeat Player	OS vs. RP III	RP vs. RP IV

Reprinted by permission of the Law and Society Association from "Afterword: Explaining Litigation," *Law and Society Review* 9 (1975), 347–357. Copyright © 1975. Footnotes and most references have been omitted. The *Law and Society Review* is the official publication of the Association.

TABLE 17-2
Distribution of Parties in Various Civil Courts

Type of Court	Location	Plaintiffs		Defendants		N	Nature of Population	Source
		Ind.	Org.	Ind.	Org.			
Civil Courts of General Jurisdiction	Baltimore, Cleveland, Milwaukee	42% (34%)*	58% (65%)*	67% (62%)*	33% (37%)*	7254 (6454)	*Excludes divorce-related cases	Wanner (1974:431)
	Clarke County, Georgia	71% (43%)*	29% (57%)*	84% (69%)*	16% (31%)*	1987** (1034)	*Excludes marital breakup cases	Owen (1971:67)
	Oconee County, Georgia	43% (23%)*	57% (77%)*	88% (83%)*	12% (17%)*	322** (240)	*Excludes marital breakup cases	Owen (1971:66)
Justice of the Peace	Arizona	34%	66%	86%	14%	556		Bruff (1973:13)
Small Claims	Alameda County, California	35%	65%	86%	14%	386		Pagter, et al. (1964:893)
	California, 4 Small Towns	16%	84%	93%	7%	400		Moulton (1969:166)
	Champaign County, Illinois	14%	86%*	87%	13%	498	*Includes landlords	Smith (1971:15, 18)
	Two Florida Counties	14%	85%	85%	14%	427		Levar (1973)
	Cambridge, Massachusetts	43%*	57%	79%	21%	1578	*Includes doctors, dentists, landlords, etc.	Small Claims Study Group (1972:127)

Worcester, Massachusetts	22%*	78%	94%	6%	125	*Includes doctors, dentists, landlords, etc.	Small Claims Study Group (1972:127)
Sacramento, California	55%*	45%	78%	22%	445	*Includes doctors, dentists, landlords, etc.	Small Claims Study Group (1972:127)
Hamilton County, Ohio	26%	74%	78%	22%	400		Hollingsworth, et al. (1974:509)
Clermont County, Ohio	11%	89%	85%	15%	100		Hollingsworth, et al. (1974:509)
Boston, Massachusetts	51%	49%*	44%	56%*	1260	*Includes professionals	NICJ (1972:378)
Ann Arbor, Michigan	57%	43%*	62%	38%**	226**	*Includes professionals, landlords, etc.	NICJ (1972:630)
Foreign							
Amtsgericht, Freiburg	36%	64%	72%	28%	489*	*Excludes cases concerning rent, housing and child support.	Blankenburg, et al. (1972:82)
Six English County Courts	9%	91%	71%	29%	1238*	*Excludes suits for possession of land or premises.	Consumer Council (1970:13-14)
Five English County Courts	25%	75%	87%	13%	451*	*Excludes judgment summonses.	Zander and Glasser (1967:815)

** Whole population, not a sample.

TABLE 17-3
Configuration of Parties in Civil Courts of General Jurisdiction in Three American Cities

Plaintiffs

	Individuals	Organizations	
Individuals	I 28% (1988)	II 40% (2854)	68%
Organizations	III 14% (1000)	IV 19% (1337)	33%
	42%	59%	N = 7179

Defendants (row label spanning Individuals / Organizations)

Source: Wanner, 1974, table 6.

Note: The figure in Box IV is an overstatement (and that in Box II correspondingly an understatement) since it includes garnishment in which the employer is technically the defendant, but in which the real party of interest is an individual.

. . . enjoys a number of advantages in the litigation process. Briefly, these advantages include: ability to structure the transaction; expertise, economies of scale, low start-up costs; informal relations with institutional incumbents; bargaining credibility; ability to adopt optimal strategies; ability to play for rules in both political forums and in litigation itself by litigation strategy and settlement policy; and ability to invest to secure penetration of favorable rules.

We may visualize litigation in terms of various combinations of OSs and RPs as depicted in Table 17-1. On the basis of our notions about the cluster of advantages enjoyed by RPs, we might speculate that RPs, equipped with these advantages, would be more successful in their encounters with OSs; on the other hand, we would expect OSs to be less successful. They face a costly and risky uphill battle in using courts to vindicate claims against RPs. We would expect litigation by RPs against OSs to be relatively frequent, that by OSs against RPs to be relatively infrequent. . . . I would like to consider these expectations in the light of data made available by [the recent literature]. . . .

Who Sues Whom?

Usable quantitative data on the configuration of parties to litigation are scarce. But the data that are available seem to confirm our surmises about the distribution of litigation. Figures from a variety of courts suggest that plaintiffs are predominantly business or governmental units, while defendants are overwhelmingly individuals. Table 17-2 summarizes the data available at this writing.

The most ample data are to be found in Wanner's study of civil courts of general jurisdiction in three large American cities. He found that business and governmental units

TABLE 17-4
Party Configurations in Courts of General Jurisdiction Excluding Marital Breakup Cases

Wanner: three cities
(excluding 800 cases
he codes as
divorce-related)

I	II
19%	45%
III	IV
16%	21%

N = 6379

Owen: Clarke County
(excluding 953 cases
of divorce, support,
child support, annulment
and alimony)

I	II
27%	42%
III	IV
16%	14%

N = 1034

Owen: Oconee County
(excluding 82 cases
of divorce, support
and alimony)

I	II
19%	64%
III	IV
4%	13%

N = 240

were plaintiffs in 58% of the cases filed in these courts, but defendants in only 33%. If we assume that in the American setting individuals roughly fit our notion of OSs and that organizations roughly correspond to RPs, we can represent his data on "who sues whom" in terms of our boxes. [Table 17-3] The only other American courts of general jurisdiction for which comparable data are available are the Clarke and Oconee County, Georgia courts. The raw totals suggest a somewhat different pattern of court use. But if we omit . . . cases related to marital breakup we find a pattern of party configuration remarkably similar to that found in Wanner's three city courts. [Table 17-4]

Small claims courts handle a very substantial portion of the total civil caseload in American courts. Yngvesson and Hennessy's (1975) review of the literature leaves little

TABLE 17-5
Configuration of Parties in Small-Claims Courts in Two Florida Counties

Plaintiffs

	Individuals	Business, Government	
Individuals	I 9% (40)	II 75% (322)	84%
Business, Government	III 5% (21)	IV 10% (44)	15%
	14%	85%	N = 427

Defendants (row label)

Source: Levar (1973).

doubt that the typical configuration of parties in these courts is organizational plaintiff versus individual defendant. Of all the small claims studies only Levar's study of two Florida counties and the NICJ studies of Boston and Ann Arbor provide data that can be arranged in our boxes. The Florida data present an exaggerated version of our expected pattern. [Table 17-5]. Figures (in Table 17-2) for other courts suggest that such a pro-

TABLE 17-6
Configuration of Parties in Amtsgericht Freiburg

Plaintiffs

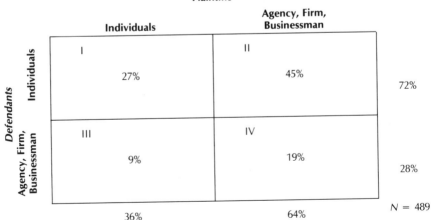

	Individuals	Agency, Firm, Businessman	
Individuals	I 27%	II 45%	72%
Agency, Firm, Businessman	III 9%	IV 19%	28%
	36%	64%	N = 489

Defendants (row label)

Source: Blankenburg, et al., 1972:82.
Note: Suits concerning rent, housing and child-support excluded (Blankenburg, 1975).

nounced concentration of cases in Box II is characteristic of most small claims courts. . . . If we take into account that criminal courts handle a vastly larger number of cases than do the civil courts and that criminal cases fall almost entirely into Box II, we can guess that in something in excess of two-thirds of all litigation in American courts the strategic configuration of the parties is RP v. OS.

There is reason to think that this pattern may not be distinctively American. Blankenburg, et al. (1972) classified a sample of 489 civil cases in the Amtsgericht [lower civil court] Freiburg in a similar fashion. The results bear a remarkable resemblance to the American data. [Table 17-6] . . .

References

Blankenburg, Erhard (1975) "Studying the Frequency of Civil Litigation in Germany," 9 *Law & Society Review* 307.

Blankenburg, Erhard, Viola Blankenburg and Hellmut Morason (1972) "Der lange Weg in die Berufung," in Rolf Bender, (ed.), *Tatsachen Forschung in der Justiz*. Tubingen: C.B. Mohr.

Bruff, Harold H. (1973) "Arizona's Inferior Courts," 1973 *Law and the Social Order* 1.

Consumer Council (1970) *Justice Out of Reach: A Case for Small Claims Courts*. London: Her Majesty's Stationery Office.

Hollingsworth, Robert J., William B. Feldman and David C. Clark (1974) "The Ohio Small Claims Court: An Empirical Study," 42 *University of Cincinnati Law Review* 469.

Levar, C. Jeddy (1973) "The Small Claims Court: A Case Study of Process, Politics, Outputs and Factors Associated with Businessmen Usage." Unpublished paper.

Moulton, Beatrice A. (1969) "The Persecution and Intimidation of the Low-Income Litigant as Performed by the Small Claims Court in California," 21 *Stanford Law Review* 1657.

National Institute for Consumer Justice, Staff and Subcontract Reports (1972) Vol. III: Staff Studies prepared for the National Institute for Consumer Justice on Small Claims Courts. Boston, Mass.

Owen, Harold J., Jr. (1971) *The Role of Trial Courts in the Local Political System: A Comparison of Two Georgia Counties*. Unpublished dissertation, University of Georgia.

Pagter, C.R., R. McCloskey and M. Reinis (1964) "The California Small Claims Court," 52 *California Law Review* 876.

Small Claims Study Group (1972) *Little Injustices: Small Claims Courts and the American Consumer. A Preliminary Report to the Center for Auto Safety*. Cambridge, Massachusetts.

Smith, Regan G. (1970) *The Small Claims Court: A Sociological Interpretation*. Unpublished dissertation, University of Illinois.

Wanner, Craig (1973) "A Harvest of Profits: Exploring the Symbiotic Relationship between Urban Civil Trial Courts and the Business Community." Paper prepared for delivery at the 1973 Annual Meeting of the American Political Science Association.

—— (1974) "The Public Ordering of Private Relations: Part I: Initiating Civil Cases in Urban Trial Courts," 8 *Law & Society Review* 421.

—— (1975) "The Public Ordering of Private Relations: Part II: Winning Civil Court Cases," 9 *Law & Society Review* 293.

Yngvesson, Barbara and Patricia Hennessey (1975) "Small Claims, Complex Disputes: A Review of the Small Claims Literature," 9 *Law & Society Review* 219.

Zander, Michael and Cyril Glasser (1967) "A Study in Representation," 117 *New Law Journal* 815 (July 27).

18

Lobbying the Supreme Court

Nathan Hakman

I. Introduction

. . .

Lobbying in judicial affairs refers to the organization and management of influence by persons and groups who are not necessarily the principals in a litigation. These parties differ from the ordinary litigant in terms of their interest in developing long range policy rather than merely winning a given case.

While lobbying or pressure in the judicial process is believed to be widespread, writers are usually careful to note important differences in the ways lobbyists behave in the judicial and legislative arenas. Judges are ordinarily not contacted directly, correspondence is definitely discouraged, and picketing, demonstrations, and even milder forms of outside pressure seldom accompany pending cases. All forms of persuasion are pursued with a maximum regard for judicial dignity and protocol.

The tactics of judicial lobbying are assumed to be of a different order, and they are frequently listed as follows: (1) the "class action" replacing individual litigants; (2) the test case; (3) *amicus curiae* participation; (4) the granting by an outsider (usually an organization) of advice, information, and service; (5) the providing of expert testimony and research assistance by a non-principal; (6) the granting of financial assistance by a non-principal; (7) the outsider assuming control of a litigation.

Besides describing these techniques, commentators on Supreme Court litigation also describe the use of other strategies and tactics. These include: (1) bringing alternative litigations in different judicial forums; (2) "broadening the issues" through research and publication; (3) engaging in other kinds of litigation planning.

In the published literature, the bringing of alternative litigations is reported to be used to achieve the following objectives: (1) achieving the most favorable forum; (2) emphasizing issues differently in different courts; (3) taking advantage of the differences in procedure and rulings in state and federal courts; (4) dropping or compromising cases with unfavorable records; (5) stalling some cases, and pushing others to ensure that the "good ones" reach the Supreme Court first; (6) creating conflicts among courts in order to encourage assumption of jurisdiction by the Supreme Court.

Reprinted by permission of copyright holder from Nathan Hakman, "Lobbying the Supreme Court—An Appraisal of 'Political Science Folklore,'" *Fordham Law Review* 35 (1966), 15–50. Business office: Fordham Law Review, Lincoln Square, New York, N.Y. 10023. © 1966 by Fordham University Press. Footnotes have been omitted.

According to this kind of political folklore the judicial lobbyist reinforces conventional legal argument by broadening the issues through a "Brandeis" or "sociological" brief, or includes policy arguments in his briefs or oral presentations. Participants in Supreme Court cases are expected to secure the help of research organizations and similar groups in presenting new social theories before the highest court. Since courts do not decide cases in a vacuum, a large dose of planned publicity is sometimes deemed desirable. This publicity is occasionally secured by "flooding" law reviews with articles presenting an interest group's general point of view. In consequence of this and other complex litigation tasks, it is also assumed that the planning of Supreme Court litigation is too great a task for the "small" or moderate-sized law firm. Success in the Supreme Court, it is argued, "is no longer the result of a fortuitous series of accidents." Instead "groups plan their forays into litigation just as meticulously as they do in other political areas."

II. Sources and Methods of Investigation

A great deal of information about parties, attorneys, *amici curiae,* and arguments, are matters of public record. Until now, these records have not been used to study these data and to challenge important assumptions about Supreme Court litigation. One must go beyond the records, however, to get information about litigation finance, sponsorship, cooperation, research, coordination, planned publicity, and other litigation strategies. . . .

To "test" the propositions . . . information was gathered in 837 cases in which the Supreme Court rendered signed or *per curiam* opinions. The cases, covering seven Supreme Court terms from 1958 to 1964, were classified both in terms of their basic subject matter and the clientele interests involved. Commercial litigations included antitrust, public utilities, transportation, public lands, tax, labor relations, government law suits (private property transactions), private litigations, and private personal injury cases. Non-commercial cases included criminal cases (involving serious anti-social crimes), civil liberties cases (governmental or government supported infringements of individual liberties), cases involving political offenders (communist and internal security cases) and cases involving race relations. The survey provided data about the types of formal parties, the *amici curiae* involved [see Table 18-1] and in many instances the reasons given for participating as *amici curiae.*

For more detailed information about litigation support and strategies in Supreme Court cases questionnaires were sent to more than 500 attorneys who participated in 127 opinion cases during the 1960–1961 Supreme Court Term. Many of the attorneys contributed very little to the survey because their participation was confined to giving general advice or merely commenting on the legal briefs. However, a definitive reply was received from attorneys in 78 cases. The comments that follow are essentially the author's own interpretations derived from responses to questionnaires, unstructured interviews, and exact tabulations.

III. The Findings

A. Formal Parties: The Role of Governments in Supreme Court Litigation

Before commenting on activity in support of litigation, a few remarks about the role of governments and government attorneys seem appropriate. Although the fact is seldom

TABLE 18-1
Participation as Principals and Amici Curiae in Supreme Court Litigation (1958–1964)

Type of Litigant	Commercial Cases (499 cases)		Non-Commercial Cases (349 cases)	
	Principal	Amicus	Principal	Amicus
United States Government and Administrative Agencies	273	38	137	23
States, Agencies, and Their Political Subdivisions	82	26	203	18
Private Companies and Corporations	375	30	13	1
Trade and Business Associations	20	69	—	—
Professions	—	17	—	28
Labor Unions	81	32	1	2
Social Defense Organizations	—	—	13	65
Individuals	117	22	310	5
TOTAL	948	234	677	142

stressed in the political science literature, the United States Department of Justice and attorneys from other federal agencies, primarily the ICC, NLRB, FPC, and FTC, participate in well over half the cases on the Supreme Court's opinion docket. In their prescribed supervisory roles in the Federal legal system, the Supreme Court and administrative agencies are preoccupied with settling technical questions in administrative law. Occasionally substantive policy issues emerge. . . .

In administrative law cases, especially those involving the regulatory processes, state and local governments often appear among the formal legal adversaries. Intergovernmental conflict is also involved in constitutional cases where issues surrounding the limits of state taxation, state regulation of labor, problems of intergovernmental tax immunity, and national-state confrontations concerning private property transactions (e.g., bankruptcy proceedings in which questions of national supremacy or priority arise) are involved. Information about Court-state and other federal relationships growing out of litigations remains largely unexplored by political scientists.

In its *amicus curiae* activity, the federal government behaves very much like a private litigant. Most of its participation in commercial cases is designed to promote narrow proprietary or operational interests that would otherwise be pursued in government litigations. For example, the Antitrust Division of the Department of Justice may instruct the Court on how a statute or patent should be construed because of the way it affects the Department's patent enforcement program. Other regulatory agencies use the device to maximize their administrative efficiency. State Department views are interposed in state and private litigation to avoid embarrassing the Federal government. Sometimes the government participates as *amicus curiae* to pursue even narrower proprietary interests. In personal injury cases, for example, the government's role as land owner, shipper, or banker comes in conflict with other private claims.

The participation of state and local governments in Supreme Court cases differs from that of the federal government in the role of both principal and amicus. When its activity is viewed in relation to other states, each state can be observed pursuing independent interests though degrees of cooperation among them are sometimes achieved in specific cases. In commercial cases, for example, states having "right to work" laws have occasionally cooperated in joining or supporting another state's amicus brief. Similar cooperation was achieved in "off-shore oil cases," cases involving agricultural regulation, and in public utility cases. This cooperation is, on very rare occasions, facilitated through the National Association of Attorneys General, but more frequently through informal exchanges of briefs and correspondence.

. . .

B. Other Formal Parties in Commercial Cases

Court records reveal little or nothing about litigation costs in commercial cases, but a study of the formal parties involved casts doubt on widely held views about the "representational character" of Supreme Court cases. This doubt is further strengthened by questionnaires and interview responses indicating that the costs in almost every commercial case were "borne exclusively by the clients."

Self-financing is to be expected among the types of corporations or public utilities that get involved in business regulation cases—e.g., antitrust, public utility, securities and exchange cases, etc. However, in cases involving taxation, government law suits, private law suits, and personal injury cases the client is more likely to be an individual with limited financial resources. The breakdown of principals classified as "individuals" in Table 18-2 shows that they appear as parties most frequently in commercial cases involving taxation, government law suits, private law suits, and personal injury cases. Though the results and implications of these cases are watched by claimants' attorneys, and attorneys from insurance companies, banks, and specialized bar associations, none of the participating attorneys reported any direct financial help from any of these sources. In most of the commercial cases in which individuals, or small business interests, participated, the stakes were sufficiently inviting to justify clients "going all the way." Some of the attorneys noted the availability of "contingent fee" arrangements and economies which aided them in getting their cases to the Supreme Court as cheaply as possible. Trial records in most Supreme Court cases are short with the legal or constitutional issues clearly defined. By keeping records short, or by having the government assume the printing costs, the expense of appellate litigation can be made economically feasible to a broader spectrum of social and economic interests.

The so-called big commercial cases usually involved, as party principals, a plethora of governments, utilities, corporations, and private companies. The complexity of the formal party interests is usually too great to be unravelled meaningfully. Yet a casual glance at transcripts and records shows that interests are combined and consolidated through various formal and informal procedures. Few of the attorneys listed in the records participate significantly at the trial, administrative, or appellate levels though usually all the principals involved in a litigation are at one stage or another represented by counsel. As a matter of common practice locally retained attorneys begin the work, and they are subsequently joined by corporation "house counsel," and finally by "outside counsel" brought in from the major law firms. The lawyers in the sample reported that the preparation of briefs and other legal materials is carried on by correspondence, conferences, and consultations. These kinds of arrangements, it was noted, are familiar procedure in all kinds of litigation.

1. *Private Companies and Corporations.* The largest group of principals participating in commercial cases are private companies and corporations. Even though information about the size and wealth of these parties has not been gathered, the prominence of many of the companies involved, and the amounts of money in controversy, should convince anyone that cost is not a controlling factor in the planning of most Supreme Court cases.

Attorneys in only two cases indicated that they had solicited trade associations for financial support in behalf of their clients, and there were only four occasions reported in which the United States Solicitor General was asked to participate in behalf of a litigating party. Those who requested such aid gave as their reasons a desire to "broaden the issues," "make a show of strength," or "educate the court on related aspects of public policy." Several attorneys mentioned "the preferred status that government attorneys deservedly enjoy" with the Supreme Court.

2. *Trade and Business Associations.* In political life, trade associations can be expected to represent their members in a variety of ways. Some are in a position to control the standards and practices of an industry or trade. Truckers, railroads, banks, and others have associations which behave in this way. Others like insurance underwriters, stock exchanges, industrial information bureaus and similar agencies specialize in providing advice, information and service to their members and other interested parties. Finally, there is a type of association that gives the business or industrial viewpoint on a variety of broader business issues. The Chamber of Commerce and the National Association of

TABLE 18-2
Participation as Principals in Supreme Court Litigation (1958-1964)

Type of Litigation	Number of Cases	Social Defense Organizations	United States Government	Trade Associations	Professional Organizations (Including Bar Associations)	State and Local Governments	Labor Unions	Private Companies and Corporations	Individual and *Ad Hoc* Groups
Commercial									
Labor Relations	100	—	54	—	—	7	72	77	8
Trade and Business Regulation	38	—	35	3	—	11	—	39	4
Taxation	93	—	68	1	—	28	1	62	21
Torts, Public Contracts and Other Civil Actions Involving Governments	33	—	24	1	—	9	—	8	15
Power-Utility Regulations	22	—	21	—	—	9	1	20	—
Transportation	36	—	31	6	—	4	3	32	—
Anti-Trust	43	—	26	2	—	—	4	38	—
Public Lands	21	—	14	—	—	14	—	8	9
Private Law Suits	48	—	—	—	—	—	—	39	14
Personal Injury	55	—	—	—	—	—	—	52	46
Total Commercial	499	—	273	13	—	82	81	375	117
Non-Commercial									
Civil Liberties	98	—	24	2	—	76	—	9	84
Political Offender Cases	57	5	34	—	—	15	1	—	46
Race Relations	60	8	10	—	—	47	—	4	46
Criminal	134	—	69	—	—	65	—	—	134
Total Non-Commercial	349	13	137	2	—	203	1	13	310
TOTAL	848	13	410	15	—	285	82	388	427

Manufacturers seem to fit this pattern. While these organizations on rare occasions participate as principals it is the amicus role of these groups that is of greater concern to the political observer.

If trade associations behaved politically one would expect more *amicus curiae* activity than the public records indicate. (See Table 18-3 *infra.*) The low rate of participation is probably explained by the fact that it is difficult to achieve consensus within an important range of an association's clientele. A broad consensus is occasionally achieved in labor relations "right to work" cases and other issues where an association can unite broad segments within an industrial community. The absence of trade association participation in most commercial cases suggests, however, that the issues are too specialized for such groups to participate in a politically meaningful way. When an association is formed along narrow and specialized lines, participation is more likely, but the number of times this happens is relatively rare.

3. *The Professions.* If the litigation practices of trade associations do not comport with a political view of litigation, professional groups, as indicated by their formal or *amicus* activity, are even less political. These groups in fact are barely visible. In the seven years of litigation studied they did not appear as formal parties and they appeared as *amicus curiae* in only seventeen commercial cases. Most of the appearances were occasioned by professional bar groups or by individual lawyers seeking technical clarification of laws governing taxes, government contracts, or specific business regulations. To this observer it is somewhat remarkable that so few professional groups play any role in Supreme Court cases. Accountants, engineers, teachers, bankers, economists, and others may individually appear as expert witnesses but rarely provide policy appraisal to guide the Supreme Court. Apparently the issues in most commercial cases are considered too narrow or private to encourage even that kind of participation.

4. *Labor Unions.* . . . [A]n examination of the unions' formal and *amici* appearances shows that their participation is confined almost exclusively to representing the union as an organizational entity. An individual worker having a grievance against the union or a "non-contractual" grievance against a company will usually have to go elsewhere for legal assistance. The cases involving unions concerning "unfair labor practices" under the Labor Management Relations Act included activities such as strikes, lockouts, illegal picketing, use of hiring halls, and suits against unions and companies in their representational or institutional capacities. In cases where individuals pressed grievances, personal injury cases, or other problems, the individuals had to get their legal support from other sources.

While international unions sometimes assume the litigation burdens of their local affiliates, the unions as a whole generally stick to their own knitting and rarely intervene in the litigation of others. Unions participated as amici in only 32 cases, but half of this participation was by the house counsel of the AFL-CIO Federation. Within the labor law, and in other business fields, there is specialization in the way amicus curiae activity is conducted. A so-called narrow labor relations issue, such as the specific use of a hiring hall, may bring another union into the case because the second union has a similar litigation pending. The arguing of broader policy issues, however, is generally left to the counsel of the federation.

This survey of the formal side of commercial litigation suggests a portrait of litigation activity that is quite different than the one presented in political science literature. It suggests that Supreme Court cases are not representational but narrowly focused private controversies. Companies, individuals, unions, and others pursue narrow interests confined to the immediate litigation. Although more than forty percent of the cases have *amici curiae* of some kind, much of this activity is conducted in pursuit of narrow private interests. If broader types of organized interests do participate in judicial processes they are more likely to be found "behind the scenes" supporting the formal party litigants.

C. Other Supporting Activity in Commercial Cases

To secure information about other kinds of lobbying that may be present, attorneys were asked "whether all significant social or economic interests" were adequately represented in the trial of their cases, and if not, "what significant social or economic interests were not represented?" Questions were also asked about sponsorship and finance as well as other tactics described earlier. While the purport of some of these questions may not have been fully understood by all the attorneys, the responses provided no support to a theory of judicial lobbying. Instead the response verified a not unexpected ethnocentricity or "egotism" within most of the Supreme Court's practicing bar. Attorneys participating in commercial cases frequently volunteered the comment that their litigation was a "straight out economic battle between the parties" or that the "important" or "garden variety" cases involved "solely legal or financial issues." In several instances the attorneys noted that their cases were "not a landmark in any social or economic sense" even though the case was "of great interest to lawyers." Many attorneys stressed the fact that the cases concerned only the parties and were conducted without any "behind the scenes" groups or interests.

In a number of cases attorneys representing commercial litigants were antagonistic or even hostile to *amicus curiae* participation arguing that opposing interests such as state governments, labor unions, or other opponents had adequate opportunities to participate at earlier stages of the proceeding. They indicated that they were opposed to persons or groups who stand aside at the trial or administrative stages only to appear with new arguments at the appellate level. Even where attorneys perceived an important social impact to their cases, they noted that the character of the parties and the amounts of money in controversy made the litigation stand on its own bottom. In these cases, it was argued, other interests were "too remote" from the specific issues involved.

Even in cases where smaller financial stakes were involved, the attorneys almost always regarded their cases as private fights. A few of them lamented the fact that policy issues were not developed at the trial or pleading stage, and occasionally an attorney criticized lawyer colleagues for "narrow legalistic viewpoints." Nevertheless, most responses cited technical legal requirements, the attitudes of judges, and of opposing counsel as justifications for strictly legalistic approaches to litigation. A few attorneys warned that policy considerations interposed at trial or pleading stages of litigation would make litigations unduly expensive, introduce irrelevancies, and obscure the resolution of specific issues. From a lawyer's point of view, litigation is a very private form of conflict, and from all indications they expect to keep it that way.

. . .

Further support for a private or legalistic view of litigation is also suggested by the observations of some attorneys that those affected by their litigations were too poorly organized and too isolated to be helpful. In one case an attorney, engaged in self-criticism, noted his own egotism and his failure to solicit such help from trade and business associations. "It might have helped," he said, "but I just didn't think of it." Thus, in tax cases, private litigations, personal injury cases, and other instances where concerted action may have been helpful, the attorneys gave no hint that they availed themselves of the assistance of "behind the scenes" interests.

Though evidence of lobbying in the judicial process can be found in appearances and briefs contributed by *amici curiae,* such participations seem rare and, more often than not, the amicus has a specific and separate pecuniary interest in the litigation itself. In some of these cases, the *amici* are themselves parties to pending litigations. Attorneys representing trade associations, labor unions and individual taxpayers were among the most frequent amici but in this capacity they were pursuing specific institutional or individual interests and not really supporting the litigations of others (see Table 18-3). While occasionally a policy-minded bystander would participate in a commercial case, such participation was criticized or even ridiculed as introducing irrelevant and confusing considerations.

If commercial litigants behaved politically, their attorneys, together with others representing similarly situated clients, would coordinate their activities to establish more effective litigation strategy. Multiple litigations involving similar issues were found to occur most frequently in the taxation and labor relations fields, and attorneys in these litigations sometimes reported that they managed more than one case at a time. However, even if the circumstances and mutuality of interests made coordination feasible, the situations never permitted litigants to "pick their own cases for Supreme Court review." "Even where cases are managed," said an experienced union attorney, "an unmanaged case gets there first."

Most attorneys reported that the case "most ripe for review" or "most advanced in the legal mill" was the one that the Supreme Court reviewed first. During the interviews, lawyers occasionally complained that "the case selected turns out, from our point of view, to be the wrong one." Counsel from international labor unions, or house counsel of large corporations, may carefully pick their own cases—they may even anticipate the probability of Supreme Court review—but it seems unlikely that any attorney can ensure that a particular case will get there.

Among the cases studied none were found in which attorneys and others planned substantial public relations campaigns in connection with a pending litigation. The usual news handouts and house organ publicity accompanied some cases, and contact with other interested parties followed the conventional pathways of correspondence and informal exchange of ideas.

In summary, attorneys representing commercial litigants seem unable or unwilling to become political actors in the judicial process. In a few instances *amici curiae,* expert witnesses, or conventional legal argument may broaden the issues involved, but most Supreme Court commercial litigation is conducted in a purely private manner, and public consequences apparently flow from "a series of fortuitous circumstances."

D. Non-Commercial Cases: Formal Parties and Amici

Though the distinction is not stressed in political science literature, it may be that the "theory of the judicial lobby" is intended to apply exclusively to non-commercial cases. In these cases, individuals representing political, cultural, religious, and social minorities are more likely to need the financial and legal backing of others. While considerations of this kind are sometimes pertinent, few of the cases clearly present this situation. Business interests are often commingled with civil liberties issues and the cases are processed in a manner similar to other private commercial litigations. In some of these cases civil liber-

TABLE 18-3
Distribution of *Amicus Curiae* Interest Activity in Supreme Court Litigation (1958-1965)

Types of Litigation	Number of Cases	Social Defense Organizations	United States Government	Trade Associations	Professional Organizations (Including Bar Associations)	State and Local Governments	Labor Unions	Private Companies and Corporations	Individuals and Ad Hoc Groups
Commercial									
Labor Relations	100	—	7	20	4	3	28	5	1
Trade and Business Regulation	38	—	3	15	3	6	—	10	1
Taxation	93	1	4	6	3	5	—	5	13
Torts, Public Contracts and Other Civil Actions Involving Governments	33	—	10	2	1	2	—	—	1
Power-Utility Regulations	22	—	2	2	1	6	—	2	1
Transportation	36	1	1	3	2	1	4	—	—
Anti-Trust	43	—	8	—	—	—	—	2	1
Public Lands	21	—	3	4	2	3	—	1	2
Private Law Suits	48	2	—	5	1	—	—	3	1
Personal Injury	55	—	—	7	—	—	—	2	1
Total Commercial	499	4	38	64	17	26	32	30	22
Non-Commercial									
Civil Liberties	98	26	8	5	12	8	—	—	1
Political Offender Cases	57	13	—	—	9	1	2	—	3
Race Relations	60	5	15	—	1	5	—	1	—
Criminal	134	14	—	—	6	4	—	—	1
Total Non-Commercial	349	58	23	5	28	18	2	1	5
TOTAL	848	62	61	69	45	44	34	31	27

ties organizations participate, but when they do so their activity is usually confined to *amicus curiae* activity at the appellate level. Also, a large number of Supreme Court cases classified as "noncommercial" do not involve issues that stimulate the activity of organized civil libertarians. Thus, immigration cases, military cases, criminal cases, and others are frequently decided on technical procedural grounds without arousing the interest of others. Unless the litigant is affiliated with, or has some special connection with an organization, he or she is unlikely to get this type of assistance. The litigant is thus forced to finance the case himself, or enlist the aid of friends and relatives. Finally, there are some litigants who do not get financial or other legal support simply because they do not ask for it.

1.   *Civil Liberties Cases.* In a number of cases, individuals, business, and organizations of various kinds invoke constitutional and legal principles against the actions of public officials. Though the American Civil Liberties Union is known for its work in this area, its spokesmen maintain that the group is not a legal aid society, or a general social defense organization, but an organization solely devoted to constitutional principles. As such, it sponsors only a few cases in which constitutional issues are clearly presented.

This organization, like other social defense groups, operates with a small legal staff and a large network of "cooperating" and consulting attorneys. Local affiliates of the organization decide if and when to intervene in a case, and also decide the character and the amount of legal aid to be rendered. In the case of weaker affiliates the litigation program, if any, is augmented by assistance from the national organization. In its circulating memoranda and official statements emphasis is placed upon the organization's policy of referring prospective litigants to "cooperating attorneys" who control the cases under organization sponsorship. Even if the organization chooses not to sponsor a given case, an attorney recommended by the ACLU may decide to press the litigation forward unilaterally.

Though cooperating attorneys participate in an increasing number of cases, there are many more cases involving civil liberties issues in which the organizations do not participate. Even including those in which they participate as *amici,* the activity of organizations is visible in only one-third of the civil liberties cases.

2.   *Political Offender Cases.* Another somewhat different pattern of activity is found in cases involving political offenders. In these cases—especially those involving Communists or "fellow travelers"—litigations are handled by a small and decreasing number of attorneys associated with or cooperating with *ad hoc* defense committees, or small radical defense organizations. Those cases are occasionally supported by civil liberties foundations, and the lawyers retained are frequently associated with the National Lawyers Guild.

. . .

The most common political offender cases involve naturalization and deportation proceedings, non-Communist affidavit cases, employment security (loyalty), passports and travel, registration or membership in the Communist Party or front organizations, contempt charges in congressional investigations, and civil disabilities imposed on Communists and other political dissenters. The ACLU sometimes sponsors cases of this kind but only if the constitutional issue is the dominant issue in the litigation.

3.   *Race Relations Cases.* After more than a decade and a half of harassment in the southern states, the NAACP and its Legal Defense and Education Fund legal staff have established constitutional legitimacy for the main lines of its "representational" litigation activity. In a line of cases culminating in *NAACP* v. *Button,* the Supreme Court majority's dicta have sanctioned at least some forms of litigation sponsorship and management. . . .

At the present time the NAACP staffs and their "cooperating" attorneys control most of the race relations cases that reach the Supreme Court. Questions surrounding legal tactics may, however, become moot due to the surge of litigation connected with more recent race relations activity. Picketing, demonstrations, sit-ins, and other forms of protest have substantially changed the litigation picture. The NAACP lawyers are no longer alone in defense of the movement for racial reform. Their tactical approaches once characterized as "radical" by some or "slow" by others now compete with those being developed by attorneys representing the National Lawyers Guild, the American Bar Association, and the American Civil Liberties Union. It is not yet possible to evaluate the behavior of each of these groups of lawyers, but preliminary indications are that each set of attorneys operates more or less at arms length from the other. The ABA-sponsored attorneys operate in the tradition of legal aid societies and "of counsel" to overtaxed trial attorneys in race cases. While occasionally cooperating with the Committee to Aid Southern Lawyers of the National Lawyers Guild, it is almost certain that this kind of volunteer did not enlist to "defend the movement" or to "avoid tactics of individualized defense and litigation which will wind up in the Supreme Court three years from now." Lawyer spokesmen from the National Lawyers Guild speak the language of collective militancy though their actual legal practices may reflect more attention to conventional lawyer-client procedures. Finally, if past behavior is precedent, lawyers representing the American Civil Liberties Union and affiliated groups will avoid direct identification with the Negro protest by supporting and seeking out selected constitutional cases for ultimate Supreme Court test.

4. *Criminal Cases.* A separate pattern of lawyer activity involving an essentially separate set of attorneys is observable in the case histories of criminal litigations which reach the Supreme Court. The largest number of cases result from prisoner applications and cases brought forward by public defenders or court appointed attorneys. Most of the attorneys in these criminal cases had no connection with the American Civil Liberties Union or similar groups, and according to their responses, they did not request aid from that organization or any similar group. Other criminal lawyers were financed exclusively by their clients and litigated their cases in the manner that private law practice would dictate. The patterns of activities described provide some degree of regularity in the Supreme Court Bar's non-commercial cases. . . .

Any taxonomy of litigation routes to the Supreme Court cannot, of course, overlook the conventional and sometimes idiosyncratic paths that some cases take. As already noted, cases classified as "non-commercial," particularly those involving civil liberties, turn out in some cases to be pocketbook actions with constitutional by-products. In other instances determined individuals press their own principles against organizational advice and at high cost to themselves. Finally, lawyers take cases for sport, and the prestige of arguing before the highest tribunal. Attorneys in all kinds of cases often state that their case was their fight in which they alone had to carry the major burden.

E. Supporting Activity in Non-Commercial Cases

One would expect that a different breed of attorney inhabits the world of non-commercial Supreme Court litigations. This belief is only partially justified because most of the non-commercial litigations involve private complaints about the use of public authority. Most of the cases that reach the Supreme Court involve the troubles of public servants, lawyers, home owners, soldiers, union officials, civilians in military posts, and a variety of other persons complaining about official actions. Though the cases are considered "important" enough for Supreme Court review, they ordinarily do not qualify for support by organized civil libertarians. In any event, the parties in civil liberties cases usually secure their own attorneys without soliciting or receiving help from any outside source. Only a few lawyers handling civil liberties cases see their cases as representing the interests of large classes of citizens.

In civil liberties cases involving movie censorship and church-state relationships, the litigation was primarily commercial with constitutional overtones. Though many cases were brought "simultaneously," local censorship statutes differed in detail and any important degree of coordination was not feasible. Also, litigation enthusiasm varied with different commercial litigants who brought cases of this kind.

. . .

Though opinions differ on other techniques, there is widespread agreement among non-commercial lawyers on the value of amicus curiae briefs. In non-commercial cases other social defense organizations are occasionally represented, but the ACLU is far and away the most active organization. From 1958 to 1964 it participated in 20 civil liberties cases, 12 criminal cases, 11 political offender cases and 3 cases involving race relations. The distribution of *amici* activity is shown in Table 18-3.

As one would expect, the forces at work in criminal cases are markedly different than those involved in civil liberties, political offender and race relations cases. Criminal cases are almost never regarded as "representative" proceedings in any sense. The ACLU over the past seven years has participated in only a dozen criminal cases which resulted in Supreme Court opinions. Attorneys handling criminal cases often regard themselves as "lone wolves" and "independent operators" who feel they are "perfectly capable" of handling their own cases. Some of the attorneys indicated that they were opposed to seeking or getting outside help, and in two interviews the attorneys complained that the "ACLU was trying to take my case away." While some criminal cases involved notorious clients and presumably large fees, a much larger number of cases involved attorneys who had "assumed a lonely burden of fighting a cause without pay and without help from any source."

IV. Conclusion

. . . [This] picture of Supreme Court litigation is at odds with that usually presented in political science literature. The actual judicial process appears to be a close approximation of the traditional *legal* model in which judicial policy-making emerges through *ad hoc* private controversies. The parties, attorneys, and issues in Supreme Court cases, more often than not, remain narrowly private so as to prevent irrelevancies and outside pressure.

. . .

If "lobbying" of litigation were to become widespread as "a form of political or pressure group activity," a fundamental change in thinking about judicial process would be necessary. Businessmen, companies, unions and corporations would have to abandon traditional attorney-client relationships and interpose trade associations and labor federations between themselves and their attorneys. In social and political litigations, "social defense" or defense by civil liberties organizations would have to supersede the limited functions performed by legal aid and public defender groups, and members of the organized bar would have to abandon traditional notions about the "independence of the bar" and "attorney-client relationships and privileges" in order to recognize their collective group responsibility for the making of public policy. The individual who seeks to vindicate his private rights in the Supreme Court would have to recognize that the judicial process is no place for idiosyncratic notions of public policy.

The evidence suggests, however, that neither the legalistic world of individual attorney-client relationships nor a world of organized or "managed" litigations reflects the actualities of Supreme Court litigation processes.

Almost all lower court litigations raise important issues of law and policy but few attract the participation of outside groups because the principles involved are too closely intermingled with the private interests of the litigants. As we move from the lower to the higher courts, we find that most of the judicial work has a narrower scope and that it is carried forward, beyond the trial stage, only insofar as the litigant is able to pay for it. Most of the issues that receive judicial attention in appellate court opinions are those involving technical legal matters. These issues are often interlocutory in nature, and are usually confined to the clarification of legal tasks.

The private parties involved in Supreme Court cases usually represent individual, commercial, proprietary or pecuniary interests. The "real party in interest" in these cases is the same as the formal party, and there are usually no "behind the scenes" groups intervening between the attorney and his business client. Sponsorship of such litigation by persons other than the formal parties is rare, but it occurs most frequently in cases involving political offenders or racial discrimination.

The lawyer's role in influencing governmental policymaking is even more apparent in the judicial sphere than in connection with lobbying in the legislative and administrative processes. Large bureaucratically sophisticated commercial law firms are particularly sensitive to the possibilities of raising new issues, whether for offensive or defensive purposes, and they have the ability to bring to bear resources such as money, files, organization, and expertise in order to respond quickly and sensitively before significant judicial decisions are made.

Criminal defense attorneys prefer to work alone and to insulate the case within the narrow confines of their client's private interests. Social defense organizations, on the other hand, participate in support of litigants whose cases provide "public relations" or "educational value." In cases involving the politically unpopular, these attributes provide the basis for the raising of funds for legal expenses and attorney's fees. Civil liberties organizations, and most private organizations supporting civil liberties causes, do not usually intervene at the trial level unless the issues are clearly focused and disentangled from other legal and evidentiary considerations.

Though coordination or management of multiple litigations is theoretically possible, there are too many intervening variables to prevent its success. Litigation management involves problems of timing, the choice of a litigant, selection of judicial forum, the strategic choice of pleadings, and the cooperation of the attorneys. Despite these obstacles, coordination is sometimes attempted. Lawyers exchange briefs and extend courtesies, but unless there is a common client, there is likely to be very little planning or coordination even among litigants who are similarly situated.

Participation in the role of *amicus curiae* is generally aimed at furthering independent pecuniary or proprietary interests, but, in commercial cases, there is evidence that the participation of the United States government is sought to strengthen the legal position of the formal party. In social and political litigations, the ACLU plays an *amicus* role similar to, but less effective than, the role assumed by the United States government in commercial cases. Other *amici* in social and political litigations participate primarily as advocates on behalf of the general position advanced by the party litigant. Some coordination of *amicus curiae* activity among private groups is achieved through clearance procedures which include conferences and exchanges of information and briefs. In social and political cases a great deal of effort is expended in enlisting endorsements to "strengthen" a litigant's position and in avoiding duplicative and unnecessary "me too" briefs. In the last analysis, however, *amicus curiae* briefs reflect the independent work products of individual attorneys or law firms.

On the basis of this study, organized interest groups would appear to play a relatively minor role in Supreme Court decision-making. . . .

19

The New Public Interest Lawyers

Robert Borosage, Barbara Brown, Paul Friedman,
Paul Gewirtz, William Jeffress, and
William Kelly

. . .

. . . In this section, an attempt will be made to suggest the full range of public interest work by describing the differing activities engaged in and clients and substantive interests represented, as well as the various theories of social change informing specific choices of clients and modes of action. . . .

. . .

A. Lawyers for the Poor

Legal services programs are one response to the dilemma of the poor. The neighborhood legal services office usually assists individual clients with occasional crises; landlord/tenant, welfare, consumer credit, wage garnishments, and family law problems predominate. Legal services, in theory, are to be provided without cost to every "eligible" poor person who walks through the door. Assuming that the political and economic order are basically sound, but that some people are cut off, legal service efforts attempt to supply more lawyers so that more cases can get into the legal system. The goal is to make the legal system available to more people, so that their grievances can be heard and channeled.

The benefits of these programs are obvious. Poor individuals are endlessly victimized, and their rights are often violated. Legal services programs serve a great need by attempting to remedy those individual wrongs perpetrated against poor people that make their day-to-day plight even more miserable. Second, lawyers in these programs must be credited with developing much of the law of the poor; in addition to evolving new forms of action and new remedies, legal services lawyers have, through their work, had the secondary effect of bringing an awareness of the problems of the poor to the law schools, to the legal profession, and to the general public. Finally, these programs provide a training ground for lawyers who then move on to other kinds of work for the poor.

Reprinted by permission of The Yale Law Journal Company and Fred B. Rothman & Company from *The Yale Law Journal,* Vol. 79, pp. 1072–1074, 1091–1098, 1103–1105, 1145–1147. © 1970. The authors were students at Yale Law School.

The shortcomings of the legal services programs as a way of dealing with the problems of the poor have become increasingly apparent over time. The ideal of service for all has led to extremely heavy caseloads, with a necessary effect on the quality and comprehensiveness of the representation given; the only realistic way to begin to cope with the quantity problem is to push for increased standardization of legal forms and procedures, and for greater use of lay people in furnishing legal service. In addition, legal services programs may fundamentally misconceive the plight of the poor and the relation of the law to that plight. A program focused upon services to individuals will fail to deal with the legal and institutional sources of the grievances of the poor. . . . In the legal services office, overwhelmed by individual cases, reform of laws and institutions—reforms that would affect the poor as a group and would deal with the depressed state of their day-to-day existence—is neglected in the rush of small, individual matters the office must handle. . . .

. . . The lawyers for the poor whom we interviewed are all in some way attempting to meet perceived weaknesses in the legal service approach. One goal is to provide more creative and comprehensive service to individual clients with specific legal difficulties. . . .

. . .

Aside from more comprehensive service for specific clients, the emphasis of most public interest lawyers is on having a wide impact on the poor, usually through representing groups rather than individuals and through attempting to achieve changes in legal rules and in the behavior of governmental agencies. . . .

. . .

B. Lawyers for Political and Cultural Dissidents

A number of public interest lawyers and law firms concentrate their practice upon representing political and cultural dissidents, such as student activists, underground publishers, and militant political organizations. Many so-called "political lawyers" are also lawyers for poor people, who are themselves in many senses "political dissidents"; in addition, groups such as SDS and the Black Panthers, who are frequent clients of "political lawyers," are centrally concerned with the problems of the poor. It is only because such radical groups have a wide-ranging political and cultural critique of American society, because their contacts with the legal order are significantly different from those of the poor people's groups already discussed, and because their lawyers tend to have a wide-ranging political practice, that those lawyers are treated separately in this discussion.

Traditional civil liberties lawyers, such as those who work for the ACLU, represent political, religious, and cultural dissenters of all types, from the far right to the far left. . . . For a number of decades, the ACLU has been a courageous and lonely advocate for unpopular clients. Its efforts, and those of other civil libertarian lawyers, have been devoted to furthering the values of free speech, belief and association, regardless of the particular aims of individual clients.

In contrast to the traditional civil libertarian, some political lawyers dedicate their efforts only to political and cultural dissenters with whom they are in sympathy. Thus, where speech is concerned, they will accept as clients only those people with whose political position they agree. For example, William Kunstler was recently asked if he would use the arguments with which he defended Panthers to defend Minutemen. He replied, "No, I wouldn't defend them at all. I only defend those whose goals I share. I'm not a lawyer for hire. I only defend those I love."

While the ACLU lawyer is typically a litigator in the civil liberties field, these other political lawyers often engage in a wider range of activities. In addition, while the ACLU usually represents individuals, the "new" political lawyer, like the lawyer for the poor, tends to emphasize organized groups. His relationship to those groups may take a number of forms, combining organizing, offensive representation, and criminal defense work. Ongoing contact with the groups is common. George Johnson of New Haven, for example, handles draft and drug cases as well as criminal defense work, but is also a lawyer and organizer for the American Independent Movement, a minority party active in New Haven politics. John Flym, of Flym, Zalkind and Silverglate in Boston, emphasizes a somewhat different role for a lawyer committed to social change. Although he usually represents individuals (often students with such "hassles" as draft and drug problems) and "underground" organizations (such as Sergeant Ground's Memorial Necktie, a coffeehouse), much of his time is spent in a slow process of organizing the people he lives among.
. . .

. . .

Where the political lawyers represent groups, those groups tend to be "radical" in the sense that they are committed to fundamental change in the structure of American society. The groups may not have a commitment to the theory of pluralism and interest group politics, or a faith that the existing legal system, with some reform, can achieve a just society. For these political and cultural dissidents, to a greater extent than for the groups usually served by legal services, legal institutions do not provide the primary focus for affirmative activity, and the practice of their lawyers reflects this difference. Indeed, wary of any activity that confirms or maintains "the system," some radical lawyers are hostile to the work done by "public interest lawyers"; such work is counterproductive, in their view, for while it can make the system slightly less oppressive, it defuses efforts for more radical change. Nevertheless, in one sense the lawyer for political groups shares the thrust of the lawyer for the poor: his goal is to further the viability of definable groups of people.

While this may entail servicing various legal needs of the group, and even some organizing, the most important activity of lawyers for groups such as SDS or the Black Panthers is criminal defense work. Although criminal defense work is obviously needed to keep movement groups alive, movement lawyers are at least ambivalent about the legal system, and are endlessly troubled by whether their work aids or is in fact counterproductive to radical efforts. One lawyer recounted a story told by Victor Rabinowitz at a National Lawyers Guild conference. Rabinowitz was handling a case involving GI's who had gotten in trouble for operating a coffeehouse at Fort Dix. The coffeehouse matter was highly publicized and had become the focus of GI discontent at the base, and of efforts to organize that discontent. Rabinowitz won the case, and afterwards asked someone who had been organizing GI's whether winning the case had been helpful to the organizing efforts. On the contrary, the organizer said. Because the case was won, the GI's tended to feel that they could rely on the courts, and that there was no need to get involved with the riskier business of organizing.

. . .

. . . Because the topic has been so much debated recently, a special word should be said about the so-called "political trial." Today the phrase usually applies to criminal prosecutions of such "enemies of the realm" as radical political groups and draft resisters. From the defense lawyer's point of view, a number of different conceptions are involved. A political trial may be characterized simply by the fact that public opinion and public attitudes on one or more social questions will inevitably have an effect on the decision. In this sense, a political trial is one where the defense lawyer seeks to get an acquittal by meeting the implicit political issues head-on. Thus, where the defendant is part of a mass arrest of anti-war demonstrators or campus activists, public attitudes on the war or student movements are inevitably present in the courtroom; the defense lawyer may choose to meet these attitudes directly, to present his client's political beliefs explicitly, and to make political arguments as much a part of the "defense" as any other alibi.

Furthermore, the trial may itself be used as an organizing device. The trial becomes a propaganda vehicle for the defendants, and hence a method for the group to bring its grievances and its program to the general public. Political issues and differences are raised in the courtroom and aired in the press. The goal may be to affect the outcome of the trial, but it may be more general. To a greater or lesser extent, these defendants do not have faith that the American legal system will or can grant them a just trial. In some cases defendants in political trials, and occasionally their lawyer, have engaged in disorderly tactics; these may be a response to specific perceived injustices in the handling of the trial, or may be provocative acts to draw the judge into an over-reaction, which can then be pointed to as further evidence of the impossibility of achieving a just trial. In many senses, the trial becomes a play about itself: the issue of justice for the defendants is united with issues of social justice, and the trial is conducted in such a way as to illustrate the impossibility of either in American society. The tension for the lawyer is obvious. To conduct a trial in this "political" way is to complicate the task of securing an acquittal, which goal neither he nor his clients entirely abandon. However, the defendants see the trial as part of a wider political struggle, and an opportunity to bring their larger case to the public and to expose inequities in the legal system.

C.   Value-Oriented Public Interest Lawyers

The attempt to represent consumer and environmental interests poses somewhat different problems for the public interest lawyer. Unlike lawyers who deal with the concerns of the poor or political dissidents, which often approach the level of immediate survival and are therefore very intense, the consumer or environmental lawyer deals with diffuse and, to any individual, less pressing interests held in common by all people. The vigorous labor union member is unlikely, despite his disgruntlement at the quality of the appliances he purchases, to join a consumer union. A partial explanation for his behavior is that the goals of consumer organizations, such as fair labeling and product safety, are "public goods"; that is, the labor union member knows that he cannot be denied the benefit of fair labeling even though he did not participate in securing it.

Just as there is a trend among poverty lawyers toward building political communities of the poor, so too is there a movement among environmental and consumer lawyers to build economically and politically powerful coalitions around a particular value or "secondary" interest. But there is an important difference between the organizing activities of poverty lawyers and those of consumer or environmental lawyers. The goal of the former is the enfranchisement of a relatively distinct minority: achievement of this goal involves primarily the development of group consciousness, internal leadership and organization, and political sophistication. Consumers, on the other hand, do not constitute an identifiable and politically underrepresented class. The problem is not disenfranchisement, but diffusion of power and the low visibility of corporate and regulatory agency decisions affecting the quality of American life. The primary effort in building coalitions around consumer or environmental values, therefore, is to arouse and mobilize the latent power of a potential majority.

The most straightforward method of increasing public awareness—the simple dissemination of information about substantive issues—is not a preserve of lawyers alone, as is evident from a brief look at the activities of environmentalist lawyers and laymen. The conservation movement in America has a long history, yet its character has changed dramatically in recent years. The change is well illustrated by the circumstances surrounding the formation of the Friends of the Earth Society, a group of ecology-minded professionals who emphasize education through publication. Friends of the Earth grew out of a split within the Sierra Club. Under the direction of David Brower, the Sierra Club had developed from a "professional hiking organization" with 5000 members into a radical environmental group of 80,000. Brower began to publish expensive books designed to give a vicarious wilderness experience. Additionally, the Sierra Club published a series of books about areas in danger, including one that helped to arouse popular support for saving the Grand Canyon. But Brower's activities led to policy disagreements within the Club, and he was ousted in 1969.

In response, Brower formed Friends of the Earth to carry on the activities he had pursued in the Sierra Club. It has already signed a $13 million publishing agreement with McCall's magazine for an international series and a scientific series on ecology. Although its lawyers will resort to the courts where necessary, Friends of the Earth will function primarily as an issue-oriented public relations firm, in the business of educating the public about ecology.

. . .

Corporate and governmental disregard for consumer and environmental values stems not only from the lack of public awareness of the problems, but also from a lack of public access to the decision-making process. The corporations are so large and powerful that an individual consumer or shareholder cannot expect to have any influence upon their decisions. Regulatory agencies such as the Federal Power Commission or the Federal Trade Commission, in theory the advocates of "the public interest," are both relatively insulated from the political process and relatively immune, because of their own structures and procedures, from significant inputs by consumers. A second thrust of legal activity in this field of public interest law is, therefore, to bring pressure upon corporations and agencies to make their decisions and their processes more responsive to the interests in product and environmental quality. This tactic is, of course, interrelated with the goal of increasing public awareness; without the support of a vocal public, lawyers can have little impact upon corporations, agencies, or Congress.

One technique of consumer advocacy is lobbying in Congress and state legislatures. While the most effective impact upon legislatures no doubt comes from the Ralph Nader-type exposure of corporate abuses and agency dereliction, increasing pressure by lawyers on behalf of organized consumer or environmental groups is being brought in less visible ways. . . .

. . .

While some lawyers in the consumer and environmental area have used litigation and public education to attack particular actions of corporations and agencies, other efforts have been aimed more generally at changing the decision-making processes of those institutions. With regard to corporations, a frontal attack has been mounted by the Project on Corporate Responsibility. . . .

The Campaign to Make General Motors Responsible, the first major undertaking of the Project, [first] centered on a proxy contest [in 1970] to secure adoption by the corporation of several resolutions and amendments to its bylaws. General Motors was selected as a target. . . . The Securities & Exchange Commission required GM to include in its proxy statement Campaign-sponsored proposals to enlarge the Board of Directors (in order to permit public representatives on the Board), and to create a Shareholders Committee for Corporate Responsibility, but refused to require the inclusion of resolutions on pollution, mass transit, minority employment and franchises, and insurance.

At a stockholders meeting in May [1970], the Campaign GM resolutions were rejected overwhelmingly, receiving about three per cent of the vote. Defeat of the proposals came as no surprise to the campaign coordinators, who regarded the campaign as a success in furthering the goal of corporate responsibility to the public. . . .

The Corporate Responsibility Project and other efforts aimed at pressuring corporations to heed the demands for product and environmental quality can be seen in part as a response to the failure of administrative agencies. Designed to regulate business activity "in the public interest," agencies such as the ICC, the FTC, and the FCC typically had an initial period of vigorous activity directed toward specific evils which led to their creation. In recent years, however, these agencies have notoriously failed to play the active champion of an ill-organized public. It is no exaggeration to say that consumer and environmental advocates today see the agencies less as a solution than as part of the problem.

The most publicized effort to expose and to correct the fumblings and inadequacies of administrative agencies has been that led by Ralph Nader. Nader's first crusade, on behalf of automobile safety, made him a public figure in 1966 after the attempts of General Motors to investigate and discredit him were exposed. He established the Center for Study of Responsive Law in June, 1969, institutionalizing an operation that had been growing since the 1966 investigations. . . .

Nader starts from a conviction that the basic evil in American society is concentrated corporate power. The Center's actions are directed toward making corporations and regulatory agencies give greater weight in their decision-making to the consumer interest. To that end, the Center investigates corporate and agency activity, publishes reports to embarrass officials and shock the public, badgers administrative agency personnel, and at times seeks relief in the courts.

The first major agency study criticized the Federal Trade Commission, pointing to its extreme laxity and calling for major reorganization; this report was the first of several critical studies which bore fruit in a proposal by the then-FTC Chairman Weinberger for a thorough restructuring of the agency. The Center's . . . report on the Interstate Commerce Commission went even further in its recommendations, urging the complete dismantling of the ICC and the establishment of a new regulatory apparatus. [Also conducted were] in-depth studies of the Agriculture Department, the Food and Drug Administration, the administrators of the air and water pollution control laws (Departments of the Interior and HEW), and the administrators of the occupational health and safety laws (Departments of Labor, Interior, and HEW). . . . Significantly, these investigations . . . encountered agency secrecy, enabling Nader to raise issues about citizen access to government records under the Freedom of Information Act. . . .

The focus of the Center's work, then, is less advocacy than investigation. The reason that corporate power is so vulnerable, according to Nader, is that Americans possess an underlying value system which will produce necessary changes when it is confronted by all the facts. "Who needs Marxist-Leninist rhetoric when you can get them on good old Christian ethics?" His studies document the failure of the agencies to fulfill their mandates, and shatter the consumer's confident assumption that the agencies are protecting him. Like those who publish or litigate, Nader relies on widespread public response to abuse of widely shared values to force decision-makers to respect diffuse consumer interests.

Unlike lawyers for the poor or for political and cultural dissidents, advocates of consumer and environmental causes represent values whose time seems to have come in the minds of an American majority. The developing public consciousness in these areas has produced some major changes in a relatively short period of time; the isolated protests of yesterday have become uncontroversial elements of major-party platforms today. The apparent successes of the movement, however, may pose an obstacle to the goals of those who see shoddy products and abuses of the environment as symbols of a deeper and more pressing need for public control over the institutions which have such enormous power over individual lives. It is not unrealistic to expect that as the battle becomes focused on issues affecting more significantly the distribution of power in American society, the most militant lawyers for consumer and environmental values will take on more of the forms and strategies of lawyers for political and cultural dissidents.

. . .

D.   Conclusion

Throughout . . . , we have used the term "public interest lawyer" to describe a large and diverse group of practitioners engaged in a broad range of activities. We believe that these lawyers occupy a professional role which differs both from that of the commercial lawyer, with his primarily profit-oriented practice, and from that of the government lawyer or administrator, who is charged with protecting the "public interest" but who does so without clients or a real constituency. A precise definition of this role, and certainly any evaluation of it, must be tentative at this time. The lawyers we interviewed have for the most part been out of law school less than ten years; with some exceptions, their firms have been in existence only a few years, and in some cases a few months. Although the field is varied and rapidly changing, our discussion in the previous sections does allow us to identify the forces which have created the role of public interest lawyers, to point out the most significant aspects of that role, and to speculate upon where the public interest law movement—to the extent that it can fairly be labeled a movement— is headed.

The role of the new public interest lawyer is a response to two major developments of recent years. First, the expansion of substantive and procedural guarantees, and the growth of organized and politically sensitive groups of poor people and consumers, have made new demands upon the legal process which are inadequately met by lawyers in commercial practice or by government agencies. These developments have coincided, not accidentally to be sure, with a heightened political and social consciousness on the part of many young lawyers, and an increased determination to integrate their personal values and their professional work. Both these demands—that of emerging interest groups for representation, and that of young lawyers for personally fulfilling work—have contributed to the present shape of public interest practice, but they are not necessarily complementary. In some ways, they create a tension which underlies most of the serious controversies within public interest law, and they provide two different perspectives for evaluating the role of public interest lawyers.

Public interest lawyers are significant first of all in the types of needs they serve. . . . Rather than devoting his energies to the defense of the constitutional rights of individuals, he feels that he must take more affirmative action and think in broader social, economic, and political terms. The lawyers we interviewed are committed ultimately to causes, not clients. They believe that the nation's most pressing problems cannot be attacked by professionals whose role is passive until retained by a client with a "legal problem." At the same time, many are unwilling to subject their professional efforts, their sense of what is important for society and how best to achieve it, to control by particular clients. Their efforts take on added significance because the resources available to pursue causes of social justice are limited; thus these lawyers are not only advocates in particular causes, but also arbiters of social priorities.

Public interest lawyers are also significant because of the type of representation they offer. In attacking broad problems and pursuing long-term goals, public interest lawyers have engaged in a wide range of strategies and activities, including litigation, counseling, lobbying, research and investigation, use of propaganda and the press, mobilizing community demonstrations, and organizing citizen's lobbies and community groups. Though none of these activities is novel in itself, the programmatic use of various strategies and various forums by a single lawyer or law firm in behalf of broad social causes has given new dimensions to the notion of "legal representation." As the services performed by public interest lawyers for their client groups have become more and more complex and far ranging, the increasing tendency has been to see the lawyer as a political figure. Several of our interviewees predicted that the next decade will see public interest lawyers attempting to enter the political arena directly, using their client groups as a constituency on either national or local levels.

. . .

20

The Practice of Law as Confidence Game: Organizational Cooptation of a Profession

Abraham S. Blumberg

. . .

. . . I wish to question the impact of three recent landmark decisions of the United States Supreme Court; each hailed as destined to effect profound changes in the future of criminal law administration and enforcement in America. The first of these, *Gideon v. Wainwright*, 372 U.S. 335 (1963) required states and localities henceforth to furnish counsel in the case of indigent persons charged with a felony. The Gideon ruling left several major issues unsettled, among them the vital question: What is the precise point in time at which a suspect is entitled to counsel? The answer came relatively quickly in *Escobedo v. Illinois*, 378 U.S. 478 (1964), which has aroused a storm of controversy. Danny Escobedo confessed to the murder of his brother-in-law after the police had refused to permit retained counsel to see him, although his lawyer was present in the station house and asked to confer with his client. In a 5–4 decision, the court asserted that counsel must be permitted when the process of police investigative effort shifts from merely investigatory to that of accusatory: "when its focus is on the accused and its purpose is to elicit a confession—our adversary system begins to operate, and, under the circumstances here, the accused must be permitted to consult with his lawyer."

As a consequence, Escobedo's confession was rendered inadmissible. The decision triggered a national debate among police, district attorneys, judges, lawyers, and other law enforcement officials, which continues unabated, as to the value and propriety of confessions in criminal cases. On June 13, 1966, the Supreme Court in a 5–4 decision underscored the principle enunciated in *Escobedo* in the case of *Miranda v. Arizona*. Police interrogation of any suspect in custody, without his consent, unless a defense attorney is present, is prohibited by the self-incrimination provision of the Fifth Amendment. Regardless of the relative merit of the various shades of opinion about the role of counsel in criminal cases, the issues generated thereby will be in part resolved as additional cases move toward decision in the Supreme Court in the near future. They are of peripheral interest and not of immediate concern in this paper. However, the *Gideon, Escobedo,* and *Miranda* cases pose interesting general questions. In all three decisions, the Supreme Court reiter-

ates the traditional legal conception of a defense lawyer based on the ideological perception of a criminal case as an *adversary, combative* proceeding, in which counsel for the
defense assiduously musters all the admittedly limited resources at his command to *defend*
the accused. The fundamental question remains to be answered: Does the Supreme
Court's conception of the role of counsel in a criminal case square with social reality?

The task of this paper is to furnish some preliminary evidence toward the illumination
of that question. . . . This paper is based upon observations made by the writer during
many years of legal practice in the criminal courts of a large metropolitan area. No claim
is made as to its methodological rigor, although it does reflect a conscious and sustained
effort for participant observation.

Court Structure Defines Role of Defense Lawyer

The overwhelming majority of convictions in criminal cases (usually over 90 per cent)
are not the product of a combative, trial-by-jury process at all, but instead merely involve
the sentencing of the individual after a negotiated, bargained-for plea of guilty has been
entered. Although more recently the overzealous role of police and prosecutors in producing pretrial confessions and admissions has achieved a good deal of notoriety, scant attention has been paid to the organizational structure and personnel of the criminal court
itself. Indeed, the extremely high conviction rate produced without the features of an
adversary trial in our courts would tend to suggest that the "trial" becomes a perfunctory
reiteration and validation of the pretrial interrogation and investigation.

The institutional setting of the court defines a role for the defense counsel in a criminal
case radically different from the one traditionally depicted. . . . It is grounded in pragmatic values, bureaucratic priorities, and administrative instruments. These exalt maximum production and the particularistic career designs of organizational incumbents,
whose occupational and career commitments tend to generate a set of priorities. These
priorities exert a higher claim than the stated ideological goals of "due process of law,"
and are often inconsistent with them.

Organizational goals and discipline impose a set of demands and conditions of practice
on the respective professions in the criminal court, to which they respond by abandoning
their ideological and professional commitments to the accused client, in the service of
these higher claims of the court organization. All court personnel, including the accused's
own lawyer, tend to be coopted to become agent-mediators who help the accused redefine
his situation and restructure his perceptions concomitant with a plea of guilty.

Of all the occupational roles in the court the only private individual who is officially
recognized as having a special status and concomitant obligations is the lawyer. His legal
status is that of "an officer of the court" and he is held to a standard of ethical performance and duty to his client as well as to the court. This obligation is thought to be far
higher than that expected of ordinary individuals occupying the various occupational
statuses in the court community. However, lawyers, whether privately retained or of the
legal-aid, public defender variety, have close and continuing relations with the prosecuting office and the court itself through discreet relations with the judges via their law
secretaries or "confidential" assistants. Indeed, lines of communication, influence and
contact with those offices, as well as with the Office of the Clerk of the court, Probation
Division, and with the press, are essential to present and prospective requirements of
criminal law practice. Similarly, the subtle involvement of the press and other mass media

in the court's organizational network is not readily discernible to the casual observer. Accused persons come and go in the court system schema, but the structure and its occupational incumbents remain to carry on their respective career, occupational and organizational enterprises. The individual stridencies, tensions, and conflicts a given accused person's case may present to all the participants are overcome, because the formal and informal relations of all the groups in the court setting require it. The probability of continued future relations and interaction must be preserved at all costs.

This is particularly true of the "lawyer regulars" *i.e.,* those defense lawyers, who by virtue of their continuous appearances in behalf of defendants, tend to represent the bulk of a criminal court's non-indigent case workload, and those lawyers who are not "regulars," who appear almost casually in behalf of an occasional client. Some of the "lawyer regulars" are highly visible as one moves about the major urban centers of the nation, their offices line the back streets of the courthouses, at times sharing space with bondsmen. Their political "visibility" in terms of local club house ties, reaching into the judge's chambers and prosecutor's office, are also deemed essential to successful practitioners. Previous research has indicated that the "lawyer regulars" make no effort to conceal their dependence upon police, bondsmen, jail personnel. Nor do they conceal the necessity for maintaining intimate relations with all levels of personnel in the court setting as a means of obtaining, maintaining, and building their practice. These informal relations are the *sine qua non* not only of retaining a practice, but also in the negotiation of pleas and sentences.

The client, then, is a secondary figure in the court system as in certain other bureaucratic settings. He becomes a means to other ends of the organization's incumbents. He may present doubts, contingencies, and pressures which challenge existing informal arrangements or disrupt them; but these tend to be resolved in favor of the continuance of the organization and its relations as before. There is a greater community of interest among all the principal organizational structures and their incumbents than exists elsewhere in other settings. The accused's lawyer has far greater professional, economic, intellectual and other ties to the various elements of the court system than he does to his own client. In short, the court is a closed community.

. . . Rather than any view of the matter in terms of some variation of a "conspiracy" hypothesis, the simple explanation is one of an ongoing system handling delicate tensions, managing the trauma produced by law enforcement and administration, and requiring almost pathological distrust of "outsiders" bordering on group paranoia.

The hostile attitude toward "outsiders" is in large measure engendered by a defensiveness itself produced by the inherent deficiencies of assembly line justice, so characteristic of our major criminal courts. Intolerably large caseloads of defendants which must be disposed of in an organizational context of limited resources and personnel, potentially subject the participants in the court community to harsh scrutiny from appellate courts, and other public and private sources of condemnation. As a consequence, an almost irreconcilable conflict is posed in terms of intense pressures to process large numbers of cases on the one hand, and the stringent ideological and legal requirements of "due process of law," on the other hand. A rather tenuous resolution of the dilemma has emerged in the shape of a large variety of bureaucratically ordained and controlled "work crimes," short cuts, deviations, and outright rule violations adopted as court practice in order to meet production norms. Fearfully anticipating criticism on ethical as well as legal grounds, all the significant participants in the court's social structure are bound into an organized system of complicity. This consists of a work arrangement in which the patterned, covert, informal breaches, and evasions of "due process" are institutionalized, but are, nevertheless, denied to exist.

These institutionalized evasions will be found to occur to some degree, in all criminal courts. Their nature, scope and complexity are largely determined by the size of the court, and the character of the community in which it is located, *e.g.,* whether it is a large, urban institution, or a relatively small rural county court. In addition, idiosyncratic, local conditions may contribute to a unique flavor in the character and quality of the criminal law's administration in a particular community. However, in most instances a variety of stratagems are employed—some subtle, some crude, in effectively disposing of what are often too large caseloads. A wide variety of coercive devices are employed against an accused-client, couched in a depersonalized, instrumental, bureaucratic version of due process of law, and which are in reality a perfunctory obeisance to the ideology of due process. These include some very explicit pressures which are exerted in some measure by all court personnel, including judges, to plead guilty and avoid trial. In many instances the sanction of a potentially harsh sentence is utilized as the visible alternative to pleading guilty, in the case of recalcitrants. Probation and psychiatric reports are "tailored" to organizational needs, or are at least responsive to the court organization's requirements for the refurbishment of a defendant's social biography, consonant with his new status. A resourceful judge can, through his subtle domination of the proceedings, impose his will on the final outcome of a trial. Stenographers and clerks, in their function as record keepers, are on occasion pressed into service in support of a judicial need to "rewrite" the record of a courtroom event. Bail practices are usually employed for purposes other than simply assuring a defendant's presence on the date of a hearing in connection with his case. Too often, the discretionary power as to bail is part of the arsenal of weapons available to collapse the resistance of an accused person. The foregoing is a most cursory examination of some of the more prominent "short cuts" available to any court organization. There are numerous other procedural strategies constituting due process deviations, which tend to become the work style artifacts of a court's personnel. Thus, only court "regulars" who are "bound in" are really accepted; others are treated routinely and in almost a coldly correct manner.

The defense attorneys, therefore, whether of the legal-aid, public defender variety, or privately retained, although operating in terms of pressures specific to their respective role and organizational obligations, ultimately are concerned with strategies which tend to lead to a plea. It is the rational, impersonal elements involving economies of time, labor, expense and a superior commitment of the defense counsel to these rationalistic values of maximum production of court organization that prevail, in his relationship with a client. The lawyer "regulars" are frequently former staff members of the prosecutor's office and utilize the prestige, know-how and contacts of their former affiliation as part of their stock in trade. Close and continuing relations between the lawyer "regular" and his former colleagues in the prosecutor's office generally overshadow the relationship between the regular and his client. The continuing colleagueship of supposedly adversary counsel rests on real professional and organizational needs of a *quid pro quo,* which goes beyond the limits of an accommodation or *modus vivendi* one might ordinarily expect under the circumstances of an otherwise seemingly adversary relationship. Indeed, the adversary features which are manifest are for the most part muted and exist even in their attenuated form largely for external consumption. The principals, lawyer and assistant district attorney, rely upon one another's cooperation for their continued professional existence, and so the bargaining between them tends usually to be "reasonable" rather than fierce.

Fee Collection and Fixing

The real key to understanding the role of defense counsel in a criminal case is to be found in the area of the fixing of the fee to be charged and its collection. The problem of fixing and collecting the fee tends to influence to a significant degree the criminal court process itself, and not just the relationship of the lawyer and his client. In essence, a lawyer-client "confidence game" is played. A true confidence game is unlike the case of the emperor's new clothes wherein that monarch's nakedness was a result of inordinate gullibility and credulity. In a genuine confidence game, the perpetrator manipulates the basic dishonesty of his partner, the victim or mark, toward his own (the confidence operator's) ends. Thus, "the victim of a con scheme must have some larceny in his heart."

Legal service lends itself particularly well to confidence games. . . .

. . . Much legal work is intangible either because it is simply a few words of advice, some preventive action, a telephone call, negotiation of some kind, a form filled out and filed, a hurried conference with another attorney or an official of a government agency, a letter or opinion written, or a countless variety of seemingly innocuous, and even prosaic procedures and actions. These are the basic activities, apart from any possible court appearance, of almost all lawyers, at all levels of practice. Much of the activity is not in the nature of the exercise of the traditional, precise professional skills of the attorney such as library research and oral argument in connection with appellate briefs, court motions, trial work, drafting of opinions, memoranda, contracts, and other complex documents and agreements. Instead, much legal activity, whether it is at the lowest or highest "white shoe" law firm levels, is of the brokerage, agent, sales representative, lobbyist type of activity, in which the lawyer acts for someone else in pursuing the latter's interests and designs. The service is intangible.

The large scale law firm may not speak as openly of their "contacts," their "fixing" abilities, as does the lower level lawyer. They trade instead upon a facade of thick carpeting, walnut panelling, genteel low pressure, and superficialities of traditional legal professionalism. There are occasions when even the large firm is on the defensive in connection with the fees they charge because the services rendered or results obtained do not appear to merit the fee asked. Therefore, there is a recurrent problem in the legal profession in fixing the amount of fee, and in justifying the basis for the requested fee.

Although the fee at times amounts to what the traffic and the conscience of the lawyer will bear, one further observation must be made with regard to the size of the fee and its collection. The defendant in a criminal case and the material gain he may have acquired during the course of his illicit activities are soon parted. Not infrequently the ill gotten fruits of the various modes of larceny are sequestered by a defense lawyer in payment of his fee. Inexorably, the amount of the fee is a function of the dollar value of the crime committed, and is frequently set with meticulous precision at a sum which bears an uncanny relationship to that of the net proceeds of the particular offense involved. On occasion, defendants have been known to commit additional offenses while at liberty on bail, in order to secure the requisite funds with which to meet their obligations for payment of legal fees. Defense lawyers condition even the most obtuse clients to recognize that there is a firm interconnection between fee payment and the zealous exercise of professional expertise, secret knowledge, and organizational "connections" in their behalf. Lawyers, therefore, seek to keep their clients in a proper state of tension, and to arouse in them the precise edge of anxiety which is calculated to encourage prompt fee payment. Consequently, the client attitude in the relationship between defense counsel and an accused is in many instances a precarious admixture of hostility, mistrust, dependence, and sycophancy. By keeping his client's anxieties aroused to the proper pitch, and establishing a seemingly causal relationship between a requested fee and the accused's ultimate extrication from his onerous difficulties, the lawyer will have established the necessary preliminary groundwork to assure a minimum of haggling over the fee and its eventual payment.

In varying degrees, as a consequence, all law practice involves a manipulation of the client and a stage management of the lawyer-client relationship so that at least an *appearance* of help and service will be forthcoming. This is accomplished in a variety of ways, often exercised in combination with each other. At the outset, the lawyer-professional employs with suitable variation a measure of sales-puff which may range from an air of unbounding selfconfidence, adequacy, and dominion over events, to that of complete arrogance. This will be supplemented by the affectation of a studied, faultless mode of personal attire. In the larger firms, the furnishings and office trappings will serve as the backdrop to help in impression management and client intimidation. In all firms, solo or large scale, an access to secret knowledge, and to the seats of power and influence is inferred, or presumed to a varying degree as the basic vendible commodity of the practitioners.

The lack of visible end product offers a special complication in the course of the professional life of the criminal court lawyer with respect to his fee and in his relations with his client. The plain fact is that an accused in a criminal case always "loses" even when he has been exonerated by an acquittal, discharge, or dismissal of his case. The hostility of an accused which follows as a consequence of his arrest, incarceration, possible loss of job, expense and other traumas connected with his case is directed, by means of displacement, toward his lawyer. It is in this sense that it may be said that a criminal lawyer never really "wins" a case. The really satisfied client is rare, since in the very nature of the situation even an accused's vindication leaves him with some degree of dissatisfaction and hostility. It is this state of affairs that makes for a lawyer-client relationship in the criminal court which tends to be a somewhat exaggerated version of the usual lawyer-client confidence game.

At the outset, because there are great risks of nonpayment of the fee, due to the impecuniousness of his clients, and the fact that a man who is sentenced to jail may be a singularly unappreciative client, the criminal lawyer collects his fee *in advance*. Often, because the lawyer and the accused both have questionable designs of their own upon each other, the confidence game can be played. The criminal lawyer must serve three major functions, or stated another way, he must solve three problems. First, he must arrange for his fee; second, he must prepare and then, if necessary, "cool out" his client in case of defeat (a highly likely contingency); third, he must satisfy the court organization that he has performed adequately in the process of negotiating the plea, so as to preclude the possibility of any sort of embarrassing incident which may serve to invite "outside" scrutiny.

In assuring the attainment of one of his primary objectives, his fee, the criminal lawyer will very often enter into negotiations with the accused's kin, including collateral relatives.

In many instances, the accused himself is unable to pay any sort of fee or anything more than a token fee. It then becomes important to involve as many of the accused's kin as possible in the situation. This is especially so if the attorney hopes to collect a significant part of a proposed substantial fee. . . .

A fee for a felony case which ultimately results in a plea, rather than a trial, may ordinarily range anywhere from $500 to $1,500. Should the case go to trial, the fee will be proportionately larger, depending upon the length of the trial. But the larger the fee the lawyer wishes to exact, the more impressive his performance must be, in terms of his stage managed image as a personage of great influence and power in the court organization. Court personnel are keenly aware of the extent to which a lawyer's stock in trade involves the precarious stage management of an image which goes beyond the usual professional flamboyance, and for this reason alone the lawyer is "bound in" to the authority system of the court's organizational discipline. Therefore, to some extent, court personnel will aid the lawyer in the creation and maintenance of that impression. There is a tacit commitment to the lawyer by the court organization, apart from formal etiquette, to aid him to this. Such augmentation of the lawyer's stage managed image as this affords, is the partial basis for the *quid pro quo* which exists between the lawyer and the court organization. It tends to serve as the continuing basis for the higher loyalty of the lawyer to the organization; his relationship with his client, in contrast, is transient, ephemeral and often superficial.

Defense Lawyer as Double Agent

The lawyer has often been accused of stirring up unnecessary litigation, especially in the field of negligence. He is said to acquire a vested interest in a cause of action or claim which was initially his client's. The strong incentive of possible fee motivates the lawyer to promote litigation which would otherwise never have developed. However, the criminal lawyer develops a vested interest of an entirely different nature in his client's case: to limit its scope and duration rather than do battle. Only in this way can a case be "profitable." Thus, he enlists the aid of relatives not only to assure payment of his fee, but he will also rely on these persons to help him in his agent-mediator role of convincing the accused to plead guilty, and ultimately to help in "cooling out" the accused if necessary.

It is at this point that an accused-defendant may experience his first sense of "betrayal." While he had perhaps perceived the police and prosecutor to be adversaries, or possibly even the judge, the accused is wholly unprepared for his counsel's role performance as an agent-mediator. In the same vein, it is even less likely to occur to an accused that members of his own family or other kin may become agents, albeit at the behest and urging of other agents or mediators, acting on the principle that they are in reality helping an accused negotiate the best possible plea arrangement under the circumstances. Usually, it will be the lawyer who will activate next of kin in this role, his ostensible motive being to arrange for his fee. But soon latent and unstated motives will assert themselves, with entreaties by counsel to the accused's next of kin, to appeal to the accused to "help himself" by pleading. *Gemeinschaft* sentiments are to this extent exploited by a defense lawyer (or even at times by a district attorney) to achieve specific secular ends, that is, of concluding a particular matter with all possible dispatch.

The fee is often collected in stages, each installment usually payable prior to a necessary court appearance required during the course of an accused's career journey. At each stage, in his interviews and communications with the accused, or in addition, with members of his family, if they are helping with the fee payment, the lawyer employs an air of professional confidence and "inside-dopesterism" in order to assuage anxieties on all sides. He makes the necessary bland assurances, and in effect manipulates his client, who is usually willing to do and say the things, true or not, which will help his attorney extricate him. Since the dimensions of what he is essentially selling, organizational influence and expertise, are not technically and precisely measurable, the lawyer can make extravagant claims of influence and secret knowledge with immunity. Thus, lawyers frequently claim to have inside knowledge in connection with information in the hands of the D.A., police, probation officials or to have access to these functionaries. Factually, they often do, and need only to exaggerate the nature of their relationships with them to obtain the desired effective impression upon the client. But, as in the genuine confidence game, the victim who has participated is loathe to do anything which will upset the lesser plea which his lawyer has "conned" him into accepting.

In effect, in his role as double agent, the criminal lawyer performs an extremely vital and delicate mission for the court organization and the accused. Both principals are anxious to terminate the litigation with a minimum of expense and damage to each other. There is no other personage or role incumbent in the total court structure more strategically located, who by training and in terms of his own requirements, is more ideally suited to do so than the lawyer. In recognition of this, judges will cooperate with attorneys in many important ways. For example, they will adjourn the case of an accused in jail awaiting plea or sentence if the attorney requests such action. While explicitly this may be done for some innocuous and seemingly valid reason, the tacit purpose is that pressure is being applied by the attorney for the collection of his fee, which he knows will probably not be forthcoming if the case is concluded. Judges are aware of this tactic on the part of lawyers, who, by requesting an adjournment, keep an accused incarcerated awhile longer as a not too subtle method of dunning a client for payment. However, the judges will go along with this, on the ground that important ends are being served. Often, the only end served is to protect a lawyer's fee.

The judge will help an accused's lawyer in still another way. He will lend the official aura of his office and courtroom so that a lawyer can stage manage an impression of an "all out" performance for the accused in justification of his fee. The judge and other court personnel will serve as a backdrop for a scene charged with dramatic fire, in which the accused's lawyer makes a stirring appeal in his behalf. With a show of restrained passion, the lawyer will intone the virtues of the accused and recite the social deprivations which have reduced him to his present state. The speech varies somewhat, depending on whether the accused has been convicted after trial or has pleaded guilty. In the main, however, the incongruity, superficiality, and ritualistic character of the total performance is underscored by a visibly impassive, almost bored reaction on the part of the judge and other members of the court retinue.

Afterward, there is a hearty exchange of pleasantries between the lawyer and district attorney, wholly out of context in terms of the supposed adversary nature of the preceding events. The fiery passion in defense of his client is gone, and the lawyers for both sides resume their offstage relations, chatting amiably and perhaps including the judge in their restrained banter. No other aspect of their visible conduct so effectively serves to put even a casual observer on notice, that these individuals have claims upon each other. These seemingly innocuous actions are indicative of continuing organizational and informal relations, which, in their intricacy and depth, range far beyond any priorities or claims a particular defendant may have.

Criminal law practice is a unique form of private law practice since it really only appears to be private practice. Actually it is bureaucratic practice, because of the legal practitioner's enmeshment in the authority, discipline, and perspectives of the court organization. Private practice, supposedly, in a professional sense, involves the maintenance of an organized, disciplined body of knowledge and learning; the individual practitioners are imbued with a spirit of autonomy and service, the earning of a livelihood being incidental. In the sense that the lawyer in the criminal court serves as a double agent, serving higher organizational rather than professional ends, he may be deemed to be engaged in bureaucratic rather than private practice. To some extent the lawyer-client "confidence game," in addition to its other functions, serves to conceal this fact.

The Client's Perception

The "cop-out" ceremony, in which the court process culminates, is not only invaluable for redefining the accused's perspectives of himself, but also in reiterating publicly in a formally structured ritual the accused person's guilt for the benefit of significant "others" who are observing. The accused not only is made to assert publicly his guilt of a specific crime, but also a complete recital of its details. He is further made to indicate that he is entering his plea of guilt freely, willingly, and voluntarily, and that he is not doing so because of any promises or in consideration of any commitments that may have been made to him by anyone. This last is intended as a blanket statement to shield the participants from any possible charges of "coercion" or undue influence that may have been exerted in violation of due process requirements. Its function is to preclude any later review by an appellate court on these grounds, and also to obviate any second thoughts an accused may develop in connection with his plea.

However, for the accused, the conception of self as a guilty person is in large measure a temporary role adaptation. His career socialization as an accused, if it is successful, eventuates in his acceptance and redefinition of himself as a guilty person. However, the transformation is ephemeral, in that he will, in private, quickly reassert his innocence. Of importance is that he accept his defeat, publicly proclaim it, and find some measure of pacification in it. Almost immediately after his plea, a defendant will generally be interviewed by a representative of the probation division in connection with a presentence report which is to be prepared. The very first question to be asked of him by the probation officer is: "Are you guilty of the crime to which you pleaded?" This is by way of double affirmation of the defendant's guilt. Should the defendant now begin to make bold assertions of his innocence, despite his plea of guilty, he will be asked to withdraw his plea and stand trial on the original charges. Such a threatened possibility is, in most instances, sufficient to cause an accused to let the plea stand and to request the probation officer to overlook his exclamations of innocence. The table that follows is a breakdown of the categorized responses of a random sample of male defendants in Metropolitan Court[1] during 1962, 1963, and 1964 in connection with their statements during presentence probation interviews following their plea of guilty.

TABLE 20-1
Defendant Responses as to Guilt or Innocence After Pleading Guilty
N = 724   Years—1962, 1963, 1964

Nature of Response		N of Defendants
Innocent (Manipulated)	"The lawyer or judge, police or D.A. 'conned me' "	86
Innocent (Pragmatic)	"Wanted to get it over with" "You can't beat the system" "They have you over a barrel when you have a record"	147
Innocent (Advice of counsel)	"Followed my lawyer's advice"	92
Innocent (Defiant)	"Framed"—Betrayed by "Complainant," "Police," "Squealers," "Lawyer," "Friends," "Wife," "Girlfriend"	33
Innocent (Adverse social data)	Blames probation officer or psychiatrist for "Bad Report," in cases where there was pre-pleading investigation	15
Guilty	"But I should have gotten a better deal" Blames lawyer, D.A., Police, Judge	74
Guilty	Won't say anything further	21
Fatalistic (Doesn't press his "Innocence," won't admit "Guilt")	"I did it for convenience" "My lawyer told me it was only thing I could do" "I did it because it was the best way out"	248
No response		8
Total		724

It would be well to observe at the outset, that of the 724 defendants who pleaded guilty before trial, only 43 (5.94 per cent) of the total group had confessed prior to their indictment. Thus, the ultimate judicial process was predicated upon evidence independent of any confession of the accused.

As the data indicate, only a relatively small number (95) out of the total number of defendants actually will even admit their guilt, following the "cop-out" ceremony. However, even though they have affirmed their guilt, many of these defendants felt that they should have been able to negotiate a more favorable plea. The largest aggregate of defendants (373) were those who reasserted their "innocence" following their public profession of guilt during the "cop-out" ceremony. These defendants employed differential degrees of fervor, solemnity and credibility, ranging from really mild, wavering assertions of innocence which were embroidered with a variety of stock explanations and rationalizations, to those of an adamant, "framed" nature. Thus, the "Innocent" group, for the most part, were largely concerned with underscoring for their probation interviewer their essential "goodness" and "worthiness," despite their formal plea of guilty. Assertion of his innocence at the post plea stage, resurrects a more respectable and acceptable self concept for the accused defendant who has pleaded guilty. A recital of the structural exigencies which precipitated his plea of guilt, serves to embellish a newly proffered claim of innocence, which many defendants mistakenly feel will stand them in good stead at the time of sentence, or ultimately with probation or parole authorities.

Relatively few (33) maintained their innocence in terms of having been "framed" by some person or agent-mediator, although a larger number (86) indicated that they had been manipulated or "conned" by an agent-mediator to plead guilty, but as indicated, their assertions of innocence were relatively mild.

A rather substantial group (147) preferred to stress the pragmatic aspects of their plea of guilty. They would only perfunctorily assert their innocence and would in general refer to some adverse aspect of their situation which they believed tended to negatively affect their bargaining leverage, including in some instances a prior criminal record.

One group of defendants (92), while maintaining their innocence, simply employed some variation of a theme of following "the advice of counsel" as a covering response, to explain their guilty plea in the light of their new affirmation of innocence.

The largest single group of defendants (248) were basically fatalistic. They often verbalized weak suggestions of their innocence in rather halting terms, wholly without convictions. By the same token, they would not admit guilt readily and were generally evasive as to guilt or innocence, preferring to stress aspects of their stoic submission in their decision to plead. This sizable group of defendants appeared to perceive the total court process as being caught up in a monstrous organizational apparatus, in which the defendant role expectancies were not clearly defined. Reluctant to offend anyone in authority, fearful that clear cut statements on their part as to their guilt or innocence would be negatively construed, they adopted a stance of passivity, resignation and acceptance. Interestingly, they would in most instances invoke their lawyer as being the one who crystallized the available alternatives for them, and who was therefore the critical element in their decision-making process.

In order to determine which agent-mediator was most influential in altering the accused's perspectives as to his decision to plead or go to trial (regardless of the proposed basis of the plea), the same sample of defendants were asked to indicate the person who first suggested to them that they plead guilty. They were also asked to indicate which of the persons or officials who made such suggestion, was most influential in affecting their final decision to plead.

The following table indicates the breakdown of the responses to the two questions:

TABLE 20-2
Role of Agent-Mediators in Defendant's Guilty Plea

Person or Official	First Suggested Plea of Guilty	Influenced the Accused Most in His Final Decision to Plead
Judge	4	26
District Attorney	67	116
Defense counsel	407	411
Probation officer	14	3
Psychiatrist	8	1
Wife	34	120
Friends and kin	21	14
Police	14	4
Fellow inmates	119	14
Others	28	5
No response	8	10
Total	724	724

It is popularly assumed that the police, through forced confessions, and the district attorney, employing still other pressures, are most instrumental in the inducement of an accused to plead guilty. As Table 20-2 indicates, it is actually the defendant's own counsel who is most effective in this role. Further, this phenomenon tends to reinforce the extremely rational nature of criminal law administration, for an organization could not rely upon the sort of idiosyncratic measures employed by the police to induce confessions and maintain its efficiency, high production and overall rational-legal character. The defense counsel becomes the ideal agent-mediator since, as "officer of the court" and confidant of the accused and his kin, he lives astride both worlds and can serve the ends of the two as well as his own.

While an accused's wife, for example, may be influential in making him more amenable to a plea, her agent-mediator role has, nevertheless, usually been sparked and initiated by defense counsel. Further, although a number of first suggestions of a plea came from an accused's fellow jail inmates, he tended to rely largely on his counsel as an ultimate source of influence in his final decision. The defense counsel, being a crucial figure in the total organizational scheme in constituting a new set of perspectives for the accused, the same sample of defendants were asked to indicate at which stage of their contact with counsel was the suggestion of a plea made. There are three basic kinds of defense counsel available in Metropolitan Court: Legal-aid, privately retained counsel, and counsel assigned by the court (but may eventually be privately retained by the accused).

. . .

The overwhelming majority of accused persons, regardless of type of counsel, related a specific incident which indicated an urging or suggestion, either during the course of the first or second contact, that they plead guilty to a lesser charge if this could be arranged. Of all the agent-mediators, it is the lawyer who is most effective in manipulating an accused's perspectives, notwithstanding pressures that may have been previously applied by police, district attorney, judge or any of the agent-mediators that may have been activated by them. Legal-aid and assigned counsel would apparently be more likely to suggest a possible plea at the point of initial interview as response to pressures of time. In the case of the assigned counsel, the strong possibility that there is no fee involved, may be an added impetus to such a suggestion at the first contact.

In addition, there is some further evidence . . . of the perfunctory, ministerial character of the system in Metropolitan Court and similar criminal courts. There is little real effort to individualize, and the lawyer's role as agent-mediator may be seen as unique in that he is in effect a double agent. Although, as "officer of the court" he mediates between the court organization and the defendant, his roles with respect to each are rent by conflicts of interest. Too often these must be resolved in favor of the organization which provides him with the means for his professional existence. Consequently, in order to reduce the strains and conflicts imposed in what is ultimately an over-demanding role obligation for him, the lawyer engages in the lawyer-client "confidence game" so as to structure more favorably an otherwise onerous role system.

Conclusion

Recent decisions of the Supreme Court, in the area of criminal law administration and defendant's rights, fail to take into account three crucial aspects of social structure which may tend to render the more libertarian rules as nugatory. The decisions overlook (1) the nature of courts as formal organization; (2) the relationship that the lawyer-regular *actually* has with the court organization; and (3) the character of the lawyer-client relationship in the criminal court (the routine relationships, not those unusual ones that are described in "heroic" terms in novels, movies, and TV).

Courts, like many other modern large-scale organizations possess a monstrous appetite for the cooptation of entire professional groups as well as individuals. Almost all those who come within the ambit of organizational authority, find that their definitions, perceptions and values have been refurbished, largely in terms favorable to the particular organization and its goals. As a result, recent Supreme Court decisions may have a long range effect which is radically different from that intended or anticipated. The more libertarian rules will tend to produce the rather ironic end result of augmenting the *existing* organizational arrangements, enriching court organizations with more personnel and elaborate structure, which in turn will maximize organizational goals of "efficiency" and production. Thus, many defendants will find that courts will possess an even more sophisticated apparatus for processing them toward a guilty plea!

Note

1. The name is of course fictitious. However, the actual court which served as the universe from which the data were drawn is one of the largest criminal courts in the United States, dealing with felonies only. Female defendants in the years 1950 through 1964 constituted from 7-10% of the totals for each year.

CHAPTER SEVEN

JUDGES: SELECTION AND BACKGROUNDS

On September 1, 1976, shortly after 9:30 in the morning, the Subcommittee on Nominations of the Senate Judiciary Committee convened a public hearing on three federal judicial nominations. The first two nominations went smoothly, quickly, and predictably as is typical (see selection 21 for a description of the usual hearing) but the third nomination, that of United States District Judge Harry Wellford, did not. President Ford had submitted to the Senate the nomination of Judge Wellford from Memphis, Tennessee, to fill a vacancy on the United States Court of Appeals for the Sixth Circuit. Wellford, former state chairman of the Republican party in Tennessee and one-time campaign manager for Senator Howard Baker, had in 1971 with Baker's backing received his federal district court judgeship. Now Baker and his Republican senatorial colleague William Brock wanted Wellford to fill a Sixth Circuit vacancy that had previously been filled by a Tennessean (see the description of geographical representation on the appeals courts in selection 22). The elevation of Wellford would create a vacancy on the district bench that Baker and Brock would have a strong hand in filling. The only hitch was that Judge Wellford was bitterly opposed by civil rights and poverty groups in Memphis.

Civil rights groups accused Judge Wellford of being extremely conservative politically and highly insensitive to the rights of blacks and of poor people in general. Some civil rights lawyers also seriously questioned the judge's competence by pointing to his high reversal rate (about three times the overall reversal rate in the circuit) and to instances where he allegedly garbled questions of federal jurisdiction, procedure, and statutory and constitutional law.[1] This was emphasized at the Senate hearing as several witnesses made their case against Wellford. But the judge had supporters who testified on his behalf and they included leaders of the Memphis Bar Association and the Chief Judge of the United States Court of Appeals for the Sixth Circuit, a fellow Tennessean, Judge Harry Phillips. Furthermore, it was noted at the hearing that Judge Wellford received a rating of "Qualified" from the American Bar Association's Standing Committee on Federal Judiciary (see selection 22 for a consideration of the A.B.A. and its ratings).

The Wellford nomination was particularly troublesome for the liberal members of the Senate Judiciary Committee. Coming out of the hearing, a young lawyer on Senator Kennedy's staff whose task it was to evaluate the situation for the senator remarked to one of the editors of this book that "There's got to be a better way to pick judges."

This observation, although it reflects the frustration of the moment, is a reaction that is frequently found among many lawyers and some students of the judiciary. Interestingly, it is not confined to federal judicial selection but extends as well to the different methods used by the states to choose their judiciaries—and we will briefly examine these methods in this chapter. What informs the critical appraisals of selection methods is the recognition that the judicial position is at the heart of the court system and that what continues to characterize courts as special forms of conflict-management institutions is in particular the unique role of the judge as a conflict manager acting within more or less well-defined boundaries of legality, legitimacy, and notions of due process and "guaranteed" rights. Judged by these standards, Judge Wellford apparently failed in the eyes of a substantial portion of his judicial constituency. That he nonetheless received the nomination points up the problems that the federal selection process can pose for the judicial system. The legitimacy of a court is surely in jeopardy when a major portion of a judge's constituency has no faith in the judge's fairness or competency. The Wellford nomination also highlights the political nature of the selection process that must be appreciated to understand the problem-solving abilities, potential, and limitations of the particular kinds of people who become judges. It is significant to note, however, that the controversy over Wellford's qualifications, coming as it did during the presidential election campaign, gave the Democrats on the Senate Judiciary Committee an incentive to stall the nomination on the chance that the Democrats would win the election. The members of a new administration would be able to name one of their own instead of a former Republican politician. Consequently, the Senate Judiciary Committee took no action at all on the nomination and it died with Gerald Ford's electoral defeat (and incidentally the electoral defeat of Republican Senator Brock). The vacancy was eventually filled in 1977 by a Carter appointed Democrat, Gilbert Merritt, a considerably more liberal and younger man than Wellford and a person with good ties to the black community. Merritt also had been active in party politics and, among other activities, served as Treasurer of the state Democratic Party.

Merritt's nomination in part resulted from the new procedure instituted by President Carter for screening potential appeals court nominees. On February 14, 1977, the President issued an Executive Order whereby he created at least one judicial selection panel for each judicial circuit. Each panel consists of 11 members chosen by the President and they are charged with submitting within 60 days 5 names from which the President "may" select a nominee. Mr. Merritt's name was on the list submitted by the Sixth Circuit panel to fill the vacancy. Among those on that panel who passed on Merritt's qualifications was the well-known black political leader Coleman Young, the Mayor of Detroit.

The first two selections in this chapter focus on federal judicial selection. The Jackson reading is an account of judicial selection, particularly during the Nixon Administration, written from the perspective of a trained and sophisticated political journalist. The Goldman reading is a systematic political science analysis of the selection of judges for the courts of appeals. Goldman's findings regarding appeals court selection are similar to those of students of district court selection although selection of district court judges is influenced to a greater extent by the senator of the President's party from the state in which the vacancy has occurred.[2]

Selection of Supreme Court justices, although somewhat different from selection of lower court judges, is nonetheless a political process. The reading by John Schmidhauser (selection 23), which examines the backgrounds of Supreme Court justices, tells us much about the selection process.

State judicial selection methods, like federal judicial selection, involve negotiation processes and kinds of considerations similar to those discussed in the readings in this chapter. But the participants and the weight given to the various considerations vary according to the method used. There are five principal methods in use by the states. Two are electoral methods (partisan and nonpartisan elections); one is the functional equivalent of federal selection (gubernatorial selection); another is the method vigorously pushed by bar groups and the method to which a number of states have shifted ("merit" selection); and the last and least frequently used method is a holdover from colonial days (legislative selection).

TABLE 1
Principal Methods of Judicial Selection in the States

Partisan Election	Nonpartisan Election	Legislative Election	Gubernatorial Appointment	Merit Plan
Alabama[a]	Idaho[a]	Connecticut[a]	California[b]	Alaska
Arkansas	Kentucky[a,d]	Rhode Island[b]	Delaware	Arizona[a]
Georgia[a]	Michigan[a]	South	Hawaii[a]	Colorado[a]
Illinois[a]	Minnesota	Carolina[a]	Maine[a]	Florida[a,c]
Louisiana	Montana	Virginia[a]	Maryland[a]	Indiana[b]
Mississippi[a]	Nevada[d]		Massachusetts	Iowa[a]
New Mexico	North		New Hampshire	Kansas[a]
North Carolina	Dakota[d]		New Jersey[a]	Missouri[a]
Pennsylvania	Ohio[a]			Nebraska
Tennessee[a,c]	Oregon[a]			New York[a,b,c]
Texas[a]	South			Oklahoma[a,c]
West Virginia	Dakota[a]			Utah[a]
	Washington[a]			Vermont[a]
	Wisconsin			Wyoming[a]

[a] Minor court judges chosen by other methods.

[b] Appellate judges only. Other judges selected by different methods.

[c] Most but not all major judicial positions selected this way.

[d] Interim appointments filled by merit selection.

Source: *The Book of the States 1976-1977* (Lexington, Ky.: The Council of State Governments, 1976); and *Judicature*, Vols. 59 (1975-1976) and 60 (1976-1977).

Table 1 lists the states by the method in formal use to select most or all members of the judiciary. As we can see, 24 states use electoral methods. In partisan elections, individuals run for judicial office for a fixed term under a party label. Candidates may conduct a partisan campaign and be endorsed by party leaders and other candidates running for other offices. Nonpartisan elections are those in which judicial candidates must run without a party designation and in which there are typically some restrictions as to the kind of campaign that may be waged. In practice both electoral methods are similar in that judicial elections tend to be noncompetitive, low-visibility, low-turnout elections. Furthermore, it has been repeatedly found that a majority of the judges in states that use electoral methods first came to the bench as gubernatorial interim appointees, that is, they were appointed by the governor to fill vacancies that occurred between elections.[3] Once on the bench they had the inside track for reelection.

Gubernatorial selection with the advice and consent of another political body (such as state senate, governor's council) is the method used by 8 states. This method bears many similarities to federal judicial selection. Legislative selection by the full legislature is used by only 4 states, and it should be noted that in these states the governor plays an important part in the process.

So-called merit selection has captured the fancy of the organized bar and is the method advocated by judicial reformers. The American Bar Association and the American Judicature Society have long pushed for adoption of the merit plan. Its origins date back to the 1920s,[4] but the first major success of its advocates occurred in the state of Missouri in 1940. Subsequently the merit plan has also been known as the Missouri Plan. Essentially, its sponsors seek to remove partisan considerations from judicial selection and to replace them with strictly legal qualifications as determined primarily by the bar and the bench. States that have legally adopted merit selection have a judicial nominating commission composed of members of the organized bar (selected by the bar itself), the judiciary, and the lay public (chosen by the governor). For each judicial vacancy the nominating commission has the job of screening potential candidates, selecting a small group of people (usually 3) qualified for the position, and presenting their names to the governor. The governor is legally required to make the final selection from this list of qualified people. Today 14 states have legally required merit selection. (Most of them have adopted it since 1960.) Three other states require that merit selection be used to fill vacancies that arise between elections. In some other states and in some cities there is an informal merit-type process that is voluntarily followed by the governor or mayor, but these officials are under no legal obligation to follow the commission's recommendations and occasionally they do not.

There seems to be accumulating evidence that although party politics affects merit plans less than other plans, partisan considerations still affect the thinking of many members of the commissions and many governors.[5] It also appears that bar association ties, mores, and "politicking" influence merit plans more than they do other selection methods. There is no clear evidence, however, that merit selection produces better-qualified judges or results in patterns of judicial policy making that are distinct from those of judges selected by the more partisan methods.[6]

It is thought that tenure provisions may affect the way judges manage conflicts. The United States Constitution provides for life tenure for federal judges and guarantees that their salary will not be diminished. The basis of these provisions is the belief that job security is essential for an independent judiciary insulated from partisan pressures and considerations of popular approval. On the other hand, fixed terms of judicial office that require the incumbent to be reappointed or re-elected are thought to add an important democratic element to an essentially nondemocratic institution. Presumably the knowledge that at some point in time a judge in a limited-tenure system will be held accountable for past judicial performance will induce the judge not to become too far removed from the social, political, and economic consequences of judicial decisions. The judge may thus be induced not to become trapped within a closed system of legal thought divorced from reality.

In practice, however, judges, regardless of formal method of tenure, tend to serve on the bench at their pleasure. Re-election or reappointment in most instances is routine. Merit plan tenure consists of retention elections (essentially plebiscites) in which the electorate answers the ultimate question, shall Judge X remain in office? A vote of no confidence means the judge is out of a job. In practice, here too, merit selection has not in most instances resulted in serious scrutiny of judicial performance. Thus, in the overwhelming majority of retention elections the incumbent wins a vote of confidence.

What are the social, economic, political, and professional backgrounds of the people chosen for the bench? Lower federal court judges historically have tended to come from the middle or upper classes and have tended to have a history of party identification if not activism.[7] These characteristics are highlighted at the Supreme Court level, as the reading by Schmidhauser suggests. The composite portrait of the recent lower-court appointees (the Johnson, Nixon, and Ford appointees) is similar in some respects to the collective portrait of Supreme Court appointees and is also similar to the portrait of lower-court judges suggested by the historical evidence.[8] Interestingly, there are some differences in the background characteristics of recent Democratic administration appointees and recent Republican administration appointees, as shown in Table 2. Democratic appointees were more likely than Republican appointees to be engaged in a modest law practice at the time of appointment and to be members of the minority Catholic and Jewish religions. All groups had engaged in partisan activity to some extent and tended to have had prosecutorial and/or judicial experience. Women and blacks were seriously underrepresented in all three administrations.[9] Of course, Democratic President Johnson appointed almost all Democrats, and Republican Presidents Nixon and Ford appointed almost all Republicans. Preliminary analysis of President Carter's 43 judicial nominations through April 1978 reveals a continuation of these trends. However, the proportions of blacks and women nominated exceed those of all previous administrations.

A study of the backgrounds of state supreme court justices also found that the Catholic and Jewish state supreme court justices were likely to be Democrats and that most judges had prosecutorial and/or lower-court judicial experience.[10]

Ultimately we must confront the question, why should we care about how judges are selected and what their backgrounds happen to be? The answer is complex and can be derived from a number of premises. At the outset we can look back to the example that opened this chapter, the controversial Wellford nomination to the Court of Appeals for the Sixth Circuit. If the essential job of a judge is to try, at least for the short run, to solve the problems that inevitably arise when there are conflicting social, economic, and political interests, and if the judge's objective is to manage conflict within the framework of legality and thus to maintain the stability

TABLE 2
Selected Background Characteristics of Johnson, Nixon, and Ford Appointees
to the Federal District and Appeals Courts (Percent)

Characteristic	Johnson Appointees		Nixon Appointees		Ford Appointees	
	District	Appeals	District	Appeals	District	Appeals
Major Occupation						
Politics/Government	21.3	10.0	10.7	4.4	21.2	8.3
Judiciary	31.1	57.5	28.5	53.3	34.6	75.0
Large Law Firm	21.3	20.0	39.7	24.4	34.6	16.7
Moderate Law Firm	4.9	2.5	11.7	6.7	5.8	—
Solo or Small Law Firm	18.0	7.5	6.7	2.2	3.9	—
Other	3.3	2.5	2.8	8.9	—	—
Type of Experience						
Judicial	34.3	65.0	35.1	57.8	42.3	75.0
Prosecutorial	45.8	47.5	41.9	46.7	50.0	25.0
Neither judicial nor prosecutorial experience	33.6	20.0	36.3	17.8	30.8	25.0
Party Affiliation						
Democratic	94.8	95.0	7.8	6.7	21.2	8.3
Republican	5.2	5.0	92.2	93.3	78.8	91.7
Partisan Activism						
Prominent Partisan Activism	48.4	57.5	48.6	60.0	50.0	58.3
Religion						
Protestant	57.4	60.0	72.1	75.6	73.1	58.3
Catholic	31.9	25.0	18.9	15.6	17.3	33.3
Jewish	10.7	15.0	8.9	8.9	9.6	8.3
Race						
White	96.7	95.0	97.2	97.8	90.4	100.0
Black	3.3	5.0	2.8	—	5.8	—
Asian-American	—	—	—	2.2	3.9	—
Sex						
Male	98.4	97.5	99.4	100.0	98.1	100.0
Female	1.6	2.5	0.6	—	1.9	—
Total Number of Appointees	122	40	179	45	52	12

of the political system, then it is crucial that the person who occupies the position of judge possess the qualities, *and be perceived to possess the qualities,* necessary to manage conflict fairly and competently. But if, as with Judge Wellford, a substantial proportion of the judge's constituency believes otherwise, the very legitimacy of the judiciary is thrown into doubt. Analysis of judges' backgrounds and of the ways in which selection processes may stress certain types of backgrounds over others tells us something about the kinds of people who come to the bench and hints at their potential abilities and limitations in the art of conflict management.[11]

Furthermore, as Wellford's first nomination (in 1971) to the federal bench suggested, judicial appointments provide rewards and benefits to particular individuals and, at the symbolic level, to particular groups. Analysis of selection processes and backgrounds can give us some indication of the representativeness and accessibility of the political system. Finally, it is widely believed and amply documented in numerous judicial biographies that particular configurations of backgrounds and experiences shape the judicial philosophies and subsequent decision-making propensities of future judges (although aggregate analysis poses some formidable obstacles to the attempt to uncover such linkages as might exist, as we shall see in Part Three, Chapter Eleven). Yet it should be noted that empirical analyses of backgrounds and selection methods do not indicate that markedly diverging backgrounds emerge when one selection method is employed rather than another.[12] What is more, the evidence, although limited, suggests that, at least in terms of aggregate analysis, no one selection method produces markedly different decisional results (in terms of who wins) than another selection method. These findings suggest that however backgrounds and selection processes may affect the way judges and courts go about their business—if indeed they do have an effect—the influence is subtle and requires more refined analyses than have been utilized to date.[13] Alternatively, the findings suggest that the backgrounds of the members of the American judiciary, as well as the basic selection methods, are essentially similar, and that the distinctions that are frequently made, albeit of some importance and interest, should not obscure the facts that collectively, the judges are of the Establishment, and that wide areas of consensus exist as to how problems are to be solved and what alternatives are acceptable in the management of conflict.

Notes

1. Statement of William E. Caldwell, Lawyers' Committee For Civil Rights Under Law, before the Senate Committee on the Judiciary, September 1, 1976, *Hearings on the Nomination of Harry Wellford to Fill a Vacancy on the United States Court of Appeals for the Sixth Circuit* (unpublished hearing on file at the National Archives).

2. See, in general, Harold W. Chase, *Federal Judges: The Appointing Process* (Minneapolis: University of Minnesota Press, 1972); and Joel B. Grossman, *Lawyers and Judges* (New York: Wiley, 1965). As noted earlier, President Carter has changed the procedure for appointment to the appeals courts. It is too soon to assess the magnitude of the change in the process as described in selections 21 and 22. The tentative conclusion reached by some is that political considerations continue to be important. See Timothy D. Schellhardt, "Reshaping the Federal Judiciary," *Wall Street Journal*, February 23, 1978, p. 26.

3. See James Herndon, "Appointment as a Means of Initial Accession to State Courts of Last Resort," *North Dakota Law Review* 38 (1962), 60–73.

4. See Alan Ashman and James J. Alfini, *The Key to Judicial Merit Selection: The Nominating Process* (Chicago: The American Judicature Society, 1974); Burton M. Atkins, "Merit Selection of State Judges," *Florida Bar Journal* 50 (April 1976), 203–211; and Richard Watson and Rondal Downing, *The Politics of the Bench and the Bar* (New York: Wiley, 1969).

5. See Watson and Downing, *op. cit.*; and James J. Alfini, "Partisan Pressures on the Nonpartisan Plan," *Judicature* 58 (December 1974), 216-221.

6. See Bradley C. Canon, "The Impact of Formal Selection Processes on the Characteristics of Judges—Reconsidered," *Law and Society Review* 6 (1972), 579-593; Burton M. Atkins and Henry R. Glick, "Formal Judicial Recruitment and State Supreme Court Decisions," *American Politics Quarterly* 2 (1974), 427-449. Also see, in general, Craig R. Ducat and Victor E. Flango, "In Search of Qualified Judges," paper presented at annual meeting of the American Political Science Association, 1975; and Stuart S. Nagel, *Comparing Elected and Appointed Judicial Systems* (Beverly Hills: Sage, 1973, American Politics Series).

7. See Kermit L. Hall, "101 Men: The Social Composition and Recruitment of the Antebellum Lower Federal Judiciary, 1829-1861," *Rutgers-Camden Law Journal* 7 (1976), 199-226; and his "Social Backgrounds and Judicial Recruitment: A Nineteenth Century Perspective on the Lower Federal Judiciary," *Western Political Quarterly* 29 (1976), 243.

8. *Ibid.*

9. Note that during the first year of his presidency, President Carter appointed two black Americans to appeals court positions. Black appointees constituted 20 percent of all appeals court appointments during 1977—four times the proportion appointed during the five years of Johnson's presidency. Carter will have ample opportunity to fill judgeships with blacks, other minorities, and women. In 1978 Congress enacted legislation creating more than 150 new judgeships. If to these are added the vacancies in existing judgeships, by early 1979, with half his term of office completed, Carter will have had the opportunity to appoint more than one-third of the entire judicial branch of government.

10. Bradley C. Canon, "Characteristics and Career Patterns of State Supreme Court Justices," *State Government* 45 (1972), 34-41.

11. See Nagel, *op. cit.*, and the discussion and readings in Part 3, Chapter 11.

12. Nagel, *op. cit.*, and Canon, "The Impact of Formal Selection Processes," *op. cit.*

13. Cf. the articles by Levin (selection 29), Vines (selection 32), and Giles and Walker (selection 33).

21

Federal Roulette

Donald D. Jackson

Federal judges are chosen by a sort of political roulette. The participants in the process are constant—senators, perhaps a congressman, the Justice Department, the President, campaigning candidates, the ABA—but their relative strength varies with the individual cases. Each selection is a fresh spin of the wheel.

The heaviest hand is usually the senator's, but senators approach the responsibility differently. Some are jealous of their prerogative and powerful enough to insist that their man be named. Lyndon Johnson held up the confirmation of thirteen judges in 1959 until President Eisenhower agreed to Johnson's candidate for a Texas vacancy. Johnson retained his influence as Vice President, exercising a veto over Texas nominees.

John McClellan of Arkansas, a key member of the Judiciary Committee, yields no ground once he settles on a name. The late Senator Robert Kerr of Oklahoma bulldozed the appointment of his friend Luther Bohanon, who was appointed by President Kennedy despite a "not qualified" [rating] from the ABA.

Other senators—former Senator Frank Lausche of Ohio was one—leave judicial selection to the executive branch. Hugh Scott and Richard Schweiker of Pennsylvania often sent a list of four or five to the Justice Department with no preference expressed, thus protecting themselves from the rancor of disappointed runners-up. Still other senators submit a list of names, but follow it with a discreet phone call identifying their real choice. The ABA rating becomes part of the smoke. "They'll send up a name they know will be rejected by the ABA," a Justice Department man says, "just so the candidate back home thinks the senator is looking out for him."

The balance of power shifts with each case; the importance of ideology, professional qualifications, and cronyism ebbs and flows with senatorial attitudes and those of the President's men. If there are two administration-party senators in the same state, they may make the decision jointly (like Scott and Schweiker), or take turns picking judges (like New York Senators Jacob Javits and James Buckley), or divide the state in half (like ex-Senator John Sherman Cooper and Marlow Cook of Kentucky). With no administration-party senator in the state, the Justice Department men will usually have a freer hand, although a powerful congressman, a governor, or a state chairman may fill the vacuum.

"Nobody likes to talk about it," a senatorial aide told me. "They all appoint their guy for personal reasons and they don't want to say that. It's because somewhere, sometime, he did something for the senator or he's a friend of the senator."

An astute judicial candidate knows where the levers of power are, and knows how to play them. Judge J. Sam Perry of Illinois, now semi-retired, is one of the few who have candidly described the machinations.

"I gambled," he said. "I saw a man—Paul Douglas—who looked as though he might be elected to the Senate. I backed him, and as a result I had his support. . . . I tried to obtain the appointment once before and learned that it requires not one but two senators. . . . I was out of politics and they did not need me. I decided I had better get back into politics, which I did. I learned that everyone shoots at the number-one choice, so I told each of the senators not to make me first. . . . That proved to be pretty good strategy because everybody else was shot off and, no use lying about it, I helped to shoot them off. The result was I landed on top."

The process begins when a senator submits a name, or names, to the Justice Department. He may consult powerful politicians back home (Mayor Daley of Chicago had enough influence to get appointments for his close friends Abraham Marovitz and William Lynch), his state bar association, colleagues in Congress, or his list of contributors. The Justice Department turns the names over to the FBI and ABA, both of which commence investigations. A negative FBI report can be fatal, but senators are not permitted to see the reports; a Justice Department man summarizes them for Senator James Eastland, the Judiciary Committee chairman. The FBI is particularly alert to evidence of immorality, skirmishes with the law (one judge had three drunk-driving citations, but was appointed anyway, after he made a vow of abstinence to a Catholic bishop), and any political, business, or social associations (membership in segregated clubs, involvement in left-wing causes) the agents consider significant.

At the same time the ABA judiciary committee checks the nominee out with lawyers, judges, and others to get a bead on his professional qualifications. If the FBI and ABA reports are both positive and the senator agrees with the administration on a single name, the President then announces the nomination and submits it to the Senate. The Senate Judiciary Committee holds a perfunctory hearing, followed by a vote to confirm and congratulations all around. The Senate fulfills its duty of advice and consent, says University of Chicago law professor Philip Kurland, "by paying less attention to the confirmation process of a federal judge than to the price of bean soup in the Senate restaurant." Thirty-two new judges were routinely confirmed within six days in 1970.

John Duffner, executive assistant to the deputy attorney general, briefs judicial nominees on their hearing. "I can write the script for the hearing," he says. "I tell them that the only senators likely to be there are Eastland, McClellan, and Hruska [a Nebraska Republican]. I tell them to volunteer nothing, that it's like the Army—the longer you keep the first sergeant from knowing your last name, the better off you are. I suggest that they answer questions only and don't bring any witnesses.

"The committee will refer to the ABA report, and then they'll recognize the senator or whoever the man's sponsor is. Then Eastland asks if the biographical sketch they have is accurate, and he'll ask the nature of the man's practice—I tell them to hold it down to a minute and emphasize their trial experience. Then McClellan will give a lecture about how judges have to think of protecting society as well as the individual. I tell them to listen politely and to watch for a question at the end of it, but don't volunteer anything unless there's a question. Hruska will ask if he's an officer or director in a profit-making corporation and point out that he's supposed to resign if he is.

"Then Eastland will ask if the candidate has anything to say. I suggest that they say thanks and that they'll do their best. The senators get impatient if a man brings his family and friends along—one did one time and Eastland got irritated. They don't go into the judge's philosophy. It's all over in about ten minutes."

"I have the impression that the Justice Department is juggling so many things that there isn't much deliberate thought given to judicial selection," says Professor Sheldon Goldman. . . . "Even the deputy attorney general doesn't think that much about it; the assistants run the show. There's not much thinking through and consideration of who might be best. The politicians usually take the initiative." Another scholar, political scientist Richard Burke, investigated judicial appointments between 1929 and 1955 and identified the major elements in the selection equation as personal friendship, partisan service, and the system itself. "Professional merit and qualifications," he concluded, "have ranked with other secondary factors such as age, race, religion, philosophy and ideology. Superior judicial temperament and professional qualifications have seldom been the basis for selection."

Presidents will occasionally cross party lines to appoint a judge, but the reasons, again, have more to do with politics than professional ability. Eisenhower's appointments were 95 percent Republican, Kennedy's were 92 percent Democratic, and Johnson's 94 percent Democratic. Nixon's first-term selections were 93 percent Republican. Opposite-party appointments are likely to be low on an administration's priority list.

President Kennedy named Republican Harold Tyler to a seat in New York. "I remember Bobby Kennedy saying we had to appoint a Republican," a member of the Kennedy Justice Department recalled. "Tyler was head of the civil-rights division in the department under Ike, and he stayed on after the Kennedys came in. That really impressed Bob, so he picked him after checking it out with the senators."

The Nixon administration's arrangement with California Democratic Senators John Tunney and Alan Cranston ensures that every fourth California appointment is a Democrat. The *quid pro quo* is said to be the Californians' support of the administration's judicial nominees. Democratic Senator Abraham Ribicoff of Connecticut was able to negotiate the nomination of Jon Newman, his former administrative assistant, through some accommodation of power, perhaps involving Ribicoff's support of ex-FBI director (and Connecticut resident) L. Patrick Gray.

An intense personal campaign may sometimes net a judgeship. Robert Grant of Indiana lined up support from eight congressmen. Myron Gordon of Wisconsin lobbied his senators and the Johnson administration for several months. And once in a while, just often enough to forestall abject cynicism, a judge reaches the bench for no good reason other than his pre-eminent qualifications. New York's Marvin Frankel was sought out by then-Senator Robert Kennedy on the recommendation of law professors. Ex-Senator Jack Miller of Iowa asked his state bar association to come up with three names, and he chose William Stuart from their list. Nixon appointments Thomas Flannery of the District of Columbia and Philip Tone of Illinois are regarded as non-political lawyers of proven ability and integrity.

. . .

Eisenhower rated "solid common sense" highly in his judicial nominees, and regarded previous judicial experience as a plus. [Attorneys General] Brownell and Rogers, both upper-echelon members of the legal Establishment, may have given less ground to senatorial sensibilities than their successors. Eisenhower-appointed judges include several, such as Edward Gignoux of Maine, Frank Johnson of Alabama, and Edward Devitt of Minnesota, who are widely admired for their courage and intelligence. He also appointed Julius Hoffman of Illinois and John Sirica of the District of Columbia.

The pre-Watergate John Sirica was generally regarded as a rigorously honest judge of modest intellectual attainments, notable chiefly for the tough criminal sentences that had earned him the nickname "Maximum John." The son of an Italian immigrant, he was an amateur boxer while working his way through Georgetown law school. (He accompanied former heavyweight champion Jack Dempsey, who was best man at his wedding, on a bond-selling tour during World War II.) . . . It was Sirica's threat of a heavy sentence, together with his rigid non-partisanship, which propelled James McCord into the disclosures that broke the Watergate case.

"I want for our courts individuals with respected professional skill," John Kennedy said in 1961, "incorruptible character, firm judicial temperament, the rare inner quality to know when to temper justice with mercy, and the intellectual capacity to protect and illuminate the Constitution and our historic values. . . ."

But Kennedy appointments, particularly in the South, have been repeatedly faulted for falling short of that standard. Nicholas Katzenbach, a deputy attorney general under Kennedy and later Johnson's Attorney General, described the Kennedy policy as "play ball with the ABA, play ball with the senator, do the best you can, don't let anyone through who has personally attacked the President." This screen was porous enough to admit at least five Southern judges whose decisions were consistently pro-segregation— William Cox of Mississippi, E. Gordon West of Louisiana, Robert Elliott of Georgia, Clarence Allgood and Walter Gewin of Alabama. Victor Navasky, author of *Kennedy Justice*, wrote that there was an "absence of any deep, abiding and overriding Kennedy commitment to the integrity and quality of the Southern judiciary itself." Navasky found "no aspect of Robert Kennedy's attorney generalship . . . more vulnerable to criticism" than his judicial appointments in the South. Southern senators, of course, share the responsibility: Cox was Eastland's man, West was a protégé of Senator Russell Long, Elliott a close associate of Senator Herman Talmadge.

Kennedy appointed eight judges who were rated unqualified by the ABA. All but one were named in his first year in office. "The general rule is that the appointments in the first year are the worst," says a high-ranking ABA lawyer. "Presidents are more susceptible to political pressure then. They have more debts to be paid."

Political scientist Mary Curzan contends that in racial terms Eisenhower's record is overrated and Kennedy's underrated. She appraises five of JFK's 16 Southern appointments as segregationists, compared with five of 15 named by Ike. She argues that the racist Kennedy appointments received more publicity, and that the ABA and the press were biased in favor of Eisenhower.

The Kennedy men generally trusted their own judgment of a nominee's character over that of the ABA or others. Sometimes that judgment succumbed to political expediency, but, as Anthony Lewis of the *New York Times* wrote, "the nominees also include a high proportion of the best men." . . .

Lyndon Johnson's career as a judge-maker divides neatly into two periods; before and after Morrissey. Francis X. Morrissey was the Kennedy family retainer backed by Senator Edward Kennedy and nominated to a Massachusetts federal judgeship by Johnson in 1965. Morrissey had received a law degree from a Georgia "diploma mill," then twice failed to pass the bar examination. His pathetically weak credentials inspired the ABA to put up a fight. In a rare breach of the judicial curtain, a sitting federal judge (Chief Judge Charles Wyzanski of the Massachusetts District) publicly opposed his nomination. The Judiciary Committee voted to confirm the nomination, and there were reportedly enough votes in the Senate to get Morrissey through, but Kennedy finally withdrew his name.

Including the Morrissey nomination, six of Johnson's first fifty-six appointments drew gasps of "not qualified" from the ABA. A strong advocate of senatorial courtesy, Johnson preferred to go along with senatorial nominations. After the Morrissey debacle and a long meeting with ABA leaders, however, he changed course. From then on, all his nominees had ABA backing. . . . The Johnson judges remained partisan Democrats, but their intellectual and professional quality rose visibly. Many are among those rated most highly by constitutional lawyers: James Doyle of Wisconsin, Marvin Frankel and Jack Weinstein of New York, Robert Merhige of Virginia, Frederick Heebe of Louisiana, and William Keady of Mississippi, among others. All were named between 1965 and 1968.

Johnson brought his familiar weaving style of political maneuver to the demands of judicial selection. "There were two District Court vacancies in Virginia," a Washington lawyer recalled. "Senator [Harry] Byrd was backing Richard Kellam, Senator [William] Spong was behind John Mackenzie, and Robert Merhige had the support of the Reynolds Metal Company in Virginia, which was a big donor to the Johnson campaign. So he had three men for two spots. Johnson's contribution to the workings of democracy was to elevate Judge John Butzner to the Fourth Circuit Court of Appeals, which gave him three openings in Virginia. Everybody was happy. *Voilà*, eh?"

The twelve members of the ABA committee on the federal judiciary—a chairman and one from each of the eleven federal circuits, chosen by the ABA president—are a cadre of well-established, generally conservative old boys who patrol the summit of their profession. There has never been a black, Spanish-speaking, or female member. Most committeemen are in their fifties or sixties.

The committee moves into action as soon as a candidate for a federal judgeship is proposed. The member for the circuit where the seat is located conducts a series of interviews (often as many as twenty-five) aimed at assessing the potential judge's ability, temperament, and integrity. The choice of whom to see is up to the committeeman, but the list will usually include federal and state judges, the "leading lawyers" in the community ("anyone in the circuit will know who they are," one member says), and attorneys who have opposed the candidate in court. The circuit member also analyzes transcripts of cases the candidate has argued.

"We try to get a fair cross-section of opinion," says Lawrence Walsh of New York, a recent committee chairman and former federal judge. "The standards we apply are is he competent, does he have a [judicial] temperament, and does he have integrity—not whether we like him or not. By temperament we mean is he capable of intellectual detachment, can he hold his mind open? Integrity may be the least subjective area, except perhaps for intellectual integrity. The question is whether he is biased, whether there is crookedness in his reasoning. The lines aren't easy to draw. You approach it as if you're looking for a lawyer for your best client in that neighborhood." The committee rejects District Court candidates over sixty-three, and regards trial experience as essential.

The circuit committeeman writes a report on the candidate and recommends a rating. The full committee then votes, usually in a telephone "conference call," and the result is passed on to the Justice Department. The definitions of the ratings—qualified, well qualified, and exceptionally well qualified—are subjective, as are the committee estimates of a man's qualifications. "We each have the definition in our own minds," Walsh says. "I define qualified as meaning that nothing adverse has been found and he has the qualities to do the job and handle himself adequately. Well qualified means a man of excellence who would be among those one would seek out for the job. Exceptionally well qualified is a brilliant, enormously capable man."

The ABA's influence has oscillated from President to President, rising when Republicans were in the oval office and dipping during Democratic rule. It established a secure foothold during the Eisenhower years, and solidified its position under Nixon, who [until his last day in office] refused to appoint candidates who lacked ABA approval.

Critics have focused on the committee's secrecy (the ABA refused to release its dossier on Otto Kerner to the Justice Department, for example, even after Kerner was indicted), its conservative orientation (it opposed Louis Brandeis in 1916, but rated G. Harrold Carswell well qualified for the Fifth Circuit Court of Appeals in 1969), and its willingness to accept the marginally qualified.

"Their standards are minimal," says Harvard [Law Professor Alan] Dershowitz. "They don't begin to approach what they should be. There is a strong presumption of suitability. There should be public hearings. The ABA doesn't really get a cross-section—I know of an appointment in Massachusetts where there was all kinds of opposition, but none of the opponents was approached by the ABA." "My impression," adds Stanford [Law Professor Anthony] Amsterdam, "is that screening for the lower courts is a matter of asking round over the lunch table at whatever restaurant gets the carriage trade for the local commercial lawyers."

. . .

Walsh concedes that a "presumption of suitability" exists. "If it's a criticism, it's valid," he says. "It's true. It's hard to turn the other way. We have no sanctions except our own powers of persuasion. We can't block a nomination. An opponent of a nomination has the burden of proof."

Walsh and other committeemen deny that ideological bias enters the process. "We avoid passing judgment on a candidate's political views or philosophy," he says. "It may be a factor," another member allows, "but it's unconscious if it is. If you're concerned about built-in prejudices, the whole thing starts to fall apart. I feel strongly that lawyers won't do that, that they'll be efficient and honest. Am I naïve?"

. . .

. . . Richard Nixon . . . appointed more judges to federal courts than any previous President. In his first four years he named 142 District Court and 37 appellate-court judges, plus four Supreme Court justices. In his second term he [passed] the record 194 federal-court appointments made by Franklin Roosevelt.

. . .

Nixon's selections have brought the partisan lineup of the federal bench close to parity. In 1969, Democratic district judges outnumbered Republicans by more than two to one. By the end of a first term in which he named 132 Republicans and 10 Democrats to District Court seats, Nixon had brought the total to 209 Democrats and 180 Republicans.

. . .

As a presidential candidate in 1960, Nixon endorsed an ABA proposal that both parties pledge to maintain the then equal political alignment on the bench. "I believe it is essential," he said, "that the best qualified lawyers and judges available be appointed to judicial office, and . . . that the number of judges in federal courts from each of the major political parties be approximately equal." John Kennedy and the Democrats disagreed, and the ensuing imbalance was the result.

Between then and now, however, "law and order" became an important political issue, with Nixon its most ardent advocate. A stout-hearted identification with the "peace forces" as against the "criminal forces" became a Nixonian criterion for judicial appointments at all levels. Judges who dissented from this simplistic interpretation, or who defended the liberal and expansive decisions of the Warren Court, were classified by the President as "softheaded."

"You can't be a federal judge today," says a Washington lawyer with government experience under both parties, "unless you believe the whole hardnosed line. It's like getting ahead in the FBI—you have to be for the death penalty, you have to regard all the criminal decisions of the Warren Court as wrong. I've never seen such stereotypes. Any background of liberalism or orientation toward the Bill of Rights is a disqualifier. Or a philosophical kinship with Learned Hand, say, the idea that better one guilty man go free than an innocent man be hanged—if you feel that way, you don't make it. There are some exceptions, where you have liberal Republican senators like [Charles] Percy or Javits. But if there's no liberal senator, then you get one-hundred-percent law and order [in Nixon's Washington]."

. . .

In California, the three-to-one trade with Democratic senators gave Nixon's men an unchecked hand in the appointment of fourteen other judges in his first term. One was Samuel Conti, a former state judge, who believes that "if judges don't have the intestinal fortitude to send someone to jail, they should get out of the judge business. This is too good a country," he declared in a 1971 interview, "to go down the drain with permissiveness." One of Conti's first acts on the bench was to deny bail to defendants in a Selective Service case, in defiance of the federal bail-reform act.

Another California appointment, Lawrence T. Lydick, is a former Nixon law partner. A third, Spencer Williams, was a losing candidate for state attorney general on the ticket headed by Governor Ronald Reagan. Williams won a qualified rating from the ABA despite minimal legal experience. He dismissed without a hearing charges that San Quentin prisoners were beaten by guards after a shooting at the penitentiary.

. . .

In the South, where there are few Republican senators to impede him (and the few are conservatives like J. Strom Thurmond of South Carolina and John Tower of Texas), Nixon's selections have followed a similar pattern. "The essential requirement seems to be strong services to the conservative wing of the Republican party and an anti-Bill of Rights position," says a Duke University law professor.

Charles Clark, a Nixon appointment to the Fifth Circuit appellate court in the South, once defended former Mississippi Governor Ross Barnett in a case arising out of Barnett's refusal to permit James Meredith to attend the state university. Joe Ingraham compiled a pro-segregation record as a Texas District Court judge before Nixon promoted him to the Fifth Circuit. Robert Varner of Alabama, a friend of former Postmaster General Winton Blount, had been president of a segregated bar association in Montgomery. At one trial Varner asked that blacks be removed from the jury because "white people in the area have not accepted the idea of eating with Negroes." He expressed the view that "a judge should not commit himself one way or the other on segregation. It is a political philosophy, isn't it?"

Friends at the top were helpful to several other Nixon appointees. Ozell Trask of the Ninth Circuit Court of Appeals was a former law partner of Richard Kleindienst. Eugene Wright, also chosen for the Ninth Circuit, is a close friend of John Ehrlichman. Stanley Blair of Maryland was once Spiro Agnew's administrative assistant. Charles Richey of the District of Columbia was another pal of Agnew's.

Richard McLaren's appointment was interesting because of its haste. McLaren, as head of the anti-trust division in the Justice Department, approved the controversial settlement of an anti-trust action against ITT after originally favoring prosecution. A promised $400,000 contribution to the 1972 Republican convention was allegedly related to the settlement. McLaren's appointment to the district bench in Chicago was one of the speediest on record. He was nominated, approved by the Judiciary Committee, and confirmed by the Senate all in one day—December 2, 1971. The process normally takes [considerably longer]. . . .

The nomination of William Frey of Arizona followed a bizarre chain of events. Frey was the choice of the state's Republican leaders, but the bar association had doubts about his temperament. Senator Paul Fannin tried to finesse the situation by endorsing another man more acceptable to the bar. He called Frey an outstanding candidate, but said the other man was "even more outstanding." The other man then underwent a physical examination and learned that he had cancer. A short time later he committed suicide. Since Fannin had committed himself to Frey as a second choice, the appointment was his.

"I've heard other lawyers say that Nixon's judges are all law-and-order-minded," says F. Lee Bailey, "but I haven't seen evidence of a general pattern to back that up." Bailey's is a minority view among the dozens of lawyers I spoke with, but it may be related to where he sits—in Massachusetts. Where liberal Republican senators share the appointing power with the administration—in Massachusetts, Illinois, New York, New Jersey, and Oregon, for example—the quality of Nixon's judges has been higher.

"We draw a line here between appointments before and since Percy," says an attorney in Chicago. "His appointments are head and shoulders above what's been done around here before." Percy works with the Chicago Council of Lawyers, a band of liberal-minded young attorneys, in screening candidates. "He tested us by asking what we thought about some liberal judges who were ideologically pure but lousy judges," a council officer says. "He hasn't named any flaming liberals, but they are all solid and capable men." At least two, Frank McGarr and Philip Tone, are ranked among the best on the federal bench.

The highly regarded Levin Campbell of Massachusetts, now on the First Circuit Court of Appeals, was supported by Senator Edward Brooke. Jacob Javits sponsored several highly rated appointments, including Circuit Judge Walter Mansfield and District Judges Arnold Bauman and Murray Gurfein. Frederick Lacey of New Jersey was backed by liberal Senator Clifford Case.

Nixon's appointments across party lines have generally been either Southern Democrats whose ideology is indistinguishable from his, or the beneficiaries of trade-offs with Democratic senators. Eldon Mahon of Texas (a nephew of Congressman George Mahon), Solomon Blatt, Jr., of South Carolina, and James King of Florida are all Nixon's kind of Democrat.

L. Clure Morton of Tennessee, whose brother was a campaign aide to Senator Howard Baker, was considered safely conservative until he surprised the administration by ordering an increase in busing to desegregate Nashville schools. Agnew's friend Charles Richey may have been another surprise. He eschewed the law-and-order line and urged instead that judges become experts in behavioral science. He spent one four-week vacation touring federal prisons to show inmates that "at least one federal judge" considered them "human beings." Richey's name came up in the testimony of Watergate witness John Dean, who said White House aides had covertly pressured the judge to get a delay in the civil trial arising out of the Watergate burglary.

The longest-standing federal-court vacancy as of 1973 was in Wisconsin, where Nixon tried for two years to gain ABA approval for Congressman Glenn Davis. The ABA's rejection was based on his lack of trial experience. A Nixon candidate in Illinois was withdrawn after he was accused of anti-Semitism; another, in South Carolina, was dropped after charges of race prejudice were made.

22

Judicial Appointments to the United States Courts of Appeals

Sheldon Goldman

This article explores the complex judicial selection process for appointments to the United States Courts of Appeals. The data have been largely gathered from a systematic study of certain Justice Department files for each of the eighty-four judges in active service on the appeals courts during part or all of the period between 1961 and 1964. The object of this paper is to analyze the various components of the selection process and, in particular, to examine the role of politics and ideology in the process and thus the kind of people appointed. Our attention is focused on the Eisenhower and Kennedy Administrations. . . .

I

The judges on the United States Courts of Appeals were nominated for their positions by the President and were appointed by him after the United States Senate had given its advice and consent. Behind this simple statement lies a complex reality of customs, pressures, expectations, and constraints that operate on the participants in the appointment process. The first reality—and an obvious one to casual observers of the process—is that the President's men in the Justice Department, *i.e.* the Attorney General and especially the Deputy Attorney General and his assistants, are primarily responsible for judicial selection. Thus, our attention must focus on the Justice Department rather than the White House.

The appointment process "begins" (at least analytically) by the President's men considering various lawyers or judges for a particular vacancy. The sources of names of prospective candidates for appeals court judgeships are varied. The President occasionally will have his personal choice whom the Justice Department will then promote. But, in more cases, the Deputy, or, indeed, the Attorney General, will take the initiative and activate candidacies of those thought to be well suited for the particular vacancy. . . .

Justice officials use their vast network of friends, acquaintances, and friends of friends as a source for possible appointees. This is not done out of personal favoritism but out of a desire to insure the selection of highly competent people who will reflect credit on the administration. Illustrative of the personal involvement of a high Justice official is a letter to the Attorney General from a candidate who was later appointed to the bench. The candidate had been extremely active in the preceding presidential campaign and had made the acquaintance of the Attorney General, who had also been active in the campaign. The letter began with a first name salutation and continued.

> Further in connection with our conversation of last week regarding the vacancy on the United States Court of Appeals for the—Circuit, this is to advise that both Senators—and—will support me. You will be receiving letters from them within a few days, and I told them, as you suggested, to send copies to [the deputy].
>
> Enjoyed visiting with you and hope to see you again before too long.

It is hard to determine the number of appeals court judges who were initially selected and promoted by the Justice Department officials on their own or at the instigation of the President. The difficulty is that for political reasons the department prefers its suggestions to become the recommendations of the senators of the President's party from the appointee's state. However, it is probably no exaggeration to suggest that close to one out of five Eisenhower or Kennedy appeals court appointees had his nomination initiated by the Justice Department.

The next obvious source of names of potential judicial candidates is the senator or senators from the President's party representing the state for which the appointment is slated. . . .

Another source of suggestions for candidates is the political leaders in the President's party, such as veteran congressmen, state party chairmen, governors, national committeemen, and mayors of large cities. Prospective candidates are also often suggested by high-level administration men, by law school deans responding to queries from Justice officials or writing on their own initiative, by friends of Justice officials, and by friends of friends. Indeed, those desiring their own appointment have been known to directly inform the Justice Department of their availability. Still another source of suggestions is the judiciary; about forty percent of the Justice Department files of the Eisenhower and Kennedy appointees contained letters of recommendation from state or federal judges.

When a vacancy occurs on an appeals court due to death or retirement, the sources mentioned will readily suggest candidates to fill the vacancy. The Justice Department maintains files on some of the likely candidates. Usually the Department will consider those candidates proposed by the senators and the party organization before promoting their own. Often it turns out that the varied sources will independently recommend the same individual for a particular vacancy. This is ordinarily taken as evidence of a strong candidacy.

The problem for the President's men is to investigate informally and evaluate the proposed candidates in the light of certain expectations and constraints. . . .

When the senator(s) and party leaders from the state scheduled to receive the appointment agree on one candidate who subsequently appears qualified by the Justice Department's standards, that candidate's nomination is virtually certain, and confirmation by the Senate is only a matter of time. However, when Justice officials select a man from many submitted names, or have their own candidate to promote and are willing to challenge the senator(s) and state party's nominee, extensive negotiations have to be undertaken with these political leaders. Once the Justice officials have secured the necessary political clearance for the selected candidate, the FBI is instructed to investigate the candidate. When the FBI report is in and nothing adverse has unexpectedly been uncovered, the Attorney General makes his recommendation to the President. Shortly thereafter, the nomination is announced from the White House and sent to the Senate.

The Senate Judiciary Committee is usually briefed on impending nominations, and committee members, particularly the chairman, may indicate what trouble, if any, there will be in having the committee render its approval. The committee meets in closed sessions to discuss the nominations and to decide when to hold hearings. . . .

In all, it is not unusual for the time span between the opening of a vacancy and the administration of the judicial oath to the appointee to be approximately one year or longer. The average time it took to appoint the eighty-four appeals judges actively serving during part or all of the 1961–1964 period was seven months. The process is long and involved, yet, for appointments to the appeals courts, the Justice Department ordinarily has much leeway in determining who will finally be appointed. Therefore, it is useful to focus our attention on the expectations and constraints, some of which have been mentioned in passing, within which the President's men in the Justice Department operate.

II

A. Qualified Appointees

The President's men in the Justice Department strive to appoint competent people to appeals court posts. They strive because they wish to do a "good" job, *i.e.*, to support these important courts, and, in general, avoid the damaging image of "playing politics" with the judiciary. The criteria for being "qualified" or "well qualified" are ambiguous and difficult to define but include being a "respected" lawyer or judge and having the professional competence and judicial temperament thought to befit an appointee to the appeals courts. Trial court experience is usually a plus mark in the evaluation of candidates. Public legal experience seems to be prominent in the backgrounds of the appointees.

There are also external pressures to appoint unquestionably qualified people to appeals court posts. Newspaper editorial writers are fond of delivering sermons on the necessity of "high quality" judicial appointments. By lauding good appointments, newspapers help cultivate an image that most administrations presumably seek.

While Justice officials would like to appoint the "magnas" and "summas" of the legal-judicial profession, they often find that only "cums" have survived the hurdles of the appointment process. The American Bar Association, through its Standing Committee on Federal Judiciary, believes it can discern the "magnas" and "summas" of the profession and has taken upon itself the task of promoting such candidates for federal court appointments. The committee has played an active role in the appointment process since the Eisenhower Administration. Lawyers and judges from the states of the leading contenders (whose names are supplied by Justice officials) are canvassed, and the candidates are given ratings. A sample survey of lawyers indicated that only 7.7 percent of the sample had actually been contacted by the ABA committee, and, of these, 70 percent held national, state, or local bar association positions. From 1957 through 1960 Judge Walsh was Deputy Attorney General and was on exceptionally cordial terms with committee chairman Bernard Segal. The committee and the Kennedy Administration were also on friendly terms, but members of the Justice Department, in several instances, would find that only the "Wall Street type" lawyers in the large cities were being initially contacted by the committee. "Wall Street types" are presumably different in attitudes or values from labor union or individually practicing lawyers.

The problem, ultimately, is the large degree of subjectivity involved in separating the "cums" from the "summas." At times the ABA committee itself has had difficulty reaching a consensus for a rating. On those occasions when both the committee and the President's men agree that among the contenders there are many "cums" but only one "summa," other constraints on Justice officials might encourage them to bypass the "summa" and support a "cum." In such cases, the committee can help Justice officials withstand the political pressures to bypass the "summa" by exerting and rallying outside pressure in favor of the "summa." The committee, it would then seem, could define its role as that of providing countervailing power to the political pressures inherent in the appointment process that might be impelling the Justice Department towards the nomination of a "cum" instead of an acknowledged "summa."

In practice, the ABA committee works with Justice officials and often strengthens the hand of the Department in dealings with senators and other political actors. . . .

In sum, there is often great difficulty in defining not only who is qualified, but who is *best* qualified for a particular post. In the final analysis, the ABA committee provides the major external pressure on the Justice Department to appoint obviously qualified people to the federal courts. . . .

B. Political Considerations: Party as a Factor

Of the 84 judges in active service during part or all of the 1961–1964 period, 79 (ninety-four percent) were affiliated with the same political party as the President who appointed them. Furthermore, about 4 out of 5 appointees, during some portion of their pre-judicial careers, were political activists. It is evident that party organizations expect that qualified lawyers or judges with some record of partisan activism and party affiliation be given preferential consideration for appointment. The Justice Department files, in fact, contain letters from party officials exhorting Justice officials to remember their partisans. . . .

On occasion, the President's supporters in the state from which the appointee is to be chosen will remind Justice officials of the stakes involved in ignoring their wishes. The following excerpt is from a letter written by a state leader to the Attorney General:

> If [X] is not named this would damage seriously the Kennedy forces in [the state]. [X] was openly for Kennedy before L.A. and stood strong and voted there. He is known as one of my closest friends. He is an excellent lawyer—and on the merits alone, better qualified than Judge [Y].
>
> The Senators will give you no trouble, but we have put this on the line in public and if [X] is not appointed it will be a mortal blow.

X was appointed. . . .

While there has not been an administration in our history whose judicial appointments were equally divided between both political parties, there is still the tradition that a few appointments to the federal courts are made to persons affiliated with the opposition party. Both the Eisenhower and Kennedy administrations attempted to make such "nonpartisan" appointments to both the federal district courts and the appeals courts. The "nonpartisan" appointments occurred when there were multiple vacancies, almost all of which involved the elevation of a district judge to an appeals court vacancy. In many cases the Justice Department had to negotiate "package" arrangements with the political actors in the process so that "nonpartisan" appointments could be made.

C. Political Considerations: Political Clearance

. . . The formal procedures for judicial appointments imply a negotiations process involving senators and administration. In practice, senators have a veto power in the appointment process so that judicial appointments, at the very least, must be "cleared" with the senator(s) of the President's party from whose state the appointee will be picked. In addition the state party organization and party leaders will, in some situations, also "clear" the prospective nominee. . . .

In some cases, shortly after a vacancy occurs, the congressional delegation and the state's political leaders will meet for the purpose of choosing one candidate to support. Such a united front is usually very persuasive when the backed candidate is clearly qualified. In such situations, of course, "clearance" is but a euphemism for a more powerful role played in the selection process. But, typically, the state's political leaders and congressional delegation cannot agree on one candidate to support. . . .

Political clearance is not necessarily synonymous with active support of particular candidacies. Rather, political clearance is considered an exercise of patronage and it is important for the prestige and power of the senator and other party leaders of the President's party to be able to "clear" all appointments made to individuals from their state. That senators, and in many cases, state party leaders of the President's party expect to be able to "clear"—and conversely veto—prospective appointees, provides a major constraint upon the President's men at Justice.

D. State Representation

Party leaders expect that their state will be represented on their federal court of appeals by a citizen of their state. . . .

Justice officials readily acknowledged in interviews that state claims for "representation" are usually accepted. However, there are several situations when the state of the retired or deceased judge may not receive the subsequent appointment. One such situation occurs when the retired or deceased judge was not the only representative of his state on the court. If another state in the circuit does not have a representative on the court and at least one of the senators is of the President's party, that state will receive the appointment. . . .

When the senators are not of the President's party, their state's claim can be ignored by the Justice Department. However, this can bring unforeseen and unwanted consequences, as was demonstrated by the Eisenhower Administration's appointment of Simon Sobeloff of Maryland to the Fourth Circuit Court of Appeals. South Carolina had been in line for that appointment. The Democratic controlled Senate Judiciary Committee obliged the Democratic senators from South Carolina by delaying confirmation proceedings for close to one year. The nomination was finally forced out of committee and onto the floor, where it was approved, although not without a bitter fight. Apparently the Eisenhower Administration got the point, for the next vacancy on the Fourth Circuit was filled by a South Carolinian.

The custom of state representation on the appeals courts, then, places a constraint upon the President's men in their efforts to find a suitable candidate for nomination. The efficacy of this custom is underscored by the fact that close to seventy percent of the judges in active service during 1961–1964 (filling other than newly created seats) came from the same states as the judges they replaced.

E. Pressures from Contenders

The prospective nominees themselves are a source of pressure on Justice officials. Most typically they urge their senators, their friends, and their friends' friends to write letters of recommendation to the Justice Department. Frequently, when urged by the candidates, local bar associations will issue endorsements or circulate petitions supporting candidates for judicial office. The candidates expect that such activity will encourage the Justice Department to consider them seriously.

. . .

In general, when judicial candidates themselves initiate their candidacies by encouraging a barrage of recommendations from lawyers, political activists, and judges to the Justice Department, the resulting pressures provide another constraint on the Justice officials. This constraint may result in prolonging the appointment process. An avalanche of recommendations for one serious contender cannot be tactfully answered by the immediate appointment of another serious contender. The Justice Department officials may feel it important for each serious contender to make his move and articulate his backing so that they can then better grasp the politics involved as well as assess the qualifications of the candidates.

F. Quasi-Ideology and Policy Orientation

In general, Justice officials from both administrations stood ready to reject "extremists," but "extremism" was somewhat differently defined by the two administrations. The Kennedy Administration, a Justice official revealed, would not consider a Democrat who was a "Goldwater Conservative" type. Although candidates during the Kennedy Administration, according to one official, were not given "a saliva test for their liberalism," judicial philosophy was an important consideration in the evaluation of candidates, especially for candidates on the "leading" circuits. A close observer of the Kennedy Administration noted that the President's men wanted to appoint Democrats with the "liberal" point of view of the administration but in many cases were not able to do so—or else made some bad guesses.

The Justice Department files yield some evidence that quasi-ideology was an articulated consideration for a few appointments made by the Kennedy Administration. For example, the following was written to Attorney General Robert Kennedy by a federal district judge concerning a particular candidate (subsequently appointed): "He is our kind of Democrat . . . I am well acquainted with his views for we have had many occasions upon which to exchange them."

The quasi-ideological assessment of candidates is, of course, a tricky business, and such assessments are usually made under the general standard of "our kind" of Democrat (or Republican). There was one appointment made by the Kennedy Administration for which quasi-ideology was the decisive consideration. The Democratic senators and the Justice officials had narrowed the list of candidates to two, and the senators (friends of both candidates) decided to leave the final selection to the President's men. A Washington, D.C., attorney, himself once a member of the Justice Department, wrote a letter to the Attorney General that undoubtedly crystallized the alternatives faced by the President's men. The letter began by noting that the choice of candidates involved two: "X" and "Y".

. . .

Assuming that I exaggerate and that these men are actually comparable in competence and judicial temperament, there are I think the intangibles which weigh more heavily in favor of [X] than [Y]. I must tread softly here for, by definition, intangibles are hard to weigh. Nonetheless, I submit the trend as toward [X] and against [Y]:

First, not only is the—Circuit a weak bench, it is a conservative bench quite out of step with the premises of the New Frontier as almost all of us understand those premises. In the great run of cases it does not matter whether a judge is liberal or conservative if he is a good judge. There are a handful of cases, however,—and, Heaven knows, they always seem to be the important ones!—where the judicial mind can go either way, with probity, with honor, self-discipline and even with precedent. This is where the "liberal" cast of mind (we all know it, few of us can define it) can move this nation forward, just as the conservative mind can and does hold it back. This is intangible truth, but every lawyer knows it as reality! [X] would go forward, [Y] would hold back.

Second, the political point of view of a candidate deserves weight when other things are equal, or almost equal. . . . I know of [X]'s devotion to the Democratic Party. . . . I personally know that over the years he has contributed vast amounts of time and money to good Democrats. On this point, both of his Senators will strongly attest. . . .

[Y] is entitled, as aren't we all, to his convictions and if his convictions in the 1950's happened to be Eisenhower that was not only his privilege, it was his duty. But I also think privilege and duty carry with them the consequences of their acts. I do not think it is unduly partisan of me if I feel a good man cannot and should not live in both worlds.

The President's men chose "X".

In general, however, the Kennedy Administration probably did not use a "liberalism" checklist as part of the selection process. Indeed, the President's men would probably have scorned any suggestion that only the most ideological "liberal" should be chosen. However, there is an indication that the President's men were alert to the candidacies of those harboring a "conservative" orientation. In practice, those appointed by the Kennedy Administration were likely to be categorized as "liberal" in newspaper articles, while the Eisenhower appointees were more likely to be labeled "conservative."

It seems evident from an inspection of the files of the Eisenhower appointees that President Eisenhower's men in the Justice Department proceeded cautiously when considering candidates with a "liberal" orientation, although again it should be emphasized that the Justice officials were not interested in using a candidate's "conservatism" as a criterion. However, just as with the Kennedy Administration, friends of the administration would write letters recommending certain candidates and espouse quasi-ideological reasons for so doing. For example, one letter on behalf of a candidate contained the following: "His [the candidate's] great belief in the democratic form of Government and its protection through the courts is something that is greatly needed in our judicial system today after twenty years of neglect." Or note the following from a former senator:

> [X] is conservative in politics and one who would not have radical social theories that would influence his interpretations of the Constitution. . . . I sincerely believe that the administration wants to appoint to all of our courts young men of good quality who will hold the fort against New Dealism as it develops in the future.

In a few cases, apparently, the President's men made special efforts to discover the orientation of particular candidates. In one case, for example, this was done by an appeals judge who, at the request of the Attorney General, made some discreet inquiries and

TABLE 22-1
Number of Justice Department Files of Appeals Judges Serving Between 1961 and 1964
Containing References to Quasi-Ideology and Specific Policy Outlook

Administration	Number of Files Containing References							
	Quasi-Ideology		Policies		Both Ideology and Policies		Total References	
	No.	%	No.	%	No.	%	No.	%
Kennedy	4	19.0	4	19.0	1	4.7	9	42.7[a]
Eisenhower	7	18.4	1	2.6	2	5.2	10	26.2[b]
Truman	2	14.3	—	—	—	—	2	14.3[c]
Roosevelt	4	40.0	—	—	3	30.0	7	70.0[d]

[a] Out of 21 Kennedy appointees in active service during part or all of 1961–1964.

[b] Out of 38 Eisenhower appointees in active service during part or all of 1961–1964.

[c] Out of 14 Truman appointees in active service during part or all of 1961–1964.

[d] Out of 10 Roosevelt appointees in active service during part or all of 1961–1964.

reported that the candidate's views "are not those of [Y, a quasi-ideological liberal] and are quite different."

Quasi-ideological considerations are difficult to discern, but the preceding data suggest that consciously or inarticulately they played some role, perhaps a very limited one, in the appointment process of at least two administrations. Table 22-1 presents in tabular form the number of files of appeals judges on the bench between 1961 and 1964 that contained references to quasi-ideology or specific policies. To be sure, a large part of the appointment process is conducted over the phone or in person and undoubtedly much does not find its way into the files. Nonetheless, such references, whether by Justice people, by those close to the administration, or in newspaper clippings inserted in the files, are suggestive.

Table 22-1 indicates that the Roosevelt group had the largest and the Truman appointees the smallest percentage of judges whose files contained general references to quasi-ideology. About the same percentages of Eisenhower and Kennedy appointees' files included quasi-ideological references. However, more Kennedy than Eisenhower appointees' files indicated a concern with specific policy areas.

The candidates' views on specific policies are likely to be ascertained by the Department's informal investigation or, if the candidate is a federal district judge or state judge, by at least a perusal of his decisions. . . .

. . . [T]here is some indication that in the Eisenhower Administration, as well as the Kennedy Administration, one specific policy area, that of criminal law, was of concern because of the Justice Department's own organizational maintenance and enhancement needs. . . .

The specific policy area that occupied most, if not all, of the attention of the Kennedy people in the Justice Department was that of segregation. The Kennedy Administration appointed six men to appeals courts who were citizens of southern states. In every case, the administration sought to discover the candidate's views on racial segregation. A Justice official emphasized that it was policy of the Department not to appoint a racist to the Fourth or Fifth Circuits. Concern with the candidates' views was in evidence in the southern candidates' files. Consider, for example, this memo to the Attorney General in reference to a candidate: "The contact says that he has no doubt whatever that [X] will be all right on civil rights questions." The Justice official noted in his memo that he had met with the candidate who "volunteered that he has no feelings of racial bias or prejudice whatever, and that if appointed he would apply the law in the civil rights field as laid down by the Supreme Court without any hesitation, and would feel quite comfortable about it."

The files of the Eisenhower southern appointees do not yield any evidence that the candidates' views of segregation were investigated, but probably such views were known. Several of the appointees had close ties with the administration (for example, Judges Soboloff, Tuttle, and Wisdom), and their federal supremacy and anti-racist attitudes were undoubtedly important for their appointments to the Fourth and Fifth Circuits. . . .

On balance, it seems that the candidate's quasi-ideological viewpoint or his position on specific policy areas occasionally plays a decisive role in the appointment process. To some extent it is probably an inarticulate force operating to favor "our kind," other things being nearly equal. However, because quasi-ideology and specific policy areas usually do not explicitly concern the political actors involved in the process (with Negro civil rights as a possible exception), quasi-ideology and specific policy views are not a pronounced feature of the selection process.

III

Any assessment of the relative importance of the components of the appointment process—particularly the six expectations and constraints discussed in this article—must be tentative and imprecise. An analysis of unsuccessful candidates for appeals posts would contribute to a more precise knowledge of the process, but even if such an analysis were made (assuming access to these files) the findings would still be incomplete. The appointment process is highly complex, with each appointment involving a different combination of participants, circumstances, and considerations. In addition, those responsible for the crucial decisions in the process (notably the Attorney General, the Deputy Attorney General, and his assistants) base their decisions upon their perceptions and weightings of the qualifications of the candidates, the political situation involved, the extent to which the candidates are "our kind" of Democrat or Republican, and the needs of the various circuits (as they see them). Different Justice officials perceive and weigh the factors involved somewhat differently. Thus, while it is possible to isolate what appear to be the most important aspects of the process, it is extremely difficult to assess the relative importance of these aspects. Nonetheless, a few tentative generalizations will be attempted.

The custom of state representation is an important custom. When a vacancy occurs on an appeals court, the state of the judge responsible for the vacancy or an unrepresented state on the circuit is generally the one from which the appointee will be chosen. The choice of candidates is thus narrowed.

A fundamental prerequisite for appeals court appointments seems to be that Justice officials must be convinced of the candidate's professional competence. The standards of the Justice Department, as we have seen, compare favorably with the ABA committee's standards. However, while the ABA officials strive to promote the candidacies of those that they believe are the "magnas" and "summas" of the legal profession, Justice officials tend to be satisfied with the "cums" if the other components of the process favor them.

Two types of appointment situations seem to be typical: (1) where one or both senators of the state from which the appointee will be selected belong to the President's party; and (2) where both senators belong to the opposition party. In the first situation, senatorial clearance is of overriding importance, and senators generally narrow the range of candidates to be considered. In the second situation, clearance with important congressmen, or party leaders is considered "good politics," but unless there is a united front of the state party leaders and congressmen, Justice officials can select their own candidate and can ordinarily secure "clearance" for that candidate.

In both types of appointment situations (and especially the second type) the Justice officials can choose among several qualified candidates. Other considerations then come into play: Is the candidate "our kind" as evidenced by past partisan activism or quasi-ideological outlook? Who (party organizations, politicians, bar groups, newspapers) will be happy or unhappy with a particular appointment? If the elevation of a district judge is involved, is the elevation part of a "package" that must be worked out with local party leaders or senators? Could a particular circuit bench be strengthened by a certain kind of appointment (such as a legal scholar or a lawyer with extensive trial experience)? Which of these considerations will carry more weight than the others depends entirely upon specific circumstances. In general, though (and with some exceptions), political considerations have taken precedence over quasi-ideological considerations, and "our kind" considerations have been more important than the appointment of brilliant legal scholars or ABA designated "summas." No doubt Justice officials are delighted to appoint brilliant or "summa" type lawyers or judges who have strong political backing and are "our kind." But the process tends to produce the appointment of qualified people who best satisfy the particular political requirements of the specific situation.

Generally, then, the judges on the appeals courts were appointed largely due to fortuitous circumstances; they were in the right place at the right time. Many had the right contacts, or friends with contacts, who could influence Justice officials to consider seriously their candidacies. Some received their appointments through a process of elimination. In general, the appointment process can be characterized as a highly complex negotiations process consisting of several components. Those selected for appointment have tended to be political activists reflecting (to some extent) the values and outlook of the appointing administration. This undoubtedly has far-reaching consequences for judicial decisional behavior and for the development of law in the United States.

23

The Social and Political Backgrounds of the Justices of the Supreme Court: 1789–1959

John R. Schmidhauser

From what levels of American society have the ninety-two individuals who served on the Supreme Court been chosen? . . . Among the diverse criteria available for the establishment of social status, paternal occupations, patterns of occupational heredity, individual career patterns, ethnic origin, religion, and education have been considered most useful by social scientists. Of these, paternal occupation has been accepted as the most trustworthy clue to the determination of social origin. The great amount of work in judicial biography completed in the last three decades has resulted in the accumulation in readily available form of much of the material necessary for such a synthesis.

Paternal Occupations

Throughout the entire history of the Supreme Court, only a handful of its members were of essentially humble origin. Nine persons selected in widely scattered historical periods comprise the total. The remaining 83 (91 per cent) not only were from families in comfortable economic circumstances but were chosen overwhelmingly from the socially prestigeful and politically influential gentry class in the late eighteenth and early nineteenth century or the professionalized upper-middle class thereafter. A large number of justices (55, comprising 60 per cent of the total) came from politically active families. The politically active families were essentially those enjoying high social status (99 per cent of the political activity was concentrated in families of high social status).

. . .

After 1862, a definite shift in the occupational emphasis of high social status families took place. The trend began in the Jacksonian period, but before the 1860's the preponderance of high social status families had been engaged in nonprofessional occupations such as farming or manufacturing. A rather high percentage of the heads of these families had pursued active and successful political careers. After 1862, the majority of fathers of

Reprinted by permission from John R. Schmidhauser, *The Supreme Court: Its Politics, Personalities and Procedures,* pp. 31–39, 42–49, 51–52, 54–59. Copyright © 1960 by John R. Schmidhauser. Footnotes have been omitted.

justices selected from high social status backgrounds were engaged in professional activities, largely in the fields of law, medicine, and religion, and occasionally in higher education. In social composition, the over-all tendency was a gradual transition from selection largely from the families of the aristocratic landholding and mercantile class of the late eighteenth and early nineteenth century to choice from among members of the professionalized upper-middle class. Lest this transition from selection from the old gentry class to predominant influence by the upper-middle class be interpreted as a liberalizing trend, it might be noted that the appointees from professionalized upper-middle class families were firmly in the ascendancy from 1889 through 1937, a period in which the Court virtually surpassed John Marshall's Court in its decisions in support of economic conservatism.

Occupational "Heredity"

The social transmission of attitudes, beliefs, values, and aspirations has as its most effective vehicle the family. Since political participation of a very advanced kind appears as a crucial ingredient in the life careers of all but one of the members of the Supreme Court, the nature and extent of family conditioning for such participation deserves special attention.

The United States has never produced an aristocracy comparable to Namier's "inevitable Parliament men," but it has developed, especially in local and state politics, families with consistent and frequently successful records of political involvement. America's "political families" have been able to transmit intangible, yet real advantages to their children. These advantages have included not only the prestige of possession of a "political" name and family connections in a local, state, or even national political organization, but also a true political education which is derived from the practice and familiarity with political activity, the encouragement of political ambitions, expectations, and perhaps a veritable sense of destiny respecting high political achievement.

Nearly two thirds of the members of the Supreme Court were raised in this far from commonplace type of American family. . . .

. . . To an even greater extent than the function of over-all political participation, that of judicial service is exceedingly rare in America. Yet twelve justices were the sons of prominent judges (usually of the highest court of a state). Six (including one of the above) married the daughters of judges. An additional fifteen were related to prominent jurists. Excluding duplication, thirty-two members of the Supreme Court (over one third) were related to jurists and intimately connected with families possessing a tradition of judicial service.

Several of these families have had members or close relations on the Supreme Court for periods extending over a half century. For example, Sarah Williamson of Georgia was the grandmother of Justice John Archibald Campbell (who served on the Court from 1853–1861) and the great-grandmother of Justice Lucius Q. C. Lamar (1888–1893). Later Joseph Ruckner Lamar, a cousin of Lucius, also served on the Court from 1910–1916. The Livingston family of New York and New Jersey has also had an intimate relation to Supreme Court service through many generations. John Jay, the first Chief Justice (1789–1795), was married to a Livingston whose father was a prominent colonial judge. Jay's wife's brother, Brockholst Livingston, served on the Court from 1806 to 1823. And Brockholst was succeeded on the Supreme Court by Smith Thompson, who had married into the Livingston family. Thompson served on the highest court from 1823 to 1843.

. . .

. . . This . . . does not imply that a deliberate effort has been made by successive Presidents to choose Supreme Court justices from such families; rather, that it frequently was very advantageous for a successful lawyer and a member of the President's political party to be a member of a family with a political background, and especially with a strong tradition of judicial service. This situation was as true in 1955 for John Marshall Harlan, the namesake and grandson of the famed dissenter in *Plessy* v. *Ferguson,* as it was in 1799 for Alfred Moore, the son of a well-known colonial judge of North Carolina, or in 1874 for Morrison R. Waite, the son of a former Chief Justice of the Supreme Court of Connecticut.

Where Were the Justices Born?

Closely related to the question of the determination of social origins and the nature of the relation of family background to social outlook is the additional environmental factor of place of birth and the setting for the formative years of the justices. Even in the earliest period, a greater number of the justices (75 per cent) were born (and usually reared) in cities or towns. Because most of the families of the justices possessed unusual social and economic advantages, the justices who were born in an urban environment were not subject to the tensions and crowded conditions of the tenement areas and slums. For many the fact that they lived in a city brought all the urban cultural advantages but maintained the serenity and security also enjoyed by the justices living on plantations and town or country estates.

In a few instances, place of birth also had a special relation to United States citizenship. An overwhelming number (94.6 per cent) of the justices were, of course, born in the United States of parents who were citizens of the United States. Six justices were born abroad, Justice David Brewer in Turkey of American missionaries. Three of the foreign-born justices were chosen for the Supreme Court by President Washington: James Iredell (England), James Wilson (Scotland), and William Paterson (Ireland). The remaining two, George Sutherland (England) and Felix Frankfurter (Austria), were chosen in modern times. Leaving aside Washington's appointees, both Sutherland and Frankfurter came to America at an early age. Their childhood experiences were similar to those of first-generation Americans rather than aliens. Although nativists raised objections to Frankfurter's appointment, other factors were present to assure presidential nomination and to assure senatorial confirmation.

. . .

Ethnic Origins of the Justices

The ethnic origins of members of the Supreme Court represent another important source of data available for the determination of their social background. Throughout the entire history of the Supreme Court, judicial recruitment has granted a virtual monopoly to natives or the descendants of natives of northwestern Europe. And among those selected, individuals of English, Welsh, Scotch, or Irish ethnic origin have predominated, comprising 88 per cent of the appointees. . . .

. . .

The patterns of ethnic representation are additional evidences of the virtual monopolization of Supreme Court appointments by the socially privileged segment of the population dubbed the "old Americans."

Religious Affiliation of the Justices

Religious diversity in America has at its root a social basis as well as a doctrinal rationale. To some denominations are attached factors of prestige and social status, while others are viewed socially as "churches of the disinherited," of unpopular immigrant groups, or of ethnic groups which, because of color, have not been fully accepted. In keeping with the fact that most of the justices were selected from among socially advantaged families was the heavy incidence of affiliation with high social status religious groups by the justices. An overwhelming majority were Protestant. A substantial majority of the justices were affiliated with the Episcopalian, Presbyterian (or French Calvinist), Congregational, and Unitarian churches. Slightly over 10 per cent were affiliated with Protestant religious groups which historically were considered of lower social status. In a special category were the slightly less than 10 per cent of the justices who were either Roman Catholic, Jewish, or Quaker. Only one Quaker, Noah Swayne, has been appointed to the Supreme Court. Since the Roman Catholic and Jewish groups in America have frequently been subjected to nativist and religious criticism and attack, members of these groups have, historically, been at a considerable disadvantage in the competition for Supreme Court appointments.

In recent years there has been considerable discussion of the existence of a custom of maintaining on the Supreme Court a member of the Roman Catholic and Jewish religious faiths. . . . The very controversy over the existence of the "custom" has political significance, and it may be assumed that . . . religious representation, whether accepted or not, must play a part in subsequent presidential considerations of judicial selections.

Educational Background of the Justices

Of all the advantages which were incidental to birth into the early gentry class or the professionalized upper-middle class, that of the opportunity to acquire a good education was perhaps of greatest importance to the later formative period in the career patterns of a majority of the justices. A college education has, until comparatively recent times, been a prize available only to a small minority of American adults. An advanced education in a college or university of high standing has been even more rare. And finally, such an education coupled with professional training in law has been exceedingly difficult to attain. A rather large number of justices have been able to acquire such education, usually in the better colleges and universities. Over a third did their college work in the Ivy League schools, while nearly a third did their law studies in them. Aside from the manifest professional advantages which might be derived from such educational opportunities, the personal associations which were established and the notions of social responsibility and civic leadership inculcated at these educational institutions must all be taken into account as aids in the individual career patterns of the justices and as factors conditioning their attitudes toward the challenges and responsibilities of judicial decision making in later maturity.

The justices who studied under private tutors and who served law apprenticeships were not recipients of inferior types of education. In fact, these justices were often afforded several unique advantages from this educational opportunity, for in most instances the tutors or law teachers not only were unusually talented but were leading practitioners of law in the community or state, and were among the top political leaders in the contemporary scene. One may conclude that in the period before the full development of law schools, members of the Supreme Court who were taught law by outstanding legal and political leaders gained incalculable educational and political advantages in the process. Throughout the history of the Supreme Court, the recruitment process has generally rewarded those whose educational backgrounds, both legal and nonlegal, have comprised the rare combination of intellectual, social, and political opportunities which have generally been available only to the economically comfortable and socially prominent segment of the American population.

The Nonpolitical Occupations of the Court Members

. . . All of the ninety-two justices of the Supreme Court had legal training of some kind. All practiced law at some stage in their careers. For eighty-eight of the total (97 per cent), law was a major nonpolitical occupation. The justices who had not practiced law as a major nonpolitical occupation (Stone, Frankfurter, Douglas, and Rutledge) were all law school professors or deans. With the exception of Stone, all were chosen by President Franklin Roosevelt and were, in essence, instruments of constitutional protest against the highly restrictive attitude of earlier appointees. . . .

. . .

. . . [A]n overwhelming number of Supreme Court appointees selected in the first two historical periods (1789-1828 and 1828-1861) pursued primarily political careers. . . . After 1862 a substantial, but not large, number of corporation lawyers were appointed to the Supreme Court, constituting 19 per cent in 1862-1888, 22 per cent in 1889-1919, 29 per cent in 1920-1932, and then declining to 14 per cent in 1933-1959. Although all except the last of these periods corresponded with historical eras in which corporate influence was, with brief contrary interludes, ascendant in the national government, it would appear at first glance that the process of appointing members of the Supreme Court had remained relatively immune from such influence. This was not true, however, because ideological soundness, from the corporate point of view, actually found its most reliable advocates among the appointees with extensive judicial careers.

The number of appointees who had pursued primarily political careers took a sharp decline after 1862, dropping from 63 per cent in the Jacksonian era to 32 per cent in 1862-1888, 33 per cent in 1889-1919, and 29 per cent in 1920-1932. In the final period, 1933-1959, political careerists on the Court rose to 62 per cent. None of these periods rivaled the original one, 1789-1828, in which 85 per cent of the Court appointees were lawyers who had pursued primarily political careers. It should be noted, however, that with only one exception, George Shiras, every member of the Supreme Court had actively participated in politics before his appointment to the nation's highest tribunal.

In actuality, the most important change in the pattern of judicial selection which occurred after 1862 was the great increase in the percentage of men chosen who had primarily judicial careers. For two periods, judges from state courts or inferior federal courts constituted the largest single group of appointees, totaling 45 per cent in 1862–1888 and 1889–1919, declining to 29 per cent in 1920–1932 and then dropping sharply to a mere 6 per cent in the final period, 1933–1959. Not all the members of the Supreme Court who had prior judicial experience were included in this group. It was felt to be more realistic to include only those whose prior judicial experience represented a major portion of their adult careers. For example, from among the Eisenhower appointees only William Brennan pursued primarily a judicial career. Harlan, Whittaker, and Stewart had short federal judicial tenures before appointment to the Supreme Court, but through most of their adult careers they were corporation lawyers.

The very fact that all the members of the Supreme Court were members of the legal profession in itself merits consideration as a conditioner of social, economic, and political attitudes. Whether one accepts the belief of Alexis de Tocqueville that "the seat of the American aristocracy is with the judges on the bench and the lawyers at the bar" or the contradictory view of a contemporary critic that "the members of the legal profession . . . are not the aristocracy but the agents of the aristocracy . . . [which] is constituted by the owners of accumulated wealth," there has been rather general agreement that the influence of the bar in America has been essentially conservative. This does not imply that every lawyer appointed to the Supreme Court has succumbed to this conservative influence, but it is clear that all are exposed to it. There is considerable evidence to indicate that many lawyers on the high bench willingly espoused the sort of legal conservatism exemplified in the leadership and ideology of the American Bar Association. Furthermore, a number of the members of the Court, such as William Howard Taft and George Sutherland, were among the leaders of the bar, both before and after their appointments to the Supreme Court, who developed and cherished its conservative traditions and attitudes.

Political Party and Ideological Constancy

The mere recitation of the changing patterns of legal careers represented on the Supreme Court lacks meaningfulness except as a descriptive contribution. When considered in connection with the most important of the customary "rules" of the judicial selection process, however, these patterns assume greater significance. The choice of men ideologically committed or thought to be committed to the values of the President making the selection has been the policy most rigidly adhered to throughout American history.

One clue to the explanation for the pre-Civil War tendency toward choice of lawyers who pursued primarily political careers lay in the fact that during much of this period party affiliation generally included acceptance of certain clearly defined social, economic, and constitutional attitudes. One need consider only the following statement of Thomas Jefferson to recognize the clarity with which early party leaders identified party loyalty and "right thinking" on philosophical, social, and economic ideas. Jefferson, writing to President Madison's Postmaster, Gideon Granger, suggested that the old Federalist justice William Cushing be replaced with "a firm unequivocal republican, whose principles are born with him, and not an occasion ingraftment, as necessary to complete the great reformation in our government to which the nation gave its fiat ten years ago." Even in the pre-Civil War era, this identity of party and values was not always present, as the appointment of Joseph Story so amply demonstrated, but after 1862, the relation between party affiliation and ideological commitment became, if anything, increasingly less clear.

The judicial selection process reveals rather convincingly that the selection of individuals of the President's political affiliation served not only as a method of rewarding political supporters but also as one of several means of identification of a judicial candidate's ideology, although there has usually been strong pressure for both party and ideological consistency. To be sure, presidents have occasionally paid off political debts (as may have been true in the appointment of Justice Catron), or perhaps have "kicked upstairs" bothersome cabinet officers (as has been alleged in the selection of Justice McLean), but the so-called crasser political motives have not generally been determinative in the appointment of members of the Supreme Court. During historical periods when party attachment actually meant commitment to certain recognizable social, economic, or philosophical values, the choice of justices rather consistently followed party lines. When the identity of party label and ideology was uncertain, presidents usually exercised greater care in their assessment of ideological consistency.

Among the biographical materials on presidents, the frank correspondence between Theodore Roosevelt and Senator Henry Cabot Lodge . . . concerning Horace Lurton, a Democrat, and a federal judge, is . . . precise with reference to the ideological prerequisites of his appointees. Wrote Roosevelt,

> Nothing has been so strongly born in on me concerning lawyers on the bench as that the nominal politics of the man has nothing to do with his actions on the bench. His *real* politics are all-important. In Lurton's case, Taft and Day, his two former associates, are very desirous of having him on. He is right on the Negro question; he is right on the power of the federal government; he is right on the Insular business; he is right about corporations, he is right about labor. On every question that would come before the bench, he has so far shown himself to be in much closer touch with the policies in which you and I believe than even White because he has been right about corporations where White has been wrong.

It is rather important to note that Democrat Horace Lurton, despite his ideological soundness, *did not* get this appointment. (Lurton was, however, later chosen for the Supreme Court by Theodore Roosevelt's successor, William Howard Taft.) Instead, Roosevent appointed his Republican Attorney General, William Henry Moody. In all probability, Senator Lodge's reply to the letter quoted above contains both the explanation for Roosevelt's failure to appoint Lurton and further insight regarding the traditional balancing of factors in the judicial selection process. Lodge wrote,

> I am glad that Lurton holds all the opinions that you say he does and that you are so familiar with his views. I need hardly say that those are the very questions on which I am just as anxious as you that judges should hold what we consider sound opinions, *but I do not see why Republicans cannot be found who hold those opinions as well as Democrats.* . . .
>
> Of course you know my high opinion of Moody. . . . Nothing would give me greater pleasure than to see him on the bench.

. . .

It is interesting to note that presidents and their Senates have always had nominees whose political *bona fides* were matters of wide knowledge. Every member of the Supreme

Court except George Shiras held a political post of some kind prior to his appointment to the high bench. Several of the justices had also been unsuccessful candidates for political offices which were of greater importance than those which they actually attained prior to their appointment to the Supreme Court.

Since state or federal judicial service is included among the political posts categorized, special consideration should be given to the factor of prior judicial experience.

The Prior Judicial Experience of Members of the Supreme Court

. . . Well over 50 per cent of the justices had served in a judicial capacity at some time before appointment to the Supreme Court, but only slightly more than 25 per cent had had really extensive judicial careers. It is upon this latter group of justices whose life careers prior to appointment to the Supreme Court had been primarily judicial that attention will be centered.

The considerations which governed the choice of these judicially trained men varied according to changing circumstances. During the period of Jeffersonian and Jacksonian dominance of the national administration, Supreme Court appointments were often viewed with an eye to the local responsibilities of the justices while on circuit duty. Thus, acquaintance with the peculiarities of the land laws of the states within a circuit was occasionally considered a prerequisite, as, for example, in the choices of Thomas Todd and Robert Trimble. Particularly before 1891, experience in the "federal specialities," such as admiralty law, was also of importance. However, it is not at all clear that experience on an inferior federal court or a state court is necessary to or intimately related to the sort of service performed on the nation's highest court. . . .

. . .

There is little in the history of the Supreme Court to suggest that justices with prior judicial experience were more objective or better qualified than those who lacked such experience. As a matter of fact, despite the examples of Holmes and Cardozo, some of the Supreme Court's most distinguished members, notably Marshall, Taney, Curtis, Campbell, Miller, Bradley, Hughes, Brandeis, and Stone, were totally lacking in this experience before their appointments to the Supreme Court.

The Significance of Social and Political Background Factors

. . .

Throughout American history there has been an overwhelming tendency for presidents to choose nominees for the Supreme Court from among the socially advantaged families. The typical Supreme Court justice has invariably been white, generally Protestant with a penchant for a high social status denomination, usually of ethnic stock originating in the British Isles, and born in comfortable circumstances in an urban or small town environment. In the earlier history of the Court, he very likely was born in the aristocratic gentry class, although later he tended to come from the professionalized upper-middle class.

Whereas nearly two thirds of his fellows were selected from politically active families, a third of his fellows were chosen from families having a tradition of judicial service. In college and legal education, the average justice was afforded opportunities for training and associations which were most advantageous. It seems reasonable to assume that very few sons of families outside the upper, or upper-middle, social and economic classes have been able to acquire the particular type of education and the subsequent professional, and especially political, associations which appear to be unwritten prerequisites for appointment to the nation's highest tribunal.

Educational opportunity emerges as a crucial ingredient in judicial recruitment. Every member of the Supreme Court was the recipient of law training and a great number were afforded college or university educations prior to their law training. Law training not only fulfilled an unwritten educational requirement for judicial appointment but frequently represented an important stage in the development of individual political careers. Especially during the periods before the widespread acceptance of law schools as the primary centers for legal education, the internship of subsequent members of the Supreme Court in the law offices of prominent practitioners afforded the student not only a unique educational opportunity and valuable professional associations, but frequently the political sponsorship of men who held high office or were influential in the councils of their political organizations.

The influence of family background, while less tangible in certain respects, may be considered of great importance. In an economic sense, birth in a family in comfortable circumstances was generally a precondition for the advanced educational opportunities afforded most Supreme Court members. However, it is important to note that the families of the justices generally were not the type one identifies with the modern middle class, a type which has become increasingly apolitical, interested more in comfort and economic security than in the assumption of social responsibility. On the contrary, a high percentage of the families of the justices demonstrated a very deep sense of social responsibility and political involvement. It would be a gross oversimplification to assume a direct transferal of the particular political attachments of these families to their sons. Yet the biographical data on the justices evidences a considerable conditioning of broad attitudes toward social and political participation.

. . . Just as training in law has been a necessary educational step in the achievement of a Supreme Court appointment, so has political activism been a virtual precondition for such an appointment. The degree of political involvement of aspirants to the Supreme Court has, of course, varied considerably. In a large number of instances the justices, prior to their appointments, not only held high political office but were deeply involved in party and campaign management and had close political associations and personal ties with the men who later nominated and appointed them. Thus, political activism of a rather intense kind emerges as a necessary stage in career ascent to the Supreme Court.

. . .

The appointment of men with prior judicial experience, especially those with extensive careers in the inferior federal courts or the state courts, was of great importance in particular historical periods. These appointments frequently served the practical function of identifying ideological partisans, as did selection from the ranks of the openly avowed political activists.

The picture that emerges in the pattern of recruitment of Supreme Court justices is one which emphasizes the intimacy of judicial and political affairs. Since the most important function of the Supreme Court is the settlement of fundamentally political issues through the medium of judicial review, the political background of the justices undoubtedly represents a very necessary and valuable source of experience and training.

It is not at all clear that the social and political background factors in themselves may serve as reliable indicators of precise patterns of judicial behavior. Explanations based entirely upon the causal influence of such factors as family, economic and social status, ethnic background, or religious affiliation could scarcely take into account such important considerations as the impact upon individual justices of the traditions of the Supreme Court itself or of the interaction of intelligent and frequently forceful personalities which has been an integral part of the internal procedure of the Court. Complete dependence upon background factors would also ignore the complexity and subtlety of intellect and motivation which is part of the collective picture of the ninety-two individuals who have sat on the high bench.

The difficulty is illustrated by looking at the over-all judicial reputations of the nine justices of humble origin. It might be argued, for example, that the choice of men of humble origin for the Supreme Court could scarcely be considered dangerous to the rights of private property because the group included James Wilson, John McLean, John Catron, Pierce Butler, and James Byrnes. Perhaps one would be tempted to accept the acid comment, made by a contemporary concerning Catron's personal characteristics, as a sociological explanation of the decision-making predilections of these justices. Catron was described as "profoundly aristocratic in all his habits and bearing *as all men raised to wealth and station by concurrence of accidents.*" Yet as appealing as such a pat explanation seems, there are certain difficulties inherent in the unqualified use of such biographical data. For one thing, the over-all judicial reputations of the other four justices of humble origin—Henry Baldwin, Samuel F. Miller, Sherman Minton, and Earl Warren—can hardly be accounted for by this explanation. Furthermore, a variety of other explanations involving such things as political associations, educational conditioning, or ideological commitments to nationalism or states' rights might appear just as plausible as the emphasis upon family background.

It would be a serious mistake, however, to conclude that the background factors have had no influence upon judicial behavior whatsoever. The social attitudes of families in the gentry class or professionalized upper-middle class, and particularly the traditions of the families with judicial associations, may be accounted subtle factors influencing the tone and temper of judicial decision making. While such influence cannot ordinarily be traced in cause-and-effect formulas in specific decisions, it frequently emerges in the careers of individual justices as setting implicit limits on the scope of theoretical decision-making possibilities. Justice Frankfurter once wrote that "by the very nature of the functions of the Supreme Court, each member of it is subject only to his own sense of trusteeship of what are perhaps the most revered traditions in our national system." If it is in this sense that the Supreme Court is the keeper of the American conscience, it is essentially the conscience of the American upper-middle class sharpened by the imperative of individual social responsibility and political activism, and conditioned by the conservative impact of legal training and professional legal attitudes and associations.

CHAPTER EIGHT
JURIES

The Sixth and Seventh Amendments to the United States Constitution guarantee the right to a trial by jury in all serious criminal cases processed by the federal courts and in certain types of civil suits. These constitutional guarantees provide for the participation in the processing of disputes by judicial institutions of a group of citizens drawn from the community in which they live—a group given the responsibility for finding facts and making determinations of fault, blame, guilt, or innocence. Giving ordinary citizens an institutionalized role in the judicial process has always been understood as a device for democratizing the law.[1] The jury, reflecting a democratic suspicion of public authority, has traditionally been regarded as a means of checking and preventing the abuse of power by judges. The presence of a jury ensures, at least in theory, that the purposes of the state will be subjected to the common-sense judgment of citizens having no official public position.[2]

Juries are employed exclusively in trial courts. Dispute processing in trial courts centers on two generic types of issues: issues of law and issues of fact. Issues of law arise as the parties to a dispute seek to identify and interpret norms that will legitimize their behavior. A trial is, to some extent, a contest of interpretation and legal reasoning. The judge, with spe-

cial training and expertise in matters of law, has the authority and responsibility to determine which interpretations of law are proper and
acceptable. But a trial is more than an argument over applicable norms; it
also provides the occasion for a reconstruction, description, and interpretation of events. The purpose of a trial is to answer the question of who
did what to whom as well as the question of whether such conduct is
legal. It is the special province of juries to listen to and decide among
competing and conflicting versions of events. The jury is to use its collective judgment to referee an adversary contest in which the truth is expected to emerge from the presentation of differing versions of the same
occurrence. In the division of labor in a trial court, the jury is the authority
on facts; the judge is the authority on law.

Although this distinction is generally accurate, there is a blurring of it in
contemporary American courts. Judges have the power to determine what
evidence can properly be presented to the jury, and they have the power
in certain circumstances to direct a verdict or to set aside the verdict of a
jury if they believe it not to be one that reasonable people would have
returned if they had understood the evidence presented to them and the
law as interpreted to them by the judge. On the other hand, American
practice allows for "jury nullification," that is, juries are permitted to refuse
to convict if they believe that the law at issue in a case is unfair or arbitrary. Despite these practices the major role of the jury remains one of
determining facts.

Several important issues surround the participation of jurors in the processing of disputes by American courts.[3] The first is whether juries are
effective checks on government power. There is, in fact, no way of determining whether the institution of jury trials ensures that public officials
will be more restrained in using their power than they would otherwise be.
We cannot know how many more political prosecutions would be initiated were it not for the realization on the part of public officials that such
prosecutions are subject to the scrutiny of a group of private citizens. The
famous Chicago Jury Project, from which selection 24 is drawn, attempted
to determine the effectiveness of the jury in checking official power by
examining the percentage of cases in which the judges and juries involved
in the same cases agreed as to the appropriate verdict. The authors, Kalven
and Zeisel, found a high degree of agreement between judge and jury—
approximately 75 percent. Furthermore, in almost all criminal cases in
which judge and jury disagreed, Kalven and Zeisel found the jury to be
more lenient. Whether the leniency of the jury can be construed as limiting the exercise of official power is open to question; it does, however,
indicate that the participation of laymen in the making of decisions does
make a difference in the results of court processing of disputes.

A second issue frequently discussed in the academic literature on juries
is whether they typically are or need to be representative of the commu-

nity. The legitimacy of the jury as a democratic influence in the trial court is largely a function of its representativeness. The assumption is sometimes made, although it is frequently subject to challenge, that a jury that is representative of the community it serves is one that provides judgment by peers. Several studies, however, have revealed that American juries are not always representative,[4] mainly because the sources from which lists of potential jurors are drawn—typically voter registration lists or telephone directories—do not include people from all segments of the community. The representativeness of such lists is important not only because of the need to maintain the legitimacy of the jury but also because different kinds of people bring different attitudes and values to their service on a jury. If particular groups of people are underrepresented, then their attitudes and values are systematically underrepresented, and different types of decisions are reached than would be reached by more fully representative juries. Selection 25, by Edward Beiser, is concerned with the representativeness of juries.

A third issue is the question of juror competence.[5] Critics of the jury system suggest that the disputes that typically reach courts are so complex that the average citizen is capable of understanding neither them nor the issues raised by them. Defenders argue that jurors are as able as judges to comprehend the factual issues presented in most lawsuits. They cite the high level of agreement between judges and juries reported in the Chicago Jury Project as support for their contention. Furthermore, although there is evidence that jurors are influenced by such "irrelevant" factors as the order and manner in which evidence is presented, there is no evidence that jurors are any more susceptible to such influences than judges or other legal experts.

Finally, the participation of citizens in the American judicial process may be important not only because it affects the way in which the state exercises its power and the way in which disputes are processed but also because it affects the individuals who participate. Service on a jury may be an important experience in participatory democracy as well as an important experience in exercising the responsibilities of judgment. Alexis de Tocqueville, writing in the early 1800s, described jury service as follows:

> [Jury service] . . . imbues all classes with a respect for the thing judged and with the notion of right. . . . It teaches men to practice equity; every man learns to judge his neighbor as he would himself be judged. . . . The jury teaches every man not to recoil before the responsibility of his own actions. . . . By obliging men to turn their attention to other affairs than their own, it rubs off that private selfishness which is the rust of society.[6]

However, in American trial courts today the jury is seldom used, since most criminal and civil cases are decided without trial. Of the small percentage of cases that go to trial, many are tried by the judge alone without the use of a jury. Ultimately the importance of the jury may lie in the anticipation of both sides to a dispute of what a jury might do if the case were to go before a jury. And in a broader sense the value of the jury may lie in its democratic symbolism.

Notes

1. Alexis de Tocqueville, *Democracy in America,* Vol. 1 (New York: Vintage Books, 1954), Chap. 16.

2. Recent events have called into question the utility of the grand jury as a device for checking government power. The function of the grand jury is to make a judgment as to whether there is sufficient evidence to justify putting an individual on trial. Like the petit or trial jury, it is composed of citizens chosen from the state and district in which the alleged offense was committed. However, the argument has recently been advanced that the grand jury is little more than a tool of the prosecutor. See Richard Harris, *Freedom Spent* (Boston: Little, Brown, 1976). Also see Marvin E. Frankel and Gary P. Naftalis, *The Grand Jury* (New York: Hill and Wang, 1977); Robert A. Carp, "The Behavior of Grand Juries: Acquiescence or Justice?," *Social Science Quarterly* 55 (1975), 853.

3. On the general role of jurors and the function of juries, see Rita James Simon, ed., *The Jury System in America* (Beverly Hills: Sage, 1975).

4. See Howard Erlanger, "Jury Research in America," *Law and Society Review* 4 (1970), 345; Hayward R. Alker, Jr., Carl Hosticka, and Michael Mitchell, "Jury Selection as a Biased Social Process," *Law and Society Review* 11 (1976), 9.

5. Broadly encompassed under this concern is the question of whether jury verdicts ought to be unanimous. Supreme Court decisions, particularly *Apodaca* v. *Oregon,* 406 U.S. 404 (1972), have established the principle that the fairness or validity of jury verdicts may be unrelated to the question of unanimity.

6. Tocqueville, *op. cit.,* note 1, p. 295.

24

The American Jury: Some General Observations

Harry Kalven, Jr., and Hans Zeisel

. . .

In the large, the mind of the jury in criminal cases might perhaps be said to exhibit four dominant traits. First, there is the niceness of its calculus of equities; it will treat provocation as justifying defensive moves by the victim but only to the extent of the one-punch battery; it may even treat injury to the victim as punishment for the actor, but only where the relationship is close and the conduct is inadvertent. Second, there is the jury's broad tendency to see little difference between tort and crime and thus to see the victim rather than the state as the other party to the case, with the consequence that the public controversy is appraised largely as though it were a private quarrel. Third, there is a comparably broad tendency to merge at several points considerations of penalty with those of guilt. Finally, . . . there is a quality of formal symmetry about the jury's responses. In what we have called the simple rape cases the jury seems to say, whatever kind of offense the defendant had committed, it just was not rape; conversely, in the cases of sexual approach to children, it says that whatever the defendant did, even though far short of rape, it was some kind of offense. Thus while the jury is often moved to leniency by adding a distinction the law does not make, it is at times moved to be more severe than the judge because it wishes to override a distinction the law does make.

. . .

Although a substantial part of the jury's work is the finding of facts, this, as has long been suspected, is not its total function in the real world. As a fact-finder it is not in any interesting way different from the judge, although it will not always reach the same conclusion. When only pure fact-finding is involved the jury tends to give more weight than the judge to the norm that there should be no conviction without proof beyond a reasonable doubt. And there is every indication that the jury follows the evidence and understands the case.

The more interesting and controversial aspects of the jury's performance emerge in cases in which it does more than find facts; where, depending on how one looks at it, the jury can be said to do equity, to legislate interstitially, to implement its own norms, or to exhibit bias.

Reprinted by permission of the publisher from Harry Kalven, Jr., and Hans Zeisel, *The American Jury* (Boston: Little, Brown and Company, 1966), pp. 493–498.

All this is fairly familiar. The distinctive bite of this study resides in the following supplementary propositions about the jury as legislator.

First, we can estimate with some precision how frequently the jury engages in more than fact-finding. . . . [A]bout three quarters of the time it agrees with the judge; and that most, but not all of the time it agrees with him, it is not importing values of its own into the case. But roughly two thirds of the disagreements with the judge are marked by some jury response to values.

Second, the jury imports its values into the law not so much by open revolt in the teeth of the law and the facts, although in a minority of cases it does do this. . . . The jury, in the guise of resolving doubts about the issues of fact, gives reign to its sense of values. It will not often be doing this consciously; as the equities of the case press, the jury may, as one judge put it, "hunt for doubts." Its war with the law is thus both modest and subtle. The upshot is that when the jury reaches a different conclusion from the judge on the same evidence, it does so not because it is a sloppy or inaccurate finder of facts, but because it gives recognition to values which fall outside the official rules.

Third, we suspect there is little or no intrinsic directionality in the jury's response. It is not fundamentally defendant-prone, rather it is non-rule minded; it will move where the equities are. And where the equities are at any given time will depend on both the state of the law and the climate of public opinion.

Fourth, the extent to which the jury will disagree with the judge will depend on the selection of cases that come before the jury. Since, under current waiver rules and practice, the defendant in effect has the final say on whether there is to be a jury trial or a bench trial, the cases coming before the jury will be skewed and include a disproportionate number in which there are factors that appeal to the jury. The selection will be affected also by pleas of guilty and, to a lesser degree, by decisions of the prosecutor not to prosecute, and even in some instances by decisions of the police not to arrest. Thus the commonplace impression that the criminal jury is defendant-prone may be largely an artifact of the dynamics by which the cases are sorted out for jury trial.

Fifth, we have said, the jury's reaction will in part depend on the lay of public sentiment on any given point. The extensive agreement between judge and jury indicates that there is in our society at this time widespread consensus on the values embodied in the law. As a result, a jury drawn at random from the public, does not often have representatives of a dissenting view.

On some points there is sufficient dissent so that the random drawing will at times place on the jury representatives of a view contrary to the existing law. Indeed on some matters the public will even be ambivalent, with factions that deviate from the law in opposite directions.

Thus, it makes a good deal of difference in this decision-making who the personnel are. The consequence of the fact that no two juries are alike is that statements about trends in jury decision-making are probabilistic at best. We cannot assert that all juries will always feel that a man who has suffered personal disasters since committing the crime has been punished enough. We can only say that this idea is prevalent enough so that it has some chance of moving the jury away from the judge in any given instance in which it is present.

Sixth, the explanation of how a disagreement is generated requires one more fundamental point. The thesis is that to a substantial degree the jury verdict is determined by the posture of the vote at the start of the deliberation process and not by the impact of this

process as rational persuasion. The jury tends to decide in the end whichever way the initial majority lies. The result is that a sentiment need be spread only so widely among the public as to produce enough representatives on the jury to yield the initial majority.
. . .

Seventh, and as a corollary, the deliberation process although rich in human interest and color appears not to be at the heart of jury decision-making. Rather, deliberation is the route by which small group pressures produce consensus out of the initial majority.

. . .

As we attempt to step back and gain some distance from the detail of the study, it may be useful to put two quite general and interrelated questions: Why do judge and jury ever disagree, and why do they not disagree more often?

Judge and jury have experienced the same case and received the same rules of law to apply to it; why do these two deciders ever disagree? We seek for the moment an explanation more general than that [previously] offered . . . in terms of specific factors of evidence, sentiment, and defendant. Why do they not react the same way to the stimuli? Why does the judge not move over to the jury view, or the jury stay with the judge?

The answer must turn on the intrinsic differences between the two institutions. The judge very often perceives the stimulus that moves the jury, but does not yield to it. Indeed it is interesting how often the judge describes with sensitivity a factor which he then excludes from his own considerations. Somehow the combination of official role, tradition, discipline, and repeated experience with the task make of the judge one kind of decider. The perennial amateur, layman jury cannot be so quickly domesticated to official role and tradition; it remains accessible to stimuli which the judge will exclude.

The better question is the second. Since the jury does at times recognize and use its de facto freedom, why does it not deviate from the judge more often? Why is it not more of a wildcat operation? In many ways our single most basic finding is that the jury, despite its autonomy, spins so close to the legal baseline.

. . . As just noted, the official law has done pretty well in adjusting to the equities, and there is therefore no great gap between the official values and the popular. Again, the group nature of the jury decision will moderate and brake eccentric views. Lastly, the jury is not simply a corner gang picked from the street; it has been invested with a public task, brought under the influence of a judge, and put to work in solemn surroundings. Perhaps one reason why the jury exercises its very real power so sparingly is because it is officially told it has none.

The jury thus represents a uniquely subtle distribution of official power, an unusual arrangement of checks and balances. It represents also an impressive way of building discretion, equity, and flexibility into a legal system. Not the least of the advantages is that the jury, relieved of the burdens of creating precedent, can bend the law without breaking it.

. . .

25

Are Juries Representative?

Edward N. Beiser

A fundamental requirement of a fair jury system is that no person or class of persons may be excluded from jury service on account of race, color, religion, sex, national origin or economic status. This principle is clearly stated in the federal Jury Selection and Service Act of 1968 and has been specifically endorsed by the American Bar Association's Project on Minimum Standards for Criminal Justice.

A specific jury panel need not represent the entire community exactly. . . . [Rather] the basic pool or list must be genuinely representative. Jurors must then be selected strictly at random from the representative list. And how is such a representative list to be secured? The ABA committee concluded that "there is reason to believe that voter registration lists will usually be the most representative comprehensive lists of names available."

Recent data gathered in the state and federal courts of the state of Rhode Island cast significant doubt on the easy assumption of the ABA and others that voter registration lists do in fact accurately represent the total population. This article will endeavor to document some of the areas in which voter registration lists differ from the population as a whole.

The United States District Court for the District of Rhode Island, which includes the entire state within its jurisdiction, selects its jurors at random from the voter registration lists. The Superior Court of Rhode Island, the basic trial court of the state and the only state court which uses juries, also draws its jurors from the voter registration lists. The two selection processes are completely independent.

The state's system differs significantly from the one employed in federal court in that, once names are drawn at random, the office of the jury commissioner sends out a mail-back questionnaire. A number of potential jurors are disqualified at this point. The jury commissioner maintains a staff of investigators who then visit each potential juror at his home or place of business to administer the same questionnaire a second time. This element of individual investigation naturally raises questions as to the impact of the investigator's discretionary evaluation.

The Federal District Court maintains a Qualified Jury Wheel from which the names of jurors are selected as they are needed. This study uses the official questionnaires administered by the clerk of the Federal Court to the 400 persons whose names were in the

Reprinted from *Judicature* 57 (1973), 194–199, by permission of the American Judicature Society, publisher of *Judicature*. Footnotes have been omitted.

Qualified Jury Wheel during two terms: October 1970 and April 1971. This is the total venire from which juries were drawn during these two terms of court.

The state jury commissioner mails out approximately 8,000 questionnaires annually. This study uses 10 per cent of the official questionnaires of those who are ultimately found to be qualified and who were called and sworn as veniremen between the second Monday in July 1970 and the second Monday in July 1971.

The state questionnaires did not include a question as to race. In order to obtain this information, we observed the swearing in of veniremen in Providence and Bristol Counties for the first five months of 1972. (Providence/Bristol accounted for 70 per cent of the jurors in our 10 per cent random sample.)

Finally, the characteristics of the general population are based on the published results of the 1970 census. Thus census data and jury data were gathered during the same year.

Random Selection

Both the state and federal procedures claim to rest on the same base—random selection from the list of registered voters. However, the state introduces individual investigation. Also, the state statute allows numerous exemptions from service which the jury commissioner interprets to mean mandatory exclusion. (This list includes the automatic exemption of any woman who states that she chooses not to serve.) The federal court has adopted a more limited set of exemptions which it interprets as voluntary. Persons so exempted may decline to serve, if they wish.

The available data permit us to address ourselves to two basic questions. First, can it be shown that the different selection processes employed by the state and federal courts produce venires with different characteristics? And second, to what extent do venires selected from lists of registered voters provide a true cross section of the adult population of the state?

. . .

Jury venires were found to be disproportionately male. Interestingly, there is virtually no difference between the state and federal venires in this respect. Thus 56.9 per cent of the federal veniremen and 56 per cent of the state veniremen were male, while males constitute only 48.2 per cent of the population above age 18. The fact that the state and federal figures are virtually identical strongly suggests that the bias is the result not of the method of selection, but of the use of voter lists as the source of jurors. And indeed, survey research has demonstrated that men are more likely to register to vote than women.

The close similarity between the proportion of women on the state and federal venires is of further interest because, as noted above, the state statute grants an automatic exemption to any woman who claims it. The rules of the Federal District Court, however, grant an automatic exemption only to women who are caring for children under 16 years of age. The data suggest that the impact of the automatic exemption of women who do not wish to serve is not significant, although it is not obvious why this should be so.

The data reveal substantial differences between the average age of the venires and those of the total population. However, state and federal venires also differ somewhat with respect to age.

Young persons are clearly under-represented in both state and federal venires. . . . Venires selected from voting lists would be expected to under-represent the young, as

TABLE 25-1
Statistical Analysis of Venires in the Rhode Island Federal District Court,
and the Rhode Island Superior Court, 1970*

Characteristic	Federal Veniremen	State Veniremen	Adult Population
Sex**			
Male	56.9%	56.0%	48.2%
Female	43.1	44.0	51.8
Age†			
21–29	12.6%	5.3%	21.5%
30–39	16.5	15.9	16.0
40–49	27.3 } 53.1	36.0 } 61.1	19.6 } 37.5
50–59	25.8	25.1	17.9
60–69	15.6	13.7	13.3
70 and above	2.3	4.2	11.7
Years of Education‡			
0–8	17.3%	19.2%	30.2%
9–11	19.8	25.6	23.5
12 (H.S. grad.)	42.4	37.9	29.0
13–15	10.5	7.5	8.0
College grad.	7.0	8.1	5.4
Post graduate work	2.5	1.4	4.0
Occupation§			
Not in labor force	19.0%	22.3%	37.9%
Professional, technical and managers	20.5	18.1	13.1
Clerical, sales	19.1	19.5	15.0
Craftsmen, laborers, service workers	40.0	39.8	33.7

* For federal veniremen, $N = 399$. For state veniremen, $N = 359$. The number of "no responses" is trivial for all variables, except occupation, where 16 per cent of the federal sample did not respond. They are excluded from this table. Their inclusion would not change the basic pattern.

** Total population for this variable includes persons age 18 and above.

† Total population for this variable includes persons age 21 and above.

‡ Total population for this variable includes persons age 25 and above.

§ Total population for this variable includes persons age 16 and above.

numerous studies have shown age to be positively related to voter registration. The data support this assumption.

The difference between the state and federal venires is due, in part, to the fact that, during the period under study, the state statute disqualified persons under 25 years of age. But this is only a partial explanation. For the census data indicate that the age group 25–29 included 10 per cent of the adult population; 8.8 per cent of the federal veniremen were aged 25–29, but only 5.3 per cent of the state veniremen fell into this category. Thus persons under 30 were less likely to serve on state than on federal venires, even when eligible under the statute. The difference is small—only 3.5 percentage points. It might be taken as evidence of some impact of the discretionary element in the state's selection process.

Clearly middle-aged persons are grossly over-represented on both state and federal venires. . . . This phenomenon is not surprising in view of the known characteristics of registered voters.

Education

In general, members of both state and federal venires are better educated than they would be were they strictly representative of the total population. Some differences between the two venires also appear in this connection.

Slightly more than 30 per cent of Rhode Island's adult population (age 25 and above) has no high school education, as contrasted with 17.3 per cent of the federal veniremen and 19.2 per cent of the state veniremen. Whereas 46.4 per cent of the population had earned at least a high school diploma, 54.9 per cent of the state veniremen and 62.4 per cent of the federal veniremen had such certification. Since level of education has been shown to be positively correlated with voter registration, this result is not surprising.

Interestingly, persons who have graduated from college (including those with graduate education) are represented on federal and state venires in their exact proportion to the adult population. Superficially this is surprising, since the college educated are more likely to register to vote than those with less formal education. The countervailing factor which should be noted, however, is the automatic exclusion of many professionals from jury service. Lawyers, doctors, dentists and clergymen are routinely exempted, (as are university teachers from state juries), thus significantly decreasing the pool of college graduates who are eligible to serve.

Some Rhode Island lawyers have suggested that one encounters a better educated juror in the federal court than in the state court. If "better educated" is taken to mean college graduate, the data contradict the folk wisdom. If "better educated" refers to those who have completed high school, there is some support for this view. Clearly, members of both state and federal venires are better educated (in terms of formal schooling) than is the general public.

. . .

Occupation

. . . The data reported in the table demonstrate that state and federal venires are virtually identical in terms of occupations. Upper status positions—professional, technical, and managerial—are more common among the veniremen than among the total population. But the most striking difference between the venires and the population involves those who are not part of the labor force. Such persons are much less likely to be called for jury service than their numbers in the population would indicate. In part this results from the fact that the published census data include all persons over age 16. (Persons aged 16–21 are less likely to be a part of the labor force than are older persons.) In part this reflects the under-representation of women, who are less likely to be employed than men. And in part it probably reflects the fact that the unemployed are less likely to register to vote.

. . .

Rhode Island is not the best state in which to attempt to demonstrate equal or unequal representation of members of racial minorities on juries, for blacks constitute only 3.4 per cent of the population over age 21. Only 1.3 per cent of the federal veniremen were non-white (with 5 per cent not responding to the question). Given the size of the sample, it is difficult to draw meaningful conclusions from these figures.

Comparative data as to race are available for Providence and Bristol Counties (which accounted for 70 per cent of all jurors in our sample). Of the 1,279 persons who were qualified as state veniremen during the first five months of 1972, 2.3 per cent were black; blacks constitute 2.5 per cent of the adult population (over 21) of these two counties. Clearly blacks appear in state venires in representative numbers. . . .

[Other Variables]

Partial data concerning three other variables shed some light on the make-up of the state and federal venires. While the data require further refinement, there is evidence that venires are disproportionately composed of long-term residents. Only 29 per cent of the federal veniremen and 15 per cent of the state veniremen have lived in their present homes for fewer than four years. In contrast, 49 per cent of the total population (of all ages) have occupied their present residences for fewer than five years.

Data regarding military service were available for state but not federal veniremen. The results are striking: 70 per cent of the male veniremen reported having served in the armed forces, as compared with 48.6 per cent of the total male population over age 16. Presumably this reflects the substantial over-representation of the 40–59 year age group on the state venire.

Finally, information about marital status was available for the federal but not the state veniremen. Whereas 68.6 per cent of the total population aged 20 and above is married, 83.7 per cent of the veniremen are married. Again, this may well reflect the over-representation of the middle aged on the venire.

These three variables should be handled with great caution. Nevertheless, if one is prepared to regard length of tenure in residence, military service, and marriage, as some evidence of a "stable" and/or "conventional" citizen, then the data are consistent with the hypothesis that the veniremen are overly "stable" and "conventional." Again, all three factors may well be another way of saying that a venireman is significantly more likely to be middle-aged than is the average citizen.

The data demonstrate marked differences between the characteristics of venires (both state and federal) and the characteristics of the adult population. Venires are disproportionately male, middle aged, educated, and employed. These are all results which could have been predicted on the basis of the existing literature about voter registration.

The characteristics of the state and federal venires were found to be quite similar, despite the fact that the state's selection process introduces the element of human discretion (individual investigation in the potential venireman's home), and despite the fact that the state statute includes explicit exemptions which are regarded as mandatory, while the federal rules provide a much more limited list of exemptions which potential jurors may claim if they wish.

. . .

JUDICIAL DECISION MAKING

CHAPTER NINE

FACTS AS BASES
FOR DECISIONS

In Part Three we turn our attention to the way in which disputes, once translated into lawsuits, are dealt with by judges. We are concerned with how judges decide cases and why they make particular decisions. The decision-making behavior of judges is of critical importance in any inquiry into the nature of dispute processing by courts. Such dispute processing should proceed, at least in theory, in a principled and impartial manner. Judicial decision making may be distinguished from the decision making of other public officials because it is expected to be guided rather strictly by clearly articulated rules and to proceed with reference solely to the facts in dispute. In this part the extent to which American judges, in fact, live up to this expectation is described and analyzed.

The traditional model of dispute resolution by trial courts suggests that the judge applies the relevant law to the relevant facts that have been established by the jury or the judge during the trial. The outcome of the case is thus considered to follow, routinely and indeed mechanically, determination of facts and law. The model, of course, assumes that legally relevant facts as well as the applicable law can be determined as a result of the trial. However, we have already seen that the traditional model's assumption that trials are the ordinary vehicle for dispute resolution is simply not true. In terms of the total business of trial courts, the fact-finding role of judges and juries is minimal.

We shall also be observing in subsequent chapters that the determination and application of "the law" is far from the straightforward technical process the traditional model suggests it is, particularly when disputes raise new questions of public policy. Our task now is to examine the traditional model's assumptions about "facts" and the place they have in judicial decision making in those cases that involve the full scope of the judicial process.

First, the traditional model of dispute resolution assumes that the facts of the case *can* be established by the judicial process. There is the underlying assumption that the adversary system, whereby opposing counsel present their respective sides of the dispute and have the opportunity to closely scrutinize each other's evidence and witnesses, facilitates the emergence of the truth. The beliefs that facts can be discovered and that the adversary system aids in their discovery are cornerstones of the traditional model.

Second, there is the assumption in the traditional model that only certain kinds of facts are legally relevant and can potentially be established and taken into account in decision making. This means, for example, that ordinarily the race or sex of the criminal defendant, or his or her socioeconomic status, or the type of lawyer defending the accused are *not* legally relevant but are rather legally irrelevant and should have no bearing on the resolution of the dispute. Judges and jurors who take such "irrelevant" facts into consideration are thought to violate basic legal norms. This second assumption, in effect, suggests a distinction between (1) the facts of the dispute, that is, what happened (most of which is legally relevant); (2) the facts about the personal attributes of the disputants, that is, their race, sex, age, class, and so on (most of which is legally irrelevant); and (3) the facts concerning the processing of the litigation itself, such as the type of lawyer involved—for example, privately retained or court appointed—and whether a plea bargain has been made (also generally not legally relevant).

A third traditional assumption is that judges give the same weight to the same legally relevant facts and that the result is individual decisional consistency as well as uniformity in decision making among different judges. Sentencing disparity among judges, where similar facts in similar cases produce different results, is considered to be an indication of judicial pathology. This underscores a related assumption that there is predictability and hence continuity in the law. There is the expectation that judges apply the same law to similar factual situations, thereby producing similar decisional results. Lawyers expect to be able to tell their clients what "the law" is and what it requires. Individuals, organizations, and governments expect to be able to know in advance the legal consequences of their actions. The concept of settled law is simply the expectation that any competent judge in a court of law will behave predictably given certain facts and the law as it is widely understood.

There is the fourth assumption that the facts of the case are important only at the trial court level. Once established by the trial court the facts are not supposed to be questioned at all by appellate courts. The traditional model considers trial courts as triers of fact and appellate courts as being concerned only with questions of law.

How do these assumptions concerning "facts" as the bases for decisions stand up against what we know of the experiences of judges and the studies of their behavior? The answer in brief: not very well. Each of the previously discussed assumptions, in one form or another, is considered in the three readings in this chapter.

Selection 26, by Jerome Frank (who himself had a distinguished career on the United States Court of Appeals for the Second Circuit), raises fundamental questions about the nature of fact finding by means of the judicial process. Frank's position, usually referred to by the shorthand expression "fact skepticism," is one of doubt about the ability of the adversary system to determine the truth. Ultimately it questions whether it is *ever* possible to objectively determine "facts." For Frank, the fact-finding enterprise is so subjective that it is impossible to predict in advance how a dispute is going to be resolved in court.

Partridge, Eldridge, and Kort, as well as other researchers who focus attention on the relationship of facts to judicial behavior, ignore the subjectivity of the fact-finding process. They assume that most facts can be objectively determined. But the fact-oriented researchers do not make the distinction between legally relevant and legally irrelevant facts made by the traditional model. Rather they consider as fair game *all* facts—those pertaining to the dispute *and* disputants as well as those concerning the processing of the litigation. Studies of both trial courts and appellate courts have suggested that the race of the defendant, although usually legally irrelevant, may affect case outcomes.[1] Some have argued that the nature of the crime and the socioeconomic status of the criminal may be tied to decisional behavior in that white-collar crime and criminals may be treated less severely than blue-collar crime and criminals.[2] Other legally irrelevant facts that have been linked with judicial behavior include whether a plea bargain was negotiated,[3] and whether the lawyer was privately retained or assigned by the Court.[4]

The third assumption, that judges give approximately the same weight to the same facts, was rigorously tested by Partridge and Eldridge (selection 27). These researchers were not concerned with the question of whether individual judges were consistent from one case to the next but rather with the question of whether different judges would make similar sentencing decisions when confronted with the same facts. The not unexpected finding of wide sentencing disparity should definitively dispel this mythical aspect of the traditional model.[5] However, the traditionalist assumption that individual judges are consistent in the weight they give certain facts is seemingly supported by fact-pattern studies of appellate courts. In these studies researchers have been able to calculate weights of facts to enable the prediction of how a dispute will be resolved on appeal. Also it has been possible to specify what combinations of facts are necessary to produce particular results. Kort discusses these concerns in selection 28. Obviously, if individual judges on a collegial court were inconsistent in the weights they gave the facts from one case to the next, fact-pattern analysis, as discussed by Kort, would result in the disproving of the fact-pattern hypothesis that particular configurations of both legally relevant and legally irrelevant facts are associated with particular case outcomes.

Finally, the traditionalist assumption that the facts of the dispute are not questioned by the appellate courts is apparently undermined by the successful application of the fact-pattern approach, as noted by Kort. Of course, witnesses and physical evidence are not presented before appellate courts. Yet appellate judges on occasion differ with trial judges over the weight and interpretation given certain facts.

Although the traditional model's assumptions about the relationship of facts to judicial decisions can be effectively challenged, it is interesting to note that both the traditional model and its challengers place great importance on the facts. With the exception of fact skeptics such as Jerome Frank, there seems to be widespread agreement that facts can be objectively determined and that predictable patterns of judicial behavior can be expected. Where there is disagreement, it is over what facts are to be considered, whether appellate courts consider them, why judges weigh and weight them the way they do, and how the "law" is applied to the facts.

We have already suggested that the traditional model's treatment of "facts" is inadequate. The other side of the coin is the traditional model's treatment of "law." Here we find prominent challenges going back to the so-called legal realists of the 1920s and 1930s. Legal realists argued that the legal rules and principles cited by judges, particularly appellate court judges, as the bases for their decisions are largely a smokescreen for the furtherance of their own views on social and economic policy. The realists argued that this occurs because inherent in judicial decision making is a large amount of discretion in choosing which precedents or principles to follow. These realists emphasized judicial discretion and played down law and the nature of judicial institutions. In subsequent chapters we will consider a number of variables that have been thought by legal realists and others to be related to decision making. We will begin with environmental variables and consider in turn backgrounds of judges, judicial attitudes and values, the judicial role, and the small-group influence on collegial court decision making.[6] The extent to which these variables are shown to be associated with decision making is the extent to which the traditional model's assumptions about the place and uses of law are inadequate.

Notes

1. See, for example, Fred Kort, "Content Analysis of Judicial Opinions and Rules of Law," in Glendon Schubert, ed., *Judicial Decision-Making* (New York: Free Press, 1963), pp. 133-197; S. Sidney Ulmer, "The Discriminant Function and a Theoretical Context for Its Use in Estimating the Votes of Judges," in Joel Grossman and Joseph Tanenhaus, eds., *Frontiers of Judicial Research* (New York: Wiley, 1969), pp. 335-369; Marvin E. Wolfgang and Marc Riedel, "Race, Judicial Discretion, and the Death Penalty," *The Annals of the American Academy of Political and Social Science* 407 (1973), 119-133; Walter G. Markham, "Chromatic Justice: Color as an Element of the Offense," paper presented at the annual meeting of the American Political Science Association, 1974. But compare John Hagan, "Extra-Legal Attributes and Criminal Sentencing: An Assessment of a Sociological Viewpoint," *Law and Society Review* 8 (1974), 357-383; Herbert Jacob and James Eisenstein, "Sentences and Other Sanctions Imposed on Felony Defendants in Baltimore, Chicago, and Detroit," paper presented at the annual meeting of the American Political Science Association, 1974; and Stevens H. Clarke and Gary G. Koch, "The Influence of Income and other Factors on whether Criminal Defendants go to Prison," *Law and Society Review* 11 (1976), 57-92.

2. See, for example, *Federal Offenders in United States District Courts, 1971* (Washington, D.C.: Administrative Office of the U.S. Courts, 1973), pp. 149, 157. Also see Marvin Frankel, *Criminal Sentences: Law Without Order* (New York: Hill and Wang, 1973), pp. 23-24.

3. See, for example, *Federal Offenders, 1971*, pp. 14-15.

4. See, for example, *ibid.*, pp. 8-9. Also see Stuart S. Nagel, "Effects of Alternative Types of Counsel on Criminal Procedure Treatment," *Indiana Law Journal* 48 (1973), 404-426.

5. Also see the findings and discussion in Shari S. Diamond and Hans Zeisel, "Sentencing Councils: A Study of Sentence Disparity and its Reduction," *University of Chicago Law Review* 43 (1975), 109.

6. There are other variables that may be relevant to decision making. For example, some scholars have suggested that the personality of the judge should be treated as a decision-making variable. See Harold D. Lasswell, *Power and Personality* (Norton: 1948), pp. 59-88; and Willard Gaylin, *Partial Justice: A Study of Bias in Sentencing* (New York: Random House, 1974).

26

Facts Are Guesses

Jerome Frank

If you scrutinize a legal rule, you will see that it is a conditional statement referring to facts. Such a rule seems to say, in effect, "If such and such a fact exists, then this or that legal consequence should follow." It seems to say, for example, "If a trustee, for his own purposes, uses money he holds in trust, he must repay it." Or, "If a man, without provocation, kills another, the killer must be punished." In other words, a legal rule directs that (if properly asked to do so) a court should attach knowable consequences to certain facts, if and whenever there are such facts. That is what is meant by the conventional statement, used in describing the decisional process, that courts apply legal rules to the facts of law-suits.

For convenience, let us symbolize a legal rule by the letter R, the facts of a case by the letter F, and the court's decision of that case by the letter D. We can then crudely schematize the conventional theory of how courts operate by saying

$$R \times F = D$$

In other words, according to the conventional theory, a decision is a product of an R and an F. If, as to any law-suit, you know the R and the F, you should, then, know what the D will be.

In a simple, stable society, most of the R's are moderately well stabilized. Which legal rules that society will enforce it is not difficult for men —or at any rate, for the lawyer, the professional court-man—to know in advance of any trial. In such a society, the R—one of the two factors in the $R \times F = D$ formula—is usually fixed.

In our society, however, with the rapid changes brought about by modern life, many of the R's have become unstable. Accordingly, in our times, legal uncertainty—uncertainty about future decisions and therefore about legal rights—is generally ascribed to the indefiniteness of the R's. The increasing multiplicity of the rules, the conflicts between rules, and the flexibility of some of the rules, have arrested the attention of most legal thinkers. Those thinkers, perceiving the absence of rigidity in some rules, have assumed that the certainty or uncertainty of the D's, in the $R \times F = D$ equation, stems principally from the certainty or uncertainty of the R's.

Reprinted from "Facts Are Guesses," in Jerome Frank, *Courts on Trial: Myth and Reality in American Justice* (Copyright© 1949 by Jerome Frank; published by Princeton University Press; Princeton Paperback, 1973), pp. 14-24, 26-27, 32, by permission of Princeton University Press. Footnotes have been omitted.

That assumption leads to a grave miscomprehension of court-house government and to the neglect by most legal scholars of the more difficult part of the courts' undertaking. I refer to the courts' task with respect to the factor in the $R \times F = D$ formula, the F. The courts, as we saw, are supposed to ascertain the facts in the disputes which become law-suits. That is, a court is supposed to determine the actual, objective acts of the parties, to find out just what they did or did not do, before the law-suit began, so far as those facts bear on the compliance with, or the violation of, some legal rule. If there is uncertainty as to whether the court will find the true relevant facts—if it is uncertain whether the court's F will match the real, objective F—then what? Then, since the decision, the D, is presumably the joint product of an R and an F, the D is bound to be uncertain. To put it differently: No matter how certain the legal rules may be, the decisions remain at the mercy of the courts' fact-finding. If there is doubt about what a court, in a law-suit, will find were the facts, then there is at least equal doubt about its decision.

Go back now to Mr. Sensible and his lawyer. [Earlier there was presented an example of a lawsuit between Mr. Sensible and Mr. Smart] Suppose that the lawyer knows the pertinent R's, and that they are as fixed as fixed can be, as precise as a table of logarithms. But, I ask again, how can the lawyer in 1946 prophesy what will be the D in 1950, unless he also knows the F that, in 1950, the trial judge (or jury) will use in the $R \times F = D$?

What is the F? Is it what actually happened between Sensible and Smart? Most emphatically not. At best, it is only what the trial court—the trial judge or jury—thinks happened. What the trial court thinks happened may, however, be hopelessly incorrect. But that does not matter—legally speaking. For court purposes, what the court thinks about the facts is all that matters. The actual events, the real objective acts and words of Sensible and Smart, happened in the past. They do not walk into court. The court usually learns about these real, objective, past facts only through the oral testimony of fallible witnesses. Accordingly, the court, from hearing the testimony, must guess at the actual, past facts. Judicially, the facts consist of the reaction of the judge or jury to the testimony. The F is merely a guess about the actual facts. There can be no assurance that that F, that guess, will coincide with those actual, past facts.

To be sure, this difficulty becomes of no importance when the parties to the suit do not dispute about the facts, when their sole difference concerns the proper R. Then the R will settle the court fight. In other words, if Smart agrees to the facts as Sensible tells them, then the only question for the court will be whether the R is as Sensible claims it to be. With reference to that sort of law-suit, the trained lawyer, as a specialist in the R's, is frequently an excellent predictor of decisions. For often (although not always) the applicable R is fairly certain and knowable, or sufficiently so that a competent lawyer can foretell what the court will say it is.

But usually, when men "go to law," the facts are not admitted, and the testimony is oral and in conflict. For convenience, call such suits "contested" cases. It cannot be known in advance which cases will be "contested." To predict a decision in a suit not yet begun, about a dispute which has not yet occurred, requires, then, the most extensive guessing. For whenever there is a question of the credibility of witnesses—of the believeability, the reliability, of their testimony—then, unavoidably, the trial judge or jury must make a guess about the facts. The lawyer, accordingly, must make a guess about those guesses. The uncertainty of many "legal rights" corresponds to the correctness or incorrectness of such lawyer-guesses.

2

Let me bring out that point more sharply. When, in 1946, the Sensible-Smart contract is signed, no dispute has yet arisen. The lawyer, in making his guess at that time, must attempt to take into account what may be the future acts of Sensible and Smart, the acts they may do in the interval between 1946 and the date of a future law-suit. Patently, that contingency makes the guessing pretty difficult.

Suppose, however, that Sensible consults his lawyer in 1948, after a dispute has arisen, so that all the actual facts have already happened. It may seem to you that if the client, Sensible, accurately reports all those facts to his lawyer, the latter can undoubtedly tell his client just what a court will decide. I'm sorry to say you are wrong. The lawyer must still cope with many elusive, uncontrollable, wayward factors which may upset any prediction. Trials are often full of surprises. The adversary introduces unanticipated testimony. Witnesses, on whom the lawyer relied, change their stories when they take the witness-stand. The facts as they appeared to the lawyer when, before a trial, he conferred with his client and his witnesses, frequently are not at all like the facts as they later show up in the court-room.

But perhaps you believe that the trial judge or jury will surely learn the truth about the facts. If so, you are adopting an axiom, implied in the conventional theory of how courts decide cases, the "Truth-Will-Out axiom." But often that "axiom" does not jibe with reality. For reflect on the following: When a witness testifies, what is he doing? He is reporting his present memory of something he observed in the past, something he saw or heard. A witness is not a photographic plate or phonographic disc. Let us suppose that he is entirely honest. Nevertheless, note these sources of possible error: (1) The witness may erroneously have observed the past event at the time it occurred. . . . (2) But suppose a witness made no error in his original observation of an event. He may, nevertheless, erroneously remember that correct observation. . . . (3) Now we come to the stage where the witness reports in the court-room his present recollection of his original observation. Here again, error may enter. The honest witness, due to a variety of causes, may inadvertently misstate his recollection, may inaccurately report his story. . . .

Thus far, I have posited an honest and unprejudiced witness. But many witnesses are neither. Some are downright liars. Aside from perjurers, there are the innumerable biased witnesses, whose narratives, although honest, have been markedly affected by their prejudices for or against one of the parties to the suit. A court has said that a biased witness, out of sympathy for a litigant he regards as having been wronged, "with entire innocence may recall things that have never occurred, or forget important instances that have occurred. . . ."

A story is told of a trial judge who, after hearing the testimony and the lawyer's arguments, announced: "Gentlemen, if Humphrey, the deceased, said—in the light of these Missouri decisions—'Daughter, if you'll come and live with me, I'll give you this house,' then I'll decide for the plaintiff. Now just what was the testimony?" Unfortunately the court reporter had boggled his notes. The judge impatiently asked if the principal witness, the plaintiff's maid, was present, and, learning that she was in the courtroom, asked her again to take the stand and repeat her testimony. This is what she said: "I remember very well what happened. It was a cold and stormy night. We were all sitting around the fire. Old Mr. Humphrey said to Mrs. Quinn, 'In the light of these Missouri decisions, daughter, if you'll come and live with me, I'll give you this house.' " Of course, in that case it was obvious enough to the judge that the witness had a convenient and partisan recollection. But there are hundreds of cases where that kind of memory and that kind of testimony are not exposed but believed.

The axiom or assumption that, in all or most trials, the truth will out, ignores, then, the several elements of subjectivity and chance. It ignores perjury and bias; ignores the false impression made on the judge or jury by the honest witness who seems untruthful because he is frightened in the court-room or because he is irascible or over-scrupulous or given to exaggeration. It ignores the mistaken witness who honestly and convincingly testifies that he remembers acts or conversations that happened quite differently than as he narrates them in court. It neglects, also, the dead or missing witness without whose testimony a crucial fact cannot be brought out, or an important opposing witness cannot be successfully contradicted. Finally it neglects the missing or destroyed letter, or receipt, or cancelled check.

Nor is it true that trial courts will be sure to detect lies or mistakes in testimony. That is clearly not so when a jury tries a case. Many experienced persons believe that of all the possible ways that could be devised to get at the falsity or truth of testimony, none could be conceived that would be more ineffective than trial by jury.

Judges, too, when they try cases without juries, are often fallible in getting at the true facts of a "contested" case. Partly that is due to our faulty way of trying cases in which we hamstring the judge. But even with the best system that could be devised, there would be no way to ensure that the judge will know infallibly which witnesses are accurately reporting the facts. As yet we have no lie-detector for which all responsible psychologists will vouch and which most courts will regard as reliable. But even a perfect lie-detector will not reveal mistakes in a witness' original observation of the facts to which he testifies, and probably will not disclose his mistakes due to his unconscious prejudices.

Lacking any adequate mechanical means of detecting such matters, the courts resort to a common-sense technique: All of us know that, in everyday life, the way a man behaves when he tells a story—his intonations, his fidgetings or composure, his yawns, the use of his eyes, his air of candor or of evasiveness—may furnish valuable clues to his reliability. Such clues are by no means impeccable guides, but they are often immensely helpful. So the courts have concluded. "The appearance and manner of a witness," many courts have said, "is often a complete antidote to what he testifies." . . .

3

Having in mind this significance properly attached to close observation of the witnesses, I now must emphasize an element in the decisional process which, curiously, has seldom been considered: Trial judges and juries, in trying to get at the past facts through the witnesses, are themselves witnesses of what goes on in court-rooms. They must determine the facts from what they see and hear, from the gestures and other conduct of the testifying witnesses as well as from their words. Now, as silent witnesses of the witnesses, the trial judges and juries suffer from the same human weaknesses as other witnesses. They, too, are not photographic plates or phonographic discs. If the testifying witnesses make errors of observation, are subject to lapses of memory, or contrive mistaken, imaginative reconstruction of events they observed, in the same way trial judges or juries are subject to defects in their apprehension and their recollection of what the witnesses said and how they behaved.

The facts as they actually happened are therefore twice refracted—first by the witnesses, and second by those who must "find" the facts. The reactions of trial judges or juries to the testimony are shot through with subjectivity. Thus we have subjectivity piled on subjectivity. It is surely proper, then, to say that the facts as "found" by a trial court are subjective.

When Jack Spratt, as a witness, testifies to a fact, he is merely stating his belief or opinion about that past fact. When he says, "I saw McCarthy hit Schmidt," he means, "I believe that is what happened." When a trial judge or jury, after hearing that testimony, finds as a fact that McCarthy hit Schmidt, the finding means no more than the judge's or jury's belief that the belief of the witness Spratt is an honest belief, and that his belief accurately reflects what actually happened. A trial court's findings of fact is, then, at best, its belief or opinion about someone else's belief or opinion.

. . .

4

And now I come to a major matter, one which most non-lawyers do not understand, and one which puts the trial courts at the heart of our judicial system: An upper court can seldom do anything to correct a trial court's mistaken belief about the facts. Where, as happens in most cases, the testimony at the trial was oral, the upper court usually feels obliged to adopt the trial court's determination of the facts. Why? Because in such a case the trial court heard and saw the witnesses as they testified, but the upper court did not. The upper court has only a typewritten or printed record of the testimony. The trial court alone is in a position to interpret the demeanor-clues, this "language without words. . . ." That is why, when testimony is taken in a trial court, an upper court, on appeal, in most instances accepts the facts as found by the trial court, when those findings can be supported by reasonable inferences from some witness's testimony, even if it is flatly contradicted in the testimony of other witnesses.

Considering how a trial court reaches its determination as to the facts, it is most misleading to talk, as we lawyers do, of a trial court "finding" the facts. The trial court's facts are not "data," not something that is "given"; they are not waiting somewhere, ready made, for the court to discover, to "find." More accurately, they are processed by the trial court—are, so to speak, "made " by it, on the basis of its subjective reactions to the witnesses' stories. Most legal scholars fail to consider that subjectivity, because, when they think of courts, they think almost exclusively of upper courts and of their written opinions. For, in these opinions, the facts are largely "given" to the upper courts—given to those courts by the trial courts.

It should now be obvious that the conventional description of the decisional process needs alteration. For that description implies that the F, in the $R \times F = D$ equation, is an objective fact—what might be called an OF—so that, seemingly, $R \times OF = D$. But, as the F is subjective—what might therefore be called an SF—the formula should read: $R \times SF = D$.

5

I can feel that at this moment some lawyer-critic, reading this book, is itching to reply: "Doubtless, decisions in 'contested' cases turn on the judge's or jury's belief, and that belief may be mistaken. Court-orders may depend upon such beliefs of the trial judges or the juries who happen to try the cases. But a man's legal rights are what they are, even if a trial court, through an erroneous belief about the facts, decides against him."

That I deny. At any rate, I deny that the words "legal rights" have any practical meaning, if used as my critic uses them. If a court decides that Smart has, in fact, done no legal wrong to Sensible, then Sensible has no meaningful legal right against Smart. Not on this earth, not in this life. If a court, after listening to conflicting oral testimony, mistakes the facts and decides for Smart, and Sensible appeals, losing his appeal, that's all there is to Sensible's legal rights—there isn't any more. His legal rights, so far as the courts are concerned, consist precisely of what he can persuade a court to make Smart do. If Sensible wins the court-fight, then he'll have a legal right; if he loses, he won't. There is no middle ground, no judicial Purgatory. If Sensible loses in court, I think it plain nonsense to say that nevertheless he still has a right against Smart, or that Smart owes him a legal duty. Please note that I say nothing of moral rights. Moral considerations should, and unquestionably do, play a part in many court decisions. But when a court, once and for all, holds that a man is without a legal right, his remaining moral rights are usually of no interest to the courts, for usually the courts will do nothing more for him.

. . .

6

Let me summarize: Law-suits are fights. They are legal battles fought in a court-room. They are historically (and contemporaneously) substitutes for private gun-fights and knife-fights. Instead of using your knife or gun to make Robinson do what you want him to do, you fight in a court-house with non-lethal weapons, with implements of persuasion, to induce a court to enter an order directing Robinson to do what you want—fight to produce a court-order which will direct the sheriff, if necessary, to use his gun to make Robinson do what you want. And law-suits alone—nothing else—ultimately fix tested legal rights. If Robinson, voluntarily—or because he is ashamed not to, or afraid not to— does what you want, you haven't tested out your legal rights against him, or his legal obligations to you. It is only if he doesn't do what you want, and if you try to get a court to order him to do so, that you really learn what those legal rights and duties are. Jones's tested legal rights against Smith on a mortgage, a lease, an employment contract, or because of an automobile accident, are unknown until Jones sues Smith and a court decides that suit.

We are all Smiths and Joneses. You can't really know your legal rights (your court-enforceable rights) against any other person, about anything, until you obtain an enforceable decision in a specific law-suit brought against that other person. No law-suits, no tested legal rights. Until there has been an enforceable court-order in a specific law-suit, there can be only guesses about any legal rights or duties. And those guesses—even if they are lawyers' guesses—are not always too good, especially before a law-suit arises. For court-decisions in law-suits depend on at least two things (Rules and Facts) and one of those is peculiarly unguessable—namely what the trial court (judge or jury) will believe were the facts. Guessing legal rights, before litigation occurs, is, then, guessing what judges or juries will guess were the facts, and that is by no means easy. Legal rights and duties are, then, often guessy, if-y.

See what this means: Most legal rights turn on the facts as "proved" in a future law-suit, and proof of those facts, in "contested" cases, is at the mercy of such matters as mistaken witnesses, perjured witnesses, missing or dead witnesses, mistaken judges, in-attentive judges, biased judges, inattentive juries, and biased juries. In short, a legal right is usually a bet, a wager, on the chancy outcome of a possible future law-suit.

. . .

7

Many non-lawyers and some lawyers, when they talk of "facts" in litigation, refer not to the kind of facts I have been considering (i.e., whether Jones ran over young Tommy Smith), but to what might be called "background" or "social and economic" facts, often of a statistical character—the sort of facts presented to the courts in the famous "Brandeis briefs." Facts of that sort do not involve witnesses' credibility. But the great majority of actual law-suits do involve some crucial fact issues which turn on determinations by the trial courts of orally-testifying witnesses' credibility. There the trial court usually has the final say about the facts. . . . With that in mind, Judge Olson recently suggested that law-suits are misnamed: They should be called "fact suits."

. . .

27

The Second Circuit Sentencing Study

Anthony Partridge and William B. Eldridge

I. Introduction

This is a report of a sentencing experiment conducted by the district judges of the Second Circuit to determine the extent of disparity in the sentencing of criminal defendants within the circuit. . . . In the course of it, the district judges of the Second Circuit—all forty-three of the active judges and seven of the senior judges—rendered roughly as many sentences as they normally do in half a year. The experiment thus represented a major effort at self-evaluation, initiated and carried out principally by the judges themselves.

The unique quality of this experiment, which sets it apart from all previous studies of disparity, is the opportunity it provides to observe a large number of judges rendering sentences in identical cases. Earlier studies have all been based on the observation of sentences rendered by different judges in different cases. The obvious problem for such studies is how to determine whether observed differences in sentences result from differences in judges or differences in cases. The solution is inevitably a statistical one: the analysis is based on groups of cases and relies upon group measures such as the percentage of cases in which different judges give prison sentences. The current study, by contrast, deals directly with differences in judges' sentencing behavior, without the complications introduced by differences in the underlying cases. For the first time, we are able to observe the extent of agreement among many judges on a case-by-case basis. . . .

Thirty presentence reports were sent to the judges at a rate of five reports a week over a six-week period beginning March 16, 1974. The first twenty of them were actual presentence reports, drawn from the files of probation offices within the Second Circuit, but edited to alter identifying facts such as names, places, identification numbers, and dates. These twenty cases were selected to be broadly representative of the sentencing business of the circuit.

Each of the last ten presentence reports was prepared in two versions which differed from one another with respect to some characteristic that might be relevant to the sentencing process. In Case 26, for example, the defendant pleaded guilty in one version and was found guilty after trial in the other, but the versions were otherwise identical. The

Reprinted from *A Report to the Judges of the Second Circuit*, published by the Federal Judicial Center, August 1974.

judges were randomly divided into two groups, so that half the judges got one version and half got the other. Through this technique, it was hoped that we might learn whether certain case characteristics were more likely than others to be productive of disagreement about the appropriate sentence. These last ten presentence reports were not selected to represent the sentencing business of the circuit; rather, they were selected so that certain characteristics might be tested. Nine of them were actual presentence reports drawn from the files of probation offices within the Second Circuit, although one version of each was of course modified to produce the desired variation, and occasional other modifications were made to sharpen the issues being studied. The tenth presentence report in this group was an invention of the Federal Judicial Center staff.

The analysis of the sentences returned is predicated on the assumption that all the judges sentencing in a particular case were acting on the basis of the same information— that is, the information contained in the presentence report. To avoid introducing information gained from other sources, a judge who had actually sentenced a defendant (or who had participated in a sentencing council considering the case) was not asked to sentence that defendant for the purposes of the experiment. About half of the judges therefore received somewhat fewer than the full series of thirty cases. The total number of presentence reports mailed was 1,465, not counting those mailed to one senior judge who was unable to participate because of illness. 1,442 responses were received, with all but two of the nonresponses being in the last ten cases.

For the purposes of the study, disparity is defined as dissimilar treatment by different judges of defendants who are similarly situated. Stated differently, disparity is departure from the principle that the defendant's sentence shouldn't depend on which judge he gets. It should be noted that this definition excludes two other phenomena that are sometimes referred to as disparity. First, it excludes dissimilar treatment of similarly situated defendants by the *same* judge—that is, departure from the principle that the sentence shouldn't depend on such legally irrelevant factors as the judge's mood or racial prejudices. Second, the definition used here excludes disproportionately dissimilar treatment of unlike situations: we do not deal with the question whether sentences for stealing government checks are unduly harsh when compared with sentences for income-tax evasion. In view of the somewhat flexible content of the word "disparity," it is important to keep those limitations in mind.

II.   The Extent of Disparity

A. Disparity in Sentences Rendered in the Experiment

For each case in the group of twenty that was selected as representing the sentencing business of the circuit, the sentences rendered have been ranked from most severe to least severe. Table 27-1 shows, for each of these twenty cases, selected points on the rank list: the two extreme sentences, the median sentence, the sixth most severe and sixth least severe sentences, and the twelfth most severe and twelfth least severe sentences. Thus, for Case 1, the median sentence was 10 years' imprisonment and a $50,000 fine, and the sentences ranged from 3 years' imprisonment to 20 years' imprisonment and a $65,000 fine. Twelve judges sentenced to 15 years' imprisonment or more; twelve judges sentenced to 8 years' imprisonment and a $20,000 fine or less; and so on. In Cases 3 and 5, special parole terms under 21 U.S.C. §841 are included in the term "probation."

The construction of a rank list of sentences of course assumes a set of rules for determining when one sentence is more severe than another. In many cases, there would be no likelihood of disagreement on that question, but there are points at which different observers may disagree on whether one sentence or another is the more severe. . . .

The rules that have been used for ranking in this study are based on the assumption that imprisonment of any length is more severe than probation or a fine, that supervised probation is more severe than a fine or unsupervised probation, and that a fine is more severe than unsupervised probation. They also give some weight to the authority under which a prison sentence or probation is imposed. . . .

The ranking is not affected by the length of any prison sentence whose execution was suspended, or by any requirement such as restitution, participation in a drug program, etc.

. . .

Table 27-1 clearly shows a wide range of disagreement among Second Circuit judges about the appropriate sentences in the twenty cases. Substantial disagreement persists, moreover, even if the extremes of the distribution are ignored. In both Cases 1 and 2, for example, at least six judges imposed prison terms of 15 years or longer, while at least six others imposed prison terms of 5 years or shorter. Indeed, in many of the cases the disagreement remains substantial even if we compare the twelfth most severe and twelfth least severe sentences. For the most part, the pattern displayed is not one of substantial consensus with a few sentences falling outside the area of agreement. Rather, it would appear that absence of consensus is the norm.

. . .

In short, the consistent tenor of the data presented in the table is one of substantial disparity . . . .

B. The Representative Character of the Presentence Reports Studied

It was stated earlier that the twenty cases included in Table 27-1 were selected to be broadly representative of the sentencing business of the circuit. It should be understood, however, that they were not selected to be a statistically valid cross-section of that business. Moreover, it is important for readers to understand that no single case in the table is in any sense representative of any class of cases. Case 2, for example, was a bank robbery case. But there is no reason to assume that the pattern of sentences displayed for that case is typical of bank robbery cases. The sentences in the case were the product of judicial reactions to a collection of facts that included not only the title of the offense, but the circumstances under which it was committed, the defendant's other involvement with the law, and a variety of other matters. It would be erroneous to conclude that the range of sentences for bank robbery among the participating judges is 5 years to 18 years, or that sentences in bank robbery cases are highly disparate, or anything else about bank robbery cases as a class. The case can properly be viewed only as one case in a group of twenty that were selected through a process designed to achieve a reasonably representative group.

. . .

After the twenty crime categories had been selected they were assigned to districts, and the chief probation officers were asked to select presentence reports. The study included one presentence report from Vermont, two each from Connecticut, Northern New York, and Western New York, five from Eastern New York, and eight from Southern New

TABLE 27-1
Sentences in Twenty Cases

	Case #1	Case #2	Case #3	Case #4	Case #5	Case #6	Case #7	Case #8	Case #9	Case #10
Most severe sentence	20 yrs pris; $65,000.	18 yrs pris; $5,000.	10 yrs pris; 5 yrs prob.	7½ yrs pris.	5 yrs pris; 3 yrs prob.	3 yrs pris; $5,000.	2 yrs pris.	YCA indet.	3 yrs pris.	1 yr pris.
6th most severe sentence	15 yrs pris; $50,000.	15 yrs pris.	6 yrs pris; 5 yrs prob.	5 yrs pris.	3 yrs pris; 3 yrs prob.	3 yrs pris; $5,000.	2 yrs pris.	YCA indet.	6 mos pris; 2 yrs unsup prob.	6 mos pris; 1 yr prob.
12th most severe sentence	15 yrs pris.	15 yrs pris.	5 yrs pris; 5 yrs prob.	4 yrs pris.	3 yrs pris; 3 yrs prob.	2 yrs pris; $5,000.	1½ yrs pris.	6 mos pris; 5 yrs prob. [§4209]	6 mos pris.	3 mos pris; 27 mos prob.
Median sentence	10 yrs pris; $50,000.	10 yrs pris.	5 yrs pris; 3 yrs prob.	3 yrs pris.	2 yrs pris; 3 yrs prob.	1 yr pris; $5,000.	1 yr pris.	5 mos pris; 5 yrs prob. [§4209]	3 mos pris; 21 mos unsup prob.	2 mos pris; 1 yr prob.
12th least severe sentence	8 yrs pris; $20,000.	7½ yrs pris.	3 yrs pris; 3 yrs prob.	3 yrs pris.	1½ yrs pris; 3 yrs prob.	6 mos pris; 2½ yrs prob; $3,000.	6 mos pris; 18 mos prob.	2 mos pris; 2 yrs prob. [§4209]	1 mo pris; 2 yrs unsup prob.	3 yrs prob.
6th least severe sentence	5 yrs pris; 3 yrs prob; $10,000.	5 yrs pris.	3 yrs pris; 3 yrs prob.	2 yrs pris.	5 yrs prob; $500.	6 mos pris; $5,000.	3 mos pris.	3 yrs prob.	2 yrs unsup prob.	2 yrs prob.
Least severe sentence	3 yrs pris.	5 yrs pris.	1 yr pris; 5 yrs prob.	4 yrs prob.	2 yrs prob.	3 mos pris; $5,000.	1 yr prob.	1 yr prob.	Susp. if leave U.S.	1 yr prob.
No. of sentences ranked	45	48	46	45	42	48	39	41	49	48

	Case #11	Case #12	Case #13	Case #14	Case #15	Case #16	Case #17	Case #18	Case #19	Case #20
Most severe sentence	6 mos pris; 6 mos prob; $5,000.	1 yr pris.	1½ yrs pris.	YCA indet.	1 yr pris; $3,000.	YCA Indet.	3 yrs pris.	6 mos pris; 18 mos prob.	2 yrs pris; $2,500.	1 yr pris; $1,000.
6th most severe sentence	6 mos pris; $2,500.	6 mos pris; 3 yrs prob.	6 mos pris; 2 yrs prob.	YCA indet.	6 mos pris; 3 yrs prob; $10,000.	5 yrs prob.	6 mos pris; 4½ yrs prob.	5 yrs prob.	6 mos pris; 2 yrs prob.	3 mos pris; $1,000.
12th most severe sentence	2 mos pris; 22 mos prob; $5,000.	3 mos pris; 21 mos prob.	6 mos pris; 18 mos prob.	1 yr pris.	3 mos pris; 2 yrs prob; $5,000.	3 yrs prob.	6 mos pris.	3 yrs prob; $100.	3 mos pris; 33 mos prob; $7,500.	3 yrs prob; $1,000.
Median sentence	1 mo pris; 11 mos prob; $5,000.	1 mo pris; 11 mos prob.	5 yrs prob.	4 yrs prob.	3 yrs prob; $10,000.	3 yrs prob.	3 yrs prob.	3 yrs prob.	2 yrs prob; $15,000.	2 yrs prob; $500.
12th least severe sentence	2 yrs prob; $7,500.	2 yrs prob.	2 yrs prob.	2 yrs prob.	2 yrs prob; $5,000.	2 yrs prob.	3 yrs prob.	2 yrs prob.	2 yrs prob; $400.	1 yr prob; $1,500.
6th least severe sentence	$7,500; 2 yrs unsup prob.	1 yr prob.	2 yrs prob.	2 yrs prob.	2 yrs prob; $1,000.	2 yrs prob.	2 yrs prob.	2 yrs prob.	1 yr prob: $7,500.	1 yr prob; $500.
Least severe sentence	$2,500.	6 mos prob.	2 yrs prob.	1 yr prob.	1 yr prob; $1,000.	2 yrs unsup prob.	1 yr prob.	1 yr prob.	$2,500.	$1,000.
No. of sentences ranked	43	44	48	39	45	42	46	48	47	48

YCA = Youth Corrections Act

York. The instructions to the chief probation officers were to seek reports in cases that would not strike judges as unusual. The chief probation officers of the Eastern and Southern districts undertook to assure that the cases would include both convictions on [guilty] pleas and convictions after trial, and also that there would be a diversity of defendant characteristics such as prior record, age, narcotics history, and family background. Corporate and other organizational defendants were excluded because of the narrow range of sentencing alternatives available, but with that exception the objective was to obtain a variety of circumstances within the mainstream of the sentencing experience of participating judges.

. . .

III.   Patterns of Sentences

In [Part] II, the focus was on the question whether substantial disparity exists among the district judges of the Second Circuit. [Here] an effort is made to analyze the disparity that has been observed by looking for patterns in the data that may increase our understanding of it. The analysis here is based on the same sentences that formed the basis for [Part] II.

A. Disparity Within Districts

The first question treated is whether the disparity observed previously is primarily a result of disagreement among judges within individual districts or primarily a result of differences in sentencing practices among districts. . . . [After analysis of sentences by districts] it is concluded that substantial disparity exists *within* districts, and that differences among districts are of secondary importance. In addition, the disparity found among judges of the Eastern District of New York casts doubt on the theory that sentencing councils tend to generate common approaches to sentencing among the judges who participate.

B. The Effect of Experience on the Federal Bench

The second question considered is whether experience on the Federal bench tends to bring judges closer together in their sentences. . . .

. . .

It might be thought that experience on the bench would tend to be a moderating factor in sentencing disparity—that experienced judges, as a consequence not only of their experience in actual sentencing but also of their greater opportunities to consider sentencing problems in sentencing institutes and other forums, would have developed greater consensus among themselves than the judges with less experience. If this were true, it would suggest that disparity in sentencing might be somewhat moderated through efforts to find training substitutes for the experience that the more recently appointed judges lack. An analysis was therefore undertaken to determine whether a greater consensus was in fact exhibited in the twenty cases by the more experienced judges.

For the purposes of this analysis, the judges were divided into two groups: those who entered on duty in July 1971 or later, and those who entered on duty in August 1968 or earlier. Since none of the participating judges entered on duty in the three years between those two dates, this division followed a natural break in the data. For the circuit as a whole, 32 of the participating judges were in the more experienced group and 18 in the less experienced group. For the Southern District of New York, which was also analyzed separately, 17 judges were in the more experienced group and 13 in the less experienced.

[Statistical tests] indicate that there are no statistically significant differences in the rank lists of sentences when the experienced and inexperienced judges are compared, either at the circuit level or within the Southern District. . . . Another way of examining the effect of experience is to ask whether the sentences of experienced judges are often found among both the most severe and the least severe sentences on the rank list. . . .

At the circuit level, half or more of the most severe sentences were rendered by experienced judges in every one of the 20 cases. Half or more of the least severe sentences were rendered by experienced judges in 14 of the 20 cases. Within the Southern District, half or more of the most severe sentences were rendered by experienced judges in 19 of the 20; half or more of the least severe in 11 of the 20. Within the circuit, some 64 percent of the participating judges were classified as experienced; within the Southern District, 57 percent.

. . .

C. Consistency Among Judges

The final question addressed [here] . . . is whether the disparity that exists reflects a consistent tendency of some judges to impose severe sentences and of others to impose light ones.

The analytical technique used to deal with this question required ranking the sentences in each case in order of severity and then, for each judge, comparing the ranks assigned to his sentences in different cases. The most severe sentence in a case was given a rank of 1, the next most severe was given a rank of 2, and so on. Since different numbers of judges sentenced in the various cases . . . a judge who did not sentence in a particular case was arbitrarily put into the rank list for that case at a point suggested by his average rank in the cases in which he did sentence, with the result that every judge had a rank in each case.

Each time a judge is given an arbitrary rank by this procedure, it of course tends to increase the apparent consistency of his sentencing. The effect of the data for the other judges is less clear, however. Since ranks are relative, their places in the rank list would be affected by the arbitrary ranking of another judge, but the direction of that effect might be expected to vary from judge to judge and case to case. To reduce the impact of this factor, only the sentences in the thirteen cases having 45 sentences or more were included in the analysis. Of the 650 ranks analyzed for these thirteen cases, only 39, or 6 percent, were arbitrary; not more than 5, or 10 per cent, were arbitrary in any single case.

Table 27-2 shows, for each of the 50 judges, his average rank in the thirteen cases, and also his lowest and highest ranks. The table is arranged in declining order of judge severity as indicated by the average rank. Thus, Judge #1 was the most severe judge, with an average rank of 5.4. His lowest rank was 1, indicating that he gave the most severe sentence in at least one case. His highest rank was 11.

. . .

For any given case, the average rank is 25.5, as is the median. If a judge were exactly in the middle of the rank list for each case, therefore, the average rank for that judge

TABLE 27-2
Ranks of Sentences of Individual Judges in Thirteen Cases

(A rank of 1 represents the most severe sentence given in a case;
a rank of 50 the least severe.)

Judge	Average Rank	Lowest Rank	Highest Rank
1	5.4	1	11
2	10.6	3.5	23
3	12.1	1	47
4	15.3	1	44
5	19.2	1.5	48.5
6	19.2	2	46
7	19.6	6	39
8	19.6	2	45.5
9	20.8	1	49.5
10	22.7	2	45
11	22.8	3	44
12	23.0	3	44.5
13	23.4	4	37.5
14	24.3	3	47
15	24.5	4	46
16	24.5	2	46
17	24.6	10	44.5
18	24.6	7	44.5
19	24.6	2	43
20	24.7	3	44.5
21	25.0	1.5	47
22	25.2	2	47
23	25.5	6.5	48
24	25.7	3.5	48
25	25.8	1	44.5
26	25.9	8	47
27	26.0	3.5	44
28	26.0	5.5	48.5
29	26.1	12	43
30	26.7	5.5	48.5
31	26.7	14.5	38
32	26.8	7	44.5
33	27.0	2	50
34	27.6	7.5	41
35	27.8	5	45.5
36	27.8	10	50
37	27.9	5.5	50
38	28.3	5	50
39	29.3	4.5	49
40	30.0	12.5	49
41	30.1	7.5	45.5
42	31.5	3.5	47.5
43	31.8	11.5	47
44	32.1	1	50
45	32.7	5.5	50

TABLE 27-2 (Continued)

Judge	Average Rank	Lowest Rank	Highest Rank
46	33.0	17	50
47	33.4	5.5	50
48	34.7	10.5	50
49	36.1	3.5	49.5
50	36.9	26.5	48.5

would be 25.5. If his average rank was less than 25.5 he may be said, on the whole, to have been somewhat more severe than his fellow judges in these thirteen cases; if more than 25.5, somewhat less severe.

Table 27-2 shows that most of the judges had average ranks quite close to the center. Some 29 of the 50 judges had average ranks within three points of 25.5. But the table also shows that these closely grouped average ranks are averages of widely differing ranks in individual cases. Judge #33, for example, with an average rank of 27.0, rendered the least severe sentence in at least one case and the second most severe in another. Of the 29 judges with averages between 22.5 and 28.5, 26 judges had a sentence that ranked among the ten most severe in at least one case and a sentence that ranked among the ten least severe in at least one other. Thus, relative to one another, individual judges appear sometimes lenient and sometimes severe. The pattern persists even with the judges whose average ranks are outside the middle group. Of the judges at the more severe end of the scale, only the first two can be said to have been consistently severe; of those at the more lenient end, only one appears to be consistent. Consistency of relative position is thus very much the exception.

This should not be interpreted as implying that judges are not individually consistent in their sentencing. To say that judges' sentencing cannot be explained by simply characterizing the judges as "hanging" or "soft" is not to say that the judges are behaving irrationally. On the contrary, it suggests only that their individual approaches to sentencing are more complex than is widely believed. The data is wholly consistent with the proposition that each judge could give a rational and consistent explanation of his sentences in these thirteen cases. There would, however, have to be a number of different rational and consistent explanations to choose from.

. . .

IV.   Effect of Particular Case Characteristics

While the first twenty cases were chosen for their representative qualities, the last ten cases sent to the judges participating in the experiment were designed to test specific hypotheses about case characteristics that might tend to be productive either of sentencing disparity or of consensus. In the first twenty cases, the effect of a single characteristic could not be tested because each case differed from the others with respect to many characteristics. In the last ten cases, limited and controlled variations in the presentence reports were used to permit some testing of such effects.

Presentence reports in each of the last ten cases were produced in two versions—an "A" version and "B" version—which differed from one another with respect to a single characteristic. The judges were divided into two groups, which remained fixed for the series of ten cases. The "A" judges received the "A" versions of these cases; the "B" judges received the "B" versions. Judges were randomly assigned to the two groups, so it was expected that the two groups would be similar to one another in their sentencing predilections. Differences in the sentences imposed by the two groups of judges in a particular case could thus be attributed to the difference between the two versions of the case.

In addition, in three of the last ten cases the judges were explicitly asked, after sentencing on the facts as presented to them, what their sentences would have been if a particular fact had changed. These questions created an additional opportunity to assess the impact of particular case characteristics on sentencing disparity.

Using these techniques, efforts were made to determine whether the degree of disparity was affected by the following matters:

1. Whether or not the probation office offered a recommended sentence.
2. Whether or not the defendant was addicted to heroin.
3. Whether the defendant stood trial or pleaded guilty.
4. Whether the defendant's prior arrests had resulted in convictions.
5. Whether the offense was "blue collar" or "white collar."

. . .

A. Effect of Probation Office Recommendation

Cases 21 and 22 dealt with the effect of sentence recommendations by the probation office. Recommendations were included in the presentence reports as follows:

21A: "It is therefore felt that he merits some consideration for probation combined with the imposition of a fine."
21B: None.
22A: None.
22B: "We respectfully recommend that this defendant be sentenced to three years imprisonment."

In both of these cases, the sentences of the judges who received the probation recommendation conformed with that recommendation somewhat more frequently than the sentences of the judges who did not receive it. But in both cases, . . . there is no statistically significant difference in the distributions of the "A" and "B" sentences. In other words, the observed differences could be simply the result of the operation of chance in the division of the judges into the "A" and "B" groups. There is therefore no sound basis in the data for concluding that the probation recommendation served as a vehicle for enlarging the area of consensus about the appropriate sentence.

. . .

B. Effect of Heroin Addiction

Cases 23 and 24 dealt with heroin addiction. The defendant's status in this respect was as follows:

23A: Currently addicted to heroin. Was in a drug treatment program at the time of the crime, and person in charge of the program believed him to be drug-free at that time.
23B: Formerly addicted, but currently appears to be drug-free. Was in a drug treatment program at the time of the crime, and person in charge of the program believed him to be drug-free at that time.
24A: No record of addiction.
24B: Currently addicted, and addicted at the time of the crime.

Among the judges who sentenced in these two cases, there was no discernible pattern of differences between the "A" and "B" judges. Indeed, in each of the two cases, the median sentences of the "A" and the "B" judges were identical. Statistical testing indicates that any differences in the sentences of "A" and "B" judges could well be due to chance.

. . .

C. Effect of Method of Conviction

In Case 26, an effort was made to determine whether the degree of disparity among the judges might be influenced by whether the defendant pleaded guilty or stood trial. In the "A" version of this case the defendant was convicted upon a plea [of guilty]; in the "B" version he was convicted after a bench trial. No statistically significant difference was found in the sentences rendered on the two versions.

The effect of plea or trial was also examined with questions in Cases 24 and 30. In Case 24, the defendant was presented in both versions as having pleaded guilty, the two versions differing with respect to heroin addiction. The judges were then asked what their sentences would have been "if, instead of pleading guilty and admitting his offense, the defendant had been convicted of this offense in a bench trial and had continued to maintain a posture of non-involvement." In Case 30, the defendant was presented in both versions as having been convicted in a jury trial; the difference between the versions was that in one version the crime was a fraud against the government while in the other it was transportation of stolen securities. The judges were then asked what the sentence would have been "if, instead of being convicted by a jury, the defendant had pleaded guilty."

The responses to these questions . . . indicate, as might be expected, that there are differences among judges, about whether sentences should be less severe if the defendant is convicted upon a plea. For reasons that are not immediately apparent, many judges who considered a lighter sentence appropriate in Case 30 if the defendant pleaded guilty did not consider a similar concession appropriate in Case 24. It is possible that this was a function of the way the questions were asked, but that is not a probable explanation. The questions appeared prominently on the same sheets on which the judges were asked to render their sentences on the facts as presented in the presentence reports, and the judges are likely in both cases to have been aware before entering their sentences that they were being asked to consider both the trial and plea assumptions.

Although it is clear that judges disagree on whether a concession should be given to defendants who plead [guilty] and, if so, how large a one, there is no discernible pattern that would suggest that one method of conviction or the other is likely to produce more disparate sentences. The median sentence necessarily tends to be lower in cases in which the conviction is by plea, reflecting lower sentences being given by those judges who do make concessions. But there is no suggestion in the data of any substantial impact on the range of sentences rendered in a particular case.

D. Effect of Prior Record

Cases 27 and 28 dealt with differences in the defendant's prior record. The hypothesis was that disparity might be greater if there was only a record of arrests than if the arrests had resulted in convictions, since judges might disagree on the effect to be given to an arrest record where there were no prior convictions. The defendants' prior records were as follows:

27A: Four arrests: one resulting in a small fine, one in dismissal, one in a year's probation, and one in a one-month jail term.

27B: Same four arrests: one resulting in a small fine, the other three in dismissal.

28A: Three arrests: one resulting in acquittal, one in dismissal, and one pending.

28B: Same three arrests: one resulting in a three-year prison term, one in a small fine, and one in a three-month prison term.

In case 27, there was a statistically significant difference at the 95-percent confidence level between the sentences of the "A" judges and those of the "B" judges. The "B" judges, sentencing a defendant with no convictions, gave markedly lighter sentences. Indeed, 9 of the 23 "A" sentences that were ranked were more severe than any of the 23 "B" sentences. But it is also true that 7 of the "B" sentences were less severe than all but one of the "A" sentences. It is therefore hard to infer from the data any tendency for one version to bring the judges closer together than the other. It would appear, as expected, that judges give more severe sentences to defendants who have records of convictions than to those who merely have records of arrests; it does not appear that they give less disparate sentences to either group, however.

In Case 28, the defendant was a narcotics addict, a fact that caused many judges to decline to sentence in the absence of more information. Only 14 "A" judges and 8 "B" judges were ranked, and no statistically significant difference appeared.

E. Effect of Socio-Economic Considerations

Cases 29 and 30 represented an attempt to develop some insight on whether disparity is greater in white-collar cases than in blue-collar cases.

The judiciary has come in for a good deal of criticism in recent years for giving white-collar criminals sentences that are thought by some to be too light when compared to sentences given to blue-collar criminals. The validity of that criticism is outside the scope of this study: we are concerned here with whether judges disagree with one another about similar cases, and not with the appropriate relationships between sentences for defendants in dissimilar cases. But if the appropriate handling of white-collar cases is a subject of public controversy, it might also be expected that it would be a subject on which judges had differing views, and that there might therefore be a tendency for sentences to be more disparate in white-collar than in blue-collar cases.

Obviously, this problem is too complex to be tested simply. The phrases "white collar" and "blue collar" are shorthand expressions that sum up a great variety of characteristics, and there is no typical white-collar or blue-collar situation. Indeed, it isn't always clear whether the phrases are used to refer to the type of crime or to the personal characteristics of the defendant. Without any pretensions of completeness, it was decided to include in this study one case in which the crime was varied and one in which the personal characteristics were varied. The differences in the versions of these two cases were as follows:

29A: Sale of heroin. Defendant was from a stable working-class home in which both parents worked, but the defendant was a high-school drop-out. Since high school, he had had alternate periods of short-term jobs and unemployment.

29B: Same transaction. Defendant was the son of a successful businessman, and was a college student.

30A: Presenting false claims to the government and conspiracy to defraud, involving Medicare claims by the defendant physician.

30B: Transportation of stolen Treasury securities and conspiracy to sell them, by the same defendant physician. (The value of the securities was the same as the amount of the false claims in the "A" version.)

In both of these cases, the "A" judge tended to be somewhat more severe. This tendency was not statistically significant in either case, however, and it may reflect only chance factors. There is no discernible tendency in either case for the sentences based on one version to be closer to each other than those based on the other. Thus, insofar as these two cases are adequate to test the proposition, they do not suggest either that district judges in the Second Circuit are more severe in blue-collar cases or that they are more disparate in white-collar cases.

28

Quantitative Analysis of Fact-Patterns in Cases and Their Impact on Judicial Decisions

Fred Kort

Studying the dependence of court decisions on facts can be clearly associated with traditional conceptions of the judicial process. There are, however, salient problems in the relationship between facts and decisions which cannot be solved by conventional methods. Such problems must be attacked by mathematical and statistical methods which have been extensively employed in the behavioral sciences. These methods are not limited to research on social backgrounds of judges, their values, and their individual positions as members of appellate courts. It has recently been suggested that the process of decision-making on the basis of relevant facts involves an attitude of the judge toward his responsibility which may be examined in the same manner as other judicial attitudes. If this view is accepted, the study of the dependence of decisions on facts could rely on methods that are also appropriate for the study of other aspects of judicial behavior. But even if traditional conceptions of the relationship of court decisions to facts are preferred, mathematical and statistical methods provide insights which otherwise cannot be obtained.

The use of mathematical and statistical methods yields such insights in areas of law where comprehensive sets of facts have been specified by appellate courts as relevant and controlling for reaching decisions. In such areas of law, it has been stated by courts that some combinations of the facts would lead to decisions in favor of one party to the dispute and that other combinations would result in decisions for the opposing party. Beyond the association of *some* combinations of facts with decisions which already have been reached, it is not known, however, what decisions can be expected on the basis of *other* combinations of the specified facts. For example, in the involuntary confession cases under the due process clause of the fourteenth amendment, the Supreme Court has clearly stated that each decision depends on the particular circumstances surrounding the interrogation of each petitioner. Workmen's compensation cases provide another example: reviewing courts have indicated that an award or denial of compensation must be decided on the basis of such facts as the nature of the injury, the circumstances under which the accident occurred and became known, and the health record of the claimant prior to the injury. In both of these areas of adjudication recurring relationships between certain fact configurations and decisional patterns can be identified. A more difficult question is to predict the decisions that other combinations of these facts would justify.

In recent years several studies have attempted to predict decisions by using mathematical and statistical techniques. But a serious problem confronts the scholar in this area: he must identify which facts appellate courts accept as controlling from lower court records and appellate briefs. The problem thus presents two aspects: (1) the acceptance or rejection of facts by appellate courts from lower court records and appellate briefs, and (2) the dependence of the decisions of appellate courts on facts that have been accepted as controlling.

I. The Acceptance or Rejection of Facts That Control Judicial Decisions from Lower Court Records and Appellate Briefs

Many legal realists argue that the acceptance or rejection of facts by appellate courts cannot be reduced to regular patterns. If the contrary can be shown, however, the prediction of the acceptance or rejection of facts, and ultimately the prediction of decisions, will become possible. As an initial hypothesis, it can be stated that the acceptance of a fact by an appellate court depends upon identifiable conditions surrounding the presentation of the fact in the briefs and record below. These conditions can be stated as follows: the appellate court will accept the fact *if and only if* it appears at one or more of the stages which the lower court records and appellate briefs represent, *or* is not denied at one or more of these stages, *or* one or a combination of other facts also is accepted by the appellate court. A specific application of this compound statement may be exemplified by the involuntary confession cases decided by the Supreme Court. The alleged fact that the defendant had not been advised of his right to remain silent is accepted by the Supreme Court *if and only if* (a) the fact appears in a dissenting opinion of the lower appellate court *and* in the respondent's brief to the Supreme Court *and* is not denied in the allegations of the respondent in the transcript of the record *and* in the opinion of the lower court, *or* (b) it appears in the allegations of the respondent in the transcript of the record *and* in a dissenting opinion of the lower court *and* in the brief of the petitioner to the Supreme Court *and* is not denied in the respondent's brief, *or* (c) it appears in the petitioner's brief to the Supreme Court *and* is not denied in the opinion of the lower court *and* in a dissenting opinion, *and* the alleged fact that the petitioner was not advised of his right to counsel also is accepted by the Supreme Court. [This example, of course, applies to involuntary confession cases decided before the 1966 ruling in *Miranda* v. *Arizona*.]

The complexity of this statement directs attention to the need for a more concise formulation. Such a formulation can be obtained by using the algebraic notation devised by the nineteenth century British mathematician George Boole—Boolean algebra—first applied to the analysis of judicial decisions by Reed C. Lawlor. The notation also can be regarded as a form of symbolic logic. The purpose of the concise formulation is not merely the convenience of relative brevity, but the important objective of reducing the compound statement to a form which permits further analysis.

The compound statement which specifies the conditions under which a fact is accepted by an appellate court—the acceptance rule—can vary considerably for different facts. Initially it is not known which combination of appearances, nonappearances, or denials of a fact, as well as the acceptance of other facts, provides the acceptance rule for the fact.

For example, in both the involuntary confession cases and the Connecticut workmen's compensation cases over one billion such combinations are possible for each relevant fact. Although not every possible combination needs to be examined to determine which compound statement can be correctly inferred for each fact from the applicable case, the number of combinations which must be examined makes human inspection prohibitive. However, the systematic search for the applicable compound statement can be performed by a digital computer—in fact, it was in this way that results for the Connecticut workmen's compensation cases and for the involuntary confession cases were obtained.

. . .

[Another] method employs a system of equations. Each case is represented by an equation, in which an index denoting the acceptance or rejection of a fact by an appellate court is set equal to the combination of appearances, nonappearances, and denials of the fact at the preceding stages. The weights of the fact at the various stages—in the sense of how persuasive its appearance at the respective stages is toward its acceptance by the appellate court—are the *unknowns* in the equations. As the equations are solved, the weights are determined. To be sure, the complex procedures which are required for the solution of the equations again necessitate the use of a computer, especially because there is a separate system of equations for each fact. By using the weights in a case not previously encountered, one can predict for each fact an acceptance or rejection that would be consistent with the established pattern of past cases. . . .

II.   The Dependence of Appellate Court Decisions on Facts That Have Been Accepted as Controlling

The methods which can be used for analyzing the acceptance or rejection of facts by appellate courts also can be employed in examining the dependence of the decisions of these courts on the facts that they have accepted as controlling. The initial approach is essentially the same. Starting from the hypothesis that a decision in favor of the aggrieved party requires the occurrence of specified conditions regarding the facts accepted by the appellate court, the following compound statement can be formulated. The decision is in favor of the aggrieved party *if and only if* facts in one of several specified combinations have been accepted by the appellate court. In its specific applications this compound statement can assume forms amounting to several billions. But, through the use of a computer, it becomes possible to provide a basis for predicting decisions by deriving the correct compound statement from past cases.

The alternative method of a system of equations also has to be considered here. Again, each case is represented by an equation. In this instance, an index which denotes the decision (in favor or against the party seeking redress) is set equal to the combination of facts that have been accepted by the appellate court. The weights of the accepted facts— in the sense of how persuasive they are toward a decision in favor of the aggrieved party— are the *unknowns* in the equations. It may be impossible, for want of sufficient available data, to solve these equations. This problem can be attacked, however, by restating the facts in terms of *factors,* and by employing *factor analysis*. In the involuntary confession cases, for example, some of the facts which have been accepted as controlling by the Supreme Court include a delay in the formal presentation of charges, the incommunicado detention of the defendant, and the failure to advise the defendant of his right to remain silent or his right to counsel. These facts can be restated in terms of a factor described as "a tactic to keep the defendant in isolation and uninformed about the proceeding against him." This would be an example of the intuitive meaning of restating facts in terms of factors. It should be noted, however, that applicable factors actually are found by relying *exclusively* on the mathematical technique which factor analysis employs. It also should be noted that—in addition to solving the problem encountered in the original equations— factor analysis fully explores the mutual dependence or independence of the facts. For this reason, it always is advisable to attempt to restate the facts in terms of factors. For the same reason, it also would be irrelevant to say that factor analysis does not increase the predictability of the decisions.

On the basis of the restatement of the accepted facts in terms of factors, the original equations now can be restated as new equations, with indices denoting the decisions set equal to the various combinations of factors in the cases. The weights of the factors—again in the sense of how persuasive they are toward a decision in favor or against the aggrieved party—are the *unknowns* in the equations. The weights of the factors are found by solving the equations. As new cases arise, the applicable facts can be reduced to the factors which have been identified, and the decisions can be predicted.

Of primary interest to the present discussion is the combination of the methods for analyzing the acceptance of facts and the methods for exploring the dependence of decisions on facts. Such a combination of methods makes it possible to predict first the acceptance or rejection of facts by appellate courts from lower court records and appellate briefs, and then the decisions of the appellate courts on the basis of the accepted facts. . . .

III.   Purposes, Limitations, and Implications of the Proposed Methods

The purposes of the proposed methods must be understood not only in terms of their effective combination for prediction, but also in terms of their potentials for analyzing separately the two aspects of the problem under discussion. With regard to the acceptance and rejection of facts by appellate courts, the methods offer insights into matters about which there has been considerable speculation. Since the emergence of "fact-skepticism" in the framework of legal realism, there has been a widespread belief that courts pay relatively little attention to facts. The application of the proposed methods has refuted such a belief in at least some areas of law.

With regard to the dependence of decisions on facts, the proposed methods provide a precise and exhaustive distinction between combinations of facts that lead to decisions in favor of one party to the dispute and combinations of facts that lead to decisions in favor of the opposing party. Thus, the methods offer information about the content and the application of rules of law which verbal statements of these rules do not provide. The given examples show that courts employ rules which state that the decisions shall be made on the basis of combinations of facts. The verbal statements of these rules specify which facts shall be regarded as relevant but do not specify which combinations of these facts call for a decision in favor of the party seeking redress and which do not. This is the information which the proposed methods can provide.

It already has been seen that prediction is another purpose of the proposed methods. Prediction is possible only if it can be assumed that the patterns of consistency in past cases—with regard to the acceptance of facts as well as with regard to the decisions—will continue in the future. The proposed methods are not designed to predict doctrinal changes and the adoption of new rules of law. Furthermore, prediction does not apply to a case in which a fact *not previously encountered* appears, although a series of such cases provides a basis for the prediction of subsequent decisions. Thus the methods can demonstrate their validity, provided that their limitations are clearly recognized and understood, and that claims never made on their behalf are not carelessly attributed to them.

It should be noted that, in examining past cases by means of the proposed methods, no assumption is made regarding the existence or nonexistence of consistent patterns in the acceptance of facts or in decisions based on facts. Whether or not consistency does exist in a given area of adjudication is determined by the use of the methods. If consistent patterns cannot be identified, it must be concluded that judicial action in the given area of law cannot be understood in terms of the dependence of decisions on facts. If, on the other hand, consistent patterns are found, an important implication of the proposed methods is apparent. Should it be possible to predict only later cases from earlier cases, the underlying pattern of consistency could be explained in terms of stare decisis. But if earlier cases could be predicted from later ones, adherence to precedent would have to be explained in terms of an independent—although convergent—recognition and acceptance of similar standards of justice by different judges at different times. Thus not only the existence of consistent patterns but also the basis for their consistency can be evaluated.

Where patterns of consistency in the acceptance of facts and in corresponding decisions appear to be absent, other explanations of judicial action obviously must be given. Such explanations could be obtained from studies concerned with other aspects of the judicial process, such as the characteristics and changes in the attitudes and values of judges, their social backgrounds, and their individual positions as members of appellate courts. The possibility of effective coordination of these various endeavors remains an open question. Gustav Bergmann called attention to the fact that free-falling bodies, the inclined plane, and the pendulum originally were explained in terms of three separate empirical laws. Later, these three phenomena were regarded as special cases of a set of general laws—the laws of mechanics—and a scientific theory replaced the empirical laws. It is not inconceivable that similar developments will eventually lead to a scientific theory of the judicial process.

CHAPTER TEN

ENVIRONMENTAL INFLUENCES

In this chapter we examine environmental influences on judicial decision making—influences that are peculiar to the geographic area in which courts are located. American courts have well-defined geographic jurisdictions. What this means is that they can only process disputes occurring in the area they serve or between a resident of that area and a resident of another area. Courts thus may be said to have relatively definable and distinct constituencies and clienteles. It may seem strange to refer to judicial "constituencies," since that word is most often used to describe legislatures and other representative institutions. Judges, on the other hand, are expected to supply an impartial evaluation of conduct and behavior—an evaluation that is generally supposed not to consider the wishes of the parties to a dispute or of those living within the geographic jurisdiction of the court.

Nevertheless, there are audiences for most disputes that come to courts—audiences that are more or less clearly defined and more or less attentive. In order to guard against the pressures these audiences might generate, American courts have been insulated through the idea that judges must be independent in order to be impartial. Judicial independence implies institutions that are formally separate from and not subservient to any other branch of government. Furthermore, judicial independence may be associated with particular types of judicial selection and with long and secure tenure for judges. Essentially, independence exists when judges feel that they need not take account of the wishes of the audiences to a dispute or those of their geographic constituents.

The establishment of particular geographic loci for courts and of norms of judicial independence results in a paradox for judges. They are expected to act without reference to environmental influences, yet the localism of the organization of the American judiciary operates to enhance such influences. How might environmental pressures influence judicial decision making? First, environmental factors, such as the relative wealth or poverty of an area, influence the kinds of disputes that come to court and impose limits on what judges can require in their decisions. Second, environmental influences affect judicial decision making through the process of judicial selection, which works to ensure that lawyers with strong local connections become judges in courts serving the local area. What this means is that judges typically share the attitudes and values peculiar to the culture of the area they serve. To the extent that those cultures vary, the way the judges perceive and decide disputes may also vary. The readings in this chapter explore these points.

A third explanation of environmental influences on judges involves the judge's sense of what will be acceptable to his "significant others," that is, to those people whom the judge respects and looks to for approval. Among the most important of these people are the local lawyers comprising the local bar. Judges may exercise their discretion in such a way as to try to win the respect of local lawyers and other politically significant people and groups. This is, according to the article by Beverly Cook (selection 31), especially true of trial court judges in the exercise of their sentencing powers, and it is especially true in visible, controversial cases. Cook, elsewhere, has demonstrated the linkage of changing public opinion on the Vietnam War from 1967 to 1975 to changing sentencing patterns of selective service law violators.[1] As public opinion turned against the war, sentences by judges became more lenient. This linkage of an environmental variable to behavior was also demonstrated in a study by James Gibson of the sentencing behavior of trial court judges in Iowa. Gibson found that judges' sentencing behavior can be explained in terms of their perception of local opinion, that is, judges appear to increase or decrease the severity of the criminal sentences they impose in accord with their own impression of how the public views the seriousness of the crime in question.[2]

The article by Martin Levin (selection 29) focuses on state court systems[3]; those by Richard Richardson and Kenneth Vines (selection 30) and by Cook concern federal courts. Each suggests that environmental influences affect judicial decision making, and each suggests the extent to which American courts overtly resemble political institutions.[4]

Notes

1. Beverly B. Cook, "Public Opinion and Federal Judicial Policy," *American Journal of Political Science* 21 (1977), 567-600. Also see, in general, Herbert M. Kritzer, "Political Correlates of the Behavior of Federal District Judges: A 'Best Case' Analysis," *Journal of Politics* 40 (1978), 25-58.

2. James L. Gibson, "Judges as Representatives: Constituency Influence on Trial Courts," paper presented at the annual meeting of the American Political Science Association, 1976.

3. Also see Martin A. Levin, *Urban Politics and the Criminal Courts* (Chicago: University of Chicago Press, 1977).

4. Also see Wolf V. Heydebrand, "The Context of Public Bureaucracies: An Organizational Analysis of Federal District Courts," *Law and Society Review* 11 (1977), 759-821.

29

Urban Politics and Judicial Behavior

Martin A. Levin

This paper presents an empirical analysis of the consequences of different political systems on the sentencing decisions of criminal court judges in Minneapolis and Pittsburgh. These cities represent polar models of urban political systems and judicial selection.

Some large cities have a traditional political system. This involves a formally partisan city government, with (in varying degree) strong parties that rely on material rewards rather than issues to attract members, have a generally working-class orientation toward politics, emphasize the conferral of material benefits upon individuals, identify with local areas of the city rather than with the city as a whole, and centralize influence. Other large cities have a "good government" or reform political system. This involves a formally nonpartisan city government and weak parties that rely on nonmaterial rewards (primarily issues or personalities), have a generally middle-class orientation toward politics, emphasize the maximization of such values as efficiency, honesty, impartiality, professionalism and identification with the city "as a whole," and decentralize influence. . . .

. . .

Pittsburgh has a formally partisan and highly centralized city government. In 1966, when this research was begun, the Democratic party organization was strong, hierarchical, disciplined and highly cohesive, and attracted workers by means of material incentives. It had dominated city politics since the early 1930's and had been influential in state and national politics. Public and party offices in Pittsburgh are filled by party professionals who patiently "wait in line" because of the party's desire to maintain ethnic and religious "balance," even on a judicial ticket. The citizens tend to accept pro-union and liberal social welfare policies. There is wide acceptance of partisanship and party activity in almost every sphere of Pittsburgh local government. The public has displayed little enthusiasm for efforts to take the selection of judges "out of politics," and parties view positions on the courts and their related agencies as primary sources of rewards for their workers.

There are nineteen judges on the Allegheny County (Pittsburgh) common pleas court, the trial court for both criminal and civil cases, and they are elected, on a partisan basis, for ten-year terms. Party designation appears on the ballot. The political parties, especial-

Reprinted by permission of author and publisher from *Journal of Legal Studies* 3 (1974), 339–375. Most footnotes have been omitted.

ly the Democratic party, dominate both the primaries and the general elections for judicial positions in Pittsburgh; the bar association usually plays a very limited role. When a court vacancy occurs, the governor appoints a successor who must stand for reelection at the next general election. Ten of the nineteen incumbent judges in 1965 had first reached the bench in this way. These appointments have been controlled by the local parties.

The Pittsburgh judges' career patterns also reflect the dominance of the parties and the limited role of the bar association in judicial selection. At the time of appointment or election almost all of the judges held a government position, such as city solicitor, assistant prosecutor, city councilman, state legislator, or congressman (all partisan offices, and all controlled by the parties), and were active members of the party organization.

Minneapolis has a formally nonpartisan and structurally fragmented city government. The Democratic-Farmer-Labor (DFL) party and the Republican party play a significant role in city politics, but one that is both formally (because of nonpartisan elections) and informally (because of the wide acceptance of nonpartisanship) limited. The parties are weak, undisciplined, loosely organized, and highly democratic. They attract workers through nonmaterial incentives. The parties do not overcome the formal decentralization of authority in the city. Individuals (including "amateur" politicians) with the ability and willingness to work, but with little seniority in the party, can and do rise rapidly in the party and in city government. The citizens tend to be disposed toward conservative city policies. Nonpartisanship in city politics is accepted by the people (and even by many party workers and some party leaders). Indeed, the electorate has had a strong negative response to candidates or incumbents who violate, or seem to violate, the ideal of nonpartisanship. This is especially true with respect to the courts and their related agencies, and consequently party leaders and workers tend not to regard them as a source of party rewards.

There are sixteen judges on the Hennepin County (Minneapolis) district court, the trial court for both criminal and civil cases. They are elected for six-year terms on a nonpartisan basis. The political parties play almost no role in the selection of judges in Minneapolis; the local bar association plays a major role. Prior to a judicial election the Minneapolis bar association polls its members and publicizes the results. The "winner" of the poll (or the second or third highest candidate) almost always wins the ensuing election. The governor makes appointments to interim vacancies, and fourteen of the sixteen incumbent judges in 1965 had first reached the bench in this manner. When vacancies occur, the Minneapolis bar association again conducts a poll, and the Minnesota governors have adhered closely to the bar's preferences. . . .

The Minneapolis judges' career patterns also reflect the minor role of the parties and the major role of the bar association in judicial selection. Prior to coming to the bench fourteen of the eighteen Minneapolis judges in this study had been exclusively or predominantly in private legal practice (usually business-oriented, and often corporate, practices). Those who held public positions before coming to the bench did not hold elective positions (with one exception) and were generally not active in either party.

This paper focuses on the criminal court division of the courts in the two cities, in part because judges typically have a very high degree of discretion in criminal court sentencing decisions. Criminal statutes in Pennsylvania and Minnesota, as in most states, allow the judge the choice of incarcerating a convicted defendant or of granting probation in most felony cases. If he chooses the former, the statutes also allow him, within prescribed limits, to fix the term of imprisonment. The high degree of discretion in sentencing decisions presents an opportunity to study judicial behavior that is shaped by the fewest external variables, such as the actual degree of the defendant's guilt and the quality of police investigation and prosecution.

To understand typical judicial behavior in each city, sentencing decisions were compared statistically for the nine most common felony offenses.[1] To understand the judges' attitudes, decision-making processes and courtroom behavior, interviews were conducted with all but one of the judges in both cities, and trials and courtroom proceedings were observed over a period of several months in 1966. The judges' interview statements were cross-validated on the basis of their actual sentencing decisions, observation of their courtroom behavior, and interviews with more than twenty criminal court participants in each city.[2]

There are significant differences in the sentencing decisions of the judges in each city. Table 29-1 compares the percentage of probation in both cities for all nine offenses in one subset of defendants—whites with a prior criminal record. In this subset, there is a greater percentage of probation in Pittsburgh for all nine offenses. . . . [O]n the whole, the decisions are more lenient in Pittsburgh than in Minneapolis. Both white and black defendants receive probation more frequently and shorter prison terms in Pittsburgh. . . . [T]his pattern persists when the defendant's previous record, plea, and age are controlled, and it is generally consistent for all of the offenses compared. For probation, when the sentencing decisions are controlled for type of prior record and race, there is a sufficient number of cases to compare the nine offenses in each city for twenty-five specific categories of offender. In 22 categories the percentage of probation is greater in Pittsburgh; in two it is greater in Minneapolis; in one there is no significant difference. For incarceration, we can perform the same analysis of sixteen categories, and we find that in thirteen of these the length of incarceration is less in Pittsburgh; in two categories it is less in Minneapolis; in one there is no significant difference between the cities.

Although both white and black defendants receive more lenient sentences in Pittsburgh, in both cities whites receive probation more frequently than blacks in most categories. In Minneapolis whites also receive shorter prison terms than blacks in most categories. In Pittsburgh, however, blacks receive shorter prison terms than whites in almost all offenses. On the whole, . . . sentencing decisions are more favorable to blacks in Pittsburgh than in Minneapolis, both in absolute terms and relative to whites.

A comparison of sentencing decisions by type of plea (Table 29-2) reveals that the Minneapolis judges give defendants who plead not guilty more severe sentences more frequently than do the Pittsburgh judges. In Pittsburgh the sentences of such defendants are, on the whole, only slightly more severe than those of defendants who plead guilty; in Minneapolis they are much more severe.

There is much more uniformity in the length of prison terms in Minneapolis than in Pittsburgh. In Minneapolis, white and black defendants with the same type of prior record receive the identical or nearly identical median term of incarceration in five of the seven offenses in which there is a sufficient number of cases for comparison. Not so in Pittsburgh. There white and black defendants with the same type of prior record receive a nearly identical median term of incarceration in only two of the nine offenses in which there are sufficient cases for meaningful comparison.

Turning to the attitudes and decision-making processes of the judges in the two cities, we find that the Minneapolis judges tend to be more oriented toward "society" and its needs and protection, and toward the goals of their professional peers, than toward the defendant. Their decision-making is also formalistic in character. The Pittsburgh judges

TABLE 29-1*

Detailed Comparison of Pittsburgh and Minneapolis Percentage Probation (White, Prior Record)

	Burglary	Grand Larceny	Aggravated Assault	Aggravated Robbery	Simple Robbery	Indecent Assault	Aggravated Forgery	Non-Sufficient Funds	Possession of Narcotics
Pittsburgh	59.4	62.1	47.4	26.1	33.3	72.4	54.6	56.2	77.8
	(227)	(103)	(19)	(23)	(21)	(47)	(11)	(16)	(9)
Minneapolis	22.0	34.8	15.4	2.8	27.8	28.6	25.5	35.7	55.6
	(159)	(69)	(13)	(36)	(18)	(28)	(106)	(70)	(9)
Ratio**	2.7	1.78	3.08	9.32	1.20	2.53	2.14	1.57	1.40

* Data on sentencing decisions and defendants' race, prior record, age and type of plea were collected from records at the offices of the Minnesota Bureau of Criminal Apprehension, the Allegheny County Clerk of Courts, and the Allegheny County District Attorney.

** The ratio is calculated by dividing the greater percentage of probation in the two cities by the lesser percentage of probation in the cities. When the percentage of probation is greater in Pittsburgh, the ratio is a positive number; when it is greater in Minneapolis, the ratio is a negative number. When the percentage of probation is zero in one city it is impossible to calculate the ratio, and the term "NR" (signifying no ratio) is used.

TABLE 29-2
Summary of Comparison of Sentencing Decisions by Type of Plea
in Pittsburgh and Minneapolis

Percentage of Probation: Comparison Between Types of Plea for Offenses
with Sufficient Cases

	Number of offenses in which defendants who plead guilty receive a greater percentage of probation		Number of offenses in which defendants who plead not guilty receive a greater percentage of probation		Number of offenses in which there is no significant difference between types of plea	
	Pitts	**Minn**	**Pitts**	**Minn**	**Pitts**	**Minn**
No Prior Record, Whites	0	5	1	0	1	0
No Prior Record, Blacks	2	0	0	1	0	0
Prior Record, Whites	5	2	1	0	1	1
Prior Record, Blacks	5	1	2	0	0	0
Total	12	8	4	1	2	1

Length of Incarceration: Comparison Between Types of Plea for Offenses
with Sufficient Cases

	Number of offenses in which defendants who plead guilty receive a shorter length of incarceration		Number of offenses in which defendants who plead not guilty receive a shorter length of incarceration		Number of offenses in which there is no significant difference between types of plea	
	Pitts	**Minn**	**Pitts**	**Minn**	**Pitts**	**Minn**
No Prior Record, Whites	1	2	0	0	0	0
No Prior Record, Blacks	0	0	0	0	1	0
Prior Record, Whites	1	1	1	0	1	1
Prior Record, Blacks	1	0	3	0	0	0
Total	3	3	4	0	2	1

typically are oriented toward the defendant rather than toward punishment or deterrence. Their decision-making is particularistic and pragmatic.

There are also significant differences in the judges' courtroom behavior prior to sentencing. Most nonjury trials in Pittsburgh are informal (for example, the witnesses stand at the front bar) and abbreviated. Most of the judges prefer this arrangement, and they also prefer informal procedures for obtaining information concerning defendants (the defense attorney's trial presentation, individuals intervening with the judge outside of court, the court staff's knowledge about the defendant) to the presentence investigations of the probation department. Trials in Minneapolis are formal, deliberate, and unabbreviated, and all of the judges prefer this arrangement. Presentence investigations are conducted in almost every case and most of the judges dislike utilizing any informal sources of information concerning the defendant. In both cities plea bargaining is infrequent.

The Minneapolis and Pittsburgh judges' views, decision-making processes, and sentencing behavior approximate two general models of decision-making: a judicial decision-making model (Minneapolis) and an administrative decision-making model (Pittsburgh). In the judicial model, decisions are made on the basis of the evidence of record developed by the adversary system. The judge feels that he must maintain an image of detached objectivity. The judge's decisions are dichotomous (yes-no) and assign legal wrong to one of the two parties. The judge arrives at his decision by a formal line of reasoning from legal principles. He is more concerned with satisfying the requirements of "the law" conceived as an abstract ideal than producing "just" settlements of individual cases.

In the administrative model of decision-making, decisions are made on the basis of the kind of evidence on which reasonable men customarily base day-to-day decisions, evidence frequently gathered by the administrator's own investigation. The length and depth of the investigation is determined by the resources available to him. An administrator believes that he must seek intimate contact with the real world in order to be able to administer effectively, and that this is more important than maintaining an image of detached objectivity. He may adopt dichotomous (yes-no) or intermediate decisions (such as compromise decisions or delay in enforcement of a decision). He reasons to his decision, pragmatically and inductively, from the policy goals embodied in the program he administers. He has greater concern for arriving at "just" settlements based on the particular merits of individual cases than for adherence to abstract notions of justice and the law. He seeks to give individuals what he feels they "deserve," and he bases his decisions in large part on the needs of those individuals; in some instances he may perceive that one of their needs is exemption from the treatment involved in his program. He has greater concern for substantive issues than for procedure, and measures his success by the way the program he administers "fits" real-world demands and supports.

. . .

Let us look more closely at some of the differences in judicial attitude between the Minneapolis and Pittsburgh criminal courts. Thirteen of the seventeen Minneapolis judges appear to have little empathy for defendants, whom they describe as "coming from low intelligence groups," "crummy people," "congenital criminals," "not learning from their mistakes," "not able to consider the consequences before they act." They tend to be resigned to the "criminality" of most defendants and often seem inclined to "give up" on them. The Minneapolis judges' tendency to penalize with more severe sentences defendants who plead not guilty seems to be an indication of their greater concern for what they consider the needs of society than for the defendant.

At the same time, thirteen of the seventeen judges are also oriented toward their professional peers (such as correction authorities and law enforcement officials) and their goals. They are willing to sacrifice the exercise of some of their own discretion in order to achieve both greater consistency in their own sentencing and the goals of some of these peers (such as "professional expertise" and "better law enforcement"). In almost all instances in recent years, the effect of pursuing these goals has been more severe sentences. These judges tend to be enlightened in terms of professional doctrine rather than benevolent toward the defendant. . . .

Twelve of the seventeen Minneapolis judges believe in the effectiveness of institutional rehabilitation and penal deterrence, and thus are not reluctant to punish defendants by incarcerating them. . . .

These . . . Minneapolis judges feel little "closeness" to the defendant. Rather than act as a buffer between him and the law, they act as if they *are* the law. The nature of the offense dominates these judges' considerations ("the offense itself is an indication of the man and his motives"), especially when the offense is a crime against the person. Thus, although sentences for all offenses are more severe in Minneapolis than in Pittsburgh, the differential is greater for armed robbery than for crimes against property. Still, ten of the seventeen Minneapolis judges consider most crimes against property "serious crimes."

Universalistic criteria dominate these judges' decision-making. They rarely regard individual characteristics (age, whether only property is involved in the crime, a black defendant's environment, a favorable family or employment situation, or addiction to alcohol or narcotics) as legitimate bases for making exceptions. . . .

Sixteen of the eighteen Pittsburgh judges seem to be oriented toward the defendant. Their view of most defendants is benevolent, and they describe their decision-making as "giving the benefit of the doubt" to the defendant, "taking a chance on the defendant," or "err[ing] in the direction of being too soft." They feel that "chances" are worth taking despite getting "taken in sometimes" because "some are rehabilitated." They seek to "help" defendants, especially by "emphasiz[ing] probation and parole." Moreover, they tend to feel that they have a "closeness" and "kinship with the people that come into criminal court," that they are "more human" than the judges of the past and that they have a "greater empathy and awareness of the [defendant's] problems" and "more insight into the different types of people" that come before them. Several judges explain this empathy and "closeness" as part of a general attachment to the "underdog"; others explain it as a product of experience in their previous careers in political parties and government; some say it stems from their own minority ethnic and lower-income backgrounds.

The Pittsburgh judges' sentencing decisions for defendants who plead not guilty, which on the whole are only slightly more severe than for defendants who plead guilty (in sharp contrast to Minneapolis), seems to be a manifestation of their greater orientation toward the defendant and his needs than toward "society." Their preference for using informal sources of information concerning the defendant—individuals' intervention with the judge, the defense attorney's trial presentation, and the court staff—also seems to be a manifestation of this orientation. These informal sources focus almost exclusively on mitigating circumstances. By contrast, the presentence report is made by a "third party," the probation officer, whose professional ethos stresses objectivity; and it includes both mitigating and aggravating information.

The Pittsburgh judges' closeness to and empathy with the defendant cause them to stand apart from the law and act as a buffer between it and the people upon whom it is enforced. Most of them act as if they view the law primarily as a constraint within which they have to operate to achieve substantive justice for the defendant. They are critical of the law's inflexibilities and resist standardization of any of their sentencing decisions (even in offenses such as drunken driving and gambling).

The Pittsburgh judges tend to reject legalistic criteria in favor of policy considerations derived from criteria of "realism," and "practicality." Fourteen of the eighteen judges do not seem to be oriented toward institutional rehabilitation, punishment, or deterrence in their sentencing decisions because of their "realistic" attitudes concerning deterrence and the actual quality and effectiveness of prisons. They believe that prisons today are usually ineffective in achieving rehabilitation or discouraging recidivism because of their low quality ("not much is done for [defendants] in jail," "it's not helpful," the jails do "more damage" and defendants leave "worse off"); and that this consideration is relevant to their sentencing decisions.

The judges' views on the gravity of offenses also seem to be based on "realistic" criteria. Twelve of the eighteen judges tend to view criminal behavior as often a manifestation of a dispute between two private parties rather than as a conflict between an individual and society. From this perspective many acts appear less serious to the judges, especially where there is a special relationship between the defendant and the victim. Similarly, thirteen of the eighteen Pittsburgh judges believe that many crimes against property that do not involve violence are "minor," involve "only money," and are "less serious than [harm to] a human being."

Thirteen of the eighteen judges indicate they should consider such "practical" factors as "how the defendants live," the heterogeneity of the city's population, and particularly the "mill town" character of the population, in ascertaining the standards of proper conduct. They seem often to base their sentencing decisions on frankly extra-legal standards, notably the standards of the group in which the offense occurred (youths, blacks, lower-income persons, homosexuals). . . .

Sixteen of the eighteen judges base their sentencing decisions on a very wide range of individual and personal characteristics as well. They feel that "everything counts"; it is the "whole system" and the "complete picture" that must be considered. They describe their decision-making as "intuitive," "impressionistic," "unscientific," and "without rules of thumb." In part they seem to base sentencing decisions on such general criteria as the defendant's offense and the "type of person" he is, but they also act as if no general norm could cover all individuals within the criteria. Thus they give weight to such diffuse and particularistic considerations as "how the defendant conducted himself" during the commission of the offense, how "cooperative" he was when arrested, and the culpability and background of the victim (for example, the degree of actual consent, provocation, and the previous "purity" of a victim, in a rape case).

. . .

The behavior of the Pittsburgh and Minneapolis judges appears to be the indirect product of the cities' political systems. These systems influence judicial selection, leading to differential patterns of socialization and recruitment that in turn influence the judges' views and decision-making processes. The pre-judicial careers of most of the Pittsburgh judges in political parties and government, and their ethnic minority and lower-income backgrounds, seem to have contributed to the development of the characteristic that many successful local politicians possess—the ability to understand the motives of other people by entering imaginatively into their feelings. Their political experience and—a frequent concomitant—lack of much legal experience seem to have contributed to the highly particularistic character of the judges' decision-making and their emphasis on policy. In party and policy-oriented government positions, general rules are usually subordinated to more immediate ends (such as the desires of a constituent), and personal relationships—rather than abstractions such as "the good of society as a whole"—are emphasized. . . .

The predominantly legal-practitioner pre-judicial careers of most of the Minneapolis judges, and their dominantly middle-class Northern-European-Protestant backgrounds, seem to have contributed to their development of a greater orientation toward "society." In their careers few had contact with individuals from lower-income backgrounds. Their experience in predominantly business-oriented private practice typically involved major social institutions, such as the "law," corporations, and commercial transactions.

Their pre-judicial experience (reinforced by their lack of party or policy-oriented experiences) may also explain the more formalistic character of their decision-making and their eschewal of policy and personal considerations. In their milieu, rules were generally emphasized, especially legal ones. These rules were used to maintain and protect the social institutions with which they were involved. Learning to "get around" required a skill in operating in a context of rules. Their success seems to have depended more on their objective achievements and skills than on personal relationships. Furthermore, the predominantly middle-class background of these judges may in itself have contributed directly to their emphasis on the importance of laws.

The decision-making of the few judges in both cities with cross-cutting backgrounds and experiences in effect serves as a control, and it seems to indicate that pre-judicial career experiences are a more important influence than social background. The decision-making of the few Pittsburgh judges with middle-class Protestant backgrounds who also had careers in party and government positions tends to be much like that of their ethnic-minority and lower-class-background colleagues. The decision-making of the few Minneapolis judges with middle-class Northern-European-Protestant backgrounds who had pre-judicial careers less oriented toward legal practice tends to be less oriented toward "society" and less formalistic than that of most of the other Minneapolis judges.

The covariation of the dominant socialization and recruitment patterns of the judges in each city and their decision-making processes suggests a causal linkage. This is especially suggested by the deviant socialization and recruitment patterns, which in effect serve as controls: In each city, interview and sentencing data indicate that the decision-making of the judges whose socialization and recruitment patterns deviate from the dominant pattern also tends to deviate significantly from the decision-making of most of the city's judges. In Pittsburgh the few judges with little party or government experience tend to be less oriented toward the defendant, less particularistic, less pragmatic, and less policy-oriented than most of the other Pittsburgh judges. In Minneapolis the few judges with less legal experience and more political experience than most of their colleagues tend to be less oriented toward society and their professional peers and less formalistic than most of the other Minneapolis judges.

. . .

Finally, several similarities in the political systems of Pittsburgh and Minneapolis and their judges' behavior are indirectly and tentatively suggestive of the linkage between the two factors. The formal trial procedures and formal sources of information concerning the defendant which the Minneapolis judges use are generally advocated by professional and reform judicial organizations. By contrast, the informal trial procedures and informal sources of information concerning the defendant which the Pittsburgh judges use are generally criticized by professional and reform judicial organizations. Patterns somewhat similar to these forms of judicial behavior seem to exist in each city's political system. Minneapolis' political system is characterized by procedures advocated by professional and reform organizations in city government (nonpartisan elections, widespread popular participation in governmental and party decision-making, frequent referenda and grass roots party-nomination procedures, merit recruitment and appointments, and an emphasis on procedures as important ends in themselves). In contrast, Pittsburgh's political system is characterized by procedures that are generally criticized by most of these professional and reform organizations (partisan elections, hierarchical control of government and party decision-making, and party recruitment and appointments). The relationship between these patterns in each city's political and judicial systems is indirect; indeed, both may be the product of a more general factor such as a common political culture.

. . .

Studies have also suggested that judges' social or ethnic backgrounds significantly shape their decisions. Thus it is possible that the Pittsburgh judges are lenient primarily because of their predominantly minority ethnic backgrounds and the Minneapolis judges more severe primarily because of their Northern-European-Protestant backgrounds. As already pointed out, however, our data show that while both the judges' pre-judicial career experiences and social backgrounds influence decision-making, in both cities the former seems to be the more important influence. Moreover, any relationship between the judges' background characteristics and their decision-making seems to be indirect. The crucial intervening variable is the city's political system: judges with a particular social and career background that may affect their decisions are recruited by the city's political and judicial selection systems. The ethnic composition of the bench in each city can serve as a partial test of the intervening impact of the judicial selection system on judicial decision-making. Significantly, that composition is more reflective of the influence of particular groups in the city's political system than it is of the ethnic composition of the city's population.

. . .

Notes

1. Burglary, grand larceny, aggravated robbery, simple robbery, aggravated assault, indecent assault, aggravated forgery, non-sufficient funds, and possession of narcotics. A random sample of all cases of these offenses for a particular set of years was compared (1959 to 1965 for Minneapolis and 1960 to 1965 for Pittsburgh).

2. The court participants included public and private defense attorneys, prosecutors, probation officers, court attendants, newspaper reporters and editors, and police officers. Sixteen incumbent judges were interviewed in Pittsburgh. Three of the recently elected incumbents had never sat on the criminal bench at the time of this study and thus were not interviewed. (In both cities the judges rotate between the civil and criminal bench.) Two recently retired judges whose sentencing decisions are included in this study's data were also interviewed. Fourteen of the fifteen incumbent judges who sit on the criminal court were interviewed in Minneapolis. (One district court judge sits exclusively on the juvenile court and one judge refused to be interviewed.) Three recently retired judges whose sentencing decisions are included in this study's data were also interviewed. Here it should be mentioned that, unless otherwise stated, all quotations in this paper are based on interviews, personal observations, and personal correspondence with the individual quoted. . . .

30

Judicial Constituencies: The Politics of Structure

Richard J. Richardson and Kenneth N. Vines

Constituencies of political officials often mold their behavior in significant ways. Although one usually thinks of constituencies simply in terms of their location and organization, or as a group of people, their political effects are actually far-ranging. They structure the flow of power; they help to define the character of political clienteles; they determine the boundaries of political activities of institutions; and, finally, constituencies influence the patterns of decision making within political institutions.

Although representative functions of courts have rarely been recognized in traditional legal theory, the linkage between political officials and the territory they serve is not just a legislative phenomenon. It follows that a systematic theory of the judiciary must include an examination of the relationship between judicial officials and the formal units within which they act. This relationship has been spelled out by . . . [one] federal judge who observed that "the district judge is personally accountable to the local community and to the local bar" and that the federal judge is tied to the territory in which he performs by a wide range of interactions.

. . . [T]he history of lower court organization has largely stemmed from efforts by nationalists and states' rights advocates to organize the federal courts after their own desires. Accordingly, both sides have often been sensitive to the relationship between judicial constituencies and the policies coming from them. Legal groups, on the other hand, although they have given attention to court organization, have primarily been concerned with the physical size and distribution of the federal courts and the courts' adequacy to carry on the business of law.

District Constituencies

In line with informal tradition and by repeatedly affirmed statutory practice, the organization of district courts follows state lines because, historically, federal judicial activities are deeply rooted within the states, which act as basic containers for federal courts. Except for the Supreme Court, whose constituency is the nation, neither the district nor the appeals courts' boundaries violate the wholeness of state territories. A district court

Reprinted by permission of the authors from *The Politics of Federal Courts* (Boston: Little, Brown and Co., 1970), Chap. 3. Footnotes have been omitted.

TABLE 30-1
Districts and Divisions

Number of Districts	Number of States
1	25
2	15
3	8
4	2

Number of Divisions	Number of States
Less than 5	37
5–10	9
Over 10	4

may encompass the whole state or a portion of a state, however, because the number of districts in a state varies. Further organizational detail is often added by splitting the districts into smaller units called divisions. Here, again, structure varies among the states, and a district may contain no divisions or it may contain several. As a result, the varying district and division lines make a complex judicial structure characterized by uneven and irregular geographic forms, and suggest, on the surface, a kind of super-gerrymandering practice.

Most federal litigation is heard initially in 88 (in 1965) *district* courts. The districts and divisions are distributed among the states as shown in Table 30-1. Apart from the consistent structuring along state lines, the organization of district constituencies does not appear to follow any rational plan. District constituency boundaries seem not to be related to any of the factors that normally determine legislative district boundaries, such as size or population. The twenty-five states where judicial affairs are conducted within a single district include such spacious and sparsely populated states as Alaska, Montana, and Colorado, but also include such compact and populous states as Connecticut, Rhode Island, and Massachusetts. Divisions are also inconsistent, for Georgia contains seventeen, Alabama twelve, and Texas twenty-five, whereas New York has four, California five, and New Jersey one. More than half the states have no special divisions, and constituency organization follows district lines.

District boundaries are very clearly drawn and determine where federal litigation shall take place within the state. On the other hand, divisions are said to be rather "frail" limits on where litigation is conducted within the district. Divisions do determine where particular judges regularly hold court within the district. Because of multi-judge districts, in only about half the instances is there a single judge in a particular district or division and quite clearly the district judiciary does not constitute a single member district system. For that reason, the relation of judge to constituency tends to be more blurred than the relations in many legislative systems where there is one legislator per district. Nonetheless, district judges are linked to definite territorial divisions within the state for the performance of their judicial functions.

The inconsistencies in structure are examined in more detail in Table 30-2, which compares the constituency characteristics of six states and lists the district population, number of judgeships, and case loads. It is clear that judicial constituencies differ not only in boundary structure but also in such fundamental features as district population, population per judgeship, and case load per judge. . . .

. . .

TABLE 30-2
Constituency Characteristics of Selected District Courts, 1966

State	Population per District	Number of Judges in State	Population per Judgeship	Number of Divisions	Case Load per Judge
Alabama	N: 1,860,672	6	620,224	12	359
	M: 774,655		516,437		259
	S: 631,413		420,942		313
California	N: 5,586,518	22	620,724	5	322
	S:10,130,686		779,283		346
Connecticut	2,535,234	4	633,808	1	187
Georgia	N: 1,819,920	6	606,640	17	396
	M: 1,281,705		640,852		258
	S: 841,491		841,491		409
Michigan	E: 5,540,674	10	692,584	2	244
	W: 2,282,520		1,141,260		240
Wisconsin	E: 2,421,275	4	807,079	2	152
	W: 1,530,502		1,530,502		233

N—Northern District; S—Southern District; M—Middle District; E—Eastern District; W—Western District.

Sources: United States Code; United States Census, 1960; Annual Report of the Director of the Administrative Office of the United States Courts, 1966.

Appeals Court Constituencies

Most appeals from the district courts are heard in one of eleven appeals courts, one located within each circuit. The appeals courts . . . have stable constituencies, their own institutional identity, and a separate judiciary. . . .

Table 30-3 describes the characteristics of the eleven appeals courts. Considered according to geographical patterns, the circuits have a pronounced regional character, following important sectional lines that mark off historical, social, and political differences. Some of the circuits are exclusively regional, such as the First which contains only New England states (except for Puerto Rico), the Fifth (only Southern states except for the Canal Zone), and the Seventh (only Midwestern states). Others are predominantly regional but include one or more outside states, such as the Eighth, which includes six Midwestern states and also a border state (Missouri) and a Southern state (Arkansas).

. . .

It is also clear from Table 30-3 that the appeals courts in the different circuits vary as to size, number of judges, population, and district judges per appeals judge. (The population of the District of Columbia is irrelevant to the size of that court, since the court gets its appellate business from government institutions situated there.) Although there are undoubtedly differences in litigation potential for different populations, there is no indication that the circuit courts are arranged according to such factors. A clear indication is the small population size of the Tenth Circuit which contains few highly urban and industrialized sections, populations generally associated with high litigation potential.

. . .

TABLE 30-3
Characteristics of the Appeals Constituencies, 1966

Circuit	Population 1960 (in thousands)	Number of Judges	Regional Character	Population per Judge (in thousands)	District Judges per Appeals Judge
First	10,202	3	New England and Puerto Rico	3,401	3.7
Second	21,086	9	Middle Atlantic (N.Y.) and New England (Conn. and Vt.)	2,343	4.6
Third	18,664	8	Middle Atlantic and Virgin Islands	2,333	4.1
Fourth	17,014	5	Border and South	3,403	4.4
Fifth	29,627	9	Deep South and Canal Zone	3,270	5.0
Sixth	25,155	6	Middle West (Mich. and Ohio) and Border (Tenn. and Ky.)	4,193	5.0
Seventh	19,421	7	Middle West	2,774	3.3
Eighth	15,459	7	Middle West, Border (Mo.), and South (Ark.)	2,208	3.4
Ninth	27,343	9	Pacific Coast and Mountain (Ariz., Mont., and Idaho), Guam, and Hawaii	3,038	4.8
Tenth	8,999	6	Mountain and Middle West	1,500	2.8
District of Columbia	808	9	District of Columbia	90	1.7

Malapportionment in the Courts?

Traditionally, malapportionment is not a concept used to describe judicial institutions, although the problems of access and representation, both features of malapportionment, are relevant to judicial problems. In legislatures and courts alike, clienteles seek access to the courts for the purpose of making claims and demands upon the political system and both institutions are located in districts, states, and regions for the convenience of their clienteles. Policy statements by the courts themselves recognize the representational function of judicial institutions. It may be assumed that courts are part of the on-going political process of the constituency in which they are located and function as part of the representational system. One can argue, therefore, that any inequality or inadequacy in judicial facilities violates fundamental democratic values.

. . .

Given the fundamental role of court constituencies in the judicial process, there is considerable justification for thinking of a "judicial malapportionment." Certainly the adequacy of judicial staff helps determine both accessibility to and effectiveness of courts, and inequalities in judicial staff may affect the expectations of litigants as well as create unfavorable environments for the presentation of policy demands. For these reasons, figures on case litigation are not an entirely satisfactory measure of institutional adequacy. The number of judges available for actions, it can be argued, might well create conditions favorable for litigation and increase it substantially. A constituency deprived of institutional representation in the judiciary may suffer some of the same ills as similarly situated constituencies in legislative malapportionment.

Constituency Social and Economic Differences

Irregularities in districting of federal district courts have resulted in some important social and political differences. Since the districts always follow state boundaries, judicial constituencies usually reflect the distinctive characteristics of state political and social systems. Thus, for example, the two districts in Mississippi take on many of the characteristics of that state simply by being within the state, staffed by local court personnel, serving a state clientele, and handling controversies that grow out of the political and social milieu.

Until recently [1960s], federal district courts in the South segregated Negroes and whites in the courtroom, even when litigation was over civil rights and was carried on by Negroes. Southern federal courts have also followed regional custom by not employing Negroes except in custodial and service jobs. As a consequence, the federal courts in the South have been called "frankly white dominated institutions" by the Southern Regional Council. In a [1965] . . . study of Negro employment in Southern federal courts, the council found that of 1,224 positions only 14 (1.14 per cent) were held by Negroes. Non-custodial and non-service positions held by Negroes consisted of nine deputy United States marshals and five assistant United States attorneys, but no jobs were held in the categories of referee in bankruptcy, United States commissioner, United States clerk, deputy United States clerk, or jury commissioner. . . .

Racial segregation in the administration of the courts raises interesting questions about the policy-making process. What practical effects do conditions in the courts have on the settlement of issues that themselves involve civil rights? Does the due process conception of "peer equals" have relevance to the way in which courts are administered? Few social scientists would maintain that the decision-making process is indifferent to the context in which it is formulated.

Many important local differences among the district judiciaries may be observed within states. Districts sometimes capture sectional features of the state, and these differences are significant because they influence the character of the district court process. Policies are formulated by judges with strong local connections, are administered by a locally appointed and sanctioned court staff, and serve a clientele usually drawn from the district. Juries, selected according to district rules, reflect the social character of the particular district. . . .

Table 30-4 illustrates how districts capture important social and economic differences. Judging from the manner in which districts are created, we see no deliberate effort to capture certain populations. The differences result rather from the drawing of district lines along sectional contours. An excellent example of this is the divisions of the Tennessee districts. There, the low Negro population of eastern Tennessee is reflected in the

TABLE 30-4
Negro-White Population Differences among Judicial Districts in the South

Per cent Negro Population	Districts in South
0–9	Middle Tennessee, eastern Tennessee, western North Carolina, western Texas, northern Texas
10–19	Western Arkansas, northern Georgia, eastern Texas, western Virginia, northern Alabama
20–29	Southern Florida, northern Florida, middle North Carolina, eastern Arkansas, western Tennessee, southern Texas
30–39	Western South Carolina, western Louisiana, eastern Louisiana, southern Georgia
40–49	Middle Alabama, eastern North Carolina, southern Mississippi, northern Mississippi, eastern Virginia, middle Georgia
Over 50	Southern Alabama, eastern South Carolina

eastern and middle districts, and the western district mirrors the much larger Negro population of the western part of the state bordering on Mississippi. In similar fashion, sectional Negro-white population differences are followed in the districts of Alabama, Georgia, Texas, Arkansas, North Carolina, and Virginia. Closer examination of the districts reveals other differences as well. For example, some districts contain cities and others have a predominantly rural population. There are also differences among labor union populations, income and occupational groups, and socio-economic features. Although constituency differences are grosser than they are among most legislative districts because of greater size of judicial districts, variations are still distinct enough to merit attention.

The impact of district social differences on judicial decision making can be seen clearly in civil rights litigation in the South. Civil rights litigants, the Justice Department, and the appeals courts have all encountered hostility in the district courts of the deep South. In a direct commentary on the hostile environment of Southern district courts, some congressmen advocated that the District of Columbia court, rather than local Southern district courts, be given powers under the 1965 Civil Rights Act to enforce voting rights. Indeed, the act as passed gives the District of Columbia court some special powers of enforcement not given to the district courts.

. . .

Inevitably tensions have existed between legal and democratic norms, particularly when controversial issues have been involved in litigation. The most visible tension has occurred in Southern judges' handling of race relations. When district judges have been responsive to Southern racial values, conflicts with such agencies as the appellate courts and the Justice Department have occurred. On other occasions, issues such as labor relations have also come into public view. It is clear that the basic nature of judicial constituencies makes for continuing conflict in the judicial process. . . .

31

Sentencing Behavior of Federal Judges: Draft Cases—1972

Beverly Blair Cook

Judicial decision-making is of interest to the political scientist and the lawyer, and of significance to the public, where the judge exercises choice: at the appellate level in making new law and at the trial level in making discretionary decisions. In areas of discretion such as the management of the trial and the selection of the sentence, the trial judge utilizes his own experiences, preferences, and common sense. Where law and precedent provide weak guidelines rather than mandates, the chief factors associated with the judge's choice may be discovered in his personal history and in his political and social environment. This study seeks such explanations for judicial discretionary behavior by examining the choice of sentences for 1,852 draft offenders by 304 federal district judges in 1972.

Sentences are treated as policy decisions. Judges can support or impede policies developed by legislative or administrative bodies through sentence selection. Federal judges do perceive the relationship between their draft sentences and public policy. One judge wrote: "Public policy considerations militate against probation, and in many cases probation would serve to permit the defendant to enjoy the fruit of his crime—that is, he would escape military service and punishment."[1] The policy reflected in draft cases is the conscription of young men for military service. Consequently, a severe draft sentence may serve as an indicator of judicial support for selective service policy and a mild sentence for judicial nonsupport.

Judges exercise wide discretion over decisions on penalties. Within the limits prescribed by law, a judge can suspend sentence at one extreme, or give a combination of prison, fine, and supervised probation at the other. . . . In the absence of appellate precedent or supervision, what accounts for the wide variance in sentences?

The location of the policy-making authority at the level of the individual judge reflects the historical decentralization of the federal court system. . . .

Although federal judges admit that variation occurs "in cases in which the nature of the offense, the gravity of public injury, the history of criminal behavior and motivation are substantially comparable," the identification of such cases for analysis poses practical problems. The realities of plea bargaining, the scope of acts chargeable under several sections of the criminal code, the human diversity of offenders, and the sectional concen-

Reprinted by permission from *University of Cincinnati Law Review* 42 (1973), 597-633. Most footnotes have been omitted.

tration of certain offenses hamper the selection of similar cases. However, these problems are not associated with the study of selective service cases since first, the offense is of national significance; second, the offenders and the corpus delicti are practically identical; and third, the purpose of the sentence is to symbolize national defense requirements rather than to rehabilitate individual offenders.

Refusal to report for military or civilian duty in the national defense is a crime deemed harmful to the country as a whole and not to a particular locality. Draft delinquency is distributed throughout the country as a result of the processing of draftees through decentralized local draft boards. Federal jurisdiction is exclusive. Differences among sentences, then, cannot logically be explained in terms of the unique interests or conditions within judicial circuits or districts. In 99 percent of the cases, violators of the Selective Service Act are young males whose offense is refusal to obey a lawful order of their draft board.[2] Half of the federal judges in a recent survey perceived these cases as "all alike." Given the isomorphism of the cases, differences in sentence cannot be explained by unique factors of the criminal act or, in most cases, the defendant.

There are four primary functions of sentencing—restraint, rehabilitation, deterrence and retribution. The first three do not apply in draft cases. Since he does not fit any criminal type, society is neither endangered by the release on probation, nor protected by the incarceration of the offender. Rehabilitation is not a sensible basis for a prison sentence for young men motivated by conscience to resist the draft, who are firm in their convictions and not otherwise socially or economically maladjusted. The third purpose for sentencing is deterrence, which Judge Kaufman calls the "teaching function." The criminal behaviors which society strongly proscribes are singled out and dealt with severely. However, obedience to selective service orders is a prescribed noncriminal obligation, information relative to the duty is widely disseminated, and deviance insignificant. Deterrence of the offender is not a reasonable expectation when dealing with acts of conscience.

The final purpose of sentencing is punishment, simple retribution by society upon the nonconformist. Some judges have formulated a rough justice by sentencing offenders to a prison term of the same duration as the contemporary enlistment or expected war period. While the notion of individualization of sentences makes sense with respect to protective, rehabilitative, and perhaps even deterrence goals, individualization of retribution for identical crimes does not commend itself to justice. The fact that individualization is not a rational basis for draft sentences allows the political scientist to assume that idiosyncratic, unknown factors relative to the offenders are not properly involved in the sentence choice. Visible and measurable characteristics of the defendant, the court and its environment, and the judge can then be proposed as explanations for sentencing decisions.

I. The Sentence as Dependent Variable

"Dependent variable" is the term used for the behavior to be explained: in this study the 1972 set of draft sentences. In order to employ certain statistical tests in accord with their underlying assumption, the dependent variable should be continuous rather than dichotomous. Judicial dispositions (sentences in criminal cases and awards in civil cases) are obviously more compatible with the requirement of such tests than are judicial opinions on constitutional or statutory issues. A particular sentence may be described in terms of the number of months of probation or prison, or the amount of the fine. A set of sentences may be described in terms of percentage of probation or prison terms, or average length of sentence. . . .

The set of draft sentences treated as the dependent variable in this study are those decided in the forty-eight continental states in 1972 by federal trial judges sitting in their own districts. District judges serving as visiting judges heard 95 cases. Since some propositions in the research required the judge to act within his local environment, these cases were excluded from the analysis. During 1972 seven appellate judges on assignment decided draft cases in district courts. Their sentences also were eliminated from the set, leaving 1,852 cases.

Data on the cases was supplied by the Administrative Office of the United States Courts. The Administrative Office collects data from the clerk of each district court on criminal case forms and transfers the data to tape for computer analysis. . . .

A severity index of draft sentences ranging from 1 to 99 is the specific dependent variable employed in this study. The index is based on the weighting scale first developed by the Administrative Office in 1964. The weighting of each kind of sentence, whether fine, probation, prison, or other, allows the formation of a single scale. The draft severity index was created by the multiplication of the Administrative Office weights by four and the assignment to the highest statutory sentence for a draft offense, five years in prison, the value of 99. The two scales are reproduced in appendix A. The translation of a sentence into an index can be followed in this example: a draft sentence of three years in prison and a $500 fine with one year of probation upon release involves the addition of the weights of 48 and 3 and 12 to form an index of 63.

The analyses in this study use case indices and judge indices as dependent variables (*i.e.*, measures of the sentencing events to be explained). Each judge has a severity index which is the average of all his case indices for the year. The range of the case and judge indices is shown in Table 31-1. The table indicates that ten percent of the judges have routinely issued a nominal sentence which appears to be a rejection of the legislative and bureaucratic draft policy. Six of the trial judges followed a settled policy of five-year prison terms and two judges a pattern of four-year terms, both likely indicators of strong support for the selective service system and its affective penumbra of patriotism and national security consciousness.

A majority of the judges limit their sentences to probation only. Approximately the same percentage of judges and cases are in the index category of 10-19, which gives only lip-service to the draft policy. One-third of the judges employed a range of sentences between the moderate majority and the extremely punitive minority. Evidently these judges were individualizing punishment of the offender according to some pattern. The "correlates" of factors associated with these various sentence choices will be the topic of the next section.

II.   Independent Variables: Proposed Explanations for Sentencing Behavior

"Independent variable" is the term used for a factor which is believed to vary with the event the social scientist seeks to understand. It can be an explanatory factor for the dependent variable, here, the severity of draft sentences. Judge George Boldt suggested a number of explanatory factors for sentence variation: "by area, by court, by judge, by defendant, and by every conceivable criterion of comparison."[3] Models of decision-mak-

TABLE 31-1
Disparities of Draft Sentences, 1972

Severity Index	Number of Cases	Percent of Cases	Percent of Judges	Number of Judges
Under 10	326	18%	10%	29
10–19	938	50%	51%	156
20–29	203	11%	20%	61
30–39	164	9%	7%	22
40–49	140	8%	6%	18
50–59	66	3%	3%	10
60–69	1	—	—	1
70–79	0	—	—	1
80–89	0	—	—	0
99	14	1%	2%	6

ing include five major classes of variables: precedent; case attributes; features of the environment; structural or systemic processes; and characteristics of the decision-maker.

A. Precedent and Public Opinion

. . .

Precedent is of little predictive value in an area of broad judicial discretion such as sentencing, where by definition the judge must exercise his own judgment. Such areas of judicial discretion invite investigation with the concepts and indicators of the social sciences. Where appellate courts have defined abuse of discretion in a particular area, their guidelines could serve to improve the utility of the predictive equation by limiting its parameters. For example, one might predict that the range of future draft sentences in the Sixth and Eighth Circuits would not include the maximum five-year prison term.

In the absence of precedent to explain decision-making, a systemic support variable, new to judicial behavior but familiar in studies of voting behavior, fills the explanatory vacuum. Public opinion correlates to a high degree with the changing pattern of draft sentences over time and with the regional variation in draft sentences in a single year. . . . Opinion may explain from 60 to 85 percent of sentencing choices. . . . If the [public opinion] model approaches reality, the other four types of variables need only explain from 15 to 40 percent of the variance in judicial decisions.

B. Case Attributes

In several statistical studies the attributes of the case have been treated as cues which trigger the response of the judge. Race, class, sex, and nationality are some of the ascriptive, and therefore nominal, characteristics of defendants which have been employed as predictors of sentences. The criminal record of the defendant is another factor often proposed as an explanation for apparent sentence disparity. There have been strong differences of opinion, based on data selection and the controls used in analysis, over the validity of studies using such independent variables.

Certain characteristics of draft defendants—age, sex, nationality, and criminal record—are held constant, but race is a distinguishing feature. Of the defendants identified by race in Markham's five-year set of offenders, 19 percent were non-white. The black

TABLE 31-2
Pleas and Trials in Draft Cases, 1965–1972*

	Plea			Sentence After			
		Not Guilty Trial			Conviction		Average Prison
Year	Guilty	To Court	To Jury	Guilty Plea	By Judge	By Jury	Sentence in Months
1965	72%	64%	36%	81%	12%	7%	21.0
1966	69%	71%	29%	71%	20%	9%	26.4
1967	70%	70%	30%	72%	19%	9%	32.1
1968	62%	77%	23%	66%	25%	9%	37.3
1969	51%	70%	30%	57%	28%	15%	36.3
1970	45%	78%	22%	56%	32%	13%	33.3
1971	46%	83%	17%	57%	34%	9%	29.1
1972	47%	84%	16%	57%	35%	8%	22.0

* Federal Offenders in the U.S. District Courts, 1970, Table H-10, p. 166, Table X-15, p. 185; Annual Report of the Director, 1972, Administrative Office of the U.S. Courts, Table D-4, p. A-55, Table D-5, p. A-57.

defendants received an average prison sentence 1.38 months longer than the white defendants, although the difference was not statistically significant. However, the difference in the average percentage of non-whites (75.8 percent) and whites (71.6 percent) imprisoned by district could not be explained by chance.[4] Moreover, the variation in imprisonment by race did not disappear even when Markham held constant the probation report, the defendant's criminal record, and the type of counsel.[5] Seventy white offenders, or three percent of those found guilty, received a lighter sentence than statistically expected. Ten black offenders, or three percent of those sent to prison, could have expected milder sentences. Consequently, race cannot be discounted as part of the explanation for sentence severity, but evidently its contribution to sentence variation is limited.

. . .

The type of crime and charge, the plea, the kind of trial and the type of counsel are other independent variables often tested for correlation with conviction rates and sentencing severity. Since there are usually no evidentiary issues in draft cases, either the guilty plea or the not guilty plea (with trial to the judge on legal issues) are typical. The trend in draft pleas has varied according to the war environment and the related sentencing patterns of the judges. As the average sentence increases, the percentage of guilty pleas decreases. The nadir of guilty pleas in draft cases in 1970 (45 percent) probably reflects the severe sentences passed in 1968 and 1969. The percentage of guilty pleas has since leveled off, still remaining below 50 percent in 1972. (See Table 31-2.) Another factor is at work in depressing the guilty plea rate. The backlog of criminal cases insures a long delay before trial or even a dismissal on constitutional grounds, while the guilty pleader goes to a speedy sentencing hearing.

In all ordinary criminal cases, the average sentence differs by plea and by type of trial. For fiscal 1970, the Administrative Office's weighted average sentence in federal district courts upon original guilty pleas was 4.6; but after a change of plea from not guilty to guilty, the sentence was 37 percent higher. The average sentence after trial by the court was 6.7, but after trial by jury, the sentence was 90 percent higher.

Of the draft defendants sentenced in 1972, 57 percent had pled guilty, 35 percent were convicted by a judge, and 8 percent were convicted by a jury. In light of this distribution

TABLE 31-3
Sentence Severity by Type of Plea and Trial

	Percentage of Defendants	Mean Severity Index
Guilty Plea (No Trial)	64% (1183)	15.6
Not Guilty Plea		
Trial to Court	29% (545)	24.5
Trial to Jury	7% (124)	29.1

it is possible that some of the variance in 1972 sentences is attributable to the judges' patterns of sentencing according to plea and type of trial. Table 31-3 shows that defendants who pled guilty and thereby waived their "day in court" on the factual and legal issues received an average severity index sentence almost nine points lower than those who went to trial. Those who pled not guilty and were tried before the court received an average index sentence over 4.5 points lower than defendants who did not waive the jury. The difference of the means and of the distribution of the sentences in each category is statistically significant.

The type of counsel who assists the defendant might also affect the sentence choice. . . . Of the draft cases in this study, 51 percent had appointed lawyers, 44 percent retained counsel, and 5 percent had no counsel. . . .

In 1972 the type of lawyer in the draft case made no significant difference in the sentence. This is in sharp contrast to Markham's findings. Classification of counsel as appointed or retained provides nominal factors which are less powerful in statistical analyses. However, if some technique of identification and quantification of ability was discovered, a variable of legal competence might contribute to an explanation of sentencing as well as other judicial outputs.

The statistical analyses in the research reported here do not include the nominal variables of defendant's race or type of trial or counsel. These case attributes are predicted to contribute from five to ten percent of the explanation for sentence disparity.

C. Environment

Social, economic, demographic and political variables of the environment within which the court operates have seldom been used as predictors of criminal case output, although they have been utilized extensively in studies of legislative output. Students of judicial behavior have tended to treat judges as if they worked in a subsystem with impermeable boundaries, isolated from any outside pressures, affected only by their internalized norms and the review power of the appellate judges. Although the interrelatedness of the judicial and political subsystems, with their entrenchment in a social milieu, have often been discussed in a theoretical context, research designs have seldom incorporated such environmental variables. Environmental factors have been treated in an impressionistic way in conventional studies dealing with periods of executive or congressional attack on the Supreme Court and apparent changes in the direction of common law development. Only a few attempts have been made to study the effect of environmental variables on trial courts.

1. Economic-Social Variables

. . .

In the study of the 1972 cases reported here, two economic-social variables are introduced: Poor, operationalized by the percentage of families with less than $5000 per year income in the city where the case was decided; and Crime, operationalized by the 1971 FBI crime index for that city. In every analysis the same relationship appeared: the more poor families in the city, the more severe the sentence; the more crime in the city, the more mild the sentence. The correlations, however, were very low, and the two variables combined contributed only one percent to the explanation of severity.

Evidently, the environmental variables are more useful in a comparison of district performance . . . than individual judicial performance. These variables may belong in a causal chain, their vitality not obvious without a subset analysis. The sentence severity of judges with Republican party affiliation showed a strong correlation with the environmental variables. The explanatory power increased to two percent. Subset analysis revealed that Democratic judges' severity varied only slightly with Crime, and the environmental variables had no explanatory power. Judges serving in metropolitan areas (over 500,000 population) were examined separately and the severity of their sentences varied significantly only in relation to the poverty of the city. It should be noted, however, that their populations included more blacks and more criminals than the cities with a lower Poor factor. The Poor variable added four percent to the explanation of the sentencing severity of metropolitan judges. It is possible that poor draft offenders are treated like ordinary criminals, particularly by Republican judges in metropolitan areas.

2. Demographic Variables. The two demographic variables of concern in this study are the size of the population and the size of the black population. Markham discovered that the size of the district population correlated positively and significantly with the percentage of offenders sentenced to prison, but not with the length of the prison term nor the disparity of sentences within the district.[6] With a single severity index, the present study tends to support the opposite conclusion. The severity indices of the judges themselves differed according to the population of the city in which they decided the case, with the judges in the smallest cities giving the most severe sentences. [Table 31-4]

. . .

In this study a variable, Black, was operationalized by the percentage of the black population of the city where the case was decided. Since federal judges, particularly in the more decentralized Southern districts, often sit at different court locations within the district, this indicator measures more precisely the immediate demographic setting of the deliberating magistrate. On a regression analysis of all 1,852 cases, the Black variable did not correlate at all with severity of sentences. The results . . . suggest that the racial variable comes into play only in cases with black defendants and perhaps with particular judges.

. . .

3. Political. The thesis that judges respond to the political culture is part of our conventional wisdom, but selected features of the political system have not been measured and related to judicial output. . . .

In this 1972 study two political variables are introduced: one, an indicator of political party dominance; and another, an indicator of pressure group strength. The party indicator is based on the party affiliation and percentage of voters for the United States senato-

TABLE 31-4
Severity of Sentencing by Population

Number of Judges	City Population	Average Severity Index
20	Under 50,000	29.9
117	50–500,000	23.5
167	Over 500,000	20.2

rial candidate who received a plurality in the city where the case was decided. The preappointment party affiliation of each judge is compared with that of the winning local candidate to generate four subsets for analysis: Republican judges in congruent and incongruent partisan milieus; and Democratic judges in congruent and incongruent partisan milieus. The percentage of voter support is used as a variable to test the impact of the intensity of local partisanship upon the judge's sentencing.

Table 31-5 shows that judges vary their sentences to some extent in relation to the political dominance in their environment. About one-third of the Democratic judges sit in a Republican environment and two-thirds of the Republican judges sit in a Democratic environment. The severity of the sentences given by Democratic judges is two points higher in Republican territory. Apparently, the Democratic judge responds to the poll power of the Republican party with more severe sentences. The Republican judges, however, do not temper their severity to suit the Democratic milieu and the correlation between severity and the size of the vote for the opposite party shows that they are not influenced by the strength of the opposition. The judges were not affected by the relative strength of their own parties among the voters.

The second political culture variable, AmLeg, was intended to measure the strength of political pressure groups. The American Legion, a pressure group with an intense commitment to national security was chosen as an indicator for the variable. The supportive attitude of the American Legion toward the selective service system is exemplified by the fact that more than 70 percent of the local draft board members came from the Legion. The indicator was operationalized by the percentage of veterans in the state who belonged to the Legion. A positive correlation between the AmLeg variable and the severity index was expected based on the hypothesis that local judges would adjust their behavior to the preferences of the most relevant organized interest in the policy area of the case.

The correlates showed that the size of American Legion membership in the state did not vary significantly with the severity indices of most judges. There was no correlation for the universe of cases. . . . Only Democratic judges serving in a Republican environment revealed a significant relationship between severe sentences and state Legion size. On the

TABLE 31-5
Severity of Draft Sentences by Political Environment, 1972

	Democratic Judges (165)		Republican Judges (128)	
	Democratic Environment	Republican Environment	Republican Environment	Democratic Environment
Percent of Judges	65%	35%	31%	69%
Mean Severity Index	19.6	21.7	19.9	23.4

whole, the judges appeared unaffected by pressure group preferences. The Legion evidently provides policy cues only to judges without other sources of input, *e.g.*, from their political party, court cohort group, service experiences, or local reference groups.

D. Court Structure

The structural feature of courts which has most stimulated the curiosity of judicial behavioralists is collegial decision-making on the appellate level. The single judge in the trial court has received less attention. Studies of collegial decision-making have examined the influence of leadership and the interaction of members in these small groups. The impact of access rules and decision rules on output has been more rigorously examined. Judicial selection processes, socialization techniques, communication patterns, and hierarchical and districting arrangements have also been proposed as useful concepts to understand judicial decisions.

. . .

The present study employed a number of structural variables—three were nominal and two ordinal.[7] The three categories used for the creation of subsets were circuit organization, case distribution, and senior status. The two variables were PerCase, the share of district draft cases handled by each judge, and JudLead, an index of judicial leadership.

1. Circuit Organization. The federal judicial system is organized by circuits, which include a number of districts. Some of these circuits are more compact and identifiable with geographical regions than others. Internal relations among the district judges and with their circuit judges are much closer within the circuit boundaries. Table 31-6 displays the sentencing severity in the six circuits which processed 100 or more draft cases in 1972. The Fifth Circuit, in the South, has the highest severity index and the Sixth Circuit, in the East-Central region, the lowest. The variables which are related to severity differ in each circuit. In the Sixth Circuit, the heavier the judge's caseload, the more severe the sentence; but in the Seventh Circuit a light caseload correlates with severity.

2. Case Distribution. Judicial districts are not apportioned by population. Through historical accident and subsequent growth patterns they have come to serve various population sizes. For example, the Southern District of New York had 19 judges deciding draft cases in 1972 while the District of Maine had only one. In some districts the judges sit together in the same federal building and in other districts they serve subdivisions from benches in different cities.

The result of this structuring is that cases are distributed unevenly. Where judges are scattered, the single judicial officer in the jurisdiction handles all of the draft cases,

TABLE 31-6
Severity of Sentencing by Circuit, 1972

Circuit	Number of Cases	Mean Severity Index
3d	130	18.5
5th	108	22.8
6th	172	17.4
7th	176	20.8
8th	163	18.5
9th	792	17.8

TABLE 31-7
Severity of Draft Sentencing by Case Distribution, 1972

	Judges Handling One or Two Cases	Judges Handling Three or More Cases
Number of Judges	122	182
Mean Severity Index	25.3	19.4

whether many or few. In the multijudge districts with a single location, the clerk assigns criminal cases by some objective procedure. Unless the executive committee of the district chooses to make a special assignment of the majority of draft cases to a senior judge, as occurred in the Northern District of Illinois in 1972, the judges will probably have an even number of cases inside the district.

The number of draft cases disposed in 1972 ranged from one to 62 per judge. Only one case was handled by 72, or 24 percent of the judges, and two cases each by 50, or 16 percent of the judges. Approximately one hundred active judges had no draft cases. At the other extreme, six judges decided more than forty draft cases in that single year. If the cases were divided equally among the 304 judges who heard draft cases, each would have heard six cases. If all active district judges had divided the cases, then each would have managed four or five cases. The decentralized and malapportioned structure together with internal court rules resulted in an erratic distribution of cases.

The significant difference between the mean severity indices of judges with light and heavy caseloads suggests that the judges for whom a draft case is a unique event during the year are more severe. (See Table 31-7.) It is possible that only one or two draft evasion cases are more visible to the attentive public than a large number of such cases. Although the subset correlation with the AmLeg variable was not significant, the direction is suggestive. The severity index for judges with few cases correlated positively with the state size of the American Legion, while the judges with heavier caseloads reacted inversely to Legion presence.

For the universe of cases there was a significant correlation between severity and percentage of the draft caseload handled by the judge. The judge who handled the largest proportion or even monopolized the selective service docket was severe. This association suggests that judges sitting alone are more harsh. The data may also suggest that in some districts where assignments are not made randomly, draft cases were turned over to the more unbending judges.

. . .

3. Senior Status. Judges who have served for 10 to 15 years and have reached the age of 65 to 70, but do not wish to retire entirely from their judicial service, may take senior judge status. Senior status allows the experienced but older judge to handle cases upon assignment by active judges, while giving him freedom to refuse assignments, accept visiting judgeships, and relief from administrative responsibilities. . . .

The overwhelming pressure of cases filed in federal courts encourages reliance upon the services of the senior brethren. Of the 1,852 draft cases decided by trial judges in their own districts in 1972, [33] senior judges decided 168 cases or nine percent of the total. . . .

The mean [severity] indices of the two subsets [active and senior judges] are very similar. Evidently the use of senior judges as a technique of judicial administration does not skew the pattern of sentencing. . . .

4. Judicial Leadership. Within the court organization only a small proportion of judges accept national level responsibilities. Those who do might be expected to identify with the nation-state and accept the role of protector of the political system more fervently than other judges. In their special capacity as judicial leaders they would be likely to sentence draft offenders severely even after the majority of judges had begun to reduce their penalties. In fact, the 56 judicial leaders have an average severity index two points higher than the universe of judges.

E. Characteristics of the Judge

The field of judicial behavior, with its focus on the judge as decision-maker rather than on the court as an institution or public law as rationally developed, is relatively new. The original question was asked in the 1950's by Glendon Schubert: How do the attitudes and belief systems of the judge, as an individual, affect his choices? This basic inquiry led to the examination of the backgrounds, education, career experiences, political associations, and religious affiliations of appellate court judges as a descriptive prerequisite to the testing of propositions about their votes in cases.

The research which has appeared since examines four characteristics of appellate and trial judges: attributes both ascribed and achieved; reference groups; judicial role definitions; and judicial values and attitudes. The background characteristics, particularly ascribed attributes of the judges such as age, religion, place of birth and ethnicity, have been tested in a number of studies because the information is readily available in standard biographical sources. Most of these suggested predictors are nominal and therefore less useful in statistical tests than an interval or ordinal variable such as age. However, locations such as birthplace can be translated into an ordinal measure by calculating the number of miles between the judge's birthplace and the city where his court is located.

The "achieved" attributes of the judge include his educational history, his legal practice, and his public service career, elective and appointive. Prior judicial experience is a predictor commonly used by federal appointing authorities as well as by social scientists. The remoteness of attribute factors from the context of current policy-making suggests that their explanatory power would be small.

Testing group affiliation in relation to judicial decisions rests upon the hypothesis that the decision-maker selects his associations on the basis of his preexisting personal attitudes, and further, that these attitudes are reinforced by continuing contact. The reference groups may be family, social, cultural, economic, political, or "policy specific." The judicial system recognizes the possibility of a real or apparent relationship between group membership and judicial choices in its ethical code. The Judicial Code of Ethics proscribes sitting on cases involving one's family, law firm or investment portfolio; and requires divestment of directorships and certain properties.

Political party membership (nominal) and more importantly the degree of prior active participation in party business (ordinal) are the variables of most interest in political science research. Party has proved to be the most significant variable in relation to judicial output in a number of studies. . . .

The judge's own definition of his appropriate role is a new variable in judicial research developed within the last five years. It is adapted from role studies of legislative behavior. Judicial attitudes and values were the first type of predictor employed in modern judicial behavior research. . . .

. . .

1. Judicial Attributes. The ascribed judicial attribute employed in this research is age. Age is expected to correlate positively with any question regarding the status quo. It is hypothesized that the older judge, with patriotic notions of earlier generations and memories of two great wars, is likely to give more severe sentences. Age was used first to divide the judges into nominal categories: those under 65 and those 65 and over. Age was also used as an interval variable in relation to the severity index.

Age per se did not affect the severity of sentencing according to the correlation tests. Within the nominal category of active judges, age had no predictive utility. But . . . within the category of senior judges, the range in age from 65 to 90 did vary with severity.

The older judges as a group have a mean severity index over three points higher than the younger judges. Moreover, the response of the two age groups to reference group variables differs. Reaction to the number of American Legion members in the community, an environmental variable, also differed. The younger judges were not affected, but the older judges sentenced more severely in such a climate. Perhaps the reason for the difference lies in history. The roots of the Legion are in World War I and the older judges would be contemporaries of the founding fathers. It may be that the important concept here is not age, but membership in a particular age-cohort group with common life experiences.

The "achieved" judicial attributes employed in this study involve prior personal experiences in military service and public office experiences in the legal process. The career data on the judge's occupation prior to ascending the federal bench allows a separate examination of the judges whose "penultimate office" was in public office in the judicial process. This nominal classification will be employed in a multivariate analysis in the next section dealing with reference groups.

The Service index is based first, on the participation of the judge in World War I or II, Korea or Vietnam, or in the regular service between wars; second, his highest rank; and third, the number of medals he received. Eight of these 304 judges served in World War I and nine served during two wars. One general and a number of Army colonels and Navy captains are represented. A high Service index was expected to correlate with high severity.

The Service index correlations produced an unexpected result. (See Table 31-8.) Judges with a high Service index were less severe than the judges who had no service at all by 3.3 index points. The direction of correlation on the high service judges was negative, and on the no service judges positive. Memberships in veterans organizations varied with severity among the high service judges, but not at a significant level. Membership in such groups had no relation to the sentencing severity of low service judges.

Evidently the judges who served in the armed forces were less reliant upon reference groups for cues as to the proper stance toward the draft issue. The high service judge made up his own mind on the basis of personal experience. Moreover, he had no motivation to prove his devotion to national security by giving severe sentences since he already

TABLE 31-8
Severity of Draft Sentencing by Military Service, 1972

	No Service	Low Service Index (5 to 45)	High Service Index (50 and above)
Number of Judges	137	109	55
Mean Severity Index Per Judge	23.8	20.6	20.5

had earned his credentials. It is possible that his more lenient sentences are compensation for his known association with the military. The same argument seems persuasive when applied to the high severity index of no service judges: are they displaying their own patriotism by requiring obedience and service from others?

2. *Reference Groups*. Four kinds of reference group variables—family, civic, "policy specific" and political party—are tested to discern whether they affect sentencing. The family reference group is composed of the sons in the judge's family. They are perceived as agents of communication between the judge and the new generation with its liberal attitudes toward war and draft resistance. Moreover, paternal affection for a draft age son was predicted to carry over to other young men who appeared before the judge as draft offenders. Consequently, the hypothesis was that the judge's acquaintance with a contemporary viewpoint, plus his emotional attachment to his sons, would lead to a lenient sentencing policy.

The son index was constructed by assigning five points for each son, plus five points if the son were of draftable age (18 to 26) between 1962 and 1972. The variable performed exactly opposite to the prediction. The more sons, and sons of draftable age, the more severe the judge. Perhaps the judge's sons were in service and he was only demanding a similar sacrifice of other young men, but without data this remains pure speculation.

The impact of the family reference group on judges operated in peculiar fashion. There were associations with greater severity for judges with high military service, for Democratic judges in metropolitan areas, and for older judges; but associations with leniency for judges in the Seventh Circuit.

The civic reference group variables were used to separate the judges into the "parochials," the "nationals," and the "altruists." Parochial judges belonged only to local groups, such as fraternal clubs (Lions, Elks, Eagles, Woodmen); social clubs (country, city and yacht); and booster clubs (Chamber of Commerce, Rotary, Kiwanis, Civitan). They had attended state law schools and participated in local partisan and business activities. National judges, in addition to local activities, also participated in national political and legal organizations, took their law degrees outside the state where their district is located, or served in the national government in Washington, D.C. The altruistic judges were either parochial or national but, in addition, belonged to reference groups devoted to charitable, health, or cultural pursuits, such as hospital, museum, or law school boards of trustees.

The hypothesis was that parochial judges would reflect the "law and order" concerns of their local associates, that national judges would reflect a concern with national security, and that altruistic judges would sympathize with personal moral commitments of draft resisters. Therefore, it was expected that the severity indices of the parochial judges would be higher than nationals, and nationals higher than altruists. The summary table of average indices, Table 31-12, shows that these predictions were verified. Further, the regression analysis revealed a significant relationship between the intensity of the judge's participation in altruistic activities and the mildness of his sentences. Active judges, senior judges, metropolitan judges, judicial leaders, and judges with small caseloads all had a significant correlation between a high altruist index and a low severity index.

The severity of altruist judges who had different career experiences prior to appointment was tested in a multivariate analysis. The career category described in an earlier section as public office in the justice system was used to separate judges according to their last office prior to appointment. It was expected that this penultimate experience would tend to moderate sentencing due to recognition of the limitations of sentencing as an

TABLE 31-9
Sentencing of "Libertarian" and "Patriotic" Judges

Severity Index	Universe	Judges in Civil Liberties Organizations	Judges in Veterans Organizations
Under 10	10%	22%	4%
10–19	51%	61%	61%
20–29	20%	17%	12%
39 up	18%	0	21%

instrument of social policy or individual change. [The findings are] that only 10 percent of the altruistic judges with penultimate office in the justice system gave high sentences in comparison with 32 percent of the non-altruistic judges without such experience. . . .

The third kind of reference groups examined are those "policy specific" to the draft issue. Only six percent (18) of the district judges in this universe belonged to civil liberties associations. Forty-nine, or 16 percent, belonged to veterans organizations. The civil liberties organizations included the ACLU, NAACP, National Council of Christians and Jews, Urban League, and various human relations councils and commissions. The veterans' organizations included, among others, the American Legion, VFW, 40 & 8, DAV, AmVets, Military Order of World Wars, Navy League, West Point Society, and Catholic, Republican, and Jewish war veteran societies. The judges who belonged to civil liberties groups were predicted to give mild sentences and members of veterans' organizations harsh sentences. Table 31-9 shows that the indices varied as expected. However, the number of judges belonging to relevant groups was not large enough for a meaningful test of relationships.

The fourth reference group is the political party of the judge. The party affiliation of political decision makers has been established as a powerful but not sufficient explanation of public choice. Earlier studies have indicated that judges who belonged to the Democratic party tended to be more sympathetic to the underdog and the civil rights claimant. This would suggest that Democratic federal judges act less severely than Republican judges toward draft offenders.

Since party is not an ordinal variable, it was used to dichotomize the cases and judges for subset comparisons. The mean severity index of all cases decided by Democratic judges was only 1.3 points lower than that of Republican judges. The variance in distribution of the indices within each party was significant, however, suggesting that party affiliation does have some bearing on the draft sentence decision.

As individuals, the Democratic judges had a mean severity index 1.2 points lower than Republican judges. The distribution of individual indices described by Table 31-10 ranged from 1 to 99 for judges of both parties. At the lower range, 63 percent of the Democratic judges and 58 percent of the Republican judges had indices below 20; and at the higher range, 18 percent of the Democratic judges and 22 percent of the Republican judges had indices of 30 or higher. The leniency of the Democratic judges is evident only at the tails of the curve.

F. Explanatory Power of the Variables

A number of variables together, environmental, structural, and personal (but not public opinion or case attributes), in a regression analysis explain only five percent of the vari-

TABLE 31-10
Severity of Draft Sentences by Party Affiliation

Severity Index	Democratic Judges	Republican Judges
0–9	10%	9%
10–19	53%	49%
20–29	19%	21%
30–39	7%	7%
40–49	5%	8%
50–59	4%	3%
60–69	0	1%
70–79	0.	1%
99	2%	2%

ation in the universe of 1,852 draft cases. However, the variables were much more useful in understanding the sentence choices of subsets of judges. For instance, a group of variables could explain 14 percent of the variation in cases decided by older judges, 15 percent of Seventh Circuit cases, 24 percent of the judicial leader decisions, 34 percent of senior judges' decisions, 35 percent of small town cases, and 36 percent of Sixth Circuit cases.

If the model is correct in claiming that precedent and public opinion can explain 60 to 85 percent of the sentence choice variance, and if case attributes (type of defendant, trial, etc.) can explain 5 to 10 percent, then the regression analysis using the other three kinds of variables does not need to explain more than 35 percent of the variation at most.

. . .

III.   Conclusion

The differences between the judges who gave very light sentences (suspended or short probation) and those who gave very harsh sentences (four to five years in prison) may be instructive. Table 31-11 confirms the earlier discoveries that mild judges are altruists who have served in the military and belong to civil liberties organizations, while stern judges are parochials or nationals and work in a community with a large Legionnaire membership. The Seventh and Tenth circuits have average to harsh judges, while the Second, Fourth, Fifth and Ninth Circuits have average to mild judges. Both harsh and mild judges are found in the Third, Sixth and Eighth Circuits.

From the entire analysis it is possible to extract models of the severe draft judge and the mild draft judge. These models may be particularly interesting in comparison with local

TABLE 31-11
Characteristics of Severe and Mild Judges, 1972

	Mild Judges (29)	Severe Judges (8)
"Altruist"	100%	25%
Democrat	62%	50%
Military Service	45%	12.5%
Libertarian	17%	0%
Strong Legion Environment	3%	25%

TABLE 31-12
Summary of Mean Severity Indices of Subsets of Draft Judges, 1972

Type of Judge	Mean Index
Small Town	29.9
Parochial	26.4
Small Caseload	25.3
Older	24.4
Judicial Leader	24.1
Non-Military	23.8
City	23.5
National	23.1
Republican	22.6
Senior	22.6
Universe	**22.0**
Active	21.8
Democrat	21.4
Younger	21.0
Altruist	21.0
Military Service	20.5
Metro	20.2
Large Caseload	19.4
Libertarian	14.7

folklore about individual judges. Table 31-12 lists the indices discussed in the body of the paper in order of severity.

A. Model of the Severe Judge

He sits in the South, in the Fifth Circuit, in a poor small town. He is a Republican in a Democratic area, 67 years old with several sons. He has just taken senior status but the regular seat is vacant so he sits alone in his division and handles only one or two draft cases per year. He never served in the armed forces, and his associations are exclusively with his local fraternal, business, and country clubs. He once gave a lecture at a seminar for new judges.

B. Model of the Mild Judge

He sits in the East, in a metropolitan area with a high crime rate. He is a Democrat in a Democratic area, 60 years old, with no sons in his family. He sits on a multijudge court and handles a large but equal share of the draft caseload. He served in World War II as a major and has a nominal membership in the American Legion. His organizational affiliations are with the ACLU and the symphony association. He has not been tapped for work on any national judicial committees.

C. Some Useful Generalizations

These stereotypes may not be useful in predicting the future decisions of a particular judge, but they do suggest some clear findings which emerge from the analyses undertaken in this study.

1. Sentencing behavior varies with the strength of the relevant pressure group in the environment only when the judge lacks other cues to appropriate choices.
2. Judges who handle three or more cases per year on a multijudge court are less severe than judges who handle few cases of that type and serve alone.
3. Older judges and judicial leaders (cross correlation .304) are significantly more severe than younger nonleaders, but senior judges perform much like active judges.
4. Judges whose only reference groups are local are more severe than judges with national associations.
5. Judges give milder sentences in proportion to the number of their altruistic associations.
6. Democratic judges give milder sentences than Republican judges, but party affiliation is not the major factor in severity.
7. Democratic judges give harsher sentences in a Republican environment than in a Democratic environment.
8. Trial judges who belong to "policy specific" groups decide in the direction of the group commitment.
9. Trial judges are not biased by personal allegiances, *i.e.*, by paternal affection or by military service.

. . .

APPENDIX A, TABLE 31-13
Weighting Scales for Federal Criminal Sentences

Administrative Office Scale		Selective Service Scale	
Sentence	Weight	Weight	Sentence
Suspended	0	1	Suspended
Probation without			Probation without
Supervision	0	1	Supervision
Fine Only	1	2	$1–$249
		3	$250–$999
		4	$1000–$4999
		5	$5000–$50,000
Probation:			
1–12 months	1	4	1 month
		5	3
		6	6
		7	9
13–36 months	2	8	12
		9	15
		10	18
		12	24
		14	30
Over 36 months	4	16	36
		17	42
		18	48
		19	54
		20	60
Imprisonment:			
1–6 months	3	12	1 month
		15	3
		16	4
		18	5

APPENDIX A, TABLE 31-13 1-13 (Continued)

Administrative Office Scale		Selective Service Scale	
Sentence	Weight	Weight	Sentence
7–12 months	5	20	6
		24	8
		26	9
		28	10
13–24 months	8	32	12
		34	15
		36	18
25–36 months	10	40	24
		44	30
37–48 months	12	48	36
		52	42
49–60 months	14	56	48
		80	54
61–120 months	25	99	60

* "Federal Offenders in the U.S. District Courts, 1970," Administrative Office of the U.S. Courts, Table 14, p. 57.

Notes

1. Comment, "Sentencing Selective Service Violators: A Judicial Wheel of Fortune," 5 *Colum. J.L. & Social Prob.* 164, 173 (Aug. 1969).

2. W. Markham, "Draft Offenders in the Federal Courts: A Search for the Social Correlates of Justice" at 106, 1971 (unpublished Ph.D. thesis in University of Pennsylvania Library).

3. Boldt, "Recent Trends in Criminal Sentencing," 27 *Fed. Probation* 3 (Mar. 1963).

4. Markham, *supra* at 145.

5. Markham, *supra* at 146, 148, 155.

6. Markham, at 179–180.

7. A nominal scale is one in which the categories function as labels. In an ordinal scale the categories are labeled and ordered. A typical nominal scale would be religion, e.g., Protestant, Catholic or Jewish. An ordinal scale might be illustrated by social class: upper, middle, and lower, or an interval scale by age: 1–99.

CHAPTER ELEVEN

BACKGROUNDS AND DECISIONS

Why do judges decide cases the way they do? Thus far we have examined how particular facts may affect the outcomes of particular cases and how environmental influences affect the way judges and courts function. We have seen that the traditional model of dispute processing is inconsistent with the research findings. Continuing our testing of the traditional model and our examination of alternative perspectives, we now consider the personal attributes and backgrounds of judges.

How does a judge's socioeconomic, political, and ethnic-religious background influence judicial decision making, if at all? Assuming that it does and that a judge's background is known, how well does it explain judicial behavior? These questions have puzzled more than one generation of scholars and have stimulated much research effort, some of it producing conflicting results. Judicial biographies have typically traced what appear to be the formative background influences and experiences that have shaped the future judge's personality and philosophy. The intriguing research question has been whether there are regularities in the linkages between certain background characteristics and judicial decision making or whether each judge is idiosyncratic and to be understood in terms of a unique configuration of backgrounds and life experiences.

If regularities of behavior were linked to certain attributes or background characteristics, then a sociological model of decision making could be established, and it, in turn, would have broad implications for the judicial selection process. If it were conclusively demonstrated that there are distinctive decisional tendencies for judges with certain attributes or background characteristics (for example, age, sex, race, political party affiliation and activism, religion, education, group memberships, type of law practice), then a number of arguments could be made about the sorts of people who should be selected for judgeships. Those with certain demographic and personal attributes could argue that some of their kind are entitled to "representation" on the bench not only to assure justice for these people but also to counter the biases or insensitivities of others already on the bench. Supporters of merit selection of judges could argue that merit selection results in the selection of the best legal minds and that such people can transcend their backgrounds and behave more in line with the traditional model of judicial behavior. Merit plan supporters could also argue that in the long run, selection on the basis of merit, assuming that there are no demographic or attribute biases in selection and that there is a random distribution of skill and intelligence among those with different attributes, should result in a mix of backgrounds that would emerge on the bench. Party officials could argue that since party is linked with judicial behavior, it can reasonably and legitimately be considered in the selection process. And so on.

One of the first and most widely cited background-behavior studies was a study of state supreme court judges conducted by Stuart Nagel. Nagel found that political party affiliation was associated with decisional propensities. Democratic judges were more liberal than Republican judges and more often found for the criminal defendant in criminal cases, for the employee or union in labor-management cases, for the economic underdog in a wide variety of economic cases, and for the injured in personal injury cases.[1] In other articles he presented findings that suggested that religion was also somewhat related to decisional propensities. Catholic judges tended to be more liberal than Protestants.[2] Other researchers soon undertook similar studies, and a considerable literature developed. (Some of it is cited in the Goldman reading, selection 34.)

The first of the initially raised questions concerned the influence on decision making of a judge's background. Kenneth Vines pursued this question with reference to the decisional behavior of Southern judges during the era of the civil rights revolution. Vines' study (selection 32) persuasively portrays the interlocking web of social-political-economic backgrounds that molded those who became segregationist judges as opposed to those who became integrationists on the bench. Giles and Walker (selection 33) conducted a follow-up study at a later point in time and, using somewhat different methods, found that indeed times had changed and that their findings differed from those of the earlier period studied by Vines. These two studies taken together suggest both the promise and the difficulties of backgrounds research. At certain points in time, backgrounds can be shown to be associated with certain behavioral patterns. But at later points in time, those same backgrounds may represent different socialization and cultural experiences and result in different behavioral syndromes.

The Goldman study of appeals court judges (selection 34) puts to the test a series of background-behavior hypotheses. Goldman, for appeals court judges, and Ulmer, for Supreme Court judges (selection 35), seek to answer the second question posed initially: how well can certain background variables explain judicial decision-making behavior? Goldman found that, with the exception of party affiliation and to some extent age, the answer is "not very well." Ulmer found that three background variables seemed to explain a major part of the variation in Supreme Court voting behavior.[3]

In general, the background-behavior studies of aggregates of judges have not satisfactorily established clear-cut linkages between most background variables and decision making. The reason for this is that taken literally, the sociological model of decision making does not make sense. It is inaccurate to assert that someone behaves in a certain way *because* that person is black, female, Catholic, Democrat, old, Harvard educated, in solo law practice, and so forth. Rather what is essentially being argued is that the fact that one has certain attributes means that one will have had certain socializing experiences that have stimulated the development of certain attitudes and values or even conceptions of the judicial role. But in reality each of the background or attribute variables tested using aggregates of judges is too crude to be associated with the same or similar experiences; hence each of the variables is not easily linked to just one set of attitudes and values. There are some weak-to-moderate associations between a few attributes and certain types of behavior; however, the background-behavior model has not been conclusively proven, and for the reasons just suggested it is unlikely that it can be. But this does not mean that we should return to the traditional model. Rather, we should conclude that taken together, the judicial biographies and the aggregate analyses are inconsistent with the traditional model. They suggest that a judge cannot be divorced from his or her life experiences and that detailed knowledge of backgrounds may be crucial for our understanding of the development of attitudes and values and ultimately the judicial behavior of the *individual* judge. The studies of aggregates of judges warn us that the crudely drawn classifications of attributes or background characteristics mask a variety of individual experiences. But they should not blind us to the linkage of attributes to attitudes and attitudes to behavior. It is this second linkage to which we shall turn in the next chapter.

Notes

1. Stuart S. Nagel, "Political Party Affiliation and Judges' Decisions," *American Political Science Review* 55 (1961), 843–850. For a retest see Nagel's study, "Multiple Correlation of Judicial Backgrounds and Decisions," *Florida State University Law Review* 2 (1974), 258–280.

2. Stuart S. Nagel, "Ethnic Affiliations and Judicial Propensities," *Journal of Politics* 24 (1962), 92–110.

3. Ulmer's article was discussed by James L. Payne and James A. Dyer in "Betting After the Race is Over: The Perils of Post Hoc Hypothesizing," *American Journal of Political Science* 19 (1975), 559–564. In a persuasive rejoinder Ulmer presented the results of newer and even more extensive testing that support his original findings and conclusions. See his "H_0: Post Hoc Con-Straw-Man Con $= 0$," *American Journal of Political Science* 19 (1975), 565–570.

32

Federal District Judges and Race Relations Cases in the South

Kenneth N. Vines

The purpose of this paper is to explore the political activities of officials operating within a judicial environment, in a sensitive, crucial area of Southern politics. This will be done by an examination of race relations cases in Southern federal district courts. The disposition of cases will be described and the distribution of decisions related to judicial districts and to deciding judges. Finally, an attempt will be made to explain the similarities and differences in the decisions. The cases examined will include all race relations cases decided in the federal district courts of the eleven states of the traditional South from May 1954 to October 1962. Data concerning the disposition of these cases will be used in conjunction with information on the backgrounds and experiences of Southern district judges and with certain information on the judicial districts in which the cases were decided.

Political scientists have shown that a variety of political institutions are molded by their economic and social environment and that political behavior is related to the social backgrounds and political experiences of the participants. Legal theory supposes, however, that courts and judges, because of the myth of legal objectivity and the quasi-insulated position of the courts from the remainder of the political system, are not similarly influenced, except perhaps by their legal environment. Judicial analysts have frequently shown that judges do vary in their behavior but have not often attempted to explain the variations in judicial behavior. Through investigation of a homogeneous group of cases decided by judges in the context of a region with both social similarities and social differences, we have an opportunity to examine the behavior of judges against their social and political environment. Then we may see whether judges and courts are also molded by their social and political environment or whether legal theory correctly describes judicial behavior.

The analysis of cases in this paper is based upon quantitative treatment of cases rather than the more usual qualitative treatments to be found in constitutional law. In constitutional law each case is treated more or less as a distinct phenomenon, related to other cases by precedent, by treatment of similar subject matters, or by legal concepts. Cases on

Reprinted by permission of author and publisher from Kenneth N. Vines, "Federal District Judges and Race Relations Cases in the South," *Journal of Politics* 26 (1964), 338-340, 343-344, 348-357. Footnotes have been omitted.

similar subject matters often involve quite different legal formulations of the issues. Thus cases on the desegregation of the schools may involve not just the issue of whether the school should be desegregated, but whether pupil placement plans should be used, how pupil placement plans should be used, and whether states may legislate methods of avoiding school desegregation such as closing the public schools.

The quantitative treatment of cases, which considers cases as part of groups even though they may involve quite different legal statements of the issue, can be justified in political analysis. Let us consider education cases in the federal courts as an example. Even though the cases may be stated legally in quite different ways, as above, the cases are all part of a common political issue conflict. This policy conflict centers on the efforts of Negro interests in the South to secure desegregation of public schools and the attempts of white groups, private and governmental, to thwart these efforts or limit their effectiveness. Litigation of the issue in terms of the conception of pupil placement does not change the basic policy conflict, since white communities have tried to use the technique of pupil placement to curtail desegregation of schools and Negro interests have objected to its use on the grounds that it slows down the process of desegregation. Hence, though legally variable, education and other race relations cases are basically similar politically.

. . .

The Districts

An important characteristic of the federal district courts is their dispersion in different states and in different sections of the same state. Twenty-eight of the more than one hundred districts in the nation are located in the eleven states of the traditional South; each of these states is then divided into two, three, or four districts. The boundaries of federal court districts are hardly systematic, following from time to time the needs of different district case loads and the political exigencies of acts of Congress. However, sectional interests are often fortuitously embodied in some districts. For example, Tennessee is divided into an Eastern, a Middle, and a Western judicial district, corresponding roughly to important sectional differences found within that state; the division of Georgia and Alabama into Northern, Middle, and Southern districts encompasses some of the distinctive social and political characteristics of those states.

Federal district judges commonly come from the district which they serve. Not only do federal judges live in the district but in 51.3 per cent of all cases they were born in that same district. Often (in 56.1 per cent of the cases) they have attended law school in the state in which the district is located, and (in 89 per cent of the cases) they have held government positions in the state. Their ties with the judicial district in which they serve are consequently deep and of long standing. Moreover, while in office, judges are required by statute to continue living in the district of appointment.

. . .

It is fair to point out that certain characteristics of the district judiciary may also reduce the influence of local political values. While predominantly local influences prepare and bring the judges into office, local influences are not necessary to keep him there. Appointed for life during good behavior, the Southern district judge does not depend for tenure in office upon his success in winning office; the district judge does not have to win the Democratic primary with all the campaigning, contacts with local politicians, and

TABLE 32-1
Disposition of Cases by Judicial Districts

Percentage Favoring Negroes	Number of Districts
90–100	3
80–89	2
70–79	1
60–69	5
50–59	5
40–49	2
30–39	3
20–29	2
10–19	0
Below 10	5
	28

interaction with Southern public opinion that are implied in competition in party prima-ries. Neither does the federal judge depend in the performance of his duties upon coopera-tion and good working relationships with local politicians and groups. The operating independence of the federal judiciary can largely insulate the judge from the effects of local and regional political values and practices if he desires it.

. . .

There is considerable variation in the way different judicial districts disposed of race relation cases, as described by Table 32-1. In dealing with similar political problems often stated in similar legal ways, Southern district courts evidenced quite wide differences in their decisions. Given the differences among the districts in Negro-white population bal-ance, we can find whether or not the two variables are related. A measure of relationship would provide one test of the proposition that courts are influenced by their social envi-ronment.

The coefficient of correlation between the two factors is $R = -.48$. That is, the propor-tion of Negroes in the population of Southern judicial districts is negatively related to the percentage of cases decided in favor of Negroes in the district. The higher the proportion of Negroes in a district, the less apt, at least to the extent of $R = -.48$, is the court to decide the cases in favor of Negroes.

A comparison of the degree of influence exercised by Negro-white population balance in another political situation is instructive. Matthews and Prothro have shown that in Southern counties the proportion of Negroes in the population correlates negatively, $R = -.46$, with the level of Negro registration in the county. The similarity of the correlations in the two situations indicates that a large Negro population has about the same impact on Southern federal judges in district courts as it does upon county officials in the South who register Negroes. In both instances the relationship, though of some significance, explains about twenty-two per cent of the total amount of variance. However, we may infer from the data that localism is of some influence in the district courts since Negro-white population balances affect decision-making in the district courts of the South.

The District Judges—Influential Factors

Among the 60 judges who sat in the Southern district courts on race relations cases from 1954–1962 there were 23 who participated in fewer than 3 decisions. These included

TABLE 32-2
Disposition of Cases by Active District Judges

Per Cent of Cases Favorable for Negroes	Number of Judges	Number of Cases Decided by Judges in Each Category
90–100	4	35
80–89	3	25
70–79	0	0
60–69	12	85
50–59	1	4
40–49	2	12
30–39	3	25
20–29	3	19
10–19	2	19
0–9	7	43
	37	267

judges who died or resigned during the period, those newly appointed, and some who sat in districts such as the West Texas district that simply had few race relations cases. There were 37 judges who sat on 3 or more cases and among them these judges decided 267 cases. These judges are ranked in Table 32-2 according to disposition of cases.

The 37 judges who were active in the decision of race relations cases reacted to them with varying degrees of favor toward the Negroes involved, as Table 32-2 shows. There is no outstanding mode which locates a large proportion of judges. Only 18 judges, or about half of them, decided cases in the large middle range of 30 to 79 per cent. Moreover, significant groups may be found at both extreme ends of the distribution. Nine judges who decided 62 cases ranked less than 20 per cent, while seven judges who decided 60 cases attained a percentage rank of more than 80 per cent in deciding cases favorably towards Negroes.

The extreme differences among the judges in the disposition of race relations cases can be indicated by the fact that there were seven judges who handled 43 cases and who decided no cases in favor of Negroes; but there were four who handled 35 cases and who decided more than 90 per cent of the time for the Negro litigants. We may conclude from this description that the average performance is made up, in part, of extreme pro-Negro decision records in combination with extreme anti-Negro decision records.

Ranked according to the disposition of cases for and against Negroes, the judges fall into three groups: the first group we may call the "Segregationists," and they decided in favor of Negroes in less than one-third of the cases; the second group who decided in favor of Negroes in 34–67 per cent of all cases handled, we call the "Moderates"; the third group whose record in favor of Negro claimants was better than 67 per cent of all cases, we call the "Integrationists." These terms are doubtless not an accurate description of the judicial philosophies of the respective groups, but they can serve as identifications for the three groups and as rough indicators of their roles in Southern politics.

One possibility of the difference among the three groups is that the different policy positions can be explained by reference to the kinds of districts they serve. Thus, those judges from the deep South where Negro populations are proportionately large might be expected to regard Negro interests less favorably than those judges in the hills and mountains outside the black belt areas where there are comparatively few Negroes. Table 32-3 indicates the differences among the three groups; the Integrationists hear cases in districts

TABLE 32-3
**Relationship of Percent of Cases Decided in Favor of Negroes
to the Percentage of Negroes in District of Judge**

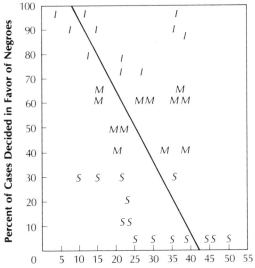

Percent of Negroes in District

I = Integrationists, *M* = Moderates,
and *S* = Segregationists

which have somewhat fewer Negroes than the two others while Segregationist judges have more Negroes in their districts. Although there is some relationship as indicated by the estimated line of regression, there are some clearly exogenous cases.

The factor of Negro-white population balance, we have seen, has limited explanatory power in accounting for the differences in the disposition of cases within the various districts. For further information on the factors associated with the differential judicial behavior, we may turn to the judges themselves, their backgrounds and experiences. Some studies of judicial behavior in various courts have indicated that judicial behavior is related to the social backgrounds and political experiences of the judges. The general thesis in all these studies is that social and political factors are related to judicial behavior in much the same fashion that social and political characteristics are related to the political behavior of voters and nonjudicial policymakers.

One way in which the personnel of Southern federal courts differ from other Southern politicians is in the larger number of Republicans on the district courts. Of the 37 judges in the three groups, 15 or 40.1 per cent are Republicans. Officeholders who must seek office through popular elections can rarely be identified as Republicans in the South and still win election. For appointments to the Southern judiciary, however, Republican presidents generally seek out Southern Republicans. Because of the appointments of both Republican and Democratic presidents the Southern district judiciary contains judges of both Republican and Democratic affiliation. Historically, the Democratic party in the South has been identified with the maintenance of segregation and white supremacy,

TABLE 32-4
Party Affiliations of Three Groups of Southern Judges*

Affiliation	Segregationists	Moderates	Integrationists
Democratic	78.6%	50.0%	45.4%
Republican	21.4	50.0	54.6
	100.0 (N = 14)	100.0 (N = 12)	100.0 (N = 11)

* X^2 indicates marginal significance at .08 level.

while the Southern Republican party has a tradition of a more permissive attitude in race relations. Consequently, we might wonder whether judicial behavior in the South is related to partisan affiliation.

The figures in Table 32-4 indicate that the Republican judges are located disproportionately among the Moderates and Integrationists, half of whose members are Republicans. Only 3 out of 14, or 21.4 per cent of the Segregationist judges, are Republicans. Republican candidates in the South today are often as enthusiastically in favor of segregation and as racially demagogic as their Democratic opponents. Yet, there is some evidence here that the traditions of the Southern Republican party still have some impact upon political behavior. The relative isolation of Southern Republicans may also contribute to their more permissive attitude toward Negroes in race relations cases. Even if active and politically involved, Southern Republicans are apt to have fewer occasions to seek state political office, to attend regional political meetings, and publicly to defend Southern political values. The political roles which result in white supremacy among the Democratic office seekers and party workers are often lacking in the more restricted political lives of Southern Republicans. A further possible explanation may be found in the character of the Republican judges appointed by Eisenhower. Not restricted by senatorial courtesy, the President was able to appoint with relative freedom and his appointments include the "new" Republicans with urban backgrounds.

The Judges' relationships to their districts, states, and the Southern region is investigated in Tables 32-5, 32-6, and 32-7.

Southern judges like other federal judges, we see in Table 32-5, tend to be born in the district they serve. A similar number of Integrationists and Segregationists hold court in the same district in which they were born. Few of any group were born outside the Southern region although a slightly greater number of Moderates had non-Southern birth places.

TABLE 32-5
Place of Birth of Southern Judges*

Place of Birth	Segregationists	Moderates	Integrationists
In His District	64.3%	50.0%	63.6%
In His State but Not District	7.1	8.3	9.1
Other Southern State	0.0	8.3	9.1
Outside South	14.3	25.0	9.1
Don't Know	14.3	8.4	9.1
	100.0% (N = 14)	100.0% (N = 12)	100.0% (N = 11)

* X^2 indicates relationship not significant.

TABLE 32-6
Location of Law School of Southern Judges*

Location of Law School	Segregationists	Moderates	Integrationists
South	71.4%	50.0%	63.6%
Border State	28.6	16.7	0.0
Outside South	0.0	8.3	18.2
Don't Know	0.0	25.0	18.2
	100.0% (N = 14)	100.0% (N = 12)	100.0% (N = 11)

* X^2 indicates relationship not significant.

The local attachments of Southern judges are strengthened in their training and practice of the law. While there is a common core of values and practices in legal training wherever it is taught in the United States, state and regional law schools and particularly state universities have strong ties with the state political system. Lawyers who practice in one state meet only the political values of that state, contact only local politicians, and gain practice only in the political process of that state. On the other hand, lawyers who have gone to law school outside the state or region of their association, receive training in other political symbols and meet a different set of political values. Lawyers who practice in more than one state have an opportunity for contact with several state political structures; they meet different kinds of litigants and may gain a more cosmopolitan perception of law and political life.

Southern judges have had, as a group, few opportunities for such cosmopolitan development in their legal training and practice, as shown in Tables 32-6 and 32-7. The legal development of Southern judges has taken place within the framework of the Southern political system and very largely within the state containing the district of their appointment. Moreover, there are few significant differences among the group of judges. The Moderates have undergone slightly more broadening experiences than the two other groups. The Moderates have attended law schools in the South less frequently (50.0 per cent compared to 71.4 per cent and 63.6 per cent) and have practiced outside the state of their court district more often (25.0 per cent compared to 7.1 per cent and 9.1 per cent). The Integrationists have attended non-Southern law schools slightly more often (18.2 per cent compared to 0.0 per cent and 8.3 per cent). But these differences are not remarkable and the fact remains that Southern judges have received their professional training and experiences very largely within the locality of the court over which they preside.

Religious affiliation, while it cannot be considered of great significance in itself, may provide a clue to the relationship of the judge to the Southern social structure. Very largely (except in quite restricted areas such as Southern Louisiana), Southern society is

TABLE 32-7
Location of Law Practice of Southern Judges*

Location of Law Practice	Segregationists	Moderates	Integrationists
In State of District	85.8%	58.3%	81.8%
In Other State	7.1	25.0	9.1
No Practice Listed	7.1	16.7	9.1
	100.0% (N = 14)	100.0% (N = 12)	100.0% (N = 11)

* X^2 indicates relationship not significant.

TABLE 32-8
Religious Affiliation of Groups of Southern Judges*

Religious Affiliation	Segregationists	Moderates	Integrationists
Orthodox Protestant	71.4%	66.7%	36.4%
Catholic	0.0	0.0	18.2
None Listed	21.4	25.0	45.4
Don't Know	7.2	8.3	0.0
	100.0% (N = 14)	100.0% (N = 12)	100.0% (N = 11)

* X^2 indicates significance at .05 level.

Protestant and orthodox. The Protestant church, far from providing an exception to the structure of a segregated society, remains an almost totally segregated institution and must be regarded as one of the important institutional supports of traditional Southern values.

The data in Table 32-8 indicate that there are significant differences among the groups of judges on the matter of religious affiliation. Only about one-third of the Integrationists list orthodox Protestant religions (36.4 per cent) while two-thirds or more of the Moderates (66.7 per cent) and the Segregationists (71.4 per cent) list such religion. The few Catholic judges are found among the Integrationists and almost half of the Integrationists (45.4 per cent) list no religion. We may speculate that the non-affiliation of the Integrationists with orthodox Protestant religions provides suggestive evidence that these judges are not closely related to the conventional social structure; this may be one of the sources of their unorthodox conduct of race relations cases.

The path to the district judiciary in the South, as Table 32-9 shows, has often involved holding public office. Experience in public office has been important in the careers of judges in all three groups, but there are some important differences in the types of experiences. No office, federal or state, judicial or non-judicial, has dominated the political experiences of all three groups with uniform frequency. While close to one-half of the Segregationists (57.1 per cent) and the Moderates (41.7 per cent) have held state office, only 9.1 per cent of the Integrationists have. Federal offices have been occupied by nearly half the Segregationists (42.9 per cent) and the Integrationists (45.5 per cent) but by only 8.4 per cent of the Moderates.

Looking at the variation in the types of offices held by the three groups, we may advance some suggestions concerning the relationship between political experience on the way to the bench and judicial behavior. Since about half of both the Segregationists and

TABLE 32-9*
Previous Public Offices Held by Southern Judges**

Public Office	Segregationists (N = 14)	Moderates (N = 12)	Integrationists (N = 11)
State Political Office	57.1%	41.7%	9.1%
Federal Political Office	42.9	8.4	45.5
State Judicial Office	50.0	33.3	9.1
Federal Judicial Office	28.6	8.4	45.5
State and Local Judgeship	35.7	33.3	0.0

* Columns do not add up to 100.0 per cent because some judges held more than one office.
** X^2 indicates significance at .01 level.

the Integrationists held federal office before coming to the court, we may conclude that political experiences gained in the services of the federal government do not function as an educational experience for the judge steeped in the values of Southern society. As a district attorney or assistant district attorney, the judicial candidate prosecutes cases involving various national political values, meets numerous kinds of litigants and serves in many political situations. Such experiences might be expected to broaden the outlook of prospective judges inducing respect for national values when these conflict with regional ones. However, federal political experience is apparently not enough, by itself, to accomplish this.

Tenure in a state political position, on the other hand, could strengthen the identification of the judge with Southern norms. As a legislator, state administrator, or state judge, he is often called upon to enact or enforce policies which implement the Southern point of view and sometimes to defend these values against what is called federal encroachment. Moreover, in seeking office, regional symbols may be invoked, or at least, paid lip service. The difference between Segregationist and Integrationist judges here is striking. Well over half the Segregationists (57.1 per cent) have held state political office while only 9.1 per cent of the Integrationists or less than one-tenth have held state office.

The Segregationist group is clearly distinguished from the Integrationist group by prejudicial experiences in state government. Both in policy making and campaigning the Southern state officeholder can rarely remain indifferent to the issues involving the political and social position of the Negro. The frequency with which Segregationist judges have held state office suggests that state political experience corroborates Southern values. Integrationists, on the other hand, have seldom held state political positions. When they have held public office, it has been a federal one and in all cases also a federal judicial office. Here the service of judicial candidates as federal attorneys, when not combined with officeholding in the state political structure, seems to have marked out many members of the Integrationist group for deviation from traditional Southern values. It is important that the future judge has not undergone commitment to the state political system. Not identified with the state political system the judge may be more sympathetic toward national values and less sympathetic toward Southern state efforts to resist federal policies.

When the district judge has been a state judge before his ascent, his objectivity does not seem to be strengthened. About one-third of both the Segregationists (35.7 per cent) and the Moderates (33.3 per cent) have been judges but none of the Integrationists. We tend to associate dispassionate behavior with judges because of the security and insulation of their position in the political structure. However, the judges of most Southern states are elected. They must seek reelection, they must undergo campaigns and secure nominations from political parties, and they must maintain good relationships with the rest of the state political structure. State judges . . . must master the technique and the symbols of the state political system to obtain and to retain office. As a state judge, the future district judge may be called upon to handle cases involving race relations. In his behavior the judge must be constantly wary, like all elected Southern officials, of the effects of his actions upon his chances for reelection. Usually the safe course of behavior for the elected Southern official is adherence to the traditional Southern norms in political situations involving race relations. Considering these aspects of the role of state judges, we could hardly expect experience gained on the state bench to train Southern officials toward greater objectivity in race relations cases.

Conclusions

. . .

The judicial behavior of district judges was . . . examined in the context of the judges' social and political backgrounds. Few differences were found in the location of births, legal training, or law practices of different judges. All were about equally tied to the region by their pre-judicial experiences. In connection with the social and political structures, however, significant differences were discovered among judges, grouped by their disposition of cases. Segregationist judges were more closely linked to the Southern social system, as measured by religious affiliations, and to the political structures by their more frequent experiences in state government. Integrationist judges had few experiences in government, and what experiences they had were in federal officeholding.

Construed broadly, linkage with the local social and political system can be considered a variety of localism. From this viewpoint we can say that Southern district courts are influenced by local factors: pro-Negro decisions in the courts are negatively correlated to the proportion of Negroes in the districts' population, and district judges are more apt to hold against Negro litigants if these judges have experiences in their backgrounds tying them to the social and political structure of Southern states.

The evidence points to the conclusion that Southern federal judges in district courts are influenced by their social and political environment. In this they join other Southern politicians, state legislators, Congressmen, and state executives, who also respond to local factors. To this extent, we can say that judges, though ostensibly "different," react to environmental factors like other policy makers. We do not exclude the possibility of the influence of the legal environment upon the behavior of judges, but suggest that if legalistic influences are operative, they must be considered along with social and political factors.

33

Judicial Policy-Making and Southern School Segregation

Micheal W. Giles and Thomas G. Walker

In *Brown v. Board of Education* the United States Supreme Court set new constitutional standards in the field of race relations law by declaring that in public education the doctrine of "separate but equal" was no longer valid. The effect of this decision was to establish a new national policy calling for massive desegregation throughout the country, and particularly in the Southern region. The primary responsibility for implementing the national policy at the local level was given to school authorities, who were to remain under the surveillance of the equity jurisdiction of the federal district courts. . . .

The events which transpired in the South during the two decades following the *Brown* decision have been well chronicled in the popular and academic press. The partnership of school authorities and the district courts has been an uneasy one. Public school officials have not been eager to design or carry out plans intended to accomplish immediate and acceptable levels of desegregation. Faced with school authorities unwilling to comply voluntarily with the *Brown* mandate, district courts have had to confront the issue of applying to local situations the national policy set by the Supreme Court. . . . While the general constitutional policy is clear (i.e., racially defined dual school systems are in violation of the Equal Protection Clause of the Fourteenth Amendment), questions of defining racially segregated systems, approving remedies to alleviate public school segregation, designating timetables for adhering to court directives, and deciding when a school district is in full compliance are left to the initial discretion of the trial judge. Mandates from the Supreme Court and the various circuit courts provide a great deal of discretion and a wide range of choice. . . . In each instance in which a district judge confronts a school segregation case, he is called upon to forge legal policy. The degree of desegregation he enforces, the remedies he imposes, and the time period within which he demands compliance are clearly policy decisions which can be made only upon a consideration of local circumstances and of the constitutional guarantees the judge is sworn to uphold. Not surprisingly, the great degree of discretion allowed a federal judge has resulted in a lack of uniformity in the judicial decisions reached.

Attempting to understand and explain the policy choices of the Southern federal judges in race relations cases has been the objective of several studies. Inevitably this body of

Reprinted by permission from *Journal of Politics* 37 (1975), 917–936. Most footnotes have been omitted.

research has focused upon the traditional segregationist political culture as the major factor behind the massive Southern resistance to the commands of *Brown*. . . .

. . .

The study reported here is an attempt to contribute to our understanding of judicial policy-making in the desegregation controversy in three basic ways. First, the dependent variable employed in the present study will provide a meaningful measure of judicial desegregation policy which is more comparable across judges and judicial districts than desegregation measures used in previous studies. . . . Second, we will examine desegregation policy as it existed when the nation entered the 1970s. Previous studies in the desegregation area have concentrated on the original attempts to implement Supreme Court policy in the South. Yet there is considerable evidence to indicate that much of what we know about the first decade post-*Brown* may not be applicable in the second decade following that decision. The Civil Rights Act of 1964, the Voting Rights Act of 1965, the activity of the Justice Department in behalf of Black litigants, and the emergence of the "New South" have made the situation in the 1970s much different from what it was in the years immediately following 1954. Third, we will present the results of a multivariate analysis of the impact of several sets of variables on the desegregation policies of Southern district judges. Included in this analysis are several variables repeatedly mentioned in the literature (but not previously subjected to rigorous empirical study), as well as additional variables examined here for the first time.

Data

In this study we will examine the policy-making behavior of Southern federal judges in school segregation controversies in 1970. The desegregation of public schools provides an excellent subject for study because this category includes the most frequently heard and publicly sensitive of the race relations disputes. In 1954, Southern school systems were totally segregated by law, but by 1970 some level of desegregation was evident in every school system in the region.

As the judiciary learned from painful experience the school segregation question was not one which could often be resolved by a single hearing or judicial decree. In most instances once a school district's desegregation efforts were challenged in court as being inadequate it marked only the beginning of long and continuous litigation lasting in some districts for more than a decade. In such circumstances the district judge having jurisdiction over the case maintained constant surveillance over the district to insure adequate compliance with constitutional standards.

The basic unit of analysis in the present study was the combination of a school district and its supervising judge. In order to gather the necessary data to conduct the designed research, we began with the approximately 400 Southern school districts listed by the U.S. Department of Health, Education and Welfare as being in compliance with court ordered desegregation in 1970.[1] Officials in each of these school districts were contacted and asked to supply information regarding the legal status of desegregation disputes in their districts in 1970. A total of 288 school districts responded and of these 151 provided complete information including verification that they were operating under active court supervision in 1970 and the name of the district judge involved.

The basic unit of analysis, therefore, became the 151 school district/supervising federal judge combinations. Of the 95 United States district judges serving the South in 1970, 42 (44 percent) were supervising at least one school district in the sample.

Dependent Variable

To measure the level of enforcement of desegregation an index of school segregation was computed for each of the 151 school districts. This index was adopted from Taeuber's index of residential segregation.[2] The index measures the amount of departure of each school in a school district from the racial balance for the entire district. The index varies from zero, signifying that each school in the district mirrors the racial balance of the district as a whole, to 1.00, indicating that a school district is totally segregated with no racial heterogeneity in any of its schools. The value that the index attains between these extremes may be interpreted as the percentage of Black and/or White students who must be transferred in order to obtain district wide racial balance.[3] The information necessary to compute the index for each of the 151 districts was drawn from racial/ethnic surveys of the public schools conducted in 1970 by the U.S. Department of Health, Education and Welfare.

The dependent variable, then, represents the degree of segregation remaining in the sampled Southern school districts in 1970. Because each of these districts was operating under court issued desegregation orders, the dependent variable also represents the amount of deviation from perfect racial balance which the supervising judge has allowed. This can be interpreted as the district judge's policy decision in implementing the *Brown* mandate at the local level. Operationalized in this manner, judicial policy-making is studied not in terms of the words the judge uses in his opinions but on the basis of the actual level of desegregation he enforces on the litigated school district.

The dependent variable improves upon previous research in two ways. First, it provides an exact measurement of desegregation levels within the litigated school districts. This procedure is superior to a simple "pro/con" measurement of a judge's decisions as employed in several previous studies. Second, the dependent variable is restricted to a single type of desegregation controversy, i.e., public schools. This allows a more accurate analysis than occurs when all race relations cases are grouped together (e.g., public accommodations, employment, juries, voting rights, etc.). These improvements, however, do not absolutely insure comparability across judges and judicial districts. Obviously there may be systematic differences in the conditions within the schools, as well as variation in local resistance to desegregation efforts; and these are factors which necessarily will be taken into account by the supervising judge. In order to compensate for this variation, the impact of school district and environmental variables will be included in the analysis presented below.

For the 151 sampled school districts the mean index of segregation was .3227, with a standard deviation of .2145. Individual school district segregation levels ranged from a low index score of .0111 to a high of .8640.

Independent Variables

In order to explain the desegregation policies imposed by district judges in the sampled school districts we tested the impact of twelve independent variables which have been suggested as possible determinants of judicial behavior in this area of litigation. These independent variables can be classified into four categories: social background variables, environmental variables, community linkage variables and school district variables.

(1) *Social Background Variables.* . . . [S]ocial background experiences which indicate a judge's degree of association with the traditional Southern culture may be related to how vigorously he enforces desegregation policy. In order to test this proposition we selected six judicial social background variables for analysis: birthplace, location of higher education, religious affiliation, political party identification, local political office held, and state political office held. These factors have been suggested by Peltason and others and have been empirically tested with varying success by Vines. We have generally followed the standard treatment of these variables in the literature in regard to the predicted association of each with desegregation policy. Judges who were expected to be less favorable toward massive desegregation were those who were born and educated in the South, were closely tied to (frequently racist) state and local politics, were aligned with the Democratic Party, and held membership in a fundamentalist Protestant faith. Judges without such ties to the traditional Southern culture were hypothesized to be more sympathetic to the desegregation policy established in *Brown*. Relatively complete social background information was collected from standard biographical sources for all of the 42 judges in the sample.

For purposes of analysis birthplace was coded "0" for judges born outside the South and "1" for those born within the region.[4] Judges receiving neither college nor law school training in the South were given a "0" on the education variable, while those attending *either* college or law school in the Southern region received a "1", and those who attended *both* a Southern college and law school were coded "2". Fundamentalist Protestant religion, Democratic Party affiliation, local and state political offices held were similarly scored with the judge receiving a "1" if the variable was present and a "0" if it was not.

(2) *Environmental Variables.* In order to consider the impact of community opinion on desegregation policy, some measure needed to be devised to tap the local cultural ethos within a judge's jurisdiction. Given the importance in the literature placed on this variable, a study of Southern desegregation would be incomplete without including it. For this reason we examined the impact of two environmental variables. The first of these was the proportion of Blacks among the general population in the judge's district or division.[5] The literature has consistently indicated that the percentage Black within a population is related to the racial climate. The presumed linkage between percent Black and resistance to desegregation is through the social, economic or political threat perceived by Whites who reside in greater concentrations of Blacks. The greater the percent Black, the greater the perceived threat and the greater the resistance to school desegregation. . . . The second environmental variable was the percentage of total 1968 presidential election votes within the judicial district or division which were cast for George Wallace. The degree of support for the Wallace candidacy would appear to give a good indication of public attitudes toward desegregation. As Wallace support increases so too should a lack of community sympathy for court imposed desegregation.

(3) *Community Linkage Variables.* If we assume a generally negative community climate toward court ordered integration in the South, it does not necessarily follow that all district judges will be similarly affected by this public sentiment. Some judges tend to be more vulnerable to public opinion than others. While there may be several plausible

reasons for the differential impact of local sentiment, a particularly important one may be the strength of the judge's linkage to the community. For purposes of analysis we isolated two possible indicators of a judge's relationship with the community. First, a judge's linkage to local attitudes may be reflected in the number of associational memberships he holds within the community. Based upon information provided in standard biographical sources, each judge was given an organizational score equal to the number of civic and fraternal groups in which he listed membership (i.e., Elks, Lions, Chamber of Commerce, country clubs, etc.). There was a wide range of scores on this variable with several judges listing no organizational memberships and three listing ten or more. As the number of associational ties increases we would expect the district judge to pay more attention to community pressure. The second community linkage variable involved the location of the judge's court vis-à-vis the school district being desegregated. A judge's regular jurisdiction, be it an entire district or a division, generally encompasses several cities and counties and, therefore, several school districts. A judge, however, will usually hold his court in a single location within the judicial district, although he may occasionally hear cases throughout his jurisdiction. Judges are likely to live and develop associations in the area immediately surrounding the established locations of their courts. Therefore, we might expect that a judge would be more reluctant to impose activist desegregation policies on school districts which envelop the judge's court than if the schools are located in an outlying area. The pressure of the local community would appear more immediate and pertinent to the judge if it originated from his "home" area than if it came from a more remote portion of his jurisdiction. In order to test this variable, each school district/judge combination was coded "0" if the judge's court was not held within the litigated school district, and "1" if the locus of the court fell within the school district.

(4) *School District Variables.* . . . Two school system variables were used in the present study. The first was the percentage of students in the school district who were Black. The influence of this variable theoretically is similar to that of percent Black among the general population. As the concentration of Blacks increases in the schools so, too, may White fear of the consequences of integration. . . .

The second school district variable examined was the size of the educational system (measured in terms of total district enrollment). . . . School district size is primarily a technical variable. The logistics of desegregation in a small district are simply less complex than in a large one. For this reason we would expect judges to tolerate somewhat higher levels of segregation in larger districts than in smaller ones.

Findings

In order to evaluate the explanatory power of our independent variables, we first tested the association of each with the levels of segregation which existed in the 151 school systems and then analyzed the combined impact of these variables.

Zero-Order Relationships

For the most part, our analysis of social background characteristics contributed little to an increased understanding of judicially imposed desegregation policy. The expectation that those judges most closely tied to the South would allow the highest levels of school

TABLE 33-1

Zero-Order Correlations (r) of Social Background, Environmental, Community Linkage, and School District Variables to Segregation in 1970

Social Background Variables	
Birthplace	.022
Education	.160[a]
Religion	−.028
Political Party	.086
Local Political Office	−.026
State Political Office	−.032
Environmental Variables	
Percent Black	.095
Percent Wallace Vote	−.096
Community Linkage Variables	
Organizational Memberships	−.018
Court Location	.448[b]
School District Variables	
Percent Black Enrollment	.125
School District Size (in hundreds)	.537[b]

[a] p < .05
[b] p < .01

segregation received little support. The relationships between two of the social background variables (birthplace and party identification) and level of school segregation are in the predicted direction, but fail to reach statistical significance. The level of segregation in school districts under the surveillance of judges born outside the South is only slightly lower than that allowed in districts supervised by judges of Southern origin. The utility of the birthplace variable, however, is severely restricted by its lack of variation. Only four of the 42 judges were born outside the South. Similarly, the correlation between party identification and school segregation is in the expected direction with Democrats approving higher levels of segregation than non-Democrats, but the relationship is quite weak. The analysis of three social background variables yielded unanticipated results. Although not statistically significant, holding a state or local political office and membership in a low status Protestant faith are negatively correlated with segregation. What makes this result particularly important is that Vines previously found the political office and religious affiliation variables to have a significant *positive* relationship with segregationist decisions.

Among the background variables only the location of a judge's education is related to school segregation in the predicted direction and at a statistically significant level. The mean level of segregation allowed by the policies of judges who received non-South college *and* law school education is .233; for judges attending non-Southern schools for *either* college *or* law school the segregation level rises to .304; and the segregation index increases to .345 for judges obtaining *all* of their advanced education from institutions within the region. From these data we may conclude that the years spent by judges in non-Southern educational institutions expose them to national norms of race relations and mollify social attitudes acquired during the course of a Southern upbringing. This, of course, does not mean that Southern schools indoctrinate their students with racist attitudes; rather it indicates that Southern judges who attend only schools within the region receive less exposure to non-Southern views toward race.

The environmental variables fare little better than the social background characteristics in predicting desegregation policies. Black concentration within the judicial district or division is positively associated with segregation levels, but the relationship may easily be attributable to chance. The community's support for the 1968 Wallace candidacy, surprisingly, is negatively associated with the amount of school segregation tolerated by federal judges, albeit the association fails to reach conventional levels of statistical significance.

The lack of predictive ability provided by the environmental variables does not necessarily preclude the possibility that the analysis of community linkage may yield productive results. The first community linkage variable analyzed, the number of local organizational memberships held by the supervising judge, exhibited no relationship whatever to the level of segregation permitted. The court location variable, however, provided altogether different results. As hypothesized, a judge's policy will allow significantly higher levels of segregation if the court is located within the school district under supervision than it will if the school system is geographically divorced from the location of the court. This demonstrates that federal judges tend to be more vigilant in enforcing national desegregation standards in remote areas than when similar issues arise within the judge's immediate work/residence locale. This finding might lead one to speculate that while a judge may not generally be affected by hostile community pressures, such factors are relevant when a judge must desegregate his own community. This, however, is not the case. When we examined only those school district/judge combinations in which the court was located within the school system, the percent Black, Wallace vote and organization membership variables remained non-significant.

There are three possible explanations for the significance of the court location variable. First, the court location variable may link the judge to environmental forces not included in the present study. Second, a judge's personal attitudes against massive social change may be greatly activated when he is desegregating his own community, whereas he is able to maintain greater detachment in litigation involving communities in which he has little personal stake. Finally, when faced with desegregating his own community a judge may be more concerned with public reaction than when dealing with an outlying area. Consequently, he may perceive a hostile environment—which may or may not exist.

School district variables provided additional insight into the desegregation policy process. While the percentage of Black enrollment in the school district was positively associated with segregation, the relationship failed to attain statistically meaningful levels. However, the size of the school district was substantially associated with the level of desegregation enforced by the supervising judge. As the size of the school district increases so too does the existing level of racial segregation within that education system.

The Combined Model

While the zero-order relationships tell us a great deal about possible determinants of court ordered desegregation policy, they do not provide a complete account of the explanatory power of the variables under analysis. First, zero-order relationships do not demonstrate the combined impact of the independent variables on Southern school segregation. And second, zero-order relationships fail to give adequate warning of the possible effects of inter-correlation among the independent variables. For example, two independent variables used in the present analysis, court location and school district size, are significantly correlated ($r = .575$). This should not be surprising because of the fact that

TABLE 33-2
Partial Regression Coefficients and Standardized Betas
for Selected Variables with Segregation in 1970

		Standardized	
	b	Beta	F
School district size (in hundreds)	.00048	.42000	26.861 [b]
Percent Black enrollment	.00251	.25914	14.923 [b]
Court location	.13949	.23861	8.936 [b]
Education	.04946	.15490	5.273 [a]
(constant)	.05518		

[a]$p < .05$ $R = .624$ $R^2 = .389$
[b]$p < .01$

most district courts are located in urban centers with large school systems. Therefore, the previously discussed relationship between court location and school segregation levels may simply be an artifact of the size of the school districts in which the courts are located. In order to deal with the question of spuriousness and assess the combined explanatory power of the independent variables, the data were examined using multiple regression. The results are presented in Table 33-2.

With one exception the results of this analysis are consistent with the zero-order correlations presented in Table 33-1. Percent Black enrollment is not statistically significant in Table 33-1, but does make a significant contribution to the multiple regression. This inconsistency arises from the fact that Black enrollment and school district size are negatively correlated and, therefore, the size variable suppresses the zero-order correlation between Black enrollment and segregation. Apart from Black enrollment, none of the independent variables which had non-significant zero-order correlations with segregation make a significant contribution to the regression equation.

The combined efforts of school district size, Black enrollment, court location, and judicial education explain 39 percent of the variance in Southern school segregation. An examination of the standardized betas shows school district size to have the largest independent effect of any of these four variables. But even with the effects of size accounted for, court location remains significantly related to segregation levels. Indeed, court location, a previously unexplored variable, appears to have independent effect comparable to percent Black enrollment, a variable that has received considerable attention. Southern education, while making a significant contribution to the regression equation, is the least helpful of the four independent variables in explaining the desegregation policies of federal judges.

Although explained variance is the most common means for interpreting regression, the "dummy" variable structure of the court location variable permits another interpretation. The regression coefficient for court location is the difference between the mean segregation index scores for the dichotomized observations on this variable, adjusted for the effects of school district size, Black enrollment, and judicial education. Thus, when the school district encompasses the location of the district court, the level of segregation averages 14 index points higher than when the court is not held within the school district boundaries. This means that in these school districts an average of 14 percent more of the Black and/or White students would need to be transferred to achieve racial balance than in those school districts geographically separated from the supervising judge.[6] Similarly, the adjusted average difference between judges who received college and law school training in the South and those who received both outside the region is ten index points.[7] These are not trivial differences from either a practical or statistical standpoint.

Conclusion

. . .

A number of conclusions may be drawn from the data analyzed in the present study, especially when considered in light of previous research. First, the influence of judicial social background characteristics, which were found to be significantly related to district court race relations decisions by Vines, was minimal on the desegregation policies examined here. This may well be due to the fact that by 1970 a new generation of federal judges was staffing the Southern courts. Of the judges in our sample, a full two-thirds took office after the period studied by Vines. . . . Apart from the education variable, none of the social background factors were found to be significantly related to school desegregation levels.

Second, the environmental factors examined in the present study demonstrated no substantial relationship with school district segregation. This again is in conflict with studies conducted during the years immediately following *Brown* which generally linked the district's racial climate and public attitudes to race relations decisions of local federal judges.

Third, the community linkage variables yielded mixed results. The number of organizational ties which the judge had with his community showed no relationship to the degree of school desegregation imposed. Once again much of the literature on Southern school integration efforts would predict otherwise. The linkage variable which does have a demonstrated impact is court location. Judges tend to allow substantially more segregation in their own communities than when implementing desegregation policy in other areas. What makes this variable particularly intriguing is that its influence occurs independent of environmental factors or the number of community associational memberships held by the judge. The differential application of law indeed appears to be worthy of more extensive analysis than we are able to provide here.

Finally, the school district variables yielded the greatest amount of explained variance. Both the Black concentration within the schools and the size of the school district were significantly related to the level of segregation allowed by district court orders. The Black enrollment variable may suggest the continuing impact of public resistance to desegregation. On the other hand, the combined importance of Black enrollment and school district size may well signify a substantial change from the original round of Southern desegregation efforts. Emphasis appears to have shifted from intense battles over the principle of integration to a judicial analysis of conditions within the schools. The prominence of these variables indicates that desegregation may be in the process of becoming a more technical procedure. The primary question (both legally and behaviorally) may now focus on how much desegregation can be practically ordered by the judge given extant school district characteristics, rather than whether integration should occur at all. This interpretation is consistent with the tone of Supreme Court desegregation precedents handed down in the late 1960s and early 1970s. The evolution of the desegregation process may be following the same pattern as exhibited in the reapportionment cases—that is, an intensely political question gradually eroding into technical applications of Supreme Court established national legal policy. The history of desegregation, however, has been a much more lengthy and painful one.

Notes

1. To receive federal education funds H.E.W. requires under Title VI of the Civil Rights Act of 1964 that a school district either comply with H.E.W. desegregation guidelines or have a desegregation plan accepted by a U.S. district court. In 1970, approximately 400 Southern school districts indicated their compliance with Title VI by means of court ordered desegregation. In some districts the order to desegregate was issued in 1969 or before. Thus, many of the 400 districts listed would not be under active supervision by a federal district judge in 1970.

2. Karl E. Taeuber and Alma F. Taeuber, *Negroes in Cities* (Chicago: Aldine, 1965), 195-245. For a more complete explanation of the application of the Taeuber index to school districts see Micheal W. Giles, "Measuring School Segregation," *Journal of Negro Education*, in press.

3. For example, if the index value for a district was .60 this would indicate that either 60 percent of the Black students or 60 percent of the White students or some combination thereof would have to change schools in order to achieve racial balance.

4. In using dichotomized or ordinal variables in correlation and regression analysis we are following the lead of Ulmer, Tanenhaus, and others. See Ulmer, "Social Background as an Indicator"; Joseph Tanenhaus, et al., "The Supreme Court's Certiorari Jurisdiction: Cue Theory." . . .

5. The basic unit of the federal court system is the judicial district which is comprised of one or more counties. In some instances a judicial district will be subdivided into divisions. Where a judge serves a district the environmental variable data are aggregated across all counties constituting the district. Similarly, if a judge serves a division of a district, the environmental variable data are aggregated across the counties comprising the division.

6. The unadjusted mean segregation index for those school districts having the district court located within their boundaries is .543; whereas, those school districts separated from the court retaining jurisdiction have an unadjusted mean of .281. Clearly a good deal of this raw difference is attributable to size differences between the two groups of school districts.

7. This figure is derived by multiplying the regression coefficient for education (.04946) by the "2" code for those judges receiving all of their advanced education in the South. The education variable most properly should be broken down into two "dummy" variables—one measuring the difference between its "0" and "1" categories and one to measure the difference between its "1" and "2" categories. The present procedure is simpler, but does not give misleading results. The difference between the unadjusted means of categories "0" and "2" is .112. Since education has low correlations with school district size, Black enrollment, and court location, it is not surprising that the adjusted differences differ little from the unadjusted.

34

Voting Behavior on the United States Courts of Appeals Revisited

Sheldon Goldman

Students of judicial behavior have devoted much attention over the past decade to mapping and documenting political decision making of judges on various courts by examining the exercise of judicial discretion. Among other concerns, research has focused on the attitudinal patterns that are uncovered by quantitative analysis of voting behavior and the relationship of judges' backgrounds to their decisional behavior. These concerns have been among those pursued by researchers who have studied judicial decision making on the United States Courts of Appeals.[1] The objective here is to explore some facets of judicial behavior on the appeals courts with particular reference to the . . . backgrounds-behavior research problems. In an earlier study of the appeals courts, voting behavior along these lines was investigated covering a three-fiscal-year period (fiscal 1962, 1963, 1964).[2] In this revisit, the earlier findings were treated as hypotheses with a new case population encompassing the subsequent seven fiscal years (fiscal 1965 through fiscal 1971).

Research Design

For present purposes, judicial voting behavior is examined in basic political terms of who wins and who loses and by implication what political values are seemingly being fostered. All decisions rendered nonunanimously (i.e., with dissent as to what happens to the litigants) by the courts of appeals during fiscal 1965 through fiscal 1971 were coded for one or more issues. Some for which there were few cases or small numbers of judges with sufficient cases to justify the calculation of scores were combined with other issues. Some decisions concerned issues (e.g., patent, shipowner-stevedore indemnity, and other commercial cases) that were not included in the issue analyses; however, the voting behavior was included in separately conducted bloc analyses. In total, there were 2,115 nonunanimous decisions of the appeals courts. Multi-issue cases were coded by treating each issue as if it were a separate case. Thus, in total, there were 2,312 "cases." The issues are presented in Table 34-1. Note that cases were not coded directly on the political liberal-

Reprinted by permission from *American Political Science Review* 69 (1975), 491–493, 496–506. Most footnotes have been omitted.

TABLE 34-1
Voting Positions Assigned Higher Numerical Values

Issue or Category	Voting Position
Criminal Procedures	For the claims of criminal defendants or prisoners (excluding selective service violations and white collar crimes such as income tax evasion, fraud, embezzlement)
Civil Liberties	For the civil rights claims of Black Americans
	For civil libertarian claims of aliens, conscientious objectors, and others
Labor	For the labor union and employees in labor-management and NLRB decisions
Private Economic	For the claims of the insured as opposed to the insurance company
	For the claims of the small business or subcontractor when opposed by large business or contractor
	Opposed to alleged anti-trust law violators
	For the tenant in landlord-tenant cases
	For the debtor or bankrupt
	For the buyer of goods as opposed to seller
	For the stockholder in stockholder suits
Government Fiscal	For the government in tax, eminent domain, and other fiscal cases
Injured Persons	For the claims of injured workers
	For the injured or the fatally injured's estate in automobile or other accidents
	For the injured in federal tort cases
Political Liberalism	Includes the above voting positions on Criminal Procedures and Civil Liberties issues and includes votes for the claims of white collar criminal defendants or prisoners
Economic Liberalism	Includes the above voting positions on Labor, Private Economic, and Injured Persons issues. Also includes votes for the governmental agency in regulation of business cases
Activism	For federal court jurisdiction and the imposition of federal standards on the states in criminal procedures and other cases
Dissents	Dissenting votes

ism, economic liberalism, and dissents dimensions but that scores were derived from the voting behavior coded on other issues.

Quantification of voting behavior was accomplished by the method utilized in the earlier study to calculate and determine the scores of the judges. Table 34-1 specifies the voting position assigned a "higher" numerical value in terms of each issue or category. These issues are the same used in the earlier study, with two exceptions. First, government regulation of business was dropped here as a separate issue because there were not enough cases to enable the calculation of scores for a sufficient number of judges. Second, in the earlier study there was one composite liberalism category; as is shown in Table 34-1, *two* liberalism categories, political liberalism and economic liberalism, were now used in order to make the categories comparable to the C and E scale cases found in other studies of judicial behavior. The issues as defined in Table 34-1 can be considered to represent political attitudes and values rather than narrowly defined technical legal issues. In the direction in which the voting position is scored higher, they can be conceptualized (with the exception of the dissents category and perhaps activism and government fiscal) as representing politically liberal attitudes.

In scoring, the numerical value of 2.0 was assigned to the voting positions specified in Table 34-1; and the value of 0.0 to the opposite voting positions. Where three different

TABLE 34-2
Dissension on the Eleven Courts of Appeals, Fiscal 1965 Through Fiscal 1971

	Circuit											
	1st	2nd	3rd	4th	5th	6th	7th	8th	9th	10th	D.C.	Total
Number of Split Decisions	15	288	178	179	294	151	232	79	231	52	416	2115
Split Decisions as % of Total No. of Cases Decided*	1.4	7.4	7.6	7.6	3.9	4.3	9.5	4.1	4.9	1.8	13.2	5.9

* The total numbers of cases are listed in Table B-1 (total cases disposed of after hearing or submission), *Annual Report of the Director of the Administrative Office of the United States Courts* (Washington, D.C.: U.S. Government Printing Office), for fiscal years 1965, 1966, 1967, 1968, 1969, 1970, and 1971.

voting positions were evident, the value of 1.0 was assigned to a vote which in part adhered to the Table 34-1 positions. A judge's score was derived by calculating the arithmetic mean of the numerical values given to all of that judge's votes for the particular issue.[3] Scores could range from 0.00 (complete opposition to the claims specified in Table 34-1) to 2.00 (complete support for those positions).

Because the eleven United States Courts of Appeals conduct their business for the most part by panels of three judges whose membership shifts,[4] the scores of the judges were primarily based on different cases; nevertheless, the basic political and broad public policy issues concerned with "who wins" were considered to be similar across cases within the circuits and across the circuits (although circuit was controlled for in some of the analyses which follow). This is by now a convention of judicial research on lower courts.[5]

Unlike the earlier study which combined unanimously decided reversals of district court cases with nonunanimously decided cases for purposes of analysis, this study only considered nonunanimously decided cases. Table 34-2 presents the rates of dissent on the eleven appeals courts during the seven year period surveyed and shows that most cases were decided unanimously. Indeed, the maximum dissent rate (split decisions as percentage of the total number of cases decided after hearing or submission) was 13.2 per cent (District of Columbia circuit). The range of dissent was like that of the earlier fiscal 1962 through 1964 years. Although the variables associated with the variation in circuit dissent rates were not systematically explored here, size of court and rate of termination of appeals were found to be related.[6] No doubt the explanation of variation in dissent rates requires investigation of more variables and their interrelationships.

· · ·

[In this section the author presents evidence and argues that a variety of methods—correlation analyses, bloc analyses of panel voting, and scaling of *en banc* decisions—point to the same basic finding, that interrelated politically defined attitudes could meaningfully describe the voting behavior of appeals judges in nonunanimously decided cases.]

Background Variables and Voting Behavior

While the importance of politically defined interrelated attitudes for the understanding of judicial voting behavior is likely to be accepted by students of judicial behavior, the same cannot be said about the relationship of background variables to judicial voting behavior. In a multitude of studies, particularly since Nagel's study of state supreme court justices, the results have been mixed. One of the difficulties in this area has been the emphasis on demonstrating statistical relationships between and among certain background variables and voting behavior without being guided by a theoretical framework that would reasonably lead one to hypothesize such relationships. Some theorizing about backgrounds and the judicial decision-making process treats background variables as precursors of political attitudes and values, with the implication by some scholars that background variables for the most part mask too wide a variety of conditioning experiences for us to expect them to be directly and clearly associated with voting behavior and thus to be able to account for a significant portion of the variation of the behavior under scrutiny.

Party affiliation is the background characteristic that has been shown to have the strongest direct link of all background variables to voting behavior. Studies of national politics and elite behavior make it reasonable to expect that party affiliation will be associated with voting behavior. In the earlier study of appeals judges it was found that the party variable was the most potent of the numerous background variables tested. . . . For present purposes, the hypotheses were that Democratic and Republican judges would be found to behave as they had earlier; Table 34-3 presents the results.

As Table 34-3 indicates, the Democratic affiliated appeals judges were found to have higher median scores than the Republican affiliated judges on seven of the ten issues and categories. The spread between the Democratic and Republican groups was greatest on two of the three economic issues (labor and injured persons) and the distribution of scores on the economic liberalism issue showed the highest statistical significance. The difference in medians and the distribution of the scores on the criminal procedures, civil liberties, and political liberalism issues also make it clear that on the whole Democratic judges tended to be more liberal than Republican judges. The smallest statistically significant difference in medians and the distribution of the scores was on the private economic issue. No differences were found for the government fiscal, activism, and dissents categories.

How can we account for the findings concerning criminal procedures and civil liberties? . . . A possible . . . explanation may be related to the apparent politicizing of civil liberties issues in the mid through late 1960s. The Republican party first under Goldwater and then under the leadership of President Nixon moved to the decidedly conservative side of these issues. It may be that the Johnson and Nixon judicial appointees also reflected in part the partisan split on these issues.[7] Certainly the judicial selection process during the Nixon administration involved taking into account whether a person under consideration was "soft on crime."[8]

The analysis of difference of medians and distribution of the scores of the two party groups was based on all appeals judges combined for purposes of analysis. It could be argued that such a method may unwittingly conceal what in fact occurs circuit by circuit. Surely, it might be observed, southern Democrats were more likely than nonsouthern Democrats to be conservative, while some of the Eisenhower Republican appointees to the southern circuits (particularly Judges Sobeloff, Wisdom, Tuttle, and Brown) were widely recognized liberals. Inclusion of the southern judges may thereby undermine the analysis of the party variable. To test for this possibility, median scores were calculated, and tests for the difference in the distribution of scores were run for Democrats and Republicans with the judges from the two southern circuits (the fourth and fifth circuits) excluded. The results showed the Democrats with higher medians (than when southern Democrats were included) on the civil liberties, labor, injury, economic liberalism, and activism issues. The Republicans had lower median scores (than when southern Republicans were included) on the criminal procedures, civil liberties, injury, political liberalism, and activism issues.

TABLE 34-3
Party Affiliation and Median Scores of Judges on Issues and Categories

Issue or Category	Democrats (1) Median	(2) (N)	Republicans (3) Median	(4) (N)	Difference in Medians (5)	Significance Level (6)	% Democrats Above Own Circuit Median (7)	% Republicans Above Own Circuit Median (8)	% Difference (9)
Criminal Procedures	1.07	(68)	0.67	(41)	0.40	.001	57.3	31.7	25.6
Civil Liberties	1.38	(51)	0.70	(28)	0.68	.007	52.9	32.1	20.8
Labor	1.43	(41)	0.46	(23)	0.97	.0006	58.5	21.7	36.8
Private Economic	1.27	(35)	1.04	(16)	0.23	.037	51.4	31.2	20.2
Government Fiscal	1.00	(36)	1.07	(16)	0.07	n.s.*	44.4	50.0	5.6
Injured Persons	1.20	(45)	0.50	(19)	0.70	.002	53.3	26.3	27.0
Political Liberalism	1.15	(76)	0.65	(49)	0.50	.0003	59.2	31.2	28.0
Economic Liberalism	1.09	(76)	0.74	(40)	0.35	.00001	63.2	17.5	45.7
Activism	1.14	(37)	1.14	(28)	0.00	n.s.	45.9	42.9	3.0
Dissents	0.60	(80)	0.56	(50)	0.04	n.s.	51.2	42.0	9.2

* Not statistically significant at the .05 level.

With the southerners excluded, the Democrats had a higher median (1.29) on the activism dimension than did the Republicans (0.75) and the difference was statistically significant at the .01 level. But aside from the activism issue, excluding the southern judges from our measures did not basically change the thrust of the findings of all circuits combined reported in Table 34-3. Even more to the point, a circuit-by-circuit analysis (see columns 7–9 of Table 34-3) further supported the results concerning the party variable reported in columns 1–6 of the same table. The two issues for which the largest number of judges decided enough cases to warrant the calculation of scores were the political liberalism and economic liberalism issues. The findings, circuit-by-circuit, for political liberalism were that in only the fifth circuit of all eleven circuits was there a higher proportion of Republicans than Democrats above the circuit median. In the third and tenth circuits the Democrats and Republicans were evenly split above and below the circuit median. But in all other circuits, the proportion of Democratic judges above the circuit median was greater than the proportion of Republican judges. For the economic liberalism measure, in *all* eleven circuits there was a higher proportion of Democrats than Republicans above the circuit median.[9] Once again controlling for circuit led to essentially the same basic finding observed when all circuits were combined for analysis.

The religious affiliation of judges is another background variable that has been examined in terms of its association with their voting behavior. The assumption is that those of minority faiths, principally the Catholic and Jewish religions, are not only more likely to be affiliated with the Democratic party than those of the various Protestant denominations, but that members of minority religious groups are or have been outsiders in American society having never fully received widespread social, economic, and political acceptability. Because of the historical and perhaps even their personal experiences as minority group members these judges may have been socialized to favor the underdog. On the other hand, it could also be argued that religious affiliation is much too broad a variable encompassing a multitude of individual experiences and thus is affected by a host of intervening variables. The earlier study of appeals courts contained a test of the religion variable and the results showed that on only one issue was there a statistically significant difference in medians; Catholic judges had the greatest tendency to oppose the government's claims in fiscal cases. Because one had to strain to explain this finding it seemed more prudent to hypothesize in the current study simply that no religious differences would be found on any of the issues. . . .

Surprisingly, statistically significant differences were found on two issues; injured persons and economic liberalism, with Catholic judges voting more liberally for the economic underdog.[10] This finding held true on a circuit-by-circuit basis for those circuits with more than one Catholic judge serving (with the sole exception of the sixth circuit on economic liberalism). When party was brought in as a control, it was found that only on economic liberalism and only for the Democrats was there still a statistically significant difference in medians and distribution of the scores. Democratic Catholics emerged as more liberal than Democratic Protestants on the economic liberalism dimension. For the Republicans there was no difference between Protestants and Catholics on these issues but it should be kept in mind that the number of Republican Catholics was small (only four individuals).

. . .

. . . In the current retest of the age variable simple correlations were run between the ages of the judges (age being defined as of January 1, 1968) and their scores on the ten issues and categories. Because there has not been solid evidence in the judicial behavior

TABLE 34-4
Relationship of Age and Years on Appeals Court to Scores of Judges on Issues and Categories

	Age			Years on Appeals Court		
	Simple Correlation	N	Significance Level	Simple Correlation	N	Significance Level
Criminal Procedures	−.29	(109)	.002	−.08	(109)	n.s.
Civil Liberties	−.30	(79)	.004	−.12	(79)	n.s.
Labor	−.39	(64)	.001	−.31	(64)	.006
Private Economic	.04	(51)	n.s.	.15	(51)	n.s.
Government Fiscal	−.05	(52)	n.s.	−.14	(52)	n.s.
Injured Persons	−.24	(64)	.026	−.04	(64)	n.s.
Political Liberalism	−.27	(125)	.002	−.08	(125)	n.s.
Economic Liberalism	−.26	(116)	.003	−.14	(116)	n.s.
Activism	−.22	(65)	.039	−.17	(65)	n.s.
Dissents	−.03	(130)	n.s.	.09	(130)	n.s.

literature concerning American judges to support an association between age and voting behavior, the hypotheses were that no such relationship would be found. These hypotheses were proved wrong for seven of the ten issues as reported in Table 34-4.

. . . [Y]ears of judicial experience . . . was defined as number of years served on the appeals court as of January 1, 1971 (or with deceased judges, at time of death). This variable, as expected, was positively correlated (.72) with age. It was assumed, however, to test a dimension somewhat different from age; to test hardening not of the biological arteries but rather of the bureaucratic judicial arteries. The simple correlations with the scores on the issues are also presented in Table 34-4. Just as with the age variable, the initial hypotheses were that no relationship would be found, but unlike the results with the age variable, the hypotheses were supported except on the labor issue.

Older judges simply tended to be more conservative on the criminal procedures, civil liberties, labor, injured persons, political liberalism, economic liberalism, and activism dimensions than did younger judges. They did not tend to dissent either more or less than younger judges. There were also no statistically significant correlations with the private economic and the government fiscal categories. The number of years on the appeals court was negatively related to support for the causes of employees in their battles with management.

Three other background variables were put to the test: (1) judicial experience on other courts at any time prior to appointment on the appeals courts; (2) experience as a candidate before the electorate for public office; and (3) public prosecutorial experience. It could be argued that such backgrounds reflect socializing experiences in the course of a judicial career on other courts or in the course of being a candidate in the hurly-burly of partisan politics or as a prosecutor in the law enforcement milieu any or all of which might affect the development of political attitudes and values. Because this researcher was skeptical that such experiences could be sufficiently uniform to produce approximately the same conditioning experiences for all sorts of people, the hypotheses were that no statistically significant association with voting behavior on the ten issues and categories would be found.

The results on the whole confirmed these hypotheses. There was, however, a statistically significant difference in medians and distribution of scores (at the .021 level) on the dissents category and the prior judicial experience variable, which suggested that judges *without* previous judicial experience tended to dissent at a higher rate than those *with* such experience. There was also a large difference in medians on the labor issue between those *with* prior judicial experience (median score of 0.58) and those *without* (median score of 1.25). This largest difference in medians for the judicial experience variable approached statistical significance (.060). When party was held constant, the relationship seemed to hold but only for the Democrats. The only other statistically significant finding was for the candidate variable with the group of those having been candidates for public office having lower median scores on the labor issue (.037 significance level) than the group of those who never were candidates. By holding party constant, however, statistical significance disappeared.

With the exception of age and years on appeals, nonparametric tests were used in the backgrounds-behavior analyses thus far discussed. The use of party as a control was helpful in the analysis of the other independent and nominal measured variables. But party was not held constant for age and years on appeals. Obviously, it would be useful to be able to assess the effect of each of the independent variables on the dependent variables with all other independent variables held constant. Don Bowen did precisely this in his study of backgrounds and judicial voting behavior.[11] He made the assumptions of interval measurement and normal distribution of his independent and dependent variables and undertook partial correlation analyses and stepwise multiple regression. He found that party was most important but that other backgrounds also accounted for the variance above and below the mean. All of the background variables together, however, seldom accounted for more than 30 per cent of the variance. The big exception occurred with labor cases that pitted a large business against a union. In these cases about 44 per cent of the variance was explained by background variables. Despite the formidable assumptions about the nature of the independent and dependent variables that had to be made, the decision was taken to follow Bowen and similarly test the relationships of the variables. Although these findings must therefore be treated cautiously, they nevertheless provide a needed perspective on the backgrounds-behavior of appeals judges. They also are for the most part consistent with Bowen's findings and are presented in Tables 34-5 and 34-6.

Table 34-5 reports the results of the stepwise multiple regression with the seven background (independent) variables and the scores on the ten issues (the dependent variables). The total variance accounted for by all the independent variables ranged from 5½ per cent for the dissent scores to about 37 per cent for the labor issue scores. After the dissents category, the government fiscal issue had the lowest percentage of the variance explained by the seven background variables (only about 8 per cent) followed by the activism and private economic categories, each of which had between 12 and 13 per cent of the variance accounted for. These findings were generally consistent with the previous analyses of the background variables undertaken individually (and reported in Tables 34-3 and 34-4 and in the text) in which dissent behavior and government fiscal voting were for the most part not associated with the background variables, and the activism and private economic voting (as compared to the other economic and political issues) produced much less statistically significant results for distribution of the scores and medians. The amount of variance of the scores on the other issues attributable to the background variables, however, was far from spectacular. The explained variance of the scores on the criminal procedures, civil liberties, and political liberalism issues was about 20 per cent, while the remaining economic issues yielded a higher proportion of explained variance—37 per cent for the labor issue, 31 per cent for the injured persons issue, but only about 22 per cent for the economic liberalism scores. Since party and age were the two variables determined by previous analyses to be most associated with the issue voting, they were first fed into the regression analysis with the other variables following.

TABLE 34-5
Stepwise Multiple Regression Analysis of Background Variables and Scores

Issue	Variable in Order of Entry in Regression	Multiple R	% of Explained Variance
Criminal Procedures	Political Party	.304	9.2
	Age	.377	14.2
	Religion	.427	18.2
	Candidate	.429	18.5
	Prior Judicial	.431	18.6
	Years on Appeals	.447	20.0
	Prosecutorial Exper.	.453	20.6
Civil Liberties	Age	.297	8.8
	Political Party	.365	13.3
	Religion	.411	16.9
	Candidate	.417	17.4
	Years on Appeals	.440	19.4
	Prosecutorial Exper.	.447	19.9
	Prior Judicial	.447	19.9
Labor	Political Party	.421	17.7
	Age	.491	24.1
	Religion	.551	30.3
	Prior Judicial	.581	33.8
	Candidate	.582	33.9
	Years on Appeals	.606	36.8
	Prosecutorial Exper.	.609	37.1
Private Economic	Political Party	.265	7.0
	Age	.294	8.6
	Religion	.304	9.2
	Prior Judicial	.335	11.2
	Candidate	.347	12.1
	Years on Appeals	.355	12.6
	Prosecutorial Exper.	.357	12.8
Gov't Fiscal	Political Party	.062	0.4
	Age	.098	0.9
	Candidate	.228	5.2
	Religion	.232	5.4
	Prior Judicial	.238	5.7
	Years on Appeals	.275	7.5
	Prosecutorial Exper.	.278	7.7
Injured Persons	Political Party	.379	14.3
	Age	.397	15.8
	Religion	.528	27.8
	Candidate	.530	28.1
	Prior Judicial	.532	28.3
	Years on Appeals	.553	30.6
	Prosecutorial Exper.	.557	31.0
Political Liberalism	Political Party	.316	9.9
	Age	.383	14.7
	Religion	.419	17.6
	Candidate	.424	17.9
	Prior Judicial	.424	18.0
	Years on Appeals	.438	19.2
	Prosecutorial Exper.	.446	19.9

TABLE 34-5 (Continued)

Issue	Variable in Order of Entry in Regression	Multiple R	% of Explained Variance
Economic Liberalism	Political Party	.389	15.2
	Age	.426	18.2
	Religion	.469	21.9
	Candidate	.471	22.2
	Prior Judicial	.472	22.3
	Years on Appeals	.474	22.5
	Prosecutorial Exper.	.475	22.5
Activism	Age	.220	4.9
	Political Party	.260	6.8
	Religion	.342	11.7
	Candidate	.345	11.9
	Prior Judicial	.346	12.0
	Prosecutorial Exper.	.352	12.4
	Years on Appeals	.353	12.4
Dissents	Political Party	.063	0.4
	Age	.065	0.4
	Religion	.066	0.4
	Prior Judicial	.194	3.8
	Candidate	.198	3.9
	Years on Appeals	.222	4.9
	Prosecutorial Exper.	.234	5.5

Note that Democrats, Protestants, candidates, those with prior judicial experience, and those with previous prosecutorial experience were assigned a higher numerical value than those who were not in those groups. Age was determined as of January 1, 1968. Years on appeals was as of January, 1971.

Table 34-5 suggests that the party variable was the single most important of the seven background variables in accounting for the variation of the scores for the criminal procedures, labor, private economic, injured persons, political liberalism, and economic liberalism issues. Age appears to have been the single most important background variable for civil liberties and (along with religion) the voting on activism. Table 34-5 also suggests that prior judicial experience was the most important variable for the dissents category and that the candidate for public office variable contributed the most to explaining the variation of the government fiscal scores. Since the stepwise routine requires us to specify the order in which the independent variables are to be entered and tells us only what happens to the variance when we successively add another variable, we cannot precisely account for the contribution of each variable acting by itself with all other variables held constant. Therefore, partial correlation analyses were undertaken in order to specify more accurately the unique contribution of each variable. Table 34-6 reports the results.

As is apparent from Table 34-6, the background variables emerge somewhat differently than they did previously. The party variable is seen as of less importance than the age and religion variables for voting on criminal procedures and civil liberties issues and of about the same importance as age on the political liberalism dimension. Only on three of the four economic underdog-type issues (labor, private economic and economic liberalism) does party emerge as the most important background variable when all other variables are held constant. The age variable is superior to the party variable in accounting for the

TABLE 34-6
Correlation Analysis of Background Variables and Scores on Issues

Issue	Background Variable	Zero-Order Correlation with Issue	Partial Correlation (Sixth Order) with Issue	% of Variance Explained
Criminal Procedures	Political Party	.304	.198	3.9
	Age	−.285	−.231	5.3
	Religion	−.253	−.220	4.8
	Candidate	−.117	−.032	0.1
	Prior Judicial	−.054	−.002	0.0
	Years on Appeals	−.082	.126	1.6
	Prosecutorial Exper.	−.109	−.080	0.6
Civil Liberties	Age	−.297	−.286	8.2
	Political Party	.286	.174	3.0
	Religion	−.185	−.203	4.1
	Candidate	−.080	.017	0.0
	Years on Appeals	−.122	.150	2.2
	Prosecutorial Exper.	−.112	−.084	0.7
	Prior Judicial	.085	.131	1.7
Labor	Political Party	.421	.346	12.0
	Age	−.389	.009	0.0
	Religion	−.298	−.268	7.2
	Prior Judicial	−.207	−.266	7.1
	Candidate	−.215	−.094	0.9
	Years on Appeals	−.312	−.216	4.7
	Prosecutorial Exper.	−.004	.076	0.6
Private Economic	Political Party	.265	.277	7.7
	Age	.035	.003	0.0
	Religion	−.141	−.113	1.3
	Prior Judicial	−.107	−.111	1.2
	Candidate	.016	.087	0.8
	Years on Appeals	.152	.084	0.7
	Prosecutorial Exper.	−.010	.046	0.2
Gov't Fiscal	Political Party	−.062	−.045	0.2
	Age	−.050	.087	0.8
	Candidate	−.215	−.204	4.2
	Religion	.042	.030	0.1
	Prior Judicial	−.024	−.014	0.0
	Years on Appeals	−.142	−.146	2.1
	Prosecutorial Exper.	−.038	−.044	0.2
Injured Persons	Political Party	.379	.220	4.8
	Age	−.244	−.267	7.1
	Religion	−.357	−.402	16.2
	Candidate	−.034	.077	0.6
	Prior Judicial	.056	.003	0.0
	Years on Appeals	−.043	.162	2.6
	Prosecutorial Exper.	−.145	−.082	0.7
Political Liberalism	Political Party	.316	.228	5.2
	Age	−.266	−.224	5.0
	Religion	−.223	−.199	4.0
	Candidate	−.107	−.048	0.2
	Prior Judicial	−.031	.042	0.2
	Prosecutorial Exper.	−.107	−.090	0.8
	Years on Appeals	−.079	.112	1.2

TABLE 34-6 (Continued)

Issue	Background Variable	Zero-Order Correlation with Issue	Partial Correlation (Sixth Order) with Issue	% of Variance Explained
Economic Liberalism	Political Party	.390	.319	10.2
	Age	−.262	−.152	2.3
	Religion	−.255	−.222	4.9
	Candidate	−.023	.064	0.4
	Years on Appeals	−.143	.044	0.2
	Prosecutorial Exper.	−.043	−.023	0.0
	Prior Judicial	−.065	−.030	0.1
Activism	Age	−.220	−.103	1.1
	Political Party	.202	.102	1.0
	Religion	−.245	−.213	4.5
	Candidate	−.177	−.038	0.1
	Prior Judicial	−.032	−.046	0.2
	Prosecutorial Exper.	.014	.059	0.4
	Years on Appeals	−.169	−.029	0.1
Dissents	Political Party	.063	.037	0.1
	Age	−.027	−.073	0.5
	Religion	.001	.018	0.0
	Prior Judicial	−.182	−.154	2.4
	Candidate	−.059	−.044	0.2
	Years on Appeals	.087	.113	1.3
	Prosecutorial Exper.	.040	.073	0.5

variance of the criminal procedures, civil liberties, and injured persons scores. Religion is the most important variable for the injured persons and activism issues; second most important (more than party) for the criminal procedures and civil liberties issues; and second only to party on the labor, private economic, and economic liberalism issues. The prior judicial experience variable was essentially tied with religion as second most important variable for the labor issue and was the most important of the seven variables for the dissents category (although accounting for a negligible proportion of the variance, only 2.4 per cent). The candidate variable was the most important one for the government fiscal issue.

The principal findings, however, were that Democrats, Catholics and younger judges tended to be more liberal (i.e., had higher scores) than Republicans, Protestants and older judges. Judges who had previous judicial experience tended to be more conservative on the labor issue and to dissent less than those who did not have such experience. Those who did not have the experience of being a candidate for public office tended to support the government more in fiscal cases than did those who had run for elective office. But none of these variables individually accounted for more than 16 per cent of the variance of the voting on any of the issues. The party variable's contribution ranged from essentially zero for government fiscal and dissents to 12 per cent for the labor issue. The age variable's contribution ranged from zero on labor, private economic, and dissents to 8 per cent for civil liberties. Religion varied from zero for government fiscal and dissents to 16 per cent for injured persons.

Multiple regression and partial correlations were also run with the southern circuits excluded and the proportion of explained variance was found to be greater. All seven background variables explained about 58 per cent of the variance of the labor scores and this was the largest amount of explained variance. In general, with the South excluded, background variables explained *up to twice* as much of the variance with the exception of the dissents category which remained virtually unchanged.[12] The party variable's biggest contribution was on the labor issue with 37 per cent of the explained variance. The age variable's contribution ranged from zero on the labor, private economic, government fiscal, and dissents categories to about 18 per cent for civil liberties (the most important of the variables on that issue). Interestingly, the religion variable lost its potency on all issues with the most dramatic change with the injured persons issue where the explained variance fell to 3.7 per cent.

In some ways this study was a more rigorous test of the backgrounds-behavior hypotheses than the earlier study of voting behavior of appeals court judges. This study utilized only nonunanimous cases decided during twice the time span covered by the earlier research. More sophisticated methods were used to test the hypotheses. In the final analysis, however, it was found that basically a principal conclusion of the earlier study has held up. The party variable is apparently best associated with voting on issues concerning economic liberalism. More rigorous methods, to be sure, permitted the detection of the effects of other variables, notably age and to an extent religion (however relatively minor the effect), not previously suspected. Perhaps most important, by in part replicating Bowen's study and coming up with some findings similar to his, we find that the background variables tested including the party variable cannot account for much of judicial voting behavior.

Summary and Conclusions

Investigation of voting behavior of judges on the eleven courts of appeals in 2,115 nonunanimous decisions during a seven-year period revealed the following:

(1) Voting patterns on the circuits suggested the existence of interrelated political attitudes and values held by judges. This finding was also supported by separately conducted bloc analyses and the scaling of *en banc* decisions and was the same as that of the earlier study of appeals courts. It therefore appears reasonable that the judicial behavior of appeals court judges be interpreted as representing gradations of broadly defined political and economic liberal-conservative attitudes. This in turn implies that to some extent the outcome of a case will be determined by who sits on the three member appeals panel. Furthermore, the difference in dissent rates of the circuits is also likely to result from the different attitudinal predispositions of the judges and the particular combinations of judges on the panels.

(2) Among the seven background variables tested for their association with voting behavior, party and age emerged as the most important. Party was seen as dividing the judges on most issues, with the Democrats tending to be more liberal than the Republicans. Circuit-by-circuit analysis suggested that the party split was most pronounced on economic issues. Partial correlational analyses also suggested that party was most important for the economic liberalism issues. Older judges tended to be more conservative than younger judges on most issues, but the partial correlations suggested that age was most important for the political liberalism issues. Religion was associated particularly with the injury and economic liberalism issues, with Catholic judges tending to be more liberal than Protestant judges (but the partial correlations also suggested some association of

religion with other issues). The multiple correlations, however, were generally low; indeed, 37 per cent was the largest proportion of the variance accounted for by the background variables and that was only for the labor issue (although with the South excluded this rose to 58 per cent). On balance, party and age seemed to have some limited importance in explaining the variance in judicial behavior, and the other background variables appeared negligible (with the possible exception of religion).

These findings lend some slight encouragement to backgrounds-behavior research at the aggregate level. If such research is pursued, a theoretical framework should be developed that will suggest which of the background variables one should attempt to relate to behavior. The party variable, which has been accorded theoretical treatment of this kind, should probably be considered, along with the regional variable (recall the findings when the southern circuits were excluded). . . . The age variable presents a special challenge for judicial behavior. The variable, after all, is a dynamic one, and the age hypothesis seems to suggest that judges grow more conservative as they grow older.[13] This proposition deserves closer scrutiny using the voting records of individual judges. . . .

· · ·

The findings reported here might be considered in terms of the judicial selection process. For example, one could take the position that as long as the party variable does not account for all or almost all of the variance in voting behavior there is little reason to oppose the traditional political appointment process. On the other hand, the increased ideological polarization in our national politics during the past decade should alert us to how this polarization is affecting the selection process and what sorts of judges are coming onto the bench. It may be useful, therefore, to have continual monitoring of the exercise of discretion of appeals judges with reference to what values are allocated and what are the broader societal consequences of those allocations. In sum, then, such research can provide insight into why judicial authorities allocate values the way they do as well as helping students of the judiciary and others evaluate judicial systemic mechanisms and processes, including judicial selection.

Notes

1. See the citations contained in Sheldon Goldman, "Voting Behavior on the United States Courts of Appeals, 1961–1964," *American Political Science Review* 60 (June 1966), 375, n. 6; and Sheldon Goldman, "Conflict on the U.S. Courts of Appeals 1965–1971: A Quantitative Analysis," *University of Cincinnati Law Review* 42 (No. 4, 1973), 636, n. 3. . . .

2. Goldman, "Voting Behavior," pp. 374–383. To aid comparability with the earlier study, much of the original research design and format of the presentation of the findings are employed here.

3. A judge had to decide a minimum of five cases on a particular issue in order for a score to be calculated and utilized. In practice, for most issues, at least three or four times the minimum number of cases were utilized for most judges. There were some judges, however, who did not decide a sufficient number of cases on all issues; thus the N for each issue varied. The private economic issue had the smallest number of judges, 51, for whom scores were calculated. The second, third, fifth, ninth, and District of Columbia circuits accounted for 41 judges on that issue. The fourth, sixth, and seventh circuits contributed the balance. No judge on the first, eighth, and tenth circuits was included on this issue because none decided the minimum number of cases.

4. Occasionally, cases are decided by the entire court sitting *en banc*. During the seven-year period under study, there were only 202 nonunanimously decided *en banc* decisions accounting for little more than one half of 1 per cent of all cases decided after hearing or submission.

5. See, for example, Stuart S. Nagel, "Political Party Affiliation and Judges' Decisions," *American Political Science Review* 55 (December 1961), 843-850; Kenneth N. Vines, "The Role of Circuit Courts of Appeal in the Federal Judicial Process: A Case Study," *Midwest Journal of Political Science* 7 (November 1963), 305-319; Don R. Bowen, "The Explanation of Judicial Voting Behavior from Sociological Characteristics of Judges" (Ph.D. Dissertation, Yale University, 1965); Burton M. Atkins, "Decision-Making Rules and Judicial Strategy on the United States Courts of Appeals," *Western Political Quarterly* 25 (December 1972), 626-642; Thomas G. Walker, "A Note Concerning Partisan Influences on Trial-Judge Decision Making," *Law and Society Review* 6 (May 1972), 645-649.

6. A positive correlation (.24) was found between circuit dissent rate and size of court (i.e., the number of judges serving on the appeals court), suggesting some tendency for the larger circuits to be more contentious than the smaller ones. A negative correlation (−.44) was found between circuit dissent rate and per judgeship terminated appeals rate, suggesting that circuits with more dissent tended to be those that were less efficient in the disposition of their business. It might be thought that circuits with the heaviest workload pressures might be those with a tendency to dissent less but the correlation analyses lent little support for this hypothesis (the correlation between dissent rate and per judgeship civil appeals rate was −.09, the correlation between dissent rate and total appeals filed per judgeship was .17). Per judgeship rates were taken from *Management Statistics for United States Courts* (Washington, D.C.: Administrative Office of the United States Courts, 1972). Sources of dissent are explored in Goldman, "Conflict," pp. 637-642. . . .

7. Note that when the judges were categorized by appointing administration, the median score of the Nixon appointees on the criminal procedures issue was the lowest of all groups, 0.53. In contrast, the median score of the Johnson appointees on the criminal procedures issue was the highest of all groups, 1.20. Appointees of other Republican administrations had a median of 0.67 and appointees of other Democratic administrations had a median of 0.82. On the civil liberties issue, the Nixon appointees again had the lowest median score (0.57) and the Johnson appointees the highest (1.50). Appointees of other Republican administrations had a median of 0.61 and appointees of other Democratic administrations had a median of 0.86. For this analysis, a judge's political liberalism score was used when no separate criminal or civil liberties scores could be constructed because of participation in too few cases. For an in-depth study of the Nixon appointees, see Jon Gottschall, "The Nixon Appointments to the United States Courts of Appeals: The Impact of the Law and Order Issue on the Rights of the Accused" (Ph.D. Dissertation, University of Massachusetts, 1976).

8. *Congressional Quarterly,* December 16, 1972, p. 3160.

9. Circuit-by-circuit analysis of the other issues revealed that only in the fifth circuit was there a higher proportion of Republicans than Democrats above the circuit median for the criminal procedures, civil liberties, and labor issues. For the injured persons category, the fifth circuit was joined by the eighth circuit. For the activism issue the fifth circuit was joined by the third and fourth circuits. On the private economic issue only on the fourth and sixth circuits was there a higher proportion of Republicans above the circuit median than Democrats.

10. Note that because there was only a small number of Jewish judges (13) and they were concentrated on the second and third circuits (8 of the 13), they were not included in the analysis of the religion variable. Their median scores on the issues were: criminal procedures 1.60 ($N = 13$); civil liberties 1.50 ($N = 10$); labor 1.73 ($N = 7$); private

economic 1.17 ($N = 7$); government fiscal 1.17 ($N = 5$); injured persons 1.39 ($N = 8$); political liberalism 1.47 ($N = 13$); economic liberalism 1.19 ($N = 13$); activism 1.62 ($N = 8$); dissents 0.56 ($N = 13$).

11. Bowen, "The Explanation of Judicial Voting Behavior."

12. The proportion of explained variance of the remaining categories follows: criminal procedures, 30 per cent; civil liberties, 42 per cent; private economic, 23 per cent; government fiscal, 13 per cent; injured persons, 47 per cent; political liberalism, 30 per cent; economic liberalism, 29 per cent; and activism, 26 per cent.

13. See the excellent summary of the literature concerning the age hypothesis in Norval D. Glenn, "Aging and Conservatism," in *Political Consequences of Aging*, Frederick R. Eisele, ed., *The Annals* (Philadelphia: Academy of Political and Social Science, September 1974), pp. 176-186.

35

Social Background as an Indicator to the Votes of Supreme Court Justices in Criminal Cases: 1947–1956 Terms

S. Sidney Ulmer

. . .

The present author, in a 1970 paper, suggested that attitudes/values are a consequence of social/experiential background.[1] But attempts . . . to connect the social backgrounds of judges to their voting behavior have produced mixed results.

In the present note, we wish to add to the picture some results from research on 14 justices who sat in the Court in the ten terms, 1947–56.

The selection of the decade, 1947–57, for analysis was an artifact of a separate research project for which this period was relevant. In that separate project it was found that the justices varied considerably in the rates at which they supported government and failed to support individuals in criminal cases decided during the decade. Using rate of support for government as a dependent variable, we selected (from social background studies) 12 possible indicators to support rate. These were the following: age at appointment, highest degree received, status of school granting LL.B., size of place of birth, size of place of last law practice, state legislative experience, federal legislative experience, prior service on an appellate bench, federal administrative experience, religious affiliation, public office immediately prior to appointment, and party affiliation.

These 12 variables, collectively, were found to account for 91.8 percent of the variance in support for state and federal governments in criminal cases. But since the number of independent variables almost equalled the number of observations, this finding is of no great moment. Close analysis, however, led to the identification of three factors that appear to have some explanatory power. These variables are age at appointment, federal administrative experience, and religious affiliation.

Age at appointment was operationalized in years; federal administrative experience was coded as present or absent; a similar dichotomization was used to separate Protestants from non-Protestants on variable three. For the dependent variable, we calculated the

Reprinted from *American Journal of Political Science,* 17 (1973), pp. 622–630. Most footnotes omitted. Reprinted by permission of the Wayne State University Press. Copyright © 1973 by Wayne State University Press.

TABLE 35-1
Raw Data Matrix*

Justices	x_1	x_2	x_3	y	N
Douglas	40	2	2	19	217
Rutledge	48	1	2	22	58
Jackson	48	2	2	56	149
Murphy	50	2	1	20	58
Brennan	50	1	1	23	38
Clark	50	2	2	59	174
Black	51	1	2	21	237
Reed	54	2	2	67	214
Harlan	55	1	2	50	62
Frankfurter	56	2	1	39	239
Vinson	56	2	2	69	136
Burton	57	1	2	64	238
Minton	58	2	2	77	133
Warren	62	1	2	32	93

* Variable identification: (x_1) age at appointment; (x_2) federal administrative experience, 1 if absent, 2 if present; (x_3) religious affiliation, 1 if non-Protestant, 2 if Protestant; (y) percentage of criminal cases decided favorably for state or federal government, 1947–56 terms; N = total number of cases.

percentage of criminal cases, per year, in which each justice supported government. Table 35-1 portrays the raw data matrix to which a step-wise multiple regression routine was applied.

As shown in Table 35-2, our three independent variables, collectively, can account for 70 percent of the variance in the rate at which these 14 justices supported state or federal governments in criminal cases during the 1947–56 terms of the Supreme Court. Initially, the variable most highly correlated with support for government is age at appointment. By starting with that variable, adding additional variables one at a time, and observing the changes in R^2, we find a fairly sizable jump in the "explained variance" at each step. Each of our three independent variables makes a contribution. Using age at appointment and federal administrative experience, we can explain 49 percent of the variance. And if we also consider whether the justice's religious denomination is Protestant or non-Protestant, we improve our level of explained variance another 21 percentage points.

. . .

In the stepwise multiple regression analysis, the variable—age at appointment—was entered first since it exhibited the highest simple correlation (.506) with the dependent variable. But that does not indicate that age at appointment was, relatively, the most important of the social background characteristics examined. The reason is that the simple correlation between any single factor and decision is affected by the extent to which

TABLE 35-2
Multiple Regression Analysis of Data in Table 35-1

Variables Entered in Equation	Multiple R	R^2
x_1	.51	.26
x_1, x_2	.70	.49
x_1, x_2, x_3	.83	.70

TABLE 35-3
Correlation Analysis of Data in Table 35-1

Variable	Pearson r (rx_1y, rx_2y, etc.)	Partials ($rx_1y \cdot x_2x_3$, $rx_2y \cdot x_1x_3$, etc.)	Percent Reduction in Unexplained Variance
x_1	.51	.88	.77
x_2	.37	.81	.66
x_3	.43	.63	.40

other factors influence output. In terms of the ability of any single variable to reduce the variance left unexplained by any combination of two variables, the order of importance is: (1) age at appointment, (2) federal administrative experience, and (3) religious affiliation. The data supporting this conclusion are presented in Table 35-3.

Table 35-3 shows that if we control for various combinations of two variables, age at appointment alone will reduce unexplained variance by 77 percent while federal administrative experience, after other variables have accounted for all the variance they can, will account for 66 percent of the remaining variance. In these terms, then, religious affiliation is the least important of our independent variables, age at appointment the most important, with federal administrative experience between the two extremes.

The same order of relative importance is maintained when we determine the proportion of the variance explained by each of the input factors in the regression equation. This determination is made by utilizing net regression coefficients, standard partial regression coefficients, standard deviations and Pearson product moment coefficients.[2] Application of the appropriate formula shows that in the prediction equation, 30 percent of the variance is explained by age at appointment, 20 percent by federal administrative experience, and 19 percent by religious affiliation.

When the same analysis was applied to state and federal cases separately, similar results were produced. In federal criminal cases only, our three factors accounted for 70 percent of the variance in support for the federal government. In state cases, R^2 was reduced to 58 percent. Calculation of the relative contribution of the input variables to the regression equation revealed the same relative importance of the variables in federal cases as in combined cases. But a separate analysis of state cases ranked federal administrative experience as most important, accounting for 27 percent of the variance as against 22 percent for age at appointment and 10 percent for religious affiliation. Thus, a "federalism" variable appears to exert some influence. But our overall finding is not appreciably disturbed.

There is no attempt in this note to suggest that starting from some complete theory, we have derived three empirical indicators to decision patterns in criminal cases and successfully confirmed a theory. The effort reported here is strictly exploratory. It is reported for two reasons. First, recent writing dealing with social background theory seems sufficiently pessimistic to risk premature closure of this kind of research in the judicial area. We do not believe such closure is warranted at this time. Second, we subscribe to the view that attitudes influence decisions of judges and that socialization patterns help determine attitudinal structure. Consequently, our inquiry is not without a theoretical base. It is legitimate, however, to ask whether the exploration reported here is suggestive.

If "age at appointment," "federal administrative experience," and "religious affiliation" are indicators to socialization patterns which shape attitudes, it should be possible to identify plausible linkages. Nagel has shown that, in 11 state supreme courts, Protestants were more likely than Catholics to support government in criminal cases. This is consistent with our findings for the 13 Supreme Court justices who fall in these two categories. Nagel also reports that Protestants from the "high income" denominations are more likely than "low income Protestants" to support government in criminal cases.[3] This, also, is consistent with our findings. Of eight Protestants from high income denominations, six supported government between 50 and 77 percent of the time. Of three Protestants from low income denominations, two supported government at rates of 21 and 32 percent. The linkage between religious affiliation and voting in criminal cases may, therefore, be socio-economic class and the influences emanating from the disparate socialization patterns which characterize different classes.

Federal administrative experience may progressively socialize the bureaucrat to support the government which employs him and, via metastasization, governmental authority in general when in conflict with alleged criminals. For every Ramsey Clark that comes to mind, there are a number of Tom Clarks, J. Edgar Hoovers, and Robert Jacksons. Serving the federal establishment is not known to be a liberalizing experience. One can surmise, of course, that ardent activists for individual rights against government are not rewarded with high federal administrative posts in the first place. Thus, the possibility exists that federal administrative experience is a surrogate for other earlier socialization patterns yet to be identified.

Age at appointment is not the same as age at point of decision. And the same theoretical considerations do not apply. If one assumes that, subsequent to appointment to the Court, all justices undergo common in-Court socializing experiences, then differences in certain areas of judicial behavior may result from initial differences in the "subjects." One such initial difference is age at appointment—a rough measure of the total impact of other socializing experiences prior to those encountered in the Court. Our data suggest that the greater the number of years to which the individual is subjected to these "other" experiences before coming to the Court, the more likely he will support government in criminal cases after getting there.

The discrepancies between the high level of explanation offered here (in terms of variance explained) and the relatively low levels produced by earlier studies underline our 1970 suggestion: i.e., that it is premature to rule out the social background model as a useful device for explaining judicial behavior. The minimal results obtained in some studies resulted from several possible causes. One, of course, is that the relationship sought between background and decisional behavior was simply absent. But that is not the last word on the point. Other factors may have intervened.

Some of the earlier researchers have dichotomized continuous variables when it was unnecessary to do so for any reasons of methodology. . . .

Additional possible reasons for the failure to explain variation in voting behavior with background factors—other than minimally—lies in the imagination of those working in the subfield. Perhaps we have been inadequate in identifying appropriate dependent and independent variables. As we move from one court system to another, from one level of court to another, from the courts of one nation to those of another, it may be necessary to alter variables on both sides of the equation if the extent to which social background impinges on judicial behavior is to be more systematically revealed.

It should be noted that studies attempting to relate social background to judicial behavior have usually dealt with some limited population of judges across a limited time span.

This may be necessitated by data set or other conditions. Consequently, we do not condemn the practice where conditions require it. . . .

As for the present analysis of 14 Supreme Court justices, the time period is a decade, but the number of justices studied is small. Were we analyzing a random sample of justices, our results would be statistically significant at .01. But since the decade used was not randomly selected, we make no pretense of generalizing beyond these particular justices. Our findings regarding this limited subset of judges are considered suggestive for broader studies and are viewed as supportive of the view that the social background model warrants further exploration in the judicial subfield of political science.

Finally, there is no intention here to suggest that knowledge of the social background of judges will *ever* enable one to predict judicial responses in individual cases. The decision making process is complex and many factors may intervene to mute whatever tendencies background and experience may predispose a judge to exhibit. The questions are (a) what kinds of experiences produce what kinds of predispositions, (b) under what conditions are those predispositions determinative or influential, and (c) to what extent are socially induced predispositions stable over time.

Notes

1. S. Sidney Ulmer, "Dissent Behavior and the Social Background of Supreme Court Justices," *Journal of Politics* 32 (August 1970), 580–598.

2. For appropriate formulae, see J. P. Guilford, *Fundamental Statistics in Psychology and Education* (New York: McGraw-Hill, 1956), pp. 393–398. . . .

3. Stuart S. Nagel, *The Legal Process from a Behavioral Perspective* (Homewood, Ill.: Dorsey Press, 1969) p. 233. . . .

CHAPTER TWELVE

ATTITUDES, VALUES, AND DECISIONS

Thus far we have examined the relation of fact-pattern, environmental, and background variables to judicial decision making. These variables are external to the judge in that they can be directly identified by the researcher independently of the judge. We have suggested that they are somehow associated with the development of attitudes and values and can therefore be linked to the decisional behavior of the judge. Now we explicitly focus our attention on variables internal to the judge—those attitudes and values—and why and how scholars have sought to discover and identify them.

By focusing on attitudes and values we once again test the traditional model of judicial decision making. If a significant proportion of judicial behavior can be shown to be linked with political attitudes and values, we must then consider judges to be *political* actors and courts to be *political* institutions. Judicial selection and the evaluation of judicial policy making must then take into account the reality of the decisional process. The judicial process, although distinctive in many important ways, must be seen as closely linked to the political system.

To understand contemporary judicial behavior research focusing on attitudes and values, one must appreciate its intellectual origins in the political behavioralism and legal realism movements of the 1920s and 1930s. Within the political science discipline, behavioralism provided a radically new perspective on the study of politics and consequently a major new research agenda for the field. Behavioralism shifted the focus of political science from legalistic institutional description and normative prescription to the analysis of empirical reality—what really happens in political life— and the search for underlying regularities or patterns in the behavior of political actors and participants, thus facilitating an understanding of why and how people behave politically. This meant a concern with the development of methods and procedures that would allow systematic analyses and objective interpretation of political phenomena.

Among students of courts and law, a parallel movement arose—legal realism—whose adherents were profoundly skeptical of the legal rules and principles that appellate court judges (especially Supreme Court justices) were offering as the bases for their decision making. (Recall our discussion of legal realism in Chapter Nine.) Political science professor C. Herman Pritchett linked political behavioralism to legal realism, although he rejected the extremist position of some of the rule skeptics—that law was merely the political preferences of judges.[1] Pritchett appreciated the fact that courts of law are unique institutions and that judges occupy a very special position within them. He took the view that only under some circumstances can we reasonably infer that judges had sufficient discretion (given certain ambiguities in the factual situation, statute, constitutional provision and precedents) so that disputes could be resolved in markedly different ways. With regard to a collegial court like the United States Supreme Court, it is the nonunanimously decided cases that should be studied, for here the judges are in open disagreement and there is no doubt that there are alternative paths to dispute resolution. Pritchett theorized that by studying the votes of the justices in nonunanimously decided cases, it is possible to discover whether there are underlying patterns of voting behavior and if so, what those patterns represent. The article by Pritchett (selection 36) is one of the landmark judicial behavior studies.

Pritchett's methodology involved the calculation of agreement scores (the proportion of all nonunanimously decided cases in which a pair of judges voted together) and the determination of voting blocs (of like-voting judges). By examining the opinions as well as the votes of the justices, Pritchett was able to identify liberal and conservative blocs on the Court. Although there have been methodological refinements since Pritchett did his studies, bloc analysis remains a tool for the identification of voting alignments on collegial courts. Table 1 shows the bloc voting of the Nixon-Burger Supreme Court through the 1976 Term. The blocs are derived from an analysis of voting patterns in all nonunanimously decided civil liberties cases. Table 2 presents the proportion of justices' votes in all civil liberties cases (both nonunanimously and unanimously decided) in favor

TABLE 1
Bloc Voting in Nonunanimously Decided Civil Liberties Cases: 1969-1976 Terms of the United States Supreme Court

Term	Bloc	Type
1969	Douglas-Brennan-Marshall	Liberal
	White-Harlan	Conservative
	Burger-Stewart-Black	Conservative
1970	Douglas-Brennan-Marshall	Liberal
	Burger-Blackmun-Black-White-Stewart-Harlan	Conservative
1971	Douglas-Brennan-Marshall-Stewart	Liberal
	Burger-Blackmun-Rehnquist-Powell-White	Conservative
1972	Douglas-Brennan-Marshall	Liberal
	Burger-Blackmun-Rehnquist-Powell-White-Stewart	Conservative
1973	Douglas-Brennan-Marshall	Liberal
	Stewart-White-Powell	Conservative
	Burger-Blackmun-Rehnquist	Conservative
1974	Douglas-Brennan-Marshall	Liberal
	Burger-Blackmun-Rehnquist-Powell-White-Stewart	Conservative
1975	Brennan-Marshall	Liberal
	Burger-Blackmun-Rehnquist-Powell-White-Stewart-Stevens	Conservative
1976	Brennan-Marshall-Stevens	Liberal
	Burger-Blackmun-Rehnquist-Powell-White-Stewart	Conservative

of the civil liberties claim. The findings in Table 2 are the basis for the classification of the blocs in Table 1.

For a considerable number of years, Pritchett stood virtually alone in political science as a practitioner of systematic empirical analysis of judicial behavior. Eventually in the mid-1950s, as political behavioralism was conquering the other subfields within political science, renewed interest in judicial behavior emerged. A leading figure in the more recent judicial behavior movement was and is Professor Glendon Schubert. Schubert took the initiative in developing the methodological apparatus that today is largely at the foundation of the study of judicial attitudes. One of the earliest and major demonstrations of the new methodology used to map the basic attitudes and values underlying Supreme Court decision making is Schubert's article (selection 37) on the 1960 Term of the Supreme Court. Although Schubert went on to make some complex and sophisticated refinements in his methods,[2] his essential approach is presented in this article, and a basic general understanding of it should be within reach of the student.

One of the principal building blocks of the Schubert methodology that has subsequently been used by many others as well to study collegial court behavior is Guttman (or cumulative) scaling. Devised by social psychologist Louis Guttman, cumulative scaling tests whether a series of questions and responses tap a single dimension underlying those questions. Questions and responses are placed in a certain order according to the direction

TABLE 2
Proportion of All Votes in Civil Liberties Cases (Nonunanimous and Unanimous Decisions) in Favor of Civil Liberties Claims: 1969-1976 Terms of the United States Supreme Court (Percent)

Justice	Term							
	1969	1970	1971	1972	1973	1974	1975	1976
Douglas	86	90	96	91	92	92	—	—
Brennan	79	77	84	86	87	76	85	70
Marshall	70	80	88	89	85	75	83	72
Black	58	51	—	—	—	—	—	—
Stewart	45	47	72	58	50	54	41	34
Stevens	—	—	—	—	—	—	44	55
White	57	46	58	33	42	42	31	33
Burger	37	35	36	28	28	32	18	16
Blackmun	—	35	42	36	34	39	27	30
Harlan	53	43	—	—	—	—	—	—
Powell	—	—	36	37	42	40	28	30
Rehnquist	—	—	27	16	21	26	13	8
Court	63	50	56	41	44	44	31	33

of the total number of responses and the minimization of "inconsistent" responses. If a pattern of response emerges that meets certain criteria such as reproducibility and scalability (these tests are described in the Schubert reading), then the questions and responses scale. It is recognized that with attitudinal questioning there may well be a nonscalar or inconsistent (in terms of the scale pattern) response. Inconsistent responses can occur because the respondent has misunderstood the question, or because the question has been faultily communicated to that individual, or because the individual is responding to that question on another dimension. Obviously only a limited proportion of inconsistent responses can be tolerated before an array of questions and responses no longer scale, hence the necessity for such criteria as reproducibility and scalability. If a set of questions and responses is found to scale, then certain statements can be made about the questions and the respondents (such as, the questions are linked to an underlying attitudinal dimension; one can "predict" the response of a respondent simply by knowing the respondent's scale position; one can "predict" the response of a respondent who did not respond to a question on the scale).

When scaling is applied to the United States Supreme Court, the cases are treated as questions and the votes of the justices are treated as responses. The number of respondents at any one time never exceeds nine. Schubert and others have hypothesized that cases raising various issues of civil liberties have in common an underlying civil liberties attitudinal dimension to which the justices may be responding. A similar hypothesis for issues involving economic liberalism has repeatedly been formulated and tested. C (civil liberties) and E (economic liberalism) scales for various terms of the Supreme Court have been found, and the accumulated weight of the evidence strongly suggests that the attitudes and values of the justices are directly and inextricably linked to their votes in cases decided nonunanimously by the Supreme Court.

But the existence of so-called inconsistent or nonscalar responses in these and other scales has troubled some scholars. Harold Spaeth and David Peterson, in particular, have argued that more refined scales representing more than one or two basic dimensions provide a more accurate description of Supreme Court behavior.[3]

There is clearly a difference of opinion among students of judicial behavior. Leading judicial behavioralists such as Schubert and S. Sidney Ulmer have argued that those engaged in the scientific enterprise look for the most parsimonious explanation of the phenomena under investigation. If much of judicial behavior can be "explained" by a small number of attitudinal dimensions, then that is a better and more satisfying explanation than that provided by a larger number of dimensions, such as proposed by Spaeth and Peterson. These contradictory positions are resolved in a later work by Spaeth and David Rohde,[4] in which attitude and value theory were applied and a large number of issue- and litigant-oriented scales were utilized, but most of them were then found to be clustered into one of three groupings. These clusters were considered to represent certain values: Freedom, Equality, and New Dealism (economics). The Freedom cluster is akin to the older civil liberties scale except that it does not include disputes that center around equal protection of the law, racial and sexual discrimination, and poverty law. These issues are related to the Equality value dimension. New Dealism is similar to the old economic liberalism scale. Thus it would seem that although a more thorough understanding of judicial behavior requires knowledge of the numerous attitudes of justices concerning different issues and different types of litigants, as few as three (or perhaps even two) major value clusters can be found that explain much of that behavior.

Table 3 presents scale scores of the justices for the 1975 and 1976 Terms of the Supreme Court on a Freedom scale (the old C scale without the equality cases) and an Equality scale. The scale scores (derivation of which is explained in the Schubert reading) range from +1.000 (complete support for the freedom and equality claims raised in the disputes) to −1.000 (complete opposition to those claims). It is interesting to note the relationship of the scale scores to the indicators of voting behavior presented in Tables 1 and 2. It is also of interest to note the similarity in the voting behavior of the justices in terms of the two scales, the most pronounced exceptions being in the 1975 Term (Justices Stewart and Stevens) and in the 1976 Term (Justices Stewart, White, and Powell). The emergence of these exceptions when two different civil liberties-oriented scales are used sug-

TABLE 3
Supreme Court Justices' Scale Scores on the Freedom and Equality Scales:
1975 and 1976 Terms

Justice	1975 Term		1976 Term	
	Freedom	Equality	Freedom	Equality
Brennan	+1.000	+0.913	+0.700	+0.909
Marshall	+0.949	+1.000	+0.750	+0.909
Stewart	+0.026	−0.391	+0.000	−0.739
Stevens	−0.333	−0.043	+0.300	+0.182
White	−0.539	−0.739	−0.600	−0.091
Powell	−0.590	−0.478	−0.350	−0.826
Blackmun	−0.641	−0.826	−0.700	−0.565
Burger	−0.744	−0.826	−0.850	−0.913
Rehnquist	−0.897	−1.000	−1.000	−1.000

gests the possible usefulness of two rather than simply one broadly defined attitudinal or value dimension.

We have been employing the terms "attitude" and "value" without explicitly defining them. It is reasonable to ask whether these terms are synonymous. (If so, is it not redundant to use both?) In much of the literature
they are used interchangeably, although the implication is that the term
"value" is more comprehensive, encompassing clusters of "attitudes." One
leading scholar, David Danelski, undertook a major exploration of values
in his study of "Values as Variables in Judicial Decision-Making" (selection
38). He drew upon the social psychological literature and made a distinction between evaluations (what we have called attitudes) and values (categories or clusters of evaluations).

Harold Spaeth and David Rohde were also concerned with a more precise definition of attitudes and values, and they utilized the attitudinal
theory of Milton Rokeach.[5] Spaeth and Rohde suggested that basic to an
attitude is a "belief," which is "any simple proposition, conscious or unconscious, inferred from what a person says or does, capable of being
preceded by the phrase 'I believe that. . . .' "[6] An attitude, then, "is nothing
more than a set of interrelated beliefs about at least one object and the
situation in which it is encountered."[7] A value is "an interrelated set of
attitudes."[8] Spaeth and Rohde argued that a further distinction can be
made between attitudes toward objects, or the litigants *(AO)* and attitudes
toward situations, or the legal issues of the cases *(AS)*, and that judicial
behavior is considered "a function of the interaction of *AO* and *AS.*"[9]
Their theory of judicial decision making is fleshed out by the construction
of numerous attitude scales and the correlations of judges' rankings on
those scales to determine which attitude scales are highly correlated. These
interrelated attitudes are then categorized as values.

One final point. It is appropriate briefly to confront one persisting criticism of the attitudinal studies of judicial behavior: the allegation that be-

havioralists use attitudes to explain votes but that those attitudes are derived from the very same votes they purport to explain. Thus critics accuse
the attitudinalists of circular reasoning and argue that, absent any independent measure of attitudes and values, one cannot offer an attitudinal
explanation of voting phenomena. It is of interest to note that, as described in the "Values as Variables" reading, David Danelski did employ an
independent measure of values[10] (based on a content analysis of off-the-
bench speeches) and that his findings were similar to those of scholars
who only examined votes. But even more to the point, it is fair to observe
that the continued finding of patterns of voting (by Supreme Court justices, and lower-court judges) that can be interpreted as representing attitudes and values puts the overwhelming weight of evidence on the side of
the attitudinalists. However, it would be more prudent for behavioralists to
claim that judges behave as if they held certain attitudes and values. It is
impossible to demonstrate conclusively that judges hold particular attitudes and values, for they are not things or events to be observed. But the
voting patterns can certainly imply the existence of such attitudes and
values, and it is the more modest as if qualification that is perhaps the most
persuasive response to the critics.

Notes

1. Robert C. Welsh, "C. Herman Pritchett and Public Law: Toward an Understanding of the Political Role of the Supreme Court," paper presented at the annual meeting
of the American Political Science Association, 1976, pp. 11–27.

2. See Glendon Schubert, *The Judicial Mind* (Evanston, Ill.: Northwestern University
Press, 1965); and his *The Judicial Mind Revisited* (New York: Oxford University Press,
1974).

3. Harold J. Spaeth and David J. Peterson, "The Analysis and Interpretation of
Dimensionality: The Case of Civil Liberties Decision Making," *Midwest Journal of Political
Science* 15 (1971), 415.

4. See David W. Rohde and Harold J. Spaeth, *Supreme Court Decision Making* (San
Francisco: Freeman, 1976).

5. Milton Rokeach, *Beliefs, Attitudes and Values* (San Francisco: Jossey-Bass, 1968).

6. Rohde and Spaeth, *op. cit.*, p. 76.

7. *Ibid.*

8. *Ibid.*, p. 77.

9. *Ibid.*

10. Also see Stuart Nagel, "Judicial Backgrounds and Criminal Cases," *Journal of
Criminal Law, Criminology and Police Science* 53 (1962), 335.

36

Voting Behavior on the United States Supreme Court

C. Herman Pritchett

"We are under a Constitution," said Charles Evans Hughes when he was governor of New York, "but the Constitution is what the judges say it is. . . ." Several theories of jurisprudence have arisen which attempt to take into account this personal element in the judicial interpretation and making of law. The so-called "realistic" school has argued that law is simply the behavior of the judge, that law is secreted by judges as pearls are secreted by oysters.[1] A less extreme position was taken by the late Justice Holmes, who said: "What I mean by law is nothing more or less than the prediction of what a court will do." While these views go rather far in eliminating any idea of law as a "normative, conceptual system of rules," no one doubts that many judicial determinations are made on some basis other than the application of settled rules to the facts, or that Justices of the United States Supreme Court, in deciding controversial cases involving important issues of public policy, are influenced by biases and philosophies of government, by "inarticulate major premises," which to a large degree predetermine the position they will take on a given question. Private attitudes, in other words, become public law.

More precisely, it is the private attitudes of the majority of the Court which become public law. As an inexact science, issues at law are settled by counting the noses of jurors and justices. About 150 times every term the judges of the Supreme Court announce to the world in a formal written opinion the result of their balloting on the questions raised by a legal controversy before the Court. Happily, in the great majority of these ballots the decision is unanimous. In such cases, presumably the facts and the law are so clear that no opportunity is allowed for the autobiographies of the justices to lead them to opposing conclusions. It is always possible that the members of the Court may be agreeing for different reasons, but no hint of that fact is given unless concurring opinions are written.

In a substantial number of cases, however, the nine members of the Court are not able to see eye to eye on the issues involved. Working with an identical set of facts, and with roughly comparable training in the law, they come to different conclusions. If our thesis is correct, these divisions of opinion grow out of the conscious or unconscious preferences and prejudices of the Justices, and an examination of these disagreements should afford an interesting approach to the problem of judicial motivation. These cases in which dissent is expressed are particularly deserving of study because they furnish data which are not

Reprinted by permission of author and publisher from C. Herman Pritchett, "Divisions of Opinion Among Justices of the U.S. Supreme Court, 1939-1941," *American Political Science Review* 35 (1941), 890-898. Most footnotes have been omitted.

TABLE 36-1
Participation of Supreme Court Justices in Dissenting Opinions, 1939 and 1940 Terms

Justice	Number of Dissents			Opinions Participated In	Per Cent Dissents
	1939	1940	Total		
McReynolds*	32	9	41	184	22
Roberts	23	31	54	300	18
Hughes	14	24	38	305	12
Black	4	15	19	306	6
Douglas	4	15	19	303	6
Stone	4	7	11	303	4
Reed	1	8	9	302	3
Murphy**	1	6	7	215	3
Frankfurter	2	2	4	309	1

 * Resigned February 1, 1941.
 ** Began service February 5, 1940.

simply the verbalizations of Justices, to be handled by the typical process of interpretation, analysis, comparison, search for inconsistencies, and general legal exegesis. Instead, they contribute the tangible data of a series of yes and no votes on a variety of issues. Analysis of this voting behavior should be of value in explaining Supreme Court action, in revealing basic relationships among the justices, and, in short, in "predicting" the law.

It may be suggested that the nature of the division of opinion on the Supreme Court at any given time is a matter of common knowledge among those who follow Supreme Court thinking. In the hope, however, that a more precise analysis might have some value, the divisions of opinion in Supreme Court decisions during the past two years (the October terms, 1939 and 1940) have been analyzed. This period was one in which the membership of the Court was fairly stable. The only changes in its composition came when Butler died soon after the beginning of the 1939 Term (without having participated in any cases) and was replaced by Murphy, and when McReynolds resigned during the 1940 Term.

During this two-year period, dissent was registered to more than one-fourth of the decisions rendered by the Court. In the 1939 term, the rate was 30 per cent (42 dissents in a total of 140 decisions), and for the 1940 term it dropped slightly to 28 per cent (47 dissents out of 169 decisions). There were thus 89 decisions during the period in which one or more of the Justices dissented, at least in part, from the conclusion reached by the majority. Table 36-1 shows the extent of each justice's participation in these dissents. The judge most persistent in disagreement was McReynolds, who took a minority stand in 22 per cent of the decisions in which he participated. Justices Roberts and Hughes were next in order, with records of 18 per cent and 12 per cent respectively. On the other hand, Frankfurter found himself on the losing side in only four of the 309 decisions rendered by the Court, a fact which calls attention to the central position which he appears to occupy on the Court. It should also be noted that he was the only justice whose dissents did not increase in number from 1939 to 1940 (with the exception of McReynolds, who did not serve out the 1940 term). Justices Reed, Murphy, and Stone are also shown by the data to be consistently members of the Court's majority.

Of these 89 dissents, 25 were one-man affairs. McReynolds dissented alone in 13 cases, Roberts in 10, and Reed and Stone once each. In the other 64 dissents, the concurrence of two, three, or four Justices in deviation from the majority view raises interesting problems of judicial interrelationships. Was there a regular pattern of dissent? Did certain Justices tend to agree with each other in expressing dissent? Table 36-2 attempts to

TABLE 36-2
Agreements among Supreme Court Justices in Dissenting Opinions, 1939 and 1940 Terms

Justice	McReynolds	Roberts	Hughes	Stone	Reed	Frankfurter	Murphy	Black	Douglas
McReynolds	(13)	26	20	4	2			2	2
Roberts	26	(10)	33	5	3				
Hughes	20	33	—	10	3				
Stone	4	5	10	(1)	1				
Reed	2	3	3	1	(1)				
Frankfurter						—	1	4	4
Murphy						1	—	7	7
Black		2				4	7	—	19
Douglas		2				4	7	19	—

answer such questions by showing the number of times each justice joined each other Justice in a dissenting opinion. A well-defined pattern of relationships was found to exist on the Court, and the names have been arranged in the table so as to bring out this relationship most clearly. Figures on the one-man dissents have been included in parentheses.

The table appears to reveal a marked division of the Justices into two wings or groups. The first is composed of McReynolds, Roberts, Hughes and Stone; the other includes Murphy, Frankfurter, Black, and Douglas. With the exception of two cases, no Justice in one of these groups ever joined in a dissenting opinion with a Justice from the other group. While every one of the eight Justices on occasion dissented in company with other members of his own bloc, in only two out of 89 dissents was there fraternization with the enemy. Both of these exceptional cases saw Roberts crossing the line to vote with Black and Douglas.[2] Justice Reed presents a special problem, since he was found in company with justices from both groups. His nine dissents included four with judges from each wing, and one lone dissent. He thus appeared to have one foot in each camp.

To the extent that Table 36-2 appears to show the existence of two self-contained blocs of opinion on the Court, it obviously misrepresents the situation. The pattern of relationships which begins to emerge from the table needs to be made clearer by presenting more complete data which will show all judicial agreements, whether on the majority or minority side. Table 36-2 reveals that Frankfurter and Hughes were never in dissent together, but it does not tell us how often they agreed with each other when other justices were in dissent. Table 36-3, consequently, is arranged to show the extent of agreement between each pair of Justices in the 89 controversial cases (or rather, in so many of them as were participated in by that pair). The number of agreements is expressed in percentages of total cases participated in by each pair.

The table reveals some interesting facts. Justices Black and Douglas are shown never to have been on opposite sides of a decision during the entire period. On the other hand, McReynolds disagreed with them in three-fourths of all the decisions in which there was division of opinion. Chief Justice Hughes was closer to Stone than to any other Justice, Stone found himself most often in agreement with Frankfurter, and Frankfurter's views coincided most often with those of Murphy. The most important fact about this complex of individual relationships, however, is that it conforms to a basic underlying pattern. Examination of the table shows that the Justices ranked as they are, every member of the Court is placed next to or between the Justice or Justices with whom he is most completely identified in agreement, and farthest away from those with whom he has least in common. The only important exceptions to this rule are found in the McReynolds-Murphy and the Stone-Frankfurter relationships.

The division of opinion thus takes the form of Figure 36-1, which locates the Justices along a continuum from one extreme to the other according to the direction and intensity of their deviation from the normal majority position of the Court, represented by the zero point on the scale. Frankfurter is closest to this point, since he dissented from only one per cent of the Court's decisions. Reed is given a position on both sides of the zero point, since his dissents were divided between the two wings. The scale makes apparent the existence of a fairly cohesive six-judge majority, most of the dissents being entered by the right-wing minority of McReynolds, Roberts, and Hughes.

This use of the term "right-wing" assumes that the division of opinion on the Court results from differences of opinion as to desirable public policy. It assumes that the above

TABLE 36-3
Agreements among Supreme Court Justices in Controversial Cases, 1939 and 1940 Terms (In Percentages)

Justice	McReynolds	Roberts	Hughes	Stone	Reed	Frankfurter	Murphy	Black	Douglas
McReynolds	—	64	64	41	35	31	38	24	24
Roberts	64	—	75	51	45	45	39	37	36
Hughes	64	75	—	78	63	64	53	49	49
Stone	41	51	78	—	81	84	75	69	68
Reed	35	45	63	81	—	86	80	79	79
Frankfurter	31	45	64	84	86	—	91	85	84
Murphy	38	39	53	75	80	91	—	89	89
Black	24	37	49	69	79	85	89	—	100
Douglas	24	36	49	68	79	84	89	100	—

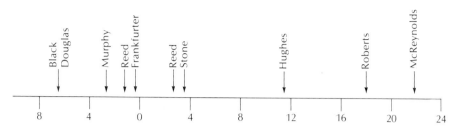

Figure 36-1. Deviations expressed in percentages.

scale reflects relative "liberalism" and "conservatism" as those terms are understood by the man in the street. This assumption should be checked by an examination of the issues actually involved in the cases where dissents were filed. Did all of these cases present issues of public policy on which liberals and conservatives might well be expected to differ, or did a number of them involve "purely legal" questions? A proper answer on this point would require the setting up of elaborate criteria for distinguishing between these two kinds of issues, and application of the criteria in a detailed analysis of each case. Such an analysis has been attempted here to only a limited degree, and covering only the dissents of the 1939 term.

A case which requires a decision as to the extent of governmental powers, or presents an issue between the government and an individual, is obviously one in which the result may be affected by the judges' views on public policy. Our present stereotypes picture the conservative as anti-government (in the sense of opposing new or more effective forms of governmental control over individuals or corporations), and the liberal or New Dealer as pro-government. An examination of the 1939 Term's 42 dissents shows that in at least 36 an issue was presented which required the Justices to vote for or against the government, to uphold or deny a government contention, to approve or disapprove an exercise of governmental authority. The voting record of the Justices in these 36 cases shows that in 27 the dissenters were right-wingers taking an anti-government position; in three more cases, the dissenters were left-wing Justices voting for the government. Thus in 30 of the cases judicial action ran true to form.

Of the six remaining cases in this group, four saw the situation exactly reversed, with the government's support coming from the right wing. The explanation is simple, however. All four were civil liberties cases (involving free speech, the right to picket, and freedom from wire-tapping), and in all four McReynolds was the lone dissenter voting to uphold government restrictions on individuals. His action was in line with the traditional conservative position on the Court. It will be recalled that in 1931 the famous free press case of *Near v. Minnesota* brought out a perfect conservative dissenting lineup of Butler, Van Devanter, McReynolds, and Sutherland. By the 1939 Term, only one of this old guard remained to take a stand against civil liberties.

In the remaining two of these 36 dissents, the vote is completely inexplicable in terms of the scale positions of the Justices. One dissent was that of Justice Stone in the well-known flag salute case,[3] in which he alone maintained a strict civil liberties position in the face of the justification for the compulsory salute which the rest of the Court found compelling. The other exception came in a case presenting the thorny question of taxability of trust income, and saw Reed alone voting for the government's contention.[4] Apart from these cases, however, the judicial reaction to a "government" issue was so consistent that it must be considered a definite factor in the Court's divisions of opinion.

Examining the 42 dissents of the 1939 Term from another point of view, we find 18 cases in which the Court was required to make a decision for or against "business." The issue was presented in many forms—the validity of a business tax, an alleged violation of the antitrust laws, the constitutionality of a federal or state regulatory scheme. But wherever the issue was present, the reaction pattern was consistent, support for business coming always from the conservative end of the Court. Specifically, there were 15 dissents by right-wingers taking the side of business, and three by liberals voting against a majority decision favorable to business. Again, in five cases during the 1939 term the Court was dealing with a "labor" issue, and here also the reaction was uniform. There were four conservative dissents to decisions favoring labor, and one dissent by Douglas and Black from a majority decision slightly weakening the effect of a N.L.R.B. order.

The 1939 dissents included seven cases in which state or local action was attacked as violating provisions of the federal Constitution; for example, state and local taxes were resisted as burdening interstate commerce or contrary to due process or infringing a privilege of national citizenship. Here the consistent policy of the Justices at the Black-Douglas end of the Court was to uphold state action, in line with the traditional liberal belief that state legislative powers should be left as unrestricted by federal constitutional limitations as possible. It may also be noted that an issue involving the extent of judicial review was raised in some form in four cases; the left-wing wanted to narrow review, and the right-wing opposed any narrowing. Public operation of a power system was an issue in one case; McReynolds opposed it.[5] The rights of a debtor under the Frazier-Lemke Act were involved in another case; a liberal minority voted in his favor.[6]

One or more of the seven issues just considered was present in every one of the cases where opinion was divided during the 1939 term. In other words, none of these cases appears to present a "purely legal" question, for in each instance the observer can find a facet of the case which might offer an opportunity for the decision to be influenced by judicial views as to desirable public policy. It is not contended, of course, that the decisions were motivated wholly by the personal views of the Justices, but the data clearly indicate that these views had a considerable effect in the process of making up the judicial mind.

It would be interesting to discuss the records of several of the individual Justices in the light of the information which this analysis has supplied. The case of the Court's new Chief Justice is particularly worthy of notice. The participation of Justice Stone in right-wing dissents may seem strange, in view of his reputation as one of the soundest and ablest liberals on the Court. Two explanations suggest themselves. One is that he has deviated slightly to the right in his views with the passage of time. The other is that he has maintained very nearly his original position, but that the Court has with recent appointments moved so substantially leftward that views which put Stone to the left of the Court ten years ago now occasionally leave him exposed in dissent on the right. Whatever the cause, the process appears to be accelerating, for Stone's dissents with the conservative group numbered three in the 1939 Term and six in the 1940 Term.

The general result of this study has been to emphasize the influence of personal attitudes in the making of judicial decisions and the interpretation of law. To prevent overemphasis on this point, it would be well to recall that even in a Court representing as wide a range of views as has been found during the last two terms, 71 per cent of the cases were decided by unanimous vote. Where there were divisions of opinion, however, they appear to be for the most part explicable in terms of the opinions of the respective judges on public policy. This conclusion hardly comes as a surprise. For few are likely to deny that Justices of the Supreme Court have always, to paraphrase Justice Frankfurter, "read the laws of Congress through the distorting lenses" ground by their own experience. On the other hand, there are many who agree that the Supreme Court's vision is better today than it has been for many years past.

Notes

1. This figure and the quotations following are taken from Francis D. Wormuth, "The Dilemma of Jurisprudence," *A.P.S.R.* 35 (1941), 44.

2. The cases are *Neuberger* v. *Commissioner of Internal Revenue*, 61 S.C. 97 (1940); and *Union Pacific R. Co.* v. *U.S.*, 61 S.C. 1064 (1941).

3. *Minersville School District* v. *Gobitis*, 310 U.S. 586 (1940).

4. *Helvering* v. *Fuller*, 310 U.S. 69 (1940).

5. *U.S.* v. *San Francisco*, 310 U.S. 16 (1940).

6. *Union Joint Stock Land Bank* v. *Byerly*, 310 U.S. 1 (1940).

37

A Psychological Analysis
of the Warren Court

Glendon Schubert

Much recent research in the decision-making of the United States Supreme Court has been characterized by a pronounced emphasis upon the invocation of sociopsychological theory and statistical methods of data processing in lieu of exclusive reliance upon the legal-historical theory and methods typical of most research in this field of study. Symbolic of this development is the increasing tendency of political scientists to consider constitutional law as an aspect of political behavior as well as a branch of law, and correspondingly, to study the subject matter as judicial behavior. Naturally, this recent work has evinced a preoccupation with unidimensional analysis, since it is less complicated to work with one variable than with many, and the experience so gained no doubt is a prerequisite to multivariate study. Nevertheless, students who remain committed to the more traditional workways in constitutional law are quite right in insisting, as they do, that most Supreme Court cases raise what at least appear prima facie to be many issues for decision, and that their more subjective and impressionistic mode of analysis retains the great virtue of not oversimplifying the rich complexity of many Supreme Court cases to the extent that inescapably seems to be required by the newer theories and methods. Clearly, further advances in the behavioral study of Supreme Court decision-making depend upon the development of multidimensional models of Court action, which will make possible the observation and measurement of interrelationships among the significant major variables that in combination provide the basis for an adequate explanation of the manifest differences in the voting and opinion behavior of the justices.

The purpose of this article is to describe one such multidimensional model of the Court, and to explain its theory and application to the empirical data of the most recent session of the United States Supreme Court, which terminated only a month prior to the time when this was written. Substantively, the purpose is to demonstrate that the psychological approach to be proposed leads to more significant, more comprehensible, and more valid insights into the political behavior of the Supreme Court than seem to be provided by the case-by-case approach—an approach that attempts to realize the same ends by the quite different means of a series of précis upon what are inevitably (since there must be some space limitations in professional journals) a fraction of the hundred-odd cases that the

Reprinted by permission from "The 1960 Term of the Supreme Court: A Psychological Analysis," *American Political Science Review* 56 (1962), 90–107. Most footnotes have been omitted.

Court decides nonunanimously on the merits each term. The specific hypothesis to be tested is that most of the *variance* in the voting behavior of the justices can be accounted for by the differences in their individual attitudes toward a small number of fundamental issues of public policy. These public policy issues constitute the variables of this study.

I. A Brief Description of the Model

Since both a general statement of the theory and a technical description of the method have been published elsewhere, only the essentials needed for comprehension of the substantive findings will be presented here. In accordance with modern psychometric theory which generalizes the basic stimulus-response point relationship, Supreme Court cases are treated as raw psychological data which embody the choices of the individual justices among a variety of stimuli. Each case before the Court for decision is conceptualized as being represented by a stimulus (j) point, which is located somewhere in a psychological space of the relevant dimensions, depending upon the number and intensity of issues that it raises. The combination of the attitudes of each justice toward these same issues also may be represented by an ideal (i) point, located in the same psychological space. In each decision of the Court, what is observed is the relationship between the i-point of each justice and the j-point for the case. The relationship that is measured is one of dominance; that is, whether the position of the i-point in the dimensions that define the space equals or exceeds, or is less than, the position of the j-point in these dimensions. Technically, an individual-compensatory composition model is assumed: for an i-point to dominate a j-point, it is not essential that the individual equal or exceed the stimulus on *all* of the relevant dimensions, since an individual may (in appropriate instances) be able to compensate for his deficiency on one (or more) dimensions by an excess on other dimensions. To take a specific example, let us assume a simple two-dimensional space, where the relevant dimensions are judicial attitudes toward "civilian control over the military" and "stare decisis." A justice like Clark, whose attitude toward the civilian control variable was relatively negative or unsympathetic, might nevertheless be induced to vote in support of this value in a particular decision, because his relatively positive attitude toward stare decisis might lead him to follow a recent precedent, even though he had disagreed with the decision establishing it. Thus, his deficiency (in relationship to the degree of support for civil liberties demanded by the later case) might be compensated for by his strongly pro-stare decisis views. Conversely, a justice like Frankfurter, whose attitude toward civilian control was more positive than Clark's, might nevertheless vote against this value because of his slight regard for the value of stare decisis.[1]

Next let us consider the conjoint relationship between the i-points of all nine justices, assuming full participation in the decision, and a particular j-point. Obviously, how the case will be decided will depend upon whether a majority or a minority of the i-points dominate the j-point. If a majority of i-points dominate, then the value or values raised by the case will be upheld or supported by the decision "of the Court"; and if, to the contrary, the j-point dominates a majority of the i-points, then the value or values raised by the case will be rejected—"the Court" will refuse to support them. To take a concrete example, let us assume the general value "civil liberty," and the specific question whether "the Fourteenth Amendment requires" the Supreme Court to reverse a state court conviction of a criminal defendant, based in part upon evidence procured as the result of an unreasonable search or seizure. According to the theory proposed, it would be assumed that the *i*-points of no more than three justices dominated the *j*-point representing this issue at the time of the decision in *Wolf* v. *Colorado,* and that no more than four did so throughout the following decade. As a consequence of Stewart's appointment and of Black's explicitly avowed shift in attitude toward this issue, a majority of *i*-points did dominate when the issue arose once again for disposition in *Mapp* v. *Ohio,* a decision announced on the closing decision day of the 1960 Term; and consequently, *Wolf* v. *Colorado* was overruled. Actually, the voting division in *Mapp* v. *Ohio* was 6–3, with Clark both supplying the extra favorable vote and writing the opinion of the Court; Clark's position should have occasioned no surprise, however, because it was in precise accord with the intention that he had announced seven years earlier when concurring in *Irvine* v. *California.* Clark considered himself bound by the *Wolf* precedent unless and until a majority could be formed that would agree to overrule that decision—an event that was forestalled for several more years, apparently, by Black's idiosyncratic blind spot for the Fourth Amendment.

We can now consider an operational definition of the Court's decision-making. In one dimension, the voting division of the Court is precisely determined by the intersection of the *j*-point with a line along which are arrayed the *i*-points of the justices. (This definition, it should be noted, is the one which applies for cumulative [or Guttman] scaling of Supreme Court cases.) In two dimensions, a decision is determined by the line orthogonal to the *j*-point vector; all justices whose *i*-points fall on the orthogonal line, or beyond it (in the positive direction of the variable) will vote in support of the value, and the remaining justices whose *i*-points lie on the negative side of the line will vote to reject it; while unanimous decisions occur, of course, when all *i*-points lie on, or on the positive side of, the orthogonal line, or else when all *i*-points lie on the negative side of this line. In three dimensions, the decision is determined by the plane which intersects the space orthogonally to the *j*-point vector; and more generally, in *r*-dimensions by a hyperplane of $r - 1$ dimensionality which intersects the *r*-dimensional space in a similar manner.

Thus, we conceive of both *i*-points representing the composite attitudes of individual justices, and *j*-points, representing the composite issues raised by individual cases, as sets of vectors terminating in points, each with a unique position in the same psychological space. Hereinafter we shall assume that this space is three-dimensional, since we shall work in three-space in the empirical application which follows. Cases in a set which raises questions of differing degrees of valuation about the same variable (e.g., sympathy for the constitutional claims of the right to counsel in state criminal trials) are located at various points in the space, but in an approximately linear relationship to each other; thus, each such point may be conceived of as lying upon or near a scale axis, representing the subvariable, which transects the space. Through the centroid of a set of scale axes, representing a set of civil liberties subvariables, would pass an axis representing a broadly defined heterogeneous major variable (such as "all civil liberties" issues for a given term); and this scale axis would follow the trace of the mean of the projections from all of the relevant *j*-points. But the *i*-points also project upon any scale axis; and therefore, a one-dimensional solution for the Court's decision-making function may be achieved by measuring the relationship between the projections from *j*-points and from *i*-points upon a scale axis representing any variable that is of interest. This, in effect, is precisely what is happening, in theory, when an analyst constructs a cumulative scale of a set of decisions that are postulated as pertaining to a single dominant variable, and positions the scale as an axis in the space. It is apparent that if the model is adapted for analysis invoking this particular definition of the decision-making function, as we shall do in the discussion which follows, the Court's decision-making is still being measured in unidimensional terms. But the model itself is multidimensional and, as we shall demonstrate, makes possible measurement of the interrelationship among several variables within a common frame of reference. . . .

In order to utilize the model that has been described, what we require are procedures to locate both i-points and j-points in three-dimensional space, and to measure the dominance relationship for any dyad, with each dyad consisting of a j-point and an i-point. Factor analysis affords a readily available technique for locating the set of i-points for a given set of decisions, such as a term of the Court, in a fixed spatial configuration. But the raw data come in a form that preclude the use of factor analysis, at least in the same manner, in order to locate the j-points. The reason for this is that, in a typical recent term, the Court divides in about a hundred decisions on the merits. Consequently it is possible to make a relatively large number of observations—about one hundred—of the location of a relatively small number of i-points—never more than nine. But more than nine observations of the location of any specific j-point are never possible, because there are never more than nine votes recorded in a single case. One hundred observations are ample to locate the i-points, by factor analytic techniques, with considerable precision; but nine observations are far too few to permit the same thing to be done for j-points. As we shall exemplify presently, factor analysis is essentially a statistical method for breaking down a correlation matrix into its principal component elements; and it can never be more reliable than the matrix upon which it works. No single Supreme Court decision contains enough votes to allow the computation of reliable correlation coefficients. If we had a hundred justices participating in the decision of each of, say, a dozen cases in the typical term, factor analysis could serve very well to locate a configuration of j-points, but it would then be incapable of locating the i-points. If there were a hundred justices participating in the decision of a hundred or more cases in each term, factor analysis could be used to locate both types of points with what ought to be good precision. This implies that the model here described may very well find application for study of the attitudes of United States senators or for state legislators, as well as for other smaller decision-making groups like the Supreme Court.

Although it is not possible to locate j-points in the space as precisely as i-points, at least by factor analysis, it is possible to locate *sets* of j-points in the same space with the i-points. This is done by cumulative scaling of sets of cases. Each cumulative scale measures the one-dimensional alignment of the attitudes of the justices toward a single variable. If most of the Court's decisions can be associated with a set of cumulative scales, and if the set of scales can be passed through the space as axes in such a way that the projections from the i-points on the scale axes are consistent with the alignments of the justices on the cumulative scales, then it will be assumed that the scale axes are indeed the counterparts of their analogue cumulative scales; and that the variance in the voting behavior of the justices is adequately accounted for by the manifest differences in the attitudes of the justices toward the cumulative scale variables. The procedure for fitting scales in the factor space will be explained in greater detail in connection with specific empirical data, in a later section of this article.

II.   The Universe of Raw Data

The sample of decisions to be analyzed consists of all cases in which the Supreme Court divided on the merits during the period of the 1960 Term, which extended from October 10, 1960, through June 19, 1961. Both formal and per curiam decisions accordingly are included, but unanimous and jurisdictional decisions were excluded. As Table 37-1 indicates, almost three-fourths of the Court's formal decisions were reached over the disagreement of one or more justices, while this was true of less than one-fourth of the per curiam decisions. These results were in line with previous experience. It has not been unusual either, in recent years, for the justices to disagree in a majority of their decisions on the merits, as they did during the 1960 Term. The average annual number of split decisions over the past fifteen terms was 97, and the average number of unanimous decisions on the merits was 79; in this respect, the 1960 Term was quite typical.

TABLE 37-1
Summary of Decisions on the Merits, 1960 Term

Decision	Formal	Per curiam	Totals
Split	87	12	99
Unanimous	34	41	75
Totals	121	53	174

For purposes of this study, each *case*, to which the Court had assigned a unique docket number and for which the Court had made a disposition on the merits, was a unit for voting analysis. As a unit of content, the docketed case offers the advantages of being specifically and uniquely identifiable, and of providing what with very rare exceptions is an unambiguous basis for voting attribution which can readily be replicated by other analysts. (Those familiar with earlier studies of judicial voting behavior will recognize that some scholars have worked with less explicit units of measurement, such as the "opinion of the Court" or the "decision" of the Court.) There are also disadvantages to the use of the case as a unit, but none relevant to the empirical data with which we presently are concerned.

For each case, one set of nine votes was counted. In each of eleven cases, one justice did not participate in the decision on the merits; and in one other, two justices did not. There were also two Federal Employers' Liability Act evidentiary cases and one Jones Act case in which Frankfurter, according to his custom, persisted in jurisdictional dissent at the time when his colleagues voted on the merits; these three jurisdictional dissents were classified as nonparticipations, for purposes of the present analysis. Eight votes could not be specified, in one case in which the Court divided equally, without opinion. After these nonparticipations and unspecifiable votes were deducted, a total of 867 votes remained; they constituted the basis for the factor analysis and the cumulative scaling.

III.   The Factor Analysis

Computation of the Correlation Matrix

The initial task in any factor analysis is the construction of a correlation matrix. In the present study, the correlation matrix was based upon a set of fourfold tables which, in

TABLE 37-2
Fourfold Table of Agreement-Disagreement, Douglas-Black, 1960 Term

		Black +	Black −	Totals
Douglas	+	41	5	46
	−	23	29	52
Totals		64	34	98

Note: The total of joint votes counted for this dyad is 98 rather than 99, although both Black and Douglas participated in all split decisions on the merits during this term, because of the lack of any objective basis for identifying the partition of the votes in the one case, already noted, in which the Court divided equally.

turn, were constructed directly from the 867 votes just described. These votes were tabulated to show the totals of agreement and disagreement with the majority, in the decision of each case, for every pair of justices. For any such pair, each case holds five possibilities: (1) both may agree in the majority; (2) both may agree in dissent; (3) the first member of the pair may vote with the majority, while the second dissents; (4) the second member of the pair may vote with the majority, while the first dissents; or (5) either or both members may fail to participate, in which event there is no score for the pair for that case. In the tabulation of votes for the factor analysis, no attention is paid to the substantive variables to which the decisions relate; the sole criterion for the attribution of votes in each case is agreement or disagreement with the majority.

It is most convenient to arrange the summary tabulation of agreement-disagreement, for each judicial dyad, in the form of a fourfold table such as Table 37-2. The table shows that Black and Douglas dissented together 29 times; this dis/dis $(-/-)$ cell is the one that contains the kind of information utilized in some earlier studies of "dissenting blocs" of the Court. Similarly, Black and Douglas agreed in 70 of these 98 sets of votes; this is the sum of the major or positive diagonal (i.e., the $+/+$ and the $-/-$ cells), and this is the kind of information that was the basis for the "interagreement" bloc analysis of the studies just cited. The weakness of these earlier approaches was that, by concentrating upon the *agreement* between pairs of justices, the analysts ignored what is at least an equally important aspect of judicial voting behavior, that is, the *ways in which justices disagree*. Table 37-2, for instance, shows that not only did Douglas and Black disagree in over a fourth of these decisions, they tended to disagree in a particular way. In over 80 percent of these instances of disagreement, it was Douglas who dissented while Black adhered to the majority. This finding certainly suggests that Douglas was more extreme in his dissenting behavior than Black (or, as we shall observe presently in Table 37-3, than any other member of the Court during this term). Moreover, the correlation coefficients, which are computed from the fourfold tables, are very sensitive to how votes are partitioned between the two cells of a diagonal, as well as to differences between the diagonals.

In order to measure precisely the relationship among the four cells of a fourfold table, phi correlation coefficients are computed.[2] In the correlation matrix shown in Table 37-3, phi ranges from $+.745$ (for Harlan and Frankfurter) to $-.602$ (for Douglas and Harlan). Harlan, therefore, was the most extreme justice in the range of his agreement and disagreement; and he voted most frequently the same as Frankfurter, and least often in agreement with Douglas.

Since there are nine justices on the Court, there are fourfold tables and correlation coefficients for each of the thirty-six dyads. For purposes of this study, all data were placed on punch cards, and both the computation of phi coefficients and the factor analysis were programmed for computer analysis. Since both matrices are symmetrical, and in order to conserve space, Table 37-3 presents the fourfold tables above the major diagonal, and the correlation coefficients below.

Before turning to the results of the factor analysis of the correlation matrix, some interesting findings may be observed from a mere inspection of Table 37-3. The most obvious is the sharp demarcation of the justices into what appear to be two opposing blocs. Douglas, Black, Warren, and Brennan all correlate positively with each other, and negatively with the five remaining justices. With the exception of Stewart's marginally negative correlation with Clark, these remaining five justices—Frankfurter, Harlan, Whittaker, Clark, and Stewart—all correlate positively with each other, and negatively with the first group. Stewart clearly was the most independent member of the Court in his voting behavior: his highest correlation with any other justice, in either direction, was less than .35; and his voting was almost perfectly independent, statistically, from what are otherwise the most marginal members of each group, since his correlation was approximately − .03 with both Brennan and Clark. As the fourfold tables indicate, Black and Warren often dissented together, as did Frankfurter or Harlan also; but neither Black nor Warren even joined either Frankfurter or Harlan in dissent. It is obvious that these two pairs of justices, and the respective groups with which each tended to associate, were in pretty sharp and basic disagreement over something; and unless we are prepared to accept the somewhat fatuous notion that they couldn't get together over the meaning or application of the principle of stare decisis, as some students of the Court seem to believe, then it may not be implausible to entertain the hypothesis that these groups may have been in disagreement about the social, economic, and political values that the Court upholds in its decisions.

The Factor Loadings

The initial product of a factor analysis is a set of derived correlations (or "loadings," as they customarily are called) which purport to measure the extent to which each element, of whatever has been associated in the correlation matrix, is related to the components or dimensions into which the basic correlation matrix has been broken down. In the present study, the elements are the justices, and the factor loadings purport to express the correlation of each justice with the basic underlying dimensions of the phi matrix. Although it is technically possible to extract as many factors as there are elements intercorrelated in the phi matrix—nine, in the instant case—only six factors actually were computed, and of these, only three will be used for purposes of testing the principal hypothesis. The reason for so limiting the number of factors is twofold: (1) the residual matrix, representing the amount of variance unaccounted for by the first three factors, was very small, and less, indeed, than the estimated error variance; and (2) most readers of the *American Political Science Review* are accustomed to thinking in terms of three-dimensional space, and three factors can be given a Euclidean graphical representation which accords with the spatial intuitions, and therefore the comprehension, of most readers.

The usual procedure in factor analysis is to rotate the orthogonal factor axes, which are the direct product of a complete centroid routine, to oblique positions that are presumed to correspond to some criterion related to empirical reality, and thus to make possible a

TABLE 37-3
Fourfold Tables and Phi Correlation Matrix, 1960 Term

	D		Bl		Wa		Br		S		C		Wh		F		H	
	+	−	+	−	+	−	+	−	+	−	+	−	+	−	+	−	+	−
D +			+41	5	42	4	44	2	31	14	23	22	20	26	16	23	20	25
−			−23	29	31	21	33	19	43	6	51	1	45	7	47	3	50	1
Bl +	.471				+61	3	58	6	41	19	40	23	32	32	31	26	37	26
−					−12	22	19	15	33	1	34	0	33	1	32	0	33	0
Wa +	.363		.655				+69	4	51	18	50	22	41	32	39	26	45	26
−							−8	17	23	2	24	1	24	1	24	0	25	0
Br +	.392		.403		.664				+57	16	55	21	45	32	44	25	49	26
−									−17	4	19	2	20	1	19	1	21	0
S +	−.230		−.337		−.195		−.029				+56	18	52	22	51	15	56	17
−											−15	4	11	9	10	9	11	8
C +	−.551		−.410		−.273		−.175		−.031				+56	18	55	14	59	14
−													−9	14	8	11	11	12
Wh +	−.455		−.474		−.367		−.319		.133		.331				+51	12	53	11
−															−12	14	17	15
F +	−.578		−.481		−.390		−.287		.228		.343		.348				+58	5
−																	−4	20
H	−.602		−.441		−.362		−.322		.171		.317		.315		.745			

Note: The justices are coded as follows: D (Douglas), Bl (Black), Wa (Warren), Br (Brennan), S (Stewart), C (Clark), Wh (Whittaker), F (Frankfurter), H (Harlan).

TABLE 37-4
Factor Loadings for Judicial Ideal-Points, 1960 Term

Justices	Factors		
	I	II	III
D	.754	.283	.170
Bl	.769	−.259	−.130
Wa	.699	−.456	.089
Br	.578	−.298	.291
S	−.289	.126	.363
Wh	−.571	.065	−.108
H	−.714	−.373	.226
F	−.736	−.338	.270
C	−.519	−.245	−.309

more meaningful psychological interpretation than would usually be possible if the orthogonal axes were retained.[3] The orthogonal axes have not been rotated in the present study, but for the reason that, contrary to the usual procedure, no reliance is placed upon the association of substantive meaning with the factors. Substantive meaning is associated, instead, with the scale axes which are passed through the space defined by the orthogonal factor axes; and thus the scale axes—which are oblique—perform the same function, for purposes of interpretation, that is usually accomplished by rotation of the orthogonal axes. The orthogonal axes are used, therefore, only as a set of reference axes to define the three-dimensional space in which the i-points of the justices and the j-points of the cases are located. And the factor loadings, shown in Table 37-4, function as Cartesian coordinates which locate the i-points of the justices in the factor space.

Factor loadings can vary, in principle, from $+1$ to -1; in practice, their variance is bounded by the extremity of the correlation coefficients upon which they are based. It will be observed that, on the average, the highest loadings (both positive and negative) are on the first factor, and that the mean magnitude of the third factor loadings is smallest. This is inherent in the centroid routine, which assumes that the first factor, to which the largest portion of the variance is attributed, is the most important factor, and so on. The loadings on the first factor range from a high of approximately $+.77$, for Black, to a low of $-.74$, for Frankfurter. Evidently, the justices are partitioned on the first factor into the same two groups that were manifest in the phi matrix; but evidently also the groupings on the second and third factors are quite different. Mere inspection of the factor matrix of Table 37-4 suggests that the multidimensional relationships among the justices are going to be somewhat different, and certainly more complex, than the simple bifurcation of a single dimension which will account for much, but not enough, of the variance in the voting behavior of the justices. For a fuller understanding than a single dimension—even when it is overwhelmingly the most important one—can afford, we must turn to an examination of relationships made possible by work with the three-dimensional factor space.

IV.   The Cumulative Scales

Cumulative scaling is a research operation completely independent of the factor analysis, and so may be undertaken before, at the same time, or after the factor analysis is completed. In cumulative (or Guttman) scaling, the same universe of raw data is used as for the factor analysis. But instead of tabulating votes by dyads and in terms of agreement with the majority, for scaling purposes votes are tabulated by cases, and are classified as being either in support of, or in opposition to, certain defined scale variables. The variables employed here were identified on the basis of experimental work in previous terms of the Warren Court. The basic procedures for cumulative scaling have been discussed elsewhere, although the format of Figures 37-1-3 differs somewhat in the presentation of results.

Consistent votes in support of the scale variable are denoted by the symbol x, and inconsistent positive votes by x̲. A blank space indicates a consistent negative vote, and the symbol − is used to signify an inconsistent negative vote. An asterisk signifies nonparticipation. Scale scores are simple functions of scale positions, and a justice's scale position is defined as being fixed by his last consistent positive vote. Where one or more nonparticipations separate a justice's consistent positive and negative votes, his scale position is assumed to be at the midpoint of the nonparticipation or nonparticipations, since it cannot be determined how he might have voted. A justice's scale score is computed by the formula:

$$s = \frac{2p}{n} - 1, \tag{1}$$

where s is his score, p his scale position, and n equals the number of cases in the scale. Scale scores, like correlation coefficients and factor loadings, can range in value from $+1$ to -1, with the significant difference in practice that scale scores frequently attain these extreme values, reflecting the extremity of attitude of several of the justices in each of the scales shown in Figures 37-1, 37-2, and 37-3.

The C Scale

Figure 37-1 is a cumulative scale of the fifty-one civil liberties cases that the Court decided by divided votes on the merits during the 1960 Term. In content, the C variable was defined broadly to include all cases in which the primary issue involved a conflict between personal rights and claims to liberty, and governmental authority. The number of cases included in the scale—over half of the total—was somewhat larger than in other recent terms; but the ranking of justices on the scale was very similar to that of the 1959 Term, and precisely the same as in 1958, which was Stewart's first term on the Court.

The scale accords with common knowledge that Douglas, Black, Warren, and Brennan are more sympathetic to civil liberties claims than the other members of the present Court. But there are definite gradations among the attitudes of these four "libertarian" justices toward the civil liberties claims of this term, and the scale distance separating Douglas and Brennan is just as great as the scale distance separating Whittaker and Clark. The mean rate of support for civil liberties claims of the four justices with high positive scale scores (the liberals on this issue) is 85 percent; the mean rate of opposition for the four justices with high negative scale scores (the conservatives on this issue) is 86 percent. This differentiation of the Warren Court into a set of liberal justices and a much more conservative group agrees with Pritchett's findings[4] for the Vinson Court, except that Frankfurter now appears as a conservative rather than as an exponent of "libertarian restraint."

It is certainly noteworthy that Douglas, over a wide range of specific issues, supported civil liberties claims in all except two out of fifty-one cases. His two inconsistent (and C −)

Figure 37-1 Judicial Attitudes Toward Civil Liberties, 1960 Term

Cases	D	Bl	Wa	Br	S	Wh	F	H	C	Totals
				1960 Term, C Scale Justices						
5/762	x									1–8
6/308	x									1–8
6/420	x									1–8
6/582	x									1–8
4778:200	x	x								2–7
5/265	x	x						*		2–6
4/507	—	x	x							2–7
4/611	—	x	x							2–7
5/458	x	—	x							2–7
4/388	x	x	x							3–6
3370:685	x	x	x							3–6
4839:122	x	x	x							3–6
5/381	x	—	x	x						3–6
4/372	x	x	x	x						4–5
4/426	x	x	x	x						4–5
5/43	x	x	x	x						4–5
5/301:70	x	x	x	x						4–5
5/301:179	x	x	x	x						4–5
5/399	x	x	x	x						4–5
5/431	x	x	x	x						4–5
6/36	x	x	x	x						4–5
6/82	x	x	x	x						4–5
6/117	x	x	x	x						4–5
4581:1	x	x	x	x						4–5
4623:12	x	x	x	x						4–5
4719:486	x	x	x	x						4–5
6/617	x	—	—	x	x					3–6
6/599	x	—	—	x	x		$\underline{x}$			4–5
4/587	x	x	x	—	x					4–5
4/479:14	x	x	x	x	x					5–4
4/479:83	x	x	x	x	x					5–4
5/85	x	x	x	x	x					5–4
5/551	x	x	x	x	x					5–4
6/1	x	x	x	x	x					5–4
4694:233	x	x	x	x	x					5–4
4842:161	x	x	x	x	x		$\underline{x}$			6–3
5/715	x	x	x	x	x				$\underline{x}$	6–3
4798:236	x	x	x	x	x				$\underline{x}$	6–3
4/631	x	x	x	x	x	x				6–3
5/312	x	x	x	x	x	x				6–3
6/213	x	x	x	x	x	x				6–3
6/418	x	x	x	x	*	x				5–3
4703:238	x	x	x	x	—	x				5–4
4754:4	x	x	x	x	x	x			$\underline{x}$	7–2
4577:669	x	x	x	x	—	x			$\underline{x}$	6–3
4/350	x	x	x	x	—	—	x	x		6–3
5/534	x	x	x	x	—	x	x	x		7–2
4/454	x	x	x	x	x	—	x	x		7–2
4687:181	x	x	x	x	x	—	x	x		7–2
5/610	x	x	x	x	x	x	x	x		8–1
5/167	x	x	x	x	x	x	—	x	x	8–1

221–236

Figure 37-1 Judicial Attitudes Toward Civil Liberties, 1960 Term *(Continued)*

					1960 Term, C Scale Justices					
Cases	D	Bl	Wa	Br	S	Wh	F	H	C	Totals
Totals										
Pros	49	43	43	38	20	10	7	6	5	221
Cons	2	8	8	13	30	41	44	44	46	236
Scale positions	51	47	45	39	25	13	6	6	1	
Scale scores	1.00	.84	.76	.53	−.02	−.49	−.76	−.76	−.96	

$$R = 1 - \frac{22}{403} = .945 \qquad S = 1 - \frac{23}{79} = .709$$

Note: In Figures 37-1, 37-2, and 37-3, cases are cited in either of two ways. Those decided prior to June 1961 are cited to the official *United States Reports:* the digit preceding the slash bar is the third digit of the volume number, and should be read as though preceded, in each case, by the digits 36; the number following the slash bar is the page cite; and if more than one case begins on the same page, a docket number follows the page cite, separated from it by a colon. Official citations are not available, at the time this is written, for cases decided during the final three weeks of the term; such cases are cited to Volume 29 of *United States Law Week, Supreme Court Section,* with a four-digit page number followed by the docket number.

Two coefficients appear at the bottom of each scale; they purport to measure the degree of consistency in the set of votes being scaled. R is Guttman's coefficient of reproducibility; .900 or better is convention-ally accepted as evidence to support the hypothesis that a single dominant variable has motivated the voting behavior of the justices in the set of cases comprising the sample. S is Menzel's coefficient of scalability; it provides a more rigid standard than R, because S (unlike R) does not capitalize upon the spurious contribution to consistency that arises from the inclusion in the scale of either cases or justices with extreme marginal distributions. Menzel has suggested that the appropriate level of acceptance for S is "somewhere between .60 and .65"; the scales presented in Figures 37-1, 37-2, and 37-3 are well above the suggested minimal levels of acceptability for both R and S. . . .

votes both came in cases that raised technical questions of procedure relating to the statutory rights of federal criminal defendants, in cases where another variable (J −: Supreme Court deference to lower courts) also was present. Douglas was the only justice to dissent alone against C − decisions of the Court; and his four solitary C + dissents identify him as the justice most sympathetic to civil liberties claims. At the opposite extreme was Clark, who found only five civil liberties claims, out of the total of fifty-one, sufficiently persuasive to gain his vote. Moreover, four of Clark's five C + votes were inconsistencies, suggesting that in these cases he may have been motivated by his attitudes toward other variables than C; there is, of course, little empirical basis for assuming that all justices perceive all issues raised by cases in the same way, or that any justice's voting behavior will be perfectly consistent. The Guttman model assumes that if in a particular scale most respondents are highly consistent most of the time, it is reasonable to infer that they are predominately motivated by their differential attachments to a common value. And it is in precise accord with the assumptions of the "individual-compensatory compo-sition model," mentioned earlier, that a justice may, in some decisions, compensate for his lack of sympathy for, say, civil liberties by his strong attachment to other appropriate values that he may perceive to be present in the decisions. This theory seems to provide a plausible explanation for Clark's inconsistencies. His most inconsistent votes, for instance, came in two cases, *Burton* v. *Wilmington Parking Authority* and *Mapp.* v. *Ohio,* where he joined C + majorities against the dissents of Harlan, Frankfurter, and Whittaker. The first case involved racial discrimination in a restaurant in a publicly owned building; and the second was the decision, already mentioned, which overruled *Wolf* v. *Colorado.* In both cases, Clark's strong attachment to stare decisis appeared to overcome his basically C −

attitude sufficiently to cause him to support the majority, although such a consideration obviously did not forestall the more activist conservatives from voting as dictated by their convictions about libertarian claims.

The key decision-maker in C cases during the 1960 Term, however, was Stewart, whose propensity to function as the swing man in an otherwise well-balanced Court was sufficiently obvious to attract journalistic comment. Although Stewart tied with Clark for inconsistency with four such votes, he nevertheless voted consistently over 90 percent of the time, and his scale score of $-.02$ indicates the close balance of his voting on civil liberties issues. Stewart was in the majority far more often than any of his colleagues, dissenting in only seven of the fifty cases in which he participated; and in nineteen 5–4 decisions, Stewart's vote was determinative. Slightly less than half (43 percent) of the cases on the scale were decided C +, but the failure of the cases to break evenly cannot be attributed to Stewart. The division between C plus and minus decisions would have corresponded precisely to Stewart's scale position, except for the inconsistent negative votes of Black, Warren, and Brennan, in the bottom three C − cases near the middle of the scale. Brennan's inconsistency is of no particular interest; it occurred in a routine case of statutory interpretation involving the imposition of multiple sentences upon a federal criminal defendant. But the Black and Warren inconsistencies appeared in two of the "Sunday Closing Law Cases," *Gallagher* v. *Crown Kosher Super Market* and *Braunfeld* v. *Brown,* both decided on May 29, 1961. Many dispassionate observers will agree that the Black and Warren votes in these cases to uphold the constitutionality of the Massachusetts and Pennsylvania "blue laws," which upheld the principle of majority transgression of both the religious and the economic claims of the defendants, were clearly illiberal; and the fact that such votes appear as inconsistencies in the C scale should enhance confidence in the proposition that the C scale provides an adequate general measure of the civil libertarian sympathies of the justices.

The E Scale

One finding, which has resulted from applying the research approach of this paper to a much longer period—fifteen terms—has been that political scientists have been living with a somewhat distorted image of the Court during the past two decades. The pronounced emphasis upon the Court's civil liberties decisions, reflecting, perhaps, the no-doubt laudable bias with which students of the Court approached their subject, has tended to obscure the significance of the Court's decisions relating to *economic* liberalism. The usual impression that one receives from reading the literature is that the traumatic events of 1937 resolved the problems of economic liberalism for our generation; and that since that time, the economic liberalism of the New Deal has motivated at least a clear majority of successively later Courts in supplanting the economically conservative precedents established by a majority of the "Nine Old Men" and their predecessors of the Taft Court. The real issues of public policy on the Court, it has seemed, have related to civil rights and liberties. But a careful and systematic examination of all of the Court's decisions on the merits contradicts the impressions that the Court is preoccupied with questions of constitutional interpretation, and that statutory interpretation—which the economic cases characteristically involve—is a policy-making function of lesser importance to the Court.

Taking the decade of the 1950s as the most relevant recent sample, there were more cases on the E scale than on the C scale in half of the terms. Specifically, there were more

E than C cases in both the 1958 and 1959 Terms, so the clear preponderance of C cases in the 1960 Term is atypical. Counting, of course, is no substitute for thinking; and a quantitative measure of the relative importance of the Court's decision-making on the issues of civil liberty and economic liberalism does not foreclose a qualitative judgment on this question. But the mere assumption that constitutional questions are qualitatively more important than statutory questions is no proof; and absent acceptable criteria in terms of which it can be demonstrated that the Court's civil liberties questions generally— not just the School Segregation Cases—have had a greater impact upon American society during the past two decades than have the Court's decisions involving economic issues, it does not seem too unreasonable to accept at least tentatively findings based upon quantitative criteria.

In content, the E scale is just as broadly and heterogeneously defined as the C scale. The basic value that permeates the issues of economic liberalism is that of favoring claims of underprivileged economic interests as against those of affluence and monopoly power. Thus, E + is prolabor in union-management conflicts, pro-small business as against big business, pro-competition and antioligopoly, pro-governmental economic regulation "in the public interest" of special, "private" economic interests, and, most characteristically, economic liberalism means to favor the claims of injured railroad workers and seamen against their corporate employers and insurers.

As Figure 37-2 shows, the four justices who are civil libertarians are also the ones who score highest on the E scale. But the remaining five members of the Court vote quite differently upon the two kinds of issues. Clark, who was least sympathetic to civil liberties, appears in the role of an economic liberal, scoring only slightly lower than Warren and Brennan, and definitely emerging as the fulcrum of the Court on E issues. Nor is this a matter of recent conversion; Clark also ranked fifth (and again, after Douglas, Black, Warren, and Brennan) on the E scales for both the 1958 and 1959 Terms. Neither fact should be surprising; Clark's judicial voting record is quite consistent with the political position of the Texas "Fair Dealer" who served as Truman's Attorney General at the time of his appointment to the Court.

Stewart scores much lower on the E scale than on C; and Whittaker, who was the most moderate of the four C − conservatives, is identified as the anchor man of the Court in terms of his economic conservativism. Of particular interest is the fact that Frankfurter, who was tied with Harlan at the next to the bottom rank on C, also is in the second lowest rank on E. If we consider, as may seem intuitively justifiable, that the C and E scales taken together provide a good test of liberalism as a generalized range of attitudes, then it seems quite clear that Frankfurter was the most illiberal justice in the 1960 Term: he voted only nine out of sixty-seven times in support of the liberal position. The necessary inference that one would draw, on the basis of cumulative scaling theory, from Frankfurter's low scale scores of −.76 on C and of −.68 on E is that he voted conservatively because of his conservative attitudes. Any inference must be evaluated, however, in the light of Mr. Justice Frankfurter's own explanations, frequently proffered, which contradict the assumption that, for him at least, these two scales each involve a single dominant variable. According to Frankfurter, who often has admitted his passionate personal sympathy for the down-trodden and oppressed among the Court's litigants, many of his illiberal votes in these cases must be attributed to his deference to federalism or to judicial restraint, or to the wise judges who sit on lower courts of the present or the Supreme Court of the past.

**Figure 37-2 Judicial Attitudes Toward
Economic Liberalism, 1960 Term**

Cases	D	Bl	Wa	Br	C	H	S	F	Wh	Totals
				1960 Term, E Scale Justices						
6/169	x									1–8
5/320	x	x								2–7
4/441	x	x						*		2–6
4614:284	x	x								2–7
4618:306	x	x								2–7
4618:307	x	x								2–7
4713:392	x	x								2–7
4743:97	x	x	x	x						4–5
5/705	x	x	x	x				*		4–4
4/325	x	x	x	x	x			*		5–3
4/520	x	x	x	x	x			x̲		6–3
5/1:45	x	x	x	x	x				x̲	6–3
5/1:46	x	x	x	x	x				x̲	6–3
5/336	x	x	x	x	x				x̲	6–3
6/316	x	x	x	x	*	*				4–3
6/276	—	x	x	x	x	x				5–4
5/731	x	x	x	x	x	x ˌ				6–3
4/642	—	x	x	x	x	x	*			5–3
5/160	x	x	x	x	x	—	x	*		6–2
5/667:64	x	x	x	x	—	x	x	*		6–2
5/667:85	x	x	x	x	—	x	x	*		6–2
5/695	x	x	x	x	—	x	x	*		6–2
5/705	x	x	x	x	—	x	x	*		6–2
5/651	x	x	x	x	x	x	x	*		7–1
6/28	x	x	x	—	x	x	—	x		6–3
										113–100
Totals										
Pros	23	24	18	17	11	9	6	2	3	113
Cons	2	1	7	8	13	15	18	14	22	100
Scale positions	25	24	18	18	16	10.5	7.5	4	0	
Scale scores	1.00	.92	.44	.44	.28	−.16	−.40	−.68	−.100	

$$R = 1 - \frac{13}{196} = .934 \quad S = 1 - \frac{13}{49} = .735$$

The F Scale

The third most important variable, in recent terms, has been the F scale, which deals with monetary conflicts of interest between private individuals and government. Thus, F + means to uphold the position of the government (national, state, or local) in tax and eminent domain cases, and in other matters where fiscal claims are at issue. In a sense, therefore, F is a closer analogue to C than is E, since C also is concerned with conflicts of interest between private individuals and governmental authority. But an examination of the voting and opinion behavior of the justices makes it apparent that for *most* of them, the issues of the F scale are more closely related to issues of economic liberalism than of civil liberties. This is hardly surprising, since F is differentiable from E primarily in terms of

**Figure 37-3 Judicial Attitudes Toward
Governmental Fiscal Claims, 1960 Term**

Cases	Bl	Wa	C	Br	F	H	S	Wh	D	Totals
	1960 Term, F Scale Justices									
4/443	x									1–8
5/624	x	x						x̲		3–6
4811:288	x	x	x	x	x					5–4
4/361	x	x	x	x	x	x				6–3
5/467	x	x	x	x	x	x	*			6–2
4/310	x	x	x	x	x	x	x			7–2
4469:533	x	x	x	x	x	x	*	x		7–1
4/289	x	x	x	x	x	x	x	x		8–1
4/446	x	x	x	x	x	x	x	x		8–1
5/753	x	x	x	x	x	x	x	x		8–1
3381:629	x	x	x	x	x	x	x	x		8–1
3381:843	x	x	x	x	x	x	x	x		8–1
4/410	x	x	—	—	x	x	x	x		6–3
6/99	x	x	x	x	x	—	x	x	x	8–1
										89–35
Totals										
Pros	14	13	11	11	12	10	8	9	1	89
Cons	0	1	3	3	2	4	4	5	13	35
Scale positions	14	13	12	12	12	11	9.5	8	1	
Scale scores	1.00	.86	.71	.71	.71	.57	.36	.14	−.89	

$$R = 1 - \frac{3}{53} = .943 \qquad S = 1 - \frac{4}{23} = .826$$

the parties whose interests are in conflict. Yet this difference in the identity of the parties may make a considerable difference to particular justices, depending upon how far they regard the government as a fiscal trustee acting in the "public interest" of the commonwealth, or as the largest single combination of monopolistic economic power.

The F variable was discovered in the process of empirically examining the voting patterns in several preceding terms. Several justices, and in particular Douglas, voted differently in some cases to which the government was a party from their behavior in most other cases involving economic issues. As Figure 37-3 shows, Douglas and Black, who ranked first and second on both of the liberalism scales, are at opposite ends of the F scale. In all fourteen cases which comprise the scale for this term, Black voted to uphold the position of the government, while Douglas voted in the opposite way in all except one case—which would have been decided unanimously, and thus would not have appeared upon the scale, if it had not been for Harlan's inconsistent vote. On the other hand, Frankfurter, who ranked near the bottom of the Court on the C and E scales, is tied with Brennan and Clark for the fourth rank on the F scale. Clearly, the ranking of the justices on F is different from their rankings on either C or E. Moreover, the government won twelve of these fourteen cases, and Douglas was the only member of the Court who did not vote to support the position of the government in at least a majority of the cases.

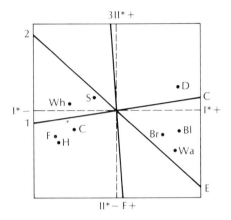

a.   Reference axes I and II

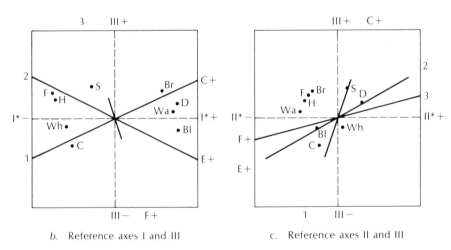

b.   Reference axes I and III   c.   Reference axes II and III

Figure 37-4. Scale axes and the judicial point configuration in the orthogonal factor space.
Note: In part *a,* the direction of orthogonal factor axes extracted by the complete centroid method is arbitrary; the asterisks following the identifying numbers for the first and second axes (i.e., I* and II*) signify that the polarity of these two axes was reversed to facilitate uniformity in inter-term comparisons in the larger study to which this article relates.

In terms of content, six of these cases raised questions of national taxation; four were state or local tax cases; and the remaining four were concerned with fiscal claims against the national government: one in eminent domain, one in tort, and two others. It is convenient to postpone, until the next section of this paper where it can be discussed in the context of Figure 37-4 the question *why* Douglas voted more often in the company of Whittaker and Stewart, than with Black and Warren, on the issues comprising the F scale.

This scale does not meet one of the recommended minimal standards for a Guttman scale, in that fewer than ten of the cases include two or more dissenting votes. But this requirement of Guttman scaling was established in order to avoid the spurious inflation of the coefficient R; and . . . the coefficient S is computed in a way that precludes that possibility. Since the value of S is quite high (.83, or about .20 above the acceptability level), and the ranking of the justices is similar to those of the immediately preceding terms, it seems justifiable to consider F to be scalable for this term, and to accept the scale.

The Minor Scale Variables

In addition to the three major variables so far discussed, three other minor variables have been tentatively identified on the basis of similar research in other recent terms of the Court. These include A (judicial activism in reviewing the decisions of the Congress, the president, and administrative agencies); N (federalism, and conflict between the national and state governments); and J (the supervisory authority of the Supreme Court over the decision-making of lower courts). Too few cases have been associated with any of these variables in recent years, to permit scaling them. In the 1960 Term there were four cases on A, two on N, two on J, besides the one 4-4 decision in which the votes were not identified. Therefore, ninety-one of the ninety-nine split decisions of the 1960 Term are included on the scales of the three major variables; and together, the C, E, and F scales account for the variance in the voting behavior of the justices in 91 percent of the decisions of the Term.

V.   Scale Axes in the Factor Space

The next step is to position the scale axes, which are considered to be the psychological analogues of the cumulative scales, in the space defined by the factorial reference axes. It will be recalled that the configuration of i-points for the justices is uniquely determined by the set of factor loadings given in Table 37-4. The problem now is to determine whether it is possible to pass a set of axes through the factor space in such a manner that the rankings of the projections, from the i-points onto the axes, are equivalent, in a statistically acceptable sense, to the rankings of the justices on the scale axes. What is required mathematically in order to accomplish this are sets of weights which will determine the position of the axes in the space, and the points on each axis where the projections from the i-points fall. Given such data, it will then be possible to compare the rankings of the justices, on the cumulative scales, with the rankings of the projections from their i-points on the counterpart scale axes.

It is helpful to prepare a set of two-dimensional plots of the i-points against the reference axes, similar to Figure 37-4 but without the scale axes. Initial estimates of weights can be made from an examination of such two-dimensional plots. More precise determination of a set of acceptable weights requires mathematical analysis of the factor matrix of Table 37-4, and the use of a calculating machine. The distance from the origin of the factor space to the point which is closest to a given i-point, on any scale axis, is computed by the formula,

$$d = \frac{\alpha x + \beta y + \gamma z}{(\alpha^2 + \beta^2 + \gamma^2)^{1/2}}, \tag{2}$$

where d is the distance from the origin to the point on the scale axis where it is orthogonal to the projection from the i-point; $x, y,$ and z are coordinates of the factorial reference axes

TABLE 37-5
Reference Axis Coordinates, Coefficients, and Cosines for Scale Axes

Scale axes	C 1	E 2	F 3
Coordinates/coefficients			
I/α	1.00	1.00	.08
II/β	.15	$-.86$	-1.00
III/γ	.43	$-.47$	$-.25$
Cosines			
Figure 37-4a	$+08\frac{1}{2}°$	$-40\frac{1}{2}°$	$-85\frac{1}{2}°$
Figure 37-4b	$+23\frac{1}{2}°$	$-25°$	$-72°$
Figure 37-4c	$+71°$	$-151\frac{1}{2}°$	$-166°$

for the i-point; and α, β, and γ are the coefficients which determine the position of the scale axis in the three-dimensional factor space. The same set of coefficients also provides the reference axis coordinates for the positive terminus of the scale axis.

The positions in which the scale axes have been placed in Figure 37-4 do not necessarily constitute a uniquely "best" fit to the configuration of i-points; but it is assumed that as defined in Table 37-5 and shown in Figure 37-4 they furnish an appropriate and approximately correct solution. One way to visualize this solution is to think of a cone intercepting a relatively quite small circular area on the surface of a unit sphere; any axis lying within the cone will array the projections from i-points so as to produce the same set of rankings of the justices as will be produced by any other axis within the cone.

The three plots of Figure 37-4 may be thought of as three views of a cube: Figure 37-4a is a top view, Figure 37-4b is a side view and Figure 37-4c is an end view. With relationship to reference axis I, the C scale axis enters from the lower right octant of the cube, passes through the origin, and emerges at the end through the upper left octant. The E scale axis passes downward and to the right of I. Reference axis I, it should be noted, is approximately the centroid, or arithmetic mean, of the C and E scale axes. The C axis clearly passes closest to Douglas, who also appears to have the most extreme projection on the positive segment of the axis. (Such a projection would correspond to Douglas' position with the highest score on the C cumulative scale.) Black, Warren, and Brennan project upon the positive segment of the C axis too, but we cannot be certain from an examination of Figure 37-4 precisely what the sequence of their rankings will be. Stewart clearly will project upon the C axis somewhere near the origin, which means that his "loading" on the axis will be close to zero. And the remaining four justices all will project upon the negative segment of the C axis, corresponding to their negative scores on the C cumulative scale.

Douglas, Black, Warren, and Brennan all will project positively upon the E axis, although it looks as though Douglas will rank lower on the axis than he does on the cumulative scale. Clark, who ranked fifth on the E cumulative scale, also will project to the fifth position on the E axis; and the remaining justices will project negatively, corresponding to their negative scale scores for this variable.

Douglas is somewhat separated from the other three so-called libertarians, and the reason for this becomes apparent when we consider the F scale axis, which cuts across the center of the space to emerge through the front face, with only slight deviation toward the end (at I +) and downward. Particularly in Figure 37-4a, which includes the two most important dimensions, it can be seen that the relationship of the F axis to the C and E axes is such that the justices who project upon the negative segment of F are Stewart and Whittaker, who have the most negative projections on E, and Douglas, who has the most positive loading on C, in these two dimensions. This suggests that F presents issues that pull together the justices who project at opposite extremes on the two liberalism scales. Douglas, in other words, might vote in opposition to governmental fiscal claims because of a strong and generalized antagonism to governmental regulation and control; this could help to explain the extremity of his support for civil liberties claims, which are also claims of private persons in opposition to governmental regulation and control. Whittaker and Stewart, on the other hand, might vote F − because of their strong economic conservativism, and their corresponding sympathy for "free enterprise" and antipathy for public fiscal controls. The converse argument would explain why the remaining justices all would project positively on the F axis. Economic liberalism, as understood by Black, Warren, and Brennan, frequently involves support of governmental regulation and control "in the public interest"; and both liberals and conservatives agree that taxation is necessary to support positive programs of governmental regulation of the economy. Douglas' action appears to have been reciprocated by Frankfurter, Harlan, and Clark, whose support of the government against claims of personal right seems to carry over to the support of the government against claims of private fiscal right. In any event, the position of the F axis in Figure 37-4 is such that, from a statistical and geometric point of view, F appears to be essentially orthogonal to—that is independent of—the C axis, and moderately correlated positively with the E scale. The suggested psychological explanation is at least not inconsistent with the mathematical relationships that are evident in the data.

VI.   A Test of the Basic Hypothesis

The principal hypothesis underlying this study is that differences in the attitudes of the justices toward the basic issues raised by the cases that the Court decides account for the differences in their voting. In short, Supreme Court justices vote as they do because of their attitudes toward the public policy issues that come before them. We are now in a position to make a statistical test of this hypothesis.

The i-points of the justices are separated in the factor space because of variance in the extent of majority participation of individual justices; but the factor analysis routine knows absolutely nothing about the subject matter of the values to which the decisions relate. The relative degrees of support by the justices of the key substantive issues can be determined by cumulative scaling; but cumulative scaling is a unidimensional measurement device, and each such scale is based upon a different universe of content, and is quite independent *methodologically* (as distinguished from psychologically) from every other scale. Moreover, the cumulative scale data are inadequate to permit the recovery of the configuration of the i-points in multidimensional space. We shall assume, therefore, that if the cumulative scales can be reconstituted as a set of scale axes whose position is consistent with the configuration of i-points in the factor space, then the attitudinal differences of the justices on the cumulative scales account for the variance in the voting behavior of the justices, which is represented by the spatial separation of their ideal-points in the multidimensional factor space. If the correspondence between the set of cumulative scales and their scale axis analogues can be established in accordance with accepted procedures of

TABLE 37-6
Correlation of Judicial Ranks on Scales and Scale Axes

C				E				F			
Axis	Ranks		Scale	Axis	Ranks		Scale	Axis	Ranks		Scale
.791	1 D	1	1.00	.308	4* D	1	1.00	.341	2* Bl	1	1.00
.614	2 Bl	2	.84	.752	1 Bl	2	.92	.474	1* Wa	2	.86
.609	3 Wa	3	.76	.749	2 Wa	3½	.44	.272	3 C	4	.71
.599	4 Br	4	.53	.498	3 Br	3½	.44	.263	4 Br	4	.71
−.104	5 S	5	−.02	−.116	5 C	5	.28	.205	6* F	4	.71
−.553	6 Wh	6	−.49	−.357	6 H	6	−.16	.251	5* H	6	.57
−.610	7 F	7½	−.76	−.406	7 S	7	−.40	−.232	8* S	7	.36
−.612	8 H	7½	−.76	−.409	8 F	8	−.68	−.081	7* Wh	8	.14
−.627	9 C	9	−.96	−.411	9 Wh	9	−1.00	−.256	9 D	9	−.89
Rank correlation coefficient (tau)			.986				.901				.870
Significance level, 1-tailed (p)			<.000025				.00012				.00043

* Inconsistent rankings.

statistical proof, then we shall have proved, in a mathematical sense, that the justices of the Supreme Court vary in their voting behavior according to the differences in their attitudes toward the scale variables.

Table 37-6 presents a comparison of the cumulative scale scores, and the distances along the counterpart scale axes at which the i-points project (as determined by formula 2), together with the corresponding sets of rankings, for all justices on each of the three major variables. Although both scale scores and axis loadings range in value, in principle, from $+1$ to -1, so that some meaning can be attached to direct comparisons of pairs of corresponding scores and loadings, it will be recalled that, for mathematical reasons relating to the marginal distributions of the fourfold tables, the intervals on the two types of continua are not genuinely commensurable. Moreover, it has been determined experimentally that the error variance in the factor analysis routine is usually around 10 percent; while the error variance in the cumulative scales is only slightly less; and there are other sources of error variance implicit in the general method. Therefore, it seems reasonable to employ the nonparametric rank correlation test for the purpose of making the comparison. In spite of the seeming precision of coefficients carried to the third decimal place, it would be fatuous to pretend that the measurement employed in this study can hope to be more than a rough approximation of empirical reality.

As Table 37-6 indicates, there are no inconsistencies in the two sets of rankings for C. The correlation coefficient is less than $+1.00$ because of the tie in the scale scores of Frankfurter and Harlan, which increased very slightly the probability of perfect agreement with another set of rankings. The correspondence between the two sets of rankings for E also is perfect, except for Douglas, whose loading on the scale axis is much too low to correspond well with his maximal scale score. We can readily observe, from Figure 37-4, that with the point configuration given by the factor analysis, it would be impossible to position the E axis in such a way as to accommodate both Douglas' position, and those of the remaining justices. It has, therefore, seemed preferable to position the E axis in the way that best reflects the attitudinal alignment of the other eight justices, and to consider

Douglas' *i*-point to be located inconsistently with his manifest attitude toward E. There are several possible explanations for Douglas' apparent inconsistency. The problem might be one of error variance, since the factor routine knows nothing of Guttman scale inconsistencies, and Douglas' two E − inconsistencies would tend to pull him below Black, at least, in projection on E, in the attribution of variance by the centroid factor routine; to this we could add the imponderable effect of the error variance inherent in the factor analysis itself. But an alternative psychological explanation might be that the *i*-point configuration is correct, and that it *is* inconsistent for a justice, who is as hostile to governmental fiscal control as Douglas, at the same time to be the Court's strongest supporter of claims of economic liberalism.

The two sets of rankings for F are generally in close accord, since a tau of .87 is considered to be very high. There are three reversed pairs in the axis rankings: Black and Warren, Frankfurter and Harlan, and Stewart and Whittaker. Reference to Figure 37-3 shows that the reversal, for each of these pairs, was occasioned by the difference of a single vote; and the value of tau was lowered by the triple tie in the scale ranks. It seems quite likely that the F scale, which is marginally acceptable in any event, is based upon too few (and too extreme) cases to constitute an adequate sampling of the attitudes of the justices toward this value; and that a scale based upon twice as many cases might result in a much closer correspondence between the cumulative scale and the point configuration. In other words, it seems most likely that in the case of F, the inconsistency between the two sets of rankings should be attributed to the inadequacies of the scale, rather than to errors in the point configuration. This question could be resolved only by an examination of the justices' voting behavior in a term in which they chose to accept for decision a considerably larger number of cases dealing with the issue of governmental fiscal powers than they have dealt with in recent years; or, as might well be done, by pooling the data for several terms of the Court.

Nevertheless, the correlation between all three sets of rankings is very high, with or without the above explanations. From a statistical point of view, it should be noted that the probabilities shown in Table 37-6 relate to the probability of producing, by chance alone, the indicated congruence between any *one* scale and the point configuration. The prospect of chance replication of as good a fit for all three scales simultaneously, with the same fixed point configuration, is of course very much more remote; indeed, the joint probability, which is the product of the three discrete probabilities, is a truly astronomical number: $< .0^{11}129$, or approximately one chance in a trillion. It seems warranted, under these circumstances, to accept the hypothesis that the variance in the voting behavior of the justices during the 1960 Term can be adequately accounted for by the differences in their attitudes toward the fundamental issues of civil liberty, economic liberalism, and governmental fiscal authority.

VII.   The Psychological Distance Separating the Justices

Taking the judicial ideal-points in the factor space as reasonably adequate symbolizations of the respective attitude syndromes of the individual justices, we can use them to examine one final question. Discussion about the justices frequently revolves around such questions as which ones tend to share the "same point of view," and which ones are "furthest apart" in their thinking. The factor space provides a convenient basis for objective measurement of the psychological distance which separates each justice from each of the others.

Since the measurement of these psychological distances is purely mathematical, we shall carry it out in five-dimensional space. This will afford a slightly more accurate basis for measurement than the three-dimensional space depicted in Figure 37-4, since the fourth and fifth factors will permit us to consider, presumably, the effect of the minor variables (such as A, N, and J) which, although not scalable in the Guttman sense, nevertheless must be considered to be a part of the attitude syndrome of each justice. The psychological distance will be measured on the same scale as that employed for the three-dimensional factor space: along orthogonal reference axes, each of which extends from -1 to $+1$. The standard formula for computing the distance between any two points in orthogonal five-space is:

$$d_{(i_1 - i_2)} = [(v_1 - v_2)^2 + (w_1 - w_2)^2 + (x_1 - x_2)^2 + (y_1 - y_2)^2 + (z_1 - z_2)^2]^{1/2}, \qquad (3)$$

where d is the distance, i_1 and i_2 are the ideal-points of a pair of justices, and v, w, x, y, and z are the coordinates (or "loadings") of the justices on factors I-V. Much more simply, one can use the computing formula

$$d = 1 - \phi, \qquad (4)$$

where phi (ϕ) is the correlation between the two points.

The result of computations according to formula (3) are shown in Table 37-7. Harlan and Frankfurter are by far the closest two justices, in terms of their attitudes toward the policy issues that the Court decided in the 1960 Term; they are separated by a distance of only .14 in the five-dimensional factor space. Contrary to what even many close observers of the work of the Court seem to believe, however, it is Warren and Brennan—not Douglas and Black—who are next most similar in attitude, at a distance of .42. In fact, there are five other pairs (Wh-C, .52; Bl-Wa, .53; Wh-S, .57; Wh-F, .67; and Wh-H, .70) with "ideational identity" closer than that of Douglas and Black, who are separated by a distance of .75. On the other hand, the greatest difference in attitude is that between Douglas and Black, on the one hand, and Frankfurter and Harlan, on the other; the average distance separating these two pairs of justices is 1.60. Moreover, Douglas, Black, Warren, and Brennan all agree that Frankfurter and Harlan are the justices whose point of view is most different from their own; and, conversely, Harlan, Frankfurter, Whittaker, Clark, and Stewart all agree that Douglas and Black are the justices most distant psychologically from themselves.

TABLE 37-7
Attitudinal Distances among Judicial Ideal-Points, 1960 Term

	D	Bl	Wa	Br	S	C	Wh	F	H
D		.75	.93	.83	1.21	1.53	1.44	1.63	1.63
Bl	.75		.53	.80	1.30	1.47	1.44	1.58	1.54
Wa	.93	.53		.42	1.18	1.38	1.39	1.52	1.50
Br	.83	.80	.42		1.02	1.27	1.29	1.42	1.44
S	1.21	1.30	1.18	1.02		.93	.57	.78	.82
C	1.53	1.47	1.38	1.27	.93		.52	.80	.85
Wh	1.44	1.44	1.39	1.29	.57	.52		.67	.70
F	1.63	1.58	1.52	1.42	.78	.80	.67		.14
H	1.63	1.54	1.50	1.44	.82	.85	.70	.14	

If we seek an "average" justice whose point of view best typifies that of the Court as a whole, he is clearly Stewart at an average distance of .98. The variation of Stewart's separation from his colleagues also is confined to the smallest range. Such a finding is perfectly consistent, of course, with the findings of scale analysis, and with the configuration shown in the three-dimensional space of Figure 37-4. In similar accord with expectations is the finding that the most atypical justice was Douglas who, separated by an average distance of 1.24 from his colleagues, entertained the most generally extreme views of any of the justices.

Although Stewart and Clark are adjacent to each other in the two-dimensional matrix of Table 37-7 since the pattern shown is the most generally consistent one, these two justices are not very close to each other in five-space (as a glance at three-dimensional Figure 37-4 suggests). Stewart and Clark both are closer to Whittaker, Frankfurter, and Harlan than they are to each other. Finally, it is noteworthy that Whittaker—not Frankfurter—is the most typical of the group who, at least in relationship to the C and E variables, are the conservative justices; Whittaker's average distance from the other four justices at the "right wing" of Table 37-7 was only .62. And it is Warren—not Black—who is the most typical of the four liberal justices, with an average distance of .63 separating him from the other three.

VIII.   Summary

The objective of this paper has been to demonstrate the utility, for a more accurate insight into the basic factors that underlie disagreement among Supreme Court justices, of a more rigorous psychological approach than has been characteristic of most discussion of their attitudes. The attention of scholars always has focused upon the values articulated in the opinions of the justices, and particularly in majority opinions; but much less attention has been given to the possibility that an examination of the voting behavior of the justices might provide a better and more reliable approach to the understanding of their attitudes than the study of opinions. Research during the last two decades has turned increasingly to the analysis of judicial voting records, in addition to opinion language; and reliance understandably has been placed, during what might well be termed the pioneering stages of the development of a science of judicial behavior, upon unidimensional models. These necessarily are limited in their capacity to represent adequately the complex interplay of attitudes in the mind of any human being. The time has now come when it may be appropriate for students of judicial behavior to consider the advantages to be gained by utilization of multidimensional models of the behavior of Supreme Court justices.

One such model, exemplified here, is suggested by recent (and ongoing) research in psychometrics. It proceeds on the premise that a justice reacts in his voting behavior to the stimuli presented by cases before the Court in accordance with his attitudes toward the issues raised for decision. This article has presented what is believed to be persuasive evidence that this is precisely what the justices were doing when they voted in the decisions of the 1960 Term.

Notes

1. See *Kinsella* v. *Singleton, Grisham* v. *Hagan, McElroy* v. *Guagliardo,* and *Wilson* v. *Bohlender,* all decided January 18, 1960. . . .

2. The phi coefficient is an approximation of the Pearsonian r correlation coefficient, and is appropriate to use when, as here, the two distributions to be correlated reflect a genuine dichotomy. . . .

3. Perhaps it should be noted, for the benefit of readers not familiar with the method, that orthogonal axes are statistically independent, while oblique axes are correlated with each other; therefore, making a factor interpretation based directly upon a system of orthogonal axes implies an assumption that there is no relationship among the factors, which must be conceived to be independent of each other. Applied to the present data, this would involve the assumption that there was no relationship, at least in the minds of the justices, among the major issues of public policy toward which they responded in their voting.

4. *Civil Liberties and the Vinson Court* (Chicago: University of Chicago Press, 1954), p. 227.

38

Values as Variables in Judicial Decision-Making

David J. Danelski

. . .

I. A Scientific Conception of Values

Values are viewed here as constructs anchored in quantifiable human behavior. Such behavior may be either verbal or nonverbal. In ordinary discourse, we move quickly—almost automatically—from the empirical to the abstract in asserting that a man or a judge possesses certain values. This value-labeling process merits close examination so that we might understand more precisely what we mean when we use the term "values." To begin with, value constructs can be anchored only in a certain class of human behavior—behavior that is perceived and labeled as "evaluations" or "value-facts." Evaluations are defined as units of human behavior indicating that an individual regards a thing, condition, property, event, action, or idea as good, useful, or desirable, in itself, or for the achievement of some purpose he is actually pursuing or may eventually pursue. After evaluations are designated, they are labeled in terms of specific value constructs such as freedom, equality, and tradition. Finally, on the basis of certain criteria—such as the number of evaluations in a specific value category or indication of preference for one value over another—an inference is made that the individual whose behavior is under inquiry possesses certain values, some of which are more salient than others. Values and their relative saliency, it is stressed, are always postulated. They are constructs, not empirical entities; their scientific status hinges entirely upon whether they are validly anchored in evaluations and whether the evaluations are validly designated.

For purposes of developing a theory of judicial decision-making, values are viewed as being anchored in individual evaluations. Although we sometimes speak of the values of a group—we say, for example, that freedom is an important value of the Supreme Court—we are actually either making a complex statement about the values of individual Court members, or inferring and postulating values from group evaluations (court decisions and opinions), which are the end products of a process we are trying to explain. In either case, we are driven back to the evaluations of individuals. This point has important implications not only in terms of theory building, but also in the selection of data for value analysis.

Evaluations always occur within particular situations—"transactions"—which are circumscribed in time and space. Therefore, any inference leading to the postulation of values must be made in the light of the entire transaction in which evaluations occur. Further, the time-space boundaries of transactions limit generalization of the postulated values to future transactions. If, for example, a judge addresses a group in wartime, a number of evaluations indicating patriotism would be expected; and their presence probably would be relevant in analyzing his judicial behavior at that time. But whether patriotism retained the same high place in his value hierarchy after the war is a matter that would bear inquiry. Other situational considerations must also be taken into account in making inferences from evaluations.

II. Identification of Values

The conception of values presented above provides a guide for their identification. Evaluations of individual judges constitute the universe of behavior for observation. Once evaluations are designated, specific values can be inferred and postulated. Personal interviews and written questionnaires are possible research techniques in gathering such value data, as well as content analysis of personal documents, speeches, autobiographies, articles, and books. In this regard, the techniques developed by Ralph K. White ("value-analysis") and Charles E. Osgood ("evaluative assertive analysis") are useful.[1]

For purposes of illustration, White's method of value-analysis will be used to identify the top values of Justices Brandeis and Butler. These Justices have been selected as examples because they were known to have had fairly well-defined, stable value systems.[2] In addition, they were perceived by their colleagues as leading proponents of divergent views on the Supreme Court. The basic hypothesis here is that their disagreement was rooted in a fundamental conflict of values—values to which they had been committed long before they came to the Supreme Court.

The universe selected for value-analysis consisted of two addresses by Louis D. Brandeis given in 1915 and 1916 and two addresses given by Pierce Butler in the same years. The 1915 addresses were on essentially the same subject: Brandeis' address, given on the Fourth of July, was entitled "True Americanism"; Butler's address was entitled "Educating for Citizenship: Duties the Citizen Owes the State."[3] The 1916 addresses were both given to bar associations in the Midwest: Brandeis' address was entitled "The Living Law," and Butler's was entitled "There Is Important Work for Lawyers as Citizens."[4] Brandeis was appointed to the Supreme Court in 1916; Butler was appointed in 1922.

The results of the value-analysis are reported in Table 38-1. They appear reliable in that they are consistent with independent estimates by contemporaries and scholars. . . .

The value of patriotism in Table 38-1 merits special comment. In view of the fact that the speeches were given during the World War I period, and that one of them was a Fourth of July speech, patriotism may have been disproportionately emphasized. Therefore, one might suspect that, if a larger universe of evaluations from other time periods were analyzed, the importance of that value would diminish. A cursory check of subsequent public statements by both men indicates that this was the case in regard to Brandeis

TABLE 38-1
Ten Top Values

Brandeis		Butler	
Value	(N = 208) %	Value	(N = 544) %
Individual Freedom	15	Morality	12
Practicality	7	Patriotism	10
Change	7	Tradition	10
Patriotism	7	Individual Freedom	8
Justice	6	Laissez Faire (+)	8
Laissez Faire (−)	5	Religion	5
Social Justice	5	Law	5
Knowledge	5	Safety	4
Unity	4	Justice	4
Equality	3	Order	3

N equals number of evaluation units disclosed by the value-analysis of the speeches mentioned in the text.

but not to Butler. Patriotism was a recurrent value in Butler's addresses even after he came to the Supreme Court.

Table 38-1 indicates what appears to be a significant conflict between Justices Brandeis and Butler in regard to laissez faire. Proceeding upon the hypothesis that this value conflict was important in Supreme Court decisions while these two Justices were on the bench, an attempt was made to verify the findings by analyzing individual evaluations of each Justice in the judicial process. This was done by examining the lone dissenting votes of Justices Brandeis and Butler during the period they were together on the Court. If the findings in Table 38-1 regarding their respective valuings of laissez faire are correct, the following could be expected: (1) Brandeis would never dissent in favor of laissez faire (+), (2) Butler would never dissent in favor of laissez faire (−), (3) a substantial number of Brandeis' lone dissents would indicate the value of laissez faire (−), and (4) the precise opposite would be true of Butler. That is what Table 38-2 shows.

TABLE 38-2
Lone Dissents, 1923–1939

Value	Brandeis (N = 15) %	Butler (N = 10) %
Laissez Faire (+)	0	40
Laissez Faire (−)	40	0

N equals the number of cases in which the named Justice was the lone dissenter.

III.   Dimensions of Values

Values are conceptualized as being multidimensional. Although there is no limit to the number of dimensions in which they can be viewed, other than the researcher's verifiable insights, only three dimensions—intensity, congruency, and cognitive completeness—are postulated here for purposes of illustration. . . .

Figure 38-1
Illustrations of High Congruency

Brandeis	Butler
Change	Tradition
↓	↓
Laissez Faire (−)	Laissez Faire (+)
↗ ↖	↗ ↖
Equality Social Justice	Law Individual Freedom

→ = reinforcement

The analyses reported in Tables 38-1 and 38-2 were based, in large part, upon assumptions about the intensity of Justices Brandeis' and Butler's values. The assumption in the value-analysis was that intensely held values are articulated in speech more frequently than values not intensely held. The assumption in the lone-dissent analysis was that generally a justice does not dissent by himself unless he is expressing some intensely held value.

Although intensity appears to be the most significant value dimension, other dimensions could assume an importance rivaling that of intensity. One such dimension appears to be congruency, which refers to the harmony between a specific value and other values held by a judge. If a specific value is reinforced by a number of other values and is not in conflict with any other value, then it is said to possess high congruency. Butler's value of laissez faire (+), for instance, possessed higher congruency than his value of individual freedom, because in the former there was only reinforcement and no conflict with other top values, whereas in certain cases the latter appears to have been in conflict with the value of patriotism. Those situations involved the freedom of speech or conscience of Communists, members of the Industrial Workers of the World (I.W.W.), and aliens who refused to swear unqualified allegiance to the United States. In every such divided case before the Supreme Court from 1923 to 1939, Butler's vote was inconsistent with his value of individual freedom but consistent with his value of patriotism. This did not mean, however, that he did not highly value freedom; in criminal cases involving issues of due process, no Justice, not even Brandeis, equalled Butler's libertarian record. This is not surprising when one remembers that Butler was the only conservative Justice to dissent in the wiretapping case of *Olmstead* v. *United States*[5] and the only Justice to dissent in the double-jeopardy case of *Palko* v. *Connecticut*.[6]

Laissez faire (−) and laissez faire (+) were highly congruent values for Justices Brandeis and Butler, respectively. As Figure 38-1 shows, both values were highly reinforced and completely absent of conflict. Hence, viewing laissez faire (−) and laissez faire (+) on two continua, each Justice again is positioned well on the plus side of his continuum.

The dimension of cognitive completeness refers to a judge's readiness to perceive a set of phenomena in terms of a specific value—this readiness being based upon his breadth and depth of experience concerning that value. If, for example, a judge, in his years at the bar, had defended a substantial number of persons accused of crime, his value of due process is apt to be more cognitively complete at the time he ascends the bench than that of a judge who had spent his legal career in corporate practice. The experience that makes for cognitive completeness of a value frequently occurs in the judicial process itself. Thus, as an increasing number of due process cases are argued before the latter judge and decided by him, his value of due process is apt to become more cognitively complete. This dimension may provide the basis for explaining why first-term behavior of Supreme Court Justices does not always square with their subsequent judicial behavior.

The cognitive completeness of Justices Brandeis' and Butler's respective values of laissez faire (−) and laissez faire (+) was high. Brandeis had argued the laissez-faire (−) position before the Supreme Court in *Muller* v. *Oregon*[7] in 1908, and Butler argued what amounted to a laissez-faire (+) position in the *Minnesota Rate Cases*[8] before the same tribunal in 1912. Their value positions on laissez faire were so well known before they came to the Supreme Court that their appointments were opposed in part because of them. Moreover, during their tenure on the Court, laissez faire was the dominant issue. From 1923 to 1939, Justices Butler and Brandeis often confronted each other over the conference table in arguments over laissez faire cases. Hence, each of them was well on the plus side of his cognitive-completeness continuum for laissez-faire.

Intensity, congruity, and cognitive completeness are dimensions of "value spaces" corresponding to postulated values. All judges holding a specific value, such as laissez faire (+), have their positions located somewhere in the laissez-faire (+) value space. . . .

IV.   Value Verification in the Decisional Process

The conception of values of individual judges being located in space is similar to Coombs' conception of individuals' ideal points in his theory of data which Schubert has applied in his factor analytic studies of the Supreme Court. According to Coombs, ideal points can be located in single-stimulus data unidimensionally by scalogram analysis and multidimensionally by factor analysis. Situations yielding single-stimulus data are those in which a number of individuals are confronted with the same stimuli eliciting either a positive or negative response. The decision-making process in collegial courts yields this kind of data. Hence, factor analysis and cumulative scaling appear to be useful techniques for verifying the presence of postulated values.

If the value of laissez faire was ever salient in the Supreme Court, it was during the 1935 and 1936 terms. The proponents of laissez faire had fought a determined rear-guard action during the 1935 Term, chalking up such victories as *Morehead* v. *New York ex rel Tipaldo*,[9] the New York minimum-wage case. Then in the 1936 Term, President Roosevelt announced his "court-packing plan," and the so-called "switch in time" occurred: Justice Roberts defected from the conservative majority in *Morehead* and voted with the liberals to sustain the Washington minimum-wage law in *West Coast Hotel Co.* v. *Parrish.*[10] If factor analysis and cumulative scaling are useful techniques for value verification, the divided decisions in the 1935 and 1936 terms appear to provide the data for proving it.

Thus the votes of each Justice in the fifty-seven divided cases decided during those two terms were correlated with the votes of every other Justice,[11] and the correlation coefficients obtained were arranged in a nine-by-nine matrix. McQuitty's elementary factor analysis was then used to determine the number of types in the Court and the most representative Justice of each type.[12] This was done because of some comments made by Mr. Chief Justice Charles Evans Hughes in his "Biographical Notes" indicating that he perceived Justices Brandeis and Butler to be the leading proponents of divergent points of view in the Court during that period. It was assumed that these divergent views concerned the value of laissez faire. The first step in the McQuitty analysis revealed the types shown in Figure 38-2.

Figure 38-2
Judicial Types, 1935–1936 Terms

| Sutherland | ⇌ | Van Devanter | | Cardozo | ⇌ | Stone | | Roberts |

Sutherland   ⇌   Van Devanter   Cardozo   ⇌   Stone   Roberts
↑   ↑   ↑
Butler   Brandeis Hughes
↑
McReynolds

Type I   Type II   Type III

→   Means Justice at the tail of the arrow is most highly correlated with the Justice at the head, but the one at the head not most highly correlated with the one at the tail.

⇌   Means recriprocal pairs of Justices most highly correlated with each other.

The second step of the analysis revealed that Mr. Justice Butler was slightly more representative of Type I than Mr. Justice Sutherland. Mr. Justice Cardozo was clearly the most representative of Type II. Type III, of course, required no further analysis. Using Justices Butler, Cardozo, and Roberts as reference factors, the factor loadings indicated in Table 38-3 were obtained. Considering the high correlation of Justice Brandeis with Type II, Chief Justice Hughes' perception of the leading proponents of divergent points of view in the Court was fairly accurate.

If laissez faire was the dominant issue before the Supreme Court during the 1935 and 1936 terms, an examination of Table 38-3 would lead to an inference that Factors I and II were related to it. In an attempt to verify this, all of the cases in the universe under consideration were examined to determine whether they could be perceived in terms of laissez faire. The operational definition of a laissez-faire case was any case that could have been perceived as involving governmental activity in economic matters. The definition was broadly applied; tax cases, for example, were viewed as a part of the laissez-faire universe. A vote against government was construed as a laissez-faire ($+$) response; a vote for government was construed as a laissez-faire ($-$) response. To minimize bias, all doubtful cases were categorized as laissez-faire cases. They formed the cumulative scale shown in Figure 38-3, which seems to verify the presence of the values of laissez faire ($+$) and laissez faire ($-$).

TABLE 38-3
Elementary Factor Loadings, 1935–1936 Terms

Justices	Factors		
	I	II	III
McReynolds	.72	$-$ .78	$-$ .24
Butler	1.00	$-$ .68	$-$ .09
Sutherland	.75	$-$ .56	$-$ .02
Van Devanter	.69	$-$ .46	$-$ .21
Roberts	$-$ .09	$-$ .20	1.00
Hughes	$-$ .28	.42	$-$ .13
Brandeis	$-$ .63	.85	$-$ .06
Stone	$-$ .65	.92	$-$ .22
Cardozo	$-$ .68	1.00	$-$ .20

The numerical figures indicate the correlations of each Justice with the three Justices who are the most representative of their type.

Figure 38-3
Laissez Faire Scale, 1935–1936 Terms

Case Vol./Page	McR	Bu	Su	VD	Ro	Hu	Br	St	Ca	Pro-Con
300/297			x							1-8
301/532					x					1-8
301/540					x					1-8
297/288	x									1-8
300/216	x									1-8
301/337	x									1-8
301/402	—	x								1-8
296/268	x	x								2-7
300/308	x	x								2-7
300/577	x	x								2-7
301/619	x	x								2-7
297/88	—	x	x		x					3-6
301/412	x	x	x	*			*			3-4
(12 cases)ᵃ	x	x	x	x						4-5
(6 cases)ᵇ	x	x	x	x	x					5-4
301/459	x	x	x	x	—	x				5-4
(10 cases)ᶜ	x	x	x	x	x	x				6-3
298/393	x	x	x	x	x	x		*		6-2
299/32	x	x	x	x	x	x		*		6-2
299/280	x	x	x	x	x	x		*		6-2
298/441	x	x	x	x	x	x	x			7-2
300/352	x	x	x	x	—	x	—	x	x	7-2
301/655	x	x	x	x	x	x	x	—	—	7-2

	McR	Bu	Su	VD	Ro	Hu	Br	St	Ca		Pro-Con
Totals	43-5	42-6	38-10	35-12	24-24	17-31	2-46	1-43	1-47	203-224	203-224 / 427
Scale positions	45	42	37	35½	23	17	3	2	2		
Scale scores	.88	.75	.54	.48	-.04	-.29	-.88	-.92	-.92		

$$R = 1 - \frac{7}{364} = .980 \qquad S = 1 - \frac{11}{75} = .853$$

R = coefficient of reproducibility   S = coefficient of scalability

ᵃ 4-5 cases: 296/85, 297/251, 300/324, 300/608, 300/379, 301/1, 301/49, 301/58, 301/103, 301/468, 301/495, 301/548.
ᵇ 5-4 cases: 296/39, 296/48, 298/238, 298/513, 298/587, 300/154.
ᶜ 6-3 cases: 296/102, 296/299, 296/287, 296/113, 296/404, 297/1, 297/135, 297/266, 298/1, 298/492.

x   = vote against government.
—   = vote for government inconsistent with scale pattern.
blank   = vote for government consistent with scale pattern.
*   = nonparticipation.

TABLE 38-4
Principal-Factor Loadings, 1935-1936 Terms

Justices	Factors					
	I	II	III	I*	II*	III*
McReynolds	.86	.17	.30	.75	.32	.33
Butler	.86	.20	−.12	.48	.52	.07
Sutherland	.78	.29	−.43	.30	.86	−.03
Van Devanter	.73	.47	−.31	.27	.91	.17
Roberts	.003	−.82	−.55	.09	−.09	.98
Hughes	−.45	.36	−.35	−.22	−.09	.06
Brandeis	−.85	.20	−.17	−.88	−.22	−.01
Stone	−.87	.32	−.03	−.88	−.27	.19
Cardozo	−.91	.31	−.09	−.90	−.25	.15

* Kaiser's Varimax Rotation.

In a further effort to verify the presence of the laissez-faire values, the entire universe from which the cases in Figure 38-3 were drawn was factor analyzed by means of the principal-factor method. It was expected that a high loading would be obtained on the first factor and that each Justice would be correlated with that factor in the same order as on the laissez-faire scale. That factor, of course, would be identified as the laissez-faire value. The results of the factor analysis are indicated in Table 38-4. Factor I appears to be the expected value of laissez-faire. Varimax rotation provided a solution that is consistent with the initial interpretation.

A comparison of Factor I in Table 38-3, Factor I in Table 38-4, and the scale scores in Figure 38-3 suggests that they are measures of the same thing—namely, laissez faire (+) and laissez faire (−). Those values, it will be recalled, were conceptualized as being located in specific value spaces. The spaces were constructed in terms of the dimensions— intensity, congruency, and cognitive completeness. If these are the most significant dimensions of the laissez-faire values, Factor I in Table 38-4 could be viewed as a composite of them and positioned in . . . value-space. . . . Butler's position would be in the laissez-faire (+) space .86 from zero on all dimensions. . . . Similarly Brandeis' position would be the laissez-faire (−) space .85 from zero on all dimensions. . . .

V.   Toward a Theory of Judicial Decision-Making

Implicit in the discussion of values in this paper is a stimulus-response model of judicial decision-making. Responses are decisions of courts defined in terms of judges' behavior at the end of the decisional process. Stimuli are cases before courts for decision, but precisely what constitutes a "case" raises some difficult problems. Values and all the other postulated variables that connect stimuli and responses in some meaningful way are, of course, only theoretical constructs.

In a strict sense, a case before a collegial court is not a stimulus, but rather a set of stimuli—briefs read by judges, arguments of counsel, conference discussions, comments of law clerks, and so forth. These sets of stimuli are not identical for all judges, partly because each judge perceives stimuli uniquely in terms of his own values, experiences, and needs. Lawyers who argue before collegial courts know this intuitively. Before ascending the bench, Robert H. Jackson, reflecting on his arguments before the Supreme Court, said of Justice Butler:

> He was relentless in bringing the lawyer face to face with the issues as he saw them. I think I never knew a man who could more quickly orient a statement of facts with his own philosophy. When the facts were stated, the argument was about over with him— he could relate the case to his conceptions of legal principles without the aid of counsel.[13]

If the sets of stimuli we call cases are considerably different for each judge, it would be fruitless to use techniques such as factor analysis or cumulative scaling in explaining collegial decision-making, for such techniques assume that the sets of stimuli are the same for all the judges. Discussing this problem, Coombs has written: "An anchor point is needed, and the same stimulus being presented to different individuals provides such an anchor. If a stimulus differs in a significant way from one individual to the next, absolutely nothing can be done with just these observations. . . ." Abandoning the hypothesis that individuals differ in their responses "because they perceive the stimuli differently," Coombs concludes, "we concede that each stimulus is more or less the same thing for everyone, not just in its physical dimensions but in whatever its subjective characteristics might be."[14]

In developing a theory of judicial decision-making, the concession to which Coombs refers cannot be made because we have empirical evidence that judges do, upon occasion, perceive the same cases differently. The problem here is how to specify judges' perceptions. A first step in that direction is intensive study of the judges themselves, using data outside of the decisional process. Value analysis is important in this regard. If judges' values are located in value spaces, inferences can be made about how they perceive value phenomena; then there is some basis for determining whether perceptions overlap. Thus, the exploration of values appears to be a fruitful first step in the development of a theory of judicial decision-making.

In the example discussed in this paper—laissez faire in the 1935 and 1936 terms—it appears that there was sufficient perceptual overlap so that factor analysis and cumulative scaling were useful techniques in verifying the presence of the values under inquiry. It must be stressed, however, that the value and the period were chosen for illustrative purposes because there was considerable independent evidence of perceptual overlap in regard to laissez faire. In the study of other values in other periods, the perceptual problem must be solved if techniques like factor analysis and cumulative scaling are to be used fruitfully.

Although values are important variables in the decision-making process, other variables must be taken into account to explain the process. Anyone who has done extensive research on the manuscripts of Supreme Court Justices is aware of the great amount of evidence in certain historical periods indicating that a Justice's value position on Case A was ($-$) when in fact his recorded position in the official reports is ($+$). Obviously his voting behavior was connected with variables other than his values.

. . .

Notes

1. White, *Value-Analysis* (1953); Osgood, "The Representational Model and Relevant Research Methods," in *Trends in Content Analysis* 23–88 (Pool ed. 1959); Osgood, Saporta

& Nunnally, "Evaluative Assertion Analysis," 3 *Litera* 47-102 (1956); White, "Black Boy—A Value Analysis," 32 *Journal of Abnormal and Social Psychology* 440-61 (1947). See also Holsti, "Evaluative Assertion Analysis," *Content Analysis* 91-102 (North ed. 1963); Stone, Bales, Namenwirth & Ogilvie, "The General Inquirer," 7 *Behavioral Science* 484-97 (1962).

2. One of Brandeis' biographers has written: "[Brandeis] . . . knew where he was headed. He did not drift with wind and tide. His actions, his policies, were too sure and definite for sudden impulse or random opportunism." Mason, *Brandeis* 640 (1946). William D. Mitchell, Butler's former law partner, said of him: "He was steadfast, the roots of convictions went deep. They were founded on principles. No one who dealt with him one day was afterwards, confounded or nonplussed by any subsequent act or declaration of his on the same subject." *Proceedings of the Bar and Officers of the Supreme Court of the United States in Memory of Pierce Butler* 39 (1940).

3. Address by Justice Brandeis, Faneuil Hall, Boston, Mass., July 4, 1915, in Brandeis, *Business—A Profession* 364-74 (1925); Address by Justice Butler, Catholic Educ. Ass'n, St. Paul, Minn., 1915, in 12 *Catholic Educ. Ass'n Bull.* 123-32 (1915).

4. Address by Justice Brandeis, Chicago Bar Ass'n, 1916, in *The Curse of Bigness* 316-26 (Frankel ed. 1934); Address by Justice Butler. Minn. Bar Ass'n, 1916, in *Proceedings, Minn. State Bar Ass'n* 106-19 (1916). A part of Butler's 1916 address appears to have been taken from his 1915 address.

5. 277 U.S. 438 (1928).

6. 302 U.S. 319 (1937).

7. 208 U.S. 412 (1908).

8. 230 U.S. 352 (1912).

9. 298 U.S. 587 (1936).

10. 300 U.S. 379 (1937).

11. A case was defined as a perceived decisional unit; that is, if two or more causes were heard together, decided, and reported as a single decision, they were treated as one. In some research situations there are advantages to defining a case as each cause with a separate docket number. This is what Schubert has done.

12. McQuitty, "Elementary Factor Analysis," 9 *Psychological Reports* 71-84 (1961). For an example of the use of McQuitty's method in an earlier stage of development, see Ulmer, "The Analysis of Behavior Patterns on the United States Supreme Court," 22 *J. of Politics* 629-53 (1960).

13. Jackson, *In Memory of Mr. Justice Butler,* 310 U.S. xiv (1939).

14. Coombs, *A Theory of Data* (1964), at 8.

CHAPTER THIRTEEN

ASPECTS OF THE JUDICIAL ROLE

The concept of role has been developed by social psychologists. Role is related to the official position occupied by an individual. An individual's role concept consists of his or her views concerning the range of behavior that is compatible with the common understanding of how that role is to be performed.

Role theory has been adapted to the study of judicial decision making. There are some aspects of the judicial role about which there is a great deal of consensus among judges. For example, it is expected that (1) judges will appear to be and in fact will be impartial with respect to the disputants; (2) judges will acknowledge precedent and legally justify their decision; (3) judges will adhere to the obvious requirements and intent of the relevant statute.[1] However, there are other important facets of the judicial role about which there is considerably less agreement among judges. Our attention is focused in this chapter on one such facet, the proper scope of judicial decision making. Here, just as with judicial attitudes, the judge's view of the scope of the decision-making role can best be considered a behavioral variable.

A judge's concept of the decision-making role is manifested by his or her judicial philosophy as explicitly stated by the judge in personal interviews, written opinions, or other writings, or as inferred from behavior. However, students of judicial behavior who have employed the role perspective have for the most part investigated concepts of decision-making role by conducting personal interviews with judges. The two selections in this chapter, by Edward Beiser and J. Woodford Howard, Jr., are based primarily although not exclusively on personal interviews.

Role is considered an important variable because it is believed that an individual's role concept is tied to the exercise of discretion and that the judge's concept of role can inhibit the full flowering of political attitudes and values. Indeed, it can be argued that the special position of *judge,* with its role constraints, makes *judicial* decision making different from legislative, bureaucratic, or executive decision making. The role of the judge is thought to be an important, even crucial, variable in making courts the unique conflict-managing institutions and judges the unique conflict managers they are.

The concept of role seems to be implicit in much of the attitudinal research. After all, the focus on nonunanimously decided cases suggests that it is largely these cases rather than the unanimously decided ones that permit choices to be made within the framework of the judicial role (however it may be conceptualized by respective judges). For the attitudinalist, then, role is a given, differences in role perceptions are not explored, and the explanation of judicial behavior is in terms of *judicial* attitudes and values. For example, suppose that one judge has a self-limiting role concept and that another judge has a more expansive and creative concept of role. Both may swear to friends and colleagues alike that they are political liberals, but if the former usually is found on the negative side of civil liberties disputes while the latter primarily opts for the positive side of those same disputes, the former will emerge as a judicial conservative while the latter will be classified as a judicial liberal. Students of the judicial role have taken the position that it is important to discover voting patterns and to interpret them in terms of attitudes and values, but that in order to get a better understanding of judicial behavior, it is also important to discover how judges perceive their role.[2]

Judicial role analyses have been most highly developed by students of state courts. Nonunanimous decisions on the state supreme courts are relatively infrequent. Whereas dissent rates on the United States Supreme Court have, in recent decades, typically been over 60 percent of the decisions on the merits, most state supreme courts have dissent rates that are less than 15 percent.[3] This means that the relatively sophisticated methodology developed to study the United States Supreme Court cannot be satisfactorily utilized for the analysis of judicial behavior on most state supreme courts.

Two leading scholars of state court judicial behavior, Henry Glick and Kenneth Vines, pursued their interest in role analysis and, on the basis of the personal interviews they conducted with state supreme court judges, developed three basic role models according to which those judges could be classified:[4] the law maker, the law interpreter, and the pragmatist. These models are discussed by J. Woodford Howard (selection 40), although he uses somewhat different classifications. Howard's "innovator" is Glick's and Vines's "law maker"; Howard's "realist" is Glick's and Vines's "pragmatist." The law interpreter role model is used in both studies. Howard's study is based on interviews with judges of federal courts of appeals for three circuits. Howard, however, goes one step further than Glick and Vines and ties role concepts to judicial voting behavior.

Selection 39, by Edward Beiser, focuses on the Rhode Island Supreme Court but does not utilize the role models employed by Howard or Glick and Vines to help explain differences within and between courts. On the Rhode Island Supreme Court Beiser found not differences but overwhelming consensus, and he undertakes to explain why there was such unanimity. Common role perceptions are an important part of the answer.

Notes

1. For a discussion of these and other aspects of the judicial role about which there appears to be a broad-based consensus, see Sheldon Goldman and Thomas P. Jahnige, *The Federal Courts as a Political System*, 2d ed. (New York: Harper & Row, 1976), pp. 199–205.

2. An important empirical study along these lines is that by James Gibson, "Judges' Role Orientations, Attitudes and Decisions: An Interactive Model," *American Political Science Review* 72 (1978), in press.

3. Henry R. Glick and Kenneth N. Vines, *State Court Systems* (Englewood Cliffs, N.J.: Prentice-Hall, 1973), pp. 77–82.

4. Henry R. Glick and Kenneth N. Vines, "Law-making in the State Judiciary: A Comparative Study of the Judicial Role in Four States," *Polity* 2 (1969), 142–159.

39

The Rhode Island Supreme Court: A Well-Integrated Political System

Edward N. Beiser

Richard Fenno has suggested that: "[I]f one considers the main activity of a political system to be decision making, the acid test of its internal integration is its capacity to make collective decisions without flying apart in the process." . . .

This article seeks to explain the fact that Rhode Island Supreme Court Justices almost never disagree with one another (at least not in public)—that in Fenno's terms, the Rhode Island Supreme Court gives evidence of a high degree of integration. An explanation of this phenomenon will, it is hoped, contribute to our understanding of state supreme courts, the significance of which for the study of the legal process is now clearly appreciated. In addition, this case study of one state supreme court faces the theoretically important question of how scholars should conceive of courts. Finally it contributes to the attempt to develop general theory concerning the behavior of small groups.

The principal source of data is a series of interviews with the five members of the Rhode Island Supreme Court, which took place between January and May, 1970. The interviews ranged from one and one-half to two and one-half hours, and I was able to interview most of the justices more than once. Judicial interviews were supplemented by interviews with members of the court's staff, with members of the bar, by extensive personal observation of oral argument, and by recourse to the usual published sources.

Evidence of Integration

Compelling evidence for the proposition that the Rhode Island Supreme Court is a well-integrated political system comes from the rate of dissent. Between December 1964, and October 1967, the court decided 445 cases—402 with opinion, and 43 per curiam. During this period, a total of 25 dissenting *votes* and 5 concurring *votes* were cast. The 13 dissenting *opinions* and two concurring *opinions* appeared in 3.7% of the total number of cases decided with opinion.

The interview data provide further evidence of judicial integration. The justices place a high value on their ability to reach agreement, and stress their capacity to get along well

Reprinted by permission of the Law and Society Association from *Law and Society Review* 8 (1974), 167–186. Copyright © 1974. Most footnotes have been omitted. The *Law and Society Review* is the official publication of the Association.

together. Two of them used the identical phrase to explain the importance of internal harmony: "You spend more time with your colleagues than with your wife." Therefore, one must learn to "disagree without being disagreeable." Another spoke of the "camaraderie" within the court. "We don't like to be offensive."

The justices were asked to indicate the qualities they would look for if they were picking the next member of their court. Their responses reveal the importance they attach to this "camaraderie." One justice spoke of a judge he had known on another court: the man was a "legal genius" and a "real work horse"; but, because his personality was "horrible," he would not be a desirable member of the Rhode Island Supreme Court. A colleague commented in a similar vein: "Far more important than genius is the simple ability to get along with others." One justice responded that "a good temperament" affects the work of the court: "You're living with four men." Still another justice said that he would look for a "competent workman with the right disposition." He explained why "the right disposition" is important for a member of a collegial court: As a judge you are required to "pick your brothers' opinions apart." It is therefore crucial that it be understood that this is not personal criticism.

The court's internal harmony is made evident by what is undoubtedly the most intriguing aspect of its decision-making process—a procedure which sharply differentiates this court from the United States Supreme Court: *Opinions are assigned to individual justices on a random basis prior to oral argument.* That is, before a given case is decided, a "round robin" procedure determines who will speak for the court.[1]

Prior to 1965, there was no discussion of cases after oral argument. The justice to whom a case had been assigned worked without guidance from his colleagues, wrote his opinion, and circulated it for comment. At present, the justices hold a daily post-argument conference to review the cases just concluded. The man to the left of the opinion writer speaks first, and the discussion continues around the table with the author speaking last. Thus he has the benefit of his associates' opinions. I was told that a consensus is usually reached in conference. It sometimes happens that the man to whom a particular case is assigned will "trade off" with another. This would happen if a justice felt that he were out of step with the court's thinking, but it is said to be very infrequent.

Once the author has produced a draft, he circulates it and receives comment from the other justices. It is at this point that differences between the justices, if any exist, are most likely to come into play. The justices freely acknowledge that there is more disagreement within the court than is revealed by published dissent. A justice who is unable to convince his colleagues of the merits of his position may acquiesce in silence rather than dissent. The draft opinion is discussed at a Tuesday conference, but there may have been discussion between justices prior to the conference: "You try to iron things out before you get into conferences where you have to fish or cut bait."

One justice reported that he gets a reaction to about half of his draft opinions (mostly concerning language, or suggestions of citations to be put in or taken out). In a "substantial number" he has "substantial changes. . . . Once in a great while there is a shift of writers." Argument over a draft can become heated, but one justice claimed that it is invariably cordial. Argument is said to take the form of a "rational explanation of the rule of law." A strong effort is made to achieve unanimity: discussion in the conference may be directed at "getting a man to come aboard." Thus the interview data very strongly indicate that consensus is the goal in decision making.[2]

It has been reported that on some courts, random opinion assignment, coupled with the relatively automatic acceptance of the judgment of the author, leads to minority decision-making—that is, the "majority opinion" is supported by less than a majority. This does not appear to be the case in Rhode Island. The justices insist that, while an individual may fail to record a dissenting vote, the opinion published always represents the view of the majority. Random opinion assignment prior to oral argument is possible because of the high rate of agreement within the Rhode Island Supreme Court. In the vast majority of cases which come before them, the justices perceive that the choice of the author is essentially of no consequence. The decision-making process of the Rhode Island Supreme Court is marked by a high degree of substantive agreement. In addition, the social norms within the court promote harmony. By Fenno's standard, the court is an extremely well-integrated system.

Why Integration?

Four important characteristics which help to explain the extent to which the Rhode Island Supreme Court is a well integrated system are:

1. The existence of a common perception of the court's goals and tasks, and of the methods by which they are to be achieved;
2. The nature of the cases which come before the court;
3. The environment in which the court operates; and
4. The justices' commitment to their job.

Consensus as to Goals, Tasks, and Methods

The justices of the Rhode Island Supreme Court discuss their role in terms of reviewing what was done elsewhere, i.e., in the Rhode Island trial courts. They are basically rule-oriented rather than outcome-oriented. Their task, as they claim to see it, is to guarantee that the correct rule of law was utilized in the proper manner by the court below. "The function of the Rhode Island Supreme Court," one justice told me, "is to decide whether a trial judge committed error under the law, as it stands." The court of last resort of Connecticut, he pointed out, was once known as the Supreme Court of Errors. When he first came to the Supreme Court, it took him a while to realize that his function was not to do "justice here, but to see that justice had been done somewhere else."

The rules by which the justices measure the performance of the lower courts are derived from three principal sources—the federal Constitution, state statutes, and the judge-made rules drawn from prior cases. The justices' perception of their role varies according to which of the three is involved. In particular, the degree of creativity which they recognize in the judicial function depends on the source of the law.

When the federal Constitution is invoked, the Rhode Island justices view themselves as members of an inferior court, which must follow as precisely as possible the dictates of the United States Supreme Court: "It is the way of the state appellate courts to defer to the United States Supreme Court on constitutional matters." The justices in Rhode Island do not speak of creativity in the constitutional sphere, even in areas in which the Supreme Court has not yet spoken: their task is to await orders from above, and to follow them diligently. Said one justice: "You don't go further than the United States Supreme Court."

It would be a mistake to equate this position with a naive or mechanistic conception of the nature of constitutional law. A majority of the Rhode Island justices would probably agree with one justice's description of the Constitution as a "living, breathing, elastic document," meant to be construed as such—but not by their court! In constitutional matters, they see themselves as an intermediate appellate court, whose task is to apply the U.S. Supreme Court's rules—whatever they may think of them—to the Rhode Island legal system.

As a result of this role perception, differences in constitutional theory—and the justices do differ on constitutional questions—are not permitted to affect the harmony within the court. Since it is not within their power to be creative in constitutional matters, questions of constitutional philosophy are, by definition, irrelevant. Furthermore, although the odds that a decision by any lower court will be reviewed in Washington are very small, this role perception promotes compliance with the Supreme Court's wishes. A strong internalized norm requiring compliance with the United States Supreme Court in federal constitutional matters is probably a better guarantee of such compliance than is the fear of reversal.

The justices express a common perception of how they are to approach statutory interpretation: their task is to carry out the will of the legislature. They have a sophisticated sense of what this entails: several of them spoke of "filling the interstices" in statutes. And they are aware that interpretation tends to be subjective. "Subconsciously you say, 'this is what I would have meant if I were in the legislature.' Here's where your own prejudices come in." But despite this, when a statute is involved, they view themselves as the handmaidens of the legislature. Or at least they ought to be. "To say that we don't legislate is blind. We do. But we shouldn't defeat legislative intent." Another justice continues, "We're a state court. Our duty and function is not to make the law. We do once in a while, [but] we're supposed to carry out the law made by the legislature."

Virtually all of the justices attempted to explain their function by referring to one or more recent cases in which they had ruled that statutes achieved results to which they were personally opposed:

> There was no way to construe this as covered by the statute. The five of us thought the legislature meant to cover this [but had failed to do so] but you can't do this with a statute—any more than with a will. If the will says "my nephew Edward," you can't take it to mean "my nephew George" even if that's what the guy meant. We couldn't have reached any other conclusion. If we did, you can forget about what the legislature said in every case.

As noted below, one of the Rhode Island justices is critical of the United States Supreme Court for interpreting constitutional language to meet changing circumstances. Is this ever a problem when his court interprets statutes? "Unless I am very dense, it hasn't happened here." Such a view of the judicial function which minimizes the possibility of creativity or development, renders differences between judges relatively unimportant, and thus promotes harmony within the court.

When they are confronted with cases involving judge-made rules—and only in this instance—the Rhode Island justices are prepared to innovate. This is not to be done lightly—there is a strong presumption in favor of stability. The court is committed to the doctrine of *stare decisis*. The justices all agree that frequently it is more important that the law be settled, than that it be settled correctly. Especially with regard to commercial and property law—cases involving contracts, wills, and trusts—men act on the assumption that the rules will remain stable. The consequence of the "ad hoc" is "bad law which redounds to the loss of most people." But when a judge-made rule—especially if it is an old one—produces undesirable results, the court is prepared to change it. In doing so, it will be influenced by similar action in other jurisdictions.

It is not suggested that the foregoing describes how the Rhode Island Supreme Court actually decides cases; we do not have access to its conferences. Rather, this is how the justices describe what they are doing. What is significant is, first, that there is a very strong consensus as to the proper role of a Rhode Island justice, and, second, that they articulate a conception of the judicial role which is to a significant extent non-creative, and which provides minimal opportunity for individual differences to come into play.

Nature of the Cases

"Great cases, like hard cases, make bad law" (*Northern Securities Co. v. United States* (1904); Holmes, dissenting). Most of the cases which come before the Rhode Island Supreme Court are neither "great" nor "hard." They are of concern only to the immediate parties, and *are rarely vehicles for broader questions.* "We just don't get jazzy constitutional law cases," explained one justice. "Few of our cases raise gutsy questions." . . .

In the absence of an intermediate appellate court, the Rhode Island Supreme Court is not able to restrict the flow of business coming to it, as do the United States Supreme Court and some state high courts. Two consequences of this situation are a heavy work load, and a highly uneven pattern of cases coming before the court.

A complaint common to all of the justices is that they hear too many cases: "Once you start in October you're on a treadmill." The court decides approximately 200 cases with opinion each year, so that each justice writes about 40 opinions. In addition, they must act on various procedural matters. The justices claim that they are not able to devote as much time as they would like to individual cases, that the press of business makes it difficult to consider writing a concurring or dissenting opinion, and that much of their reading in legal periodicals and the advance sheets of other jurisdictions must be put off until the summer recess.

As the single appeals court in the state, the Supreme Court confronts a varied docket. . . . The routine nature of most of the cases before them—the repetition of "the same operations with respect to the same subject matter year after year" is an important source of stability within the court.

In his discussion of the House Appropriations Committee, Fenno suggested that committee members view themselves as a "business" rather than a "policy committee"—thus avoiding controversial programmatic concerns. The same phenomenon seems to operate within the Rhode Island Supreme Court. To the extent that the cases which come before it do not call for creative policy-making, the potential for controversy is avoided. It was from this perspective that one Rhode Island justice contrasted his court with the federal Supreme Court: "The U.S. Supreme Court gets the worst cases."

Between January and May, 1970, roughly the period of my interviews, the Rhode Island Supreme Court published opinions in 60 cases.[3] All were decided unanimously.

The cases can be sorted into the following categories:

Commercial and Property Law	13
(mortgages, trusts, title to property, breach of contract)	
Zoning (and related matters)	10
Criminal Appeals	6
Automobile Insurance Cases	6
Procedural Appeals	6
Workman's Compensation	5
Insurance Claims (non-auto)	5
Family Law	2
Negligence	1
Extradition	1
Municipal Pensions	1
Total	56

The questions raised by these 56 cases appear to have been significant to no one other than the parties. The remaining four cases were of broader interest, to varying degrees. . . .

Taken by itself, the volume of cases would not appear to be enough to explain the absence of dissent. Obviously, the press of business does not prevent a dissenting vote; a justice needs time only if he wishes to file a separate opinion. One justice who is quite proud of several dissenting opinions he wrote years ago explained that he wouldn't have time to write them today: "If you're going to dissent, you have to do it well." This explanation makes particular sense in light of the prevailing consensus within the court. It assumes that agreement is the norm. Since dissent is unusual, it requires a very careful justification.

While the routine nature of the cases seems to promote harmony, this process is also facilitated by the justices' consensus as to goals and methods. A Rhode Island justice views his function as guaranteeing that the correct rule was applied to a concrete case. The cases he reviews almost never involve challenges to the rules per se, and have limited impact on a few people. What would be the point of a dissent which would not help the parties to the case, and which would have no effect on the law? "I can think of at least 25 cases I joined in but did not agree. But to dissent solo would be of no help to the party, and had no chance of challenging a body of law." "What is a dissent unless it's going to improve the law?" "A dissent is futile; if you can't get the other four, why bother?"

Judges who held a different perception of their role might be expected to react differently when confronted with these same cases. Conversely, one wonders whether the Rhode Island justices could have developed their consensus as to goals, tasks and methods if they were responding to different stimuli. Two factors appear to be interrelated: considered together, consensus as to goals and methods, and the kinds of questions confronting the court, provide the basic explanation for the infrequency of dissenting and concurring opinions.

Environment

"Rhode Island is a compact, chummy little state." And this fact has its impact on the Supreme Court. "It is inconceivable that a man would be elevated to this court by the Grand Committee who was not known personally to the other members of the court. . . ."

. . .

The justices' work patterns maximize informal contact. They all live within easy driving distance of Providence. Their offices are adjacent, and there is a considerable amount of office-hopping. They frequently lunch together, attend civic functions together, and see each other at weddings and wakes. Several of the justices contrasted their situation with that of those state supreme courts where justices do not reside in the same city, and where there is limited contact between them.

It may be that the size of the court has an impact on the quality of social interaction. One Rhode Island justice would not like to see his court expanded to seven men, despite the need for a reduction in individual case loads, because "more men means more disagreement." . . .

Quite possibly the social setting of Rhode Island and the court's internal logistics help explain how the justices came to share a common perception of their roles and tasks. In addition to promoting general norms of harmony and courtesy, one sees how the atmosphere in which the court functions would be conducive to an extremely effective socialization process.

Commitment

The justices of the Rhode Island Supreme Court are serious, dedicated men. They have a sense of purpose, take pride in their work, and seem to derive satisfaction from it. They have a strong feeling of responsibility: the buck stops here. Like skilled craftsmen, the justices are pleased when they produce what they consider to be a good opinion: "At the trial level you can say 'Damn it, this isn't fair. I'll do X and let "upstairs" worry.' But 'upstairs' has to put it in writing and give reasons."

The justices share a common style—that of hard work. A justice has to be willing to take his work home from the office and to work on weekends. When asked about the type of man they would pick as the next member of the court, they emphasized the need for a hard worker.

In addition, the justices have made an *exclusive* commitment to their court. Upon assuming the bench, they terminated their business and many of their organizational contacts. Several even spoke of their social isolation. They are critical of judges who permit themselves to become involved in controversial extra-judicial matters, presidential commissions, for example. While it would be a mistake to view them as cut off from the world, the sense of propriety which they feel with respect to their positions sets them apart to some extent from other men, and this increases their identification with each other and with the court. . . .

Division within the Court

An important conceptual question raised in the literature is whether the integration of small groups can best be understood in terms of processes internal to the group, or external to it. For example, it might be suggested that since Rhode Island Supreme Court justices are all selected by the state legislature, and since a small state presents a relatively limited pool of candidates for judicial posts, it is natural that the level of disagreement will be very low. That is to say, the integration of the Rhode Island Supreme Court might be attributed to the characteristics of the men who are chosen to serve as judges, and to their pre-judicial experiences, rather than to the pressures of a common institutional setting after they don the robe.

During the course of the interviews, the justices were asked a number of open-ended questions which sought to identify their attitudes and values. It would be both presumptuous and incorrect to assume that, on the basis of one or two interviews, it is possible to identify the parameters of a judge's philosophy. However, one may demonstrate that they disagree significantly with respect to judicial philosophies and policy preferences. This being the case, the high degree of integration within the court must be attributed primarily to internal rather than external factors.[4]

Differences between the justices quickly became apparent when I asked questions concerning the role of the United States Supreme Court, with particular regard to constitutional law. One justice, who identified with Mr. Justice Harlan, felt strongly that the Constitution should be interpreted in light of the times in which it was written. It is not appropriate, he believed, for the Supreme Court to reinterpret the document in terms of changing conditions. The right to amend belongs to the people, not the courts. If a court misconstrues a statute, in his view, the legislature can reverse it, but if it misconstrues the Constitution, its ruling can be upset only with great difficulty:

> The liberal approach wants to keep the people up with the times. This is very dangerous. The Constitution would mean what five men say it means. Which five men? If you stick with the clear language of the Constitution you'd be on safer ground. Let the people change it if it doesn't work.

His concern flows from his basic democratic commitment and is very similar to the position expounded by the late Judge Learned Hand in *The Bill of Rights* (1962). It is not surprising that he felt that, had he been a member of the Warren Court, he would have dissented frequently.

The other members of the Rhode Island bench are more favorably disposed to the Warren Court's constitutional policies (though to varying degrees). One went so far as to wonder "if we would exist as a nation today if it were not for the Warren Court." They do not share their colleague's objection to the process of updating the Constitution:

> Courts have always been responsive to the times. . . . The Constitution is a living, breathing elastic document. Constitutional law should be settled right, not just settled.

. . .

Discussion of particular decisions of the Warren Court suggested that the Rhode Island justices differ on policy matters. For example, one was critical of *Brown v. Board of Educ.* (1954) on substantive grounds. The Court should have reaffirmed *Plessy v. Ferguson* (1896) and demanded true equality of funding, etc. *Brown* has done "real harm"—witness the pressure for bussing of school children. Other justices approved of *Brown*. One Rhode Island justice spoke of the need to support the police; he is sympathetic to their difficult task. Another told me that he knew what happened to poor kids in the back rooms of station houses.

Considering the range of their opinions, the potential for conflict and division clearly exists within the Rhode Island Supreme Court. One supposes that if these five men—as a group—became Justices of the United States Supreme Court, the unanimity which they exhibit would quickly disappear. That is to say, their behavior on this lower court would probably be a very poor basis for predicting their behavior on the U.S. Supreme Court. The fact that the Rhode Island Supreme Court is such a well-integrated system despite philosophical and substantive differences among the justices is compelling evidence of the behavioral significance of the four factors discussed earlier. . . .

. . .

. . . The integration of the Rhode Island Supreme Court appears to be a function of factors internal to, rather than external to, the small group setting.

Concluding Observations

The late Robert McCloskey reminded us that one who studies the American Supreme Court must constantly be aware that he is studying a court—that it is a supreme court—and finally that it is American. McCloskey's insistence that each of the three terms is significant applies also to this study of the Rhode Island Supreme Court.

Portions of the analysis in this article are explicitly related to characteristics of Rhode Island—the "chummy little state." Any case study suffers from the serious limitation that one does not know whether he has identified characteristics of judicial behavior which are common to many state courts, or peculiar to one. For that reason, it is particularly gratifying to note that Canon and Jaros' studies of *all* state courts of last resort (based on aggregate data and a variety of elegant statistical techniques) have identified the presence or absence of an intermediate appellate court as the most significant determinant of dissenting behavior.[5] Statistical studies of this sort are extremely useful because they make generalization possible. Descriptive case studies help us understand the nature of the connections indicated by the statistics. The combination of the two approaches would seem necessary if we are to develop a thorough understanding of the behavior of the state courts. At present, the data simply do not exist which would permit us to say with any degree of confidence whether the discussion of the judicial role in the Rhode Island setting applies to other state supreme courts as well.

This study—and those of Canon and Jaros—is limited temporally as well. We may not assume that the behavior of the present court is identical with that of the Rhode Island Supreme Court of 15, 50, or 150 years ago. Indeed, should data prove to be available, comparative analysis across time would be worthwhile.

There has been a tendency in recent years to minimize the distinctions between decision-making in courts and in other institutions. While the identification of common aspects of decision-making is important—my own heavy reliance on Fenno's study of a congressional committee is an example—one must not ignore the differences. The facts that the institution under study is a state court—that it is an appellate court rather than a trial court—and that it is the appellate court of last resort, are important, at least insofar as a study of the Rhode Island Supreme Court is concerned. The role perceptions of the justices, their specific task orientation, and the nature of the material with which they deal, are behaviorally significant consequences of the fact that these five men sit as a state supreme court, not as a legislature, nor as a commission, nor as the Rhode Island Superior Court. Finally, this study underscores the utility of the approach taken by Canon and Jaros, in treating dissent as a characteristic of courts rather than of individual judges.

It is indeed interesting that Fenno's discussion of the House Appropriations Committee provides better analogues to the Rhode Island Supreme Court than does Walter Murphy's (1964) [*Elements of Judicial Strategy*] leading study of decision-making in the United States Supreme Court. The two courts deal with different material. The outlooks of the justices on these two courts diverge in major respects and they function in distinctive social contexts. Thus, it is hardly surprising that the judicial process in Providence differs greatly from that in Washington: clearly we cannot base our understanding of state supreme courts on studies of the highest federal court. In the case of Rhode Island, and perhaps other states as well, models drawn from the United States Supreme Court are inadequate.

Important aspects of the behavior of the Rhode Island Supreme Court result from its position as an appellate court. It seems appropriate to emphasize the distinction between appellate courts and trial courts, at least until it is shown that this distinction is not significant. It may well be that the status "judge" includes a variety of kinds of political actors, who must be carefully sorted out.

The present framework of analysis was employed because it appeared to make sense for this court. The focus is one which might provide the basis for a comparative study of state supreme courts: one would wish to compare and contrast courts in terms of three variables suggested by Fenno:

1. The extent of their integration;
2. The factors which enhance or inhibit their integration;
3. The consequences of varying degrees of integration.

The last of the three is probably the most significant. In terms of its impact on public policy, the Rhode Island Supreme Court appears strongly to support the status quo. One wonders whether this is a necessary corollary of a high degree of integration? Further research may demonstrate whether state supreme courts whose justices perceive of their roles in more creative terms are less well integrated.

. . .

Notes

1. The assignments are kept secret so that counsel are not able to gear their arguments to a specific judge. One might expect that the justice to whom a case had been assigned would dominate the questioning in his case. My impression is that this is not so; as an observer in court over several months I was unable to determine which justice would write the opinion in a particular case.

2. There is no indication that the chief justice is more than the first among equals. Under the recent court reorganization, he was made the administrative head of the state court system, but it remains to be seen what this change will amount to. In terms of influence within the court, all of those interviewed agree that the chief justice's impact is a function of his personal characteristics: he enjoys no more influence than he would as an associate justice. This is not surprising, since he does not control opinion assignment, and in the initial daily conference, he does not enjoy a strategic position.

3. Based on all Rhode Island cases reported in Volumes 261, 262, 263, and 264 *Atlantic Reporter 2d,* including per curiams, but excluding memoranda.

4. By tradition, the court consists of three Democrats and two Republicans.

5. Bradley C. Canon and Dean Jaros, "External Variables, Institutional Structure and Dissent on State Supreme Courts," 4 *Polity* 185 (1970); and "Dissent on State Supreme Courts: The Differential Significance of Characteristics of Judges," 15 *Midwest Journal of Political Science* 322 (1971).

40

Role Perceptions and Behavior in Three U.S. Courts of Appeals

J. Woodford Howard, Jr.

The concept of "judicial role" refers to normative expectations shared by judges and related actors regarding how a given judicial office should be performed.[1] Scholars have long debated whether judges' perceptions of these norms influence judicial decisions. Though similar issues vex students of legislatures and foreign policy-making, the linkages among role perceptions and behavior are of special significance for the federal judiciary. Since the Supreme Court grants certiorari in less than 2% of federal appeals, internalized professional values have traditionally been regarded as essential controls binding federal courts into a system. Yet, the appropriate roles and functions of federal appellate judges have never been fixed nor universally accepted. A law explosion, trebling federal appeals in the last decade, has taxed the ability of appellate courts to maintain coherent national law in a highly decentralized judicial organization. Outside the Supreme Court empirical proofs are inconclusive that judges' prescriptions guide their decisions rather than rationalize personal preferences.[2]

The purpose of this paper is to explore the relationships among judicial role perceptions and voting behavior in three leading intermediate tribunals—United States Courts of Appeals for the Second, Fifth, and District of Columbia Circuits—against a backdrop of the political orientations of their members. . . .

The data concerning political values and role perceptions are derived from off-the-record interviews conducted by the author with 35 active and senior circuit judges of the three tribunals during 1969-71. The voting data are derived from analysis of all decisions by the three tribunals after hearing or submission during FY 1965-67 ($N = 4,941$), roughly 40% of total cases so decided by U.S. circuit courts in this period. Thirty judges, slightly less than a third of total federal circuit judges, participated in both the interviews and decisions. . . .

Role Perceptions

These judges shared a strong consensus, heavily influenced by official and professional prescriptions, that their central mission is to adjudicate appeals as agents of the national

Reprinted by permission from *Journal of Politics* 39 (1977), 916-938. Most footnotes have been omitted.

TABLE 40-1
Attitudes Toward Judicial Lawmaking

Circuit	Innovator N	Realist N	Interpreter N	Other N	Total N
Second	0	8	1	1	10
Fifth	2	9	6	0	17
D.C.	3	3	2	0	8
Sums	5	20	9	1	35

government. Little disagreement also existed about their duty to enforce the laws of Congress, Supreme Court, and their circuits. Considerable tension emerged, nonetheless, over the proper scope of judicial lawmaking in an estimated tenth of their cases having innovative potential. The appropriate limits of judicial creativity, to one judge "the stinking question," was clearly a highly salient issue, especially in the Fifth and D.C. Circuits.

Whereas studies of state legislatures and Congress indicate that role conflicts among legislators center on the purposes of representation, accumulating studies of judges suggest that the sharpest role conflicts in American appellate courts concern judges' functions as legislators. However, it is important to note that these federal circuit judges, unlike some members of state supreme courts, differed over issues of degree rather than of kind. Virtually all of them agreed that, while bold policy ventures such as *Brown* v. *Board of Education* should be left to the high court or Congress, *stare decisis* is "not an unbreakable rule." Within these extremes, their responses to questions concerning the propriety of judicial innovation fell into three broad groupings along a continuum which for convenience are summarized in Table 40-1 as ideal types.[3]

Innovator

Five judges left the impression that they felt obliged to make law "whenever the opportunity occurs." Creative opportunities were usually described as legal vacuums created by unclear precedents, unanticipated situations, and political stalemates. In aiding the Supreme Court, Innovators also emphasized their filtering or "gatekeeping" functions less than their lawmaking. As one senior circuit judge declared:

> The Supreme Court cannot be expected to be supermen. The Courts of Appeals should take a definite lead in innovating in the law—even at the risk of being overruled. Of course, we've got to be cautious, but we shouldn't leave it to the Supreme Court. . . . Courts of Appeals are a laboratory to try out ideas on a regional basis.

The most unqualified expression of this view came from a jurist who considered the best part of the job to be "launching new ideas." Did this mean that circuit courts participate in policy formation? "Certainly," he said. "And the greatest abuse of power is failure to exercise it."

Interpreter

At the opposite pole were nine judges who emphasized that judicial lawmaking should be held to a minimum. Two judges, harboring a "phobia" against "the modern trend of judicial legislation," bitterly denounced jurists who "can't wait for the people's representatives; they must seize power for themselves." "Activism," a term the interviewer avoided, was a favorite pejorative, which one judge defined as follows:

It means 15% concentration on personal justice, about 20% on sociological values, 20% on psychiatry, 15% on economics and on through the social sciences. An activist is a kind of Leonardo, a master of many crafts. Nonactivists believe courts are confined to the law of cases. I am a nonactivist, which means of course that I am a reactionary. I believe courts should confine themselves to legal problems. You know where that places me on the animal farm, among progressive sheep and reactionary goats.

Only one judge, a Southern newcomer, unqualifiedly endorsed the view that judges should merely interpret the law, a traditional conception of judicial duty still prominent on several state supreme courts and trial courts.[4] Recognizing that lacunae inevitably occur in statutes and case law, these judges objected most to courts reaching out "beyond the case" to legislate. Almost a paradigm of modern "strict constructionism" was this soliloquy from a Nixon appointee:

I certainly do have views on that. There is a lawmaking power in every judge, whether he likes it or not. It is inescapable. You can't just leave the law blank because Congress did. To that extent the judges fill in the gaps to determine the rights of parties and get on to decisions. You can't be a pink funk and do nothing!

However [with emphasis], the judge should avoid this process whenever possible. He should leave innovation within the confines of the particular case and leave wholesale innovation to the legislature, where Madison said it should be left. . . . Some judges just go way out of line beyond the case. . . . It's a grand forum, you know. The opinions get printed. Lawyers have to read them. Some judges just can't resist temptation. I call it diarrhea of the pen.

Realist

Almost two-thirds of these circuit judges, including the majority of the Fifth Circuit and all but one member of the Second Circuit, took middle positions, recognizing more demands for judicial creativity than Interpreters and more restraints than Innovators. Like Innovators, Realists saw no conflict with *stare decisis* when precedent is ambiguous or "when Congress abdicates." Like Interpreters, Realists cautioned against anticipating the Justices and emphasized "the professional way" of initiating legal change. What distinguished Realists from the other judges was their common tendency, when acknowledging legislative responsibilities, to differentiate carefully various types of judicial lawmaking and appropriate occasions for innovation. For example, several judges saw more room for creativity in civil rights than in commercial law, which requires planning and stable rules, and attributed the conservatism of the Second Circuit to its heavy commercial docket. A few judges, following Karl Llewellyn, stressed the innovative potential of "shaping the rules to the facts." Others, shading close to Interpreters, believed that judicial policy-making should be restricted to the Judicial Conference and the Supreme Court's power to define procedural rules.

. . .

This summary scarcely captures the subtlety with which these jurists pondered the dilemmas of lawmaking by intermediate courts in a federal republic. But it helps to delimit the problems of relating roles and behavior in circuit courts. On the one hand, these judges plainly shared what Chief Justice Burger has called a "basic divergence between two schools of thought among professors, lawyers and judges as to the proper role of judges," a divergence ranging from emphasis on precedent and the status quo to innovation and policy-making.[5] On the other hand, they differed over issues of degree within a relatively narrow range of creative opportunities. Despite a robust commitment to rendering justice in individual cases, and recognition that Supreme Court reversal is rare in practice, nearly all of them manifested strong precedent orientations. Most agreed further that, lacking docket control, their opportunity to fashion new legal rules seldom exceeds a tenth of their cases. Though they may disagree as to what cases properly constitute the fertile tenth, these judges felt obliged to lead as well as to follow. Hence, their conflicts over judicial lawmaking are inadequately captured by such popular dichotomies as "activism" versus "restraint," or the so-called "objective" role of adherence to precedent versus subjective preference. . . .

Because circuit judges are called upon to reconcile values of continuity and change in adjudication, usually in advance of the Justices and with little assurance that their mistakes will be corrected, tension is inherent in their positions. Strain among expectations *within* a role perhaps characterizes their situation better than does the concept of conflict *between* roles. In any event, ambiguity of appropriate limits on lawmaking by intermediate courts softens the control of received interpretations and elevates the significance of situational factors in decision-making. *Stare decisis* is thus an "open norm," to use Richard Lempert's term, which cannot specify precise forms of action in all cases.[6] When norms are open to further specification, individuals or groups can establish socially approved rules of conduct of greater particularity. That is why these jurists often illustrated their disputes over lawmaking with specific issues, e.g., problems of criminal responsibility in the D.C. Circuit or race relations in the Fifth Circuit, in which policy conflicts were sharp and the law in flux. When judges are free to choose, personalities, predilections, and group relations perforce fill the void. Open or ambiguous roles inevitably enlarge the personal discretion of judges.

Political Orientations

What then guides a circuit judge's conception of judicial duty when rules and roles are unclear? Of the welter of factors that may bear on this issue—psychological, social, institutional—we shall focus on political and professional values. Both are central to popular theories of the judicial process. According to political interpretations, judicial decisions are heavily influenced by the political philosophies that judges bring to the bench. In legal theory, contrarily, professional norms control political and other personal preferences. The trouble with these formulations is that political orientations and role conceptions are not mutually exclusive. In plumbing the sources of role conceptions among these circuit judges, for instance, we find intriguing associations among the judges' political orientations before ascending the bench and their attitudes toward judicial lawmaking. Though the relationships were less marked than those found by John Wold in four state supreme courts, the dotted squares in Table 40-2 show that role conceptions, unlike party or participation variables, ran in the same direction as self-estimated political orientations.[7] Four of the five Innovators identified themselves as having been political liberals before becoming federal judges; only one of nine Interpreters did so. A single Innovator called himself a former political conservative, perhaps as a joke. Otherwise, the large majority were men in the middle, self-styled moderates before becoming jurists, who likewise straddled the conflict over lawmaking.[8]

The fuzziness of both political and role categories, not to mention the small number of judges involved, warns against pushing attitudinal associations very far. The data do not

TABLE 40-2
Political Backgrounds of Circuit Judges and Attitudes Toward Judicial Lawmaking

Political Background Characteristic	Attitudes Toward Judicial Lawmaking			
	Innovator N (5)	Realist N (20)	Interpreter N (9)	Total N (35)*
Political Party Affiliation				
Democrat	4	13	4	22*
Republican	1	6	4	11
Other	0	1	1	2
Political Participation				
Voter only	0	3	2	5
Party worker	0	2	3	5
Party official	3	6	1	10
Candidate**	2	9	3	15*
Political Values before Appointment				
Conservative	1	0	3	4
Moderate	0	11	4	16*
Moderate-liberal	1	0	1	2
Liberal	3	5	0	8
Other	0	4	1	5

* Includes one unscorable response.
** Includes 1 Innovator and 2 Realists who were candidates for party posts only.

prove that philosophies of the judicial function are berobed political ideologies. Yet, on the whole, these jurists tended to favor conceptions of judicial role in accord with their prior political convictions. Hardly surprising given the realities of their recruitment, this connection is an important link among personal values and the judicial process. Because the socialization of American judges is largely informal and anticipatory, in contrast to jurists in France, federal circuit judges are expected to learn their roles largely via experiences prior to appointment. Their perceptions of judicial duty are likely to interact with their prior political beliefs, because both sets of values develop from the same antecedent experiences.

Political values thus pervade the world of circuit judges as well as other political elites. Their philosophies of politics and the judicial function, notwithstanding official efforts to separate the two, *are* entwined in resolving and rationalizing the normative ambiguities of their work.

Values and Votes

The proof of the pudding is whether . . . role conceptions affect adjudication. . . .

The reader should keep in mind the many pitfalls confronting efforts to answer this question. Theoretically, a person's . . . role perceptions are but single aspects of a vast cognitive network, which may be rooted in the irrational. Even discounting disparities between what people say and think, a direct relationship is seldom to be expected among an individual's social roles, role perceptions, and conduct.

Methodological problems compound the difficulty of establishing links. The most formidable are subjectivity in classifications, a multiplicity of competing variables (e.g., collegial decision-making or personality) intervening between general attitudes and specific choices, and the lack of transitivity among aggregated votes. Panel techniques were used to reduce the subjectivity of inferred role perceptions, but disagreement among the author and two assistants regarding 6 of 35 judges on both margins of the Realist category indicate that standardization of terms remains a serious problem in judicial role analysis. . . . Equally problematic is the assumption that votes accurately mirror individual attitudes on collegial courts, where "give and take" is also expected. More troublesome is violating the assumption of transitivity (i.e., that all judges participated in the same cases) for purposes of aggregation in rotating courts. Even though this study rests on a sample of over 5,000 votes, relaxation of transitivity standards proved necessary because panel rotation and low dissent rates on these courts yielded frequencies too small for conventional analysis of variance of different subjects and individuals. Finally, the difficulty of isolating the cases that comprise the creative opportunities of circuit judges precluded testing of judicial role perceptions in exclusively lawmaking situations.

. . . Still, for exploratory purposes it is useful to establish whether general . . . professional predispositions are related to aggregate voting behavior. . . . For this purpose the judges' . . . attitudes toward judicial lawmaking were compared with the policy outcomes of their votes in selected subjects.

Few concepts in the American political lexicon are more elusive than "liberal" and "conservative." While these jurists readily classified their prior political values on a liberal-conservative continuum, they often affirmed common observations that neither label describes a unitary ideology but rather a cluster of attitudes toward different policy referents. To capture some of this complexity, broad policy subjects are differentiated in Table 40-3 which compares the . . . role perceptions of these jurists with the outcome of their votes during FY 1965-67. . . .

. . .

. . . Assuming that role conceptions were in fact related to political values evident in circuit decisions, as popularly assumed during the era of the Warren Court and implied by the overlapping attitudes in Table 40-2, Innovators should have been more likely than Interpreters to favor workers and claimants in injuries cases, public rights in patent and copyright cases, and the government in NLRB and tax cases. Innovators more than other judges also would be expected to favor individuals in civil rights, prisoner petitions, and criminal cases.

The distribution of votes in Table 40-3 offers moderate support for the proposition that Innovators generally were more libertarian in voting behavior than were Realists and Interpreters. The evidence bolsters confidence especially in the distinction between Innovators and Interpreters and in the association of Innovators on the Courts of Appeals with "libertarian activism." . . . [D]ifferences among Innovators and the other judges were statistically significant when role perceptions were compared with mean percentages of liberal voting per judge. . . . [T]he direction of voting between the two groups of judges followed the liberal-conservative continuum in every field save the ideologically elusive subject of income tax. Furthermore, the strongest overlap among role conceptions and voting behavior occurred precisely in subjects, e.g., civil rights and criminal justice, with which the judges illustrated their disputes over lawmaking. In criminal appeals Innova-

TABLE 40-3
Attitudes Toward Judicial Lawmaking and Votes in Selected Subjects FY 1965-1967

Subject	Attitudes Toward Judicial Lawmaking									
	Innovator (5)		Realist (19)		Interpreter (6)		Total (30)		
	Votes %	(N)	Votes %	(N)	Votes %	(N)	Votes %	(N)	
Employee Injury pro-employee	63.5	(52)	57.8	(211)	58.5	(118)	58.8	(381)	$X^2 = 0.56$, $p > .70$* $\gamma = .038$
Other Personal Injury pro-claimant	54.2	(72)	44.2	(265)	45.2	(104)	46.0	(441)	$X^2 = 2.32$, $p > .30$ $\gamma = .085$
Patent & Copyright anti-claimant	61.5	(39)	65.9	(129)	54.3	(35)	63.1	(203)	$X^2 = 1.64$, $p > .30$ $\gamma = .078$
Labor-Management defer to agency	64.5	(110)	61.7	(311)	55.5	(108)	61.1	(529)	$X^2 = 2.0$, $p > .30$ $\gamma = .108$
Income Tax pro-government	69.1	(94)	73.9	(307)	69.8	(106)	72.2	(507)	$X^2 = 1.2$, $p > .50$ $\gamma = (-).004$
Civil Rights pro-individual	65.4	(81)	57.1	(238)	48.4	(95)	56.8	(414)	$X^2 = 5.19$, $p > .05$ $\gamma = .200$
Prisoner Petitions pro-individual	34.1	(226)	25.3	(688)	23.3	(231)	26.6	(1,145)	$X^2 = 8.29$, $p < .02$ $\gamma = .153$
Criminal pro-individual	35.6	(368)	22.0	(1,132)	17.1	(374)	23.7	(1,874)	$X^2 = 39.6$, $p < .001$ $\gamma = .282$
Sums	47.3	(1,042)	39.7	(3,281)	37.0	(1,171)	40.6	(5,494)	

df 2
γ = Goodman-Kruskal gamma

tors favored defendants more than did Interpreters by a 2 to 1 margin. The odds that this occurred by chance were less than 1-in-1,000.

Granted, judges and cases are not fungible. Given the size of the voting universe and the low levels of dissensus in these courts, even these modest relationships are among the most positive associations yet uncovered between judicial role perceptions and aggregate voting behavior.

. . .

Conclusions

A classic question in the theory of judicial decision is whether judging is "political behavior" or "judicial role behavior." The short answer from this study is a qualified neither. The basic findings are that fairly uniform political orientations and role perceptions prevailed on three major Courts of Appeals, though substantial tension flourished among circuit judges over their lawmaking roles. The judges' role perceptions and their past political orientations were related at perceptual levels, suggesting interaction among political and professional attitudes in their socialization. . . . In general, different role perceptions, though untested in exclusively lawmaking situations, were moderately associated with liberal-conservative voting behavior. . . . Especially was this so of Innovators who, on circuit courts as on the Supreme Court during this period, gravitated toward "libertarian activism" in civil rights and criminal justice. . . .

These conclusions . . . have several implications for students of the judiciary. First, judicial role perceptions in the three courts appear neither so weak as to be subsumed under personal preferences nor so strong as to be considered "the most significant single factor in the whole decisional process."[9] Federal circuit judges enjoy more discretion to make policy than presumed in deterministic theories of judicial decision, whatever the postulated control.

Second, these mixed results should not cast a plague on political or professional theories of judicial decision-making, but point up the need to refine both by developing finer measures of political and professional ideologies and by differentiating conditions under which they may be expected to affect judicial behavior in different courts. Contrasting role perceptions among the judges of these circuits and state supreme courts, for example, shake the notion that a uniform role structure controls American judges, irrespective of . jurisdiction, organizational level, or political environment. Capturing such differences will aggravate dilemmas of measurement; but the evidence suggests that the effects of political and professional values vary substantially with institutions, issues, and situations. As Glenn Stassen observed of U.S. Senators, role expectations tend to be determinative for lower-level officials and for routine questions whose rules of decision are settled.[10] So these circuit judges regarded roughly nine-tenths of their cases. Role-playing is also likely when issues are perceived in terms of victory or defeat for an organization against rivals. The self-consciousness of the Fifth Circuit in civil rights and the Second Circuit in patents offer examples. Discretion and role strain, in turn, coalesce with policy disputes on legal frontiers, where ambiguity breeds subjectivity.

Lastly, the cohesion among these circuit judges concerning the constraints of precedent and national office, which limit creative opportunities, warns against exaggerating this leeway into license. Shared normative beliefs help to institutionalize the federal judiciary. Role conflict, according to participants, is absent from the overwhelming majority of circuit cases. Ordinarily, the mutual expectations of *stare decisis*, . . . enable circuit judges to control the premises of decision of subordinates who exercise discretion in particular cases. Common policy values among judges, neglected as a source of cohesion in legal theory, likewise contribute to the integration of federal courts.

Even so, some circuit judges now consider the Supreme Court's supervision of tribunals below to be "patently inadequate."[11] The practical problem, however, is not whether the Justices can effectively monitor all federal appeals in a law explosion, but rather the creative tenth in which judicial roles and policy directions are relatively open. This study suggests that professional discipline *is* an imperfect surrogate for institutional controls in cases of greatest policy-making potential. The irony is that pragmatic and middle-of-the-road policy values, dominant among federal circuit judges by virtue of professional socialization and political recruitment, make it unlikely that circuit courts as institutions will stray far from the reservation.

Notes

1. See . . . Bruce J. Biddle and Edwin J. Thomas (eds.), *Role Theory: Concepts and Research* (New York: John Wiley and Sons, 1966).

2. [T]he effort to examine systematically the relationships among judicial role orientations and behavior began with C. Herman Pritchett's *Civil Liberties and the Vinson Court* (Chicago: University of Chicago Press, 1953). Other published attempts include: Theodore L. Becker, "A Survey of Hawaiian Judges: The Effect on Decisions of Judicial Role Variations," *American Political Science Review* 60 (1966), 677–80; Henry R. Glick, *Supreme Courts in State Politics: An Investigation of the Judicial Role* (New York: Basic Books, 1971), 42–51; Joel B. Grossman, "Role-Playing and the Analysis of Judicial Behavior: The Case of Mr. Justice Frankfurter," *Journal of Public Law* 11 (1962), 285–309; . . . Dean Jaros and Robert I. Mendelsohn, "The Judicial Role and Sentencing Behavior," *Midwest Journal of Political Science* 11 (1967), 471–88; and Kenneth N. Vines, "The Judicial Role in the American States: An Exploration," in Joel B. Grossman and Joseph Tanenhaus (eds.), *Frontiers of Judicial Research* (New York: Wiley, 1969), 461–85.

3. Role perceptions were inferred from the judges' responses to open-ended and structured questions, including the following query concerning innovation: "Some people think circuit judges should be legal innovators, thus illuminating issues for the Supreme Court; others argue that circuit judges should merely apply the law, leaving legal innovations to legislatures and the Supreme Court. What do you think?" No problems of intersubjectivity of meaning arose on this score in the interviews. . . .

4. See note 2 above. Also, Charles H. Sheldon, "Perceptions of Judicial Roles in Nevada," *Utah Law Review* (1968), 355–67; Thomas D. Ungs and Larry R. Bass, "Judicial Role Perceptions: A Q-Technique Study of Ohio Judges," *Law and Society Review* 6 (1972), 343–66; and John Wold, "Political Orientations, Social Backgrounds, and Role Perceptions of State Supreme Court Judges," *Western Political Quarterly* 27 (1974), 239–48.

5. Interview, *U.S. News & World Report*, August 21, 1972, p. 39.

6. "Norm-Making in Social Exchange: A Contract Law Model," *Law and Society Review* 7 (1972), 1–32.

7. Following Wold, *loc. cit.,* political orientations were determined by responses to the structured question: "*Before* you became a federal judge, how did you classify yourself according to political beliefs or values?"

8. In addition, though former federal district judges comprised 43% of the total, none was an Innovator. Nor did the most active former politicians become judicial activists.

Except for one Interpreter, those formerly most active in electoral politics tended to gravitate toward the moderate and Realist positions, one suspects because they were political centrists to begin with or underwent substantial resocialization as district judges.

9. Kenneth M. Dolbeare, *Trial Courts in Urban Politics* (New York: Wiley, 1968), 69.

10. Glenn H. Stassen, "Individual Preference Versus Role-Constraint in Policy-Making," *World Politics* 25 (1972), 118–119.

11. Shirley M. Hufstedler, "Courtship and Other Legal Arts," *American Bar Association Journal* 60 (1974), 547.

CHAPTER FOURTEEN

COURTS AS SMALL GROUPS

In viewing judicial decision making we have seen how several factors influence judicial behavior. Analysts of the judicial role attempt to link individual and institutional characteristics in explaining judicial behavior. Others interested in what affects judicial behavior have chosen to direct attention to a variety of structural considerations beyond those embodied in the concept of judicial role. Among these considerations are the number of judges with decisional responsibility in a particular case, that is, whether decisions are made by one judge or by a group of judges.

In the United States today both types of decision-making structures are used. However, for the most part the single-judge structure is found in the trial courts and the collegial court apparatus is common to appellate tribunals. In the federal system the judicial institutions that provide for collegial court decision making are, with some exceptions (such as the very infrequently used three-judge federal district court) appellate courts, and include the eleven regional courts of appeals, most of the specialized federal courts, and of course the United States Supreme Court. Collegial courts are also evident in the state systems, primarily at the intermediate level (the majority of states have them) and at the highest appellate levels.

The fact that decisions are made by a group rather than by an individual requires us to examine the dynamics of the group process and to seek to discover what difference it makes that decisions are a group and not an individual product. Social psychologists have utilized small experimental decision-making groups (composed of paid subjects, usually college students, who were unobtrusively observed by researchers) to study group behavior and to generate as well as to test hypotheses. One common-sense proposition about group decision making is that leadership will be exercised within a group. Consequently, leadership roles have been carefully examined by researchers. The concepts of task leadership and social leadership, discussed in the Danelski reading (selection 42), have resulted from this research.

Other hypotheses have also been formulated and put to the test. A number of findings have emerged.[1] For example, in a small group there are strong pressures to conform to the majority position (that is, deviance is discouraged). Small groups have been found to be more accurate than individuals acting alone in solving certain kinds of problems. Small groups have also been found to take greater risks than individuals.[2] The literature also suggests that the quantity and quality of communication within the small group may in themselves affect the decisional behavior of the group.

It is a fair question to ask how these and other small-group findings by social psychologists relate to collegial court decision making. We further can and should ask how we can test small-group hypotheses when we obviously cannot bring the judges to the small-group laboratory or otherwise observe the conference deliberations of collegial courts. In other words, even if we think the small-group concepts are relevant to court behavior, how can we objectively determine if indeed they are, and what data *can* be collected to test the hypotheses?

First let us consider the question of relevance. We can observe that the small-group leadership concepts directly relate to how collegial courts go about their business. In the selection by David Danelski these leadership concepts are developed with reference to the United States Supreme Court, and a convincing argument is made that the role of Chief Justice is the one that best permits the exercise of task leadership and social leadership, although it does not necessarily follow that all Chief Justices will assume these leadership roles.

The concepts of conformity and deviance are obviously applicable to the study of the dissent behavior of members of collegial courts. It has been found that, with the exception of the United States Supreme Court since 1943,[3] the overwhelming majority of the decisions of state and federal collegial courts have been unanimous. Although the dissent rates have varied,[4] it appears that the pressures to conform were there and that it is these pressures and not necessarily the characteristics of the cases that have led to so much consensus.[5] When dissents did occur, they tended to reflect attitudinal and value commitments rather than a deviant type of personality.[6] Studies of consensus (conformity) and conflict (deviance) on collegial courts reflect a continuing research interest on the part of judicial behavior scholars, and the small-group literature is certainly suggestive of hypotheses to test.

We may infer from the article by J. Woodford Howard, Jr., "On the Fluidity of Judicial Choice" (selection 41), that the accuracy of judgment finding of the social psychologists may be applicable to collegial courts. Howard demonstrates that in some of the more complex and controversial cases decided by the Supreme Court, the small-group context has caused some justices to change their initial perceptions of the issues involved; that is, had these justices not had the benefit of interchange with their fellow justices in the small-group context of Supreme Court decision making, their judicial decisions would have been different. But perhaps the importance of this small-group concept is exaggerated, for it is difficult to objectively determine that the majority view on thorny issues is necessarily more accurate than the view of the dissenters or, in the case of a unanimous court, that even a solid consensus represents the most accurate representation of reality. Because of the dynamics of the small-group interchange, Justice Douglas may indeed have been led to a more accurate perception than he had at first concerning the issues in the Terminiello case, but it is difficult to objectively demonstrate that his final view and that of the majority indeed reflected more accurate judgment than his earlier and the dissenting views.

Another small-group hypothesis that has found its way into the judicial behavior literature raises the question whether a collegial court will take more risks, that is, will be more willing to make decisions that the judges believe will provoke significant criticism, than a single-judge court. One political scientist, Thomas Walker, explored this question with reference to federal district court judges. He took advantage of the fact that although district court judges usually sit as single-court judges, on some occasions they sit as members of three-judge federal district courts. Walker assumed that a pro-civil liberties decision would tend to be more controversial than a decision limiting the scope of civil liberties. This assumption may be problematic, but it is nonetheless of interest to note that Walker examined the civil liberties decision making of the same judges in the single-judge and collegial court contexts and found that the judges were more likely to decide in favor of civil liberties, that is, they made more controversial decisions and thus took greater risks, in the group context.[7] Walker also conducted a survey of the judges and found that although a majority expressed no preference as to court context for deciding controversial cases, a large majority of those who did express a preference favored the group over the single-judge setting.[8] In 1976 Congress passed legislation restricting the use of three-judge district courts;[9] if the hypothesis about the risk-taking behavior of small groups is correct, such a change should have an important impact on policy-making behavior in the federal district courts.

As for the Supreme Court, one can argue that the Court on occasion goes further, takes greater risks, than do the lower courts. One example of a landmark controversial (and "risky") decision is *Brown* v. *Board of Education*. The interview with Chief Justice Earl Warren (selection 43) highlights not only Warren's leadership role[10] but also the shift to risk phenomenon (although as a small-group concept this must be hesitantly employed since cases such as in the *Brown* litigation generally come to the Court from lower *collegial* courts). The interview with Warren also hints at the existence of communication networks on the Court; but communication concepts have yet to demonstrate their worth for the analysis of collegial courts.

The group context of appellate court decision making is conducive to negotiation, bargaining, and the utilization of a variety of strategies of persuasion. Walter Murphy, in a classic work of political analysis, *Elements of Judicial Strategy*,[11] demonstrated the workings of these processes within the Supreme Court. The Danelski and Howard readings also offer insight into the negotiation process, as does (although more indirectly) the interview with Earl Warren.

Unlike social psychologists, students of collegial court behavior cannot directly observe the group in action, but the group is real and not experimental. Researchers must rely on accounts of group deliberations or draw inferences from the voting records of judges. Accounts of collegial court deliberations are found in the diaries and other private papers of judges and sometimes in memoirs, interviews, articles, or speeches of judges and their close relatives or associates. Danelski and Howard drew from the private papers of deceased justices and pieced together data to permit analyses of small-group processes. The interview with Chief Justice Warren is a primary source of data concerning the internal dynamics of the Court as a small group.[12]

To be sure, some small-group concepts are not readily applicable to collegial court decision making, but even those that are offer formidable problems of data collection.[13] Nevertheless, as the selections in this chapter demonstrate, insights into judicial decision making are to be gained from an examination of the dynamics inherent in the structural context of decision making. Although it is difficult to be precise, there appears to be justification for asserting that the group condition makes a difference in judicial decision making.

Notes

1. This discussion draws heavily on the review of the literature in S. Sidney Ulmer, *Courts as Small and Not so Small Groups* (New York: General Learning Press, 1971).

2. But note that there is some controversy among small-group researchers concerning the description and explanation of this phenomenon. See " 'Risky Shift' Baffles Social Scientists," *ISR Newsletter* 3 (Autumn 1975), 2-3.

3. C. Herman Pritchett, *The Roosevelt Court: A Study in Judicial Politics and Values, 1937-1947* (Chicago: Quadrangle, 1969), p. 25; and Glendon Schubert, *The Judicial Mind* (Evanston, Ill.: Northwestern University Press, 1965), p. 45.

4. See, for example, Henry R. Glick and Kenneth N. Vines, *State Court Systems* (Englewood Cliffs, N.J.: Prentice-Hall, 1973), p. 79; and Sheldon Goldman, "Voting Behavior on the United States Courts of Appeals Revisited," *American Political Science Review* 69 (1975), p. 493.

5. See, for example, Robert J. Sickels, "The Illusion of Judicial Consensus: Zoning Decisions in the Maryland Court of Appeals," *American Political Science Review* 59 (1965), 100-104; Burton M. Atkins and Justin Green, "Problems in the Measurement of Conflict on the United States Courts of Appeals," paper presented at the 1974 annual meeting of the American Political Science Association; Sheldon Goldman, "Voting Behavior on the United States Courts of Appeals, 1961-1964," *American Political Science Review* 60 (1966), 374-383; Sheldon Goldman, "Conflict and Consensus in the United States Courts of Appeals," *Wisconsin Law Review* (1968), 476-480; Donald R. Songer, "Policy Oriented Behavior of Judges in Unanimous Decisions of Appellate Courts" (unpublished manuscript, 1976).

6. See Burton M. Atkins, "Judicial Behavior and Tendencies Towards Conformity in a Three Member Small Group: A Case Study of Dissent Behavior on the U.S. Court of Appeals," *Social Science Quarterly* 54 (1973), 41-53.

7. Thomas G. Walker, "Judges in Concert: The Influence of the Group on Judicial Decision-Making," Ph.D. dissertation, University of Kentucky, 1970.

8. *Ibid.,* pp. 99-104.

9. Under the provisions of the statute, three-judge district courts are no longer required in cases in which litigants seek to enjoin enforcement of allegedly unconstitutional state or federal laws. Three-judge district courts are still mandated by several statutes, most notably the Civil Rights Act of 1964 and the 1976 renewal of the Voting Rights Act. However, their use is very limited—they hear fewer than 200 cases each year.

10. Also see S. Sidney Ulmer, "Earl Warren and the *Brown* Decision," *Journal of Politics* 33 (1971), 689-702; and Richard Kluger, *Simple Justice* (New York: Knopf, 1975), pp. 830-883.

11. (Chicago: University of Chicago Press, 1964).

12. A second major source of data for the testing of small-group hypotheses is the voting records of judges. See, for example, Atkins, *op. cit.,* where conformity and deviance hypotheses were examined by analyzing voting behavior.

13. See the discussion in Sheldon Goldman and Thomas P. Jahnige, *The Federal Courts as a Political System,* 2d ed. (New York: Harper & Row, 1976), pp. 190-192.

41

On the Fluidity of Judicial Choice

J. Woodford Howard, Jr.

. . .

I. The Evidence of Fluidity

It has long been known, of course, that judges change their votes and permit their opinions to be conduits for the ideas of others. *Causes célèbres* such as the Legal Tender and Flag Salute Cases, or the *Carolene* footnote, come quickly to mind. So does Chief Justice Hughes' pungent expression of willingness to alter language in the interest of harmony: "Justice Holmes used to say, when we asked him to excise portions of his opinions which he thought pretty good, that he was willing to be 'reasonably raped.' I feel the same way."

Walter F. Murphy's excellent *Elements of Judicial Strategy* is replete with examples of how Justices work such changes via internal bargaining. Yet it may come as some surprise to political scientists how commonplace, rather than aberrational, judicial flux actually is. The recently opened papers of Justice Murphy, which contain fairly extensive conference notes for the years 1940–49, as well as docket books for the 1947 term, give a much more plastic impression of judicial choice in the making than the rigidly stratified bloc warfare by which most of us have characterized the Roosevelt and Vinson Courts. Indeed, when meshed with the Stone and Burton papers, which overlap the same period, the Murphy papers tempt one to say that hardly any major decision in this decade was free from significant alteration of vote and language before announcement to the public. Neither was the phenomenon confined to Justices whose overt allegiances were to professional ideologies of law as reason or to philosophies of self-restraint. One of the most striking aspects of the decade is that the most important instances of judicial flux, from the doctrinal standpoint, occurred precisely among those Justices most suspected of ideological automation and in cases that stand as highpoints of their libertarian commitment. From the very human tendency to change one's mind under pressure, no one, and certainly no "libertarian activist," was immune.

Examples of fluctuating options are legion; but for convenience of illustration, certain types of flux may be distinguished from among well-known civil liberties decisions of the

Reprinted by permission from *American Political Science Review* 62 (1968), 43–57. Most footnotes have been omitted.

day. Without pretending to offer the following categories as a unified theoretical construct, we may classify fluid choices according to certain intervening variables which appear to have been at work. First is the "freshman effect"—i.e., unstable attitudes that seem to have resulted from the process of assimilation to the Court. It is not uncommon for a new Justice to undergo a period of adjustment, often about three years in duration, before his voting behavior stabilizes into observable, not to mention predictable, patterns. Biographical materials suggest the generality of this experience, irrespective of prior background and ranging from Justices as dissimilar as Cardozo and Murphy. Justice Cardozo, according to one clerk's recollection of the docket books, registered surprisingly unstable options as a newcomer. Frequently voting alone in conference before ultimately submerging himself in a group opinion, Cardozo himself confessed discomfort in adjusting from the common law world of the New York Court of Appeals to the public law orientation of the federal Supreme Court. Elsewhere I have documented a similar instability on the part of Justice Murphy. During his freshman years on the high bench, Murphy swung from the wing of Justice Frankfurter, whom he had assumed would be his intellectual mainstay and ally, to substantial agreement with Justice Black, whose views regarding the First Amendment and state criminal procedure, it should be remembered, were also shifting ground at the time. In the process of adjustment, however, Murphy had problems of craftsmanship in the picketing cases and, along with other members of the Court, groped for a coherent position regarding free speech. He drowned a dissent in *Gobitis;* he cast a decisive turnabout vote at the last minute in *Bridges* v. *California;* and he also switched sides in *Hines* v. *Davidowitz.* However contrary to preconceptions, it was the libertarian Justice Murphy who had to be talked out of publishing a concurrence in *Cantwell* v. *Connecticut* (in return for different language) which criticized Justice Roberts' Court opinion for inadequately protecting state power to preserve the peace from clashing religious sects.

Eloise Snyder's pioneering study of the Court as a small group supports the hypothesis that the "freshman effect" has been a continuing phenomenon.[1] Parallels in other decision-making groups, e.g., the socialization of freshman Senators, also indicate that the Court is not alone in creating assimilation problems for new members. What occurs is a sort of hiatus between the norms of the individual's belief system and new institutional norms which must be internalized as role expectations unfold. Still, the aggregate effects of such freshman transitions are probably more difficult to trace in the judiciary. Using the concept of cliques, Snyder hypothesized that the high court assimilates its new members through a "pivotal clique" in the ideological center, with the implication that uncommitted newcomers on stratified courts are likely to maximize influence at the outset of their judicial careers, before attitudes and bloc alignments jell. The experience of Justices Cardozo and Murphy suggests the need of refining this concept, however, especially the suggestion that fledging judges with unstable or inchoate attitudes are more influential than senior, committed members. While a pivotal Justice may have a controlling vote in a given five-four situation, the very reasons for the "freshman effect"—inexperience, feelings of inadequacy, hesitation about premature bloc identification, low seniority in assignments, strategies of playing safe, etc.—all point to the opposite direction of freshmen Justices following rather than leading. . . .

A second cluster of fluctuating choices may be grouped around the familiar strategic variables of massing the Court and of institutional loyalties. Justices frequently compromise personal opinion in order to maximize their collective force and to safeguard the power and legitimacy of the Court. . . . That personal ideology may be qualified or even defined by organizational perspectives is by no means unique to the judiciary. . . . The evidence of the 1940's suggests that all of the Justices, at one time or another, were constrained by group and institutional interests. Not only was it common for them to offer helpful suggestions and advice to adversaries, according to the official theory of collective responsibility, but they also sacrificed deeply felt views. For example, Justice Murphy stifled a powerful lone dissent in the first Japanese Relocation Case under the badgering and patriotic appeals of Justice Frankfurter; and Justice Douglas did the same in the second. After finding himself alone, and probably under advice from Justice Rutledge, Murphy also withheld an elaborate dissent in the case of runaway spy Gerhard Eisler, with the result that he left stillborn the first known assault by a Justice upon the House Un-American Activities Committee for violating the First Amendment. Similarly, Justice Rutledge swallowed personal opinion in order to avoid stalemate in *Screws* v. *United States,* an important civil rights decision which held off an attack on expansive concepts of state action at the price of enfeebling federal statutory power to punish police brutality in the states. . . .

More difficult to analyze is a third class of fluctuating options, those which appear to have resulted from the changing factual perceptions of a particular judge. In some cases, the reasons for such a shift may be indistinguishable from pressures to coalesce. Thus, Justice Douglas' acquiescence in *Korematsu* v. *United States* probably was made easier by Chief Justice Stone's continuing reminders that opportunity to challenge relocation orders still remained open to petitioners so long as orders to report to control centers and actual detention were separable. Lack of opportunity for individuals to prove their loyalty was what had troubled Douglas all along. In other cases, shifting perspectives appear to have been a function of additional thought and homework, by a clerk or a Justice, into issues that were only partially perceived at first because of inadequate argument, briefs, or time. The Supreme Court does not follow the practice in some state supreme courts of assigning cases by lot and of infrequent dissent. But it is not uncommon for a Justice assigned to express one consensus to reverse field after further analysis, and then persuade his colleagues to follow suit. Justice Murphy did so with unanimous approval in the complex Chickasaw-Choctaw land claim controversy.[2] An even neater example occurred in *Lawson* v. *Suwannee Fruit & Steamship Co.,* in 1949. There, after independent research by a clerk in a poor record showed that a workmen's compensation award for the particular petitioner might jeopardize statutory rights of longshoremen as a class, Murphy turned tail, reworked the opinion without asking the Court's leave, and won quick, eight-to-one approval at conference. Justice Frankfurter, at that point, could not resist the "dig":

> It seemed to me a compelled conclusion if due respect is to be given to legislation—if, that is, we let Congress make laws and not re-make them.
> This opinion (and change of Conference vote) ought to be a lesson that merely because a particular case is to be decided for a particular employee the result on a fair and long view may be a great disservice to labor and to Law. I could 'document' this truth.[3]

The difficulty is that the reasons for changing perceptions are not usually so obvious. One may argue that flux of this sort is inevitable in the cross-pressures of a collegial court of last resort whose main business lies at the frontier of legal development. One may speculate further about the competing values, the strategies of avoidance, the problems of obtaining linguistic consensus, the rush of business, and the just plain difficulties of substance which induce perceptual change. Occasionally, one may even suspect Justices of doing the unexpected just to confound bloc identification. . . .

But no outsider really knows why judges change their minds. Seldom do they admit, as Jackson hinted in *Everson* v. *Board of Education,* to having switched their votes. . . . Nor, it must be stressed, should judges be faulted either for changing their minds or for lack of complete candor. A major objective of the adversary system, after all, is prevention of premature classification and judgment. That judges may shift position between conference and final voting is not only well understood among themselves, but a testament to the limitations of conference and the effectiveness of the argumentation system. And it is hardly "robism" to suggest that a cloak of secrecy may be just as necessary for judges as for diplomats in making such accommodations possible.

Whatever their causes, however, shifting individual perceptions can significantly affect public policy and the ideological complexion of courts. Consider, for example, the changing positions of Justices Black and Douglas in three of the most ideology-charged decisions of the decade: *Martin* v. *Struthers, Colegrove* v. *Green,* and *Terminiello* v. *Chicago.*[4]

In *Struthers,* the Court faced the question whether an anti-doorbell ringing ordinance designed to protect sleeping night-shift workers in an industrial town violated the First Amendment rights of proselyting Jehovah's Witnesses. Although he too expressed sympathy in conference for the Sunday sleepers of Struthers, Chief Justice Stone at first was unable to attract a majority in support of "preferred freedoms." Justice Black, who saw the scales tipping toward privacy of the home and local control, expressed prophetic fears in conference that the next case might be Jehovah's Witnesses invading Roman Catholic services if no restraints were approved. That view was accepted by a five-four vote; and, after assigning himself the majority opinion, Black circulated a hard-hitting memorandum to the effect that such a community reasonably could forbid doorbell ringing altogether in order to protect privacy. Then, after answering objections in a second circulation, Justice Black suddenly reversed himself. The ordinance was overturned by a five-four vote, and the Chief Justice graciously permitted Black to write a new majority opinion which in effect invited the town to try again with a more carefully drafted ordinance that accommodated privacy and free speech. After all, as Stone argued behind the scenes, some room for accommodation remained before community action, at least until homeowners had an opportunity to listen or object.

Justice Black's about-face in *Struthers* goes far toward explaining some of the puzzles in the opinions. For one thing, it accounted for Justice Murphy's emotional concurrence which replowed the same terrain but had originated as a Murphy-Douglas-Rutledge dissent against their colleague's failure to balance interests. It also made more sense of the Frankfurter-Jackson complaints that the Court was "wanting in explicitness" and attempting to resolve tough practical issues by a "vague but fervent transcendentalism." What the Court had decided was a narrow question of judgment—whether it was possible for a community to accommodate colliding interests by more carefully framed time, place, and manner regulations. What the public read, on the other hand, were heavily rhetorical outpourings from both sides which obscured the precise rights involved and exaggerated the doctrinal split over "preferred freedoms." No one could have guessed until twenty-five years later that privacy of the home and local control loomed so high in Justice Black's scale of values. No one could have guessed that the attitudes he expressed in the sit-in and racial picketing cases of the 1960's represented, not a switch attributable to advancing age, but constancy to prime values which, for two decades, the course of litigation had left unexposed.

Likewise, from reading the opinions in *Colegrove* v. *Green,* no one could have fathomed that Justice Black, author of the three-man opinion which viewed congressional reapportionment as a justiciable issue, had initially expressed contrary conclusions in conference, along with every other Justice but one.[5] Who could have guessed that Justice Black had not only echoed the general fears about entering the apportionment thicket, but himself had attempted to express those sentiments for the Court before he once again changed his mind and wrote the powerful minority opinion which structured a fateful enlargement of judicial power as a supervisor of the electoral process? The answer, of course, is that no one could have inferred such flux from votes or opinions. Having resolved his own misgivings, Justice Black simply advanced his conclusions unencumbered by his previous doubts.

The majority opinion in *Terminiello* v. *Chicago* also provided no clue that its author, Justice Douglas, had followed a parallel course. Nevertheless, both the Murphy and Burton papers indicate that Justice Douglas had initially perceived Terminiello's speech at a volatile political rally of Gerald L. K. Smith forces in Chicago as throwing a lighted match into an explosive situation and had cast his vote accordingly. Then, after reversing position and thus the result, Justice Douglas was assigned the majority opinion and defended the choice by arguments that many contemporaries regarded as the apogee of libertarian dogma.

These examples may be extreme because the opinions acknowledged none of the doubts which had been resolved. Yet they serve to make the point. Votes can be a crude measure of attitude. So can opinions, and even the lack of them. The ideological commitments seemingly manifest in both may be lower and the basis of choice far more pragmatic than either imply on their face. Certainly that was true of the 1940's. The disparity between the rigid ideological appearance of opinions and the fluid choices behind them was sufficiently widespread as to pose genuine problems for anyone making ideological inferences, whether by analyzing opinions or by aggregating votes. After all, if it is true that even the most libertarian of Justices sweated so hard over their options, what are we to make of interpretations, advanced by both quantitative analysts and their critics, which explain libertarian judicial behavior as simply attitudinal automatism? Plainly, the data point to a deflation of the ideological component in the decision-making of this period.

II.   The Gap Between Ideology and Choice

. . . In grouping the evidence of flux around intervening variables of socialization, strategy, and personal perception, the implication is that group variables moderate personal ideologies. Yet the mediation works both ways. Ideology may be inflated as well as deflated. . . .

Besides bargaining and the intervening variables already mentioned, moderation may have resulted from: *equivocation,* in which personal ideologies were victim of novel situations and newness on the bench (Flag Salute Cases); *pragmatism,* in which ideological values were tempered by strategic judgments about what professional and lay traffics would bear (Murphy, J., in *Hirabayashi*); *cross-pressure,* in which conflicting values neutralized individual response (Rutledge, J., in *Colegrove*). Limitations of law cannot be dismissed from that equation. As Justice Rutledge once put the problem to his confrere Murphy in a tax case: "I an constrained to concur, though I wish, as I know you do, that there was some tenable way to reach the opposite result." Ideological inflation, in turn, appears to have resulted from several factors: *conversion,* in which judges who changed tack after further analysis wrote with a conviction that acknowledged none of the misgivings they had resolved . . . ; *workload,* in which busy decision-makers reached into pigeon holes and lawyers' briefs for standing arguments to support conclusions more discriminatingly reached . . . ; *evangelism*, in which desires to persuade lay publics reinforced tendencies to black-and-white argument; *a milieu of advocacy*, in which the demands of persuading colleagues and countrymen in trailblazing cases coalesced with professional habits and personal antagonisms to transform opinion-writing into argumentation and over-statement. . . .

Admittedly, these variables resist quantification and are seldom constant; but it is not unlikely that we have underestimated their effect upon judicial choice, styles of argument, and hence ideological appearances. Especially is this so of institutionalized advocacy. Among the myriad influences at work on the Roosevelt and Vinson Courts, surely advocacy by judges flowered with unaccustomed brilliance. And what advocate would willingly concede an advantage to his adversary by parading his doubts in public? Judges, all of them lawyers and many ex-politicians, commonly refer to opinion writing in terms of advocacy; "you have stated your side of the case as well as it can be put," is a routine compliment to an opponent. Neither are they impervious to Huey Long's reported tactical suggestion on the margin of a Senate speech: "Weak Point, Holler Louder!" Vigorous language, as Judge Walter V. Schaefer of Illinois once remarked, may even be psychologically necessary to cover interior doubt. Aggravating the effects of advocacy, moreover, are heavy workload and scarce time. The Justices, whatever their inclinations, simply lack the time to indulge in all the subtle philosophic calculations attributed to them by commentators. As active problem-solvers, they are sometimes, in Murphy's words, "rushed beyond belief." Pressures are especially intense at the end of term. Under the circumstances, it is understandable why busy judges may throw the book at their tasks of persuasion. And the tendency to overstate is reinforced by the prevalent professional norm that it is nobody's business how the Court's decisions are reached, that official explanations are all that count.

Whatever the reasons for the disparity between plastic deeds and hard argument in the 1940's, however, one untoward effect was exaggeration of doctrinal conflict to the point, it is tempting to say, that outside ideologues preferred. For ideology is also in the mind of the beholder, and scholarship did not escape entrapment in its own polar opposites. However useful pedagogically it may have been to depict judicial struggle of the decade as an epic clash between dichotomous ideologies, the fact is that few major issues took so simple a form. Rather, the fluidity of choice on the Roosevelt and Vinson Courts serves as a reminder that judging, like most American decision-making, is situational and that causation is apt to be more complex than the simple mirroring of precedent or principle or personal belief systems.

This observation has particular bearing on the controversy between "quantifiers" and "qualifiers" regarding the accuracy of attitude measurement. All doubtless would agree that attitudes affect action. All probably would agree with Justice Frankfurter's aphorism that general propositions do decide concrete cases if a judge's convictions are strong enough. The main issue is how to determine attitudes and to chart their effects, and that touches again upon the question whether influence should be measured by doctrines or by votes. This question, of course, has close parallels to an older conflict between aggregationists and survey researchers in the study of voting behavior. An inherent problem of voting analysis generally is that votes, of themselves, do not distinguish underlying variations of intensity, issue perception, and certainty of response among voters. Opinion sampling and scaling techniques were designed to unravel these variables in mass electoral behavior, and today few scholars would seriously dispute their efficacy or rich potential. Guttman

scaling, content analysis, and other quantitative techniques were adapted to judicial behavior as surrogates for opinion sampling. But while sampling poses problems enough in
mass populations, there is little doubt that the surrogate methods of attitude analysis face
rougher sledding in the Supreme Court. The principal reason is that the universe is a
collegial elite whose members not only make decisions in a highly structured and secret
process but also must offer persuasive collective reasons to the public. While scaling of
judicial votes in split decisions has the virtue of stressing relationships among the decision-
makers, the method excludes unanimous decisions and the power considerations which
help produce them. Further, the unit of analysis itself is under collegial influences. The
very reliance on votes to infer attitudes points to the essential problem of identifying the
intervening variables which affect those votes.

. . .

. . . [T]he intervening variables of strategy and style, in my judgment, are so critical in
judicial decision-making that they cannot be excluded from any stimulus-response model
without distorting results and reducing the reliability of the most carefully constructed
attitudinal inferences. Consider, for example, Justice Frankfurter's posture toward federal
searches and seizures. Either scaling techniques or doctrinal analysis, I daresay, would
result in a relatively high rank order for Frankfurter in libertarian responses against
searches and seizures by federal police. To assert that he felt more intensely about the
matter than even Murphy or Rutledge, on the other hand, would invite dispute. Yet
Frankfurter appears to have done just that in the *Harris* and *Trupiano* cases, a fact which
was obscured because he chose to work *through* Justice Murphy in order to maximize his
protest.[6] Confessing himself to be "nuts about" the *Harris* problem, and even apologizing
to his colleagues for excess heat in conference, Justice Frankfurter himself wrote a brilliant
dissent challenging the Court's conclusion that discovery of contraband during lawful
arrest legalized unauthorized searches and seizures in the premises. But Frankfurter had
difficulty rousing his fellow dissenters to the same level of intensity. Justice Jackson, who
had expressed doubts in conference, declined to enter a joint statement. Justice Rutledge,
who differentiated searches of automobiles and homes as well as seizures of open and
hidden contraband, refused to join Frankfurter's attempt to undermine the close *Zap* and
Davis decisions of the year before. Justice Murphy's draft dissent was routinely restrained.[7]
Once before in the Detectaphone Case, Justice Frankfurter had encouraged Murphy to
add "a little pastry," as Murphy described his rhetoric, to strengthen his dissent.[8] Because
he regarded it as "terribly important" that their *Harris* protest reach the police and lower
courts as well as their brethren, Frankfurter again prodded Murphy to stoke his fires,
which was done in an opinion that Frankfurter regarded as "none too strong." By way of
reward, Frankfurter then assigned Murphy the majority opinion in *Trupiano* the following
year, when Justice Douglas' swing gave them a temporary five-four majority.

Stylistic variations may color the problem of intensity no less than the tactical. Felix
Frankfurter, both as teacher and judge, was a scrappy and excitable intellectual with
intense convictions. But Frankfurter also valued "Doric austerity" in opinions, a trait he
lionized in Brandeis and juxtaposed to "the Blue Danube side of me." Frankfurter's
notions of style and strategy coalesced in racial discrimination cases. The former NAACP
counsel consistently cautioned his colleagues to play down anti-racist rhetoric on the
ground that "this Court should avoid exacerbating the very feelings which we seek to
allay." "And if I myself at times betray this wisdom," he added, "so much the worse for
me." Frank Murphy also was a passionate character and a pushover for appeals to evan-

gelical preachment, his most congenial style. But perceiving different responses to judicial crusading, former NAACP board-member Murphy insisted that the Court should invoke "constitutional condemnation" at every opportunity as a symbolic stroke against racism. These variations, of course, were situational as well as personal. Yet that is the point; in assessing attitudinal intensities, can we safely subsume such strategic and stylistic variables, hot or cool?

Similar reservations hold for variations of issue perception and certitude among Justices. If anything, these aspects of choice are even harder to infer than intensity. The problem for traditional analysis is that opinions seldom reveal the issue perceptions of all the Justices, and those perceptions which are revealed may reflect collegial influences more than individual cognition. In any event, we are dependent upon what the judges say their perceptions are. The problem for behavioral analysis is that quantification can reach a point of diminishing returns when multiple variables are involved. There are forces at work in the appellate process, to be sure, which are designed to narrow the issues; we also may expect that increasing sophistication in regression techniques may make the multiplicity problem more manageable. Still, the collisions of value which fracture customary blocs—*Screws* and the privacy cases, for example—also tax ideological analysis. When cases turn on clashes among multiple libertarian values, problems of classification and quantification increase. Furthermore, when past opinions have greater predictive force than current bloc configurations, as was true of Justice Black's *Adamson* opinion for his position in *Griswold* v. *Connecticut,* the lesson may be that, at this point, no one method of prediction is intrinsically superior.[9]

There are occasions of flux in narrowly divided courts, finally, which bloc and swing man notions fail to fit because of pervasive uncertainty. A case may be considered so close that one conference vote cannot be considered more stable than another. The Justices, to put the matter differently, may be proceeding on probabilities of 51-49 percent. That situation probably obtained for several Justices in the tough treaty abrogation case, *Clark* v. *Allen,* in which Justice Rutledge's description of his mental state—"in fog"—aptly caught a wider mood. Uncertainty also characterized a substantial segment of the Court in the early establishment clause case, *Everson* v. *Board of Education.* Although all the Justices readily accepted the principle of a high wall of separation between church and state, application of that principle to a parochial school bus rebate set off prolonged soul-searching and flux. Only two Justices, Frankfurter and Rutledge, would have nullified the subsidy in preliminary voting, and Frankfurter expressed his conclusion "with difficulty." Justice Jackson criticized the child benefit theory so vigorously that his vote for affirmance was doubtful. Justice Murphy, devout Catholic and "ardent Jeffersonian," passed. After Justices Jackson and Burton switched votes, Murphy's signature gave Justice Black's opinion the decisive fifth vote. Murphy thereby came closest to a classic, cross-pressured swingman; but it stretches reality to suggest that he, more than Jackson, Burton, or any other doubtful voter, "controlled" the decision. Attitude analysis becomes hazy in *Everson* because the judges were still in [the] process of determining them. Principle did not decide the concrete case.

In conference, only Justice Rutledge appears to have articulated absolutist arguments; even those reflected a pragmatic judgment that there was no other way to draw a comprehensible and consistent line. "First it has been books, now buses, next churches and teachers," Murphy recorded him as saying bluntly and presciently in conference. "Every religious institution in [the] country will be reaching into [the] hopper for help if you sustain this. We ought to stop this thing at [the] threshold of [the] public school." Rutledge's medicine—on the face, invalidation of aid to *any* private school—was too strong for the others. But as they tried to sharpen alternatives by projecting the principle into implications ahead, Chief Justice Vinson seems to have expressed a common discomfort—and lack of ideological compulsion—when he declared: "I try to think of [the] case before me." *Everson*, in short, may have been one of Justice Brandeis' "go-aheads" when the certainties are no more than 51 percent. Ideological hardening came later.

The Court's evolution in the religion field suggests that different methods of analysis may be better suited to different subjects as well as to different questions. Quantitative methods, in my opinion, have proven utility as negative tests of affirmative hypotheses; it is illuminating, for example, that the legal categories of *stare decisis* and self-restraint are difficult to scale. It also should be remembered that quantitative techniques were designed primarily for research situations in which votes and opinions are the only data available. Yet even then quantitative methods may be safer after judicial attitudes have time to set than when belief systems and doctrinal categories are still emergent. Early quantitative researchers indeed made a "lucky hit," for instance, by choosing right-to-counsel cases for scalogram analysis. The doctrinal watershed in that field and in state criminal procedure generally was reached relatively early in *Betts* v. *Brady*. Successive decisions after Betts seem to have been a matter of pumping factual situations into standing doctrinal categories rather than attempts at differentiation. Nothing really new was added after 1942 except Justice Black's historicism in *Adamson*, and even the language used in the great Black-Frankfurter debate over due process in that case was a projection of the internal dialogue in *Betts*. Religion cases, by contrast, would have been far more difficult to quantify dynamically, because in both freedom to worship and establishment cases, doctrinal motifs themselves were emergent and the threshold conclusions of judges were erratic. One has only to contemplate scaling of the Flag Salute Cases or *Everson*, *McCollum*, and *Zorach* to grasp the point.[10] Time and litigation may be necessary for implications to be perceived and attitudes to harden in a case-law system. Methods that make no explicit provision for such change are essentially static. The subject of religion, in this sense, probably could be studied more fruitfully as a form of "incrementalism," however difficult that concept may be to operationalize. For the attitudinal referents themselves evolved as the Court was forced to shift emphasis from free exercise to establishment and as successive cases exposed tension between the two which at first was only dimly perceived. Consequently, for all the rhetoric released as litigation progressed, the judgments of erstwhile libertarian absolutists remained interest-balancing and close to the vest. Whatever the merits of decisions in either field, it is no accident that the Court ventured into new pastures in state criminal procedure while in religion it still is fashioning attitudes in the old.

III. Conclusion

If the foregoing argument is persuasive that greater fluidity of choice prevailed in the Supreme Court of the 1940's than is commonly assumed, the evidence presented has several implications for the empirical and normative concerns of the discipline. First, assuming that the experience of this decade can be projected, the data point to a potential disparity between a highly complex and fluid "input" stage and a relatively simplistic official "output" in the judicial process. This disparity between choice and explanation aggravates a general analytical problem of reliably classifying hard data, votes and opinions, whether classification proceeds by a single observer or risks are cut by panel techniques. The disparity also points to the complexity of conversion processes, since presumably they too are affected by group interaction. The disparity likewise suggests the need of refining popular concepts about blocs, cliques, and attitudinal automatism which sometimes pass for causal explanations in both quantitative analyses and normative critiques of Supreme Court behavior. By no means do I conclude that the above examples of fluctuating options *refute* the findings of socio-psychological measurement, particularly the more sophisticated and careful versions as exemplified by Schubert's *The Judicial Mind,* or by Ulmer's suggestive work on the theory of sub-groups. Indeed, a surfacing latent attitude may be the very reason for the flux described; and aggregate analysis may be the most effective safeguard against the hazards of classification, particularly in the nonreplicable and highly impressionistic form in which findings such as mine are usually presented. The point is, however, *not necessarily.* Quantifiers must classify no less than qualifiers, and both should face squarely the probability and effect of fluid choices on their modal categories and attitudinal inferences. Because group theory focuses upon such variables while drawing from both behavioral and traditional resources, that approach offers a rich potential source of synthesis for analysis of judicial behavior.

Second, the evidence of the 1940's lends greater support to the lawyer's ideal of the judicial process as a system of reasoning than many legal realists would accept. Clearly, judges of all ideological persuasions pondered, bargained, and argued in the course of reaching their decisions, and they compromised their ideologies, too. No one can plow through the papers of a Stone or a Murphy without coming out with renewed respect for the give-and-take or without appreciation for the multiplicity of variables and constraints, including that old whipping-post, Law, that went into the decision-making of the era. . . .

Third, and for the same reasons, the evidence suggests the need of caution before generalizing about the so-called "role" of ideology on the high court. Especially is this so of the ever-popular dichotomy between "libertarian activism" and "judicial self-restraint." The fact that the Justices commonly identified as libertarian activists actually changed their minds so readily in the 1940's, the fact that Justices Black, Douglas, Murphy, and Rutledge arrived at libertarian conclusions only after tortuous processes of reflection and interchange in some of the most ideologically loaded decisions of the day, should cool the attraction of these worn antinomies as meaningful labels (though I doubt that any evidence will). On the other hand, the fact that the opinions lend themselves so easily to simplistic ideological explanation adds substance to continuing professional criticism of the Court for indulging in over-statement. The issue here is more than one of taste. Apart from styles of advocacy of interest mainly to lawyers, over-statement touches upon problems of credibility, of clarity of choice and inflation of doctrine, and thus of effective judicial leadership in an intricate legal system in which the Court's ultimate power is persuasion. Libertarian Justices, whatever their reasons for ideological modes of address, can be faulted for presenting their conclusions as if they never had any doubts. Oversimplification from the Court, after all, feeds its often-decried public counterpart.

Finally, the evidence presented here points to the essential unity of research techniques, in particular as traditional methods of biographical exploration may contribute fresh data and suggest conceptual refinements for newer methods that were designed for more usual research situations in which votes and opinions *are* the only hard data available. This point is worth stressing because at the present stage of inquiry the critical need is for attempts to combine the findings of aggregate analysis and microanalysis in a theoretical synthesis. Thus, if the above conclusions appear unduly negative or destructive of what passes for conventional wisdom in substantial parts of the discipline, my defense is that they are offered for the peacemaking rather than the warlike purpose of helping to sharpen the theoretical tools that will enable us collectively to cut through the judicial process' fierce complexity.

Notes

1. Eloise Snyder, "The Supreme Court as a Small Group," *Social Forces* 36 (March, 1958), 236-238.

2. *Choctaw Nation* v. *United States and Chickasaw Nation*, 318 U.S. 423 (1943). . . .

3. 336 U.S. 198 (1949). The conference vote was 5-4 in favor of reversal, with Vinson, Black, Douglas, Rutledge, and Murphy in the majority, but the last three Justices apparently had misgivings because the clerk noted question marks by their votes. The final outcome was an affirmance, Douglas, J., dissenting without opinion.

4. 319 U.S. 141 (1942); 328 U.S. 549 (1946); 337 U.S. 1 (1949).

5. On first impression, only Justice Douglas voted to intervene. Justice Murphy passed, and Justice Rutledge echoed general doubts about the political implications of the case. Rutledge later changed his mind on the justiciability issue, but cast the decisive vote against intervention because of difficulties perceived in equitable remedies. . . .

6. *Harris* v. *United States,* 331 U.S. 145 (1947); *Trupiano* v. *United States,* 334 U.S. 699 (1948).

7. *Zap* v. *United States,* 328 U.S. 624, 630 (1946); *Davis* v. *United States,* 328 U.S. 582, 594 (1946).

8. *Goldman* v. *United States,* 316 U.S. 129, 136 (1942). . . .

9. *Adamson* v. *California,* 332 U.S. 46, 68 (1947). *Griswold* v. *Connecticut,* 381 U.S. 479 (1965).

10. *McCollum* v. *Board of Education,* 333 U.S. 203 (1948); *Zorach* v. *Clauson,* 343 U.S. 306 (1952).

42

The Influence of the Chief Justice in the Decisional Process of the Supreme Court

David J. Danelski

In theory, the relationship among the Justices of the Supreme Court of the United States is one of equality, and frequently the Chief Justice is referred to as first among equals. Rarely, however, is there equality in practice. Some Justices are more able, more persuasive, or more personable than their associates, and, in the calculus of influence which lies behind every decision of the Court, these are the important factors. The Chief Justice, by virtue of his office, has a unique opportunity for leadership. He is the key figure in the Court's *certiorari* practice. He presides in open court and over the secret conferences where he usually presents each case to his associates, giving his opinion first and voting last. He assigns the opinion of the Court in virtually all cases when he votes with the majority, and, as a practical matter, he decides when the opinion will be announced. But the Chief Justiceship does not guarantee leadership. It only offers its incumbent an opportunity to lead. Optimum leadership inheres in the combination of the office and an able, persuasive, personable judge.

The Chief Justiceship has lived and grown in the shadow of judicial secrecy. Data cannot be obtained about it for purposes of analysis by direct observation of the Chief Justice's participation in the decisional process of the Court. Manuscripts, memoirs, interviews, and the Court's official reports are the chief available sources of data. Although one must be wary of coming too close to the present, lest disclosures embarrass Justices still on the bench, a study of the Chief Justiceship, to be worthwhile, must be close enough to the present to yield generalizations useful in understanding the office as it is today. In an effort to avoid both difficulties, the period 1921 to 1946—the era of Chief Justices Taft, Hughes, and Stone—was selected for analysis.

I.   Some Theoretical Considerations

Leadership in the Supreme Court is best understood in terms of influence: CJ influences J to do x to the extent that CJ performs some activity y as a result of which J chooses

Published with the permission of the author. Paper delivered at the 1960 annual meeting of the American Political Science Association. Most footnotes have been omitted.

to do *x*. Explicit in this definition are the two concepts, activity and interaction. Activity simply refers to things Court members do, for example, voting and writing opinions. Interaction refers to activity by one member of the Court to which another member responds, for example, conference discussion and opinion assignment. Interaction is indispensable to influence, for if J does not respond to CJ's activity, J cannot choose to do *x* as the result of *y*. Influence, however, implies more than surface activity and interaction, for frequently underlying these phenomena are expectations, values, and attitudes of CJ and J.

Expectations are evaluative standards applied to an incumbent of a position, such as the Chief Justice, and a set of those expectations defines his role. The term "expectation" is used in the normative sense (CJ *should* do *y*) rather than in the predictive sense (CJ *will* do *y*). Role is an important concept in the analysis of judicial behavior because the expectations the Chief Justice and Justices hold for themselves and each other affect their activity. Conversely, activity affects expectations. The Chief Justice, by his activity, can create new expectations and to some extent thereby redefine his role and even the roles of the Justices. Chief Justice Hughes, for example, did this when he established the "special list" for disposing of unmeritorious *certiorari* cases without conference discussion. Thereafter, the Chief Justice was expected to determine initially which *certioraris* should be considered in conference, and if a Justice wanted a case transferred from the "special list" so that it might be discussed and voted upon, the Chief Justice was expected to do so upon request.

Likeability is an important dimension of influence. Like other men, Court members tend to like some of their associates more than others, to be indifferent to some, and perhaps even to dislike others. Chief Justice Taft, for example, regarded Justice Van Devanter as "the closest friend [he had] on the Court . . . ," and when he was fatally ill in January, 1930, Van Devanter was the only member of the Court who was allowed to see him.[1] . . . As this paper will show, the social structure of the Court is significant in the decisional process, and likeability is an important variable in influence, for it is related to the degree and kind of interaction between Court members. Thus, the more the Chief Justice is liked, the greater is his influence potential.

Esteem is another important dimension of influence. The member who is regarded as having the best ideas in conference and being best able to handle the tough cases assigned him for opinion is ordinarily highly esteemed by his associates. Of course, there may be differences of opinion as to who is the most able member of the Court, the next most able, etc., but there is no doubt that such ranking occurs.[2] Esteem within the Court may rest on, or be increased by, prestige he carries over from previous high status positions, such as President, presidential candidate, Secretary of State, etc. The position of Chief Justice in itself, however, probably adds only a little to the esteem of its incumbent in the eyes of his associates. In the Court his esteem depends more upon his over-all ability and how well he fulfills his role as Chief Justice.

In terms of influence, then, the ideal Chief Justice is a persuasive, esteemed, able, and well-liked judge who perceives, fulfills, and even expands his role as head of the Court. One might ask: influence for what? The more important objects of influence are the attainment of: (1) a majority vote for the Chief Justice's position, (2) written opinions satisfactory to him, (3) social cohesion in the Court, and (4) unanimous decisions. In the close case, where a Justice is wavering in his vote, influence may be the difference between a decision one way or another. Since the Chief Justice assigns opinions in cases in which he votes with the majority, the content of an opinion is to some degree determined by his selection of the Court's spokesman. Unless there is minimum social cohesion among the Justices, collegial decision-making is virtually impossible. And where there is such cohesion, unanimous decisions tend to be prevalent, for unanimity arises from the give and take of compromise. Thus, the main objects of influence go to the heart of the Court's decisional process.

II.   The Decision to Make a Decision

Today, the appellate jurisdiction of the Court is almost entirely discretionary. Therefore, the threshold decision to take or not to take a case for review is crucial; six out of seven cases go no further in the Court's decisional process. Standing at the throat of the Court's discretionary jurisdiction is the Chief Justice. All the Justices examine the petitions for *certiorari* and jurisdictional statements, but the Chief Justice's examination must be particularly careful, for it is his duty to present them in conference. Chief Justice Taft's preparation of *certioraris* was like Holmes's: not done so thoroughly as to decide the cases, but thoroughly enough to decide whether or not they should be brought before the Court.[3] Chief Justice Hughes, however, made very complete and thorough preparation, usually going into the merits of each case and often deciding it "then and there in his own mind."[4] Apparently Chief Justice Stone, who was prone to defer judgment for days and even weeks after cases were argued, usually prepared the *certioraris* and jurisdictional statements only to determine whether the Court should exercise its jurisdiction.[5]

Until the middle 1930's, every petition for *certiorari* was presented in conference by the Chief Justice and voted upon by the Court. At the beginning of a term, some 250 to 300 certioraris would be awaiting disposition. Taft scheduled daily conferences to dispose of them, taking up about 50 to 60 cases a day. At first, Hughes followed Taft's procedure, presenting and disposing of as many as a hundred petitions for *certiorari* in a single afternoon.[6] Then he established a unanimous consent procedure in which the Chief Justice was the key figure. If the Chief Justice decided that a petition for *certiorari* was frivolous or ill-founded and therefore did not merit conference discussion, he placed it on a "special list" which was circulated to the Associates. Upon request, any case on the special list would be transferred to the regular take-up list, but cases remaining on the special list were automatically denied *certiorari* without discussion. Hughes disposed of about 60 per cent of the petitions for *certiorari* via the special list, and rarely did a Justice challenge his lists. Challenges were also relatively rare during Stone's Chief Justiceship.[7]

The innovation of the special list increased the influence potential of the Chief Justice. Petitions he wants discussed in conference are taken up automatically, but petitions are not so easily transferred from the special to the regular list. The Justice who challenges the special list must be well prepared and willing to disagree openly with the Chief Justice. To the extent, therefore, that a Justice does not prepare thoroughly or is hesitant to disagree with the Chief Justice, because he likes or esteems him or for some other reason, the Chief Justice's influence increases proportionately.

The Chief Justice's second opportunity for influence during this phase of the decisional process arises when he presents the petitions for *certiorari* and jurisdictional statements to the conference, for he gives his views first and usually speaks longer than any of his associates. The influence of the Chief Justice in conference is considered later, but a word as to the time spent on petitions for *certiorari* and jurisdictional statements is in order here.

Frequently when Hughes finished his presentation of those cases, his associates had nothing to add, and when there was a discussion, he limited it. In the Hughes Court, the average time devoted to the discussion of a *certiorari* case was 3.6 minutes. During Taft's Chief Justiceship, the average *certiorari* case received about 10 minutes, but Taft felt that too much time was devoted to such cases, thus limiting discussion of argued and submitted cases. During Stone's Chief Justiceship, "petitions for *certiorari* and jurisdictional statements," said Justice Douglas, "were never more fully or carefully discussed."[8]

Taft admitted that his conference activity in regard to *certioraris* was not very influential: when the Court votes on *certioraris,* he said, "I'm usually in the minority. . . ."[9] Hughes was more influential partly because of his rigorous control of discussion. In the three and one-half minutes allowed each *certiorari* petition, there could be little discussion, for usually it would take that long to present the case and vote. Thus, by virtually monopolizing the time available, he greatly influenced the *certiorari* and probable jurisdiction decisions. Conversely, Stone's influence was probably less than Hughes's because of the expanded discussion of *certioraris* and jurisdictional statements during his Chief Justiceship.

III.   Oral Argument

When the Court hears oral argument, the Chief Justice is only in a little better position than his associates to influence the decisional process. As presiding officer, he has some discretion in extending counsel's time for argument, but beyond that, his influence depends primarily upon his esteem and interaction. For oral argument is a period of deliberation in which Court members frequently arrive at tentative decisions that usually accord with their final votes.

. . .

IV.   In Conference

In conference, the Chief Justice is in a favorable position to influence his associates. In order to explain the nature of his influence at this stage of the decisional process a theory of conference leadership is necessary. Relying principally upon the empirical studies of decision-making groups by Bales, Slater, and Berkowitz, the following theory has been constructed: The primary task of the conference is the decision of cases through interaction. In making decisions, some Court members initiate and receive more interaction than others. Usually one member makes more suggestions, gives more opinions, orients the discussion more frequently, and successfully defends his ideas more often than the others. Usually, he is regarded as having the best ideas for the decision of cases and is highly esteemed by his associates. Thus, he emerges as *task leader* of the conference. He is apt to be an intense man, and, in concentrating on the Court's decisions, his response to the emotional needs of his associates is apt to be secondary. The interaction involved in deciding cases tends to cause conflict, tension, and antagonism, which, if allowed to get out of hand, would make the intelligent decision of cases virtually impossible. The negative aspects of interaction are counterbalanced by members of the conference who initiate interaction relieving tension and showing solidarity and agreement. One member usually performs more such activity than the others. He invites orientation, opinions, and suggestions, and, in general, attends to the emotional needs of his associates by affirming their value as individuals and Court members. Typically, he is the best-liked member of the conference and emerges as its *social leader*. Not only is he well liked; usually he wants to be well liked. He is apt to dislike conflict, and its avoidance may be a felt necessity for him. Thus, it is difficult for him to assume task leadership of the conference.

Yet it is possible for the Chief Justice to be both task and social leader. Although his task leadership is not primarily derived from his office, the fact that he speaks first in conference tends to maintain such leadership if he has an independent claim to it. Also his control of the conference process puts him in a favorable position to exercise social leadership, for he can minimize exchanges which contribute toward negative feelings among Court members and perform other activity which favorably disposes his associates toward him. Assuming he performs both aspects of leadership well and fulfills the important expectations of his role, his influence in conference tends to be high. Other important consequences, stated as hypotheses, are: (1) Conflict in conference tends to be minimal. (2) Court members tend to be socially cohesive. (3) Court members tend to be satisfied with the conference. (4) The conference tends to be productive in terms of the number of decisions made for the time spent. Rarely, however, are both aspects of leadership combined in a single individual. Typically, leadership is shared in conference. If it is positively shared, that is, if a Chief Justice who is social leader forms a coalition with a Justice who is task leader and they work together, a situation prevails which is similar to the one in which both aspects of leadership are combined in the Chief Justice. Such coalitions ordinarily occur where the personal relations between the Chief Justice and the task leader are fairly close. However, if leadership is negatively shared, that is, if the Chief Justice and the task leader do not work together and even compete against each other, then not only does the Chief Justice's influence in conference tend to decrease, but conflict tends to increase, and cohesion, satisfaction, and production tend to decrease.

There was positive sharing of leadership during Taft's Chief Justiceship: Taft was social leader and his good friend and appointee, Van Devanter, was task leader. Evidence of Van Devanter's esteem and task leadership is abundant. Taft, time and time again, asserted that Van Devanter was the most able Justice on the Court. If the Court were to vote, he said, that would be its judgment, too. The Chief Justice admitted that he did not know how he could get along without Van Devanter in conference, for Van Devanter kept the Court consistent with itself, and "his power of statement and his immense memory make him an antagonist in conference who generally wins against all opposition." The impression Van Devanter's contemporaries had of him was: "Here is a man with great physical vigor, a powerful intellect and a driving and dominant personality."[10] Though he was absorbed by his work, he had a sense of humor, "not of the frivolous or merry sort," but "always dignified." At times, Van Devanter's ability actually embarrassed Taft, and the Chief Justice wondered if it might not be better to have Van Devanter run the conference himself. "Still," mused the former President, "I must worry along until the end of my ten years, content to aid in the deliberation when there is a difference of opinion." In other words, Taft was content to perform the functions of social leadership. Clearly, he was the best liked member of his Court, and he wanted to be liked. His friendship with Van Devanter was especially close, but he valued the friendship of each Justice with whom he served, even that of McReynolds, whom he characterized as a "grouch." "I am old enough to know," he wrote to one of his sons after an incident with McReynolds, "that the best way to get along with people with whom you have to live always is to restrain your impatience and consider that doubtless you have peculiarities that try other people."

Discussion in the Taft-Van Devanter conference was described in 1928 as being of "the freest character," and naturally this led to some conflict. But when the Justices disagreed, it was usually, as Brandeis said, "without any ill feeling"; it was "all very friendly." . . . During his Chief Justiceship, the Justices were satisfied with the conferences. "Things go happily in the conference room," Brandeis remarked. "The judges go home less tired emotionally and less weary physically than in White's day." Despite differences of opinion, there was compromise and teamwork among the liberal and conservative Justices alike. And there was production. The Court under Taft, for the first time in more than 50 years, came close to clearing its docket. Taft's influence in conference was probably as great as it could have been, for his coalition with Van Devanter gave him power he would not have had otherwise.

Task and social leadership were combined in Hughes. Overall, he was the most esteemed member of his Court.[11] His prior high positions undoubtedly contributed to his high esteem, but primarily it was due to his performance in conference. His associates could always be sure that he was well prepared. Blessed with a photographic memory, he would summarize comprehensively and accurately the facts of each case. When he was finished, he would look up and say with a smile: "Now I will state where I come out." Then he would outline his views as to how the case should be decided. Sometimes that is all the discussion a case received, and the Justices proceeded to vote for the disposition suggested by the Chief. Where there was a discussion, the Justices gave their views in order of seniority without interruption, stating why they concurred or dissented from the views of the Chief Justice. After the Justices had their say, Hughes would review the discussion, pointing out the agreement and disagreement with the views expressed. Then he usually called for a vote. In terms of interaction, Hughes was the key figure of the conference. He made more suggestions, gave more opinions, and oriented the conference more than any other member. He not only did most of the talking; his associates' remarks were usually addressed to him, and they discussed the views he initially presented. Clearly, Hughes was conference task leader. His personality was in some respects similar to Van Devanter's. "The Chief Justice was an intense man," said Justice Roberts. "When he had serious business to transact he allowed no consideration to interfere with his operations. He was so engrossed in the vital issue that he had no time for lightness and pleasantry."

Yet Hughes's relationship with his associates was genial and cordial, and he was regarded as being "considerate, sympathetic, and responsive." Never in the eleven years that Roberts sat with Hughes in conference did he see him lose his temper. Never did he hear him pass a personal remark or even raise his voice. Never did he witness him interrupting or engaging in controversy with an associate. Despite his popular stereotype, Hughes had a "keen sense of humor" which aided in keeping differences in conference from becoming discord. On the whole, he was well liked. . . .

Justice Stone's attitude toward Hughes, however, was ambivalent. From the beginning of Hughes's Chief Justiceship, he thought Hughes did not allow adequate time for discussion in conference. Stone was also critical of Hughes' presentation of cases. The Chief Justice, he said, would greatly overelaborate "unimportant details" and then dispose of the vital questions "in a sentence or two." Stone referred to a portion of Hughes's presentation of the AAA case as "painful elaboration." Oddly enough, Hughes was not aware of Stone's attitude, for Stone never openly challenged Hughes' methods, even when he had strong feelings about them. Why did not Stone speak out? If he had pressed his views in conference, Hughes could not have stopped him. It might be suggested that Hughes' esteem among his associates tended to inhibit discussion generally; for, as Frankfurter said, the "moral authority" exerted by the Chief "inhibited irrelevance, repetition, and fruitless discussion." It might have inhibited relevant and fruitful discussion as well. Stone's ambivalence toward Hughes might be also traced to his conception of the Chief Justice's role in conference which he learned during Taft's Chief Justiceship. Since leadership was shared in the Taft Court, the Chief Justice was a more permissive presiding officer, and Stone apparently felt that Hughes should have presided in a similar manner.

Although there was some conflict in the Hughes conference, the Chief Justice used his position as presiding officer to cut off discussion that showed signs of deteriorating into wrangling. Socially, the Hughes Court was fairly cohesive. Justice Roberts said that though the Court was divided on constitutional policy, there was a feeling of "personal cordiality and comradeship" among the Justices. . . . Unquestionably, Hughes's influence in conference was great.

During Stone's Chief Justiceship, conference leadership was negatively shared. . . . Stone departed from the conference role cut out for him by Hughes. When he presented cases, he lacked the apparent certitude of his predecessor, and, at times, his statement indicated that he was still groping for a solution. In that posture, the case would be passed down to his associates. Justices would speak out of turn, and Stone did little to control their debate. Instead, like his younger associates, he would join in the debate with alacrity, "delighted to take on all comers around the conference table." "Jackson," he would say, "that's damned nonsense." "Douglas, *you* know better than that." In other words, Stone was still acting like an Associate Justice, and in the free and easy interaction of the conference, his presumptive task leadership began to slip from his grasp.

Eventually, Justice Black emerged as leading contender for task leadership of the conference. Although Stone esteemed Black, he distrusted his unorthodox approach, and no coalition occurred as in the Taft Court. Most of the Justices, having served under Hughes, probably expected that Stone should lead in conference much in the same manner as his predecessor. When he did not, a problem arose which is similar to the one studied by Heyns. Heyns's study suggests that when a designated leader of a conference group does not perform the task functions expected of him, the group will tend to accept leadership from one of its other members. But if the designated leader performs his task functions, members who act like leaders will tend to be rejected by the group. Stone's case was ambiguous, for Stone performed some task functions. That may explain why some Justices accepted Black's assertion of task leadership and others did not. Douglas, Murphy, and Rutledge esteemed and liked Black and went along with his leadership which, as senior Associate, he was able to reinforce by usually speaking before them in conference and by assigning opinions when Stone dissented. Roberts, Frankfurter, and Jackson, however, rejected Black's leadership, regarding him as a usurper of functions which were properly Stone's. Reed, who was inclined toward Black, stood in the middle as did Stone. Since Black asserted task leadership, a word might be said about his personality. His former law clerk, John P. Frank, described him in the following terms: ". . . Black is a very, very tough man. When he is convinced, he is cool hard steel. . . . His temper is usually in close control, but he fights, and his words may occasionally have a terrible edge. He can be a rough man in an argument."

Debates in conference were heated in the Stone Court and a social leader was needed to sooth ruffled tempers, relieve tensions created by interaction, and maintain solidarity.

Stone was liked and respected by all of his associates and could have performed this function well, but he did not. He did not use his control over the conference's process, as Hughes did, to cut off debate leading to irreconcilable conflict. He did not remain neutral when controversies arose so that he could be in a position to mediate them. As Professor Mason said, "He was totally unprepared to cope with the petty bickering and personal conflict in which his Court became engulfed." In sum, he did not provide the conference with effective social leadership.

The combination of negative sharing of task leadership and the failure of social leadership increased conflict in conference during Stone's Chief Justiceship. The conflict was not friendly as in Taft's day; rather it was acrimonious, and, at times, descended to the level of personalities. On one occasion, even Stone's integrity was challenged. Cohesion in the Court decreased. Satisfaction with the conference also decreased. Frankfurter warned Stone about the dangers of Justices speaking out of turn after the first conference, and a year later he was appalled at the "easy-going, almost heedless way in which views on Constitutional issues touching the whole future direction of this country were floated. . . ." Extended discussion meant extended conferences, and frequently they lasted until after six in the evening and sometimes had to be continued on Monday, Tuesday, or even Wednesday of the following week. "On more than one Saturday," Frankfurter noted, "the discussion after four-thirty gave evidence of fatigued minds and occasionally of frayed nerves." He longed for the taut four-hour conference of the Hughes Court and felt that the Justices of the Stone Court were not always well prepared for conference and discussion was not duly focused. Production decreased. The Court under Stone decided as many cases as the Hughes Court did, but the time spent in conference to do this was just about double. It is probably safe to say that Stone's influence in conference was no greater than that of some of his associates.

Hughes was probably the most influential conference leader in modern times because he was able to perform both the task and social functions of leadership. These functions are to some degree incompatible and ordinarily a Chief Justice will be predisposed to perform either the task or social function, but not both. It is possible that Taft's strong dislike of conflict and his desire to be liked would have prevented him from becoming task leader even if he had the ability and esteem of Van Devanter. This, too, may have been the reason for Stone's failure as task leader. For Justice Jackson said, "Stone dreaded conflict" and the description of Black as "a very, very tough man" could not be applied to Stone. Stone, it would seem, was made of the intellectual, but not of the emotional, stuff that task leaders are made of. By comparison, it would seem that these elements were magnificently combined in Hughes. But there was more to Hughes' success as conference leader than that. He had all the advantages of both Taft and Stone and few of their disadvantages. He apparently had more esteem than Taft when he came to the Court as Chief Justice, and on the Court he had more esteem than either Taft or Stone. Like Stone, he had the advantage of having been a Court member; but he did not have the disadvantage of disassociating himself from his former role of Associate Justice. The principal thing he learned during his service with Chief Justice White was how not to preside in conference. He felt White did not give the leadership he should have in conference and did not control and focus the discussion of the Justices. As Chief Justice, Hughes intended to act otherwise. He had a clear conception of his role in conference and acted accordingly. One might well conclude that Hughes understood the task and social functions of leadership and rationally sought to perform them to maintain his position in conference.

V.   Assignment of the Court's Opinion

In all cases in which the Chief Justice votes with the majority, he may write the Court's opinion or assign it to one of his associates who voted with him.[12] The making of assignments is significant in terms of influence because the selection of the Court's spokesman may be instrumental in:

(1)   Determining the value of a decision as a precedent, that is, depending upon the writer, an opinion may be placed on one ground rather than another or two grounds instead of one, or deal narrowly or broadly with the issues.

(2)   Making a decision as acceptable as possible to the public.

(3)   Holding the Chief Justice's majority together in a close case.

(4)   Persuading dissenting associates to join in the Court's opinion.

The Chief Justice has an opportunity to exercise such influence in a high percentage of cases. Taft and Hughes assigned more than 95 per cent of the Court's opinions during their Chief Justiceships. Stone's assignment average was slightly better than 85 per cent. Usually assignments by the Chief Justice are accepted without question by the Justices.

The Chief Justice has maximal control over an opinion if he assigns it to himself, and undoubtedly Chief Justices have retained many important cases for that reason. The Chief Justice's retention of "big cases" is generally accepted by the Justices. In fact, the expectation is that he should write in those cases so as to lend the prestige of his office to the Court's pronouncement. In varying degrees, Chief Justices have fulfilled this expectation. Taft wrote opinions in 34 per cent of the "important constitutional cases"[13] decided while he was Chief Justice. Hughes' and Stone's percentages were 28.9 and 17.9, respectively.

When the Chief Justice does not speak for the Court, his influence lies primarily in his assignment of important cases to associates who generally agree with him. From 1925 to 1930, Taft designated his fellow conservatives, Sutherland and Butler, to speak for the Court in 50 per cent of the important constitutional cases assigned to Associate Justices. From 1932 to 1937, Hughes, who agreed more with Roberts, Van Devanter, and Sutherland than the rest of his associates, assigned 44 per cent of the important constitutional cases to Roberts and Sutherland. From 1943 to 1945, Stone assigned 55 per cent of those cases to Douglas and Frankfurter. During that period, only Reed agreed more with Stone than Frankfurter, but Douglas agreed with Stone less than any other Justice except Black. Stone had high regard for Douglas' ability, and this may have been the Chief Justice's overriding consideration in his assignments to Douglas.

It is possible that the Chief Justice might seek to influence dissenting Justices to join in the Court's opinion by adhering to one or both of the following assignment rules:

Rule 1: Assign the case to the Justice whose views are the closest to the dissenters on the ground that his opinion would take a middle approach upon which both majority and minority could agree.

Rule 2: Where there are blocs on the Court and a bloc splits, assign the case to a majority member of the dissenters' bloc on the ground that he would take a middle approach upon which both majority and minority could agree and that the minority Justices would be more likely to agree with him because of general mutuality of agreement.

There is some evidence that early in Taft's Chief Justiceship he followed Rule 1 occasionally and assigned himself cases in an effort to win over dissenters. An analysis of his assignments from 1925 to 1930, however, indicates that he apparently did not adhere to either of the above rules with any consistency. Stone's assignments from 1943 to 1945 show the same thing. In other words, Taft and Stone did not generally use their assignment power to influence their associates to unanimity. However, an analysis of Hughes' assignments from 1932 to 1937 indicates that he probably did. He appears to have followed Rule 1 when either the liberal or conservative blocs dissented intact. When the liberal bloc dissented, Roberts, who was then a center judge, was assigned 46.5 per cent of the opinions. The remaining 53.5 per cent were divided among the conservatives, apparently according to their degree of conservatism: Sutherland, 25 per cent; Butler, 17.8 per cent; McReynolds, 10.7 per cent. When the conservative bloc dissented, Hughes divided 63 per cent of the opinions between himself and Roberts.

Hughes probably also followed Rule 2 to some extent. When the left bloc split, Brandeis was assigned 22 per cent of the cases he could have received, compared with his 10 per cent assignment average for unanimous cases. When the right bloc split, Sutherland was assigned 16 per cent of the decisions he could have received, compared with his 11 per cent average for unanimous cases. He received five of the six cases assigned the conservatives when their bloc was split. One of those cases was *Powell* v. *Alabama* which, it has been said, was assigned Sutherland "probably in the hope that he could bring over Justices Butler and McReynolds while some of the more 'liberal' Justices could not."

If the Chief Justice is to be well liked, he must appear to be generous, considerate, and impartial in assigning cases, particularly the important cases. Taft was considered generous in his assignments, and undoubtedly this contributed to his likeability. Hughes said he tried to assign each Justice the same proportion of important cases and especially took into account the feelings of the senior Justices. Justice Roberts thought Hughes' assignments were generous and considerate, and Justice Frankfurter believed that no Chief Justice equalled Hughes in the "skill, wisdom, and disinterestedness" with which he assigned opinions. Justice Stone, however, thought otherwise. During the early and middle Thirties, he felt that Hughes was not assigning him as many important cases as he should have received. Just as Stone felt slighted by Hughes in the matter of assignments, so did Justices Murphy and Rutledge during Stone's Chief Justiceship. Stone was aware of this, but he did little about it.

How often the Chief Justice uses his assignment power to influence activity of his associates cannot be determined with certainty. Besides influence, there are other reasons underlying opinion assignments such as equality of case distribution, ability, and expertise. Nonetheless, every assignment presents the Chief Justice with an opportunity for influence.

VI. The Final Phase: Persuasion and Unanimity

In the last stage of the decisional process, opinions are written, circulated, discussed, and approved or disapproved. Final decision near, Court members have their last chance to persuade each other. The results of interaction during this period can be highly significant: opinion modification, increase or decrease in the size of a majority, and even the reversal of a conference decision. Again the Chief Justice is in a favorable position for purposes of influence. Standing at the center of intra-Court communication, he ordinarily knows better than any of his associates the status of each case—who is having trouble writing an opinion, who is overworked, who is wavering in his vote, etc.—and if he is so inclined, he can play an active role is reconciling differences, seeking compromises, and attaining unanimity. Since, as a practical matter, he decides when an opinion will be announced, he can delay the announcement in hope of augmenting the Court's majority. What the Chief Justice actually does greatly depends upon how he views his role in this final phase of the decisional process.

Seldom has a Chief Justice had a more definite conception of his role than Taft. The Chief Justice, he said, is "expected to promote teamwork by the Court so as to give weight and solidarity to its opinions." He believed his predecessor, White, earnestly sought to avoid divisions by skillfully reconciling differences among the Justices, and he intended to do the same. His aim was unanimity, but he was willing to admit that at times dissents were justifiable and perhaps even a duty. Dissent was proper, he thought, in cases where a Court member strongly believed the majority erred in a matter involving important principle or where a dissent might serve some useful purpose, such as convincing Congress to pass certain legislation. But in other cases, a Justice should be a good member of the team, silently acquiesce in the views of the majority, and not try to make a record for himself by dissenting.

Taft's conception of the function of the dissent was shared by most of his associates, and when he sought to unite them, his efforts were accepted as proper and consistent with his role as Chief Justice. Justices joining the Taft Court were socialized in the no-dissent-unless-absolutely-necessary tradition, and most of them learned it well. Justice Butler gave it classic expression on the back of one of Stone's slip opinions:

> I voted to reverse. While this sustains your conclusion to affirm, I still think reversal would be better. But I shall in silence acquiesce. Dissents seldom aid in the right development or statement of the law. They often do harm. For myself I say: "lead us not into temptation."

Even Stone, who was not so sure about the no-dissent tradition, usually went along with it, acquiescing in the appropriate cases.

Taft enjoyed moderate success in his efforts to attain unanimity. During his first year as Chief Justice, he united the Court in a number of [controversial] cases. . . . Usually he would assign himself such cases and try to write an opinion which would bring in the dissenters. This meant he had to make concessions to Justices like Brandeis, but he was willing to exchange concessions for votes. When there were divisions in cases he assigned to others which could be reconciled, Taft would try to mediate between majority and minority (at times with the help of Van Devanter) in an effort to attain unanimity. If there was a possibility of winning over a dissenter, Taft would frequently let the case go over a few conferences with hope that time would work in his favor.

Hughes easily assumed the role of Court unifier that Taft had cut out for him, for he believed that unanimity should be sought where it could be attained without sacrificing strongly held convictions. Like Taft, he distinguished two types of cases, those involving matters of important principle and those of lesser importance. The former were dissent-worthy; the latter were not. As to the cases of lesser importance, Hughes felt it was better to have the law settled one way or the other regardless of his own ideas as to the correct disposition of the case; and if the majority voted contrary to his view, he would change his vote. For example, in a case involving statutory construction, Hughes wrote to Stone: "I choke a little at swallowing your analysis; still I do not think it would serve any useful purpose to expose my views."

Like Taft, Hughes mediated differences of opinion between contending factions, and in order to get a unanimous decision, he would try to find common ground upon which all could stand. He was willing to modify his own opinions to hold or increase his majority, and if this meant he had to put in some disconnected thoughts or sentences, in they went. In cases assigned to others, he would suggest the addition or subtraction of a paragraph if by doing so he could save a dissent or concurring opinion. According to Justice Roberts, dissents were thus avoided in some cases in which agreements seemed impossible. But unlike Taft, Hughes apparently seldom held up the delivery of an opinion in an effort to secure another vote or two. He made his attempt to secure unanimity, and if it failed, the case was usually handed down as soon as the opinions were ready.

Hughes' efforts to attain unanimity were fairly successful. During his Chief Justiceship, there was no radical increase in the number of dissents. Even in the cases that invalidated New Deal legislation, the Court was fairly intact. Of the eleven such cases, five were unanimous, and two were decided 8 to 1. The no-dissent-unless-absolutely-necessary tradition continued, and in a host of lesser cases Court members acquiesced in silence. The Roosevelt appointees, particularly, showed remarkable restraint in the matter of dissents while serving under Hughes. Frankfurter, who had the best record, registered only seven dissents in his three years with Hughes. The New Deal Justices were baptized in the old tradition concerning dissent, but whether they would retain the faith after Hughes left the Court was another matter.

As an Associate Justice, Stone prized the right to dissent and occasionally rankled under the no-dissent-unless-absolutely-necessary tradition of the Taft and Hughes Courts. As Chief Justice, he did not believe it appropriate for him to dissuade Court members, by persuasion or otherwise, from dissenting in individual cases. A Chief Justice, he thought, might admonish his associates generally to exercise restraint in the matter of dissents and seek to find common ground for decision, but beyond that he should not go. Stone usually went no further. His activity or lack of it in this matter gave rise to new expectations on the part of his associates as to their role and the role of the Chief Justice regarding unanimity and dissent. A new tradition of great freedom of individual expression displaced the tradition of the Taft and Hughes Courts. This explains in part the unprecedented number of dissents and separate opinions during Stone's Chief Justiceship.

Chief Justice Stone, nonetheless, exercised some influence in the final phase of the decisional process. In *Edwards* v. *California,* one of the first cases heard by the Court after he became Chief Justice, he persuaded Justice Byrnes to change his conference vote, and the switch resulted in a decision based on the commerce clause rather than on the privileges and immunities clause of the Constitution. He also influenced the content of many opinions, especially those of Justice Murphy, by suggesting additions and deletions. Although Justices who voted against Stone in conference would occasionally go along with his opinions, he usually made no concerted effort to attain unanimity. He recognized, however, that unanimity in certain cases was desirable, and in a few cases he sought it. . . .

The unprecedented number of dissents and concurrences during Stone's Chief Justiceship can be only partly attributed to the displacing of the old tradition of loyalty to the Court's opinion. A major source of difficulty appears to have been the free and easy expression of views in conference. Whether the Justices were sure of their grounds or not, they spoke up and many times took positions from which they could not easily retreat, and given the heated debate which sometimes occurred in the Stone conference, the commitment was not simply intellectual. What began in conference frequently ended with elaborate justification as concurring or dissenting opinions in the United States Reports. This, together with Stone's passiveness in seeking unanimity, is probably the best explanation for what Professor Pritchett characterized as "the multiplication of division" in the Supreme Court.

VII.   Conclusion

The task of the political scientist, said John Morley, is not simply to describe governmental institutions, but to penetrate to the secret of their functions. In regard to the Chief Justiceship, that is difficult, for complex relationships among the Chief Justice and Justices are involved. The office provides the Chief Justice with an opportunity for influence, but it does not guarantee it. To exercise influence, he must perform activity that results in his associates choosing to do what he wants them to do; and in this regard, his success depends largely upon his likeability and esteem in the Court and upon how he perceives and fulfills his role.

. . .

Notes

1. Taft to Charles Taft, June 8, 1927; Taft to Horace D. Taft, June 29, 1927; Taft to Van Devanter, Jan. 7, 1930, William Howard Taft Papers, Manuscript Division, Library of Congress.
2. See Henry F. Pringle, *The Life and Times of William Howard Taft* (New York, 1939), II, pp. 968–972; Alpheus Thomas Mason, *Harlan Fiske Stone: Pillar of the Law* (New York, 1956), p. 793; Charles Evans Hughes, Biographical Notes, 1930–1941, p. 12, Hughes Papers, Manuscript Division, Library of Congress; Steven T. Early, Jr., *James Clark Mc-Reynolds and the Judicial Process,* Unpublished Ph.D. dissertation, Department of Political Science, University of Virginia, 1954, p. 90. . . .
3. Holmes to Lewis Einstein, May 19, 1927, Oliver Wendell Holmes, Jr., Papers, Manuscript Division, Library of Congress.
4. Edwin McElwain, "The Business of the Supreme Court as Conducted by Chief Justice Hughes," *Harvard Law Review,* Vol. 63 (1949), p. 13. McElwain is a former law clerk of Chief Justice Hughes.
5. See Mason, *op. cit.,* p. 792; William O. Douglas, "Chief Justice Stone," *Columbia Law Review,* Vol. 46 (1946), p. 693; Alfred McCormack, "A Law Clerk's Recollections," *ibid.,* p. 716; Bennett Boskey, "Mr. Chief Justice Stone," *Harvard Law Review,* Vol. 59 (1946), p. 1200.
6. Hughes to Stone, Oct. 1, 1931, Harlan F. Stone Papers, Manuscript Division, Library of Congress; Hughes to Brandeis, Oct. 1, 1931, Louis D. Brandeis Papers, University of Louisville Law School; McElwain, *op. cit.,* p. 15.
7. Stone's Papers indicate that his special lists were challenged less than 10 times in five years.
8. Douglas, *op. cit.,* p. 695.
9. Taft to McKenna, April 20, 1923, Taft Papers.
10. Remarks of former Attorney General William D. Mitchell, 316 U.S. xvii (1941).
11. Frankfurter has said that if Hughes "made others feel his moral superiority, they merely felt a fact. . . . All who served with him recognized the extraordinary qualities possessed by the Chief Justice. . . ." *Of Law and Men* (New York, 1956), p. 148. Hughes was the only member of the Court to whom McReynolds would defer. Early, *loc. cit.,* Black said he had "more than impersonal and detached admiration" for Hughes' "extraordinary intellectual gifts." Black to Hughes, June 3, 1941. Hughes Papers.
12. One minor exception to this rule is that a newcomer to the Court is entitled to select his first case for opinion. This is a tradition of long standing. Matthews to Waite, Oct. 5, 1881, Morrison R. Waite Papers, Manuscript Division, Library of Congress.

13. The "important constitutional cases" decided by the Court from 1921 to 1946 were determined by examination of four leading works on the Constitution: Paul A. Freund, Arthur E. Sutherland, Mark De Wolfe Howe, and Ernest J. Brown, *Constitutional Law* (Boston, 1954); Alfred H. Kelly and Winfred A. Harbison, *The American Constitution: Its Origins and Development* (New York, 1948); Alpheus T. Mason and William M. Beaney, *American Constitutional Law* (Englewood Cliffs, N.J., 1959); and C. Herman Pritchett, *The American Constitution* (New York, 1959). If a case was discussed in any two of these works, it was considered an "important constitutional case."

43

A Conversation with Chief Justice Earl Warren

Interviewer: Is the Supreme Court as serene as the outside public sometimes imagines, or are there some pretty tough hassles when the decision is being talked through?

Warren: I think that it is. Conditions in the Supreme Court are far more serene than the public has an idea of. . . . Now I can say, honestly, that in the sixteen years I was there I don't believe there were sixteen times, let's say, during that period, when anyone's voice was raised above normal in that conference room. That didn't mean there wasn't serious disagreement because we did have serious disagreement, but when you are going to serve on a court of that kind for the rest of your productive days, you accustom yourself to the institution like you do to the institution of marriage, and you realize that you can't be in a brawl every day and still get any satisfaction out of life. And so it is there, if we're going to produce anything, we can't be brawling all the time in the conference room. And the men I sat with were thoroughly conscious of that and just, oh, an occasional flair of temperament, you know, maybe occurred, but it was very very rare that it did and all the rest of the time we argued the things, we debated them fully, but without any rancor or any harsh words in the conference room. Now it might be interesting to you to know just how we do that in the conference room. In every case during my time, and as I understood it traditionally, the Chief Justice opens a discussion in every case that's to be decided. And he will state in a very few moments how he views the case, and, take my own situation, I usually say, now it seems to me that the main issue in this case is such and such, and that how we are to decide it depends very largely upon this testimony in the case. And it seems to me that all things considered, that it should be decided under certain principles, in this manner, and I would either vote to affirm or reverse the case as that language might reflect. Then, after that is done, it goes around to every member of the Court, not in an argumentative way, but each one stating his own views. Now the next man, who in my time always was Justice Black, he was a senior all the time, might say,

Reprinted from pp. 5–8, 10–15 of the transcript of the television show "Brandeis Television Recollections," first telecast on May 3, 1972, produced by WGBH Educational Foundation and funded by a grant from Samuel and Minna Dretzin in association with Brandeis University. Reprinted by permission. The interviewer was Dr. Abraham Sachar, Chancellor of Brandeis University.

well I don't view it just that way, I think this is the principal issue in the case, and I think this principle determines it, and I think these facts justify it, and I would come out the other way, I would do so and so. Now, that's if he disagreed with me. If he agreed with me he might say, well, I agree with the Chief Justice, that's the way I would view it, and decide it, and so we go on until everybody has spoken without any argument of any kind until everybody has generally stated his views. And then after that has been done, if everyone is agreed that the outcome should be one way, and well agreed upon the manner in which it should be decided, there's no need of taking a vote. We just drop it there and go on to something else. But if there is a division on that court at that time, then we debate it as much as we wish, without any regulations or any rules and we never, I never had to bother about invoking Robert's Rules of Order or anything of that kind. We just debate back and forth until it looks as though everybody has spoken as much as he wants to and then I would say well, are we ready for a vote? And if they said yes, why we take the vote. And when we vote, though, we start with the junior member of the court and vote upwards instead of going from the Chief Justice down to the junior member of the court. And why the Chief Justice then votes last, why that is done we've never been able to determine satisfactorily, but it's generally believed that many years ago that that system was devised so as not to put the junior member of the court in a position of being the last member to vote and therefore having the burden of maybe deciding it, where the case would go five to four one way or the other.

Interviewer: The most important Supreme Court decision which affected education was probably the Brown v. Board of Education decision of 1954. It came out as a unanimous decision, really, to end segregation in education with all deliberate speed. The court was made up of tough individualists, they came out of very diverse backgrounds, they had very strong individual convictions, and you presided over a judgment which came out unanimously, fortunately. It needed to be unanimous in order to accomplish the purpose in an emotion-ridden climate such as we had. How did you do it?

Warren: Well, I didn't do it. It was done by nine men, nine men who were there, and who had the same belief that I did of the importance of the decision in the case. And it had been argued you know, the term before I came, and it had been put over for re-argument. They had had a long time to think about it. . . . there was some division, but I think there had been a lot of thought given to it before it was even argued during my time. But in order that we might not get polarized on the great issue and not be able to work it out in an unanimous way, we decided that for some time we would not take a vote on how we stood. Normally, every Friday after a series of arguments in the court, we go into conference and there we decide what we're going to do with each of the cases. And we take a vote on them, and we determine who's in the majority, and who's in the minority for the writing of opinions. But in this case we decided that we would just discuss the arguments that we had heard, the arguments we had studied from the briefs, and from our own knowledge of the situation, and our own research, and without committing ourselves, one way or another, we would continue to discuss it. So week after week on the agenda each week, I would find the time to discuss Brown v. Board of Education and the other cases that were heard with it. And I believe the arguments were held in the middle of November, and we didn't take a vote on it until the middle of February.

Interviewer: Were there sharp divisions at the beginning?

Warren: Well, they weren't noted if they were, but each Justice would pick out a point that he thought was debatable and that it ought to be considered and we would discuss it in that light without anybody announcing that he felt this way or felt that way. And so, by the middle of February, it seemed to me that we had thoroughly discussed it, and I inquired of them if they were ready to vote, and they said, they were. And we took a vote, and the vote was unanimous. And I think it was the fact that we did not polarize ourselves at the beginning of it that gave us more of an opportunity to come out unanimously on it than if we had done otherwise.

. . .

Interviewer: Did it take considerable work to evolve that brilliant phrase, all deliberate speed?

Warren: No, no that took no . . . that wasn't our phrase. That was used by Holmes, I think, in the case of Virginia v. West Virginia. And it's an old admiralty phrase that was used in England, oh, I think for centuries before that, but very rarely known or used in this country. But it was suggested that that would be a way to proceed in the case because we realized that under our federal system there were so many blocks preventing an immediate solution of the thing in reality, that the best we could look for would be a progression of action, and to keep it going, in a proper manner, we adopted that phrase, all deliberate speed. . . . I remember the first time we discussed how long we thought it would take, I remember someone suggested, I can't remember who it was, wouldn't it be wonderful if on the Centennial of the Fourteenth Amendment that it would be a reality all over this country. And I've always remembered that and thought about it many times. It didn't become a reality by then [1968] but still much more has been accomplished than most people realize.

PART FOUR

POLICY-MAKING: PROBLEMS OF COMPLIANCE AND IMPACT

CHAPTER FIFTEEN
WHO GETS WHAT

The results of the judicial process can be analyzed by asking three questions. The first is the question of who wins and who loses. Are there consistent patterns of winning and losing that are associated with particular characteristics of the parties and the situations in which they are involved? The second question is a question of reaction. How do those directly affected by court policy decisions respond to them? The third question is, simply, what difference do court decisions make to the parties involved in a dispute and to others? The second and third questions will be considered in the remaining chapters.

In the Introduction to this book we argued that there has been a gradual increase in the scope of the American legal system. This increase, whose origins go back at least as far as the 1930s, means that the law now regulates or reaches almost everything in American life. The scope and reach of law in turn determines the role and significance of our courts. The greater the former, the greater the latter. As new and different kinds of rights and remedies are created, new and different kinds of disputes reach courts, thus providing more opportunities to make and shape policy. Although courts decide lawsuits between particular litigants, the significance of any court decision often reaches far beyond those immediately involved. The decision may set a precedent for future litigation, and its effect may be to distribute, either directly or indirectly, tangible or intangible resources throughout society. When the Supreme Court ordered the Board of Education of Topeka, Kansas, to end de jure segregation, the "defeat" was borne not only by that city but also by the entire Southern region (including the Border States).[1] When the Court found that Roe had a constitutionally protected right to an abortion, all women found themselves with a newly recognized right.[2] Patterns of victory and defeat may have the broadest political and social ramifications.

Patterns of victory and defeat may also be important in addressing the issue of the distinctiveness of the courts as dispute-processing institutions. Unlike some types of dispute-processing institutions, courts are expected to provide impartial judgment; courts are supposed to decide disputes by reference to the facts of who did what to whom and by identifying, interpreting, and applying appropriate norms. This requires that judges remain neutral with regard to both the issues of the case and its result. We have already discussed the extent to which American judges allow themselves to be influenced by their own political attitudes and values when they feel free to exercise their discretion in making decisions. In this chapter we analyze the "result impartiality" of American courts.

When we talk about "result impartiality," we are referring to the extent to which cases are decided independently of the personal attributes of the parties involved. We assume that impartiality is displayed when both parties to a case are given the same opportunities and are shown the same consideration. Equality of consideration requires that the judge be influenced neither by a personal interest in the outcome of a case nor by positive or negative attitudes toward the people and the particular situation involved.[3] Impartiality in result cannot be determined, we believe, by analyzing a single decision. Rather, it is necessary to examine a series of decisions involving similar situations to ascertain whether, over time, different kinds of parties are equally likely to gain favorable results. If the results were perfectly impartial, then the pattern of decision should be random and should not consistently favor one type of litigant over another. If, for example, courts in custody cases sometimes rule for the mother and sometimes rule for the father, the conclusion may be drawn that they show equal regard for both sexes. If, on the other hand, courts were to favor mothers over fathers regardless of the facts or the applicable law, then their results would not be impartial.

The problem with this way of determining result impartiality is that it does not take into account the several factors responsible for variations from the standard of randomness that go beyond the attitudes and values of the judges. The first, and most obvious, is that even if courts are impartial in their procedures, they may still produce biased results if the laws that they apply favor one type of litigant. This is certainly true in our example of custody cases, since in most states divorce laws embody a strong presumption in favor of the mother. No matter how even-handed the application of such laws, the pattern of results is predetermined by the bias in their substance. Other factors producing deviations from the standard of randomness are the costs of using courts, the fact that they operate in accord with complex legal rules and procedures, and the fact that they tend to be passive in the manner in which they acquire cases.

As we have suggested several times, dispute processing by American courts is costly. The major cost affecting the result of litigation is the time it takes to obtain a judicial decision. Delay, according to Marc Galanter, favors parties who are better organized and who have more expendable resources.[4] Delay favors such parties in three ways. First, by complicating the task of challenging ongoing activities, delay advantages parties who derive benefits from the neglect of rules that favor their adversaries. Second, delay tends to protect the "possessor," that is, those who have resources that might be endangered in the course of litigation. Third, delay means that courts cannot efficiently protect all of the rights that are formally recognized by law. Since there are priorities in the allocation of judicial resources, judges tend to favor the more organized and the more attentive among their clientele. In each instance, delay benefits the well organized and the economically powerful.

The fact that courts operate in accord with legal procedures puts a premium on the ability of parties to obtain expert legal counsel. Since not all lawyers are equally skillful or committed, resource differentials result in an unequal distribution of legal talent. In addition, the reactive organization of courts gives advantage to those parties with information and a sense of legal efficacy. The passivity of courts means that the burden of instituting a lawsuit remains on the parties themselves. Parties are treated as if they were equally capable of marshaling the resources and legal skills needed to effectively present a case. When they are in fact not equally capable of doing so, the pattern of results will be imbalanced. Finally, the lack of impartiality in the results of the judicial process may be a function of the personal biases of judges. To the extent that judges are selected from among particular groups or interests, they may be expected to sympathize with the attitudes and values associated with those groups or interests when making decisions.

Each of these explanations may provide some insight into the two readings in this chapter. In selection 44, Marc Galanter summarizes the findings of a variety of empirical studies. These findings, as well as those presented in the Dolbeare article (selection 45), suggest that parties who are better organized and wealthier fare considerably better in all types of cases than those who act on their own with little in the way of organization and resources. Both articles suggest that the results produced in many American courts are not impartial and that those results tend to be predictable on the basis of the characteristics and configurations of the litigants in the situational context. Courts, then, in terms of the pattern of results they produce, cannot be said to differ greatly from other more overtly political institutions.

Notes

1. *Brown* v. *Board of Education*, 347 U.S. 483 (1954).
2. *Roe* v. *Wade*, 410 U.S. 113 (1973).
3. Torstein Eckhoff, "Impartiality, Separation of Powers and Judicial Independence," *Scandinavian Studies in Law* 9 (1965), 9.
4. Marc Galanter, "Why the 'Haves' Come Out Ahead: Speculations on the Limits of Legal Change," *Law and Society Review* 9 (1974), 98–101.

44

Who Wins?

Marc Galanter

Data on patterns of outcomes by types of parties are scarce. What data are available suggest that RPs [repeat players[1] fare better. Wanner (1975) found that business and government plaintiffs win more often (1975:Table 5) and more quickly (1975:Tables 8, 9) than do individual plaintiffs. Not only are they more successful overall, which might be attributed to differences in the kinds of cases they bring, but they are more successful in almost every one of the heavily litigated categories of cases. (Wanner, 1975:Table 9). This general pattern is confirmed in Owen's (1971) study of the two Georgia courts: individual plaintiffs win less often and individual defendants lose more often than do their organizational counterparts [Table 44-1].

In all of the studies reviewed here, the courts are overwhelmingly plaintiffs' forums and the cases are mostly of a routine nature. Dolbeare (1969) analyzed a sample of much more problematic cases, those in which Federal District Courts in twenty cities were faced with claims about urban public policy. In these cases plaintiffs were successful much less frequently. But his data suggest that organizations fared somewhat better than individuals [Table 44-2].

The combination of organizational capacity and individual incapacity produces a pattern of success which corresponds to that suggested by our analysis. Organizations are more successful as plaintiffs and as defendants than are individuals. They enjoy greater success against individual antagonists than against other organizations; individuals fare less well contending against organizations than against other individuals.

Wanner reports that business and government plaintiffs enjoy complete victory in 65% of the cases they bring against individuals, but the latter enjoy complete victory in only 20% of the cases they bring against business or government defendants. If we combine these success ratios with Wanner's earlier (1974) findings about frequency of cases, we may sum up by saying that for every hundred filings in these courts, 26 lead to complete victories for organizational plaintiffs over individuals, but only a tenth of that number (2.8) lead to complete victories by individuals over organizational defendants [Table 44-3].

TABLE 44-1
Success Rates of Types of Parties

Percentage of Cases in Which Plaintiff Wins Completely, Mostly or by Default

		Clarke County	Oconee County
Plaintiff	Individual	25%	20%
	Organization	36%	46%
Defendant	Individual	35%	44%
	Organization	23%	20%

Source: Derived from Owen, 1971: tables 4-5, 4-6, 4-7, 4-8.
Note: Marital breakup cases excluded.

We conclude then that our earlier analysis was correct in its basic outline. Litigation is undertaken mainly by organizations. They enjoy greater success at it. These data, assembled by various authors for quite different purposes, lend some plausibility to our surmises about the profile of litigation and the general tilt of the judicial forum. We cannot escape the conclusion that in gross the courts in the United States are forums which are used by organizations to extract from and discipline individuals.

TABLE 44-2
"Success Ratios" of Various Kinds of Plaintiffs in Urban Public Policy Litigation in Federal District Courts in 20 Large Cities 1960-1967

Type of Plaintiff	"Success Ratio"	N
Negro Groups	42%	12
Businesses	24%	21
White Groups	17%	6
Organizations	(28%)	(39)
Negro Individuals	14%	16
State Prisoners	14%	125
White Individuals	11%	46
Individuals	(13%)	(187)

Source: Derived from Dolbeare, 1969:398.

TABLE 44-3
Success of Plaintiffs in Different Party Configurations in Wanner's Three Courts

	Plaintiffs	
	Individuals	Organizations
Defendants Organizations	3.846	4.370
Defendants Individuals	3.092	3.906

Source: Wanner, 1975: table 7.

Note: The five-point plaintiff success scale (1 = verdict for the defendant, etc.; 2 = dismissal where defendant not found; 3 = dismissal for lack of prosecution, etc.; 4 = formal settlement; 5 = judgment for plaintiff, or "full satisfaction" recorded) is explained at Wanner, 1975:296*ff.*

Conclusion

What are we to make of this profile of the . . . outcome of litigation? Certainly no definitive answers can be teased out of the haphazard collection of data that are at hand. But there is enough there to provide some suggestive leads for a serious test of alternative explanations. Among the general explanations that suggest themselves are several clusters of hypotheses.

(1) First, there is the notion that certain kinds of parties, like our RPs, enjoy a set of strategic advantages. We may call this the party capability theory. Although the available data fit neatly, there is no direct evidence that the patterns observed result from such advantages. We shall return to party capability after examining some alternatives.

(2) Second, there is the notion that individuals fare less well because they or their causes are the target of judicial bias, conscious or unconscious. There may be some categories of cases which are explainable in terms of such bias, although persuasive demonstrations of systematic bias are few and far between (cf. Hagan, 1974). Individual propensities running counter to established role requirements of impartiality are difficult to credit as an explanation for a pattern as widespread and uniform as the one in question. There is not enough evidence of systematic judicial bias to make it a leading suspect.

(3) The differences observed may be an artifact of the selection of cases brought by RPs and OSs. That is, the courts may serve all parties in the same fashion, but organizational parties bring more cases of the kinds that are easiest to win, such as debt collections. The overall pattern then results from their well selected portfolio rather than from any difference in the rate of return. There seems to be some measure of truth in this, but it does not explain all the observed variation between individuals and organizations. Wanner (1975:Table 9) finds that organizations do better than individuals in almost every

kind of frequently-litigated case. And organizations do strikingly better not only as plaintiffs, but also as defendants. (Wanner, 1975:Table 7).

(4)   A more refined version of this selection hypothesis would say that organizations not only bring different kinds of cases, but better cases—cases in which the evidence is stronger and the claim is more firmly located within accepted lines of recovery; as defendants, their defenses are more ironclad, etc. They can avoid bad cases as plaintiffs by forbearance to bring suit or by readily accepting a low settlement. As defendants they settle the more meritorious claims against them—perhaps before filing. This version, too, awaits testing. We need to explore whether this kind of selectivity does operate. I would suggest that to some extent this is a restatement of our party capability cluster. Stronger evidence, more cut and dried claims, and unassailable defenses are the result of advance planning and good record keeping, as well as of the intrinsic merit of the claim. A calculating settlement policy reflects their skill as litigants as much as the virtues of their conduct in the underlying transaction. What I am suggesting is that in good measure "case merit" is not an alternative explanation, but a specification of one of the ways in which party capability affects the profile of litigation.

(5)   Differences in legal services. Perhaps the differences observed between organizations and individuals are explainable in terms of quantity and quality of legal services. There is evidence that legal representation makes for a massive difference both in likelihood of recovery and in amount recovered. Again, the influence of this factor needs to be tested. Let me mention a few points that suggest that much of the difference attributed to legal services is again traceable to difference in party capabilities. When we talk of differences in amount of preventive work, continuity of attention, specialized expertise, economies of scale, shrewd investment in rule development—we are talking about legal services provided to certain kinds of parties. Legal professionals in the United States can be roughly dichotomized into those who service OSs on an episodic basis and those who serve RPs on a continuing basis. Although there are many exceptions, there is a massive difference in education, skill and status between these groups. There is also a massive difference in the range and quality of services provided: the profession is organized to provide a wide range of services to RPs and a much narrower range to OSs. Fitzgerald's (1975) study of the Contract Buyers provides a dramatic example of change in the organizational state of parties bringing in its train dramatic changes in the amount, character and quality of legal services. Organization need not follow from improved legal services, but it seems likely that improved legal services ordinarily will result from organization.

Thus legal services are surely one vehicle through which differences in party capability have effect. But there are several reasons why I think it is useful to retain the broader notion of party capability. First, legal competence is not something supplied exclusively by professionals and entirely separable from the parties. Parties themselves may have different levels of capacity to utilize legal services. For example, Rosenthal (1974) finds superior results obtained by "active" personal injury plaintiffs; Moulton (1969:1662) finds that in a California small claims court in which lawyers are not permitted to appear, businesses that are frequent users "form a class of professional plaintiffs who have significant advantages over the individual." Second, it seems that major distinctions in party competence can exist quite apart from disparities in legal services. The reports of Kidder (1973, 1974) and Morrison (1974) on litigation in India suggest a distinction between the "experienced" or "chronic" litigant and the naive and casual one that seems to be quite independent of the organization of legal services.

Why am I so insistent on retaining the RP–OS distinction? Are we not just picking up differences in wealth and organization? Would it not be simpler to say merely organizations or the wealthy? Why treat the RP–OS distinction as fundamental? Basically this distinction is between the casual participant for whom the game is an emergency and the party who is equipped to do it as part of his routine activity. The sailor overboard and the shark are both swimmers, but only one is in the swimming business. The distinction overlaps, at least in the American setting, with two other distinctions—that between individuals and organizations and that between the poor and the wealthy. It is generally organizations that can be repeat players—because law in America is a complex and expensive activity requiring employment of full-time specialists. Organizations can use the law routinely because, compared to the cost of remedies, organizations are the right size and almost all individuals are too poor to play. But, as the Indian studies show, in other settings the distinction between habitual and "one-shot" users may be entirely independent of distinctions between organizations and individuals.

Hence, the RP–OS distinction seems to hold some promise of usefulness for comparative purposes. The OS–RP distinction commends itself for yet another reason. It points to an antinomy that strikes me as a fundamental feature of legal life. Presumably law is corrective and remedial in intent; it is designed to restore or promote a desired balance. But as it becomes differentiated, complex and maze-like in order to do this with increasing autonomy and precision, the law itself becomes a source of new imbalances. Some users become adept in dealing with it; those with other advantages find that those advantages can be translated into advantages in the legal arena. There arise new differences in access and competence—thus law itself can amplify the imbalances that it set out to correct. The scope and location of these differences in party capability, one expects, would vary with other features of the society.

. . .

(6) I do not mean to suggest that the RP–OS distinction, or any party capability factors, can explain everything about the distribution of litigation in a society. It seems to me that it is necessary to go beyond the characteristics of individual parties to another set of factors which seem to be clearly related to the profile of official litigation—that is to the relation between the parties. Are the parties strangers or intimates? Is their relationship episodic or enduring? Is it single-stranded or multiplex? For example, we may surmise that most litigation in the United States is between parties who are strangers to each other. Either they never had any mutually beneficial continuing relationship, or they had one and are now at the point of divorce—familial, commercial or organizational.

. . .

Note

[1. As noted in the earlier selection by Galanter, repeat-players (RPs) frequently engage in litigation, whereas one-shotters (OSs) infrequently have recourse to the courts—eds.]

References

Dolbeare, Kenneth M. (1969) "The Federal District Courts and Urban Public Policy: An Exploratory Study (1960-1967)," in J. Grossman and J. Tanenhaus (eds.), *Frontiers of Judicial Research.* New York: John Wiley.

Fitzgerald, Jeffrey M. (1975) "The Contract Buyers League and the Courts: A Case Study of Poverty Litigation," 9 *Law & Society Review* 165.

Hagan, John (1974) "Extra-Legal Attributes and Criminal Sentencing: An Assessment of a Sociological Viewpoint," 8 *Law & Society Review* 357.

Kidder, Robert L. (1973) "Courts and Conflict in an Indian City: A Study in Legal Impact," 11 *Journal of Commonwealth Political Studies* 121.

——— (1974) "Lawyers and Litigation: Understanding Litigation through its Effects on the Legal Profession," 9 *Law & Society Review* 11.

Morrison, Charles (1974) "Clerks and Clients: Paraprofessional Roles and Cultural Identities in Indian Litigation," 9 *Law & Society Review* 39.

Moulton, Beatrice A. (1969) "The Persecution and Intimidation of the Low-Income Litigant as Performed by the Small Claims Court in California," 21 *Stanford Law Review* 1657.

Owen, Harold J., Jr. (1971) *The Role of Trial Courts in the Local Political System: A Comparison of Two Georgia Counties.* Unpublished dissertation, University of Georgia.

Rosenthal, Douglas E. (1974) *Lawyer and Client: Who's in Charge?* New York: Russell Sage Foundation.

Wanner, Craig (1974) "The Public Ordering of Private Relations: Part I: Initiating Civil Cases in Urban Trial Courts," 8 *Law and Society Review* 421.

——— (1975) "The Public Ordering of Private Relations: Part II: Winning Civil Court Cases," 9 *Law and Society Review* 293.

45

The Federal District Courts and Urban Public Policy

Kenneth M. Dolbeare

This paper reports some beginning steps toward two still distant goals: assessment of the policy outcomes of federal court activity and comprehensive evaluation of the political role and policy impact of such courts. At this early stage, the focus of inquiry extends no further than a quantitative account of the decisional output of federal District Courts concerning selected public policy matters in twenty large cities of the United States. Even with this limited scope, and despite certain serious data limitations, some useful potential seems to inhere in an output focus, stemming from the fact that analysis is projected in both directions around the now-familiar systems theory circle. First, taking output as the dependent variable in the usual manner, some additional insight may be gained into the significance of particular decision-making patterns from identification of the nature and objects of the burdens and benefits allocated by the courts. Second, taking output as the independent variable, it may be possible to identify patterns of differential policy impact, reactions, and resultant feedback associated with particular policy outputs. Placing policy content at the center of theoretical interest (rather than decision making), leads, in effect, to collection of data which outline a different and as yet undefined set of causes and effects. I do not suggest that such an output-impact focus is necessarily more fruitful than one which takes the behavior of the judge as its focus, but merely that it is a useful complement in that it projects empirical inquiry toward relatively unexplored areas which are of perhaps equal importance to the building of a comprehensive theory of the part played by judges as actors and courts as institutions in the larger political system.

. . .

The Nature of the Inquiry and the Character of the Data

Three limits were imposed on the scope of this preliminary inquiry in order to maximize explanatory potential from a manageable and relevant body of data. These included *political contexts* (twenty large cities), *policy areas* (urban public policy problems), and *cases employed* (decisions made between January 1, 1960 and March 31, 1967, which are reported in the *Federal Reporter* or *Federal Supplement* series). Each category requires further elaboration.

Political Contexts

The settings selected for this inquiry included seven of the nation's ten largest cities, plus thirteen others of more than 150,000 population. Urban settings were chosen because of the range and multitude of their public policy problems, as well as their social and political importance. These particular cities were included because they were the ones which had been the subject of relatively systematic published analyses by political scientists; it was my original intention to explore relationships between the part played by the federal courts and the political (as well as socioeconomic) characteristics of the cities in which they are located.

Policy Areas

The kinds of public policy problems selected for inclusion are those which are generally perceived as such by urban scholars, publics, and public officials—and which have been acted upon by the federal government or the cities themselves. Law enforcement, civil rights, urban renewal, public housing, pollution, poverty, and transportation make up the major policy areas of urban concern which meet this standard. Not included are such general federal court matters (bearing no special relevance to the urban character of the setting) as bankruptcy, admiralty, tax, workmen's compensation, federal law enforcement, or ordinary diversity cases. The focus is the city's local urban problems—its policy practices, segregation in its schools, its slums, and air and water pollution—with regard to which it, as a political entity, has at least potential capacity to act.

Cases Employed

District Court output which meets the geographic and policy criteria of the foregoing paragraphs is only a small proportion of the total workload of such courts, although it is of important political relevance. Not all of such cases, however, are publicly reported. This inquiry includes only those cases decided between January 1, 1960 and March 31, 1967, which were reported in the *Federal Supplement* or could be reconstructed from the opinions of the Courts of Appeals as reported in the *Federal Reporter*. This limitation may be a major weakness, but several factors suggest that the resultant body of cases still may be employed, with appropriate care in certain respects, for the purposes of this inquiry.

First, the publisher of the *Federal Supplement,* the West Publishing Company of St. Paul, Minn., exercises no independent judgment as to which cases should be reported. The practice is to publish all decisions for which opinions should have been written, except for those few which are not released for publication. This means that the trial judge's decision to write an opinion or to simply render a judgment without an opinion essentially controls the content of the *Federal Supplement.* Because public bodies or officials are frequently involved in the cases of concern for this study, and because these cases are those which carry public significance, it seems likely that there is a high incidence of opinion writing in cases which fit our criteria. At the very least, it would appear that the resultant body of cases would include most of the *major* policy decisions made by federal district judges.

Second, although the reports of District Court activity emanating from the Administrative Office of the U.S. Courts do not contain detailed breakdowns in classifications reflecting our public policy concerns, it is possible to use those statistics to develop rough estimates of the total number of cases decided per year in some of our areas for some of our cities. In the case of New York, Chicago, and Philadelphia, for instance, it appears that the cases included within this study constitute between 40 and 50 percent of all those falling within our criteria which were actually decided by the relevant District Courts. Thus, while no claim can be made as to representativeness of this body of cases, the proportion is probably substantial.

. . .

Table 45-1 details the major classifications of subjects of these cases for the cities involved. The small number of cases in the "all other" category indicates that District Court public policy actions are relatively narrowly confined to those areas which rest upon constitutional interpretations or statutory extensions of constitutional rights—principally the post-Civil War Civil Rights Acts. The "all other" category includes public housing, urban renewal, and slum clearance (a total of 8 cases), city tax and regulatory powers (20 cases), and a miscellaneous remaining group of 12 cases. Few of the several federal programs for aid to urban areas, such as mass transportation, poverty, and air pollution, are included among these cases, probably as a result of the fact that they are based chiefly on grants-in-aid and potential opponents normally lack standing to challenge them in court. As might be expected, the number of cases rises in the latter years of the study. An average of 28 cases per year was decided in 1960 through 1962 while the average for the remainder of the period was nearly 60 per year. The increase, however, was due almost entirely to a rise in habeas corpus petitions, and there is very little change in any other category.

. . .

The Subjects and Results of District Court Decisions

The subjects with which the District Courts are engaged, and hence the areas in which they may have policy effects, are shaped by their jurisdiction, the substance of "federal questions," and the litigiousness of actors in the various urban political contexts—itself a product of both cultural factors and the characteristics of the particular subject areas involved. The former is both well known and relatively fixed in effect, requiring little comment. The latter two factors present empirical questions. Some extensions of the definition of a "federal question" occur from time to time as new constitutional interpretations are made or new federal statutes are passed, and considerable variability inheres in the local propensity to invoke the courts as a means of advancing one's policy goals. Thus, it is helpful to first establish the grounds on which the District Courts were called upon, the forms of action which were employed, the parties who came to court, and the purposes which animated them.

The scope of District Court policy action is practically coterminous with the reach of constitutional limitations. In more than 90 percent of the cases, a constitutional provision was the ultimate basis of the claim. In 90 of these cases (30 percent), the action was based on a federal civil rights statute which, in effect, extended legal enforceability of constitutional rights. Only 17 cases invoked provisions of the Civil Rights Act of 1964, and all the

TABLE 45-1
District Court Cases per City, Major Classifications

| City | Total Number of Cases | Major Classifications | | | | | | | |
| | | Civil Rights–Race Relations | | Civil Rights–Free Speech and Due Process in Police Practices | | Habeas Corpus–State Prisoners vs. City Police Practices | | All Others | |
		Number	Percent of City Total	Number	Percent of City Total	Number	Percent of City Total	Number	Percent of City Total
New York	85	3	4	25	29	48	56	9	11
Philadelphia	41	2	5	14	34	21	51	4	10
Chicago	39	1	3	19	48	12	31	7	18
Los Angeles	36	0	—	23	64	11	31	2	5
New Orleans	30	14	47	4	13	9	30	3	10
Houston	17	4	23	0	—	10	59	3	18
St. Louis	13	1	8	8	61	4	31	0	—
Pittsburgh	12	0	—	5	42	5	42	2	16
Denver	12	0	—	6	50	5	42	1	8
Atlanta	11	8	73	1	9	0	—	2	18
Detroit	8	1	12	3	38	1	12	3	38
Nashville	5	2	40	1	20	2	40	0	—
Boston	4	0	—	2	50	2	50	0	—
Cleveland	4	1	25	2	50	0	—	1	25
Miami	4	2	50	0	—	0	—	2	50
Milwaukee	4	0	—	2	50	2	50	0	—
All others (Salt Lake City 2, Seattle 2, Minneapolis 3, Kansas City 3)	10	2	20	6	60	2	20	0	—
	335	41	(12)	121	(36)	134	(40)	39	(12)

rest employed one or more provisions of the post-Civil War Civil Rights Acts to seek injunctions or damages from state officials who allegedly denied complainants their federally secured rights. This may be a result of the broadly inclusive nature of the applicable sections of those statutes, together with expanding definitions of constitutional rights produced by the Supreme Court. In any event, it is a fact that these Civil Rights Acts were almost the only federal statutes which came before the District Courts in these cases. Only five cases involved other statutes, and in 240 cases there was no substantive federal statute involved.

The forms of action in which these policy questions arose reflect the constitutional and statutory grounds just described. A large number (134 or 40 percent of the total number of decisions) were habeas corpus petitions in which a state prisoner contested a contemporary city police practice. The next largest proportions (20 percent and 16 percent respectively) were injunctions against present or prospective deprivations of constitutional rights or suits for damages for past violations of civil rights. Other forms of action, in order of incidence, included motions to suppress allegedly illegally obtained evidence about to be used in a state trial, actions for damages arising without statutory grounds, and miscellaneous declaratory judgment and other actions. In those areas where constitutional limitations may be applicable, at least, the District Courts are offered opportunities for varying forms of policy applications.

Those who invoke the federal courts are, not surprisingly, those who are apparently low in influence within their communities—Negroes, prisoners, marginal businessmen, and individuals whose claims have been unsuccessful elsewhere. Table 45-2 presents a composite "who sues whom" summary of the parties to these cases. About half of all cases were brought by state prisoners contesting actions of city police. The remaining cases were brought by white individuals (chiefly suits for damages against police and city officials for violations of civil rights) and Negro individuals or groups (injunctions against segregation in school districts or city facilities, plus some damage suits for violations of civil rights). Suits by businesses were for declaratory judgments as to invalidity of city tax or regulatory laws. Even if the large proportion of prisoner-generated cases is excluded, the share of cases initiated by groups is comparatively low, despite a generous definition of "group," indicating that assumptions as to group sponsorship of litigation may not hold true at the trial court level. The nature of the litigants and their goals, of course, is in part a product of the jurisdictional and state-of-the-law qualifications for access to the courts, but in part it is the product of the local environment and political structure.

This complex of forces produces a specialized set of policy issues for the District Courts. We have already seen that these issues are almost entirely reflections of constitutional limitations, and thus, our question is one of the particular distribution of subjects among the various possible constitutional dimensions. Table 45-3 presents a detailed breakdown of the actual subjects of cases before the District Courts in these cities. The preponderance of police practice-due process issues is again emphasized.

The policy actions of the District Courts are not the same in each of these subject areas. For purposes of analysis, we may include the race relations cases as a single category. Habeas corpus petitions, given their number and special character, deserve independent classification, but the remaining civil rights issues show sufficient consistency to permit consolidation. Such organization of the case classifications facilitates analysis of the *direction* of District Court policy making in a way which highlights the uniqueness of the courts' actions in the race relations area, as is indicated by the data in Table 45-4. In each major

TABLE 45-2
Plaintiffs and Defendants: A Composite Summary of Who Sues Whom in the District Courts[a]

Plaintiffs \ Defendants	School Districts	City Government	Public Officials (Not Police) Personally	Policemen, Sheriffs	Custodians of Prisoners	Law Enforcement Officials	Other Officials, Boards, Governments	Individuals	Businesses, Groups	Others	Total Suits by: Number	Percent of Total
Negro individuals	4	1	0	4	2	1	2	1	0	0	15	5
Negro groups	7	2	1	0	0	0	2	0	1	0	13	4
Businesses	0	12	2	0	0	4	2	1	0	0	21	7
State prisoners, before and after state trial	0	0	2	4	133	10	3	1	0	0	153	49
White individuals	1	15	8	19	1	8	5	0	1	1	59	19
White groups	1	1	1	0	0	0	5	0	1	0	9	3
Governments	0	0	0	0	0	0	0	33[b]	4	1	38	12
Others	0	0	0	0	0	0	1	0	2	1	4	1
Total suits against by number	13	31	14	27	136	23	20	36	9	3	312	
Total suits against by percent of total	4	10	4	9	44	7	6	12	3	1		100

[a] A total of 23 cases were unclassifiable for this purpose, either because of multiple plaintiffs or defendants, uncertainty as to character, or the preliminary nature of a motion.

[b] This category is potentially misleading: in most instances, governments were only nominal plaintiffs, such as in actions to suppress evidence or quash subpoenas, allegedly unlawfully secured by city police.

TABLE 45-3
Subjects of Cases, District Courts

Subjects	Number of Cases	Percent of Total
Civil rights—race relations—education	22	7
Civil rights—race relations—all others	19	6
Civil rights—other noncriminal due process (free speech, church/state, etc.)	38	11
Criminal law—police practices (search and seizure, confessions, interrogation, counsel, wire-tap, etc.) (includes habeas corpus)	194	58
Criminal law—other issues (practices of city officials, judges, prosecutors, etc.)	23	7
Urban renewal, slum clearance, other housing	8	2
City tax and regulatory policy	20	6
All other issues	11	3
	335	100

area, the District Courts support local city policy a high proportion of the time—with the sole exception of race relations, where the proportion is 45 percent, about half that of other areas.

For two important reasons, then, District Court policy making is narrowly channeled. The kinds of issues in which they may develop significant impact are few, and in most of

TABLE 45-4
District Court Action, Major Classifications, All Cities (Percent)

District Court Action	Total[a] Number	Percent	Major Classifications			
			Civil Rights— Race Relations	Civil Rights— Free Speech and City Police Practices	Habeas Corpus— City Police Practices	All Others
Supports present city policy or practice	224	81	45	88	84	81
Modifies or prohibits present city policy or practice	44	16	33	11	14	19
Supports present private policy or practice	6	2	12	—	2	—
Modifies or prohibits present private policy or practice	4	1	10	1	—	—
	278	100	100	100	100	100
			N = 33	N = 107	N = 106	N = 32

[a] 57 cases were unclassifiable for these purposes and are omitted from this table. Some of these involved preliminary or procedural issues which did not bring the court to the point of taking a stand for or against basic city policy, while others involved mixed results.

these areas their role is essentially supportive of local city policy and police practices. This is not to suggest that the areas or instances of District Court action are not consequential; qualitative analysis might indicate that they have substantial effects even where they modify city policy infrequently, and federal court effects on race relations can hardly be overlooked. . . .

. . .

The Policy Impact of the Federal District Courts

The concept of the "policy impact" of authoritative decisions made by the institutions of a political system, or by any particular institution of that system, is broadly inclusive of a variety of factors. Each of these factors is closely related to the characteristics of the ongoing political context and process; none is under the sole control of the decision-making institution, not even the substance of the policy which it produces. I shall attempt to identify several of these factors which together would comprise the policy impact of trial court decision making. Although the data developed in this preliminary inquiry are sufficient to provide empirical evidence in only a few of these areas, I shall try to identify a larger number of them in order to lay a base for some inordinately speculative extractions yet to follow. If data were available in each, they should add up to a characterization of the part played by the federal District Courts in the urban political system.

Preliminary to the study of policy impact, of course, is the classification of the subjects of cases on which the court makes decisions. Detailed specification of those areas in which the courts had an opportunity to develop policy effects, *and of those in which they did not,* are essential to an opening perspective on policy impact. That different subjects are brought to court in different types of political contexts may be anticipated, and considerations of policy impact must allow for varying impact in different contexts. Outcome patterns—in the sense of the results of decisions, not the effects as yet—are also an early component of policy impact. Such questions as who wins and who loses in the decisions of the courts in each of the contexts and in each of the subject areas in which the courts are active must be answered in order to establish a sense of the nature and objects of the allocations of various kinds of benefits and burdens of public policy. The results in cases may also be expressed, as we have done, in terms of the policy changes required; this is short of policy effects or impact . . . but it is a first step which permits identification of probable differing results in various contexts and subject areas. . . .

. . .

Table 45-5 summarizes the proportions of success enjoyed by various plaintiffs and defendants. Negro groups prove to be the most successful complainants; almost every instance reflects a court order to desegregate some governmental facility. Businesses trail Negro groups but are still ahead of all others. Their achievements are in the area of preventing city regulatory and taxing efforts and in voiding ordinances that would license or prevent the sale or showing of books and films. State prisoners, both before and after trial (civil actions, injunctions, and habeas corpus petitions), are no more successful than the average of all other cases in the District Courts, which casts some light on the charge that the federal courts are opening the state jails. Similar implications may be seen from the fact that law enforcement officials are almost always successful in defending themselves in these courts. Only school districts and city governments are required to change their policies more than 30 percent of the time, and this reflects the winners and effects outlined above.

TABLE 45-5
"Success Ratios" of Various Plaintiffs and Defendants in the District Courts[a]

Plaintiffs	Success Ratio (Percent)	Total Cases	Defendants	Success Ratio (Percent)	Total Cases
Negro individuals	14	16	School districts	69	13
Negro groups	42	12	City governments	69	26
Businesses	24	21	Public officials (not police) personally	100	11
State prisoners (before and after trial)	14	125			
White individuals	11	46	Policemen, sheriffs	81	21
			Custodians of prisoners	84	107
White Groups	17	6	Law enforcement officials	96	23
Others[b]	0	9	Other officials, boards, and governments	78	18
			Individuals	90	33
			Businesses, groups	75	4
			Others	67	3

[a] "Success Ratios" represent the proportion of cases in which the party emerged with substantially what he had sought from the litigation. Some close questions arose where plaintiffs received only a small part of their goals, and in some instances cases had to be eliminated from the classification.
[b] Cases in which governments were only nominal parties were eliminated.

· · ·

We lack the data to fulfill the requisites for understanding of the stages of policy impact subsequent to patterns of winners, losers, and differential policy results in varying types of cases. If possible, it would have been profitable to examine qualitative effects, political accommodations, compliance, employment of alternative means and shifts in goals, functional implications, and feedback and support effects. Even without such inquiry, however, it is possible to draw some speculative extractions out of our data and apply them to the problem of defining the part played by the federal District Courts in the political system and thereby moving toward building a more comprehensive theory of the judicial subsystem's linkage to the larger political system. In particular, it is possible to suggest some comparisons with the part played by the state trial courts in at least four respects.[1]

Users of the Courts and Their Purposes

Those who invoked the federal courts were chiefly individuals (and among them, predominately state prisoners and Negroes), with some cases brought or sponsored by voluntary associations and a few by businesses. Their motives were *offensive*, in that they sought to use the federal courts to prevent action or negate action already taken by the state or local machinery, or (frequently) to force the urban government to take action in a manner contrary to its existing policies. On the other hand, those who invoked the state courts as plaintiffs were individuals and businesses in nearly equal proportions. Their motives were more likely to be *defensive* and chiefly economic in character. They sought to defend the status quo and themselves against limitations of one form or another on the profitability of their use of their property; only a small proportion of litigants sought to force modification in established government policies. In both instances, however, the proportion of litigation initiated by organized interest groups was slight, in contrast to the assumptions of some students of higher courts.

Subject Areas of Court Activity

District Court cases were shown to be confined to narrow areas related to constitutional rights and statutory extensions therefrom. But the subjects of state trial courts are quite different: they include zoning and land use, the powers and organization of local governments, and the property rights of businessmen and others who seek to avoid local regulation. Few constitutional issues and almost no civil rights issues were litigated in the state trial courts examined.

Many important issues and problems of the urban political arena never are the subject of decision making by either set of courts. The federal courts are limited by the criteria of their jurisdiction and the fact that such federal statutes as exist are likely to be grant-in-aid or other kinds of statutes which do not give rise to standing to sue. The state courts are limited by the insulation which state legislatures frequently provide for such intimate state functions as education, welfare, utility and rate regulation, and public improvements. In many states, these functions are discharged through elaborate administrative structures which can be challenged, if at all, only in specialized courts and after exhaustion of remedies within the agency structure itself.

Policy Impact of the Courts

We have seen that the policy-change ratios of the federal courts were low, with the single exception of the race relations area. The District Courts modified local government policies less than 20 percent of the time in every area of their activity, and there was very little variation between the different subject areas in this respect. Race relations cases were the sole exception, and the ratio in these cases was 43 percent. But the policy-change ratio of the state courts was much higher overall—amounting to nearly 50 percent of all cases. And there was much greater variability between areas: in cases involving education or elections, for example, the policy-change ratio was no higher than in the federal courts, but in taxation and business regulation cases it was 67 and 57 percent respectively. If the number and proportions of reversals of local government policies are a valid measure, the state trial courts are much more intimate participants in the policy-making complex of local institutions.

Overall Effects and Functions

Each set of courts is narrow in the range of impact, though the state courts are the broader of the two and also the heavier in impact (at least in quantitative terms) in those areas where they are active. The areas of impact of the federal courts are too few and their impact too limited to do more than intimate that they are highly relevant to the content of urban public policy in the two basic areas of police practices and race relations. For the state courts, because of the larger number of areas and heavier impact (as well as a more extended and comprehensive analysis), it was possible to identify three major policy functions performed by courts within the local political system. They were found to have a "constitutional" function, in which they regularly determined the powers and legitimated the forms of local governments; a "rules of the game" function, in which they maintained the openness of the political process in a variety of ways, thereby enabling new groups to rise to power in the other arenas of politics; and an "economic rights" function, in which they defended businessmen's investments in the status quo and continuously limited local governments' efforts to regulate the uses of property in the social interest.

In Summary

Neither set of courts really overlaps the other in any frequent or recurring way, for the subjects with which they deal are demonstrably independent, except in rare instances. The state trial courts were found not to engage in any substantial number of civil rights issues but to be regularly involved in land use, regulation, taxation, and other economic rights matters. The federal courts, on the other hand, touched upon these matters rarely (except for some regulation or taxation issues, and these may be the inevitable product of the law's concern for property rights in all forms) and concentrated instead on race relations and criminal due process problems, almost never touching the structure or powers of local government.

The federal courts, not unexpectedly, appear to be less fully integrated into the ongoing political processes of the urban polity. They are relevant chiefly to certain limited (and output) areas of the urban political process, while the state trial courts had functions at the formative (and input) stages of that process as well as on the output side. The integration of the state trial courts did not depend entirely on the number of areas of activity and weight of the impact which they had in each, but also on the intimacy of engagement of local judges with the day-to-day activity of the political system and their interaction with the political parties and other decision-making elements. In neither instance, however, did the courts exercise a major influence on the ultimate shape of public policy: there are too many areas in which they are not involved—too many alternatives to the routes that their actions do foreclose for other political actors to be bound by their decisions.

The intimation that the federal courts are involved in the civil rights-law enforcement sets of policy-making actors, institutions, and processes, and that the state trial courts are in the property rights-regulation-local governments bodies of actors, institutions, and processes, could be an important cue toward theories of linkage of these courts to elements of the larger political system. If we posit disparate groupings of actors, institutions, and processes for each major policy area, or at least different distributions of power and goals among them regarding various policies, the part played by courts might be more readily defined along the lines suggested earlier in this section. From this point, comparisons of the role of courts in other contexts and with other institutions might facilitate the kind of more general theory that has so far not been achieved.

. . .

Note

1. All findings regarding state trial courts are drawn from Kenneth M. Dolbeare, *Trial Courts in Urban Politics: State Court Policy Impact and Functions in a Local Political System* (New York: Wiley, 1967).

CHAPTER SIXTEEN

COMPLIANCE

Specific problems involving particular parties come before courts, and judges seek to resolve those disputes. Appellate courts, notably the highest state courts and the United States Supreme Court, consider the broader public policy implications of the resolution of the initial dispute (of course, so may lower courts as well), but technically and legally the resolution of a legal dispute at every court level binds only the parties to that particular case (or, when government officials are involved, their successors in office). Therefore, compliance in its basic sense means adherence by the parties to the rulings and orders of the court, be it a trial court, an appeals court, or a supreme court. However, scholarly concern with compliance must go beyond the immediate parties because courts, in resolving particular disputes, frequently make broad policy declarations that are applicable to many others in society. A court, for example, may declare that certain programs, procedures, or actions of governmental authorities (within the jurisdiction of the court) are against the law and that any cases involving them will be decided accordingly if brought to that court. Compliance here is a matter of those who are not parties to a dispute following the court's policy statement and voluntarily doing or not doing whatever the court has ordered.

Compliance generally has a negative quality to it. A court says, in effect, "no, this should not be done—you should do this instead" (although the court may then take steps to implement a new policy). Students of compliance then examine what happens following such a public policy ruling by the court. Of course the "thou-shalt-not" decisions of courts are only part of the picture. Courts also say "yes," but these decisions are permissive in that they allow ongoing practices to continue and thus require no change in behavior.

The focus on the thou-shalt-not decisions means that we are concerned with court rulings that something violates *the law*. But rulings of a trial court that can be appealed to a higher court need not necessarily be obeyed while an appeal is in progress. Certainly those who are within the court's jurisdiction but are not a party to the suit need not comply with the court's decision (even though it has policy implications relevant for their behavior) as long as the possibility remains that a higher court may reverse the lower court. Thus when compliance is studied, it is compliance to the authoritative rulings in cases that have run the course of appeal. These authoritative rulings may be interpretations of state or federal statutes, state constitutions, or the United States Constitution.

Because the United States Supreme Court is the ultimate expounder of constitutionality in our political system, the compliance-to-court-decisions literature emphasizes compliance with Supreme Court decisions. Although it can be persuasively argued that such attention to the Supreme Court has resulted in the neglect of the federal circuit courts, the highest state courts, and both federal and state trial courts, many of whose policy decisions are never reviewed, it is likely that the kinds of variables and processes that affect compliance are common to most if not all courts. Also, in terms of compliance with Supreme Court decisions, other courts are frequently among those to whom the decision is applicable thus *they* are examined from the standpoint of *their* compliance.[1]

When the United States Supreme Court announces its thou-shalt-nots, it is of interest to observe who are the intended recipients or the target population of its message. The study of compliance, in the broader public policy sense and not in the narrower parties-to-the-dispute sense, then becomes largely but not solely the study of how public officials and governmental institutions respond to the Court's determination of legality. Concern is focused on compliance by the police, local prosecuting attorneys, school boards, public school teachers, administrative officials, state legislatures, and so on. It can then be noted that the study of compliance includes the study of the extensiveness of the rule of law in the United States, and the extent to which lower-court judges and other public officials and public employees adhere to the law as determined by the highest legal authority in the land.

Research on the subject of compliance has concentrated on two main areas. The first, which is the one we are concerned with, is the narrower area of compliance with *court decisions*. The second area is compliance with the *law*. Research conducted in the first area has examined courts as a source of law. Research in the second, broader area has examined *all* law regardless of source; for example, statutory law (legislature as source), executive orders (President and governors as source), and administrative regulations (bureaucracy as source). The broader area of research on compliance focuses on the behavior of individuals, private organizations, and government employees acting in their public capacity. Much research effort has been spent studying compliance with criminal law, and the field of criminology has developed a rich literature.

The study of compliance with court decisions, we have observed, centers on the United States Supreme Court, the source of the most authoritatively pronounced constitutional thou-shalt-nots, which are often aimed at the official actions of public employees. This leads us to an important question: how are those decisions communicated to the intended recipients of the Court's message?

The first link in the chain of compliance with Court policy is the communication to the intended recipients of that policy. The characteristics of the decision in which the policy is announced—such as the clarity with which the policy is presented, its complexity in terms of what is or is not to be done, and the nature of the target group at whom the policy is aimed— are among the variables that are thought to ultimately affect compliance. The relation of these and other variables to the Supreme Court's criminal procedures decisions is considered by Stephen Wasby (selection 46).

An interesting related question is whether the manner in which a Court decision is communicated can change attitudes that are incompatible with Court policy. Does accurate communication and explanation of Court policy in a controversial area stimulate a shift of opinion toward the Court's views? One student of the subject thinks it does.[2] Presumably attitudinal compatibility with Court policy is linked to compliance with that policy, although the evidence does not indicate a clear-cut relation between law, attitudinal change, and compliance of public employees and officials.[3]

Are full communication and attitudinal change, where needed, the only bases for compliance with Court decisions? Probably not, as suggested by Don Brown and Robert Stover (selection 47). Brown and Stover argue persuasively that compliance is a phenomenon that can best be understood in terms of utility theory—that is, people will or will not obey Court decisions when the benefits of compliance or noncompliance outweigh the costs. Assuming the accurate communication of the Court's policy decision, those who constitute the target population will behave rationally and will act in their own self-interest. For the Court to have its policies complied with, the costs of disobedience must outweigh the benefits, or the benefits of compliance must outweigh the costs. In selection 48, Kenneth Dolbeare and Phillip Hammond explore compliance with the Court's public school prayer and Bible reading policy. Their findings are consistent with the utilitarian view of compliance held by Brown and Stover.

We do not include in this chapter considerations of compliance by Congress and the presidency, although on occasion one or the other faces a Court decision requiring that something be done or not be done by either branch of government. More usual are Court decisions that stimulate some reaction from either or both branches even though neither may be a disputant in that particular issue area. The reactions may be positive and may facilitate compliance with Court policy, or they may be negative and may stimulate resistance. (For example, recall the treatment by Congress and the President of the busing issue in the early 1970s.) Yet these reactions of Congress and the President do not squarely fall under the term "compliance" in the sense we have used it here. Nonetheless, the student should be aware that the actions and reactions of these two branches of government may have a profound effect on compliance with Court decisions.[4]

Notes

1. See, for example, Neal Romans, "The Role of the State Supreme Courts in Judicial Policy Making: *Escobedo, Miranda,* and the Use of Judicial Impact Analysis," *Western Political Quarterly* 27 (1974), 38–59.

2. Steven Steinert, "The Quasi-Experiment as a Tool for the Study of Public Law," paper presented at the 1973 annual meeting of the American Political Science Association.

3. See William K. Muir, *Prayer in the Public Schools* (Chicago: University of Chicago Press, 1967); and Richard M. Johnson, *The Dynamics of Compliance* (Evanston, Ill.: Northwestern University Press, 1967).

4. See, in general, John R. Schmidhauser and Larry L. Berg, *The Supreme Court and Congress: Conflict and Interaction, 1945-1968* (New York: Free Press, 1972); and Robert Scigliano, *The Supreme Court and the Presidency* (New York: Free Press, 1971).

46

The Communication of the Supreme Court's Criminal Procedure Decisions: A Preliminary Mapping

Stephen L. Wasby

The policeman is supposed to protect your life, rights, and property in that order; in fact, he protects life and property, and doesn't know your rights.

—*a police training officer*

I. Introduction

Why the policeman does not know our rights, why the Supreme Court's "criminal procedure revolution" in the 1960's apparently did not reach him, or if it reached him, had little effect, is of considerable theoretical and practical importance. It is theoretically important to understand the processes of communication in a complex society; it is . . . important to know whether our police follow the law, at least as declared by our highest courts, or are a law unto themselves.

As one examines the available studies of the actual impact of decisions of the United States Supreme Court, one finds that the rates at which local officials carry out what the Court has determined to be "the law" are often relatively low. In some instances, it is clear that the officials are aware of the Court's decisions. However, there are other instances where one cannot easily attribute the lack of impact to conscious resistance. It may be, one realizes, that the decisions have never reached the place where they might be applied. . . .

While we have begun to learn something about the means by which Court decisions are transmitted, we still know very little of the process by which they get "from here to there," from the Court to the ultimate consumer of the Court's message. The increasing number of impact studies of the Court's decisions have concentrated more on the ultimate effect of the decisions than on the linkage between the process of implementation and resultant policy. . . . While communication and impact are inextricably connected, it is important to distinguish analysis of communication of decisions from analysis of the impact of those decisions or of compliance with them.

What follows is a preliminary treatment of the transmission of Supreme Court criminal procedure decisions to those concerned with law enforcement. Its purpose is to present an initial inventory of the means which might be used to move the decisions from their point of origin to their point of utilization, and of a set of factors which might affect the communications process through these channels.

. . .

II.   An Inventory of Means

In attempting to determine the various means by which Supreme Court decisions might be communicated to their ultimate audience, we might, using a model (Figure 46-1) developed by the author, begin "at the top" and work our way "down" channels of communication from the Court, to lower courts, to governmental officials, to the public.

The Supreme Court's opinions themselves obtain circulation, at least among some attorneys and a few laymen interested in the work of the Court. They are available in a number of forms, from their early publication in various unofficial reporters to the "slip opinions" published by the Government, and ultimately to the bound volumes produced both by the Government and private publishing companies. Some newspapers, but only a very few, print excerpts from what are thought to be the most important decisions. The decisions are also available in publications specializing in criminal law matters such as the *Criminal Law Reporter* which reports Supreme Court criminal procedure holdings.

Despite the multiplicity of forms in which the decisions are printed, the actual availability of the decisions at the city and county level, where law enforcement officials, whether prosecuting attorneys or policemen, might want to avail themselves of direct reference to the Court's pronouncements, is less than satisfactory. This appears to be particularly true in the more rural states, where there may be a set of *United States Reports* only in the larger cities (of which there may be only a few). For example, it has been estimated that, in Wyoming, the Reports are not available except in Casper, Laramie, and Cheyenne. A survey of clerks of the circuit court in Illinois, conducted by the author, showed that only about half of the counties had the Supreme Court's decisions available; far less had access to decisions of either the courts of appeals or the district courts. In fact, there are instances where even large-city police departments have been unable to easily obtain copies of decisions directly affecting them. . . .

The court structure, a multi-level one in this country, is one way in which decisions are communicated. Not only is there a dual court system, with a separate structure of courts for the federal and state governments, but each has several levels. Supreme Court decisions may not be communicated directly to the lowest, or trial, level, but may work their way down through intermediate appellate courts. Thus, a Supreme Court holding may be

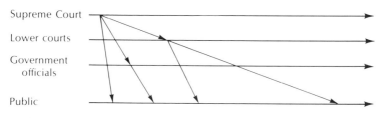

Figure 46-1.

communicated to the federal district courts by being cited in a decision of the court of appeals for the circuit in which the district court sits. At the state level, it may take a decision of a state supreme court, and then of an intermediate appellate court, before the holding reaches the state trial level, at least through this particular means of communication. In a particular case, the decision and relevant orders are generally sent by the Supreme Court to a lower court for "proceedings not inconsistent with this opinion." As a result, "[t]he formal judicial structure . . . provides an important channel through which a ruling is transmitted to those *directly under obligation to act.*"[1] However, for those lower courts in which no pending cases are affected by a Supreme Court decision, it is probably time enough to wait until the published reports become available.

Despite this picture, the court structure, or the relationship between the highest court and those below it, is *not* bureaucratic, with communications passing regularly down through channels. Even a lower court judge's knowledge of cases is not automatic, and may not come from following the actions of superior courts. The decision of the Supreme Court in a relevant case may come to the attention of a judge only by being cited by a lawyer arguing a case before him. While some judges may regularly follow what the Supreme Court does, others may wait until attorneys bring matters to their attention. Given the nature of our adversary legal system and the apparently inescapable time pressures on the judiciary, this may be a perfectly natural way for communication to occur. However, if attorneys do not cite the cases because *they* are unaware of them, the judges may never hear of them. Where the bar in a state is relatively small and unspecialized, at least as to criminal matters (*e.g.,* Rhode Island or Wyoming), this is particularly likely. To be sure, in deciding a matter presented to them, judges may do research on their own, but even then they may have waited for the issue to be presented in court rather than doing "independent research" on the off-chance that the issue might be raised before them. . . . This interplay of formal (printed/published) media and personal communication is not uncommon. This method of judges' finding out about cases may also mean that diffusion of court decisions may be horizontal—from one state or lower federal court to another court at the same level. While such decisions have no binding legal effect in a foreign jurisdiction until adopted, lawyers utilize them, and the decisions of some state courts are adopted more often than others.

Lawyers also serve as an important means of communication by helping to transmit decisions to other attorneys. Where a community contains a substantial number of criminal defense attorneys, they may be organized, either informally or formally, into a "defense bar" which circulates information about relevant cases. More formally organized bar associations, through publications, meetings, and continuing legal education "short courses," also assist in the communication process [among lawyers]. . . .

. . .

The advisory opinion of the state attorney general is of considerable importance. Usually available only on request by a public official, these documents, while not having the force of law in the courts, are given great weight by application of Supreme Court holdings to their own work. In recent years, a number of attorneys general have begun to publish bulletins prepared specifically for law enforcement officials, covering both Supreme Court cases and related state court opinions. These documents have the advantage both of coming from a state official rather than a distant federal court, thus making the decisions more "immediate," and of tying Supreme Court decisions to matters of more immediate concern to local law enforcement officers, who may not be sure of the possible relationship between the Court's pronouncements and the law in their own jurisdiction.

While the prosecutor could be a major means of communication, "the prosecutor assigned to [a] case rarely assumes it to be his duty to inform the police department of the meaning of [a] decision or of its intended impact upon current police practice,"[2] partly because he was never taught that he should do so and partly because there is little pressure from a defense-oriented bar to do so. . . . District attorneys also vary in their knowledge of higher court decisions. If they have lost cases, at trial or on appeal, they will, perhaps, have more motivation to instruct police in the law. Prosecutor's knowledge of court decisions depends in part on whether or not they are full-or part-time, the former having more time in which to become informed, and on whether or not they handle their own appeals, since district attorneys who must do so are much more likely to know about relevant appellate court holdings than are district attorneys where the attorney general's office takes appeals to higher state courts. In California, the attorney general and district attorneys hold "zone meetings" for law enforcement officers to keep them posted on important legal developments. . . . More common is the situation in which one man in the attorney general's office provides liaison with judges and district attorneys in the state. Perhaps an extreme case of this is Wisconsin, where trials have been recessed so that prosecuting attorneys might consult with the assistant attorney general who is their "contact man" in the attorney general's office. Even when the district attorneys are well-informed about the law, there is still the need for a link between them and the police department—one which often does not exist. Some prosecutors, however, including some United States Attorneys, who clearly have no responsibility for the behavior of county or municipal police, do extend themselves to carry out some teaching programs.

Even when a Supreme Court decision is utilized at the state trial court level, it often is not effectively transmitted to the police. Few departments have set up a method of having a specifically designated police officer report to the department on what has occurred in trial court, where many, if not most, of the rulings are unpublished. In most departments, no one has the responsibility to report back to the department why a particular case was lost. Even if someone were assigned the responsibility, much might not be accompanied, for "[t]he trial judge seldom explains his decision in a way likely to be understood by the police officer."[3] When the police officer does not understand what has gone on, he does not systematically transmit it, although he is likely to talk about it with some fellow officers. . . .

Of some note is the development in some police departments of a special position for lawyers, that of police legal adviser, to remedy the lack of communication between district attorneys and city attorneys on the one hand, and sheriff's officers and policemen on the other. These advisers work within the department providing legal advice, including interpretation of Supreme Court decisions. . . . Without such a member of the staff, the police department must often rely on its own nonlegal resources for assistance in interpreting cases. . . . Most departments have methods of communication of decisions which can only be called random; in other words, they have no regular system of communication.

Printed sources other than the Court decisions themselves abound. The mass media, particularly the newspapers, have been mentioned in connection with the communication of decisions, and the predominant role of the wire services in such transmission has been stressed. Television generally plays a lesser role than newspapers, because there is altogether too little time in a 30-minute newscast to say more than a few words about even major Court decisions. The substance of some of the more important decisions may also find its way into the entertainment side of television, and appear in dramas about defense attorneys and detectives. . . .

Media of general circulation are only one source of information about Court decisions; specialized magazines are another. There are quite a number of journals aimed particularly at law enforcement officials. . . .[4]

Beyond these materials, there is much material of a more scholarly sort. The law reviews published by law schools include much discussion of what the Court has said, although usually there is little to link this discussion to day-to-day problems of the policemen, and the intended audience is generally other lawyers. There are, however, some more specialized types of law reviews, of which the *Journal of Criminal Law, Criminology, and Police Science,* published at the Northwestern University School of Law, is the best known; newer journals, like the *Criminal Law Bulletin,* further increase the range of available material. . . .

Printed materials and individuals tend to come together in a variety of types of training programs for law enforcement officers. For some individuals who will enter law enforcement work, the route to such work includes a 2-year—and increasingly a 4-year—college degree program. Such programs usually contain courses in criminal law and American government in which there is some exposure to what the Supreme Court has said. In the larger cities, the police departments have police academies through which all recruits pass. As relatively few policemen have college degrees, far more pass through this form of training than are exposed to 2- or 4-year programs. For people already in law enforcement work, in-service training is extremely important. Some in-service training is no more than the reading of a bulletin at line-up before the policemen go out on the beat, the traditional method of communicating "the law" to police officers. . . .

At the beginning of this section, a very simplified model of the steps or levels down which a Supreme Court decision might pass was indicated. The means inventoried here suggest the need for a more fully developed model of the communications process. Figure 46-2 is an attempt in that direction, an attempt to portray the complexity of the relationships without totally cluttering the diagram. A number of comments may be in order about the diagram. Although there is no adequate indication of a time scale, it should be recognized that some events precede others in time. Political socialization, while a continuing phenomenon, and general background are clearly distal factors, and any police training occurring before the announcement of a particular Supreme Court decision is also a prior matter. While the court system has been shown as a vertical column, there is little question that it might also be portrayed as a series of steps, running from the Supreme Court at top left to the state trial courts at bottom right, as some indication of the time lag in transmission of a decision "down" the various levels of courts. Of the influences on the policeman outside the court system, the media, particularly those of general circulation, will be the first to have an effect, to be followed up by communications from interest groups in the police field, from his superiors, and from instructors during in-service training. These will, in turn, have received communication from agencies like the FBI and the state attorney general. The policeman will also have some contact with a case through trial judges before whom he must testify—another form of direct learning and experience for him. His reaction to all these communications is also affected by the social environment in which he is immersed. The effect of that environment may be both immediate and cumulative, making it both a distal and proximal factor.

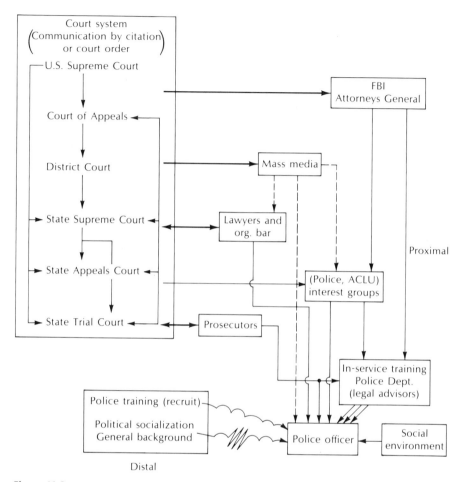

Figure 46-2.

While contact between lawyers and police departments is shown in the model, the crucial role of attorneys (other than those publicly employed) in the process is to help "move" the decisions down the various levels of the court structure, by citing the decisions to lower court judges before whom they argue cases. Clearly, defense attorneys will use particular court decisions in negotiating with prosecutors over the fate of defendants, but it would seem that the primary role of the lawyer in this process is vis-à-vis the courts, not the police directly.

The strength of the various relationships in the diagram is hard to portray at this early stage of our exploration of the subject, but a few suggestions are made by indicating basic relationships in single unbroken lines, with weaker relationships in either wavy or broken lines, and stronger ones in multiple lines.

That most of the lines are unidirectional, pointing toward the law enforcement officer as the ultimate recipient, while in part a result of the purpose of the diagram, also suggests one of the problems in communicating to the police. Those in the field of cybernetics have suggested that communication will be most complete when all the lines in a diagram of this sort have arrows pointing in both directions, indicating bilateral rather than unilateral communication. For the time being, however, given the public concern about police lack of knowledge regarding Supreme Court decisions, more attention seems to have been paid to the lines as drawn than to communication running in the other direction.

III.   Factors Affecting Communication Regardless of Means

We move next to an attempt to identify additional factors which might influence the communication of Supreme Court decisions through the indicated channels. Characteristics of the Court's decision itself, and where it fits in a pattern of decisions, give us a starting point. Whether or not a decision is unanimous is one of its most relevant characteristics; the existence of dissenting, as well as concurring, opinions increases the amount of information which has to be transmitted, in addition to giving potential opponents of the majority's view a "handle" on which to hang their opposition. If the majority cannot agree on a line of argument, leaving only a plurality of "prevailing" opinion, it becomes very difficult for those who wish to understand the case to determine what the Court has held. . . .

The clarity of the Court's decision is a characteristic to which most students of the Court point, although they are not agreed upon its effect. . . . A basic rule, like the exclusionary rule, may be clear by itself, but the circumstances under which it is to be applied may be so myriad that transmitting them is difficult. There are few decisions which, like *Miranda,* can be reduced to four (or five) warnings to be put on a *"Miranda* card." However, even with a decision apparently as clear as *Miranda,* there is divergence of opinion among law enforcement officials as to its meaning, and its clarity. . . .

Not only may a particular decision be vague and ambiguous, but a set of decisions in juxtaposition may be collectively unclear, particularly if the Court seems to move back and forth rather than following a clear doctrinal line. Certainly, the addition of more and more cases, particularly if decided on a case-by-case approach on the basis of the "totality of the circumstances," will by itself increase the amount of "noise" in the communication system.

Effects of ambiguity in communication may be several. The most orthodox position is that there is a direct relationship between clarity and compliance; the greater the clarity, the greater the compliance, so ambiguity increases noncompliance. However, it has also been suggested that ambiguity in the Court's language forces people to come back to the courts to obtain further elucidation of what the Court has been trying to say, thus increasing the Court's hold over the contestants. Still a third possibility is that ambiguity may be more likely to produce a minimal level of compliance because each recipient of a communication can perceive the decision as favoring his own cause.

Related to clarity is the visibility of a decision. The Court's decisions need to be perceived by those who might implement them. Sometimes this perception will occur only after a lower federal court or a state court has included them in its decisions. If state courts apply federal court decisions, the latter will be made more visible to law enforcement officials and may be more likely to be observed. Some cases, like *McMann v. Richardson,*[5] on counseled guilty pleas, and *Illinois v. Allen,*[6] on courtroom disruption, are of greater importance to lawyers, while others, like *Escobedo* and *Miranda,* affect on-the-beat and station-house officers as well. If a decision has to be communicated well down the various steps in the communication process, its visibility has to be high, because the more steps in the communication net through which a communication must travel, the more garbled it will become, as well as the longer it will take to reach its ultimate destination. Decisions like *McMann* and *Allen* may be transmitted more quickly because they are favorable to the law enforcement community, and may become more visible for that reason. We may hypothesize that decisions like *Escobedo* and *Miranda,* although widely publicized in the media, would be less quickly disseminated—at least less quickly than favorable decisions receiving equal publicity.

The information the Court has about the practice about which it is deciding, as reflected in its opinions, is another factor. Many law enforcement officers felt that the Court's knowledge of police procedures, or at least of the actualities of police life, vital to the *Miranda* decision, was very meager. . . . When the Court seems to be acting without reference to the actualities of the police situation, it is easier for the police to ignore what it has said. . . .

A Supreme Court decision occurs in a broad, on-going situation. Whether or not the Court plans to affect the existing social milieu, or takes the current situation into account in handing down its decisions, situational factors can affect their communication. For example, if the decision is handed down in the midst of a nationwide crisis, it is likely to receive less coverage than might otherwise be the case. If the decision is perceived as contributing to a crisis, as when it affects an emotion-laden area like race relations or perhaps law enforcement, communication about the decision may be greater. Ironically, however, communication may then be greater about reaction to the decision than about the decision itself, leading to no greater communication of what the Court has said. If changes have occurred in the law shortly before the Supreme Court's decision, obtaining further change may be quite difficult. . . .

Another part of the general situation which may affect the receipt of communication is the occurrence of relevant events in the community which may attune potential recipients to what the Court has said. A community with few major crimes may not feel that the Supreme Court's criminal procedure pronouncements are particularly important, but a murder may make policemen wake up to relevant decisions, so that they can be sure of not ruining the case they may have against the defendant. . . .

Related to the on-going situation is the "followup" to a case. As indicated earlier, much of what is communicated about a decision is the reaction of prominent officials to a decision, even if they have not yet read it. *Who* responds is extremely important. If the dominant interests in a community respond with immediate opposition, communication about the decision will fall, if not on deaf, at least plugged, ears; on the other hand, if elites indicate support for a decision, "average citizens" in the community and government employees, including policemen, may listen far more closely to communications about it. Support by an elite does not guarantee compliance, or even that communication will be adequate, because of all the other possible interfering factors, but the substantial effect of countermanding commands or comments is clear. At a Chicago Police Department staff meeting held several weeks after *Escobedo,* someone asked the Chief Judge of the Criminal Courts, the speaker at the meeting: "Judge, the Supreme Court handed down this *Escobedo* decision. What do you recommend we do?" The judge replied: "Boys, that's a decision of law. You let us lawyers worry about that sort of things. You're overworked as it is." As the person telling this story to the author remarked, when a memorandum about the case later comes to the level of the division commander who was at that meeting, "do you think he will pay attention to it?" The judge was telling policemen to ignore what the Supreme Court had done. On the other hand, given the criticism of *Miranda* by many law enforcement officers, refusal by a leading law enforcement officer to criticize could be quite important in setting the "atmosphere." For example, in Milwaukee:

> The chief of the . . . department . . . specifically refused to criticize the [*Miranda*] decision. He insisted that the crime rate would not be affected by the decision and refused to question the Court's wisdom. [Thus] Wisconsin had no police chief who, like Orlando Wilson of Chicago . . . spoke often, if not eloquently, against the Supreme Court's criminal law decisions.[7]

Another part of "followup" is the degree to which the government enforces, or attempts to enforce, the standards the Court has enunciated. Such standards are clearly not self-enforcing, and, while executive branch officials do not often directly attack Supreme Court decisions, they may kill them by ignoring them, or by refusing to . . . implement them. Similarly, for example, if law enforcement officials see no effort by prosecutors to enforce the exclusionary rule internally (instead, leaving it to defense attorneys to raise the issue of illegal search) or if they see no penalty attached by their own superiors for illegal searches, they are not likely to be deterred from those practices the Court has outlawed, nor are they likely to see much need to pay attention to the Court's decisions. Even when Supreme Court decisions have been specifically communicated to the police, supervision is necessary to see that implementation takes place. . . . Again, if the policeman knows that what he has been taught will not be followed up once he leaves the classroom, he may be less likely to listen intently to what is being conveyed to him. More than that, there are no sanctions, or only limited ones, for not knowing the law; the police officer is likely to find no reward in following Court-established procedure and no punishment for failing to do so; in fact, he may be complimented for trying his hardest *despite* the barriers the Court has established.

When messages pass through any communications network, distortions are likely to occur; the channels of communication are not "clean" and contain distortion-creating "static." . . . Among the distortions is inaccurate reporting of decisions in the media—inaccuracies which, on occasion, have been acted upon, perhaps because of the concept that decisions of the Supreme Court, the "highest court in the land," are meant to be *the law of the land* and thus final. Oversimplification, particularly, but not only, in headlines, is another distortion which occurs. That oversimplification includes not only broad overgeneralizations but also failure to report why the Supreme Court did what it did. Thus, the "*Miranda* rules" were transmitted, but not the interrogation methods which had led the Court to invalidate confessions given in the absence of the warnings. Individuals involved in cases often get more attention from the press with its "human interest" orientation than the legal substance of the cases. Also, individual cases get overemphasized, particularly in the "roundup" stories sent out by the wire services, so that equally important cases get less visibility, are buried at the bottom of a story, and are often clipped by an outcountry copy editor pressed for space. One further distortion is that reaction to the cases—immediate impact—often gets more attention than the Court's decision itself, so the public has a hard time trying to ascertain to what people are reacting.

Beyond these distortions, we can specify some others. The Police Task Force of the President's Crime Commission commented on the spirit and tone of the communication and the communicator. . . . Who the communicator is—in terms of his credibility to the recipient—would also play a part, as would his legitimacy, in the case of a Supreme Court decision being seriously questioned by many policemen. . . . If those who communicate a decision are ambivalent about it, their ambivalence is likely to show up in their communication, either through the perfunctory way in which the decision is communicated (just as policemen unhappy about *Miranda* will give the warnings in a more formalistic tone than the general pleasant conversational tone they might use to elicit a confession) or through lack of forceful assertion that compliance should be forthcoming.

Whether or not methods are provided by which policemen can actually comply with a decision is another factor related to the effectiveness of communication. . . .

. . .

Whether the details of a decision are communicated and whether communication goes beyond the details to explain the underlying philosophy, have been pointed out as other relevant factors. . . .

Whether factual details or underlying philosophy, or both, are presented, the communications embodying Supreme Court decisions have often seemed to be written more for a lawyer or law-trained person than for the average policeman, likely to have no more than a high school diploma and little special training. The lawyer's style makes it very difficult for the line officer to know what is meant. What makes this worse is that the officer seldom has lawyers available to whom he can turn for advice. The difficulty of the lawyer-written communication was well put, a number of years ago, by Victor Thompson, writing about Office of Price Administration (OPA) regulations:

> The attorneys appeared not to be concerned at all with ease in reading but only with the accuracy of the statement. . . . Consciously or subconsciously, the drafting attorneys wrote for readers who were trained or disposed to squeeze the last drop of a conventionalized logic out of a word. . . .[8]

Professor Remington, University of Wisconsin, School of Law, has suggested that lawyers, because defense attorneys outnumber prosecutors, may *want* to keep police ignorant. While prosecutors may dislike Supreme Court decisions, they have an interest in having police forces well versed in current law. . . .

The training of police officers, during which material about Supreme Court decisions might be communicated, is another factor. . . . Both the proportion of training time spent on criminal law and criminal procedure matters and the total time involved in police training are minimal in most jurisdictions. Most discussion of criminal law involves the definitions of crimes (often simply a reading from the statute book) rather than criminal procedure, about which the Supreme Court has been saying so much in the last decade. In addition, very little time is required for police training. For example, in Illinois, the minimum amount of training time required for police is now (only recently) 240 hours. By comparison, it takes approximately 3500 hours to become a beautician and 5500 hours to become a mortician. As one police-community relations expert has put it, "[w]ith that time allotment, how can the policeman know your rights?"

. . .

There are substantial differences between police departments in central cities in metropolitan areas, suburban police departments in the same metropolitan areas, and departments in small towns. One of these differences is the degree to which the departments are bureaucratized. . . . In small departments, there is not enough differentiation to be able to give to one person the responsibility for following what the Supreme Court has said and transmitting it to the rest of the men (although the problem of transmission may be less because of the possibility of face-to-face communication). In large departments, some officers may be trained in the law and/or be given specific responsibility for dealing with legal matters, although the department may be so large, and there may be so much distance (both geographical and social) between headquarters and the "field" that even the most elaborate communications system may not accomplish much. However, larger departments can clearly commit more resources to training and education, one part of which would be communication of Supreme Court decisions. . . .

Size, however, does not account for all of what we have been discussing; the location of a community in relation to a major metropolitan area is another important variable. Law enforcement officials may see Supreme Court decisions as being meant only for large cities with high crime rates, certainly not for themselves. . . . . Suburban police departments may be able to draw on the training resources of a "big-city" department, resources not available to a city of the same size in the hinterlands. Similarly, location near a university may provide access to that facility's faculty and library.

The "work situation" in which the individual policeman finds himself is related to the structure of police agencies. The man in the police department with the largest amount of discretion is not, despite the military model on which police departments are built, the man at the top, but the policeman on the beat. He must make split-second decisions, in the words of one FBI agent, as he "rounds the corner to the sound of tinkling glass." Or, in the words of another police official:

> [T]he municipal police officer is called upon to take action alone, on the street, in the face of violently developing situations, without law books, without ready authorities, without legal advice, and quite often in an atmosphere of latent or overt hostility. . . .[9]

While there are "squad-car lawyers" in a few states and cities for such things as "drug busts," the policeman is usually on his own. Some parts of his work, like the writing of traffic tickets, are more subject to "guidance from above," but his discretion on most matters is quite broad.

There are competing pressures on the police officer from the community he serves, pressures which may affect his superior in a more organized way, but with which he must live from day to day. The reward structure of his work is keyed to arrests, traffic tickets, or the "clearance rate" for robberies, but not to implementation of Supreme Court decisions. He must be more attuned to what his superiors want and the criteria by which they will judge him. The bulk of communications from them concern "catching criminals," even though much of the policeman's work may involve "social service," like helping injured people and settling (or at least "cooling") family disputes. Where there is a desire to obtain convictions, or perhaps where "feedback" from the court has occurred as the result of a case lost, policemen will be more open to communication about the law. . . .

The cues which influence the policeman in his work come not only from his superiors, but also from his fellow officers, and if they are not much concerned about what the Supreme Court has said lately, or feel that the Supreme Court is hurting their work (making it easier for criminals to stay free, or making it more difficult for them to obtain the rewards available in their own departments), the officer is not likely to want to become a "sore thumb" or deviant by attempting to follow rules none of his colleagues are following. The basic uncertainties characterizing police work drive the individual officer to look for reinforcement of his views, for camaraderie, for a source of improved morale. He gets social reinforcement from people who, like him, do not pay much attention to communications about the Court even when they are available, who, at a minimum, do not look for ways to enforce them, or who may get social reinforcement from "knocking" the Court together, something which may be triggered by communication about that body's decisions. The increasing organization of the police subculture, and the resultant increasing militancy of the police organizations—like the Patrolmen's Benevolent Association—have reinforced this point within the last several years. This occurs even during the policemen's "social life," much of which is spent in the company of other police officers who constitute much of his social environment. Thus, even if all problems concerned with communicating a decision to the officer are solved, his response is likely to be greater to such informal pressures than to the communication.

. . .

The last category of factors involves characteristics of the individual policeman. His background, including his socio-economic status and his education, would be one of the relevant characteristics. That many police come from the lower-middle or working class, precisely the stratum least happy about the Supreme Court's "criminal procedure revolution," is clearly relevant. Whether the policeman has been exposed to materials about the Supreme Court, and the sort of attitudes about the Court to which he has been socialized, would be distal factors having an effect on the immediate situation in which he receives a communication concerning a Court decision. These attitudes will affect his perceptions of what the Court has said, or of what is being said to him about what the Court has said. It is clear that education and socialization are not uniform, and that, despite internal departmental pressures, some policemen will, more than others, want to work to make their department conform to the commands of the courts. What number constitutes the "critical mass" of such men necessary to produce departmental adherence is unclear. However, there are noticeable uniformities in socialization within generations. Professor Remington has noted that judges receiving their law school training in the 1930's—judges who might have been sitting on the bench in the *Miranda* period—grew up with the Wickersham Commission's Report on police third-degree methods ringing in their ears.

Another related matter which seems to be of some importance is the individual's expectations of what the Court will do, and what effect its decisions will have. An unanticipated decision is likely to be seen as having a far greater effect than one clearly anticipated, even if negatively valued. Similarly, if a decision is seen as having substantial (particularly negative) effects, reaction will occur largely in terms of those expectations, even though, as in the case of *Miranda's* effect on use of confessions and conviction rates, such expectations are not borne out. . . . If some see a whole system of values in jeopardy, they will resist more forcefully than if they are only anxious about particular values.

Among the characteristics police bring to their work are certain personality variables, such as an orientation toward conformity. While many have alleged that at least some enter police work because they enjoy exercising authority over others and/or are sadistic, we have little firm data on the subject. One recent study, relevant to the advanced training of police officers, suggests that those policemen in a large-city department (New York) who had gone to college were "significantly less authoritarian" than those who did not attend college.[10] The authors suggested that the college-attending police will be better able to function "in accordance with the guidelines set down by the Supreme Court with respect to arrests and search and seizure." If personality is a predominant factor in police work, this may be so; however, if the *mores* of police work, and the structure of the work situation, mentioned above, predominate—which is more likely the case—this may turn out to be only of marginal significance. . . .

IV. Conclusion

In the interests of identifying the various steps through which the criminal procedure decisions of the United States Supreme Court might pass on their way to law enforcement officers at the local level, we have developed an inventory of means by which those decisions might be transmitted. While it is not bureaucratic in character, the judicial structure, both federal and state, serves as one way in which the decisions travel "downward," although lawyers often bring cases to the attention of judges, who do not always hear of cases directly from their judicial superiors. Thus, there is an interplay of formal structure and personal communication. State attorneys general and local prosecutors help to bring decisions to the attention of the police; their work is supplemented by police legal advisers, within police departments. The mass media, specialized instructional materials, and law enforcement officers' general education are also means of communication, with police training, both recruit and inservice, being of particular importance.

Turning to factors which might affect communication, we have noted that characteristics of the Supreme Court's decisions, such as the unanimity of the vote, the decision's ambiguity, and the visibility it obtains, are important factors. The situation into which the decision is injected, particularly if of a crisis nature, and the extent to which reforms in the law have taken place shortly before the decision is announced, also affect its acceptance. The "followup" to the case, through actions taken either in support or in defiance of the decision, will affect the degree to which it is communicated to law enforcement officials. As relatively few of these officials read the Court's opinion directly, the content of communications—often distorted—is quite important; for example, it is considered vital that ways of complying with the decision be communicated, along with the rationale behind the case, and not simply the bare standards the Court may have enunciated. That the communications not be written in legal jargon seems essential if they are to be understood. The limited time available for training, and the limited proportion of that time devoted to criminal law matters, serve as "natural" barriers to the communication of much information about the decisions to the individual policeman. The location of the department in which he works may assist or hinder his ability to get access to more thorough types of training. Finally, the policeman's "work situation" was stressed as a factor which, because of lateral pressures from the community and his fellow officers and the nature of the reward/sanction system in the department, may offset or neutralize any communication which may ultimately reach him through the many channels which we have identified.

Notes

1. R. Johnson, THE DYNAMICS OF COMPLIANCE 61 (1967) (emphasis supplied).

2. LaFave & Remington, *Controlling the Police: The Judge's Role in Making and Reviewing Law Enforcement Decisions,* 63 MICH. L. REV. 987, 1005 (1965).

3. LaFave & Remington, at 1005. Through personal interviews the author learned of a small town police chief in Wisconsin who lost six consecutive cases because of motions to suppress evidence which were never explained to him.

4. For a review of materials available to the police if they read their own periodicals, see Wasby, *From Supreme Court to Policeman: A Partial Inventory of Materials,* 8 CRIM. L. BULL. 587-615 (1972).

5. 397 U.S. 759 (1970).

6. 397 U.S. 337 (1970).

7. N. Milner, The Impact of the Miranda Decision on Four Wisconsin Cities 233, (1969 unpublished Ph.D. dissertation, University of Wisconsin).

8. V. Thompson, THE REGULATORY PROCESS IN OPA RATIONING 384 (1950), quoted in L. Friedman & S. Macaulay, LAW AND THE BEHAVIORAL SCIENCES 793, 801 (1969).

9. Broderick, *The Supreme Court and the Police: A Police Viewpoint,* 57 J. CRIM. L.C. & P.S. 271, 274 (1966).

10. Smith, Locke & Walker, *Authoritarianism in College and Non-College Oriented Police,* 58 J. CRIM. L.C. & P.S. 128, 132 (1967).

47

Compliance with Court Directives: A Utility Approach

Don W. Brown and Robert V. Stover

. . . [S]ome scholars have suggested the potentially broad usefulness and integrative capacity of treating individuals' compliance decisions as though they were made on the basis of a cost-benefit or utility analysis (Rodgers and Bullock, 1972; Krislov, 1965: Ch. 6). . . .

According to utility theory, human behavior is motivated by a desire to maximize positive gratification and minimize negative gratification of *subjectively* defined wants, needs, desires, and drives. The utility of any action is simply the net gratification which an individual expects from it.[1] This will be determined by the individual's *values* (conceived so as to encompass all wants, needs, desires and drives and the relative intensity with which they are felt) and *expectations* (perceived probabilities) that performing the action will positively or negatively gratify these values. Positive gratification of values can be thought of as *benefits* and negative gratification as *costs*. Thus the utility of any action is the sum of its expected benefits (a non-negative number) and its expected costs (a non-positive number).

Utility theory, as we are using it, does not imply that human beings are always rational, in the sense of being willing or able to calculate those actions which in fact would maximize net gratification. Nor does it imply that subconscious motives are unimportant or that a person's values are constant over time. It simply says that people act so as to try to satisfy their desires, regardless of the source, "rationality," or stability of those desires.

A person with the physical capacity either to comply or not comply with a given legal directive will not comply when the utility of noncompliance is greater than the utility of compliance. . . .[2] Utility theory treats compliant and noncompliant behavior as *each* having a set of costs and benefits associated therewith.

Numerous factors might contribute to the total expected costs and benefits summarized in . . . the . . . above inequality, which we will refer to as the *utility inequality*. For example, the expected benefits of noncompliance for a white school board member directed to implement a court-ordered busing plan might include the political payoffs of taking a position popular with his constituency, the symbolic and psychological gains of sending his

"Court Directives and Compliance: A Utility Approach," by Don W. Brown and Robert V. Stover, is reprinted from *American Politics Quarterly*, Vol. 5, No. 4 (October 1977), pp. 465–480, by permission of the Publisher, Sage Publications, Inc. Most footnotes and references have been omitted.

own and his white friends' children to a white "neighborhood" school, and the social rewards of acting in accord with the norms of his friends and peers. The expected costs of noncompliance might include the guilt or discomfort felt from working to subvert a court order, the possibility of being cited for contempt of court and of receiving the subsequent sanctions, and the likelihood of being involved in further litigation. The expected benefits and costs of compliance probably would be multi-faceted, as well.

Finally, it is important to recognize that utility theory does *not* imply simply that individuals will engage in noncompliant activity whenever its expected benefits exceed its expected costs. . . . For example, a hypothetical person for whom only considerations of monetary gain were important might find himself able to earn $10,000 a year through illegal activity with an extremely low probability of detection but still not do it because of the opportunity to earn $20,000 over the same period by devoting the same time and resources to some legal activity. On the other hand, a person might perform an illegal act of negative utility if the utility of compliance was even more negative. . . . [O]ne [ought not] to think [simply] in terms of punishing noncompliance and to disregard rewarding compliance as a means of influencing behavior. . . .

Compliance and Noncompliance with the Directives of Courts

The utility approach postulates that the extent of compliance with a legal directive depends on the values and expectations of the individuals to whom the directive is addressed. To affect levels of compliance, a source of law must influence either of these two variables. The low levels of compliance with many court decisions[3] can be explained in large part by the important limitations on the ways in which courts can affect the values and expectations of target populations. In exploring the court's ability to influence values and expectations, our discussion will be limited to their ability to affect compliance with their own legal directives.

Terminology

Understanding the capacity of courts to affect values and expectations can be facilitated by developing a set of terms classifying the tools available to the courts and the types to whom they may be applied. First, the term *target population* is applied to the individuals and institutions whose behavior a court wishes to influence in a given manner by making a decision. . . .

Second, target populations can consist of *primary* and *secondary recipients* of court directives. Primary recipients are the participants in a case (e.g., litigants, jurors, witnesses, etc.) for whom a directive issued by the court prescribes or proscribes a particular behavior. Secondary recipients are individuals not participants in a case, for whom certain behavior is proscribed or prescribed by a court directive. . . .

The term *sanction* is applied to the benefits and costs which a source of law may deliver to those who comply or fail to comply with its directives. For example, courts impose sanctions when they: (1) use their contempt power to fine or throw someone in jail, (2) suppress illegally obtained evidence to "punish" noncomplying police and prosecutors, and (3) reprimand a noncomplier or praise a complier in an opinion. By their very nature, sanctions are administered *after* complying or noncomplying behavior takes place. Only when a source of law can *respond* to such behavior has it the capacity to apply sanctions. However, having this capacity allows the source of law to affect expectations regarding the likelihood that it will apply the sanctions at its disposal in the future. Thus the *potential* imposition of sanctions may influence compliance through the effect it has on the expected costs and benefits of the utility inequality.

Influence Through the Threat of Judicial Sanction

. . . [T]he range of sanctions available to courts is limited. They (unlike legislatures) must rely almost exclusively upon what commonly would be called "punishments" rathern than "rewards." In terms of the utility inequality, courts have the ability to increase the costs of noncompliance (as through their contempt power) and to decrease the benefits of noncompliance (as through use of the exclusionary rule) but have very little opportunity to decrease the costs of compliance, or to increase the benefits of compliance.

Courts can administer most of the sanctions at their disposal only to the primary recipients of their directives. . . .

. . .

The limited arsenal of judicial sanctions, and the narrow scope within which courts may apply them, lead to our first hypothesis:

H₁: Holding other factors constant, the level and rapidity of compliance with any court directive will vary with the proportion of the target population comprised of primary recipients.

Nevertheless, secondary recipients are not immune totally from the *threat* of judicial sanctions. Under some conditions, secondary recipients will feel that if they do not alter their behavior so as to conform to a court ruling they might become primary recipients of the same directive in some future case in which a court could fine or imprison them for contempt. The fear of being sued and losing may stimulate their compliance. In any case, the important question is . . . "When will secondary recipients tend to feel a *threat* of judicial sanctions?"

We identify two factors: the total number of noncomplying secondary recipients in the target population and the number of persons willing to bring suit against such noncompliers. Therefore,

H₂: The smaller the total number of noncomplying secondary recipients, the greater will be their individual expectations of being sued, and the greater will be their frequency of compliance

and,

H₃: The greater the number of parties willing to bring suit against secondary recipient noncompliers, the more will secondary recipients feel a threat of judicial sanctions and the greater will be their frequency of compliance.

The first factor is important because a given number of potential litigants with finite resources will be able to only bring suit against a limited number of noncompliers. To exemplify this relationship, one can compare the reaction of state legislatures to the Supreme Court's reapportionment decisions with the response of segregated local districts to desegregation decisions or of local officials to obscenity rulings which appear to make unconstitutional their obscenity ordinances. The state legislatures, a set of secondary recipients to Reynolds v. Sims (377 U.S. 533, 1964) which numbered no more than forty-nine, complied relatively promptly with the reapportionment decisions. Had they not, most, and perhaps all, soon would have found themselves pushed into the role of primary

recipients of similar rulings. Their response contrasted with the slow move toward desegregation by the over four thousand school districts in southern and border states which
imposed racial segregation by law in 1955.

The second factor (number of persons willing to bring suit) will be affected by the way
in which courts act as "gatekeepers" on relevant litigation and by the separate cost-benefit
concerns of potential plaintiffs or appellants. The courts' gatekeeper role is exercised
through rulings on standing, justiciability, and jurisdiction, which, although variable in
application, have an important effect on the likelihood that potential litigants will bring,
and successfully complete, legal action.

Cost-benefit considerations are important because potential plaintiffs and appellants
will litigate more frequently when they feel they have the most to gain and the least to
lose in terms of their own values. . . .

Influence Without the Threat of Judicial Sanctions

In many instances, the circumstances which surround and follow an initial court directive do not allow the use or even the threatened use of judicial sanctions. Nevertheless,
courts can still affect the values and expectations represented in the utility inequality.

Influencing Expectations. Courts can affect expectations by at least two important routes,
neither of which is linked to the use of judicial sanctions. First, they can influence expectations of individuals in target populations regarding the imposition of sanctions by *other*
groups. Some studies have found that courts can do this by serving a scapegoat function.
Peltason, for example, argued that by taking a harder line in *Brown* the Supreme Court
could have promoted compliance by allowing lower court judges and school board members wanting desegregation to justify their actions on the grounds that they had no choice;
Brown II, of course, clearly gave them a great deal of choice (Peltason, 1961; 245-246).
Had the Court permitted them little or no discretion they would have found it easier to
blame their complying behavior on the nine justices and thereby to insulate themselves
from some of the political and social consequences of more rapidly implementing desegregation of educational facilities.

Returning to the language of the utility inequality, we have

H_4:   When courts fill a scapegoat function by writing opinions that precisely proscribe
or prescribe behavior, they tend to increase compliance by reducing the expected costs of compliance for target populations.

Second, the influence courts have on expectations can be totally unrelated to any kind
of sanction. Perhaps the primary way in which courts can affect expectations is by convincing members of the target population that implementation of a decision will gratify
positively their pre-existing social goals and more personal values or that failure to implement it will negatively gratify them. Of course most of a target population may either be
already convinced or virtually beyond convincing. . . . Courts might significantly affect
compliance with their decisions by using their opinions to address the empirical questions
crucial in determining a target population's expectations about the consequences of compliance. Hence,

H_5:   As courts more effectively show that compliance tends to fulfill positively, and
noncompliance negatively, important values held by members of a target population, levels of compliance will tend to increase.

Influencing Values. Influencing the values of individuals may be a good deal more difficult than influencing their expectations about empirical outcomes. Such deep-seated predispositions as a bigoted school-board member's attitudes toward racial equality, a fundamentalist teacher's views on separation of church and state, or a law-and-order policeman's orientation toward defendants' rights are not likely to be changed by any arguments a court might make in handing down an opinion.

Even so, two important ways in which courts may influence values are (1) by increasing the intensity of people's commitment to values which specific decisions or sets of decisions are seen as advancing, such as racial equality in desegregation decisions and (2) by increasing their desire to comply with court decisions as an end in itself, apart from the goals which the decisions advance.

With regard to the first, a court can use its written opinions to argue in favor of certain values, perhaps relying on its own moral authority as a source of influence. Single opinions are unlikely to have an effect on deep-seated convictions, but a consistent line of decisions handed down over a period of years might help modify the moral climate within a community. One could argue for instance, that this was the case with the Supreme Court's decisions concerning racial equality.

Courts can increase people's desire to comply as an end in itself by acting in ways that serve to increase court legitimacy. Such actions might include handing down large numbers of substantively popular decisions and conforming to existing norms of court behavior to build up a reservoir of legitimacy on which a court may draw when issuing substantively unpopular decisions (Wasby, 1970:265).

Research Directions

Two general sets of research directions are suggested by the foregoing discussion. The more specific set arises from the hypotheses proposed and the more general set from the utility framework that stimulated the hypotheses. First, how might researchers proceed to employ the five hypotheses empirically? Hypotheses one and two should be the easiest to handle. The most difficult task is to operationalize compliance, a task which is complicated by the fact that the legal directives of courts are sometimes quite ambiguous. Once the meaning of the legal directive has been determined, the target population can be specified and the level and rapidity of compliance and the number of noncompliers can be measured, subject to the everpresent restrictions that data availability impose.

The other hypotheses may prove more difficult to operationalize, yet they should still prove fruitful guides. For hypothesis three, survey techniques would probably be necessary to determine directly the number of parties willing to bring suit against secondary recipient noncompliers, although reasoned estimates at a lower level of measurement could also be made. The fourth hypothesis requires that the researcher classify the precision with which a court directs the behavior of a target population; ordinal rankings may be the most that can be expected; few analysts would disagree that the directive in Brown II was less precise than those in Miranda, but a determination of exactly how much less would surely be more arguable. With regard to the fifth hypothesis, to know *effectively* a court shows how compliance positively fulfills important values held by a target population would require measurement of the population's perceptions, a difficult and expensive task. But a researcher should be able to determine whether a court *overtly* tries to demonstrate that compliant behavior would be of greater utility in positively fulfilling the recipients' values or simply issues a command largely unsupported by such an argument.

. . .

Conclusion

Despite its present skeletal form, a utility theory approach to the study of compliance has several important virtues. First, it provides a degree of conceptual and analytical rigor that the study of compliance has often lacked. . . .

Second, utility theory serves as a framework for analyzing the variable capacity of courts to affect compliance with their own directives and gives rise to a number of hypotheses about levels of compliance with such directives.

Finally, utility theory provides a guide for research which we believe increases the likelihood that studies of compliance will be more fruitful and more cumulative.

Notes

1. It must be emphasized that *gratification,* as we are using the term, can be either positive or negative, or in other words, can involve either "pleasure" or "pain."

2. Compliance and noncompliance, as we use them, refer simply to behavior which respectively conforms and does not conform to legal directives. . . .

3. For a review of the literature on decisional areas in which compliance rates have been low see Wasby (1970): 126-135, 147-185).

References

Krislov, S. (1965) The Supreme Court in the Political Process. New York: Macmillan.

Peltason, J. (1961) Fifty-Eight Lonely Men: Southern Federal Judges and School Desegregation. New York: Harcourt, Brace and World.

Rodgers, H. R., Jr. and C. S. Bullock, III (1972) Law and Social Change: Civil Rights Laws and Their Consequences. New York: McGraw-Hill.

Wasby, S. (1970) The Impact of the United States Supreme Court. Homewood, Ill.: Dorsey.

48

Inertia in Midway: Supreme Court Decisions and Local Responses

Kenneth M. Dolbeare and Phillip E. Hammond

This is a case study of the processes by which a principle of law established in U.S. Supreme Court decisions becomes (or fails to become) part of the reality of official behavior at the local level across the country. It is now widely recognized that some Supreme Court decisions bearing upon local practices eventuate in sharply variant consequences in different parts of the nation. Some states and localities "comply" fully and enthusiastically; others display a wide range of other responses, from very limited modification of practices to outright defiance in some cases. Attentive observers might quite reasonably note that these responses can be shaped by such factors as the nature of the Court's holding, the character of the rights or obligations newly created, the pre-existing policies and practices of states and localities, the availability of remedies for noncompliance, and the general tenor of official and public reaction to the decisions. And, of course, in any given case it might be more remarkable that so many local communities complied than that they did not.

But, faced with widely variant responses in such important areas as segregation, reapportionment, defendants' rights, and schoolhouse religion, we want to go beyond such plausible if abstract generalizations. We seek to move closer to specifying precisely why responses take such varying forms, and which factors are operable under what circumstances to bring about particular types of consequences. We want to know the characteristics of attitude and behavior change in the wake of Supreme Court decisions, and to identify the forces that produce them. In short, after a change-inducing Supreme Court decision, who does what? And what are the implications for the role of the law and the courts in American society?

I. The Nature of the Study

Our choices of subject area, object of inquiry, and research method for this case study all require explanation and perhaps justification. We have taken schoolhouse religion—in particular, responses to the school prayer cases of 1962 and 1963—as our subject. Our inquiry is directed at the behavior of state and local public officials and related elites. The

Reprinted by permission from *Journal of Legal Education* 23 (1970), 106–122. Most footnotes have been omitted.

sites selected were five communities in a single Midwestern state, and our approach consisted of extensive interviewing and document search five years after the decisions were rendered. Let us provide some background on each choice in turn.

(a) Subject area

The subject of school prayers is less crucial to the workings of our political system than many other subjects, and there have been many studies of reactions to these decisions. But earlier research showed it to be highly salient among the general public as an area of Supreme Court activity, comparable only to the segregation decisions; no other area of Court decision-making (not even defendants' rights) was anywhere near as readily recognized in our 1966 survey (shortly to be described). Because we wanted to explore an area in which the general public was reasonably well informed and concerned (and because the subject was not without intrinsic interest) we chose to trace responses to Engel v. Vitale and School District of Abington Township v. Schempp. The fact that there had been several other studies of different kinds in this subject area, thus allowing some cumulation of knowledge, seemed to us a distinct advantage.[1] And, although the subject of school prayers in some ways presents an atypical compliance problem, it may be representative of those areas (segregation, local reapportionment) where enforcement must be via citizen-initiated lawsuits or other forms of pressure on officials who may be reluctant and who possess some degree of discretion. . . .

(b) The Object of Inquiry

A substantial proportion of the growing body of "judicial impact studies" has been devoted to schoolhouse religion cases, beginning with the released-time cases of the 1940s and 1950s and continuing particularly with the *Engel, Schempp,* and *Murray* cases of the 1960s. Survey research has thoroughly documented the oft-observed fact that Supreme Court decisions may produce only scattered changes in actual local practices, and imaginative case studies have examined instances of compliance in some depth. The major thrust of much of this research is to the effect that the preferences and behavior of state and local officials are highly determinative of local response. Our own prior research indicated that local elites were, in addition, far more knowledgeable and more Court-oriented than the general public. . . .

Our findings in this earlier research were drawn from mail questionnaire responses of three Wisconsin leadership groups (clergymen, newspaper editors, political party county chairmen) obtained nearly simultaneously with a statewide sample of the general public in Wisconsin in 1966. Leaders averaged twice as much information about specific Supreme Court decisions as did the general public, and stood well above comparably educated members of the general public. Although relatively small proportions of both groups saw the Court as the most important of the three branches of government, leaders were three times more likely than the public to select the Court for this status. Leaders also were sharply polarized ideologically in their ratings of the Court: among the public, the divergence between conservatives and liberals in characterizing the Court's performance as "good" or "very good" was only 6%; between conservative and liberal leaders, however, the gap was 54%.[2] And, finally, leaders were 50% more likely than the general public to express trust in the actions of the Court. Taken together, our findings led us to the conclusion that the Supreme Court is chiefly an object of leadership attention and concern, and that if there were to be local responses produced by Court decisions it would have to be through the agency of attentive (and power-holding) local leaders. The two sets of research thus converged to indicate that inquiry directed at the determinants of the behavior of local elites might shed useful light on the process shaping ultimate response to Supreme Court decisions.

(c) Research Method

We also knew from a variety of sources that there were broad regional and state patterns of response to the Court's prayer decisions. These were related to systematic variations in the actions of state-level agencies and officials, who were, in turn, responsive to state statutory and constitutional requirements, and/or local practices. In general, before 1962, many *eastern* and *southern* states had constitutional or statutory provisions requiring religious observances, and the incidence of such activities at the local level within these regions was very high. *Western* states tended to have prohibitions against such activities, and the incidence throughout was very low. *Midwestern* states had few formal provisions either way, and about half of all school districts regularly conducted religious observances. . . .

(1) *What happened:* The basic source on national patterns of schoolhouse religion is Dierenfield's 1960 survey of the practices of a national sample of school districts.[3] In 1967, we resurveyed all of the 1100 districts which had earlier reported that at least some of their schools engaged in devotional exercises. Presumably, all of these districts would have been faced with the question of what if any changes to make after the 1962 and 1963 decisions. We secured a return rate of 57%, sufficient to justify the characterization that about one-third of all districts were still not complying, and that there were sharp regional patterns in compliance. Table 48-1 shows these comparisons.

TABLE 48-1
By Region, the Percentage of School Districts in 1960
Engaged in Devotionals Which, by 1967, Had Stopped

Region	Percentage Stopped by 1967	Number of Cases
West	62%	21
Midwest	54%	164
East	93%	295
South	21%	171

(2) *Why it happened:* These regionally distinctive patterns are attributable in a general sense to the nature of established practices and preferences—and in more specific terms to the actions of state officials. In the aftermath of the decisions, the Eastern states removed their requirements (in many cases with official announcements that such actions were now proscribed), and local practices promptly followed the Court's new requirements. Southern states not only did not remove their requirements but actually in some cases added to them—and the reduction in religious activities among local districts was quite modest. The Western states were under no obligation to act, but some did anyhow, and those few districts which had conducted religious activities generally stopped. In the Midwest, very

little action was taken at the state level, and local districts' responses were mixed and widely variant. About half reported reducing their practices in some way, but many continued on much as they had before. . . .

An effort to explore the role of local actors in the compliance drama, therefore, would have to be set in a midwestern context where all communities would have been subject to the same ambivalent or non-existent state-level cues regarding response to the Court. Further, insight into the behavior of such persons could best be gained by a comparative study of several communities—some of which complied and some of which did not.

From our 1967 resurvey of school districts we selected four communities (two reporting compliance, two reporting continuation of religious activities) in one state ("Midway") where there had been no official cues given or requirements set by relevant state officials. The communities were comparable in size, averaging about 10,000 in population. All were county seats, had a daily newspaper, and served as retail shopping centers for the surrounding areas. Teams of interviewers undertook three rounds of interviewing of local educational system officials, teachers, community leaders, and others in each community in the Spring and Summer of 1968.

We should have liked to report findings based on this neat scheme. But our first finding was that neither of our "complying" communities was in fact complying. Both were saying prayers and reading the Bible, and doing many other religious-oriented things, exactly as they had before the decisions were rendered. Further, resort to our elaborate survey responses, detailed search of all the major newspapers in the state, and lengthy consultation with knowledgeable persons in the state all failed to turn up a single community (other than the major city in the state and three university towns) where—according to our subsequent investigation—there had been actual compliance or any serious official or private attempt to obtain compliance.

Rather than wholly exhaust ourselves in the pursuit of "compliance" where there was none, therefore, we adjusted to reality and undertook to understand how an entire state could so transcend the law of the land without significant protest from any of its citizens. We added another community, a slightly larger county seat where a right-wing movement had at least made some effort to enlarge on the schools' religious programs. And we made a comprehensive study of the behavior of all state-level officials and interest group leaders who might conceivably have been moved to action on this subject.

In all, our data consist of interviews with either the executive head or chief deputy (and frequently both), and some subordinate officers, in (a) each department of the state government concerned with religion in the schools, and in (b) all seven of the major statewide religious, civil liberties, or school-oriented interest groups, plus (c) more than one hundred interviews with superintendents, principals, teachers, newspaper editors, school board members, and other local notables in the five towns. Together with detailed reconstruction of school-related events from each of the local newspapers, these are the grounds on which our analysis rests.

II.   Findings: The Banality of Noncompliance

Six years after *Engel,* and five years after *Schempp* and *Murray,* Midway schools regularly engaged in every form of religious observance known to the fertile imagination of generations of teachers. While superintendents soberly answered mail questionnaires to the effect that their schools were in full compliance with the Court's interpretation of the Constitution, many teachers led their pupils in a wide variety of morning and afternoon prayers, Bible reading, and hymns. Some others regularly exhorted their pupils to attend Sunday school, posting attendance sheets on Monday morning to shame those who had not. Bible stories and religious poems were standard year-round components of the curriculum, and most schools had established forms of grace to be recited at lunch periods. Ministers conducted religious activities in assemblies near the time of religious holidays, and most schools required attendance at baccalaureate services, which were conducted on school property. On the basis of our interviewing, we estimate that at least half of the classrooms in Midway engage in some explicitly proscribed religious observance, and that nearly all schools sponsor some form of unconstitutional religious activity.

Most teachers were aware that there had been some type of decision rendered by the Court. Some acknowledged that they "should not go too far," and so had eliminated "denominational" prayers or "forcing a child to do something he doesn't want to do." But many teachers (including several who either once had or still doubled as Sunday School teachers) saw their obligations as more compelling. One elderly woman declared frankly, "I consider it my professional duty to teach religion." . . .

Principals too knew of the decisions, but were confident that teachers legally could, and generally that they should, engage in some form of religious observances. . . .

But these schoolhouse practices, clearly violative of the Court's authoritative interpretation of the Constitution (and recognized as such by all of the superintendents), did not represent strong elite or superintendent preference for religion in the schools. On the merits of the issue, superintendents opposed prayers and other religious activities, and local elites, while divided (with a majority favoring prayers), did not feel at all strongly about the matter. Nor was it a deliberate act of defiance of the Court. On this point all were in agreement. Superintendents and school board members and other local leaders alike acknowledged more than perfunctorily that the Court should be obeyed, even in this subject area. Nor was the situation in Midway the product of an aroused popular determination to maintain the status quo in the schools—because most people, even activists who were engaged in this issue, simply did not know what the actual practices were in the schools. Nor, finally, was the situation due to nonexistence of interest groups which supported the rulings. Midway had a full complement of civil liberties groups and liberally oriented religious groups such as the Anti-Defamation League of B'nai B'rith, the National Conference of Christians and Jews, and the National Council of Churches. And the leaders (and most members, we assume) of all these groups felt strongly that prayers and Bible reading should be eliminated, in accordance with the Court's ruling.

We are confronted in this setting, then, with the resounding failure of a Supreme Court decision. Here was a new national policy—an authoritative interpretation of the Constitution—requiring revision of state-sponsored practices, but it had no observable consequences whatsoever for Midway. Elsewhere, there were varying responses apparently approaching compliance. But in Midway, the many varied religious practices that had pre-existed the Court's decisions simply went on unchanged, and not just for a temporary period of adjustment. Five years after the decisions, the only thing that was different was that the practices were unconstitutional and violative of the rights of persons subject to them. And nobody did anything about it.

Explanation of the many possible forms of noncompliance may be more complex—or at least more uncertain—than that of compliance. For one thing, there may be many forms of behavior short of tangible compliance. Formal, perfunctory, or rhetorical "compliance" may be involved, as well as degrees of enthusiasm for the prescribed new behavior. This is why we have preferred to use the term "response" to refer to the actions subsequent to Court decisions. Further, we are dealing with a *process* of inaction or "nondecision," rather than a single event or a moment's profile of quantitative patterns of response. We found no courageous and independent superintendent who was willing to act decisively to eliminate prayers, as did Richard Johnson in Eastville-Westville, Illinois. Indeed, we found no evidence that there was such inclination in any of the more than 250 superintendents in Midway. Nor did we find any differentiation between school board members in law-abidingness, as did Robert Birkby among the school boards of Tennessee. No school board except those in the largest city and the three university towns, so far as we were able to ascertain, acted even perfunctorily to eliminate any religious activities. But why?

We found that avoidance of the issue and deflection of responsibility ran up and down the scale, from the highest state officials to the smallest towns' leaders and citizens. We identified four contributing explanations among the (no doubt) many which converged to establish this response pattern. The first two relate to some familiar political realities, first of the state and then of local settings. The next two have to do with the cognitive and institutional features of *both* levels of government at once.

First, there was unfocused responsibility for action and a lack of self-interest motivation on the part of officials, chiefly at the state, but also at the local level. No officeholder carried clear and unavoidable responsibility for acting to carry out the Court's rulings. Nor did any power holder, state or local, have anything significant to gain from acting to support or enforce them. Every official and every other actor in state and local politics has a kind of priority list of goals which he is seeking in the long-enduring and ongoing political process in which he is engaged. He yields on some goals in order to achieve others he considers more important. But nobody cared enough about elimination of school prayers to risk loss of his other goals; every political actor who calculated the costs and benefits of action in this sphere was immediately immobilized by his perception of dramatic costs.

These are eminently understandable reasons for inaction, and they were put forward frankly by practically every political actor whom we interviewed. State officials denied responsibility, the applicable attorney in the Office of the Attorney General suggesting that "nobody understands federal laws." Leaders of the state-wide liberal church groups perceived themselves and their groups as standing to lose much more from arousing public resentment than they could possibly gain from an effort to spur obedience, and so they remained publicly silent. They contented themselves with a joint private visit to the State Superintendent of Public Instruction, a man who had declared publicly that he saw no way to prevent schools from engaging in religious activities if they wanted to. They solemnly offered him materials for distribution to districts which might inquire about conforming to the Court's rulings—which he accepted and, no doubt, filed. Superintendents had many more pressing problems on their hands, such as consolidation of school districts, tax levels, new construction, or busing arrangements. There was no leader or official who did not have a politically understandable reason for not taking action. Indeed, the ordinary, everyday nature of these reasons suggests a kind of banality to this pattern of noncompliance: no great principles were perceived to be at stake—it was merely a case of all power-holders independently concluding that their responsibilities did not include the costly task of upholding the "law of the land." There was no reward in sight for the individual official who might be inclined to support the Court, and apparently none felt strongly enough about prayer to take a stand by himself.

Second, and perhaps most important to the status quo-without-controversy-outcome in Midway, was the effective commitment of local elites to the avoidance of conflict in their communities. In each of the five communities we examined, educational policies were shaped by a small number of people. Superintendents and school boards knew which persons to consult about any matter of importance, they conceded vetoes to key figures, and they knew that their discretionary powers extended only to certain well-defined boundaries. Paramount among all of their guiding principles was the desire to keep out of controversy, in order that they not embarrass the local power-holders whose approval was essential to the attainment of their goals. If conflict were generated, of course, public involvement would be spurred and the established gentlemanly process of accommodation, good judgment, public spiritedness, and predictability would be lost.

For this reason, it did not matter so much what local practices in an unimportant area such as school prayers were, but that they not be changed if that would provoke conflict. Both right-wing advocates of more religion and Seventh Day Adventists or Jehovah's Witnesses—or anybody who sought to conform to Supreme Court mandates—would therefore be repulsed, deflected, and dismissed if possible. It did not matter who they were, or what they sought, but what might follow. Once this pattern of conflict-depressing is established as an operating principle in at least the educational policy area of a community, it becomes an effective support for both elite decisionmaking and the status-quo. There seems little doubt, however, that if local power structures had thought the matter important enough to take up, they could have eliminated prayers and Bible reading from the schools with relatively little uproar. Too few people were aware of what was actually going on to effectively resist, and the courts would have been obliged to uphold the action anyhow. Local elites were thus the key to action, given the absence of state-created requirements; and they cared almost exclusively about managing conflict, rather than about what the schools did regarding prayer.

Third, some remarkable cognitive insulation developed among power-holders and others who might have acted to support the Court's rulings. Having once committed themselves to inaction, they apparently generated cognitive and perceptual screens against dissonance or role strain. One form taken by this phenomenon was misperception of the Court's holdings themselves: both officials and attorneys at the state and local levels proved much better informed about *Engel* than *Schempp*, and they were likely to state the Court's doctrine as prohibiting only state-drafted or -sponsored prayers. Although informed about lower court cases subsequent to *Schempp*, they resisted acknowledgment that *Schempp* and *Murray* proscribed reading of scripture or saying of prayers, and found it almost unimaginable that some might construe the holdings to outlaw other forms of religious observance conducted by the schools in the absence of formal school board policy requiring it. They were far more likely to see the Court as acting against the religious freedom of the majority than on behalf of a minority's right to be free of state-sponsored religion. In brief, most officials saw the Court as having acted on the "free exercise" rather than the "no establishment" clause.

Another form of psychological insulation, common to officials above the local level, was ignorance about actual practices in the schools. Not only did high educational system officials with decades of experience quite sincerely deny knowledge of long-established practices, but also liberal leaders who had every reason to wish to be informed found it very difficult to accept such knowledge. Many were offended that the suggestion would be put before them. After some testing, we became convinced that this was a sincere psychological phenomenon and not just a protective mechanism for use against inquisitive inter-viewers. These two phenomena may also explain why superintendents could (also appar-ently sincerely) respond to questionnaire inquiry that their districts were in full compliance with the Court's rulings: they either reduced the rulings to narrow prohibi-tions on state-sponsored prayers or against official school board requirements for prayers, or they too screened out knowledge concerning actual practices in their schools.

Another curiosity among officials was a widely shared perception of the school prayers issue as a highly controversial one. To some extent, this was probably an exaggerated estimate of what would have happened if they had taken action, developed *post hoc* as a rationale for not acting. But it was more than that: in interview after interview, we were told of the controversy that had swept the state in regard to prayers in schools. But we were unable to find a single community (again excepting the capital and the three univer-sity towns) in which there had actually been conflict over prayers in the local schools. Probing this apparent misperception with leaders at all levels, we concluded that there is a wide bifurcation between a national issue and its local application. The Court's deci-sions, and the general question of prayers and Bible reading in the schools, were a major national issue. The campaign for the Becker Amendment to permit prayers in schools was highly visible and strongly supported in Midway, with thousands of persons signing peti-tions and attending rallies. But the national issue never linked in and made contact with the local public schools. It remained one of the abstracts about which people felt deeply, but it never aroused conflict over the actual local practice. Leaders of an active right-wing prayer-seeking group were frankly amazed to learn from us that prayer had not been eliminated from their local schools, which indeed practiced many more religious obser-vances than were called for by the program which the right-wing group sought to insti-tute.

Fourth, there were no regular channels through which the issue could be raised to official visibility. Neither state nor local officials could be forced to take a stand on this question through any institutionalized procedure. At the state level, relevant interest groups such as the Civil Liberties Union or the Council of Churches saw no uncostly and available public route to put the issue onto an official agenda. At the local level, there were not even any potentially interested groups or individuals who might have raised the issue of com-pliance. Local ministers, not very well integrated into the decision-making apparatus of their communities in any event, were further neutralized by disagreement among them-selves over mechanics and by their perception of opposition from parishioners. And if the *ministers* did not take action on a religious issue, citizens were even less inclined to do so on their own initiative.

The absence of channels or arenas through which the issue might be legitimately and routinely raised means that an individual's only recourse would be to initiate a lawsuit. The social and psychological costs of doing so, and the possible isolation or ostracism which might follow, make this an unlikely course in a small town setting. The procedural opportunities for challenging the acts of a public official in Midway are not as readily invoked or as effective as they are in some states, and so the overall context would be discouraging for even the most determined advocate of separation of church and state. So far as we were able to ascertain from the admittedly sketchy reporting of trial court decisions, supplemented by newspaper search, no lawsuit was initiated in Midway on this issue during this five-year period.

III. Supreme Court Decisions, "The Law,"
and Social and Political Change

We succeeded in identifying four factors contributing to the various responses which add up to noncompliance: a banal business-as-usual adherence to established priorities; local elite conflict-avoidance; insulating misperceptions and ignorance; and a lack of institutionalized channels through which state and local officials might be routinely forced to confront the issue. The status-quo ante was preserved despite two highly salient Supreme Court decisions authoritatively interpreting the Constitution and mandating dramatic change at the local level. Nothing happened. Ironically, the same officials and leaders who did not act in furtherance of this Constitutional interpretation would probably be among those who would call most loudly for "law and order" in the cities, and for the suppression of "violations of the rights of others" on college campuses. In concrete settings, of course, "the law" is very much a question of what results power-holders happen to prefer. If nothing else, this study shows how easy it is for "respectable" people to ignore or use the law for their own ends. If others seek to do so, it may be a matter to be deplored; but under the proper circumstances of elite management, the law may be conveniently fitted to the needs of officeholders and other regular political participants. The legal profession played no distinctive part in generating support for the Court's rulings, and was indeed only marginally related to the outcome here. Where lawyers did become involved, as lawyers, their role was one of facilitating the non-compliance goals of other officials.

What was different here from elsewhere—where, apparently in many cases, compliance was achieved? As a preliminary, we may note that we have lost confidence in the validity of our initial survey evidence. Our first round of questionnaires went to more than a thousand school superintendents. Their cooperative responses produced relatively neat patterns of "compliance" and "noncompliance" from which we duly ascertained that urbanism, media exposure and religious heterogeneity might be related to compliance. But interviewing and observation in several local contexts succeeded in destroying such interpretations as based on anything more than formalism or whimsy. We are left instead with images of the resourcefulness and longevity of the actual status quo of established local practice. We see no reason to doubt quantitative surveys' reports of formal *school board* policies of noncompliance for we assume few officials will falsely report that they have an unlawful official policy. But we cannot confidently build interpretations which rely on such studies' findings of, and proferred explanations for, compliance in the classroom, because we now know how widely definitions of "compliance" can vary and how self-congratulatory superintendents can be.

Nevertheless there is solid evidence testifying to the effects of decisive action by individuals among state or local elites. Johnson and Muir at least have demonstrated that classroom compliance, even among unconcerned or opposed constituencies, may follow such action. The interesting question is when, how, and under what circumstances tangible change consistent with Supreme Court policy initiatives may be accomplished. Let us try to organize the implications of our findings with this question in mind.

Four categories of factors shaping response to Court rulings seem implicit. The first two are structural in character, in the sense of being "givens" or properties of a situation which are constant for all settings, e.g., objective components of the policy (decision) itself, or pre-existing characteristics of institutions and procedures. The next two are *behavioral* in character, varying between settings and people, e.g., the attitudes and actions of leaders and publics in the context of distinctive ongoing state and local political processes. Although the analysis which follows draws specifically on our findings here regarding the consequences of a new church-and-state policy enunciated by the Supreme Court, we speculate that similar or analogous categories apply to other types of policies generated by other institutions of the national government.

(1) *The substance of the decision.* Self-evidently, response is affected by the nature of the decision or policy involved. The allocation of a benefit is more likely to engender cooperative action among recipients than is the imposition of a burden; a clear mandate for specific action more than an ambiguous or confusing one; and incremental change more than a drastic reorganization of established relationships; and so on. Perhaps less obviously, *who* is required to act may be just as important as *what* they are to do. Where highly visible public officials carry clear responsibility for enforcement of other implementation, discretion is most confined and cooperation is most likely. Public officials at lower levels of visibility may enjoy somewhat more discretion over their subsequent behavior, although they too are subject to the responsibilities inherent in their offices and to the availability of legal maneuvers forcing them to act in some fashion. If the policy requires behavior change on the part of large segments of the general public, however, cooperation will be more dependent upon popular preferences, the nature of the inducements to conform to a new standard, and the relationship between the new policy and the established patterns of behavior in this area.

Each of these propositions is illustrated by our findings. The change called for was substantial, the mandate was somewhat ambiguous, and people were being asked to give up something they were in the habit of enjoying. There was no unavoidable obligation for visible public officials to act, local officials had discretionary capacity to avoid implementing action, and there were no inducements for the general public to change its behavior from long-established practices. The characteristics of this decision, in other words, gave especially broad scope and opportunity to the shaping capacity of participants in the post-policymaking process.

(2) *Institutional mechanisms and procedures.* The existence of a bureaucracy with the primary function of implementing policies establishes one pattern of relevant forces and raises the prospects of conformity with the policy. A bureaucracy has the capacity to reach out, investigate, and persuade or coerce the objects of the policy into appropriate behavior. Most likely to limit the power of indigenous forces to shape consequences, and therefore most likely to induce conformity, is a federal bureaucracy (such as the Social Security or Veterans Administration) and then a state bureaucracy (such as welfare agencies). Less effective for such purposes are multipurposes agencies without oversight capabilities—such as the courts. Courts must await the initiation of cases by parties with the psychic and financial capacity to challenge authoritative decision-makers, and then they must act within narrow confines of the law and its application to the particular relationships of the contending parties. Further, courts' interpretations do not necessarily bind officials or others not actually before the court. Thus, the scope of court capability is very limited, rendering policies dependent on court-induced behavioral change highly responsive to local preference and discretion. In some circumstances, of course, officials must themselves resort to the courts in order to discharge their responsibilities, and the courts may be a more effective vehicle of structuring response of national policies. Where law enforcement officials are the objects of new policies, such as in the case of the defendants' rights

decisions, for example, courts are in a relatively strong position to enforce compliance. This is because prosecutors must secure convictions of wrong doers in order to do their jobs, and judges may simply dismiss cases if defendants' rights of counsel or freedom from policy harassment have not been observed. Officials and investigators thus have little choice about conforming with constitutional interpretations in such areas.

The availability of institutional mechanisms and/or other established procedures is thus an important conditioning factor which structures the rewards and punishments influencing behavior in any particular area. In the case of school prayers, no institutional support was unavoidably available except the courts, and even their limited capabilities were contingent upon invocation by local people. With the prospect of no rewards and few punishments in store, local elements were especially free to exercise their own discretion.

(3) *The politico-cultural context.* The context of public attitudes and prior traditions and practices may vary sharply in different settings across the United States. . . . Public attitudes toward the issue, as well as public attitudes toward the Court as an institution, in other words, enter the equation. The legitimacy of the originating institution (in this case, the Supreme Court), if great in a particular context, will reduce the capacity of local forces to modify a policy initiative; correlatively, strongly held preferences (in this case, for prayer) will neutralize such feelings and restore initiative in the hands of local elites. In Midway, respect for the Court was thought to be low and preference for prayers was thought to be high; so local elites were free to act in accordance with their usual predilections.

The politico-cultural context becomes particularly important also in determining whether local efforts to shape action by local officials will be forthcoming. In a socially homogeneous, small community, it takes great psychic motivation to break out of the mold of acquiescence and conformity with the decisions of dominant local elites; starting a lawsuit or other movement to force change in a policy preferred by the local majority may cause social isolation or even ostracism, and it would not be lightly undertaken. In Midway, it appears, the context was so forbidding that no individual felt it worth the costs to seek to compel compliance with the Court's rulings.

(4) *The interests, priorities, preferences, and behavior of political actors.* State and local public officials and other powerholders in the policy context are engaged in a continuing interaction process; they have varying goals and aspirations, and different capabilities with which to attain them. The only thing that is certain about their relationship is that it has been going on for some time and will continue long after any particular policy is integrated into the subject area. Least predictable and least expressable in terms of regularities of these four categories of factors, the value-based actions of officials and leaders nevertheless may be the most determinative of ultimate policy consequences. We have seen that officials at all levels operated with a personal cost-benefit equation, seeking only those goals which they valued most highly and sacrificing others. The actions of others might have raised school prayers to a sufficiently visible level so that they would have had to take action, but until this happened they were able to go on about their business, unaffected by the '62 and '63 Court rulings. In this context, there was little to be gained and potentially much to be risked *for practically all political actors,* whether state or local and whether official or private. Nobody stood to gain in self-interest terms from acting to further the Court's policy, and so nobody did. If there had been some important payoff for some powerholder in Midway, the whole story might well have been different.

In seeking to understand why a particular policy results in certain specific consequences, all four types of factors must be considered. Ultimate consequences are the product of a complex equation of structures and behavior, and not of any single factor. On occasions, a property of a decision might be highly determinative, at other times less so. Or the role of local decision-makers might vary from case to case. We do not suggest constant importance for each factor relative to all others. But at least all of the factors we have identified as operative here are involved in practically every instance where national policy filters down towards local applications, and perhaps many more not apparent from our investigation are also involved. In this inquiry, we saw that a constitutional interpretation implying substantial change was cast adrift with very little institutional support available to induce compliance. State and local officials and elites had no self-interest reason to act in furthering it, and consequently they did nothing. Moreover, both the general context of public attitudes and the specific context of small town homogeneity discouraged any movement toward compliance. Not surprisingly, the net result was perpetuation of the status quo—even though it meant noncompliance with the law of the land.

Are these categories and interpretations limited to the circumstances of Supreme Court outlawing of school prayers, or do they extend to other Supreme Court rulings and perhaps to the acts of other policymaking institutions as well? We examined only the one situation, of course, and have evidence only on what transpired in response to two Court rulings in the schoolhouse religion area. All else is speculation, but it still seems that our findings lead to some sketchy implications of a more general nature. As for Court decisions, it appears that the capabilities of subsequent actors to alter the intended outcome is greatest when the new policy requires substantial change in the behavior patterns of numbers of people in an area where official enforcement depends on local residents' invocation of the courts. The more clearly the obligation to respond is focused upon few and identifiable public officials, and the more available are enforcement agencies (such as the Civil Rights Division of the Justice Department, or criminal courts in the case of defendants' rights issues), the more limited is the range of discretion on the part of post-policymaking forces and people. There is always some discretion on the part of political actors subsequent to any Court decision, of course, and the variation is only in the degree to which a given ruling is subject to the manipulations of others. In most cases, it seems safe to say, a large share of the shaping of ultimate results rests with political actors on the local level, rather than with the higher courts' views of the merits of issues.

Perhaps this is a point at which our findings show even greater generality. The extent of local capacity to shape policy consequences appears to be in important ways a reflection of which national institution created the particular policy. A Supreme Court-produced policy is probably much more open to discretionary implementation by a variety of domestic political forces than is a Congressional statute or an executive regulation. The availability of detailed clarifying and implementing instructions, or a bureaucracy legally to bind all persons with a single pronouncement, cannot help but reduce the opportunity for local forces to shape implementation and ultimate consequences. It does not prevent such forces from exercising power or from affecting the outcome, of course, but their opportunities are more constricted. By contrast with Court-produced policies, which depend on volunteered cooperation or a sense of obligation on the part of state and local officials, Congressional and executive actions have a ready-made corps of federal implementators waiting to convert policy into consequences. Although the Court is different, however, it is different in degree and not in kind: the same types of forces and factors apply, to some extent, to all major policy-producing institutions. Specification of the precise extent must await other studies of the consequences of such policies.

Notes

1. Patric, "The Impact of a Court Decision: Aftermath of the McCollum Case," 6 *J. Pub. L.* 455 (1957); Sorauf, "Zorach v. Clauson: The Impact of a Supreme Court Decision," 53 *Am. Pol. Sci. Rev.* 777 (1959); Katz, "Patterns of Compliance with the Schempp Decision," 14 *J. Pub. L.* 396 (1965); Birkby, "The Supreme Court and the Bible Belt: Tennessee Reaction to the 'Schempp' Decision, 10 *Midwest J. of Pol. Sci.* 304 (1966); Reich, "The Impact of Judicial Decision-Making: The School Prayer Cases," in Everson, ed., *The Supreme Court as Policy-Maker* (1968); Way, "Survey Research on Judicial Decisions: The Prayer and Bible Reading Cases," 21 *Western Pol. Q.* 189 (1968); W. Muir, *Prayer in the Public Schools: Law and Attitude Change* (1967); R. Johnson, *The Dynamics of Compliance: Supreme Court Decision Making from a New Perspective* (1967).

2. This difference may be best presented in tabular form:

Percent Evaluating the Court's Performance as "Very Good" or "Good" Among:

	Conservatives	Liberals	Difference
Public	46 (180)	52 (447)	6
Leaders	26 (97)	80 (122)	54

. . .

3. Dierenfield, "The Impact of the Supreme Court Decisions on Religion in the Public Schools," *Religious Education* 445 (September–October 1967).

CHAPTER SEVENTEEN
POLICY IMPACT

When we ask, what is the policy impact of, for example, the Supreme Court's ruling in *Brown* v. *Board of Education* (striking down legally required separation of the races in public education)?, we seek to go beyond the question of compliance. We are concerned with both short and long-range consequences, for the Court and for society, of the Court's having acted in that particular policy area.

We can ask, first of all, what have been the consequences for public education over the long run? Has the intent of the Supreme Court been realized or have unanticipated problems emerged? What have been the consequences for the Supreme Court itself, both in terms of its subsequent race relations policy and in terms of the Court's political standing? What have been the broader societal consequences of the Court's destruction of the legal basis of racism and its furtherance of the continuing struggle of racial minorities to have carried out the promises of the Declaration of Independence and the Constitution? Can we point to an event or a series of events that the Court's policy decision set in motion? In other words, our concern with impact is a concern with the question "so what?" What difference has it made that the Court ruled as it did?

As should be obvious, the sorts of questions just raised are infinitely easier to ask than to answer. Some of them lend themselves to systematic empirical investigation, as the three studies reprinted in this chapter demonstrate. But the broader questions are more difficult to answer. For example, it is possible to examine the consequences of the *Brown* policy for public education in terms of the extent of desegregated education some two decades after the policy was first announced. It is also possible to examine the effect of racially integrated education on the performance and abilities of school children of both races. The policy impact of *Brown* along these lines is discussed in the reading by Charles Bullock and Harrell Rodgers (selection 49). Although Bullock and Rodgers in the excerpt presented here do not consider the full range of Court policy in the broad race relations field, it is not difficult to demonstrate the logical connection between the end of racism in public education and the end of racism in other aspects of public life and publicly sponsored activities. By taking the major step it did in *Brown*, the Court became involved in all aspects of the law of race relations and thus established the legal basis for the civil rights revolution. Ultimately *Brown* led to an assault on officially sponsored racism in all its guises throughout the country. One can suggest, then, that the *Brown* policy ushered in the civil rights revolution in political, social, and economic terms, and that the long-run impact of *Brown* has been and continues to be immense. However, this last assertion is more difficult to demonstrate conclusively.

Concern with the policy impact of the Court's landmark reapportionment rulings means that we ask questions similar to those asked concerning the school desegregation policy—essentially, what difference has it made that the Court formulated its one person one vote policy and required the end of malapportioned legislative districts? Roger Hanson and Robert Crew attempt to answer that question in selection 50. The impact of reapportionment should be demonstrable by comparing the legislative policy outputs of fairly apportioned legislatures with those of unfairly apportioned legislatures. The Supreme Court's policy in the reapportionment field thus lends itself more easily than does its race relations policy or, for that matter, its criminal procedures policy, to a systematic empirical accounting of policy impact.

We face a host of difficult problems in assessing the impact of Court policy on criminal procedures. One criminal procedure policy area in which there has been a continuing debate over the impact of Court policy is the exclusionary rule. Under that rule, evidence illegally obtained by the police in violation of Fourth Amendment standards cannot be introduced at the trial of the criminal defendant nor can it in any way be used against the defendant. The history of the exclusionary rule goes back to a 1914 decision of the Supreme Court whereby the exclusionary rule was imposed on the federal courts to implement the Fourth Amendment's guarantees. In 1961, in the case of *Mapp* v. *Ohio,* the Supreme Court ruled that the exclusionary rule applies to the state courts as well.

Assessment of the impact of the exclusionary rule is not a simple task. First there is the problem of determining the impact of the *Mapp* policy on law enforcement in the states. Are Fourth Amendment standards difficult to follow, and if so does the rule hamper effective law enforcement? Does the rule accomplish what it is supposed to do and engender police respect for the requirements of the Fourth Amendment? Questions such as these, related to the impact of *Mapp* on law enforcement, have continued to stimulate controversy over the efficacy of the exclusionary rule. A large majority of the justices on the Nixon-Burger Court do not believe that the consequences of the rule have been beneficial for society. Before reaching that conclusion they ought to have carefully pondered the study by Bradley Canon (selection 51), in which these important questions are considered.

In a broader sense one can argue that the policy impact of the exclusionary rule has been profound. Imposition of the rule was one of the first major steps taken by the Warren Court to extend the criminal procedural guarantees of the Bill of Rights to the states. *Mapp* was part of the criminal procedures revolution that occurred in the 1960s and, just as it was the first major criminal procedural right to be extended by the liberal Warren Court, it has been the first major criminal procedural right to be narrowed by the more conservative Nixon-Burger Court of the 1970s.

It is plausible to argue (although difficult to demonstrate conclusively) that the major impact of *Mapp* was that it sensitized law enforcement officials and prodded them to show greater respect for the requirements of the Bill of Rights. The standards used in the federal criminal process, they were now being told, would be imposed on the states. No longer would states be free to "experiment" with the rights and liberties of Americans. The message sent by the Court of the 1970s, however, has been a different one. Its broader impact has yet to be analyzed.

49

School Desegregation: Successes and Failures

Charles S. Bullock, III, and Harrell R. Rodgers, Jr.

School integration is often viewed as a device for improving the academic achievement of black students. The thrust of this view is that if school desegregation does not result in higher academic achievement for blacks, it is a failure and should be abandoned. This reasoning is faulty on several counts. First, the Supreme Court's decisions on school desegregation were based on the finding that black Americans were segregated because they were considered inferior by white society. To allow such discriminatory treatment, the Court said, denied black Americans the equal protection of the law. The obligation to desegregate the public schools, then, was based on a legal principle guaranteed to all Americans by the Constitution, not on a pedagogic speculation.

Second, it would be extremely peculiar if school desegregation had to prove its value as an academic device to justify its continuation. Segregated schools existed for decades without any demands that their existence be justified on any ground other than the pernicious doctrine of white supremacy. Third, to center attention almost exclusively on the academic potential of school desegregation neglects a number of other areas in which desegregation may have important consequences for society. The more important product of school desegregation may be improved race relations and life opportunities for black students. [Here] . . . we evaluate a number of potential benefits and costs of school desegregation.

The Academic Impact

Although academic improvement is not the best standard for evaluating desegregation, available evidence indicates that under proper conditions school integration does have some potential for enhancing the academic achievement of *both* white and black children. To evaluate the academic potential of school integration we must start with an examination of the factors empirically identified as predictors of school achievement. The most important factor found by the Coleman study was the child's home environment, defined as the education and socioeconomic status of the child's parents.

Several characteristics of the school environment were also found to have some importance. High-quality classroom instruction, as measured by the presence of skilled teachers, was found to be weakly but positively related to student achievement. The socioeconomic status of the student body, however, was found to be the most important school factor affecting achievement. A middle-income environment seemed to be important because of the well-known *peer effect*. The values, aspiration levels, work habits, and achievement levels of the more socially prestigious members of a group tend to be emulated by the others. . . .

These findings are important because many black children can be placed in a middle-income milieu only in an integrated environment. Given the economic inequality between black and white Americans, most black children are in a lower-income milieu where the quality of instruction and the achievement level of their classmates may be very low. In lower-income schools, it is not uncommon for teachers to contribute to low achievement levels by averaging down their expectations, producing a self-fulfilling prophecy.

. . .

Recent School Integration Studies

A review of the more recent studies of school integration programs provides somewhat better insight into the total impact of racial mixing in the schools. Before we begin this survey, however, it should be pointed out that several analyses of recent school integration studies have revealed that most of them suffer serious methodological problems, and that the conditions for positive interracial change are rarely controlled for or investigated. . . . In addition, most studies have tried to assess the impact of integration after only one to three years, which is undoubtedly too short a time. Integration is frequently a traumatic experience and it probably takes several years for students to feel secure in, and fully adapt to, their changed environment. Only after five or six years of an integrated experience, therefore, can really solid studies be done. Despite these limitations, the studies generally reveal that black students in racially mixed schools make gains over those left in segregated schools.

The best of these research projects administer standardized achievement tests to black students in segregated schools, and then retest the same students later, making a distinction between those who were bused to integrated schools and those left in segregated schools. . . .

Even though some studies have found no improvement in the achievement of blacks and others have revealed only minor gains, no study of which we are aware has found that the achievement level of black children decreases with integration. It is also extremely rare for studies to reveal any decrease in white achievement when schools are integrated. In those schools in which significant increases in black achievement were not found, we do not know if any of the conditions for positive change were present. . . .

Another survey of recent studies concludes that racial integration is generally beneficial to black students, but suggests that the most important factors besides a positive racial environment are classroom socioeconomic integration and early desegregation. Black children who begin their integrated school experiences at the elementary level experience the greatest gains in achievement. By the junior high or high school years it may be more difficult to overcome educational disadvantages.[1]

Interestingly, a few studies report that both black and white achievement levels increase significantly in racially mixed schools. It may seem strange that the achievement of white students would improve when they are placed in a classroom with black students, many of whom may be low achievers. A logical explanation may be that a panic mentality set in motion by integration helps account for these improvements. A 1967 study found that, when integration takes place, school officials frequently try to compensate for the arrival of minority students by making special efforts to improve the curriculum and teaching for *all* students. It is also possible that when schools are integrated, both black and white parents become concerned about their childrens' performance (for fear that they may fail or that they will not learn as much) and are more conscientious about seeing that children complete their homework. . . .

A few studies have found a slight decrease in the grade averages of integrated blacks, but the decrease is never very substantial. At least one study found that the grades of black students increased with integration. These findings probably mean simply that no significant changes take place because grading standards may differ substantially among schools. Some studies also show that the aspiration levels of blacks decrease slightly after integration, but this is not necessarily a negative finding. Some black students have exaggerated and rigidly high aspiration levels. Research indicates that moderate aspiration levels are best for learning, and in some situations in which a decrease has been found, the new level may still be sufficiently high. It is not uncommon to find that black aspirations went down after integration but achievement went up. Still, there is little doubt that some black students find integration a disturbing, even defeating, experience. The important point, however, is that the academic impact of desegregation on both black and white students is usually positive.

Racial Tolerance

The impact of racial mixing in the public schools on racial tolerance is difficult to evaluate. Schools have often been desegregated under very tense and negative conditions, and this variable has rarely been examined in longitudinal studies. One study revealed that in hundreds of desegregated schools, the most invidious kinds of discrimination persist.[2] Given the number of racially mixed schools in which discrimination and tension remain, it is not surprising that some studies have found that desegregation has not led to increased interracial tolerance, or that in some cases desegregation has been viewed as disappointing by both black and white students.

Still, the available cross-sectional evidence reveals that interracial contact frequently leads to racial tolerance, especially if conditions for positive change are present. For example, one study reported the rather obvious finding that blacks attending integrated schools where no racial tensions were present were more positive in their racial attitudes than black students in racially tense desegregated schools.[3] Several studies reveal that both black and white students who had attended interracial schools are more inclined than students without this experience to prefer to attend racially mixed schools in the future. Further, students attending racially mixed schools are more inclined to say they trust and feel at ease around members of the opposite race. Additionally, a study of 252 desegregating school districts during the 1970-1971 school year found: "About 70 percent of the blacks and about 60 percent of whites agreed that both races were becoming more open-minded as a result of interracial busing."[4] A larger study of 879 schools in desegregating districts during the 1970-1971 school year also reported basically positive findings. . . .

Life Opportunities

Perhaps the one finding that all studies (both longitudinal and cross-sectional) of inter-racial schools agree on is that the life opportunities of blacks improve considerably if they attend a racially mixed school. Blacks who attended interracial schools are more likely to graduate from high school, more likely to attend college and to attend a better college, and more likely to obtain a better job and receive a higher income.[5] Crain speculates that black gains in jobs and income probably do not result primarily from the educational gains made in racially mixed schools. Instead, he argues, blacks attending interracial schools learn to deal with and trust whites, which may improve their ability to succeed in their post-school environment. Crain also points out that, because many jobs are obtained through informal social contacts, blacks in an interracial environment have an advantage in obtaining a better job.

In summary, one fact seems clear: The record for integrated schools is generally posi-tive, especially given the lack of attention to the creation of a favorable environment for interracial schools. Not only do blacks frequently achieve better in integrated schools, but blacks attending interracial schools are generally more trusting and tolerant of whites, and white attitudes are also more positive. The life opportunities for blacks are so improved that on this point alone integration would seem justified.

. . .

Summary

The ultimate goals of school integration are long range. Racial attitudes and behavior cannot be changed easily or over a short period of time. Therefore, until integration has been given a much longer and more carefully designed trial, no final conclusions can be reached about its total implications. However, the research surveyed here, although ten-tative, is basically positive. It seems clear that interracial education, especially when implemented under positive conditions, is beneficial. In many ways integration is a neces-sary preparation for interracial living. As a black parent in Rochester, N.Y., said about integrated schools: "Education . . . is preparing yourself to live and work in the world, and in this respect your education is definitely lacking if you are not being prepared to live and work with all types of people."[6] . . . A select committee of the United States Senate recently made the point even more forcefully.

> It is among our principal conclusions—as a result of more than two years of intensive study—that quality integrated education is one of the most promising educational policies that this nation and its school systems can pursue if we are to fulfill our commitment to equality of opportunity for our children. Indeed, it is essential, if we are to become a united society which is free of racial prejudice and discrimination.[7]

Besides the benefits of integration described [here] . . . changes . . . have taken place in white attitudes towards blacks since the 1940s. The evidence reveals a consistent, and sometimes dramatic, moderation. The alterations have primarily been caused by legally compelled desegregation. Despite the old saw that "you can't change men's hearts with law," experience indicates that laws that have required integration have led to changes in even deep-rooted attitudes. By requiring behavioral change, laws eventually serve as catalysts for new attitudes. Behaving differently, in other words, frequently leads to think-ing differently. In an excellent book, William Muir has reminded us that laws have always played an important role in shaping the attitudes of citizens. As Muir points out, law is a sensitive agent of social change. It educates, inculcates, and changes our attitudes.[8] Thus, the careful design and application of laws can aid considerably in achieving additional progress in race relations.

Notes

1. *Toward Equal Educational Opportunity.* The Report of the Select Committee on Equal Educational Opportunity, United States Senate (Washington, D.C.: Government Printing Office, 1972), p. 217.

2. *The Status of School Desegregation in the South 1970,* A Report by the American Friends Service Committee, et al.

3. U.S. Commission on Civil Rights, *Racial Isolation in the Public Schools,* pp. 157–158.

4. Cited in Select Committee on Equal Educational Opportunity, *Toward Equal Educational Opportunity,* p. 210.

5. Robert L. Crain, "School Integration and Occupational Achievement of Negroes," *American Journal of Sociology* 75 (January 1970), 593–606; Robert L. Crain, "School Integration and the Academic Achievement of Negroes," *Sociology of Education* 44 (Winter 1971), 1–26; Thomas F. Pettigrew, et al., "Bussing: A Review of the Evidence," *The Public Interest* 30 (Winter 1973), pp. 110–111.

6. U.S. Commission on Civil Rights, *Racial Isolation in the Public Schools,* p. 159.

7. Select Committee on Equal Educational Opportunity, *Toward Equal Educational Opportunity,* p. 3.

8. William K. Muir, Jr., *Prayer in the Public Schools: Law and Attitude Change* (Chicago: University of Chicago Press, 1967), pp. 122–138.

50

The Policy Impact
of Reapportionment

Roger A. Hanson and Robert E. Crew, Jr.

. . .

[Following the Supreme Court reapportionment decisions, some observers offered contradictory assessments about what would be the likely consequences in broad political terms of those decisions. In their introductory remarks the authors trace these different perspectives.]

. . . [U]ntil evidence is obtained about possible changes in policy outcomes after reapportionment, some scholars can remain committed to the belief that reapportionment is likely to produce cataclysmic changes while others do not anticipate even mild tremors.

The findings of the current research are that reapportionment is associated with important policy changes in the 1960's. By means of a longitudinal analysis, evidence is gathered which can be interpreted as showing that reapportionment preceded changes in the pattern of policy outcomes.

Research Design

The basic function of the design is to provide a valid test of the association between reapportionment and policy outcomes. Because the authors of prior studies claim that malapportionment index scores are not highly related to policy outcomes, it is reasonable to suppose that reapportionment might not be a causal determinant of interstate variations in such outcomes. With that presumption, a research format is developed which permits us to determine if an adjustment in apportionment precedes any major policy changes within a given state. The verification of hypothesized connections between reapportionment and variation in intrastate policy outcomes is a basic step in obtaining knowledge about the impact of the judicially ordered changes in the legislative structure.

The methodological framework selected for the purpose of examining the causal efficacy of reapportionment within the boundaries of the individual states is a before and after test. In this context, reapportionment is conceptualized as an event which occurs within the broader time frame of the ongoing process of policy-making. The before period includes observations about the policy outcomes prior to the date of the application of a

Reprinted by permission of the Law and Society Association from *Law and Society Review* 8 (1973), 72–86, 88, 90, 92–93. Copyright © 1973. Footnotes have been omitted. The *Law and Society Review* is the official publication of the Association.

reapportionment plan. The after period takes in measurable decisional outcomes which happen subsequent to the implementation of the structural reform. The first task of the empirical analysis is to ascertain whether any significant changes in policy outcomes are evident after reapportionment is introduced. The second task is to ascertain whether it is reapportionment or some other antecedent condition that is the source of any observable policy change. In order to attempt to satisfy these research goals, the data are analyzed in a manner approximating the standards of inference that have been proposed for quasi-experimental designs.

Forty-eight states (Hawaii and Alaska are excluded) are the subjects for comparisons of intra-unit variations in policy outcomes. By looking at forty-eight units, this research effort complements the scope of prior analyses of the impact of reapportionment which are close examinations of legislative roll call voting and legislative committee occupancy in a single state. Each state is examined for the *first* state election held under the guidelines of a reapportionment plan. Because reapportionment plans are not necessarily adopted simultaneously for both houses of a state legislature, we consider a change in *one* house to be sufficient for a state to be classified as reapportioned. Since state governmental expenditures are adopted as the indicators of policy outcomes, the fiscal year expenditures that are the result of legislative activity prior to reapportionment are the data set of the before period. Those fiscal year expenditures that are the result of legislative activity under the reapportioned districts form the data base of the after period.

In order to undertake appropriate quantitative analysis, there must be a sufficient number of observations of policy outcomes during both periods. This requirement eliminates most states from being classified as reapportioned because many did not hold an election under a reapportionment plan until 1968. After the election of 1968, there were, at the time that this study was completed, data for only two fiscal years. Thus, all of the states classified as reapportioned underwent the treatment of reapportionment in a state election before 1966. In spite of this common feature, not all of these states received the same dosage of reapportionment. Some states experienced major shifts in district boundaries and the number of urban legislators increased significantly while other states experienced only minor rearrangments. In future studies of the effects of reapportionment, it will be important to estimate the association between the degree of structural modification and the variation in governmental outlays. However, in this exploratory study, attention is not given to this problem. The states in which the legislatures were reapportioned to some degree are listed with the fiscal years for the respective time periods.

	Before	After
New York	1958–66	1967–69
Massachusetts	1958–63	1964–68
Oregon	1958–63	1964–68
South Carolina	1958–63	1964–68
Kentucky	1959–64	1965–68
Delaware	1959–64	1965–68
Georgia	1958–63	1964–68
Mississippi	1959–64	1965–68
Virginia	1959–66	1967–69
Kansas	1958–66	1967–69
West Virginia	1958–65	1966–69
Wisconsin	1958–66	1967–69
Michigan	1958–65	1966–69
Wyoming	1958–65	1966–69
Oklahoma	1958–66	1967–69

The non-reapportioned states are defined as those states in which a reapportioned legislature was not elected during the first five years of the 1960's. This time dimension is imposed because any state legislature elected after 1965 under a reapportionment plan would make allocations beginning with the fiscal year 1968. Since fiscal year 1969 is the last year for which data are available, the limited number of observations obviate classifying such a state legislature as "reapportioned." Instead, those states that did not experience the election of a reapportioned legislature before 1965 are utilized as a control group. Since the states are not randomly assigned to the control group, it is not possible to assume that all features of state political systems other than the dates of reapportionment are randomly distributed across all the states. The lack of random assignment of states into the control group brings impurity into an assumption about the variables that are not controlled statistically. Nevertheless, the policy outcomes of the states in the control group are analyzed in order to determine if the patterns of policy outcomes without the intervention of reapportionment are similar to, or different from, the patterns exhibited in reapportioned states. The nonreapportioned states are divided artificially into before and after periods. The control group can be examined for evidence of policy changes between the two time periods. If factors other than reapportionment are the foundation for policy changes, then such events would be equally probable in both reapportioned and nonreapportioned states. (The assumption of equal probability can not be made because of the nonrandom selection of units for the control group.) Since factors other than reapportionment, such as a sudden influx of federal aid or a social commitment by a governor to a new program area, can occur in between the before and after period, the existence of any policy changes in a reapportioned state cannot be immediately attributed to reapportionment.

The states that are included in the nonreapportioned category include Alabama, Arizona, Arkansas, California, Colorado, Connecticut, Florida, Idaho, Illinois, Indiana, Iowa, Louisiana, Maine, Maryland, Minnesota, Missouri, Montana, Nebraska, Nevada, New Hampshire, New Jersey, New Mexico, North Dakota, North Carolina, Ohio, Pennsylvania, Rhode Island, South Dakota, Tennessee, Texas, Utah, Vermont, and Washington. The before period for all of these states is 1958-63, and the after period is 1964-67. By using 1967 as the end point, there is no state in which a fiscal year expenditure is the product of a legislature reapportioned after 1965.

. . .

Some explanation is in order about the confirmatory-bases for the hypotheses. There are two sets of data to be used as the bases for tests of verification of the hypotheses. The first set consists of state governmental expenditures for various areas of policy outcomes. These data represent the total amount of state expenditures in a given fiscal year for specified functional areas. The areas selected are the following per capita spending items: higher education, inter-governmental expenditures for education (local schools), highways, public welfare, and hospitals.

There are at least two reasons for operationalizing policy outcomes as state governmental expenditures. First, some advocates of reapportionment argued that reapportionment would result in more extensive social welfare programs. Since some of these programs would require state governmental financing, the level of state expenditures is a measure of the decisional outcomes to allocate resources to these programs. Second, the conclusions drawn from existing analyses of state governmental expenditures are that levels of expenditures do not readily change over time. Incremental budgeting is inferred to be a method of decision-making which results generally in only marginal increases in expenditure levels. Hence, if there are unexpected changes in expenditures after reapportionment, the finding will be an indication that reapportionment is sufficient to overcome the established pattern of incremental changes. . . .

The second set of data is the amount of money that state governments allocate to municipal corporations. This set of data provides a more valid measure of the policy impact of reapportionment than the first set. Since the alleged effect of reapportionment is to make the legislature more responsive to urban needs and demands, it is imperative to measure the level of state expenditures committed to their major cities. Prior studies that use expenditures as measures of policy outcomes do not include any indicators of state allocations to cities. To fill that gap, the total expenditures allocated to municipal corporations over 100,000 in population by state governments are used. Specific functional areas such as welfare and education are not used since there is no one area funded by all of the states for all of the cities. The periods of the allocations to municipal corporations in the nonreapportioned states are 1959-64 for the before period and 1965-68 as the after period. For the reapportioned states, the time periods are the same as in the first set of data (1960; 1966).

There are limitations in the use of either of these data-bases. First, it is not certain that either state expenditures or state allocations to cities is a valid measure of the legislature's policy outcomes for urban areas. These indicators do not measure directly where the money is being spent. . . . The second limitation is the small number of observations. There are very few observable fiscal years for either group of states in either period. This problem is aggravated by the fact that some legislatures do not hold annual sessions. If the legislatures were to make their allocations for two fiscal years as part of one decision, the number of observations would be reduced even further. However, this problem is minimized because the legislatures of 11 of the 15 reapportioned states meet annually, as do 16 of 33 nonreapportioned states. Moreover, on the basis of our observation of legislatures which meet only biennially, the budgets for each fiscal year do not appear to be determined by the same decision. . . .

Some mention needs to be made about the meaning of the term "policy change." For both sets of data, if the trend of yearly governmental expenditures increases, a policy change occurs. Generally, the level of expenditures rises in an absolute amount year after year. Given that basic fact, important changes in expenditure patterns are evidenced by increases in the rate of change in levels of expenditures. Since the levels before and after a particular point in time are being compared, it is necessary to compute the rate of change of expenditures for the fiscal years in each period. It is not appropriate to compare rates of change for each year because there is only one breaking point (reapportionment).

Measurement Technique

The measurement technique used to determine the presence of before and after policy changes is the comparison of unstandardized regression coefficients. To ascertain the intrastate policy impact of reapportionment, regression equations are computed for each state. For every state the independent variable is the set of fiscal years included within the respective period. As an illustration, with a 6 year time period, the values of the observations of the independent variable are 1,2,3,4,5,6. The expenditure items are the dependent variables. The regression coefficients are in this instance measures of the average rate of change in the dependent variable as a function of time. They can be interpreted as trends in expenditures because the regression coefficient determines the trend line's slope which is the most important aspect of a trend line. The particular trend in expenditures for each state's before and after period is found by computing regression coefficients for each period. As an illustration, see Table 50-1. For Massachusetts there are two comparable regression coefficients each time a different dependent variable is regressed on fiscal years. In the case of the first set of data there are five dependent variables. Looking at one dependent variable, higher education expenditures, the rate of change in expenditure levels before reapportionment is .492 and after reapportionment it is 3.647. In order to determine whether or not this difference between the regression coefficients is significant, a test is made of the statistical null hypothesis that $b_1 = b_2$, where b_1 is the regression coefficient of the before period and b_2 is the regression coefficient of the after period. This procedure generates a t-value, which is a measure of the statistical difference between the two coefficients.

Applied to the substantive problem of the current research, the null hypothesis (H.O.) is as follows: H.O. for every state, the regression coefficient in the before period is equal to the regression coefficient in the after period. This hypothesis is similar to the claim that only minimal policy changes will accompany reapportionment. If the t-value generated by the analysis is not statistically significant, H.O. cannot be rejected. . . . On the other hand, those individuals who maintain that reapportionment can produce increases in expenditure levels suggest an alternative hypothesis. Their hypothesis (H.1.) is as follows: H.1. for every state, the regression coefficient in the after period is a positive increase over the previous regression coefficient. With this hypothesis, the regression coefficients are predicted to be different and the difference is in a particular direction. If the t-value obtained from the calculations is *negative* and statistically significant with a one-tailed test level of significance, then H.1. can be accepted. Let us examine briefly the findings in order to illustrate the utilization of these hypotheses. In the case of Massachusetts, a comparison of the regression coefficients .492 and 3.647 yields a t-value of -15.626, which is significant at the .01 level of significance. On the basis of the high negative t-value, we infer the existence of an important policy change.

There is a reason for employing this technique rather than others. Since the level of expenditures is likely to increase over time in every state, it is vital to work with a measure that will take this factor into account while still measuring the difference in the rate of change in expenditure levels. . . . With the comparison of regression coefficients . . . the absolute level of spending in the before period can be lower than the level in the after period, but such a difference does not affect the comparison of the average rates of change between the two periods. Hence, the existence of significant positive increases in the average rate of change after reapportionment can be established independent of the absolute levels of expenditures.

Findings

A blunt manner of interpreting the results of the regression analyses is to calculate the relative frequency of policy changes across all of the units within each of the two groups of states. The operational meaning of the term "policy change" refers to a negative t-value that is statistically significant. Such a t-value which is predicted by H.1. indicates that there is an upswing in the trend of state expenditures when compared to the trend in expenditures during a preceding period of time. These quantitative measures of policy changes are presented in Tables 50-1 and 50-2.

TABLE 50-1
Trends in Governmental Expenditures Before and After Reapportionment

State	Policy area	Higher Education b₁ b₂	Local Schools b₁ b₂	Highways b₁ b₂	Public Welfare b₁ b₂	Hospitals b₁ b₂	t-value at .01 level	Number of Policy Changes
		Higher Education b_1 b_2	Local Schools b_1 b_2	Highways b_1 b_2	Public Welfare b_1 b_2	Hospitals b_1 b_2		
Delaware		4.113 8.391	10.450 −.676	1.380 5.243	.382 1.705	−1.50 15.665	d.f. = 6	1
	t =	−2.788	1.134	−3.304*	−2.971	−.687	3.143	
Georgia		1.285 5.947	3.671 7.930	3.049 3.371	.925 1.759	3.986 15.981	d.f. = 7	3
	t =	−9.091*	−2.542	−4.141*	−1.623	−10.168*	2.896	
Kansas		3.099 5.215	2.885 1.05	1.031 6.465	.759 1.345	6.155 7.21	d.f. = 8	1
	t =	−1.227	.407	−10.417*	−1.965	−.193	2.896	
Kentucky		3.062 7.896	3.715 8.303	5.657 11.592	9.006 5.740	7.306 17.695	d.f. = 7	4
	t =	−4.916*	−3.391*	−6.063*	1.211	−6.419*	2.998	
Massachusetts		.492 3.647	.630 5.175	.371 5.194	.389 1.548	2.303 9.678	d.f. = 6	4
	t =	−15.626*	−3.027	−6.543*	−3.737*	−5.277*	3.143	
Michigan		2.709 5.314	2.23 7.459	1.155 8.764	6.28 2.603	5.095 15.095	d.f. = 8	3
	t =	−2.024	−5.378*	−15.787*	1.462	−4.876*	2.896	
Mississippi		1.496 2.921	.098 7.949	1.683 1.391	.754 1.147	1.737 12.695	d.f. = 6	2
	t =	−2.906	−9.211*	−2.783	−.861	−9.643*	3.143	

New York		1.851	.94	5.242	13.25	.2832	4.15	2.868	27.675	5.23	4.56	d.f. = 8
	t =		.79		-3.3*		-21.948*		-12.619*		-5.919*	2.896	4
Oklahoma		3.243	5.865	1.366	2.177	1.827	4.023	2.748	6.229	.612	1.722	d.f. = 8
	t =		-1.424		-1.138		-.658		-2.177		-4.742*	2.896	1
Oregon		3.605	8.440	2.023	5.291	3.205	1.044	.716	.877	5.741	14.580	d.f. = 6
	t =		-7.507*		-2.650		-.716		-.764		-5.957*	3.143	2
South Carolina		1.085	4.583	1.285	7.804	1.026	.135	.883	1.382	2.897	17.659	d.f. = 6
	t =		-6.977*		-6.115*		.980		-2.207		-9.859*	3.143	3
Virginia		1.90	6.01	2.071	11.748	.445	1.436	.329	1.799	3.481	20.559	d.f. = 8
	t =		-15.725*		-10.089*		-5.141*		-5.936*		-18.304*	2.896	5
West Virginia		1.66	9.082	1.894	5.962	3.065	2	.588	1.789	3.903	16.998	d.f. = 8
	t =		-6.596*		-7.191*		.754		-11.469*		-9.465*	2.896	4
Wisconsin		5.001	5.68	2.621	3.14	1.323	9.86	1.182	2.365	7.859	9.825	d.f. = 8
	t =		-.202		-.516		-9.787*		-1.906		-.459	2.896	1
Wyoming		3.139	5.876	2.195	2.936	.208	1.622	.266	.061	5.466	10.711	d.f. = 8
	t =		-1.153		-.500		-3.917*		.325		-1.583	2.896	1

* The results of the regression analysis for each expenditure variable are listed for each individual state. The regression coefficient in the before period is the set of numbers in the upper left hand side of a cell. In the upper right hand side is the regression coefficient in the after period. Below the two regression coefficients is the t-value. Significant t-values at the .01 level of significance are asterisked.

TABLE 50-2
Trends in Governmental Expenditures for Non-Reapportioned States

State	Policy Area	Higher Education b_1	b_2	Local Schools b_1	b_2	Highways b_1	b_2	Public Welfare b_1	b_2	Hospitals b_1	b_2	t-value at .01 level	Number of Policy Changes
Alabama		1.844	4.8	.041	7.363	1.305	1.383	.862	.128	.670	−.022	3.143	1
	t =	−1.100		−6.404*		−.032		.639		1.953			
Arizona		2.361	9.503	3.065	8.577	1.912	12.917	.503	.603	.114	.355	3.143	2
	t =	−7.092*		−2.746		−6.081*		−.353		−.769			
Arkansas		.999	4.267	.672	8.934	3.785	4.793	1.739	3.462	.655	.058	3.143	2
	t =	−3.914*		−3.791*		−.576		−2.063		2.353			
California		1.647	.670	.340	5.987	.285	3.605	1.167	15.07	2.49	.679	3.143	1
	t =	.880		−1.317		−1.752		−7.240*		−1.190			
Colorado		3.661	8.154	1.714	7.043	−.998	3.567	.605	1.793	1.318	.758	3.143	2
	t =	−2.860		−5.385*		−3.219*		−1.305		1.331			
Connecticut		.126	1.403	−9.662	1.996	−8.171	−5.959	1.559	−.442	1.539	−.11	3.143	1
	t =	−3.286*		−.959		−.226		1.989		.657			
Florida		.499	3.757	.257	10.908	.129	−1.225	−.146	1.155	.067	.737	2.896	4
	t =	−15.142*		−3.938*		1.011		−5.246*		−9.066*			
Idaho		1.999	5.174	1.907	8.044	2.838	2.411	.980	1.8	.673	.435	3.143	1
	t =	−2.870		−4.307*		.142		−.791		.571			
Illinois		2.002	3.48	2.194	6.384	−1.804	−.761	3.5466	2.011	.371	1.671	3.143	0
	t =	−2.155		−2.887		−.640		1.463		−2.568			
Indiana		2.872	5.513	1.538	6.646	3.347	.469	.484	.806	.401	1.591	3.143	2
	t =	−2.386		−6.078*		1.650		−1.900		−3.571*			
Iowa		2.885	5.889	.882	6.496	−.132	6.188	.957	1.567	.717	.993	3.143	2
	t =	−5.221*		−6.395*		−2.904		−1.437		−1.489			

Louisiana	1.317	5.994	2.038	8.178	.289	2.92	1.526	.675	7.64	1.783	3.143	2
t =		-3.214*		-5.285*		-.863		2.126		-2.267		
Maine	2.282	5.268	1.305	4.501	.867	2.418	1.618	1.672	.399	.958	3.143	2
t =		-2.100		-5.392*		-.863		.107		-3.367*		
Maryland	1.432	3.378	3.440	7.265	.251	-.276	.912	5.214	1.167	-.178	3.143	2
t =		-5.419*		-1.347		.222		-4.118*		2.337		
Minnesota	1.447	7.99	2.697	5.988	.296	5.183	1.394	3.792	.404	.699	3.143	3
t =		-15.048*		-3.901*		-2.025		-4.760*		-1.218		
Missouri	.912	5.261	2.355	6.576	2.430	-.621	.464	.957	.517	1.12	3.143	2
t =		-6.815*		-1.469		1.971		-.841		-3.880*		
Montana	1.861	5.789	1.749	5.79	3.737	-.704	-.435	1.986	-.18	.578	3.143	4
t =		-3.823*		-12.314*		1.533		-4.962*		-3.819*		
Nebraska	1.751	6.392	.260	2.231	3.807	3.359	.733	3.142	.363	2.02	3.143	3
t =		-4.187*		-2.826		.183		-5.311*		-5.323*		
Nevada	4.175	9.032	4.044	5.441	.761	-5.057	.968	2.34	.290	-.089	3.143	0
t =		-2.124		-.747		.719		-1.355		.507		
New Hampshire	.392	7.84	.419	-.32	.172	.979	1.078	2.161	.165	1.439	3.143	2
t =		-3.912*		.188		-.406		-2.037		-6.201*		
New Jersey	1.513	1.893	.452	6.688	1.903	2.486	.84	1.774	.575	1.087	3.143	2
t =		.491		-4.448*		-.671		-9.253*		-1.185		
New Mexico	3.433	12.87	2.614	11.255	-4.097	6.422	4.305	2.59	.010	11.063	3.143	3
t =		-5.657*		-3.246*		-2.089		.538		-9.303*		
North Carolina	1.569	4.904	11.502	10.053	.924	4.787	1.047	1.13	.661	.838	3.143	2
t =		-8.248*		.304		-3.165*		-.481		-1.315		
North Dakota	1.088	4.4	-.156	3.497	1.193	-1.925	3.193	-1.925	1.148	1.358	3.143	0
t =		-.689		-.982		.596		.604		-.342		

TABLE 50-2 *(Continued)*
Trends in Governmental Expenditures for Non-Reapportioned States

State	Policy Area	Higher Education b_1 b_2	Local Schools b_1 b_2	Highways b_1 b_2	Public Welfare b_1 b_2	Hospitals b_1 b_2	t-value at .01 level	Number of Policy Changes
Ohio		.965 6.754	.657 5.562	.218 3.752	1.630 1.143	-.028 .621	3.143	2
	$t =$	-4.659*	-4.043*	-2.452	.274	-2.538		
Pennsylvania		.879 2.091	1.639 5.140	2.020 3.962	2.053 1.78	.616 .828	3.143	2
	$t =$	-3.482*	-3.394*	-1.107	.983	-.433		
Rhode Island		1.264 6.325	2.471 5.312	.673 8.084	1.623 1.226	.839 2.16	3.143	4
	$t =$	-3.482*	-3.235*	-3.219*	6.783*	-2.908		
South Dakota		1.567 8.34	.44 6.422	2.165 11.231	.718 5.871	.367 .725	3.143	3
	$t =$	-6.375*	-3.354*	-1.237	3.945*	-2.243		
Tennessee		1.215 7.35	1.573 8.4	3.342 1.986	.375 2.727	-.048 1.326	3.143	2
	$t =$	-6.906*	-1.072	.748	-7.461*	-1.975		
Texas		1.09 .169	2.325 6.434	.012 1.558	.707 .185	.210 .059	3.143	0
	$t =$	.386	-.829	-.741	.829	.428		
Utah		3.772 13.202	4.374 7.258	3.835 2.113	1.059 2.557	.1 2.1	3.143	3
	$t =$	-6.884*	-1.488	.433	-3.610*	-3.552*		
Vermont		4.077 7.837	.133 5.2	7.014 15.45	1.212 2.457	.850 .472	3.143	0
	$t =$	-1.172	-1.920	-2.064	-.877	.306		
Washington		4.066 6.543	4.825 9.105	1.293 9.105	1.648 1.675	.677 .673	3.143	1
	$t =$	-3.418*	-.970	-2.347	-.952	.007		

* The results of the regression analysis for each expenditure variable are listed for each individual state. The regression coefficient in the before period is the set of numbers in the upper left hand side of a cell. In the upper right hand side is the regression coefficient in the after period. Below the two regression coefficients is the t-value. Significant t-values at the .01 level of significance are asterisked.

Tables 50-1 and 50-2 list the regression coefficients and t-values from operations performed on the five state expenditure variables for reapportioned and nonreapportioned states, respectively. *H.1.* is supported in 39 of the 75 possible instances for the reapportioned group. The 52 percent level of corroboration of *H.1.* suggests that reapportionment accounts for changes in the direction of expenditures. The occurrence of policy changes in the nonreapportioned states is not as frequent. On the basis of the figures displayed in Table 50-2, policy changes happened in 62 of the 165 possible instances. The relative frequency of policy changes among all of the nonreapportioned states is 37 percent. A comparison of the two groups of states reveals that the percentage of changes in the reapportioned states is nearly one and a half times greater than in the nonreapportioned states. While a higher proportion of policy changes exist in the reapportioned states, it is clear that reapportionment is not a necessary condition for increases in the trend of state expenditures. Policy changes, as they are defined in this research, are produced in the absence of legislative reapportionment. The fact that a higher proportion of policy changes takes place in states that are reapportioned than occur in nonreapportioned states offers the possibility that reapportionment is a sufficient condition for increases in the trend of expenditures.

. . .

Evidence [concerning state governmental expenditures to municipal corporations] supports the observed relationship above, but it indicates that reapportionment is a slightly weaker sufficient condition for policy changes. . . . The proportion of cities experiencing an increase in allocations from the states which fall into the reapportioned category is 10/29, or 34 percent. The incidence of policy changes in the nonreapportioned group of states and respective cities is 18/73 or 23 percent. The margin of difference between the percentage of policy changes in the two states is somewhat discouraging, perhaps, for the individuals who expect reapportionment to produce major policy changes. They might expect, presumably, the relative frequency of changes in the reapportioned states to be greater and the margin of difference between the two groups to be greater. While reapportionment is associated with policy changes, the lack of a stronger relationship may be interpreted as the result of reapportionment strengthening the representation of suburban areas primarily and central cities secondarily. Because inner cities are losing population while the suburbs are growing more rapidly than any other part of the states, reapportionment shifts most of the legislative seats from meager sized districts to suburban based constituencies. Hence, even if a state is reapportioned, there will be no decisive combination of central city based legislators who control policy outcomes. Under these circumstances, any increase in state governmental expenditures to municipal corporations will reflect in significant ways the desires of the citizens who live outside the immediate boundaries of the city's "core." The validity of the measure of state allocations to municipal corporations does not allow us to pursue this line of inquiry because it fails to specify the functional areas to which the state expenditures are directed. . . .

. . .

Conclusions

The foregoing research has provided empirical support for the hypothesis that legislative reapportionment is related to changes in state public policy. The nature of the data examined and the test utilized allows us to speak with some confidence to one of the major questions posed by political scientists: "How does governmental organization (and reorganization) affect governmental policy?"

The specific nature and the strength of the relationship remains unclear. Legislative reapportionment is not a necessary condition of policy change. There is a possibility that it is a sufficient condition. It clearly has different effects in different policy areas. However, there is a relationship. Future research may want to focus on the variables which intervene between the act of reapportionment and public policy change. When this line of research is pursued, we will perhaps be in a better position to explain the additional questions raised by the present research.

51

The Case of the Exclusionary Rule

Bradley C. Canon

This paper explores two things. First it attempts to measure the changes in the behavior of law enforcement officials in response to a decision of the Warren Court specifically aimed at altering such behavior. Second, it compares the relative efficacy of this decision in altering such behavior with the efficacy of rather similar decisions made by state supreme courts.

The vehicle for this exploration is the exclusionary rule—a judicially created rule which prohibits the admission in criminal trials of evidence seized in violation of the Fourth Amendment. The exclusionary rule was imposed upon the states as a constitutional requirement by the U.S. Supreme Court in *Mapp* v. *Ohio* (1961). However, 22 states had adopted the rule themselves at various times in a 40-year period preceding *Mapp*. The clear impetus behind its adoption at both the state and federal level was a strong belief that there was widespread police disregard of the restraints of the Fourth Amendment in conducting searches and seizures, and the clear purpose of the rule, in the Supreme Court's own words, "is to deter—to compel respect for the constitutional guaranty in the only effectively available way—by removing the incentive to disregard it."

. . .

Models Relating State and Federal Efficacy

By comparing the effect of *Mapp* on the search and seizure behavior of law enforcement officers in those states which had their own exclusionary rule (hereafter termed Own Rule states) with *Mapp*'s impact in those states which did not have the rule until the Court's decision (hereafter called Imposed Rule states), it is possible to draw inferences about the efficacy of the rule in Own Rule states. Such a comparison also enables us to measure more directly the effect of the federal civil liberties decision. There are four possible pure combinations or models which can occur; they are shown in Table 51-1.

In ordinary legal theory there is an assumption of compliance with judicial decisions. If the Legal Theoretical Model prevails, it would indicate that law enforcement officials positively respond to civil liberties decisions, regardless of whether they are made at the

"Testing the Effectiveness of Civil Liberties Policies at the State and Federal Levels: The Case of the Exclusionary Rule," by Bradley C. Canon, is reprinted from *American Politics Quarterly*, Vol. 5, No. 1 (January 1977), pp. 57–82, by permission of the Publisher, Sage Publications, Inc.

TABLE 51-1
Models of Impact of Mapp v. Ohio on Search & Seizure Behavior

	Impact in:	
Model	Imposed Rule States	Own Rule States
Legal theoretical	+	0
Federal impact	+	+
Non-compliance	0	0
State reinforcement	0	+

state or federal level. The non-response in Own Rule states would indicate that no change in the behavior of law enforcement officials occurred because they were already abiding by state exclusionary rules. The positive response in Imposed Rule states would reflect changes in these officials' behavior as a consequence of *Mapp.*

There is some reason to believe that the two middle models are more likely to reflect reality than is the Legal Theoretical Model. If the Federal Impact Model prevails, it would indicate that law enforcement officials respond positively *only* to civil liberties decisions coming from the federal courts. Behavior in both Imposed Rule and Own Rule states would change positively in response to *Mapp.* From the latter change we can infer that illegal searches and seizures were not much curtailed by the existence of the state's exclusionary rule. Some studies would support such a conclusion. . . . [They] suggest that state civil liberties policies may not receive much publicity or even effective dissemination through the law enforcement community and perhaps are virtually ignored even when known.

If the Non-Compliance Model occurs, it would indicate that law enforcement officials simply do not respond positively to the exclusionary rule, regardless of its source. The non-response sign in the Own Rule column does not represent absence of change due to previous impact, but rather reflects continued noncompliance despite *Mapp.* . . .

In the State Reinforcement Model there would be a positive response to *Mapp* in Own Rule states on the part of law enforcement officials, but the decision would have no impact on officials' behavior in Imposed Rule states. Its occurrence would mean that a prior state civil liberties policy paved the way psychologically for compliance with a similar Supreme Court decision; absent a pre-existing policy, local officials would not comply. An expectation of such differential compliance is not illogical, but previous findings (focusing on judges' reactions) do not support it.

To determine which of these models best reflects reality, it is necessary to obtain data on the extent to which the police conducted illegal searches in the period immediately following *Mapp* compared to that immediately preceding *Mapp.* This is impossible to do directly. Illegal searches are not recorded per se; systematic observation of them at the time would have been extremely difficult and is obviously impossible a decade later. However, a related measure is available in the form of routine records, namely police arrests for what I will term "search and seizure" offenses. These are narcotics, weapons, and gambling offenses and are so designated because arrests for them are often the consequence of a police search of the arrestee's person, property or dwelling (with conviction primarily resting on the evidence so seized). The assumption is that prior to 1961 many of these searches, in Imposed Rule states at least, were conducted illegally. . . . Thus if *Mapp* did in fact have its intended impact on police search and seizure behavior, it should be reflected by a decline in arrest rates for search and seizure offenses.[1]

There are several problems with the use of arrest figures in this capacity. First, it is possible that in some cases—particularly for weapons—the figures are inflated by their use as a secondary charge in a more serious arrest. For example, an armed robbery suspect might also be charged with carrying a dangerous weapon. Inquiries to several of the police departments whose data were being used revealed that such secondary charges were *seldom lodged by the police*, and arrests were usually recorded in the annual report only according to the most serious offense involved in an incident. Some departments could not vouch for their practices 15 years ago, but it is not likely that the figures are unduly inflated with non-search related arrests.

Second, the above offenses are usually broadly categorized in published police reports, and some particular charges within the category often do not result from a search, e.g., selling narcotics. The problem is amenable to some analysis because a breakdown by specific charges was available in three cities. These data showed that an average of 80% of the weapons arrests were for carrying a concealed weapon, and about two-thirds of the narcotics arrests were for illegal possession. Both charges are usually the result of a search. Thus, while total arrests in these categories are somewhat larger than the search related arrests, they are not greatly so and significant changes in search practices ought to be reflected in changed arrest rates. The situation is less resolvable for gambling where the specific charge is often not given to a determination of whether a search occurred. However, much previous evidence makes it clear that searches constitute a major if unquantifiable element in gambling arrests. . . .

Third, arrest rates obviously respond to many stimuli, e.g., changes in statutes, prosecutory policies, police leadership, police record keeping policies, public concerns, demands upon police manpower, to name a few of the more obvious ones. Where such stimuli were noticeable (usually changes in statutes or record keeping), I have eliminated a city from consideration. Most, however, are not discernible, especially 15 years later. But all such stimuli are based on local events. The corrective here is that I have gathered data from a score of cities; it is not likely that significant coterminous events would occur in very many of them. Moreover, there is no reason to think they would operate in only one direction. Thus, to the extent that local stimuli are operative, on an overall basis they should counteract one another and neither help nor hinder our determination of whether *Mapp* produced a decline in search and seizure related arrests.

Beyond that I use arrest data because there is evidence that the exclusionary rule has produced a decline in arrest rates. Most salient are the testimony of prominent California law enforcement officials following that state's adoption of the rule and New York City arrest statistics in the year following *Mapp*. . . . While some such testimony comes in a self-serving context (criticism of the rule), it seems clear that the data behind it are not fabricated.

In sum, arrest rates do not so closely reflect search and seizure behavior that they can serve as a surrogate measure in the scientific sense. They are a crude indicator upon which to rely. But they are the best data available; certainly at this time there is no other way of obtaining reliable information on what the police did in the years immediately surrounding *Mapp*. And considered in aggregate form I think arrest rates for these offenses are reasonably related to search and seizure practices—there is a close enough connection between the two that we can expect a major decline in inherently illegal searches to produce a noticeable decline in arrests.

Using the Quasi-Experimental Approach

The approach used to determine which of the Models is most valid is experimental logic—more particularly, the quasi-experiment. Quasi-experiments take advantage of a non-researcher introduced manipulation in the independent variable in the real world to control for confounding variables and thus probe for a causal relationship between the independent and dependent variables. I will employ a variant of a particular type of quasi-experiment known as the "control series design." In the control series design an experimental group and a control group are measured simultaneously at several points in the time before and after a given event (the independent variable), but only the experimental group is exposed to its effects. . . . The logic of the control series design is that any change occurring in the E [experimental] group but not in the C [control] group following X [the event] can be attributed to that event.

Strictly speaking, the term control series design is probably not applicable to what is being done here. This is because the control group (Own Rule states) have not been shielded from the independent variable (the *Mapp* decision), but rather were exposed to a seemingly similar event at a distinctly earlier period in time. . . .

As with the standard control series design, our variant can test for the impact of event X. . . . If event X has an impact, it should occur only in the E group. Thus, if we find a post X change in the behavior of the E group but none in the C group, the extent of the change will serve as a measure of the impact of event X. This is, of course, the Legal Theoretical Model.

Contrariwise, if it turns out that there is no difference between the post X behavior of the E and C groups, then we must conclude that . . . the C group is not really a control group in that it has not been truly exposed to the independent variable. Under these circumstances we can still test for the impact of X but our test now becomes a before and after type of test rather than a control series design. If the post-X behavior of the E and C groups changes significantly, we will conclude that the difference measures the impact of X. This is the Federal Impact Model. If there is no significant alteration in the post-X behavior in the E and C groups, we will conclude that X has no impact. This is the Non-Compliance Model.

Finally, of course, if we find that the post-X behavior of the C group changes but that of the E group does not, we would conclude that X' [the state's own rule] is a necessary requisite to X having an impact. In this case we would not be measuring the impact of event X. Rather the difference between the change in the post X behavior of the C group and its stability in the E group would represent the delayed impact of X' in a post-X situation. This is the State Impact Model.

In either a control series design or a before and after test, confidence . . . in the findings depends upon the extent to which plausible rival hypotheses do not seem viable. . . . The most common concern is that the change in the dependent variable reflects the influence of some other event occurring roughly simultaneously with the posted independent variable. A second rival hypothesis is that the dependent variable is subject to periodic trends or fluctuations, and that shifts ostensibly related to the independent variable are really part of such periodicities. In the Legal Theoretical and State Reinforcement Models, we will have controlled for these rival explanations by dividing the states into two groups. There is no imaginable event with a nationwide impact (other than *Mapp*) which would affect search and seizure arrests in one set of states but not the other. And no evidence supports a suggestion that such arrests were periodical or cyclical in one set of states but not the other. The Non-Compliance Model is the null hypothesis and gives us no concern for rival hypotheses.

The Federal Impact Model will be most exposed to the rival hypotheses. As to the first, there was no general event occurring on a nationwide scale in or around 1961 which approaches the potential magnitude of *Mapp* for effecting a decline in arrest rates for search and seizure offenses. Because of the unavailability or poor quality of long term pre-*Mapp* arrest data and changes in reporting formats over time, we cannot absolutely reject the possibility that search and seizure arrests are subject to long term cyclical fluctuations. In general, however, neither logic nor such data as exist (including post-*Mapp* arrests into the 1970s) suggest their occurrence.

We have already noted that local events may significantly affect some arrest rates. However, there is no reason to believe that this would occur in one set of states and not the other or that such events would cause only decreased arrest rates. Consequently, if we find that decreased arrest rates outnumber increased arrest rates *plus* those which are substantially unchanged in one or both sets of states, we can conclude that the rates are responding to a national event as well as a conglomeration of local ones. And the only national event around 1961 likely to affect all search and seizure offense arrests was the *Mapp* v. *Ohio* decision.

Data and Method

The data base for this test are the annual arrest figures for the three search and seizure offenses noted earlier in 19 large American cities. The figures were recorded for four or five pre-*Mapp* years (1956 or 1957-60) and for four post-*Mapp* years (1962-65).[2] It would be advantageous statistically to have more measurements before and after *Mapp*, but it is not feasible. Often no reports were available prior to 1956. While post-1965 reports are usually available, the inclusion of measurements too far removed from the subject event would allow contamination of the results from other events and seriously weaken the utility of the quasi-experiment. One obvious such event was the dramatic nationwide rise in narcotics arrests beginning in 1966; less obvious events were two Supreme Court decisions in the late 1960s (*McCray* v. *Illinois*, 1967; *Chimel* v. *California*, 1969) which may have effected considerable change in police search and seizure behavior.

A regression line was determined on the basis of the pre-*Mapp* figures for each offense for each city separately (hereafter called a city/offense). The line was then hypothetically extended into the post-*Mapp* years and a predicted arrest rate was calculated for $T + 1$ (1962), $T + 2$ (1963), etc. The difference between the predicted arrest rates and the actual arrest rates for each city/offense was then subjected to a one-tailed, single sample difference of means test (Student's t). (Blalock, *Social Statistics*, 1960: 144-49) In a sense, this test is not fully appropriate because of the small number of points used to calculate both the regression line and the difference of means, and because there is no claim that the sample is random. However, there seems to be no clearly applicable statistical test appropriate to this situation. My purpose in using a statistical test is not to be as sophisticated as possible, but to avoid possibly subjective "eyeball" judgments. This is a well-known test which accomplishes this objective. The conventional .05 level of confidence was used to determine significance.

. . .

Where possible, a test was used to check that significant declines in arrest rates were not an artifact of a general decline in arrest rates for that particular city. . . .

Findings: Mapp's General Impact

With 19 cities having three offense arrest rates each, there are 57 possible test situations. For reasons noted earlier, however, eight were eliminated from consideration. Of the 49 remaining city offenses, 18 (37%) declined significantly enough to be adjudged the result of *Mapp*, while 31 (63%) did not. *Mapp*'s impact did not vary much by offense. The percentage of city/offenses which declined significantly in each category is: weapons = 39%; gambling = 38%; narcotics = 33%.

To a considerable degree, the above results occur because *Mapp* seems to affect the entire search and seizure behavior of some police departments and does not at all affect that of others. As Table 51-2 shows, six cities were completely affected in that arrest rates for all three offenses declined significantly in the aftermath of *Mapp*.[3] By contrast, in five cities no offenses had significantly declining arrest rates, and in five others only one of the three declined significantly. We can categorize these ten cities as being largely unaffected by *Mapp*. Only three of the 19 cities occupy an ambiguous middle ground in regard to *Mapp*'s impact on police search behavior.

The clear implication of Table 51-2 is that *Mapp*'s impact largely has been mediated by differentials in attitudes and styles among police and civic leaders. While we have no data on these factors in the 19 cities, a more general discussion is possible. It seems sensible to assume that the visible attitudes and actions (or inactions) of elites in the local criminal justice systems will affect the behavior of subordinates. Put otherwise, the police are likely to behave differently in a city where the chief almost openly encourages evasion of a Supreme Court decision than in one where the chief insists on obedience. We know that in some cities the exclusionary rule was criticized virtually to the point of defiance by police leaders while in others it was accepted with equanimity. Beyond the reactions of immediate superiors, scholars have shown that compliance behavior is related to the attitudes and actions of civic elites, to variations in community cultures, and to differential political leadership-law enforcement relationships. In this context, it is noteworthy that reactions were not similar within states (Ohio and Texas), thus reinforcing speculation that local elites, cultural patterns, and politics primarily determine reactive behavior.

Other explanations are possible. For instance, police transgressions of Fourth Amendment rights may have been far greater in some cities prior to *Mapp* than in others, thus affecting the extent of reactive behavior. At any rate, *Mapp*'s differential impact across cities fairly begs for further research. This calls for reconstructing the past with all its pitfalls, but it should be possible to explore the above hypothesis through interviews and existing records or data.

TABLE 51-2
Impact of Mapp on Arrest Rates for Three Search and Seizure Type Offenses in 19 Cities

On All Offenses	On One of Two Offenses	On One of Three Offenses	No Offenses Affected
Atlanta	Houston	Boston	Baltimore
Buffalo	Jacksonville	Detroit	Dayton[a]
Columbus, Ohio[a]	Milwaukee	Kansas City, Mo.	Denver[a]
Dallas[a]		New Orleans	Louisville
Indianapolis[a]		San Antonio	Newark
Portland, Oregon			

[a] Only two offenses.

Findings: Prior State Rule and Reactions

Table 51-3 divides the results for city/offenses into Own Rule and Imposed Rule states and Table 51-4 does the same for cities.[4] The data demonstrate no dramatic differences between police reactions to *Mapp* in states where the rule already prevailed and in those where it did not. In particular, we can absolutely reject the Legal Theoretical Model. Obviously arrest rates in Own Rule states were not immunized from the impact of *Mapp* through compliance with a prior state rule as the model posits; the clear inference here is that state rules produced no particular compliance with the Fourth Amendment. The data do, however, show a slight trend in the opposite direction—to the State Reinforcement Model—but in neither table is the greater impact in Own Rule states statistically significant (or even close to it). Given the small Ns here, however, we can neither dismiss nor adopt the State Reinforcement Model, yet the trend in its direction is interesting enough to warrant further exploration.

TABLE 51-3
Mapp's Impact on City/Offenses Controlled for
Prior State Adoption of the Exclusionary Rule

	Imposed Rule States	Own Rule States	Total
Significant Impact	8 (34.8%)	10 (43.5%)	18 (37.0%)
No Significant Impact	15 (65.2%)	13 (56.5%)	31 (63.0%)
	—	—	—
	23	23	49[a]

[a] Baltimore's city/offenses were not placed in either the Imposed Rule or Own Rule category. See footnote 4.

Our choice, then, lies between the Federal Impact and Non-Compliance Models, neither of which posited a difference between Imposed Rule and Own Rule states. Obviously the data do not approximate either very well. The data clearly indicate that *Mapp* has had an impact on police search and seizure behavior in an appreciable minority of city/offenses and cities, but that the decision has had little impact in a majority of cases. There is little point in establishing criteria designed to force our findings into one or the other models. Suffice it to say that the impact of *Mapp* lies somewhere near a mid-point between the Federal Impact and the Non-Compliance Models.

TABLE 51-4
Mapp's Impact on Cities Controlled for Prior State Adoption of the Exclusionary Rule

	Imposed Rule States	Own Rule States	Total
All Offenses Affected	3 (33.3%)	3 (37.5%)	6 (31.6%)
Half of Offenses Affected	0 (0.0%)	3 (37.5%)	3 (15.8%)
Few or No Offenses Affected	6 (66.7%)	2 (25.0%)	10 (52.6%)
	—	—	—
	9	8	19[a]

[a] Detroit and Baltimore were not placed in either the Imposed Rule or the Own Rule category. See footnote 4.

Discussion of the Findings

In terms of the paper's first goal—an assessment of *Mapp*'s efficacy—our findings are obviously rather ambiguous. This is quite frustrating, but in retrospect it seems unwarranted to have expected clear-cut results. For various reasons already noted, it is now simply impossible to determine with any precision how law enforcement agencies responded to *Mapp* on any widespread scale in the 1962-65 period. The best we can do is make intelligent inferences from highly imperfect data. It is the importance of the problem and not its methodological convenience that attracts us—for it is a problem that bears directly on a highly debated issue of current public policy. Equally important, however, we should not have anticipated a clear-cut situation because there is no necessary reason to expect that all law enforcement agencies would react similarly to *Mapp*. The expectation of near uniformities of reactive behavior is a mainstay of social science research, and thus these uniformities are investigated or at least publicized far more often than mixed reactions. Nonetheless, mixed reactions are very common in the real world, and in our particular case neither the impact literature nor studies of police behavior gave us any reason to think that everyone would react alike to the imposition of the exclusionary rule.

Despite their ambiguity, our findings are not meaningless in relation to the current controversy over the efficacy of the rule. Most important, they show that the exclusionary rule can work—for it has worked dramatically in a number of cities. Obviously it has not always or even often worked. But because we know it can deter illegal police searches, the rule cannot be dismissed as being inherently unworkable, as some of its opponents have suggested. We do not know what political or environmental ingredients are necessary to allow the rule to work. But, presumably, it is possible to determine them and to some extent control them to give the rule maximum utility.

Also, these findings cover responses to *Mapp* only through 1965. Often compliance with controversial Supreme Court decisions, if it occurs, is an incremental phenomena. At first, accurate versions of what the court has said may not circulate out to stationhouses, defense lawyers, etc. And old habits and thought patterns die hard. But things do change. Educational programs, professional journals and local courts spread and refine the word while "old school" sergeants and detectives die, retire or are transferred.

Finally, however inconclusive they may be, the findings are psychologically more useful to the rule's friends because they have been on the defensive during this controversy. A new shipment of sparse empirical ammunition, even if distributed roughly equally to both sides, cannot but help bolster morale among the rule's beseiged advocates. However, the rule's protagonists can take only limited comfort. After all, the findings do show that *Mapp* had seemingly little or no impact in the majority of cases. In other words, the findings can do much to negate the sweeping claims of total inefficacy advanced by the rule's detractors. But they do not come close to supporting a claim that the rule wholly or largely works. All that can be said is that it works sometimes; it may or may not be amenable to improved efficacy.

Implications for State Civil Liberties Policies

Our second major question in this paper was whether there was a differential impact between the state and federal exclusionary rules. Because the data clearly negate the Legal Theoretical Model, it is appropriate to infer that the state's exclusionary rules had little deterrent impact on illegal searches. By contrast, the Supreme Court's *Mapp* decision produced visible if not universal inhibition on such behavior. While we cannot assert that such a differential impact between similar federal and state civil liberties policies always occurs, no noteworthy reason comes to mind why such a difference would be limited to the exclusionary rule. The reasons suggested below for the non-impact of the state exclusionary rules can well be applied beyond the exclusionary rule.

One reason may be the lack of publicity given to state civil liberties decisions. . . . More generally, the media just do not give state civil liberties decisions the same dramatic attention given to U.S. Supreme Court decisions. Perhaps this is too much to expect for decisions so limited geographically. But publicity involves more than headlines. It involves reiteration of the principle by the promulgating court, reinforcement by lower courts, and dissemination of the decision and its rationale by the legal fraternity, civil libertarians, and law enforcement officials. It is doubtful that this occurred in Own Rule states. By contrast, considerable attention and discussion accompanied *Mapp*—law journal articles, legal seminars, ACLU publicity, and the like.

Another factor may well be the differential perceptions of the decisional sources—the state versus the federal government. . . . Thus local law enforcement officers may just not take state civil liberties actions seriously, but regard them a disguise for non-civil libertarian purposes at worst or an inexplicable aberration at best. Beyond that, perhaps they perceive a difference in the judicial enforcement efforts accompanying state and federal civil liberties decisions. It is well known that civil liberties lawyers strongly prefer federal courts to state ones; federal judges are perceived as being more likely to give U.S. Supreme Court decisions an effective application. Of course, *Mapp* transferred few prosecutions involving allegedly illegal searches into federal courts. But it did open up the possibility of appeals, injunctions and habeas corpus actions in federal courts. Thus law enforcement officials in Own Rule states now had to worry about the attitudes of federal judges as well as state ones in weighing their policies and behavior.

. . .

If the findings presented along with my subsequent discussion of them are anywhere near accurate, we can only restore the states to an innovative role in civil liberties policy through encouraging the media, the legal fraternity and civil libertarians to give prominent and continuing attention to such laws or decisions as occur. More importantly, however, these same people, along with legislators and judges themselves, must be encouraged to see the states as a proper source of changes in civil liberties policies and to actually make such changes. This will not be easy, but it will be worth the effort.

Notes

1. Sometimes the police conduct illegal searches for harassment purposes rather than for arrests. Obviously arrest data will not reflect such behavior. Indeed, *Mapp* could not logically be expected to affect such behavior. Nor is *Mapp* aimed at changing the *actual behavior* of police who conduct warrantless searches where a warrant could have been obtained; the aim here is to have the police legalize such behavior. To the extent that the police can and do obtain more warrants after *Mapp*, arrest rates would not decline. Search warrant use cannot be easily measured, but it appears that police interest in obtaining them varied considerably after *Mapp*. Practically speaking, *Mapp* is aimed at changing— that is eliminating—illegal evidentiary searches that cannot be legalized by a warrant because there is not sufficient probable cause to justify its issuance. This type of search was

widespread before *Mapp* and its continued existence is at the crux of the debate about *Mapp*'s efficacy.

2. Because the Uniform Crime Reports do not report Part II arrests by city, I have relied on police department annual reports. The largest collection of these is at the Wisconsin State Criminal Justice Library in Madison. Although the Library has reports from about 60 cities, missing reports, changed offense definitions or reporting formats, and an N of less than 50 for any year or other anomalies reduced the number of testable search and seizure offenses considerably. Only cities with at least two usable offenses were included.

. . .

3. In five of these cities the decline in arrest rates for one offense approached but did not attain the .05 level of significance. Because the decline in arrest rates for the other offenses exceeded the .05 level, it seemed reasonable to infer that the arrest rate for the remaining offense so closely approaching significance, was also affected by *Mapp*.

4. Michigan's exclusionary rule did not apply to weapons and narcotics seized illegally away from the home and the Maryland rule applied only in misdemeanor trials. As nearly all seizures of weapons and perhaps a majority of those in narcotics cases are away from the defendant's home, I have put Detroit weapons and narcotics arrests in the Imposed Rule category and gambling arrests in the Own Rule category. As arrests for the three offenses involve both felonies and misdemeanors, I have not included Baltimore arrests in either category.

CHAPTER EIGHTEEN

THE IMPACT OF THE SUPREME COURT ON THE AMERICAN POLITICAL SYSTEM

The United States Supreme Court, by its exercise of judicial review, has long been thought to have a distinctive impact on the American political system. It is the exercise of this power to determine the constitutionality of any act or action of any governmental official or agency, federal or state, that has continually captured the attention of scholars. The authors of the three selections reprinted in this chapter examine certain empirical evidence in an attempt to assess the impact of the power of judicial review, particularly on the institutions of the national government.

A basic concern of scholars has been the implication of judicial review for the functioning of American democracy. Robert Dahl, in an article that has achieved the status of a "classic" in the literature (and that, in an updated version, constitutes selection 52), takes the position that the Supreme Court has historically been part of the national governing coalition and has rarely been out of step (and even then, only for the short run) with the popularly elected components of that coalition. He argues that judicial review over congressional legislation has rarely been used to substitute judicial judgments for those of stable and substantial popular majorities. Rather the most important function of judicial review is to legitimize national policy, that is, to confer legitimacy on controversial policies fashioned by the popularly elected branches of government.

The article by Jonathan Casper (selection 53) focuses on the Warren Court years of the 1960s. Casper notes that judicial review to negate the actions of government was vigorously exercised, especially when the states were concerned (and Casper stresses that Dahl's assessment was weakened because he ignored judicial review over the actions of the states). Thus the Court's exercise of judicial review is not nearly as benign as Dahl's analysis would lead us to believe. Casper also views the Court's record differently than Dahl when considering judicial review over congressional legislation.

Is judicial review justifiable? Does the Court's use of judicial review to confer legitimacy on controversial policies make the institution of judicial review an essential prop for the legitimacy of the entire political system? David Adamany (selection 54) cautions us to question the basic assumption that underlies these questions—that the Court has a legitimacy-conferring function. Adamany can find no hard evidence demonstrating the so-called legitimacy-conferring capability of the Court. (Adamany bases this conclusion on a review of public opinion-and-the-Court literature such as that presented in Part One, Chapter Five). Adamany looks at the Court during major party-realigning periods of American history and indeed finds the Court at odds with the popularly elected governing majorities. Far from legitimizing the actions of the regime, the Court does quite the reverse. The Court once again becomes part of the new governing structure only after at least some of the old justices have beaten a strategic retreat (usually as a consequence of attacks against the Court itself) and new justices, appointed by the new regime, have come to the Court. During the realigning periods the Court most assuredly flexes its judicial muscles. Despite majority opposition to the Court's policies, judicial review has always remained intact because the opponents of the Court typically become divided when the issue becomes one of whether or not to fundamentally alter Court power. The Court's legitimacy as an institution of government thus saves the day.

In some respects Casper's article can be taken as further evidence in support of Adamany's argument. The 1960s was a decade of political and partisan flux and gave many indications that the party configuration that came into being with the New Deal in the 1930s had come to an end. It was precisely during that decade that the Warren Court, with its concern for civil rights and liberties not unlike many of the concerns of the old liberal Democratic majority, was in conflict with the emerging, considerably more conservative, new governing majority. After the Nixon appointees came to dominate the Supreme Court, the Court retreated—most noticeably in the criminal procedures area, but in some others as well—and once again came to terms with the new majority. Only the incredible events of "Watergate," and the severely troubled national economy, prevented the Republicans from winning the presidency in 1976 and fully exploiting an apparent shift to a more conservative, and less party oriented, electorate.

Adamany's analysis suggests that the Supreme Court has had a broad impact on the political system and that the political system has in turn affected the Court. But Adamany, aside from his view that the Supreme Court with its power of judicial review is a legitimate branch of government, does not offer any justification for judicial review. He does not offer any view concerning how those powers should be exercised in a democracy. Perhaps, like many observers (including the editors of this book), he sees judicial review as a given, a power that is inherent in our judicial institutions. How that power should be exercised is an important question to ask but one that cannot be definitively answered. How courts in general should exercise their powers is a question that is equally difficult to answer but one that is worthwhile for the student to consider.

52

The Supreme Court's Role in National Policy-Making

Robert A. Dahl

. . . In the course of its one hundred and sixty-seven years, in eighty-five cases, the Court has struck down ninety-four different provisions of federal law as unconstitutional, and by interpretation it has significantly modified a good many more. It might be argued . . . that in all or in a very large number of these cases the Court was . . . defending the legitimate constitutional rights of some minority against a "tyrannical" majority. There are, however, some exceedingly serious difficulties with this interpretation of the Court's activities.

To begin with, it is difficult to determine when any particular Court decision has been at odds with the preferences of a national majority. Adequate evidence is not available, for scientific opinion polls are of relatively recent origin; and, strictly speaking, national elections cannot be interpreted as more than an indication of the first choice of about 40 to 60 per cent of the adult population for certain candidates for public office. The connection between preferences among candidates and preferences among alternative public policies is highly tenuous. On the basis of an election, it is almost never possible to adduce whether a majority does or does not support one of two or more *policy* alternatives about which candidates are divided. For the greater part of the Court's history, then, there is simply no way of establishing with any high degree of confidence whether a given alternative was or was not supported by a majority or a minority of adults or even of voters.

In the absence of relatively direct information, we are thrown back on indirect tests. The ninety-four provisions of federal law that have been declared unconstitutional were, of course, initially passed by majorities of those voting in the Senate and in the House. They also had the President's formal approval. One could, therefore, speak of a majority of those voting in the House and Senate, together with the President, as a "law-making majority." It is not easy to determine whether a law-making majority actually coincides with the preferences of a majority of American adults, or even with the preferences of a majority of that half of the adult population which, on the average, votes in congressional elections. Such evidence as we have from opinion polls suggests that Congress is not markedly out of line with public opinion, or at any rate with such public opinion as there is after one discards the answers of people who fall into the category, often large, labeled "no response" or "don't know." If we may, on these somewhat uncertain grounds, take a

Robert A. Dahl, *Pluralist Democracy in the United States,* © 1967 by Rand McNally & Company, Chicago, pp. 155–64. Reprinted by permission of Rand McNally College Publishing Company. This excerpt is an updated version of "Decision-Making in a Democracy: The Supreme Court as a National Policy-Maker," *Journal of Public Law* 6 (1957), 279–295.

TABLE 52-1
The Interval Between Appointments to the Supreme Court, 1789-1965

Interval in Years	Number of Appointments	Percentage of Total	Cumulative Percentage
Less than 1 year	38	41	41
1	22	24	65
2	10	11	76
3	9	10	86
4	6	6.5	92.5
5	6	6.5	99
12	1	1	100
Total	92	100	100

Note: The table excludes six Justices appointed in 1789. It includes only Justices who were appointed and confirmed and served on the Court. All data through 1964 are from *Congress and the Nation,* 1452–1453.

law-making majority as equivalent to a "national majority," then it is possible to test the hypothesis that the Supreme Court is shield and buckler for minorities against tyrannical national majorities.

Under any reasonable assumptions about the nature of the political process, it would appear to be somewhat naive to assume that the Supreme Court either would or could play the role of Galahad. Over the whole history of the Court, one new Justice has been appointed on the average of every twenty-three months. Thus a President can expect to appoint two new Justices during one term of office; and if this were not enough to tip the balance on a normally divided Court, he would be almost certain to succeed in two terms. For example, Hoover made three appointments; Roosevelt, nine; Truman, four; Eisenhower, five; Kennedy in his brief tenure, two. Presidents are not famous for appointing Justices hostile to their own views on public policy; nor could they expect to secure confirmation of a man whose stance on key questions was flagrantly at odds with that of the dominant majority in the Senate. Typically, Justices are men who, prior to appointment, have engaged in public life and have committed themselves publicly on the great questions of the day. As the late Mr. Justice Frankfurter pointed out, a surprisingly large proportion of the Justices, particularly of the great Justices who have left their stamp upon the decisions of the Court, have had little or no prior judicial experience. Nor have the Justices—certainly not the great Justices—been timid men with a passion for anonymity. Indeed, it is not too much to say that if Justices were appointed primarily for their 'judicial' qualities without regard to their basic attitudes on fundamental questions of public policy, the Court could not play the influential role in the American political system that it does in reality play.

It is reasonable to conclude, then, that the policy views dominant on the Court will never be out of line for very long with the policy views dominant among the law-making majorities of the United States. And it would be most unrealistic to suppose that the Court would, for more than a few years at most, stand against any major alternatives sought by a law-making majority. The judicial agonies of the New Deal will, of course, come quickly to mind; but President Franklin D. Roosevelt's difficulties with the Court were truly exceptional. Generalizing over the whole history of the Court, one can say that the chances are about two out of five that a President will make one appointment to the Court in less than a year, two out of three that he will make one within two years, and three out of four that he will make one within three years (Table 52-1). President Roose-

TABLE 52-2
Supreme Court Cases Holding Federal Legislation Unconstitutional:
By Time Between Legislation and Decision

Number of Years	Supreme Court Cases Involving:					
	New Deal Legislation		Other		All Federal Legislation	
	N.	%	N.	%	N.	%
2 or less	11	92	13	17.5	24	28
3–4	1	8	13	17.5	14	16
5–8	0	0	20	27	20	24
9–12	0	0	10	14	10	12
13–16	0	0	7	10	7	8
17–20	0	0	2	3	2	2
21 or more	0	0	8	11	8	10
Total	12	100%	73	100%	85	100%

velt had unusually bad luck: he had to wait four years for his first appointment; the odds against this long interval are about five to one. With average luck, his battle with the Court would never have occurred; even as it was, although his "court-packing" proposal did formally fail, by the end of his second term in 1940, Roosevelt had appointed five new Justices and he gained three more the following year: Thus by the end of 1941, Mr. Justice Roberts was the only remaining holdover from the pre-Roosevelt era.

It is to be expected, then, that the Court would be least successful in blocking a determined and persistent law-making majority on a major policy. Conversely, the Court is most likely to succeed against "weak" law-making majorities: transient majorities in Congress, fragile coalitions, coalitions weakly united upon a policy of subordinate importance or congressional coalitions no longer in existence, as might be the case when a law struck down by the Court had been passed several years earlier.

An examination of the cases in which the Court has held federal legislation unconstitutional confirms these expectations. Over the whole history of the Court, about half the decisions have been rendered more than four years after the legislation was passed (Table 52-2). Thus the congressional majorities that passed these laws went through at least two elections before the decision was handed down and may well have weakened or disappeared in the interval. In these cases, then, the Court was probably not directly challenging current law-making majorities.

Of the twenty-four laws held unconstitutional within two years, eleven were measures enacted in the early years of the New Deal. Indeed, New Deal measures comprise nearly a third of all the legislation that has ever been declared unconstitutional within four years of enactment.

It is illuminating to examine the cases where the Court has acted on legislation within four years of enactment—where the presumption is, that is to say, that the law-making majority is not a dead one. Of the twelve New Deal cases, two were, from a policy point of view, trivial; and two although perhaps not trivial, were of minor importance to the New Deal program. A fifth involved the NRA, which was to expire within three weeks of the decision. Insofar as the unconstitutional provisions allowed "codes of fair competition" to be established by industrial groups, it is fair to say that President Roosevelt and his advisors were relieved by the Court's decision of a policy that they had come to find increasingly embarrassing. In view of the tenacity with which FDR held to his major

TABLE 52-3
Number of Cases Involving Legislative Policy Other Than Those Arising Under New Deal Legislation Holding Legislation Unconstitutional Within Four Years After Enactment

Interval in Years	Major Policy	Minor Policy	Total
2 or less	11	2	13
3 to 4	4	9	13
Total	15	11	26

program, there can hardly be any doubt that, had he wanted to pursue the policy objective involved in the NRA codes, as he did for example with the labor provisions, he would not have been stopped by the Court's special theory of the Constitution. As to the seven other cases, it is entirely correct to say, I think, that whatever some of the eminent Justices might have thought during their fleeting moments of glory, they did not succeed in interposing a barrier to the achievement of the objectives of the legislation; and in a few years most of the constitutional dogma on which they rested their opposition to the New Deal had been unceremoniously swept under the rug.

The remainder of the thirty-eight cases where the Court has declared legislation unconstitutional within four years of enactment tend to fall into two rather distinct groups: those involving legislation that could reasonably be regarded as important *from the point of view of the law-making majority* [15 cases] and those involving minor legislation [11 cases]. . . . We would expect that cases involving major legislative policy would be propelled to the Court much more rapidly than cases involving minor policy, and, as the table above shows, this is in fact what happens (Table 52-3).

Thus a law-making majority with major policy objectives in mind usually has an opportunity to seek ways of overcoming the Court's veto. It is an interesting and highly significant fact that Congress and the President do generally succeed in overcoming a hostile Court on major policy issues (Table 52-4). It is particularly instructive to examine the cases involving major policy. In two cases involving legislation enacted by radical Republican Congresses to punish supporters of the Confederacy during the Civil War, the Court faced a rapidly crumbling majority whose death knell as an effective national force was sounded after the election of 1876. Three cases are difficult to classify and I have labeled them "unclear." Of these, two were decisions made in 1921 involving a 1919 amendment to the Lever Act to control prices. The legislation was important, and the provision in question was clearly struck down, but the Lever Act terminated three days after the decision and Congress did not return to the subject of price control until the Second World War, when it experienced no constitutional difficulties arising from these cases (which were primarily concerned with the lack of an ascertainable standard of guilt). The third case in this category successfully eliminated stock dividends from the scope of the Sixteenth Amendment, although a year later Congress enacted legislation taxing the actual income from such stocks.

The remaining ten cases were ultimately followed by a reversal of the actual policy results of the Court's action, although not necessarily of the specific constitutional interpretation. In four cases, the policy consequences of the Court's decision were overcome in less than a year. The other six required a long struggle. Workmen's compensation for longshoremen and harbor workers was invalidated by the Court in 1920; in 1922, Congress passed a new law which was, in its turn, knocked down by the Court in 1924; in 1927, Congress passed a third law, which was finally upheld in 1932. The notorious

TABLE 52-4

Type of Congressional Action Following Supreme Court Decisions Holding Legislation Unconstitutional Within Four Years After Enactment (Other Than New Deal Legislation)

Congressional Action	Major Policy	Minor Policy	Total
Reverses Court's Policy	10[a]	2[d]	12
Changes Own Policy	2[b]	0	2
None	0	8[e]	8
Unclear	3[c]	1[f]	4
Total	15	11	26

[a] *Pollock* v. *Farmers' Loan & Trust Co.,* 157 U.S. 429 (1895); *Employers' Liability Cases,* 207 U.S. 463 (1908); *Keller* v. *United States,* 213 U.S. 138 (1909); *Hammer* v. *Dagenhart,* 247 U.S. 251 (1918); *Bailey* v. *Drexel Furniture Co.,* 259 U.S. 20 (1922); *Trusler* v. *Crooks,* 269 U.S. 475 (1926); *Hill* v. *Wallace,* 259 U.S. 44 (1922); *Knickerbocker Ice Co.* v. *Stewart,* 253 U.S. 149 (1920); *Washington* v. *Dawson & Co.,* 264 U.S. 219 (1924).

[b] *Ex parte Garland,* 4 Wall. (U.S.) 333 (1867); *United States* v. *Klein,* 13 Wall. (U.S.) 128 (1872).

[c] *United States* v. *Cohen Grocery Co.,* 255 U.S. 81 (1921); *Weeds, Inc.* v. *United States,* 255 U.S. 109 (1921); *Eisner* v. *Macomber,* 252 U.S. 189 (1920).

[d] *Gordon* v. *United States,* 2 Wall. (U.S.) 561 (1865); *Evans* v. *Gore,* 253 U.S. 245 (1920).

[e] *United States* v. *Dewitt,* 9 Wall. (U.S.) 41 (1870); *Monongahela Navigation Co.* v. *United States,* 148 U.S. 312 (1893); *Wong Wing* v. *United States,* 163 U.S. 228 (1896); *Fairbank* v. *United States,* 181 U.S. 283 (1901); *Rassmussen* v. *United States,* 197 U.S. 516 (1905); *Muskrat* v. *United States,* 219 U.S. 346 (1911); *Choate* v. *Trapp,* 224 U.S. 665 (1912); *United States* v. *Lovett,* 328 U.S. 303 (1946).

[f] *Untermyer* v. *Anderson,* 276 U.S. 440 (1928).

income tax cases of 1895 were first somewhat narrowed by the Court itself; the Sixteenth Amendment was recommended by President Taft in 1909 and was ratified in 1913, some eighteen years after the Court's decisions. The two child labor cases represent the most effective battle ever waged by the Court against legislative policy-makers. The original legislation outlawing child labor, based on the commerce clause, was passed in 1916 as part of Wilson's New Freedom. Like Franklin Roosevelt later, Wilson was somewhat unlucky in his Supreme Court appointments; he made only three appointments during his eight years, and one of these was wasted, from a policy point of view, on Mr. Justice McReynolds. Had McReynolds voted "right," the subsequent struggle over the problem of child labor need not have occurred, for the decision in 1918 was by a Court divided five to four, McReynolds voting with the majority. Congress moved at once to circumvent the decision by means of the tax power, but in 1922, the Court blocked that approach. In 1924, Congress returned to the engagement with a constitutional amendment that was rapidly endorsed by a number of state legislatures before it began to meet so much resistance in the states remaining that the enterprise miscarried. In 1938, under a second reformist President, new legislation was passed twenty-two years after the first; this a Court with a New Deal majority finally accepted in 1941, and thereby brought to an end a battle that had lasted a full quarter-century.

The entire record of the duel between the Court and the law-making majority, in cases where the Court has held legislation unconstitutional within four years after enactment, is summarized in Table 52-5.

A consideration of the role of the Court as defender of minorities, then, suggests the following conclusions:

First, judicial review is surely inconsistent with democracy to the extent that the Court simply protects the policies of minorities from reversal or regulation by national majorities acting through regular law-making procedures.

TABLE 52-5
Type of Congressional Action After Supreme Court Decisions Holding Legislation Unconstitutional Within Four Years After Enactment (Including New Deal Legislation)

Congressional Action	Major Policy	Minor Policy	Total
Reverses Court's Policy	17	2	19
None	0	12	12
Other	6*	1	7
Total	23	15	38

* In addition to the actions in Table 52-4 under "Changes Own Policy" and "Unclear," this figure includes the NRA legislation affected by the *Schechter Poultry* case.

Second, however, the frequency and nature of appointments to the Court inhibits it from playing this role, or otherwise protecting minorities against national law-making majorities. National law-making majorities—i.e., coalitions of the President and a majority of each house of Congress—generally have their way.

Third, although the court evidently cannot hold out indefinitely against a persistent law-making majority, in a very small number of important cases it has succeeded in delaying the application of a policy for as long as twenty-five years.

53

The Supreme Court and National Policy Making

Jonathan D. Casper

The role of the Supreme Court in national policy making has long been a subject of debate among students of the American legal system and of democratic theory. The relative influence of the Court vis-à-vis other political institutions and the implications of its activities for principles of majority rule and democracy have been central issues in this discussion. One of the most influential treatments of this issue in recent years is the argument advanced by Robert A. Dahl in 1957.[1] Dahl offers a sophisticated "political" view of the role played by the Court, arguing that it is an active participant in the ruling national coalitions which dominate American politics but that the Court does not perform the task of protecting fundamental minority rights that is often attributed to it. The Court, like other political institutions, says Dahl, is a member of such ruling coalitions, and as such its decisions are typically supportive of the policies emerging from other political institutions. Dahl's account has endured so well because it frames the questions precisely and brings to bear a carefully selected body of evidence upon a dispute long characterized by anecdote and example.

I argue here that Dahl's account is not adequate for understanding the role of the Supreme Court in policy making. Consideration of the way he interprets his own evidence and of other relevant evidence that is excluded from his analysis suggests that the Court participates more significantly in national policy making than Dahl's argument suggests.

. . .

The Supreme Court and Federal Legislation, 1958-1974

Dahl's article was published in 1957, appearing at the end of a decade that had seen one of our periodic episodes of national political repression. Fear of internal subversion by Communists and fellow-travelers had produced not only intense public concern but a variety of federal and state programs aimed at control of the thought, expression, and behavior of allegedly subversive elements in our society. The rulings of the Supreme Court in this period did not mark it as a bastion of individual rights standing against a fearful

Reprinted by permission from *American Political Science Review* 70 (1976), 50-63. Most footnotes have been omitted.

TABLE 53-1
Cases in Which Federal Legislation Was Held Unconstitutional,
Arranged by Time Intervals Between Legislation and Decision

Time Interval (in years)	1789–1957[a]	1958–1974	1789–1974
2 or less	30%	7%	25%
3 to 4	18	14	17
5 to 8	24	11	20
9 to 12	11	21	13
13 to 16	6	21	10
17 to 20	1	7	3
21 or more	10	18	12
	100%	99%	100%
	(N = 78)	(N = 28)	(N = 106)

[a] See Dahl, p. 290.

and repressive national majority. The Court vacillated on the civil liberties issues raised by the loyalty-security programs and generally placed the imprimatur of legitimacy upon a variety of constitutionally questionable governmental activities (e.g., prosecutions under the Smith Act, employee loyalty-security screening programs, legislative investigations.) In this partly salient issue area, then, the Supreme Court did follow the deferential path suggested by Dahl's analysis.

Since then, we have witnessed the work of the Warren Court and are currently in the midst of the emergence of the Burger Court. The Warren Court, by general reputation at least, was quite different from most of its predecessors. Indeed, one associates with it precisely the characteristics that Dahl found lacking in the Supreme Court—activism and influence in national policy making and protection of fundamental rights of minorities against tyrannical or indifferent majorities. The first step, then, in examining Dahl's thesis is to look at what has happened since he wrote. Do events since that date suggest the possibility of a different pattern of Supreme Court participation in policy making?

With respect to the dimensions of frequency, decisiveness, and direction, the data since 1957 are somewhat mixed. During this period, the Supreme Court declared 32 provisions of federal law unconstitutional in 28 cases. In the entire previous 167-year period, 86 provisions had been declared unconstitutional in 78 cases. Putting the two sets together, we note that more than a quarter of all cases involving a declaration of unconstitutionality (28 of 106) have occurred since 1957. In terms of frequency, the Supreme Court proved more active in recent years than it typically had been in the past.

But Dahl's argument does not rest simply upon the frequency of Supreme Court holdings that federal statutes are unconstitutional. Since he focuses upon the relation of policy emerging from the Court to policy emerging from the "lawmaking majority," particular attention is paid to the period of time that occurs between passage of legislation and the declaration that it is unconstitutional. Dahl lays great stress upon declarations of unconstitutionality occurring within four years of enactment—"where the presumption is . . . that the lawmaking majority is not necessarily a dead one." Table 53-1 reproduces his findings about the time intervals between enactment and Court decisions and also brings them up to date. Recent decisions seem to follow the same pattern as before—the bulk of cases involve a Court decision somewhat removed in time from the passage of the legislation. In sum, the data suggest that although the period since 1957 did involve a substantial amount of Supreme Court activity in declaring legislation unconstitutional, only about a fifth of the cases involved clashes between what Dahl would call "live" national majorities and a Court bent upon pursuing other policy alternatives.

Dahl also pays attention to the decisiveness dimension—what happened *after* the Court declared laws unconstitutional within four years of enactment. Especially in matters involving what he calls "major policy," Dahl found that the Court policy has typically been reversed, either by legislation, constitutional amendment, or a change of heart by the Court itself. In the six cases during the 1958-74 period in which the Court held legislation unconstitutional within four years after passage, one seems clearly "major" and was reversed by a quickly passed constitutional amendment (*Oregon* v. *Mitchell*,[2] holding that the provision of the 1970 Voting Rights Act lowering the voting age in state and local elections to 18 was beyond the power of Congress). Since Dahl does not offer a definition of "major" and "minor" policy, it is difficult to classify the other five cases. They involved the residency requirement for welfare recipients in the District of Columbia, military trials for civilian dependents and employees stationed abroad with servicemen and a form of censorship of mail from Communist countries.[3] The Court's decision was not followed by reversal or a change of mind in any of these cases. The same was true with the 22 cases holding federal statutory provisions unconstitutional more than four years after enactment—all were followed either by positive congressional acceptance (e.g., amending the law to conform to the Court's holding or formal repeal) or by acquiescence. Thus, the evidence appears to support the view that the Court intervened decisively in these 22 cases holding federal legislation unconstitutional. In the next section, however, we will discuss a peculiar feature of the way in which Dahl treats his evidence—he considers the decisiveness dimension only for cases occurring within four years of enactment. Those occurring more than four years after enactment are excluded on the ground that we cannot be sure that the law-making majority continues to be "alive" and hence that the clash of preferences required to judge relative influence exists. As a result, it is not clear how to interpret the 22 cases during the 1958-1974 period. For some—particularly those dealing with internal security matters—the view that the law-making majority was no longer "alive" seems plausible; for others—those dealing with the administration of justice, citizenship rights, and welfare programs—an account attributing influence to the Court seems more plausible.

Thus, because of the nature of Dahl's coding rules, evaluation of the Court's recent work on the decisiveness dimension is difficult. Given that there has been only one instance of reversal in 28 cases, one must conclude either (1) that the ambiguity in Dahl's coding rules makes the issue unanswerable for the recent period (and, it is argued in the next section, for the period Dahl himself covers); or (2) that the recent experience does not support the Dahl thesis.

On the dimension of direction, the pattern of decisions since 1958 is clearly at variance with Dahl's findings. With the exception of *Oregon* v. *Mitchell,* all of the 28 decisions were based upon provisions of the Bill of Rights (primarily the First and Fifth Amendments) and the Fourteenth Amendment. In addition to furthering the interests of all in the society in greater freedom of expression, equal application of the laws, and procedural fairness, the decisions had special impact upon such groups as aliens, communists and other alleged subversives, criminal defendants, war protesters, and poor people. The Court attempted to extend to these groups rights and privileges that the law-making majorities had not chosen to extend. For example, a series of decisions struck down statutes that took away citizenship for such activities as voting in foreign elections, desertion from armed forces, leaving the country to avoid military service, and extended residence in country of origin. By the same token, the heart of the McCarran Act—its registration provisions and restrictions upon employment in sensitive industries for members of Communist action organizations—was struck down on Fifth and First Amendment grounds.

We have now examined the recent decisions in terms of Dahl's three dimensions. The results, while not wholly conclusive, do not tend to support Dahl's thesis. The Supreme Court has, in recent years, struck down federal legislation more frequently than in the past. The Court's decisions, with one exception, were not met with reversal by legislation, constitutional amendment, or a reversal by the Court itself (though a few have occurred sufficiently recently that this outcome may still occur). By the same token, however, the bulk of the decisions did not involve legislation passed shortly before the Court intervened, so one cannot, under Dahl's rules, be sure that the lawmaking majority on the issue was still alive. Finally, in terms of direction, the recent cases demonstrate a concern for and protection of basic liberties and rights of minorities that is different from the picture Dahl draws from past cases. With the exception of *Oregon* v. *Mitchell*, none can be adequately interpreted as protecting the privileged at the expense of the poor or a majority at the expense of an insular minority.

It would be somewhat improbable—in either a statistical or substantive sense—for the Court in 16 years to erase a pattern that had stood for nearly 170 years before. My updating of Dahl's argument does not render his conclusions invalid or totally inapplicable to more recent events. By the same token, recent experience does suggest that the Court may operate differently from the way in which Dahl suggests it has and, even more important, from the way he suggests it must.

The Evidence Considered

One of the most appealing aspects of Dahl's argument is his careful specification and gathering of evidence. In dealing with an issue that has long been the subject of discussion and argument based upon impression and example, Dahl offers a carefully developed specification of the question and of the evidence that he believes is required for an informed resolution of the conflicting views that have been offered. Yet analysis of what Dahl has done and what he has not done reveals problems both in his mode of analysis and his conclusions. The issues I wish to raise in this section deal with both the way in which he treats his own evidence and with relevant evidence that is excluded from his analysis.

Dahl considers only cases in which federal legislation has been declared unconstitutional, and offers two justifications for casting his evidentiary net in this way. The first centers around the proposition that relative influence in policy making can be determined only when there are disagreements among participants[4] and upon his selection of the "lawmaking majority" as the most useful criterion for majority preferences. The second is based upon the assertion that it is *national* (for which he substitutes *federal*) issues that defenders of the importance of the Court in policy making have in mind. . . .

Both of these justifications are plausible, but they produce a very narrow evidentiary net. Later in this section, I shall suggest a variety of relevant evidence that is excluded. First, I shall discuss the way in which Dahl analyzes the data that he does utilize.

Dahl's Evidence and Coding Rules

Dahl asks three questions about Supreme Court decisions declaring federal legislation unconstitutional: what has been their frequency, their decisiveness, and their direction? In analyzing the cases to determine whether they support the view that the Court plays an influential role in national policy making, he relies almost exclusively upon the decisiveness dimension. Thus, in dealing with two typical sequences of events, he codes them as follows on the dimension of relative influence of Court and law-making majority:

Type I (Court Influential)
(1) Law-making majority acts
(2) Court reverses policy within 4 years
(3) Court's policy stands

Thirty-eight of the 78 cases he discovered fell into one of these two categories, and, of these, 19 fell into what I shall call Type II (law-making majority influential). Moreover, applying a distinction between what he calls "major policy" and "minor policy" cases, 17 of 23 "major policy" cases fell into Type II.

He takes special note of the fact that in some of these Type II situations the overriding of the Court's policy has taken a period of many years (e.g., those dealing with child labor legislation, the federal income tax, and workman's compensation for longshoremen). But his analysis of the decisiveness dimension concludes that, particularly in cases involving "major policy" issues, the Court has not generally succeeded in resisting the law-making majority. This finding is the linchpin for his conclusion that the Court does not play the significant role in national policy making that many of its defenders have suggested.

Type II (Law-making Majority Influential)
(1) Law-making majority acts
(2) Court reverses policy within 4 years
(3) Court's policy reversed

Yet Dahl considers the decisiveness dimension *only for cases in which the Court declares federal legislation unconstitutional within four years of the enactment of the statute.* What of the forty cases in which the Court's decision came more than four years after enactment? His analysis of this group of cases—which comprises more than half of his data—is restricted to a discussion of the *direction* of the Court's policy. He notes that the bulk of the Court decisions were neither based upon provisions of the Bill of Rights nor protective of fundamental rights of minorities. He provides neither data nor discussion of the decisiveness of these decisions.

Dahl's reasons for this approach are discussed only casually. He obliquely asserts that in situations involving a period of more than four years between enactment and Court decision, the law-making majority cannot be assumed to be still viable, and hence we cannot judge relative influence. For example, he introduces his discussion of what I call here "Type I" and "Type II" cases (declarations of unconstitutionality *within* four years) by saying that in these cases "the presumption is . . . that the lawmaking majority is not necessarily a dead one." In his discussion of the cases that occurred more than four years after enactment (what I will call Type III), he asks, "Do we have evidence in these [cases] that the Court has protected fundamental or natural rights and liberties against the *dead hand of some past tyranny* by the lawmakers?" If more than four years have passed, then, we lack the evidence necessary to judge relative influence.

Type IIIa

(1) Law-making majority acts
(2) Court reverses policy more than 4 years later
(3) Court's policy stands

There is logic to this argument, but it has implications that are largely unexamined. Not only do we lack data relevant to assessing the decisiveness of Court action in nearly half the cases, but the logic of Dahl's argument seems to load the dice strongly against the possibility of discovering influence by the Court if we *did* gather such data. Consider the following sequences of events:

Type IIIb

(1) Law-making majority acts
(2) Court reverses policy more than 4 years later
(3) Court's policy reversed

Common sense would suggest that Type IIIb is one in which the law-making majority should be judged to have been influential. By the same token, Type IIIa is one in which the Court ought to be judged to have exercised influence. Assume, for example, that the Court declares an act of Congress unconstitutional more than four years after its enactment. Assume that there is no move to reverse the Court or that there is a move to reverse the decision by further legislation or a constitutional amendment but that such an effort is defeated. What are we to make of the relative influence of the Court under such circumstances? The Court appears to have played a decisive role: without its intervention, the original policy would presumably have been continued. Yet Dahl's coding scheme asserts that the law-making majority was "dead" by the time the Court acted and hence we cannot judge relative influence (and cannot conclude that the Court has intervened in an important fashion). If we did gather data on cases occurring more than four years after enactment and most of them fell into Type IIIb—if the bulk of such decisions were reversed by the law-making majority—it would be reasonable to conclude that they, like those of Type II, support Dahl's conclusion that the Court has not been able to intervene decisively against the law-making majority. But suppose most of them fell into Type IIIa? Dahl seems to assert that this would not be evidence for decisive intervention by the Court because we cannot assume that the law-making majority is still viable. Under such a view the Court *cannot* be judged to be influential in circumstances that compose more than half of his evidence. If the Court's policy is reversed, it has clearly not been influential; if the Court's policy stands without discussion or is debated but not reversed, again the Court has not been influential. With such coding rules, heads and the law-making majority wins; tails and the Court loses.

This feature may assume increasing importance as the workload of the Court becomes heavier. The time required for the typical case to get to the Supreme Court for resolution is now on the order of two to three years and seems to be growing. As a result, the probability that an issue will reach the Court in time to fall within the category when we can, under Dahl's rules, assess relative influence, is decreasing.

In sum, more than half the cases Dahl discovered fall into a category in which under his coding rules it is not possible to conclude that the Court (or law-making majority) has been influential. Not only does he fail to provide the relevant data, but he seems tacitly to assert that if such data were gathered and appeared to indicate decisive interventions by the Court (Type IIIa), such data would not be interpreted in this fashion. This feature of his treatment of the evidence suggests that the conclusions based upon his analysis, though by no means disproved, are potentially a product of an asymmetry in the coding rules as well as of the nature of the evidence itself.

The Evidence Excluded

Dahl limits his consideration to cases in which the Court held federal legislation unconstitutional. Yet cases involving tests of constitutionality of federal legislation compose only one segment of the work of the Court. Two other types of activities also stand out as particularly important arenas in which the Court contributes to national policy making. The first deals with statutory construction and the second with federal constitutional issues arising out of state and local legislation or practice.

Statutory Construction

The Court is frequently called upon to interpret the meaning of federal statutes, and in the course of doing so, important policy choices must be made. If we adopt for the moment the notion that influence in policy making is most accurately judged in situations in which various participants conflict with one another, it is clear that the interpretations that are made by the Court—even when they are based on "legislative intent"—are often quite different from those that members of Congress and the President had in mind when the legislation was passed. The Court's doctrine that it will, if at all possible, interpret a statute in such a way as to "save" it from being declared unconstitutional means that the Court will often significantly twist and change the ostensible provisions of a statute. Thus, in interpreting statutes the Court often makes important policy choices, and these choices are at least arguably quite contrary to the preferences of the law-making majority that passed the legislation. The more influence the Court exercises by virtue of statutory construction, the less influence it will appear to have in terms of Dahl's coding rules. When the Court "saves" a law by interpreting it rather than declaring it unconstitutional, its contribution to the course of public policy is excluded from consideration under Dahl's rules.

. . .

Recent years have seen a variety of . . . instances of important policy making by the Court in the context of statutory construction. The extension of conscientious objector status to those without formal religious training, restrictions upon the use of delinquency provisions against opponents of the Vietnam War, restrictions upon residency requirements for welfare recipients, limitation upon the power to use surveillance techniques without a warrant, elimination of the "man-in-the-house" rule for welfare recipients, and freedom for broadcasters to refuse to sell air time to individuals and groups wishing to speak out on public issues have all been based wholly or in important measure upon interpretations of various federal statutes.

In some of the examples cited, especially those in which attempts by Congress to reverse the interpretation offered by the Court failed to pass, the mode of Dahl's analysis might suggest that the law-making majority was no longer viable, and hence the influence of the Court not significant. Yet this argument has the peculiar implication discussed above: if the Court acts and Congress overrides, then the Court has not been influential; yet if the Court acts and Congress *fails* to override, then again, the Court has not been influential for we assume the law-making majority no longer exists.

In sum, then, one must consider the work of the Court in the area of statutory construction in any discussion of its role in policy making. Dahl's exclusion of this activity in his consideration of the role of the Court constitutes a serious omission, and its inclusion will significantly increase the scope of Court influence that one is likely to observe.

The State and Local Cases

The second major area of the Court's work that is excluded from Dahl's analysis involves constitutional issues arising in cases involving state and local statutes or practice. As suggested above, this exclusion is justified on the grounds that we lack evidence about the preferences of the lawmaking majority in such cases and that these cases have not been typically cited by defenders of the Court as the basis of their view that the Court plays a significant role in national policy making. Although there are, to be sure, difficulties in establishing the preferences of the national majority in these cases, a review of them suggests that many do indeed involve the Court in important issues of national policy.

To use the schematic device introduced above, the state and local cases deal with situations in which the Court may be conceived of as speaking first and in which the law-making majority is placed in the position of responding to the policy promulgated by the Court. Applying the type of coding rules that Dahl follows, one might code the following sequences of events in terms of relative influence:

Type IV (Law-making Majority Influential)
(1) Court promulgates policy
(2) Law-making majority reverses policy
(3) Law-making majority's policy stands

The decision in *Chisholm* v. *Georgia*[5] asserting federal jurisdiction in diversity suits against state governments and the subsequent passage of the Eleventh Amendment is an example of a Type IV sequence.

Type V situations are more significant for our purposes. Here the Court speaks "first," and its policy is not followed by reversal by the law-making majority. In the various cases discussed below, this appears to have been the pattern followed, despite frequent attempts at reversal by legislation or constitutional amendment. After a brief review of these cases, we shall return to the problem of whether they are consistent with the argument that Dahl presents and what they suggest about the role of the Court in national policy making.

In the nineteenth century, a long line of important Supreme Court decisions dealt with the development of interstate commerce and relations between the national and state governments. Cases like *McCulloch* v. *Maryland*,[6] *Gibbons* v. *Ogden*,[7] and *Cooley* v. *Board of Wardens*[8] are merely the landmarks in a gradual development of a set of rules designed to produce a national government and economy. In citing the power of Congress via the supremacy and interstate commerce clauses, the Court was not simply legitimizing assertions of power by the national government vis-à-vis the states but took the initiative in offering its own theory of the nature of the union and of the most satisfactory distribution of powers among the various levels of government. Such cases are excluded from Dahl's analysis.

In the area of individual rights and liberties during the second half of the twentieth century, the contributions of the Court are equally striking. A simple catalogue of the issue areas in which the Court has become involved suggests the breadth of its contributions to national policy that emerged in the context of state and local cases.

In the area of reapportionment, the line of decisions beginning with *Baker* v. *Carr*[9] and proceeding through *Reynolds* v. *Sims*[10] and on to the recent decisions in *Mahan* and *Gaffney*[11] have produced significant changes in the districting of local, state, and congressional districts in nearly all the states.

Type V (Court Influential)
(1) Court promulgates policy
(2) Law-making majority fails to reverse policy
(3) Court's policy stands

Although questions have been raised about the impact of such changes upon party competition and policy outputs of legislatures, it seems clear that such widespread reform in legislative apportionment would not have occurred without the Court's intervention.

In the religion cases, especially the *Engel* and *Schempp*[12] decisions, the Court set forth a policy toward devotional exercises in public schools that affected all schools, not just those in particular localities. Though the decisions were by no means greeted with total compliance, they have not been reversed and still stand as national policy. By the same token, a string of decisions dealing with aid to parochial schools has restricted the nature and types of aid that states and the federal government have been permitted to offer. Though the decisions have not cut off such aid, they have shaped these programs in ways that run contrary to the directions that they would have gone without such intervention.

A long line of confusing and confused decisions emerged as the Court attempted to define obscenity and thus to determine what enjoyed the protection of the First Amendment and what did not. Though the Court is still grappling with this problem . . . the upshot of this line of cases has been to expand greatly the range of materials available to the society.

In the area of race relations, the Supreme Court played a vital role in the development of national policy. Its decisions in the 1950s and 1960s placed a stamp of legitimacy upon claims for equality on the part of black citizens that was crucial to the development of organizations and activities that eventually succeeded not only in the streets but in the Congress as well. Though a solid consensus against *de jure* segregation did subsequently emerge, the Court played a crucial role in this process rather than merely reflecting developments in other political arenas.

In the area of criminal procedure, the Court developed a federal constitutional code of criminal justice, ranging from initial contacts of suspects with police, through the development of evidence, the adjudication of guilt or innocence, the imposition of penalties, the appellate process, and the treatment of offenders by probation and correction agencies. From a wealth of cases reflecting the diverse policies of various jurisdictions the Court produced a series of rules aimed at vindicating the adversary system and vouchsafing substantive and procedural rights ignored in many localities. Surely uniformity of treatment has not been achieved in doctrinal, much less behavioral, terms. Yet the Court has moved us toward policies that were not emerging from state legislatures or Congress. The criminal justice cases illustrate an issue area in which the Supreme Court itself took up the burden of being the major advocate for a group in the society that was politically powerless and subject to deprivation of basic procedural rights.

This brief review of some of the Court's work in the area of state and local statutes and practice suggests several issues relevant to Dahl's analysis. First and most important, the policy questions at stake in these cases are not narrow, local or regional issues. In all of these areas the policy promulgated by the Court, although emerging in the context of cases arising out of states or localities, was directly aimed at and had an effect upon governmental activities throughout the nation. *Miranda* v. *Arizona*, *Gideon* v. *Wainwright*, *Reynolds* v. *Sims*, *Abington Township* v. *Schempp*, *Cooley* v. *Board of Wardens*, *Memoirs* v. *Massachusetts*, *Brown* v. *Board of Education* all came from cities or states. Yet the policies that were enunciated had relevance to the whole nation in ways much more manifest than many of the cases involving federal legislation with which Dahl deals.

Did the Court prevail? Was it reversed by a subsequent act of the law-making majority? Did the Court itself take back what it had said? In some areas, these questions are difficult to answer at this time, for a few of the decisions are recent. In terms of one crude indicator, the Court has not been substantially reversed in any of these areas by the passage of legislation or constitutional amendment. In some areas, though, the pattern Dahl suggests does not seem apposite: unpopular decisions became part of the country's political agenda, and changes in political regimes affected recruitment to the Court. The replacement of the Warren Court by the Burger Court is to some extent verification of his thesis. Recent decisions in the areas of obscenity, reapportionment, and criminal justice suggest modifications in policy to some extent congruent with the demands of Court opponents. So the thrust of this argument is not that new evidence unambiguously indicates a role for the Court that is radically different from the one that Dahl suggests. The Court *is* a member of ruling alliances and does respond to others. But examination of the state and local cases does reveal that the arena in which the Court makes policy is substantially broader than the limited area Dahl selects for discussion. Moreover, it suggests that the Court can and does get its way a good deal more frequently than his analysis implies.

Assuming that the Court has not been reversed and has not reversed itself in several important issue areas arising out of state litigation—a plausible account of the areas of civil rights, religion, and the basic thrust of policy in criminal justice and reapportionment—what are we to make of this fact in assessing the relative influence of the Court in our political system? One of the problems with dealing with such cases—and one of the reasons why they were excluded from Dahl's analysis—is that it is, to be sure, difficult to make the determination of the preferences of the national majority that Dahl says is necessary in order to decide whether the Court's policy was influential. Yet these cases did involve issues of broad national significance, and none of the decisions was struck down by legislation or constitutional amendment, even though such efforts were attempted. Thus, in formal terms the Court seems to have "won" (setting aside for the moment the possibility that new appointments may lead the Court to step back to some degree in some issue areas). On the other hand, Dahl's analysis might suggest that the very lack of overriding legislation indicates that the Court was not acting contrary to the preferences of a law-making majority. The difficulty with this argument, of course, is that it places the Court in a no-win situation: if it acts first, regardless of what happens subsequently, it is judged not to have exercised influence.

Another facet of Dahl's argument is relevant to this issue. He suggests that, in general, the major function of the Court, as a member of the ruling alliance at any particular time, is to "confer legitimacy on the fundamental policies of the successful coalition." He goes on to note that at certain periods—when the ruling coalition in an issue domain is weakened and decaying or when a stable coalition has not emerged in the issue area—the Court may "at great risk to its legitimacy powers" intervene and even "succeed in establishing policy." The Court, in such situations, is likely to be successful only when its "action conforms to and reinforces a widespread set of explicit or implicit norms held by political leadership." Dahl refers to the work of the Court in dealing with civil rights as an example of this ability of the Court to intervene when stable coalitions do not exist.

The areas in which the Court has been particularly active in recent years—civil rights, reapportionment, criminal justice, religion, obscenity, privacy—do seem to have been characterized by substantial division both within the political stratum and in the society at large about the most preferable policy alternatives. The Court's intervention has been followed by substantial controversy and attempts to modify its policy as well as attacks on its institutional powers. Both types of opposition have been unsuccessful, and the activities of other members of the political leadership stratum have been of great importance. Lyndon Johnson's activities as majority leader during the late 1950s were crucial in thwarting attempts to modify decisions dealing with loyalty-security programs and to punish the Court for its libertarian decisions in the 1956–57 terms. John F. Kennedy's support for the bible-reading and school prayer decisions was, again, an important element in cooling off attacks on the Court as an institution and attempts to reverse its policy by constitutional amendment.

Assuming, though, that many of the Court's most important contributions to public policy in recent years have involved situations in which the Court was appealing to norms implicitly held by other influential policy makers and that the ability of the Court as an institution and the policies it has promulgated to survive have required support by others, what are we to make of these facts? Dahl's argument stresses the importance of the values and activities of other policy makers rather than the influence exercised by the Court. In one sense he is of course correct, for no institution can successfully carry the day when others are cohesively arrayed against it. But the overall impression that his analysis yields is somewhat misleading. He argues that the Court's activities are best understood by examining the constellation of other political interests willing to support its policies even though they were not united and powerful enough to promulgate such policies on their own. An equally plausible interpretation of such events would suggest that the crucial role was played by the Court, by its willingness to set forth policies that other state and federal institutions were unwilling or unable to promulgate. To be sure, support for such policies by others, or at least their grudging acquiescence, was crucial to the viability of the Court's policies (just as the Court's acquiescence is often crucial to the success of policies promulgated by the law-making majority). But if we are to identify the crucial participants in the policy-development process, to minimize the role of the Court, as Dahl is inclined to do, provides a view of policy making that does not do justice to the potential or actual contributions of the Court.

In sum, there are several difficulties with the evidence that Dahl gathers and the ways in which he utilizes it. The coding rules he employs have a certain asymmetry such that much of his own evidence is excluded from analysis and if further relevant information were gathered it would not be possible to conclude that the Court has been influential. He also excludes from consideration a large body of evidence that seems highly relevant to determining the Court's role in national policy-making. Consideration of this evidence indicates a substantially more influential role than Dahl's argument admits.

The Court and Policy Making

Dahl's analysis is based upon the premise that policy making is most fruitfully analyzed in terms of concepts like influence or power, a view that the crucial questions deal with winners and losers. The argument that Dahl sets out to confront and evaluate—the view of the Court as a protector of fundamental minority rights against majority tyranny—is itself framed in terms of influence. Moreover, Dahl's article was written at a time when he was developing and conducting his research on community power. In his article dealing with the "ruling elite model" published in 1958, Dahl asserts that "one cannot compare the relative influence of two actors who always perform identical actions with respect to the group influenced. What this means as a practical matter is that ordinarily one can test for differences in influence only where there are cases of differences in initial preferences." [13]

If one can judge relative influence of various individuals, groups, and institutions only when there are disagreements among them, focus upon Court declarations that federal legislation is unconstitutional appears to make sense. From this basic posture about the way in which to study influence, Dahl moves to a view of the policy-making process that focuses upon disputes among policy makers and determines who prevails and who does not. His view of the way to measure influence shades into a conception of policy making that stresses its zero-sum characteristics.

There are several difficulties with Dahl's account of policy making and the role of the Court in it. Some deal with his specific conclusions about the role of the Court; others center about the relatively narrow conception of policy making that underlies his argument. [14]

To begin, let us assume that the winners and losers view that Dahl utilizes is a reasonable way to conceive of the policy-making process. Dahl's basic conclusion is that, except for its important role as a legitimator, the Court does not play an especially influential role in national policy making. There are three major difficulties with this view, the first two of which may be disposed of briefly. First, as argued above, the exclusive focus upon cases in which federal statutes are declared unconstitutional ignores a good deal of what the Court in fact contributes to national policy making. Second, Dahl does not place sufficient emphasis upon those cases in which the Court succeeded in delaying policies for periods of up to 25 years. He focuses upon the dénouement—upon the ultimate rejection of the Court's policy—while an equally salient feature of these examples is the extensive period of time in which the law-making majority was prevented from working its will.

The third and most important objection to Dahl's characterization of the influence of the Court—assuming that we accept the winners and losers approach—is that he engages in a somewhat misleading contrast in comparing the influence of the Court to that of the law-making majority. Dahl concludes that the Court does not typically play a decisive role in national policy making. "Acting solely by itself with no support from the President and Congress, the Court is almost powerless to affect the course of national policy." He essentially stops here, contenting himself with an effective antidote to the mythology that the Court stands as a lonely bastion single handedly thwarting tyrannical majorities from trampling upon the rights of despised minorities.

Although he does not address the question in detail, at this level of generality such a proposition is true of all institutions of government as well as other groups and individuals in the society. Certainly this comports with Dahl's emphasis upon the building of coalitions, upon the notion of minorities' rule, and upon the great restraints that such stable coalitions place upon the policy choices that may be made at any point in time. But because he frames the question in terms of who wins or loses—Court versus President and Congress—and because he does not in this article emphasize the degree to which *no* institution is really capable of the decisive role he argues the Court fails to possess, the impression of the Court's relative insignificance is cemented. Thus, the framing of the question as one of relative influence produces a view of policy making in which such influence seems to be the touch-stone of significant participation, and this produces a view that the Court, except in its legitimizing role, simply is not a particularly important participant in national policy making.

The arguments offered above suggest that even within the framework for analyzing policy making that Dahl adopts, there is room for disagreement with his basic conclusion that the Court does not frequently exercise an important influence on the national political outcomes. There is another set of objections that center about the rather narrow conception of policy making that seems to inform Dahl's analysis.

The policy-making process involves more than clashes among political coalitions and institutions, more than winners and losers.[15] The winners-and-losers view implies that there are decisive outcomes to disputes about issues—that among the variety of policies that might be selected, one outcome ultimately prevails. It implies (1) that when interests or institutions clash, the position of one side or another prevails; (2) that the outcomes in policy making that occur as a result of such disagreements somehow "settle" disputes; and (3) that the crucial contributions to policy making consist in promulgating policies that prevail. All of these are implicit in the conception of policy making that informs Dahl's approach to the Supreme Court, and none is adequate.

Dahl argues that when the Court clashes with the law-making majority we can assess its significance in policy making by examining whose policy prevailed. The consistent "winner" in such clashes is judged to be influential and the loser to be a less significant contributor to the policy-making process. This view assumes that when such clashes occur the policy of the "winner" is adopted and the policy of the "loser" is discarded. In fact, when such clashes occur, the policies that eventually emerge are affected by the interaction among institutions that takes place.

For example, when we examine the role of the Court in policy making in the area of economic regulation in the first third of this century, Dahl's view suggests that the Court, although delaying certain policies, was ultimately not influential because its laissez-faire policy was discarded. But one could argue that the Court played a particularly important role in this episode of policy development. Not only for the period in which its decisions thwarted the law-making majority, but also for its role in leading other groups and interests in society to come to grips with laissez-faire economic policy and the interests that supported it. The laissez-faire decisions contributed to the development of the coalition that led to the election of Roosevelt, the legislation of the New Deal, and the eventual discarding of the Court's policies in favor of a conception of public welfare policy that had not heretofore enjoyed the political base it subsequently developed. In this way, both the nature of subsequent policies—their breadth, their statutory and administrative form— and the constellation of political forces in the society were shaped by the activities of the Court. What emerged at the "end" of this struggle was quite different from what had been proposed by the law-making majority at its beginning.

To suggest another example, suppose that changes in Court decisions or a constitutional amendment were to "reject" the Supreme Court's policies since 1957 dealing with the freedom to distribute and possess "obscene" materials. Two features of this hypothetical case suggest difficulties with the notion of examining winners and losers in policy making. First of all, it is hard to imagine what the supposed "winning" policy might be that we could compare with the "losing" policy of the Court. Because there was almost no federal constitutional doctrine on the subject of obscenity before 1957, almost any new "winning" policy would produce a policy outcome different from the pre-1957 status quo.

Second, suppose the new "winning" policy permitted states and localities a substantially greater discretion to restrict the dissemination of such materials. Surely events of the past 18 years affect what types of material would remain available. Experience with the availability of pornography—for example, the fact that substantial numbers of people in the society have come to enjoy it or to believe that it is less harmful than they once believed—would probably produce policies permitting substantially greater availability than existed in the pre-1957 period. Moreover, the political and economic interests with an investment in protecting the freedom to distribute and profit from such materials have greatly increased in recent years and would also operate to dampen to some degree the ability of the "anti-obscenity" interests to impose restrictive policies. In this fashion, the very enunciation of a policy by one institution is likely to affect future policies, even if the original policy is "reversed." The notion of a "winning" and a "losing" policy when institutions clash imposes an artificial distinction that obscures a dynamic process in which even "losers" contribute importantly to outcomes that eventually emerge.

The second objection is related to the first, and it simply states that many of the issues in which national political institutions become involved are not "settled" but continue to recur. Conflicts among political institutions produce not "winning" and "losing" policies, but rather tentative solutions that themselves become the basis for future policy making. Consider, for example, recent developments in national policy dealing with racial equality, legislative apportionment, the relationship between church and state, and criminal procedure. All of these were issues that had long smoldered beneath the surface of American politics. Regardless of the decisions of the Warren Court, these issues have surely not been resolved: we have not succeeded in defining, much less in embracing, racial equality; malapportionment remains a disputed issue; religious practices continue in many schools; and the typical criminal defendant does not enjoy the rights that the Court has doctrinally afforded. Yet all of these issues have become increasingly salient features of the national political agenda in the past twenty years; what was latent conflict has become manifest, and both the general public and political institutions have been forced to confront the policy questions involved. The dénouement is not clear, any more than it was twenty years ago, for these are questions that our society presumably will always have to confront. Though at various times one position or another may carry the day, ultimate resolutions are not discovered, and the Court, like other political institutions, has and will continue to make important contributions to the "solutions" that carry the day, become the subject for further debate, and are modified or rejected.

This suggests a third point. The policy-making process—and the exercise of influence within it—involves more than producing outcomes that prevail. Providing effective access to participants who wish to take part in decision making, placing issues on the agenda of public opinion and of other political institutions, providing an imprimatur of legitimacy to one side or another that may affect its ability to attract adherents, mobilize resources, and build institutions—these are all important parts of the policy-making process that may get lost if we pay attention only to winners and losers. One reason that courts may have particular importance in placing issues on the agenda of other political institutions and in development of interest groups is that "success" in a court requires only that a party convince a relatively small number of decision makers. At the trial level, success requires only a favorable decision from a single individual; at the Supreme Court level, success requires the approval of five of nine. Thus, interests that lack resources for effective influence in legislative, executive, or administrative arenas may find the legal system an attractive spot in which to attempt to influence public policy. "Success" in a court then becomes useful in participation in these other arenas—the court's decision may require other institutions to come to grips with an issue they have ignored; the legitimacy conferred by victory in court may be useful in attracting members and resources and mobilizing others. For example, the civil rights decisions culminating in *Brown* contributed to the growth of civil rights organizations like SCLC, CORE, and SNCC that became active in the streets as well as in the Congress. The right-to-counsel decisions contributed to the development of a more respectable criminal bar and widespread use of organizations like Public Defender offices that have become active in behalf of criminal defendants not only in trial courts but in appellate courts, the legal community, and legislative settings as well.

The burden of this section, then, is that the view of policy making that informs Dahl's analysis is too narrow. Even in Dahl's own terms, he does not take account of the Court's influence on public policy. Moreover, the winners-and-losers approach leads to a view of policy making that diverts attention from a variety of ways in which the Supreme Court makes significant contributions to national policy making.

Notes

1. Robert A. Dahl, "Decision-Making in a Democracy: The Supreme Court as a National Policy-Maker," *Journal of Public Law* 6 (Fall 1957), 279–295. Dahl integrated and somewhat revised this article as a chapter in two editions of his American government text. See Robert A. Dahl, *Pluralist Democracy in the United States* (Chicago: Rand McNally & Company, 1967), Chapter 6; in the 1972 edition, called *Democracy in the United States,* see chapter 16. Because the original is the clearest and most widely read version of his arguments, I shall focus upon it here.

2. 400 U.S. 112 (1970).

3. *Washington* v. *Legrant,* 394 U.S. 618 (1969). *Grisham* v. *Hagan,* 361 U.S. 278 (1960); *McElroy* v. *Guargliardo,* 360 U.S. 281 (1960); *Kinsella* v. *Singelton,* 361 U.S. 234 (1960). *Lamont* v. *Postmaster General,* 381 U.S. 301 (1965).

4. Dahl's "ruling elite model" article, published in 1958, argues that influence can only be measured effectively in such situations. See "A Critique of the Ruling Elite Model," *American Political Science Review* 52 (June 1958), 463–69.

5. 2 Dall, 419 (1793).

6. 4 Wheat 316 (1819).

7. 9 Wheat 1 (1824).

8. 12 How. 299 (1852).

9. 369 U.S. 186 (1962).

10. 377 U.S. 533 (1964).

11. *Mahan* v. *Howell,* 410 U.S. 315 (1973); *Gaffney* v. *Cummings,* 412 U.S. 735 (1973).

12. *Engel* v. *Vitale,* 370 U.S. 421 (1962); *Abington Township* v. *Schempp,* 374 U.S. 203 (1963).

13. Dahl, "A Critique of the Ruling Elite Model," p. 464.

14. I shall not discuss here the problem of taking account of "anticipated reactions" in discussing the relative influence of the Court in the policy-making process. It seems plausible to argue, though, that just as the Court in its decisions may take account of the breadth and intensity of support for various policies, members of Congress may take into account their predictions of potential rulings by the Court in making choices about what legislation to pass. For a discussion of the role of constitutional considerations in the legislative decision-making process, see Donald G. Morgan, *Congress and the Constitution* (Cambridge, Mass.: Harvard University Press, 1966); and Paul Brest, "The Conscientious Legislator's Guide to Constitutional Interpretation," *Stanford Law Review* 27 (February 1975), 585–601.

15. Much of Dahl's work is consistent with this view and has added to our understanding of the ways in which these processes operate. Yet in the article under consideration here, a narrower view of the nature of the policy-making process emerges from the fashion in which he formulates the question and gathers his data.

54

Legitimacy, Realigning
Elections, and the
Supreme Court

David Adamany

. . .

The symbolic quality of the Constitution and the Supreme Court has . . . long ago become a commonplace in the literature of law and political science. But the hands of creative scholars have recently bent it to new purposes. Jerome Frank and Thurman Arnold intended to strip away the mystery of law so that people might govern themselves free of its irrational appeals. Edward S. Corwin and Max Lerner exposed and dispelled the myth of Constitution and Court to open the way for the New Deal vehicle of popular, as opposed to judicial, will. Karl Llewellyn wanted "an intelligent reconstruction of our constitutional law theory"[1] around the view that the Constitution was an operating contemporary institution, subject to popular controls. And Alpheus T. Mason's pleas were for open criticism and debate of the merit of judge-made policy rather than awe-stricken acceptance of judicial decisions.

The unmasking of judicial power—so ardently sought by these friends of popular policymaking—has for Robert A. Dahl . . . revealed an entirely new justification for judicial review. Dahl . . . concedes that the Supreme Court is a national policymaker; dismisses on grounds of both logic and history the claim that the Court is a "democratic" vehicle for safeguarding minority rights; finds that virtually all "important" congressional policies struck down by the Court within four years of enactment, and thus presumably while the sponsoring lawmaking majority was still intact, subsequently are vindicated by further congressional action or judicial reversal; ascribes this mainly to the President's appointment power, noting that on the average a new justice is appointed every 22 months; and concludes finally that "the policy views dominant on the Court are never for long out of line with the policy views dominant among the lawmaking majorities of the United States."

This line of reasoning is not entirely free from difficulty, however. If judicial review cannot be theoretically squared with democracy and if the Court is defended mainly because it quickly harmonizes its policies with the preferences of lawmaking majorities, then why have judicial review at all? The American polity would be different without judicial review only to the extent that lawmaking majorities would never, as happens now, be delayed or, in a handful of cases, obstructed in effecting major policies.

Reprinted by permission from the *Wisconsin Law Review* (1973). Copyright © 1973 by the University of Wisconsin. Most footnotes have been omitted.

Dahl responds in several directions. "National politics in the United States, . . ." he says, "is dominated by relatively cohesive alliances that endure for long periods of time." The Supreme Court could not, except in rare cases, sustain policies at odds with those of the dominant coalition. It might, however, occasionally take policy initiatives when the coalition is so unstable on key issues that no lawmaking majority can be assembled for any policy option, or when there is adequate support to sustain the Court's decision against attempts to override it. Why judicial enactment of policies which cannot garner a law-making majority is appropriate in a democracy remains unanswered. Even where the conflict over policy is a struggle only among minorities, a situation Dahl suggests is typical, Supreme Court policymaking cannot be viewed as democratic, for it neither advances majority aspirations nor necessarily promotes the position of the most numerous minority.

The Supreme Court, Dahl goes on to say, "is an essential part of the political leadership and possesses some bases of power of its own, the most important of which is the unique legitimacy attributed to its interpretations of the Constitution." It is this special legitimacy that defines the Court's role as a national decisionmaker. "The main task of the Court is to confer legitimacy on the fundamental policies of the successful coalition." It does this, presumably, by declaring presidential and congressional actions constitutional.

But the Court's role does not stop there. . . . If . . . the Court's role [is] as a defender of minorities or an agent of external standards of justice, then there is a contradiction with Dahl's earlier concession that "no amount of tampering with democratic theory can conceal the fact that a system in which policy preferences of minorities prevail over majorities is at odds with the traditional criteria for distinguishing a democracy from other political systems."

Furthermore, Dahl's own analysis of judicial vetoes of congressional legislation does not support the proposition that the Supreme Court legitimizes basic rights. . . .

. . .

Dahl's survey, made in 1958, does not take into account the Court's recent role as a defender of disadvantaged minorities. But the minority-rights activism of the Warren Court is already fading; that one 15 year period will not counterbalance the whole of the Court's historical record recited by Dahl; and even in this modern role, judicial review will still not square with democratic theory as Dahl postulates it.

It is difficult to know, then, what Dahl means when he defends the Court as a legiti-mator of rights, liberties, restraints, and obligations which are fundamental to a democ-racy. These issues come to the Court's attention in only two situations. First, the lawmak-ing majority expands such rights by legislation (for example, the Voting Rights Act of 1965), in which case the Court's approval is indistinguishable from its usual legitimization of legislation and its disapproval, as Dahl himself concedes, has been substantially damag-ing to the cause of liberty throughout history. Second, minorities may seek judicial protec-tion from legislation which trammels rights but "legitimization" of rights, liberties, re-straints, and obligations in such instances means striking down legislation to protect freedom, which Dahl concedes is not justified by democratic theory and which has not been the Court's usual conduct in history.

Thus, neither Dahl's assertion that the Court may exercise leadership in an unstable coalition nor his admonition that the justices legitimize rights or liberties will square with his own definition of democracy and his own rendering of the Court's historical use of the power of judicial review. All that remains is Dahl's bare assertion that the Supreme Court's special role in American democracy is freighting majority policies with the special legitimacy it derives from the public reverence for its guardianship of the Constitution. Thus does the much assailed myth of Constitution and Court become the handmaiden of majority rule.

. . .

I. What is Legitimacy?

Central to the modern resurrection of that myth is the concept of legitimacy. . . .

Seymour M. Lipset defines legitimacy in political systems as "the capacity . . . to engender and maintain the belief that the existing political institutions are the most appropriate ones for the society."[2] He distinguishes this from "effectiveness," the system's performance in satisfying societal expectations. Legitimacy, then, is not instrumental, but evaluative. It lies in the eye of the beholder, who believes the Supreme Court is endowed with the "right" to make decisions because it follows the Constitution, has traditionally exercised authority, and is therefore an appropriate decisionmaking institution for his society.

This definition sets aside the content of decisions . . . which is conceptually distinct. Content legitimacy rests on agreement with the substance of policies rather than awe of the source of decision. It therefore lies between symbolic legitimacy and effectiveness. Agreement with its policy may heighten regard for an institution's "right" to act. At the same time, approval of policy may contribute to a perception that an institution is effective, that it meets felt needs.

But content legitimacy is not the "legitimacy" expounded by Black, Dahl, or Bickel, for they anticipate that the Court's legitimacy-conferring power will create acceptance of policy among those who oppose or are neutral about its substance and heighten acceptance among those already committed to its content. Robert G. McCloskey captured the distinction, saying that:

> the Supreme Court has historically been blessed with two kinds of supporters—those who venerate it and are prepared to defend it as the symbol of continuity and fairness who are attached to the idea of the rule of law; and those who happen to be gratified by the course of policy the judges are pursuing at the moment.[3]

It is the former attitude, symbolic legitimacy, rather than the latter, content legitimacy, that is the foundation upon which the elegant judicial mansions of Black, Dahl, and Bickel have been so carefully constructed.

Distinguishing these concepts—symbolic legitimacy, content legitimacy, and effectiveness—should not, however, obscure their interplay. An institution's overall influence depends on all of them. Lipset suggested this relationship when he said that ". . . prolonged effectiveness over a number of generations may give legitimacy to a political system."[4]

We might say, then, that levels of symbolic legitimacy are affected by the content and effectiveness of constitutional decisions. The individual who strongly or consistently disapproves policies of a legitimate institution may reconcile this conflict by asserting that the institution has forsaken its traditional function or that it has broken loose from the rules that gave it "legality." Similarly, an institution which is consistently ineffective in meeting deeply felt needs may ultimately be discredited as no longer appropriate for the society.

Dahl stresses the potential for such trade-offs when the Court advances its own preferences rather than legitimizing policies established by the lawmaking majority. "There are times when the coalition is unstable with respect to certain key policies; *at very great risk to its legitimacy powers,* the Court can intervene in such cases and may even succeed in establishing policy." Certainly the *Dred Scott Case* illustrates the point: So repugnant was the decision to many Northerners that the Court's "right" to make decisions was eroded in their minds.

Although they do not precisely define the concept of legitimacy on which their arguments turn, it is plain from their texts that a special kind of legitimacy—that is, symbolic legitimacy—is the Atlas holding up the constitutional worlds of Charles Black, Robert Dahl, and Alexander Bickel. . . .

. . .

Thus symbolic legitimacy—an evaluative perception by the people that Supreme Court mandates should be accepted because the justices, as guardians of the Constitution, act by legal right, because they exercise a traditional authority, and because they constitute an appropriate societal institution—coincides with the sometimes thinly, sometimes fully elaborated concept of legitimacy advanced by Black, Dahl, and Bickel.

II. Can the Court Legitimize?

Whether the legitimacy-conferring function justifies judicial review or judicial self-restraint, it rests on an assumption about the facts: That the Supreme Court has the capacity to and does throw the cloak of legitimacy over governmental actions. Yet none who bottom their arguments on the Court's legitimacy-conferring capacity offer the slightest empirical basis for its reality. . . .

Without assuming the burden of disproof, . . . review [of] the bits and pieces of evidence . . . reenforce doubt and, indeed, suggest the Court's *incapacity* to legitimize governmental action. . . . [Here follows the public opinion evidence concerning support for the Court.]

. . .

III. The Legitimizing Function and Realigning Elections

Let us suppose arguendo that scholars pondering speculatively in their studies have better insight into the public mind than do survey researchers, that the Supreme Court does indeed have a legitimacy-conferring capacity. Such a concession in no way frees the legitimacy-conferring function from theoretical and practical difficulties, especially as it is advanced by Charles Black and Robert Dahl as a stabilizing force in a democratic society. These troublesome elements become most evident when judicial review is placed in the framework of American election cycles.

Political scientists now recognize that most voters hold long-term party allegiances which create stable party divisions during long periods of American history. Elections are classified to acknowledge continuity and change in party alignments in the electorate and in party control of government. Maintaining elections are those in which the majority party retains the loyalty of its electorate and wins the presidency. A deviating election sees long-term voter allegiance unchanged but witnesses a defeat for the majority party because of short-term factors such as temporarily persuasive issues or candidate personalities. Converting elections are characterized by substantial shifts in party allegiance in the electorate, but the majority status of the dominant party is preserved and it wins at the polls. Realigning elections, finally, occur when voters revise their party loyalties in such a way as to create a new majority party and to give it control of the government.

It is realigning elections that create the gravest theoretical and historical difficulties for the asserted legitimacy-conferring function of the Supreme Court. Such elections ordinarily occur in response to major social upheavals that discredit old regimes and cause voters to shift their allegiances to an alternate set of party leaders. Those swept into office by such electoral tides attempt to respond to popular discontents by bold programs addressing the sources of unrest. At the onset of a realigning period, which may actually take several elections as groups of voters break former party ties and give their allegiances elsewhere, the effectiveness of government in meeting deeply felt public needs is low. This ineffectiveness corrodes to some extent the legitimacy of governmental arrangements and institutions; and stability is, as Seymour M. Lipset points out, endangered. The actions of the new regime are ordinarily designed to consolidate electoral gains by responding to public concerns, and they simultaneously have the result, by actual or apparent effectiveness, of increasing public confidence in government.

It is at such critical moments in history that the Supreme Court, according to its defenders, most importantly plays a legitimacy-conferring role. Charles Black points out that the Court's endorsement of the New Deal after 1937 was essential for reconciling that large minority whose reservations went beyond the merits of Rooseveltian policy to the constitutionality of the program.[5] A similar task fell to the justices in other great periods of governmental change. Dahl's analysis emphasizes the Court's legitimization of rising party coalitions. . . .

This interpretation of history in support of the legitimacy-conferring function seems flawed. I concede that eventually a new majority coalition will win control of the Court. But the moment of crisis, when stability is most impaired, occurs during the realigning period itself. The newly instituted regime is challenged to meet public needs and restore public confidence because both the effectiveness and the legitimacy of government are in doubt. Yet at precisely this moment the Supreme Court is most likely to impose a barrier to both goals. A new political coalition usually inherits a Court fully staffed by the opposition party. . . .

Even if vacancies occur at average intervals of 22 months, as calculated by Dahl, the President who leads the newly emergent majority party does not win working control on a nine member Court during the period of most severe crisis. Furthermore, there might be fewer opportunities than usual for presidential appointments if justices of the displaced majority party tend to cling to their seats, echoing the sentiment of Chief Justice William Howard Taft, expressed during Herbert Hoover's presidency, that "[A]s long as . . . I am able to answer in my place, I must stay on the Court in order to prevent the Bolsheviks from getting control. . . ."[6] And, finally, does not the new coalition find that, to respond to the turmoil in society, it must attempt to overcome the judicially created barriers, even if compelled to assail the Supreme Court itself?

The Court, then, might easily be viewed as blocking the effectiveness of government in periods of crisis by the exercise of its "checking" power. But it has an even more subtle role which implicates its presumed legitimizing capacity. Charles Black has insisted that the legitimizing function can be carried out only if the Court has and occasionally uses the power to declare laws unconstitutional. . . . But is it not also true that the capacity to legitimize is the capacity to delegitimize? And it follows that at moments of crisis and realignment, the Court's opposition to the popular branches may reach beyond checking their actions to undermining their legitimacy. Too narrow is Black's view that the Supreme Court legitimizes only when it validates actions of the popular branches, for expressions other than validation may express legitimacy. . . . And the converse is also true: It is not mere checking that delegitimizes, but any conflict which shows the guardians of the Constitution in a posture hostile to the politicians who man the elected branches.

Humpty Dumpty, once shattered, may not be so easily put back together; and it would not be surprising if fragile legitimacy too, once smashed, is difficult to repair. The new coalition's eventual appointment of a majority of the justices and their validation of its policies may not so quickly restore the legitimacy withdrawn by the court in its conflict with the popular branches in the immediate aftermath of a realigning election. Indeed, since the legitimacy-conferring function necessarily assumes a reasonably alert electorate and because the popular branches may often be compelled in realigning periods to assail a recalcitrant judiciary, the eventual coming around of the Court—its eventual validation and other approvals of popular branch policies—may have more the appearance of surrender to superior force than of legitimization.

In the main, these speculations, rather than those advanced by Professor Black, seem more nearly consistent with the history of relations between the Court and majority coalitions in realigning periods. Although electoral realignments occur during a series of elections rather than in a single balloting and despite some scholarly contentiousness about just which elections constituted realignments, the best analyses cite the election of Jefferson in 1800, of Jackson in 1828, of Lincoln in 1860, and of Franklin Delano Roosevelt in 1932 as the moments in realigning periods at which the leadership of new majority coalitions actually took public office.[7]

Thomas Jefferson swore the oath of office facing a Supreme Court of six unsympathetic Federalists. Lincoln found seven Democrats, one Whig, and one vacant seat on the high Bench. Roosevelt inherited a Court divided between five Republicans, including one unwilling to interpose judicial power against New Deal policies (Justice Harlan F. Stone) and four Democrats, of whom Pierce Butler and James C. McReynolds were steadfast conservatives. Thus he counted an unfavorable margin of six to three. Jackson was greeted by a less clear situation because the three Democratic-Republicans were not necessarily sympathetic and the three Federalists not necessarily hostile—party lines being fluid and increasingly meaningless in the period before Jackson's inauguration. It cannot be doubted, however, that the justices were not in tune in style, ideology, or regional orientation with the new "popular" coalition that Jackson was building. In each instance, therefore, new presidents correctly perceived the Court as dominated overwhelmingly by opposition partisans.

Jefferson named three justices, the third in 1807 to fill a newly created seat, never winning a Republican majority on the Court. Jackson was more fortunate; he appointed five members of a seven man bench. But three of his appointments were in the last two years of his tenure and his first, John McLean, in 1829, was a Whig. Lincoln was also fortunate: He named Samuel Miller to a vacancy existing at his inauguration, replaced three of the eight sitting justices, and named War Democrat Stephen Field to a new tenth seat. Five justices in five years constitutes an heroic exception to the ordinary pace of appointments. . . .

Democratic Justices Samuel Nelson, Robert Grier, Nathan Clifford, and, until 1865, John Catron, constituted a potential bloc which, in concert with Field and Lincoln's politically ambitious Chief Justice Salmon P. Chase, menaced the policies of lawmaking majorities, especially the Radical Congress, until 1870. In his first two terms Franklin Roosevelt actually appointed five justices, but not a single one until after the old Court's obstruction of the New Deal had led to the court-packing fight of 1937.

These "realigning presidents" actually had greater appointment opportunities than the average, but because vacancies occurred slowly and because the pre-existing membership of the Court was so dominated by the other party, their appointees constituted majorities, if at all, only very late in their second terms. Furthermore, because some justices—estimated by Robert Scigliano as one in four[8]—stray far from the general ideological position of their appointing presidents, even a slim majority attained late in the second term could not be counted upon to validate and thus legitimize the new majority's program. . . .

There is, finally, slight evidence that justices are more reluctant to resign after a realigning election. Of the 92 cases in which men have left the highest bench, 44 (48 percent) were retirements or resignations. Ten justices vacated their chairs under Jefferson, Jackson, and Lincoln, but only three (30 percent) by resignation or retirement. Roosevelt by contrast, had three resignations and one death during his first two terms; but the first retirement (Willis Van Devanter) did not occur until 1937, after the Hughes-Roberts switch that reversed the Court's policy toward the New Deal, and it was followed rapidly by the retirements of Justices Sutherland and Brandeis and the death of Justice Butler. Thus, when the President represented a newly forged majority coalition, justices have seemed somewhat more reluctant to leave the bench, at least before the point when judicial resistance to the new regime has been overwhelmed.

Command of the Court by men of the old majority, slow turnover on the bench, and the added reluctance of justices to resign after a new lawmaking majority is inaugurated all set the stage for conflict between the Supreme Court and the new, dominant electoral coalitions. There is nothing to be gained by rehearsing here all the scenes and subplots in those struggles. But a broad rendering of the scenarios . . . [shows] that each realigning election has been followed by conflict which somewhat discredited and sometimes checked the lawmaking majority. And each scenario's dénouement was a clash that left doubtful the Court's capacity ultimately to legitimize the new regime and its policies.

[The author presents detailed analyses of the Court during the realignments of 1800, 1828, 1860, and 1932.]

. . .

What conclusions are fairly drawn from these historical vignettes? First, each new party coalition took office in a condition of tension with the judiciary. Prior judicial decisions were repugnant to the ideology of the new regime. The Court—indeed, the entire judiciary—was drawn mainly from the ranks of partisan and ideological opponents. There is no evidence that "realigning presidents" were denied the same opportunity to make appointments as other chief executives; and only the scantiest support can be drummed up for the proposition that justices of the old coalition held more tenaciously to their posts after realigning elections than did other justices in other times. Nonetheless, the adherents of the repudiated party so dominated the Court that the new coalition's chief executive either was unable to appoint a majority of friendly justices or at least was unable to do so until well into his term.

Second, after two realigning elections—those of 1860 and 1932—the Court used its checking power to thwart significantly the policies of the new coalition. In all four realigning election periods the executive and legislative leadership firmly believed that the Court would disrupt their program. Certainly in the former two cases, and perhaps in all four, the capacity of the newly elected majority effectively to undertake actions they deemed necessary to relieve the national crisis and preserve the stability of our democratic system was impaired.

Third, after each realigning election there was intense and highly visible conflict between the Court and the lawmaking majority. Professor Black measures legitimization by judicial validation of popular branch programs; but it must also follow that the checking function involves "delegitimization" of the popular branches and their policies. Nor does the legitimizing aspect of judicial review end with the validating and checking activities of the Court. There are other relations between the elected branches (or the States) and the Supreme Court—not every expression of agreement or hostility need be manifested in finally adjudicated cases. And if legitimacy inheres in any of the Court's actions it inheres in them all—just as the President's ceremonial role as chief of state is implicated whenever he acts as legislative leader, administrative chief, party politician, and so forth. Thus, any conflict, whether in litigation or otherwise, between the justices and elected officials brings into play the Court's unique standing as arbiter of the Constitution, its potential to legitimize or delegitimize policies and regimes. The recurring clashes between the Court and the popular branches in realigning periods therefore erode regime legitimacy, the appearance that the popular branches are meeting the crisis within their constitutional mandate.

Finally, in each case the clash between the justices and the lawmaking majority rose to such fury that elected officials felt compelled to assail the Court. Sometimes this involved defiance, either in fact or appearance. At others it spawned attempts, twice successful, to alter the Court's size, jurisdiction, or decisional process. In 1805 it led to the only impeachment of a Supreme Court justice. I will return shortly to the diversion of energies and resources of new coalitions that accompanies these battles over judicial power. But it is enough to conclude here that the legitimacy conferring capacity of the Supreme Court is vastly reduced by these battles. When the Court finally comes into line with the new majority, it appears to capitulate to overpowering force rather than freely to legitimize. And those who disagree with the new regime's policies, who must be persuaded of its legitimacy, and who would be attentive enough to comprehend legitimizing action by the justices must certainly also be counted intelligent enough to draw the common inference that the Court has been taken by storm rather than by persuasive constitutional argument. Little legitimization is likely in such circumstances.

Thus, even conceding the dubious proposition that the Court has a legitimacy-conferring capacity, the history of realigning election periods more readily supports the view that the justices check and delegitimize popular government and constitute a force for instability than the conclusion advanced by Black and Dahl that the Court legitimizes the actions of the elected branches, reconciling recalcitrant minorities to the constitutionality of new regimes and their policies.

IV. Conclusions

Now briefly to recapitulate. The symbolic qualities of law, especially constitutional law and the Supreme Court, were expounded by the Legal Realists in the 1920's and 1930's. This was not only the development of a legal philosophy, but in the 1930's a strategem in the assault upon the old Court. The purpose was a better understanding of law and a freeing of popular government from the restraints of judicial power.

Modern constitutional scholars, however, have stood the Realists on their heads. The symbolic quality of Supreme Court adjudication is recognized as a fact, but not for the purpose of debunking. It becomes in the hands of Charles Black and Robert Dahl a justification for judicial review. The Supreme Court, because of its identification as the oracle of the Constitution, serves a valuable function in American democracy by legitimizing the actions of popular government and regime changes. . . .

What strikes one about these arguments is the absence of evidence. Not one of these commentators advances any factual support for the Supreme Court's legitimacy-conferring capacity, the linchpin in their lawyerly arguments. Indeed, a survey of the available public opinion studies suggests quite another conclusion: That the public has sufficient knowledge about neither the Court's actions nor its function to meet the conditions necessary in an operationalized definition of legitimization. Even an attempt to save the commentators from themselves, by limiting their theory of legitimization to opinion molding elites is not promising, despite the bits of evidence that might lay a foundation for such a revised approach.

But, even if the legitimacy-conferring function is conceded, it will not sustain the argument of those, especially Black and Dahl, who have put it at the center of their vision of the Supreme Court's role in American politics. At the critical moments of economic and social crisis in American history, when both government effectiveness and legitimacy are impaired, the Supreme Court is a barrier to majorities, operating through the medium of realigning elections, as they attempt to meet the emergency. This is not simply because life tenure and partisan-ideological appointments combined with the power of judicial review make the Court "the check of a preceding generation on the present one; a check of conservative legal philosophy upon a dynamic people, and nearly always the check of a rejected regime on the one in being."[9] More important, the symbolic status of the Supreme Court has the effect, when the justices and the popular branches are thrown into conflict, not simply over specific cases but in the fullness of philosophical debates and political maneuvering, of "delegitimizing" the elected branches, thus casting doubt not only on policies enacted but also on the "rightness" of the regime. And when the justices are finally brought into line, usually following bitter assaults on the Court itself, those disaffected from the new regime's substantive policy, among whom the Court might well legitimize the new leadership, certainly see that the constitutional citadel has been taken by force and that the legitimizing voices come from justices installed by the new regime or at least intimidated by it.

. . .

Finally, then I venture a speculation. . . . The Court may not, in fact, have a legitimacy-conferring capacity; but it may nevertheless command the same reverence as a constitutionally sanctioned branch that the others do. It may, in short, have legitimacy as an institution in a legitimate political system, to which it in a small way contributes, as do other institutions and centers of opinion formation. And might it also be true that the Court commands some additional reverence because of the American devotion to "law" and to the Constitution?

May not this more modest legitimacy of the Supreme Court, then, cast it in realigning election periods as the reef upon which the vessel of reform is shattered? In the early stages of each new electoral coalition party majorities tend to be inflated. Spurred by the ideological zeal common among those long out of power and by the national crisis, these large majorities move toward sweeping reform. But the Supreme Court, because of its composition and its checking power, stands in the way or seems to. Finally the new coalition's leadership, often its most reformist wing and usually the Executive, concludes that it must curb the Court.

It is at this moment that the Court's legitimacy is important, for elements of the coalition's elected elite and of its electoral base now hold back in reverence to a constitutional institution, whose actions and function they may or may not fully understand or approve. The coalition is thus divided over an issue of constitutional structure; the energies, resources, and zeal of the reformist wing of the coalition are diverted to that struggle; the leadership's hold over the loosely joined alliance is weakened; and the momentum for substantive policy change is slowed or stopped.

One can only idly speculate about the history of race relations in America if the Radical Republicans had not been diverted from their Reconstruction program by their attacks first on the Court and then on an Executive branch which had been lost to their party by assassination rather than election. Similarly, what measures toward social welfare and redistribution of wealth might have been enacted by the New Deal coalition if it had not splintered in the court-packing fight? Might poverty, again a visible issue in the 1960's, but without any effective legislative response, have been mainly alleviated by more sweeping legislation in the 1930's?

Finally, one is entitled to speculate whether a large, younger electorate, just now coming of age politically, might be the stuff from which a new political coalition will be made. Restoration of the natural environment, dramatic redistribution of wealth, sternly enforced rules against discrimination by race or sexual identity, and medical care for all citizens—to select only four examples requiring massive new governmental "regimentation" of the conduct of individuals and of such collectivities as corporations, unions, and medical associations—might be goals of such a coalition. The ideological predilections and the age of recent judicial appointees certainly presage another "old Court" which would block such reform, first by checking legislation and then by itself becoming an issue which diverts reform energies and divides a political coalition.

But this is simply speculation, an alternative definition and interpretation of Supreme Court legitimacy. Whatever the merit of this different model, there seems no question that the widely asserted legitimizing function of the Supreme Court cannot summon adequate empirical support from public opinion studies, does not square with the history of relations between the justices and the popular branches, and will not withstand a searching analysis of its assumptions. Such a formulation cannot be the foundation for elaborately structured theories about the worth, justification, or scope of judicial review in a democracy.

Notes

1. Llewellyn, *The Constitution As An Institution*, 34 COLUM. L. REV. 1, 3 (1934).
2. S. Lipset, POLITICAL MAN 77 (1959).
3. R. McCloskey, THE AMERICAN SUPREME COURT 72 (1960).
4. S. Lipset, at 82.
5. C. Black, THE PEOPLE AND THE COURT 56-69 (1960).
6. H. Pringle, THE LIFE AND TIMES OF WILLIAM HOWARD TAFT 955 (1939).
7. With two exceptions, these demarcations follow the analysis of Thomas P. Jahnige. Jahnige, *Critical Elections and Social Change*, 3 POLITY 468, 469 n. 11 (1971). I have marked 1800 as the onset of the Jeffersonian party system; Jahnige more vaguely de-

scribes the period 1789-1828 as the Federalist-Jeffersonian party period. And I have adopted Pomper's view that 1896 was a converting election, which strengthened the preexisting Republican majority, rather than a realigning election. Pomper, *Classification of Presidential Elections,* 29 J. POL. 533, 562 (1967). . . .

8. R. Scigliano, THE SUPREME COURT AND THE PRESIDENCY 125-48 (1971).

9. R. Jackson, THE STRUGGLE FOR JUDICIAL SUPREMACY (1941) at 315. After this paper was in draft, an additional commentary bearing on its historical thesis became available. Sheldon Goldman and Thomas P. Jahnige compare the nation's realigning election cycles with the successful "court-curbing" periods discovered by Stuart S. Nagel. There is a distinct coincidence, with these court-curbing periods occurring on the eve of and during realigning election periods. This seems added confirmation that conflict between the Judiciary and the popular branches accompanies these electoral upheavals, threatening effectiveness by checking programs of the new coalition and delegitimizing the new regime by subjecting it to judicial disapproval. S. Goldman & T. Jahnige, THE FEDERAL COURTS AS A POLITICAL SYSTEM 261-68 (1971); cf. S. Nagel, THE LEGAL PROCESS FROM A BEHAVIORAL PERSPECTIVE 260-279 (1969).